C0-AWN-178

CAPTAIN COOK
IN AUSTRALIA

CAPTAIN COOK IN AUSTRALIA

Extracts from the journals of
CAPTAIN JAMES COOK
giving a full account in his own words of his adventures and discoveries in Australia

EDITED BY
A. W. REED

A. H. & A. W. REED
WELLINGTON—AUCKLAND—SYDNEY—MELBOURNE

First published 1969
Reprinted 1969

A. H. & A. W. REED
182 Wakefield Street, Wellington
29 Dacre Street, Auckland
51 Whiting Street, Artarmon, Sydney
357 Little Collins Street, Melbourne

SET IN LINOTYPE JANSON

PRINTED IN AUSTRALIA BY HALSTEAD PRESS, SYDNEY

CONTENTS

ILLUSTRATIONS

(Between pages 96 and 97)

The maps were prepared by Lionel Forsdyke.

The jacket design by Beverley Buxton is based on an engraving from Hawkesworth's account of Cook's first voyage, 1773. It shows the *Endeavour* while refitting at Endeavour River.

LIST OF MAPS

INTRODUCTION

THE portion of Captain Cook's Journals relating to his discoveries in Australia is presented in this volume as a popular account of one of the most important journeys in the annals of exploration. A companion volume, *Captain Cook in New Zealand*, was published in 1951. After remaining out of print for many years it has now been reissued. The present volume continues the narrative after the departure of the *Endeavour* from New Zealand at the end of March 1770. In his own words:

> To return by the way of Cape Horn was what I most wished, because by this rout we should have been able to prove the Existance or Non-Existance of a Southern Continent, which yet remains Doubtful; but in order to Ascertain this we must have kept in a high Latitude in the very Depth of Winter, but the Condition of the Ship, in every respect, was not thought sufficient for such an undertaking. For the same reason the thoughts of proceeding directly to the Cape of Good Hope was laid aside as no discovery of any Moment could be hoped for in that rout. It was therefore resolved to return by way of the E. Indies by the following rout: upon Leaving this Coast to steer to the Westward until we fall in with the E. Coast of New Holland, and then to follow the direction it might take us, until we arrived at its Northern extremity; and if this should be found impracticable, then to Endeavour to fall in with the Land of Islands discovered by Quiros.*
> With this view, at daylight we got under Sail and put to Sea.

Captain Cook in Australia may therefore be looked on as the second book of a two-volume work; but the discovery and exploration of the eastern coast of Australia, or New Holland as it was then known, is a self-contained and self-sufficient story that justifies separate publication. The earlier book contained a short introductory account of Cook's life and travels which puts his experience both in Australia and New Zealand into proper perspective. Mr C. R. H. Taylor, sometime librarian of the Alexander Turnbull Library, Wellington, and compiler of the monumental *Pacific Bibliography*, contributed an essay on the literature relating to Captain Cook's voyages, which has been brought up to date in the latest edition of *Captain Cook in New Zealand*. Both essays may well be of value to Australian readers, but as many will have access to both volumes, their place in this book

* The New Hebrides, which were explored by Cook on his second voyage.

has been taken by a concise account of the discovery of Australia prior to Captain Cook's visit.

Admiral W. J. L. Wharton had access to a copy of the Journal written by Captain Cook's clerk Orton, the text of which has been used in this volume. It was not Cook's own Journal, but can be described as a fair copy with alterations in Cook's own hand. Wharton made slight changes in wording and spelling but the present reprint may be regarded as substantially what Cook himself wrote. The volume edited by Admiral (then Captain) Wharton in 1893 was entitled *Captain Cook's Journal during his First Voyage Round the World made in H.M. Bark "Endeavour", 1768-1771.*

To Cook's account of the country and people on pages 129-38 is added a more extensive account taken from *The Three Famous Voyages of Captain Cook* published towards the end of the nineteenth century by Ward Lock Bowden and Co. This account is an amalgam of the descriptions of Cook and Banks.

During the second voyage Cook did not visit Australia, but the text of Captain Tobias Furneaux, who made a fleeting visit to Tasmania in the *Adventure*, is taken from the Ward Lock Bowden publication, as is also Cook's record of his visit to Tasmania during the third voyage. Here again we are reading Cook's own narrative, but in an edited form with modern spelling and punctuation.

The two volumes *Captain Cook in Australia* and *Captain Cook in New Zealand* have been published in the hope that readers in both countries may welcome the simple, straightforward narrative Cook gave of the remarkable adventures that finally put Australia and New Zealand on the map and within the fold of British sovereignty.

In preparing the present edition of Cook's Journal relating to the east coast of Australia for publication, the editor has incorporated many of Wharton's excellent footnotes, which add to the value of the record, for he was himself a hydrographer. Results of later research have been added. Recourse has been made to the Hakluyt edition of the *Journals of Captain James Cook on his Voyages of Discovery*, edited by Dr J. C. Beaglehole, only for final checking of notes, for these volumes are currently available and elucidate the text in a manner that cannot be emulated; in a few cases they have provided a final and authoritative source of information for the more elusive origins of place names conferred by Cook.

Thanks are due to Mr C. R. H. Taylor for advice and for his essay on the Cook MSS.; to Mr Andrew Sharp whose invaluable book, *The Discovery of Australia*, published by the Clarendon Press, Oxford, 1963, has been used extensively in the preparation of the essay on early voyages to Australia; also to the kindness of author and publisher in giving permission to use the quotation on pages 20-1. The editor is indebted to Mr Sharp for his careful revision of the article. *The Australian Encyclopaedia*, published by the Grolier Society of Australia, has proved a useful source of information and identification. Gratitude is also expressed to Dr F. H. Talbot, Director of the Australian Museum, Sydney, to Dr G. C. Petersen of Palmerston North, and to Mr Vincent Serventy, Sydney, for assistance and advice, and to my daughter, Mrs R. E. Lane, for typing.

Special thanks are due to the following specialists for the identification of birds, reptiles, animals, plants, fish, and shellfish, the source of information being acknowledged in brackets after the appropriate footnotes: Keith Hindwood, Honorary Associate in Ornithology, Australian Museum, Sydney; K. Mair, Director and Chief Botanist, Royal Botanic Gardens and National Herbarium, Sydney; Gilbert Whitley, Honorary Associate in Ichthyology, Australian Museum, Sydney; Ellis Troughton, Honorary Associate in Mammalogy, Australian Museum, Sydney; D. McPhee, Herpetologist; also to Dr D. F. McMichael for the identification of molluscs and to Dr J. C. Yaldwyn for crustacea.

The simple line illustrations in the text are reproduced from sketches by Captain Cook, by courtesy of the Trustees of the British Museum; the engravings from the Ward Lock Bowden edition of Cook's Journals. The folding map of the east coast of Australia has been redrawn from the original engravings now in the British Museum by L. Forsdyke; the sketch of Botany Bay and plan of the Endeavour River are reproduced from the originals in the British Museum. Gratitude is also expressed to New South Wales Government Tourist Bureau; State Public Relations Bureau, Premier's Department, Brisbane, Queensland; Tasmanian Government Tourist and Immigration Department; and Qantas Airways Ltd for supplying photographs so generously; and to M. C. Smith for his endeavours to locate suitable subjects; also to Mrs Beverley Buxton for the jacket designs.

In the transformation from manuscript to published book, much time and expert knowledge are involved. The editor wishes to express gratitude to F. A. Davey and D. W. Sinclair who were responsible for the physical production of the book.

A. W. REED

GOING BACK TO THE MANUSCRIPTS

The broad outline of Captain Cook's life and voyages is covered in many books, and something of them is known to most readers. But because for a good number of us curiosity takes us more deeply into the record of events, we become conscious that Cook himself did not commit to paper every piece of information gleaned during the voyages, much less of his own life. He kept no known diaries of his personal life, and apparently only official logs and journals at sea. If he wrote many personal letters, too few have survived. For much of his official life we must go to the Admiralty documents; for his earlier years in the coal trade, to the records of the ship of John Walker, shipowner, of Whitby, and his very good friend; and for the voyages themselves, to the journals of Cook himself and quite a number of his sailing companions.

It was not to be expected that Cook would, or indeed could, cover the same ground as other members of the ship's personnel, and it was frequently the case that these latter were in a position to observe things that Cook could not have seen or fully appreciated. Several of the ship's company after each voyage published unauthorised accounts, and these often amplify or qualify Cook's and others' observations.

As noted in *Captain Cook in New Zealand*, the Admiralty required all personal diaries, journals etc. to be surrendered at the conclusion of each voyage. For the most part this was complied with, so that there is a quantity of records which, varying greatly in quality, contribute to the sum of our knowledge.

It was unfortunate that Cook's own journals of the first voyage, published officially, were "edited" and "improved" by Dr John Hawkesworth in such a way that the significance of the text was often distorted or lost. So a return to the original manuscript is sometimes revealing: but immediately the question arises, which manuscript? For there are drafts and transcripts and "fair copies", which even when appearing to be repetitious, can vary in sense or implication. Again, the modern reader, seeking clarification of some small event, or facet of the voyages, may well find that an overlooked remark in a midshipman's log or a naturalist's notes will illumine the point.

However, it is more likely that the task has already been done for him by Dr J. C. Beaglehole, editor of the compendious, scholarly and admirable edition of Cook's Journals, published by the Cambridge University Press for the Hakluyt Society. To date three (of the ultimate four) volumes have been issued, usually the final word on almost every aspect of the voyages.

The fact that this great publication has been in process since 1955 is indicative of the magnitude of the task, a considerable part of which involved the examination of all manuscripts connected with Cook and the voyages. These are not only numerous, but are scattered in a number of repositories about the world; occasionally they duplicate or overlap, some are incomplete, some unidentifiable.

There are several minor mysteries about certain Cook manuscripts, never yet resolved. How did the solitary journal page, now in the Huntingdon Library at San Marino, California, become separated from its volume? What happened to the page missing from Lieut. Hicks's log in the Turnbull Library? Dr Beaglehole, discussing the records of the second voyage, reasons that yet another manuscript, covering about three years, has totally disappeared. Again, after the third voyage, a group of miscellaneous papers, presumably drafts, vanished inexplicably before reaching the editor Dr John Douglas. Even as recently as 1960, when the "Palliser-Hudson" transcript of Cook's Journal of the second voyage was sold at Christie's in London, it went into the hands of an unknown buyer, and appears, in the meantime at least, to be lost to further researchers.

Several depositories of Cook records possess volumes or collections of amazingly heterogeneous papers, such as odd pages from logs and journals, letters, accounts, transcripts, drafts and notes, all not necessarily relating to any one voyage—or, in at least one instance, to Cook or the voyages at all.

So we realise that there is virtually no single final journal or log for any one of the voyages that gives a full clear unequivocal account of everything that happened or was learned, even from any one man's point of view. Most of these anomalies are easily explained, but not all.

The voyage of the *Endeavour* is not unlike the later ones for the diversity of texts, and problems in the manuscripts themselves. True, the two subsequent voyages, each with two vessels, meant twice as great a quantity of paper for an editor to study. These papers, scattered as they are, are really mostly in some half-dozen principal locations, as the following brief survey of the *Endeavour* records shows.

Cook's own Journal, now at the Australian National Library, Canberra, is a very good version in his own handwriting. Strangely enough, until the Hakluyt Society edition, it had not been the basis of any edition of the voyage since the time of Cook. It was purchased at auction by the Library in 1923, but how it reached an earlier sale in 1868 is not completely clear, for it was almost certainly owned till her death in 1835 by Cook's widow.

A copy of his journal made by Richard Orton, the ship's clerk, was sent to the Admiralty from Batavia. This became (with questionable right) the personal property of the then Secretary to the Admiralty, from whose descendants it came by successive sales to John Corner in 1890, from whose estate it was purchased by F. H. Dangar and presented to the Australian Museum, which in 1935 transferred it to the Mitchell Library (which is housed with the Public Library of New South Wales). It is frequently known as the "Corner copy". Cook himself had corrected and annotated it freely. This journal was used by Wharton for his edition of 1893.

Another transcript is held by the National Maritime Museum, Greenwich. It was in the Windsor Castle Library till 1935, when King George V presented it to Greenwich. It was probably written especially for King George III. It contains several handwritings and is not a complete record of the voyage; it is thus not a satisfactory text, and one suspects it was a task handed to anyone available, as something of a "chore".

The Admiralty itself received a full journal from Cook at the end of the voyage. This is again a transcript, in the hand of Richard Orton (the same whose ears were partly cut off by James Magra in a drinking bout). It was transferred to the Public Record Office probably about 1900 and is, all considered, the most satisfactory of all.

Apart from these basic texts, there are logs (as distinct from journals) by Cook himself, as well as by others such as Lieutenant Zachary Hicks, Robert Molyneux, master, Richard Pickersgill, master's mate, and William Monkhouse, the surgeon. Hicks's log is in the Alexander Turnbull Library, Monkhouse's in the Mitchell Library, the others, and more, in the Public Record Office. Beyond these again is the mass of official and unofficial papers concerning the fitting and arranging of the voyage. These are mainly in the three great English institutions, the British Museum, the Public Record Office and the Maritime Museum.

But the name of Joseph Banks is almost synonymous with the voyage of the *Endeavour*, to which he added considerable lustre, much of which was reflected upon himself. Banks contributed vastly to the success of the expedition, for he was an educated man, youthful, energetic, and a first-class observer. He wrote usually more fully and with a facile pen, not only in his capacity as naturalist, but as an alert and vigorous traveller. Others of the company were at times glad to draw upon his accounts of events, places, and peoples. Cook himself did this more than once, and his writing almost certainly benefited from the association with Banks. His journal is in the Mitchell Library, Sydney, and though much of it had been absorbed in the several "Lives" of Banks (as well as in Hawkesworth's edition of Cook), it was not till the definitive edition, prepared by Dr J. C. Beaglehole, and published by the Public Library of New South Wales, appeared in 1962, that its full text and accordingly full usefulness became available. A contemporary transcript of Banks's Journal is in the Turnbull Library, and another changed hands on the London market in 1961. There are quantities of Banks correspondence and miscellaneous papers in the British Museum, the Mitchell Library, the Sutro Library of California, the National Maritime Museum, the Australian National Library, the Turnbull Library, and Yale University Library. It is remarkable that Banks, for all his energy and enthusiasm, never came to annotating and publishing his own invaluable record of the *Endeavour* voyage.

It would be tedious to particularise the several logs and journals drawn upon for the full story of the second and third voyages. Again the principal repositories are those already mentioned, but there are other manuscripts, some considerable, some slight, in the following places: the Poverty Bay Club, Gisborne, New Zealand, the Auckland Public Library, the New Zealand General Assembly Library, the Public Libraries of Liverpool and Sheffield, the Peabody Museum, Salem, Massachusetts, Princeton University Library, the Dixson Collection in the Mitchell Library, the Whitby Museum, the Royal Observatory, Herstmonceaux, and the private collections of R. Nan Kivell, Viscount Hinchinbrooke, and the late K. A. Webster.

The record of the second voyage suffered from the separately published observations of the Forsters, perverse and querulous, father and son, naturalists to the expedition. And of course the last voyage involved some discrepancies occasioned by the deaths of first Cook, and then Clerke who succeeded him.

The last two voyages benefited to some extent from the journals, published or unpublished, of such naturally competent diarists as David Samwell, surgeon, and Heinrich Zimmermann, A.B., for their accounts which noted the circumstances of Cook's death with some particularity; John Ledyard the American corporal of marines who published a book in Boston, Massachusetts; John Rickman who published anonymously; William Anderson, also a surgeon, James Burney, and Thomas Edgar. The observations of these last three are printed in Dr Beaglehole's classic edition.

There are a few documents relating to Cook still in private hands, and one comes to light from time to time. It is probable that a good deal thus held privately has been lost, and some may yet emerge from some unsuspected family associate of a century and a half ago. Students of Cook and his achievement would welcome any such discovery as may illumine his resolution and high endeavour in those years of great adventure.

Tawa, 28 May 1968 C. R. H. TAYLOR

EARLY DISCOVERIES IN AUSTRALIA

The first known two-way visit to Australia made by Europeans did not occur until 1606. Determination of the configuration of the continent and Tasmania took another two centuries. There were several reasons for the delay.

The first major innovation in oceanic navigation was the invention of the compass, but it gave no clue to the displacement of ships from their course when out of sight of land. Then came the astrolabes, cross-staffs and other forms of the quadrant enabling the altitudes of heavenly bodies above the horizon to be determined. When used to measure the height of the sun at noon they gave a guide to latitude, when the sun's known movements to and from the north and south solstices were allowed for. These inventions helped Portuguese, Spanish, and Dutch conquerors to establish themselves in the East Indies.

The early Dutch explorers discovered the northern and western parts of the Australian continent which lie nearest the East Indies; these regions appeared to them to be arid and inhospitable. The Dutch navigators failed to penetrate Torres Strait, which lay to the east. It was left to James Cook to approach the continent from the east and so to discover the more fertile eastern area, opening up the way to the annexation of Australia by Britain.

The first European discovery is a matter of controversy. In a number of French maps compiled during the middle of the sixteenth century there appears a region known as Iave la Grande–Java the Great. Whether this is a product of imagination, or a record of a very early discovery of the western, northern, and eastern coasts, is in dispute. That a Portuguese ship at least arrived in Australian waters in early times appears to be demonstrated by the finding of two carronades on Carronade Island off the north coast by H.M.S. *Encounter* in 1916. They were of Portuguese make and are believed to have been cast in the late fifteenth or early sixteenth century.

In 1568 the first expedition of Alvaro de Mendaña discovered a number of islands in the western Pacific, this influencing later exploration, but at no time did it come within 1,200 miles of Australia. Mendaña had been sent to try to discover a great continent thought by many cosmographers to lie in the south part of the South Pacific. A Peruvian Indian story of a voyage to offshore islands where gold and silver were found had induced the Viceroy of Peru to send his nephew Mendaña to make discoveries. As a result Mendaña found the Solomons.

The first European ship to report beyond all doubt the finding of a part of Australia was the Dutch vessel *Duyfken* (Little Dove). The *Duyfken* sailed from Bantam in search of gold and spices on the south coast of New Guinea. This small three-masted vessel traversed the coast and then swung over to the west of Cape York Peninsula in or about March 1606. A chart found in the secret archives of the Dutch East India Company contains a legend at the point of contact at the mouth of the Pennefather River*: R. met het Bosch (River with Bush). Willem Jansz, the skipper of the *Duyfken*, coasted along the land as far south as Cape Keerweer, turned, and retraced his course up the coast. At the estuary of the Batavia River there was an encounter with Aborigines. Leaving the coast about thirty miles south-west of Cape York, he skirted the west side of Wallis Island and Prince of Wales Island (later named by Cook) without discovering Torres Strait, which was to be so elusive to many later mariners. He sailed north, after having discovered 200 miles of Australian coastline. The senior officers of the *Duyfken* were Willem Jansz, captain, and Jan Lodewycksz van Roossengin, supercargo or commercial agent on the ship. Neither of them realised the nature of their epoch-making discovery, thinking that the coast they had sighted was part of New Guinea.

In 1606, the same year as Jansz's discovery, Pedro Fernandez de Quiros led a Spanish expedition from Peru in search of a settlement to be established in the fabled continent, or in some suitable islands. His three ships reached the southern islands of the Banks Group, and the northern islands of the New Hebrides. He thought that the northern part of Espiritu Santo was a portion of a continent which he called Austrialia del Espiritu Santo. Quiros sailed to North America in the flagship, leaving two vessels at Espiritu Santo. The larger of the two was the *San Pedrico*, commanded by Luis Vaez de Torres. Torres proceeded south-west in search of land and then turned north-north-west. His progress was barred by land and reefs, so he turned west along the Louisiade Archipelago and in due course came to the south coast of New Guinea. History was made again as he passed through the strait subsequently named after him. There is no reason to think that he actually saw Cape York Peninsula, the nearest part of the continent of Australia. This was in September, five or six months after the *Duyfken* had passed westward of the strait. Torres demonstrated that New Guinea was an island and had no connection with the southern continent, but the significance of his discovery of the strait was not appreciated by the Dutch in the East Indies.

Ten years later the first contact with the west coast of Australia

* Possibly the Coen River, named after the Dutch Governor-General who founded Iacatia (now Jakarta) in Java.

was made by the Dutch commander Dirck Hartog in the *Eendracht*. Hartog sailed from Amsterdam for Java, taking advantage of the prevailing westerlies after rounding the Cape of Good Hope, and finally turned north for Java. This course greatly reduced the time of the voyage compared with sailing north-east from the Cape. To celebrate his discovery and sojourn of three days, Hartog fastened a sailor's pewter dish on a pole on Dirk Hartog Island, one of the islands on the leeward side of Shark Bay. This plate bore the inscription (in Dutch):

> On 25 October 1616 there arrived here the ship Eendragt of Amsterdam, the supercargo Gillis Miebais of Liege, skipper Dirck Hartog of Amsterdam; on the 27 do, it sailed for Bantam: the subcargo Jan Steyn, the mate Pieter Ledocker van Bil.

Eighty-one years later this plate was discovered by another Dutch sailor, Willem de Vlamingh, who removed the plate and replaced it with another on which the original inscription was copied together with a record of his own visit. Hartog's plate is still preserved in Amsterdam. Vlamingh's plate was recovered by a French expedition in 1801, lost, found once more and taken to Paris, where it was again lost. In 1940 its chequered career was ended for it was rediscovered and is now in a museum in Perth.

In coming north from Shark Bay, Hartog had fleeting glimpses of the west coast. A distant sighting of it was made in 1618 by skipper Haevik Claeszoon van Hillegom and supercargo Pieter Dirkszoon in the *Zeewolf* (Sea-wolf). The land was low and flat and the skipper wrote: "Whether it is the mainland or islands is known to God but I feel it is mainland, from all the signs seen." This sighting was evidently near North-west Cape. The vessel did not linger but sailed on to Java.

The practice, developed by the Dutch, of sailing westward after passing the Cape of Good Hope for some 4,000 miles and then turning northward to the East Indies was putting fragmentary pieces of the Western Australian coastline on the map. Three months after the *Zeewolf's* discovery the *Mauritius* made contact with the coast. On board the vessel was Willem Jansz, supercargo of the *Mauritius*, commanded by Lenaert Jacobszoon. On 31 July 1618 they discovered what they thought was an island. The "island" was in fact the peninsula on the west side of Exmouth Gulf, terminating in North-west Cape. On Hessel Gerritsz's map of Dutch discoveries up till 1628, the west coast of Australia is named The Land of the Eendracht, after Hartog's vessel. On it Willems Revier (William's River) is no doubt named after Willem Jansz.

The next discovery was more detailed. On 19 July 1619 Frederik de Houtman, commander of the ships *Dordrecht* and *Amsterdam*, reported that he was "suddenly confronted by land where we stood off. On the 20th we found that it was a mainland coast, stretching north and south." After spending several days in danger near the Swan River, Houtman discovered Houtman Rocks, then named Abrolhos, a Portuguese term meaning "Keep your eyes open", or "Be careful!" While sailing north Houtman saw other parts of the west coast.

An early Dutch map shows a sketchy outline of coast called "The Golden Province of Beach". Apparently it was thought that red mud in the vicinity might prove to be gold-bearing. More than two centuries later the promise of a "golden province" was fulfilled in the forbidding inland territory unseen by the Dutch.

Cape Leeuwin, on the south coast of Western Australia, is a name that commemorates a sighting by the *Leeuwin* (Lioness) in March 1622.

The story of continued Dutch discovery is interrupted at this point by the visit of a British vessel. In September 1621 the *Trial*, in command of Captain John Brooke, sailed from Plymouth for Java. On 1 May 1622 North-west Cape was sighted. On the 25th, shortly before midnight, the ship struck a rock and sank. Most of the ship's company were drowned, but the captain and one of the officers, Thomas Bright, and forty-four other survivors escaped in two boats, and eventually reached Java. When morning dawned after this terrifying experience, the survivors saw rocks and islands nearby. The men in the larger boat spent seven days on one of these islands. After many years the islands were identified as the Monte Bello Islands and Barrow Island, near the north-west coast of Australia.

The Council of the Dutch East India Company in Batavia sent Jan Carstensz in command of the *Arnhem* and the *Pera* to make contact with the native inhabitants of the islands of "Key, Arn and Tenimber, and also to make discoveries on the land of Nova-Guinea". Skirting the south coast of New Guinea in 1623, the ships followed the course of the *Duyfken* seventeen years earlier, and then attempted to sail further eastwards. Their passage was blocked by shallows and Carstensz did not find an entrance to Torres Strait. He had sighted Cape York Peninsula on 12 April 1623 and by 14 April reached Cape Keerweer, the furthest south point of Willem Jansz's course in the *Duyfken.* The two ships later became separated and Carstensz returned to the port of Ambon on 8 June, having discovered the coast from Cape Keerweer to the Staten or Gilbert River. The *Arnhem*, under the command of Willem Joosten van Colster, sailed north-west and then skirted the west of Arnhem Land (spelt Aernhem on his chart) from Cape Grey to Cape Arnhem; he may also have seen Groote Eylandt. In April-May 1623 Colster thus discovered the north-eastern extremity of Arnhem Land, the Wessel Islands, and possibly Groote Eylandt.

In 1627 another section of the coastline was unveiled by Pieter Nuyts and François Thijssen in the *Gulden Zeepaard* (Golden Seahorse), this time on the south side of the continent. The "Land of Peter Nuijts" which appears on a Dutch map of 1628 shows the south coast of Australia as far east as Nuyts Archipelago, a distance of some 900 miles.

Earlier sightings of the north coast were now extended further to the vicinity of Port Hedland. In 1628 Gerrit Frederikszoon de Witt in the *Vianen* followed the coast from the Port Hedland area for about 200 miles on a south-west course as far as the Monte Bello Islands.

A number of further fleeting contacts were made on the west coast of Australia from 1622 onwards, but no significant discoveries occurred until 4 June 1629, when the *Batavia*, commanded by François Pelsaert, was wrecked on Houtman Rocks. Leaving the passengers and most of the crew on a small islet, Pelsaert went in a small boat in search of water on nearby islands, intending to make for the mainland if necessary, and even to set sail for Java. It was a perilous voyage. Pelsaert and his men were at first unable to land. They were driven northwards by bad weather and a strong current. When they managed to find a sheltered inlet, the land was barren and without water. By this time they were several hundred miles to the north of the castaways. Pelsaert continued on to Batavia. He returned in a small vessel in time to rescue some of the people who had been left behind. This involuntary exploration of the west coast in a small boat may be said to have completed its discovery broadly.

Mr Andrew Sharp has stated that:

> It is interesting to reflect how the history of Australia might have been changed if the Dutch had followed up their discovery of the west coast by establishing on it a staging post or settlement. Dedel's hope that the shores south of Shark Bay might prove to be gold-bearing would have been doomed to disappointment, but inland exploration might have anticipated the Western Australian gold strikes by a couple of centuries. A party looking for a site for settlement would have found a superb one in the Swan River area where Fremantle and Perth now go on from strength to strength. From such a bridgehead there might well have been no limit to Dutch expansion throughout the continent. Had a settlement been made in the seventeenth century, immigration would have extended beyond those of Caucasian race, for the Dutch would surely have brought Indonesians there. There would have been

little rivalry from other nations for Australia's shores—far less, indeed, than the Dutch encountered in Manhattan and its environs, where they spent their colonizing resources only to see them taken over in due course by the British. Twenty-three years after the latter event was finally accomplished, Willem de Vlamingh, in 1697, explored the Swan River for some thirty miles. The Dutch, however, were more interested in commerce than colonization, and the aborigines of Western Australia were left undisturbed until the nineteenth century.*

During his term of office as Governor-General in Batavia, Anthony van Diemen was responsible for encouraging expeditions leading to the discovery of large portions of Australia and New Zealand. Van Diemen took up his appointment in 1636. The first exploration, made in that year, was that of the *Klein Amsterdam* and the *Wesel*, commanded by Commander Gerrit Thomasz Pool and, after his death in New Guinea, by the commercial agent, Pieter Pieterszoon. The isolated charts of earlier discoveries could not be connected, and the "Southland" was a challenge to map-makers. Were the western and southern coasts connected in any way with Cape York Peninsula which, in spite of Torres's discovery, was still regarded as a southward extension of New Guinea? The great southern land might be divided from the north-eastern portions by a channel—a suspicion, as Sharp has reminded us, that was not fully extinguished until the nineteenth century. Pieterszoon sighted the northern coast of Australia in the vicinity of Dundas Strait and skirted the north coast of Melville Island for eighty miles, without being aware that it was an island.

The year 1642 was notable, for it was then that Abel Janszoon Tasman commenced a memorable voyage which culminated in the circumnavigation of Australia. It will be noted that the discoveries of the preceding thirty-six years had been confined to parts of the northern, western, and southern coasts. There were many gaps and the continental character of the great island was still a matter of conjecture.

Abel Janszoon Tasman, a skipper in the employ of the Dutch East India Company, was put in charge of an expedition to search for new countries and avenues of trade by sailing south and then east until he fell in with land. The chief pilot, Franchoys Jacobszoon Visscher, was with Tasman on the *Heemskerck*, which was accompanied by a second vessel, the *Zeehaen*. On 24 November 1642 a mountainous land was sighted. On the previous day Tasman and Visscher assumed that they were somewhere south of New Guinea (or Cape York Peninsula, supposed to be a southward extension of

* *The Discovery of Australia*, Clarendon Press, Oxford, 1963, pp. 63 and 64.

New Guinea). "This land is the first land in the south seas that we have encountered," Tasman wrote in his Journal, "and is still known to no european people, so we have given this land the name of Anthoonij van Diemens land in honour of the Hon. the Governor General our high superior who sent us out to make this discovery, the Islands lying round it as many as are known to us we have named after the Hon. Councillors of India, as can be perceived by the chart which is made of them."

Van Diemen's Land it remained for many years. By 1823 the name Tasmania was occasionally in use, but it did not receive official endorsement until 26 November 1855 when appropriate recognition was made of its discoverer.

The vessels sailed into Storm Bay and were then driven by fierce winds round Tasman Island. On 1 December anchorage was made near Green Island, in the mouth of North Bay, on the east side of Tasmania. On 2 December Visscher was sent with an armed party to forage for vegetables, timber, and water in what is now Blackman Bay. The men reported evidence of animals and of human occupation. The following day a small company landed on the shore south-east of the anchorage, and on the following day the carpenter swam ashore through heavy surf which prevented Tasman from making a landing by boat. A slate with the company's insignia carved on it and "the prince flag" were set up and formal possession taken.

After sailing north to the vicinity of St Patrick's Head, Tasman sailed eastward on 5 December to make the notable first European discovery of New Zealand, having in less than a fortnight skirted a portion of the west, most of the south, and a part of the east coast of Tasmania. After leaving New Zealand he sailed to Tonga and Fiji, and then to New Guinea on his way to Batavia, thus circumnavigating (but at a considerable distance) the whole of Australia.

The question whether New Guinea was separated from the "Southland", i.e. the previously discovered western and northern parts of the Australian continent, was still unanswered. It was the task of Tasman and Visscher to try to solve the problem on their second great voyage. They were instructed to sail down the west coast of Cape York Peninsula in an attempt to discover a south-easterly passage that would enable them to sail south to Van Diemen's Land, although little faith was placed in the prospect of such a passage. If it could not be found, they were to traverse the northern and western coasts of the "Southland" as far as Houtman Rocks. There were several supplementary instructions.

The explorers set sail from Batavia on 29 February 1644 in three small vessels, *Limmen*, *Zeemeeus*, and *Bracq*, with a total complement of 111 sailors and soldiers. Tasman failed to discover an entrance to

Torres Strait. Obeying the alternative instructions he sailed west along the northern coast of Australia. There were some errors in the charts, but knowledge was greatly extended. Having reached the west coast, the ships turned northward and arrived at their home port five months after their departure.

No journal of this voyage has survived but in a report to the East India Company in the Netherlands, Anthony van Diemen and his councillors summed up its results after making some comments on the barrenness of the coasts and the "bad natured people" whom the explorers had encountered:

> What now is on and in said Southpart, remains unknown, as the navigators have done nothing but sail along the coast, and who shall investigate what the lands give, must walk therein and through, for which these agents say that there was not enough opportunity, in which there may be something. Meanwhile this great and till now unknown Southland has been gone round by the aforesaid Tasman in two voyages and is reckoned to contain in it 8000 miles of land as the charts drawn thereof, which we send to Your Worships, make known. That such great land lying in various climes, namely the south-east end as far as 43½° southern latitude, extending to 2½°, shall have nothing of profit to find is scarcely acceptable.

It was a prophetic remark, but its realisation was to be deferred for more than a century, to await the arrival of the greatest of all the explorers of the Southern Hemisphere. The Dutch authorities in the Netherlands were not in favour of further attempts to explore the unknown area to the east of Australia and New Zealand.

Thirty years passed by before the next arrival on the north coast—the Englishman Captain Read in the *Cygnet*. Little is known of him except that he had been forced by his crew into piracy, but much of William Dampier, the famous adventurer and buccaneer, who was also a member of the crew. They remained for some weeks in the vicinity of the western entrance of King Sound and the Buccaneer Archipelago (so named because of the roistering crew of the *Cygnet*), where the vessel was careened. Dampier reported that "New-Holland is a very large Tract of Land. This part of it that we saw is all low even Land, with sandy Banks against the Sea, only the Points are rocky, and so are some of the Islands in this Bay." Although the contact had little significance, Dampier has the honour of being the first Englishman to set foot on the mainland. He also made an amusing comment on the poverty of the Aborigines as "the miserablest people in the world. The hodmodods of Monomatapa, though a nasty people, yet for wealth are gentlemen to these."

It was not good fortune alone that guided Captain James Cook to the hitherto unvisited fertile eastern coast of the mysterious continent. His commission in 1769 was quite specific. It was first to sail to Tahiti where it was hoped that the transit of Venus across the sun might be observed; then to proceed southwards to latitude 40° to test whether the great southern continent which by now obsessed the minds of men existed in that area. There could be no doubt of the existence of the great Southland discovered by Dutch seafarers, but who could tell but that another vast continent might not extend far into the southern ocean? "There is reason to imagine that a continent, or land of great extent may be found to the southward," his instructions read. If the coast of the fabulous continent was attained, Cook was to explore it, to become familiar with its nature and products, and to establish good relations with the inhabitants. The land was to be annexed or taken possession of in the name of the King. If the continent was not found he was to set sail for New Zealand, the country discovered by Tasman in 1642-3, and to explore it as far as he was able before returning to his home port via the Cape of Good Hope or Cape Horn.

On Cook's first and second voyages he proved conclusively that the fabled continent did not exist. The more tangible achievements of the first voyage were the accurate charting of the islands of New Zealand and of the eastern coast of Australia, with a high degree of accuracy, although with a few errors. As the result of Dutch exploration, three sides of the continent had taken reasonable shape on the map. Cook's exploration of the remaining coast on the eastern side completed its broad outline, with a thoroughness that had not hitherto been achieved. The problems of the previous century were solved. The existence of Torres Strait was confirmed, together with the fact that no passage existed between the southern limits of the western shore of Cape York Peninsula and the eastern seas. The only major issue that remained unsolved was the existence of a passage between Van Diemen's Land and the mainland.

On his second voyage Cook planned to revisit the scene, but when Furneaux made a visit and reported that no strait existed, Cook had to be content with this opinion. On his third voyage he touched briefly at the island but had no opportunity of visiting the north coast.

By his own observations and those of a distinguished team of scientists, led by Sir Joseph Banks, the existence of the eastern portion of the continent, to which Cook gave the name New South Wales, was proclaimed, and its inhabitants and resources described.

Cook's discovery of the east coast of Australia, one of the most memorable events in British history, culminated in the annexation of the sixth continent of the world. Cook's Journal speaks for itself in the pages of this book, showing the commander of the *Endeavour* as an intrepid yet cautious navigator, a man of imagination and enterprise, ever zealous for the health and welfare of his men (though reputedly of quick temper), an acute observer, a meticulous recorder of information written with clarity and occasionally with touches of humour, and an ambassador in his relations with both the savage and the enlightened people with whom he came in contact.

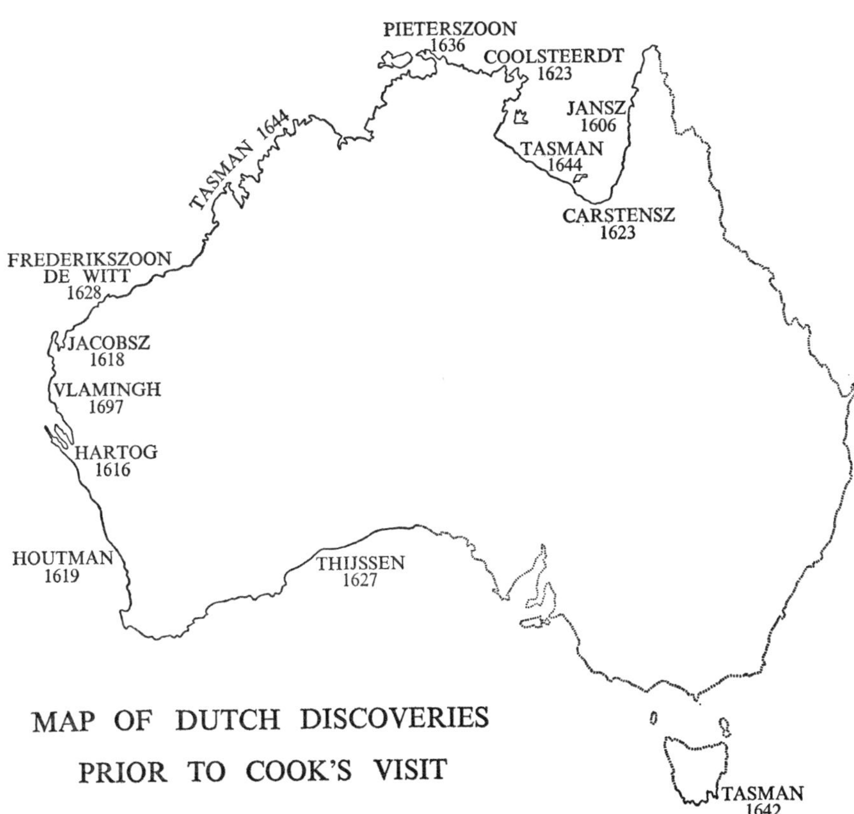

MAP OF DUTCH DISCOVERIES
PRIOR TO COOK'S VISIT

FIRST VOYAGE

MADE IN H.M. BARK *ENDEAVOUR*

1768-71

Leaving England in 1768, Cook sailed down the coast of South America, visited Tahiti and reached New Zealand in October 1769. After circumnavigating the islands, the Endeavour *sailed westward, still in search of the Southern Continent.*

FIRST VOYAGE

MADE IN H.M. BARK *ENDEAVOUR*

1768-71

1 April 1770-23 August 1770

Sunday, 1st April.–In the P.M. had a moderate breeze at E., which in the Night Veer'd to the N.E., and was attended with hazey, rainy weather. I have before made mention of our quitting New Zeland with an intention to steer to the Westward, which we accordingly did, taking our departure from Cape Farewell in the Latitude of 40° 30′ S. and Long. 185° 58′ W. from Greenwich, which bore from us at 5 p.m. W. 18° N., distance 12 Miles. After this we steer'd N.W. and W.N.W., in order to give it a good berth, until 8 o'Clock a.m., at which time we steered W., having the Advantage of a fresh Gale at N. by E. At Noon our Latitude by account was 40° 12′ S., Long. made from Cape Farewell 1° 11′ West.

Monday, 2nd.–In the P.M. had a moderate Gale at N., with thick hazey weather, attended with rain. At 8 it fell little wind, and Veer'd to W.S.W., at which time we Tack'd. At Midnight the wind came to S.S.W., and increased to a brisk gale with fair Cloudy weather, which we made the most of as soon as it was daylight. At Noon our Latitude, by Observation, was 40° 0′, and Long. made from Cape Farewell 2° 31′ W.

Tuesday, 3rd.–Cloudy weather; Winds at S.W. and S.S.W., a fresh Gale, with which we made our Course good N.W. by W., and distance run from Yesterday at Noon to this day at Noon 38½ Leagues. Latitude, by observation, 38° 56′ S.; Longitude made from Cape Farewell 4° 36′ W.

Wednesday, 4th.–Had a steady brisk Gale at S.S.W. with some flying showers of rain and large hollow Sea from the Southward. In the P.M. unbent the Maintopsail to repair, and brought another to the Yard and set it close reefed. At Noon our Lat., by Observation, was 37° 56′ S.; Course and distance since Yesterday at Noon N. 60° W., 122 Miles; Long. made from Cape Farewell 6° 54′ W.

Thursday, 5th.—Fresh Gales at S., which in the A.M. veer'd to S.E. by S. At Noon our Lat., by observation, was 37° 23′ S., Long. made from Cape Farewell 9° 10′ W.; Course and distance sail'd since Yesterday at Noon N. 73° 15′ W., 37 Leagues.

Friday, 6th.—Winds between the S. by E. and S.E., with a Continued swell from the S.S.W. At Noon our Latitude in per Observation 37° 18′ S.; Course and distance sail'd since Yesterday at Noon N. 85° W., 58 Miles. Long. made from Cape Farewell 10° 35′ W.

Saturday, 7th.—Gentle breezes at N.E., which in the A.M. Veer'd to N.W. In the P.M. found the Variation by the Mean of several Azimuths to be 13° 50′ E., being then in the Lat. of 37° 23′ S., and Long. 196° 44′ W. In the A.M. Punished Jno. Bowles, Marine, with 12 lashes for refusing to do his duty when order'd by the Boatswain's Mate and Serjeant of Marines. At Noon Lat. per Observation 37° 35′ S., Long. made from Cape Farewell 11° 34′ W.; Course and distance run since Yesterday noon S. 70° 15′ W., 50 Miles.

Sunday, 8th.—Gentle breezes from the N.W. and N. In the P.M. found the Variation to be 13° 56′ E. At Noon Lat. in per Observation 38° 0′ S., Long. made from Cape Farewell 13° 2′ W.; Course and distance sail'd since Yesterday noon S. 70° 15′ W., 74 Miles.

Monday, 9th.—Gentle breezes at N.W.; pleasant weather and a Smooth Sea. In the A.M. saw a Tropic Bird, which, I believe, is uncommon in such high Latitudes. At Noon Lat. observ'd 38° 29′ S., Long. made from Cape Farewell 14° 45′ W.; Course and distance sail'd since Yesterday noon S. 70° 15′ W., 86 Miles.

Tuesday, 10th.—Gentle breezes at N.W. by N., and clear settled weather. In the A.M. found the Variation, by the Amplitude, to be 11° 25′ E., and by Azimuth 11° 20′. At Noon the observed Lat. was 38° 51′ S., and Long. made from Cape Farewell 16° 45′; Long. in 202° 43′ W.; Course and distance sail'd since Yesterday noon S. 76° 45′ W., 96 Miles.

Wednesday, 11th.—Gentle breezes from the N.W., and pleasant weather, with some few showers of rain. In the A.M. found the Variation to be 13° 48′ E., which is 2½ degrees more than it was yesterday, altho' I should have expected to have found it less, for the observations were equally good. At Noon Lat. in 39° 7′ S., Long. made from Cape Farewell 17° 23′; and Course and distance sail'd since Yesterday noon S. 62° W., 34 Miles.

Thursday, 12th.—Calm, with now and then light Airs from the N.E. and N.W.; cloudy weather, but remarkably warm, and so it hath been for some days past. At Noon we were in the Lat. of 39° 11′, and Long. from Cape Farewell 17° 35′ W.; Course and distance sail'd since Yesterday noon S. 66° W., 10 Miles.

Friday, 13th.—Light Airs next to a Calm, with Clear pleasant weather; what little wind we had was from the N.W. quarter. In the Course of this day found the Variation to be 12° 27′ E., being at Noon, by observation, in the Lat. of 39° 23′ S., and Long. 204° 2′ W.; Course and distance since Yesterday noon S. 62° W., 26 Miles, and Long. made from Cape Farewell 18° 4′ W.

Saturday, 14th.—Calm serene weather, with sometimes light Airs from the Northward. At sun set found the Variation to be 11° 28′ E., and in the Morning to be 11° 30′ E. The Spritsail Topsail being wore to rags, it was condemn'd as not fit for its proper use, and Converted to repair the 2 Top Gallant Sails, they being of themselves so bad as not to be worth the Expence of new Canvas, but with the help of this sail may be made to last some time longer. At Noon Latitude in 39° 25′ S., Long. made from Cape Farewell 18° 21′ W.; Course and distance since Yesterday noon S. 18° W., 13 Miles.

Sunday, 15th.—In the P.M. had light Airs at N., which in the A.M. increased to a fresh Gale, with which we made the best of our way to the Westward, and by noon had run since yesterday upon a S. 86° 15′ W. Course, 79 Miles. Latitude in, by Observation, 39° 30′ S., and Long. made from Cape Farewell 20° 2′ W. Some flying fish seen this day.

Monday, 16th.—Fresh Gales at N.N.W., with Cloudy, hazey weather. In the P.M. saw an Egg Bird,[1] and yesterday a Gannet[2] was seen; these are Birds that we reckon never to go far from land. We kept the lead going all night, but found no soundings with 100 and 130 fathoms line. At noon we were in the Lat. of 39° 40′ S., and had made 22° 2′ of Longitude from Cape Farewell; course and distance sail'd since Yesterday at Noon S. 82° W., 108 Miles.

Tuesday, 17th.—At 2 p.m. the wind came to W.S.W., at which time we Tack'd and stood to the N.W. Before 5 o'Clock we were obliged to close reef our Topsails, having a Strong gale, with very

1 This name is usually given to the Sooty Tern (*Sterna fascata*) (Hindwood).

2 Probably the Australian Gannet (*Sula serrator*), a common bird both in south-east Australia and New Zealand (Hindwood).

heavy squalls; about this time a Small land bird was seen to pearch upon the rigging. We sounded, but had no ground with 120 fathoms of line. At 8 o'Clock we wore and stood to the Southward until 12 at Night, then wore and stood to the N.W. until 4 a.m., when we again stood to the Southward, having a fresh Gale at W.S.W., attended with Squalls and dark hazey unsettled weather until 9; at which time it fell little wind, and the weather soon after Clear'd up, which, a little after 11, gave us an Opportunity of taking several observations of the Sun and Moon, the Mean result of which gave 207° 56′ W. Long. from the Meridian of Greenwich. From these observations the Long. of the Ship at Noon was 207° 58′, and by the Log 208° 20′, the difference being only 22′; and this Error may as well be in the one as the other. Our Latitude at Noon was 39° 36′ S., the Long. made from Cape Farewell 22° 22′ W.

Wednesday, 18th.—Winds Southerly, a hard gale, with heavy squalls, attended with Showers of rain and a great Sea from the same Quarter. At 3 p.m. Close reeft the Topsails, handed the Main and Mizen Topsail, and got down Top Gallant Yards. At 6 the Gale increased to such a height as to oblige us to take in the Foretopsail and Mainsail, and to run under the Foresail and Mizen all night; Sounding every 2 hours, but found no ground with 120 fathoms. A 6 a.m. set the Mainsail, and soon after the Foretopsail, and before Noon the Maintopsail, both close reeft. At Noon our Latitude by observation was 38° 45′ S., Long. from Cape Farewell 23° 43′ W.; and Course and distance run since Yesterday noon N. 51° W., 82 Miles. Last night we saw a Port Egmont Hen,[3] and this morning 2 More, a Pintado bird,[4] several Albetrosses,[5] and black sheer Waters.[6] The first of these birds are Certain signs of the nearness of land; indeed we cannot be far from it. By our Longitude we are a degree to the Westward of the E. side of Van Diemen's Land, according to Tasman, the first discoverer's, Long. of it, who could not err much in so short a run as from this land to New Zeland; and by our Lat. we could not be above 50 or 55 Leagues to the Northward of the place where he took his departure from.

Thursday, 19th.—In the P.M. had fresh Gales at S.S.W. and Cloudy Squally weather, with a large Southerly Sea; at 6 took in the Topsails, and at 1 A.M. brought too and Sounded, but had no ground

[3] The Southern Skua (*Catharacta longbergi*). Some authorities consider it to be conspecific with the Great Skua (*S. skua*) of the northern hemisphere (Hindwood).

[4] Cape Petrel or Cape Pigeon (*Daption capensis*) (Hindwood).

[5] These could be of one or more species (Hindwood).

[6] Possibly one or more species of the genus *Puffinus* i.e. "mutton-birds" (Hindwood).

with 130 fathoms of line. At 5, set the Topsails close reef'd, and 6, saw land[7] extending from N.E. to W., distance 5 or 6 Leagues, having 80 fathoms, fine sandy bottom. We continued standing to the Westward with the Wind at S.S.W. until 8, at which time we got Topgallant Yards a Cross, made all sail, and bore away along shore N.E. for the Eastermost land we had in sight, being at this time in the Latitude of 37° 58′ S., and Long. of 210° 39′ W. The Southermost point of land we had in sight, which bore from us W. ¼ S., I judged to lay in the Latitude of 38° 0′ S. and in the Long. of 211° 7′ W. from the Meridian of Greenwich. I have named it Point Hicks, because Lieutenant Hicks was the first who discover'd this Land.[8] To the Southward of this point we could see no land, and yet it was clear in that Quarter, and by our Longitude compared with that of Tasman's, the body of Van Diemen's land ought to have bore due S. from us, and from the soon falling of the Sea after the wind abated I had reason to think it did; but as we did not see it, and finding the Coast to trend N.E. and S.W., or rather more to the Westward, makes me Doubtfull whether they are one land or no.[9] However, every one who compares this Journal with that of Tasman's will be as good a judge as I am; but it is necessary to observe that I do not take the Situation of Vandiemen's from the Printed Charts, but from the extract of Tasman's Journal, published by Dirk Rembrantse. At Noon we were in the Latitude of 37° 50′ and Long. of 210° 29′ W. The extreams of the

7 Cook first sighted the coast of Australia at 6 a.m. on Friday 20 April 1770, and not, as would appear from the Journal, on Thursday 19 April. Two factors have been taken into consideration in making this statement. (1) Cook used "ship's time" or "sea time", by which each day began at midday on the preceding day, according to "civil time". Thus: "*Thursday, 19th.*–In the P.M." refers to Wednesday afternoon in civil time. The A.M. that follows was therefore the morning of Thursday the 19th, according to the Journal. (2) When crossing the 180th meridian of longitude Cook made no adjustment to the dates in the log and journal. During the period spent on the east coast of Australia the dates must therefore be advanced by one full day to give the correct chronology.

8 The point of land named by Cook after Lieutenant Zachary Hicks cannot be identified with certainty, but it is generally recognised as the granite promontory at the farthest east point of the coast of Victoria, now known as Cape Everard. Although Cook's name for the point disappeared from the maps, it was preserved in later years in Point Hicks Hill, some five miles west of the cape. A monument to perpetuate the occasion of the first sighting of Australia during Cook's visit has been erected on Cape Everard. Midshipman Hicks was promoted to second lieutenant prior to the departure of the expedition from England. Hicks Bay in New Zealand also bears his name.

9 Had not the gale on the day before forced Cook to run to the northward, he would have made the north end of the Furneaux Group, and probably have discovered Bass Strait, which would have cleared up the doubt, which he evidently felt, as to whether Tasmania was an island or not. The fact was not positively known until Dr Bass sailed through the Strait in a whaleboat in 1797. Point Hicks was merely a rise in the coastline, where it dipped below the horizon to the westward, and the name of Point Hicks Hill is now borne by an elevation that seems to agree with the position (Wharton).

Land extending from N.W. to E.N.E., a remarkable point, bore N. 20° E., distant 4 Leagues. This point rises to a round hillock very much like the Ramhead[10] going into Plymouth sound, on which account I called it by the same name; Lat. 37° 39′, Long. 210° 22′ W. The Variation by an Azimuth taken this morning was 8° 7′ E. What we have as yet seen of this land appears rather low, and not very hilly, the face of the Country green and Woody, but the Sea shore is all a white Sand.

Friday, 20th.—In the P.M. and most part of the night had a fresh Gale Westerly, with Squalls, attended with Showers of rain. In the A.M. had the Wind at S.W., with Severe weather. At 1 p.m. saw 3 Water Spouts at once; 2 were between us and the Shore, and one at some distance upon our Larboard Quarter. At 6, shortned sail, and brought too for the Night, having 56 fathoms fine sandy bottom. The Northermost land in sight bore N. by E. ½ E., and a small Island[11] lying close to a point on the Main bore W., distant 2 Leagues. This point I have named Cape Howe[12]; it may be known by the Trending of the Coast, which is N. on the one Side and S.W. on the other. Lat. 37° 28′ S.; Long. 210° 3′ W. It may likewise be known by some round hills upon the main just within it. Having brought too with her head off Shore, we at 10 wore, and lay her head in until 4 a.m., at which time we made sail along shore to the Northward. At 6, the Northermost land in sight bore N., being at this time about 4 Leagues from the Land. At Noon we were in the Lat. of 36° 51′ S. and Long. of 209° 53′ W., and 3 Leagues from the land. Course sail'd along shore since Yesterday at Noon was first N. 52° E., 30 miles, then N. by E. and N. by W., 41 Miles. The weather being clear gave us an opportunity to View the Country, which had a very agreeable and promising aspect, diversified with hills, ridges, plains, and Valleys, with some few small lawns; but for the most part the whole was covered with wood, the hills and ridges rise with a gentle slope; they are not high, neither are there many of them.

Saturday, 21st.—Winds Southerly, a Gentle breeze, and Clear weather, with which we coasted along shore to the Northward. In the P.M. we saw the smoke of fire in several places; a Certain sign that the Country is inhabited. At 6, being about 2 or 3 Leagues from

[10] Now Rame Head or Ram Head.

[11] Gabo Island.

[12] Cape Howe, called after Admiral Earl Howe, is the south-east point of Australia. The position is almost exact (Wharton). Richard Howe, the first Earl Howe, was Treasurer of the Royal Navy at this time. The cape, which is actually on the border of Victoria and New South Wales, is low-lying. Howe Hill, rising to 1,292 feet, lies some five miles inland.

the land, we shortned Sail, and Sounded and found 44 fathoms, a sandy bottom. Stood on under an easey sail until 12 o'Clock, at which time we brought too until 4 A.M., when we made sail, having then 90 fathoms, 5 Leagues from the land. At 6, we were abreast of a pretty high Mountain laying near the Shore, which, on account of its figure, I named Mount Dromedary (Lat. 36° 18′ S., Long. 209° 55′ W.). The shore under the foot of the Mountain forms a point, which I have named Cape Dromedary, over which is a peaked hillock. At this time found the Variation to be 10° 42′ E. Between 10 and 11 o'Clock Mr. Green and I took several Observations of the Sun and Moon, the mean result of which gave 209° 17′ W. Longitude from the Meridian of Greenwich. By observation made yesterday we were in the Longitude 210° 9′. West 20′ gives 209° 49′ the Longitude of the Ship to-day at noon per yesterday's observation, the Mean of which and to-day's give 209° 33′ W., by which I fix the Longitude of this Coast. Our Latitude at Noon was 35° 49′ S.; Cape Dromedary bore S. 30° W., distant 12 Leagues. An Open Bay[13] wherein lay 3 or 4 Small Islands, bore N.W. by W., distant 5 or 6 Leagues. This Bay seem'd to be but very little Shelter'd from the Sea Winds, and yet it is the only likely Anchoring place I have yet seen upon the Coast.

Sunday, 22nd.—In the P.M. had a Gentle breeze at S. by W. with which we steer'd along shore N. by E. and N.N.E. at the distance of about 3 Leagues. Saw the smoke of fire in several places near the Sea beach. At 5, we were abreast of a point of land which, on account of its perpendicular Clifts, I call'd Point Upright; Lat. 35° 35′ S.; it bore from us due W., distant 2 Leagues, and in this Situation had 31 fathoms, Sandy bottom. At 6, falling little wind, we hauld off E.N.E.; at this time the Northermost land in sight bore N. by E. ½ E., and at midnight, being in 70 fathoms, we brought too until 4 A.M., at which time we made sail in for the land, and at daylight found ourselves nearly in the same Place we were at 5 o'Clock in the evening, by which it was apparent that we had been drove about 3 Leagues to the Southward by a Tide or Current in the night. After this we steer'd along shore N.N.E., having a Gentle breeze at S.W., and were so near the Shore as to distinguish several people upon the Sea beach. They appeared to be of a very dark or black Colour; but whether this was the real Colour of their skins or the Cloathes they might have on I know not. At Noon we were by Observation in the Latitude of 35° 27′ and Longitude 209° 23′; Cape Dromedary bore S. 28° W., distance 15 Leagues. A remarkable peak'd hill laying inland, the Top

[13] The inlet on which the tourist resort of Bateman's Bay now stands appears on Cook's chart as Bateman Bay, being named after Captain Nathaniel Bateman of the *Northumberland*. It continues to appear in the form Bateman Bay in Admiralty charts.

of which looked like a Pigeon house,[14] and occasioned my giving it that name, bore N. 32° 33′ W., and a small low Island,[15] laying close under the Shore, bore N.W., distance 2 or 3 Leagues; Variation of the Compass 9° 50′ E. When we first discover'd this Island in the morning I was in hopes, from its appearance, that we should have found Shelter for the Ship behind it; but when we came to approach it near I did not think that there was even security for a Boat to land. But this, I believe, I should have attempted had not the wind come on Shore, after which I did not think it safe to send a Boat from the Ship, as we had a large hollow Sea from the S.E. rowling in upon the land, which beat every where very high upon the Shore; and this we have had ever since we came upon the Coast. The land near the Sea coast still continues of a moderate height, forming alternately rocky points and Sandy beaches; but inland, between Mount Dromedary and the Pigeon house, are several pretty high Mountains, 2 only of which we saw but what were covered with Trees, and these lay inland behind the Pigeon House, and are remarkably flat a Top, with Steep rocky clifts all round them.[16] As far as we could see the Trees

A VIEW of the PIGEON HOUSE and Land adjacent

in this Country hath all the appearance of being stout and lofty. For these 2 days past the observed Latitude hath been 12 or 14 Miles to the Southward of the Ship's account given by the Log, which can be owing to nothing but a Current set to the Southward.

Monday, 23rd.—In the P.M. had a Gentle breeze at E., which in the night veer'd to N.E. and N. At ½ past 4 P.M., being about 5 Miles from the Land, we Tack'd and stood off S.E. and E. until 4 A.M., at which time we Tack'd and stood in, being then about 9 or 10 Leagues from the land. At 8, it fell little wind, and soon after Calm. At Noon we were by Observation in the Latitude of 35° 38′ and about 6 Leagues from the land, Mount Dromedary bearing S. 37° W., distant

[14] Pigeon House, 2,358 feet, is about twelve miles west of Ulladulla. Hawkesworth adds the information that Cook gave the name because the dome of the peak bore some resemblance to a dovecote.

[15] Brush Island.

[16] Budawang Range.

17 Leagues, and the Pidgeon house N. 40° W.; in this situation had 74 fathoms.

Tuesday, 24th.—In the P.M. had Variable light Airs and Calms until 6 o'Clock, at which time a breeze sprung up at N. by W.; at this time we had 70 fathoms Water, being about 4 or 5 Leagues from the land, the Pidgeon house bearing N. 40° W., Mount Dromedary S. 30° W., and the Northermost land in sight N. 19° E. Stood to the N.E. until Noon, having a Gentle breeze at N.W., at which time we Tack'd and stood to the Westward, being then, by observation, in the Latitude of 35° 10′ S. and Longitude 208° 51′ W. A point of land which I named Cape St. George, we having discovered it on that Saint's day, bore W., distant 19 Miles, and the Pidgeon house S. 7° W., the Latitude and Longitude of which I found to be 35° 19′ S. and 209° 42′ W. In the morning we found the Variation to be, by the Amplitude, 7° 50′ E., by several Azimuths 7° 54′ E.

Wednesday, 25th.—In the P.M. had a fresh breeze at N.W. until 3 o'Clock, at which time it came to West, and we Tack'd and stood to the Northward. At 5 o'Clock, being about 5 or 6 Leagues from the land, the Pidgeon house bearing W.S.W., distant 9 Leagues, sounded and had 86 fathoms. At 8, being very squally, with lightning, we close reef'd the Topsails and brought too, being then in 120 fathoms. At 3 A.M. made sail again to the Northward, having the advantage of a fresh Gale at S.W. At Noon we were about 3 or 4 Leagues from the land and in the Latitude of 34° 22′ and Longitude 208° 36′ W. Course and distance sail'd since Yesterday noon is N. by E. 49 Miles. In the Course of this day's run we saw the Smoke of fire in several places near the Sea beach. About 2 Leagues to the Northward of Cape St. George the Shore seems to form a bay,[17] which appear'd to be shelter'd from the N.E. winds; but as we had the wind it was not in my power to look into it, and the appearance was not favourable enough to induce me to loose time in beating up to it. The N. point of this bay, on account of its Figure, I nam'd Long Nose. Latitude 45° 4′ S., 8 Leagues to the Northward of this, is a point which I call'd Red Point; some part of the Land about it appeared of that Colour (Latitude 34° 29′ S., Longitude 208° 49′ W.). A little way inland to the

[17] Jervis Bay, a very fine port, but little use has been made of it up to the present time (Wharton). The bay has had an interesting history. It was named in 1791 by Lieutenant Brown of the *Atlantic*, in honour of Sir John Jervis of the Royal Navy, under whom Brown had served. With the development of the settlement at Sydney the inlet became a port for coastal vessels. By the 1915 Jervis Bay Acceptance Act an area of land on the south side of the bay was transferred from New South Wales to the Australian Commonwealth Territory to provide access by sea to the Federal capital. The Royal Australian Naval College was established here. By 1930 the inlet had become a popular holiday resort.

N.W. of this point is a round hill, the top of which look'd like the Crown of a Hatt.

Thursday, 26th.—Clear, serene weather. In the P.M. had a light breeze at N.N.W. until 5, at which time it fell Calm, we being then about 3 or 4 Leagues from the land and in 48 fathoms. Variation by Azimuth 8° 48′ E., the extreams of the land from N.E. by N. to S.W. by S. Saw several smokes along shore before dark, and 2 or 3 times a fire. In the Night we lay becalm'd, driving in before the Sea, until one o'Clock A.M., at which time we got a breeze from the land, with which we steer'd N.E., being then in 38 fathoms water. At Noon it fell little Wind, and veer'd to N.E. by N., we being then in the Latitude of 34° 10′ and Longitude 208° 27′ W., and about 5 Leagues from the land, which extended from S. 37° W. to N. ½ E. In this Latitude are some White Clifts, which rise perpendicular from the Sea to a moderate height.

Friday, 27th.—Var'ble light Airs between the N.E. and N.W., clear pleasant weather. In the P.M. stood off Shore until 2, then Tackt and Stood in till 6, at which time we tack'd and stood off, being then in 54 fathoms and about 4 or 5 miles from the land, the Extreams of which bore from S., 28° W. to N. 25° 30′ E. At 12 we tack'd and stood in until 4 A.M., then made a Trip off until day light, after which we stood in for the land; in all this time we lost ground, owing a good deal to the Variableness of the winds, for at Noon we were by Observation in the Latitude of 34° 21′ S., Red Point bearing S. 27° W., distant 3 Leagues. In this Situation we were about 4 or 5 Miles from the land, which extended from S. 19° 30′ W. to N. 29° E.

Saturday, 28th.—In the P.M. hoisted out the Pinnace and Yawl in order to attempt a landing, but the Pinnace took in the Water so fast that she was obliged to be hoisted in again to stop her leakes. At this time we saw several people a shore, 4 of whom where carrying a small Boat or Canoe, which we imagin'd they were going to put in to the Water in order to Come off to us; but in this we were mistaken. Being now not above 2 Miles from the Shore Mr. Banks, Dr. Solander, Tupia, and myself put off in the Yawl, and pull'd in for the land to a place where we saw 4 or 5 of the Natives, who took to the Woods as we approached the Shore; which disappointed us in the expectation we had of getting a near View of them, if not to speak to them. But our disappointment was heightened when we found that we no where could effect a landing by reason of the great Surff which beat everywhere upon the shore. We saw haul'd up upon the beach 3 or 4 small Canoes, which to us appeared not much unlike the Small ones of New Zeland. In the wood were several Trees of the Palm kind, and no under wood; and this was all we were able to observe from the boat, after which we return'd to the Ship about 5 in the evening.[18] At this time it fell Calm, and we were not above a Mile and a half from the Shore, in 11 fathoms, and within some breakers that lay to the Southward of us; but luckily a light breeze came off from the Land, which carried us out of danger, and with which we stood to the Northward. At daylight in the morning we discover'd a Bay,[19] which appeared to be tollerably well shelter'd from all winds, into which I resolved to go with the Ship, and with this View sent the Master in the Pinnace to sound the Entrance, while we keept turning up with the Ship, having the wind right out. At noon the Entrance bore N.N.W., distance 1 Mile.

Sunday, 29th.—In the P.M. wind Southerly and Clear weather, with which we stood into the bay and Anchored under the S. shore about 2 miles within the Entrance in 5 fathoms, the S. point bearing S.E. and the N. point E. Saw, as we came in, on both points of the bay, several of the Natives and a few hutts; Men, Women, and Children on the S. Shore abreast of the Ship, to which place I went in the Boats in hopes of speaking with them, accompanied by Mr. Banks, Dr. Solander, and Tupia.[20] As we approached the Shore they all made

[18] The place where Cook attempted to land is near Bulli, a place where there is now considerable export of coal. A large coal port, Wollongong, lies a little to the southward (Wharton). The town of Bulli is now part of the city of Wollongong.

[19] Botany Bay.

[20] Banks: Sir Joseph Banks (1743-1820), has been called "the father of Australia". As a young man with a considerable fortune he devoted himself to botanical pursuits and was elected a Fellow of the Royal Society at the unusually early age of twenty-three. About this time he met Solander. Banks accompanied Cook's expedition, and provided a staff of scientists and artists, including Dr Solander. Banks bore all the expenses of the botanical equipment and personnel, amounting to at least $20,000. His journals and the drawings of the artists provide an invaluable addition to the natural history observations made by Cook. Subsequently he took a great interest in the development of the first settlement and gave practical encouragement to Matthew Flinders, who added greatly to knowledge of the Australian coast. From 1778 until his death Banks was President of the Royal Society. An obelisk was erected to his memory at Kurnell in 1914, the place where Cook first set foot in Australia. A cape at the entrance to the bay was named in his honour by Captain Cook.

Solander: Daniel Carl Solander (1736-1782), born in Sweden, was a pupil of Linnaeus. He came to England at the age of twenty-four. As a member of Banks's staff on the *Endeavour* he collected many plant specimens, and was later associated with Banks in the preparation of *Illustrations of Australian Plants Collected in 1770 During Captain Cook's Voyage Round the World in H.M.S. Endeavour*, which was published by the British Museum at the beginning of the twentieth century. After acting as Banks's secretary and librarian for some time, Dr Solander became keeper of the Natural History Department of the British Museum.

Tupia: When the *Endeavour* left Tahiti Tupia was taken on board to act as interpreter and guide amongst the Pacific islands, for he claimed to be familiar with more than a hundred of them. Because of the affinity of Polynesian languages he proved invaluable in establishing contact with the Maoris of New Zealand, but

off, except 2 Men, who seem'd resolved to oppose our landing. As soon as I saw this I order'd the boats to lay upon their Oars, in order to speak to them; but this was to little purpose, for neither us nor Tupia could understand one word they said. We then threw them some nails, beads, etc., a shore, which they took up, and seem'd not ill pleased with, in so much that I thought that they beckon'd to us to come ashore; but in this we were mistaken, for as soon as we put the boat in they again came to oppose us, upon which I fir'd a musquet between the 2, which had no other Effect than to make them retire back, where bundles of their darts lay, and one of them took up a stone and threw at us, which caused my firing a Second Musquet,

BOTANY BAY.

load with small Shott; and altho' some of the shott struck the man, yet it had no other effect than making him lay hold on a Target. Immediately after this we landed,[21] which we had no sooner done

he could not help in interpreting the several Australian Aboriginal languages and dialects. According to the late Leslie G. Kelly, the proper rendering of his name is Tupaia. He came from the island Ra'iatea where he was high priest to Purea, the chieftainess of Ha'apape and wife of Amo, chief of Papara. He lost his influence when Purea was defeated by Teu, chief of Pare, and so was ready to accompany Cook.

21 The district where Cook first landed in Australia, near the south head of Botany Bay, is now called Kurnell, a corruption of the Aboriginal name Kundel. The first to land was probably Midshipman Isaac Smith, a cousin of Mrs Cook, who later became a rear-admiral. A tablet has been affixed to rocks to commemorate the

than they throw'd 2 darts at us; this obliged me to fire a third shott, soon after which they both made off, but not in such haste but what we might have taken one; but Mr. Banks being of Opinion that the darts were poisoned, made me cautious how I advanced into the Woods.[22] We found here a few small hutts[23] made of the Bark of Trees, in one of which were 4 or 5 Small Children, with whom we left some strings of beads, etc. A quantity of Darts lay about the Hutts; these we took away with us. 3 Canoes lay upon the beach, the worst I think I ever saw; they were about 12 or 14 feet long, made of one piece of the Bark of a Tree, drawn or tied up at each end, and the middle keept open by means of pieces of Stick by way of Thwarts.[24] After searching for fresh water without success, except a little in a Small hole dug in the Sand, we embarqued, and went over to the N. point of the bay, where in coming in we saw several people; but when we landed now there were nobody to be seen. We found here some fresh Water, which came trinkling down and stood in pools among the rocks; but as this was troublesome to come at I sent a party of men ashore in the morning to the place where we first landed to dig holes in the sand, by which means and a Small stream they found fresh Water sufficient to Water the Ship. The String of Beads, etc., we had left with the Children last night were found laying in the Hutts this morning; probably the Natives were afraid to take them away. After breakfast we sent some Empty Casks a shore and a party of Men to cut wood, and I went myself in the Pinnace to sound and explore the Bay, in the doing of which I saw some of the Natives; but they all fled at my Approach. I landed in 2 places, one of which the people had but just left, as there were small fires and fresh Muscles

---

occasion. A public reserve is known as Captain Cook's Landing Place, and Cape Solander is included in the reserve. A number of Cook monuments have been erected in the district—tablets to the honour of Cook and Banks on the cliff at the heads, monuments to honour Cook and Solander, and a memorial to Banks.

22 The "darts" were no doubt spears. Banks's warning was a sound one, but it was not the habit of the Aborigines to poison their throwing spears, as Cook himself noted the following day.

23 Huts were erected as temporary shelter. The bark variety consisted of a cross-bar on two supports with a sheet of bark folded over it in the shape of a tent-fly, or simply a bark sheet bent in two and stood on end to form a windbreak. Other kinds of hut were made of grass and branches bent into the shape of an old-fashioned beehive.

24 A good description of native canoes, which were quickly made and adequate for sheltered inlets. The method of manufacture was ingenious. Two rings circling the trunk of a stringy bark tree were cut with an axe, ten feet or more apart, and a vertical cut made between them. The complete sheet of bark was then levered off the trunk, and held over a fire to soften it. It was bent in two and the ends sewn together with fibre, pieces of wood then being placed in position to keep the sides apart. These primitive canoes were poled in shallow water, or propelled with a piece of bark as a paddle.

broiling upon them; here likewise lay Vast heaps of the largest Oyster Shells I ever saw.

Monday, 30th.—As soon as the Wooders and Waterers were come on board to Dinner 10 or 12 of the Natives came to the watering place, and took away their Canoes that lay there, but did not offer to touch any one of our Casks that had been left ashore; and in the afternoon 16 or 18 of them came boldly up to within 100 yards of our people at the watering place, and there made a stand. Mr. Hicks, who was the Officer ashore, did all in his power to intice them to him by offering them presents; but it was to no purpose, all they seem'd to want was for us to be gone. After staying a Short time they went away. They were all Arm'd with Darts and wooden Swords;[25] the darts have each 4 prongs, and pointed with fish bones. Those we have seen seem to be intended more for striking fish than offensive Weapons; neither are they poisoned, as we at first thought. After I had return'd from sounding the Bay I went over to a Cove on the N. side of the Bay, where, in 3 or 4 Hauls with the Sean, we caught about 300 pounds weight of Fish, which I caused to be equally divided among the Ship's Company. In the A.M. I went in the Pinnace to sound and explore the N. side of the bay, where I neither met with inhabitants or anything remarkable. Mr. Green took the Sun's Meridian Altitude a little within the S. Entrance of the Bay, which gave the Latitude 34° 0′ S.

Tuesday, May 1st.—Gentle breezes, Northerly. In the P.M. 10 of the Natives again visited the Watering place. I, being on board at this time, went immediately ashore, but before I got there they were going away. I follow'd them alone and unarm'd some distance along shore, but they would not stop until they got farther off than I choose to trust myself. These were armed in the same manner as those that came Yesterday. In the evening I sent some hands to haul the Saine, but they caught but a very few fish. A little after sunrise I found the Variation to be 11° 3′ E. Last night Forby Sutherland, Seaman, departed this Life, and in the A.M. his body Was buried ashore at the watering place, which occasioned my calling the south point of this bay after his name.[26] This morning a party of us went ashore to some Hutts, not far from the Watering place, where some of the Natives are daily seen; here we left several articles, such as

[25] There was no weapon that could properly be called a sword. Those mentioned may possibly have been boomerangs, but were almost certainly woomeras. In describing woomeras in some detail (page 133), Cook wrote: "These throwing sticks we at first took for wooden swords, and perhaps on some occasions they may use them as such."

[26] A tablet to his memory has been erected on Sutherland Point.

Cloth, Looking Glasses, Coombs, Beads, Nails, etc.; after this we made an Excursion into the Country, which we found diversified with Woods, Lawns, and Marshes. The woods are free from underwood of every kind, and the trees are at such a distance from one another that the whole Country, or at least great part of it, might be Cultivated without being obliged to cut down a single tree. We found the Soil every where, except in the Marshes, to be a light white sand, and produceth a quantity of good Grass, which grows in little Tufts about as big as one can hold in one's hand, and pretty close to one another; in this manner the Surface of the Ground is Coated. In the woods between the Trees Dr. Solander had a bare sight of a Small Animal something like a Rabbit,[27] and we found the Dung of an Animal which must feed upon Grass,[28] and which, we judge, could not be less than a Deer; we also saw the Track of a Dog, or some such like Animal. We met with some Hutts and places where the Natives had been, and at our first setting out one of them was seen; the others, I suppose, had fled upon our Approach. I saw some Trees that had been cut down by the Natives with some sort of a Blunt instrument, and several Trees that were barqued, the bark of which had been cut by the same instrument; in many of the Trees, especially the Palms, were cut steps of about 3 or 4 feet asunder for the conveniency of Climbing them. We found 2 Sorts of Gum, one sort of which is like Gum Dragon,[29] and is the same, I suppose, Tasman took for Gum lac; it is extracted from the largest tree in the Woods.

Wednesday, 2nd.—Between 3 and 4 in the P.M. we return'd out of the Country, and after Dinner went ashore to the watering place, where we had not been long before 17 or 18 of the Natives appeared in sight. In the morning I had sent Mr. Gore, with a boat, up to the head of the Bay to drudge for Oysters; in his return to the Ship he and another person came by land, and met with these people, who followed him at the Distance of 10 or 20 Yards. Whenever Mr. Gore made a stand and faced them they stood also, and notwithstanding they were all Arm'd, they never offer'd to Attack him; but after he had parted from them, and they were met by Dr. Monkhouse and one or 2 more, who, upon making a Sham retreat, they throw'd 3 darts

27 Possibly a kangaroo-rat, but more likely a marsupial bandicoot, of which two species could be represented (Troughton).

28 The grass-feeding animal was doubtless one of the kangaroo family, ranging from the small scrub or pademelon wallaby to the larger brush-wallaby (genus *Wallabia*) or, more probably, the Great-Grey or Forester Kangaroo, according to the size of the pellets, which Cook refers to as not less than those of a deer (Troughton).

29 Probably *Angophora costata*, Rusty Gum (sometimes called Smooth-barked Apple or Sydney Red Gum); or otherwise *Eucalyptus gummifera*, Red Bloodwood (Mair).

after them, after which they began to retire. Dr. Solander, I, and Tupia made all the haste we could after them, but could not, either by words or Actions, prevail upon them to come near us. Mr. Gore saw some up the Bay, who by signs invited him ashore, which he prudently declined. In the A.M. had the wind in the S.E. with rain, which prevented me from making an Excursion up the head of the bay as I intended.

NATIVES OF NEW HOLLAND.

Thursday, 3rd.—Winds at S.E., a Gentle breeze and fair weather. In the P.M. I made a little excursion along the Sea Coast to the Southward, accompanied by Mr. Banks and Dr. Solander. At our first entering the woods we saw 3 of the Natives, who made off as soon as they saw us; more of them were seen by others of our people, who likewise made off as soon as they found they were discover'd. In the A.M. I went in the Pinnace to the head of the bay, accompanied by Drs. Solander and Monkhouse, in order to Examine the Country, and to try to form some Connections with the Natives. In our way thither we met with 10 or 12 of them fishing, each in a Small Canoe, who retir'd into Shoald water upon our approach. Others again we saw at the first place we landed at, who took to their Canoes, and fled before we came near them; after this we took Water, and went almost to the head of the inlet, were we landed and Travel'd some distance in land. We found the face of the Country much the same as I have before described, but the land much richer for instead of sand I found in many places a deep black soil, which we thought was

Capable of producing any kind of grain.[30] At present it produceth, besides Timber, as fine Meadow as ever was seen; however, we found it not all like this, some few places were very rocky, but this, I believe, to be uncommon. The stone is sandy, and very proper for building, etc. After we had sufficiently examin'd this part we return'd to the Boat, and seeing some Smoke and Canoes at another part we went thither, in hopes of meeting with the people, but they made off as we approached. There were 6 Canoes and 6 small fires near the Shore, and Muscles roasting upon them, and a few Oysters laying near; from this we conjectured that there had been just 6 people, who had been out each in his Canoe picking up the Shell fish, and come a Shore to eat them, where each had made his fire to dress them by. We tasted of their Cheer, and left them in return Strings of beads, etc. The day being now far spent, we set out on our return to the Ship.

Friday, 4th.—Winds northerly, serene weather. Upon my return to the Ship in the evening I found that none of the Natives had Appear'd near the Watering place, but about 20 of them had been fishing in their Canoes at no great distance from us. In the A.M., as the Wind would not permit us to sail, I sent out some parties into the Country to try to form some Connections with the Natives. One of the Midshipmen met with a very old man and Woman and 2 Small Children; they were Close to the Water side, where several more were in their Canoes gathering of Shell fish, and he, being alone, was afraid to make any stay with the 2 old People least he should be discovr'd by those in the Canoes. He gave them a bird he had Shott, which they would not Touch; neither did they speak one word, but seem'd to be much frightned. They were quite Naked; even the Woman had nothing to cover her nudities. Dr. Monkhouse and another Man being in the Woods, not far from the watering place, discover'd 6 more of the Natives, who at first seem'd to wait his coming; but as he was going up to them he had a dart thrown at him out of a Tree, which narrowly escaped him. As soon as the fellow had thrown the dart he descended the Tree and made off, and with him all the rest, and these were all that were met with in the Course of this day.

Saturday, 5th.—In the P.M. I went with a party of Men over to the

30 This report was the cause of much criticism when the First Fleet arrived and subsequently had to leave Botany Bay for Port Jackson in search of more fertile land. Dr Beaglehole states that Cook was referring rather to the absence of the undergrowth and heavy timber which would require felling before cultivation could be commenced than to the fertility of the soil. Nevertheless Cook emphasised the richness of the black soil he found there, and in this he was correct for it is found in some parts of the Botany Bay district.

North Shore, and while some hands were hauling the Sean, a party of us made an Excursion of 3 or 4 Miles into the Country, or rather along the Sea Coast. We met with nothing remarkable; great part of the Country for some distance inland from the Sea Coast is mostly a barren heath, diversified with Marshes and Morasses. Upon our return to the Boat we found they had caught a great number of small fish, which the sailors call leather Jackets[31] on account of their having a very thick skin; they are known in the Wt. Indies. I had sent the Yawl in the morning to fish for Sting rays, who returned in the Evening with upwards of four hundred weight; one single one weigh'd 240 lbs. Exclusive of the entrails. In the A.M., as the wind Continued Northerly, I sent the Yawl again a fishing, and I went with a party of Men into the Country, but met with nothing extraordinary.

Sunday, 6th.—In the evening the Yawl return'd from fishing, having Caught 2 Sting rays weighing near 600 lbs. The great quantity of plants Mr. Banks and Dr. Solander found in this place occasioned my giving it the Name of Botany Bay.[32] It is situated in the Lat. of 34° 0′ S., Long. 208° 37′ W. It is capacious, safe, and

31 Most likely to be *Scobinichthys granulatus*. It is possible that there was more than one species, including *Monocanthus macrolepis* (Whitley).

32 The bay was at first called Stingray Bay. The plan of it at the Admiralty is called by this name, and none of the logs know Botany Bay. It seems probable that Cook finally settled on the name after the ship left, and when Banks had had time to examine his collections. A monument was erected in 1870 near the spot, on the southern side, where Cook first landed. Botany Bay was intended to be the site where the first settlement of convicts should be made, but on the arrival of Captain Phillip, on 18 January, 1788, he found it so unsuited for the number of his colony that he started in a boat to examine Broken Bay. On his way he went into Port Jackson, and immediately decided on settling there. On the 25th and 26th the ships went round, and Sydney was founded (Wharton).

Later research has added to Wharton's knowledge of the naming of Botany Bay. The first name was given alternatively as Sting-Ray Harbour, Sting-Rays Harbour, and Stingrays Bay. Apart from its appearance as Botany Bay on the chart of the *Endeavour*, Banks's journal recorded the name Botany Bay, but only during a later stage in the voyage. A comparatively recent discovery shows that Cook altered Sting-Rays Harbour to Botanist Bay and then to Botany Bay, because of "the great quantity of New Plants &ca. Mr Banks & Dr Solander collected in this place".

Cook himself was impressed by the promise of the vegetation on the shores, while Banks became even more enthusiastic about it with the passing of time. By 1779 we find him warmly recommending Botany Bay before a committee of the House of Commons as a suitable site for a penal colony, and subsequently supporting other schemes for settlement. When in 1786 the government decided to send convicts to this locality Banks became one of the prime movers and supporters of the scheme. He maintained correspondence with the governors of Australia for some years and was interested in all the developments of the colony.

Wharton's note reminds us that Governor Phillip found the land unsuitable for cultivation, but at least Banks's opinion was vindicated in later years when the northern and western shores of Botany Bay were largely devoted to the cultivation of vegetables. Cook's connection with his first landing place is further recalled in the name Cook's River, which flows into the north-western corner of the harbour.

Commodious; it may be known by the land on the Sea Coast, which is of a pretty even and moderate height, Rather higher than it is inland, with steep rocky Clifts next the Sea, and looks like a long Island lying close under the Shore. The Entrance of the Bay lies about the Middle of this land. In coming from the Southward it is discover'd before you are abreast of it, which you cannot do in coming from the Northward; the entrance is little more than a Quarter of a Mile broad, and lies in W.N.W. To sail into it keep the S. shore on board until within a small bare Island, which lies close under the North Shore. Being within that Island the deepest of Water is on that side, 7, 6 and 5 fathoms a good way up; there is Shoald Water a good way off from

NATIVE OF NEW HOLLAND WITH BOOMERANG.

the S. Shore—from the inner So. Point quite to the head of the harbour; but over towards the N. and N.W. Shore is a Channell of 12 or 14 feet at low Water, 3 or 4 Leagues up, to a place where there is 3 or 4 fathoms; but there I found very little fresh Water. We Anchor'd near the South Shore about a Mile within the Entrance for the Conveniency of Sailing with a Southerly wind and the getting of Fresh Water; but I afterwards found a very fine stream of fresh Water on the N. shore in the first sandy Cove within the Island, before which the Ship might lay almost land locked, and wood for fuel may be got everywhere. Although wood is here in great plenty,[33] yet there is very little Variety; the bigest trees are as large or larger than our Oaks in England, and grows a good deal like them, and Yields a reddish Gum; the wood itself is heavy, hard, and black like

[33] The forests here are mostly of the *Eucalyptus* species.

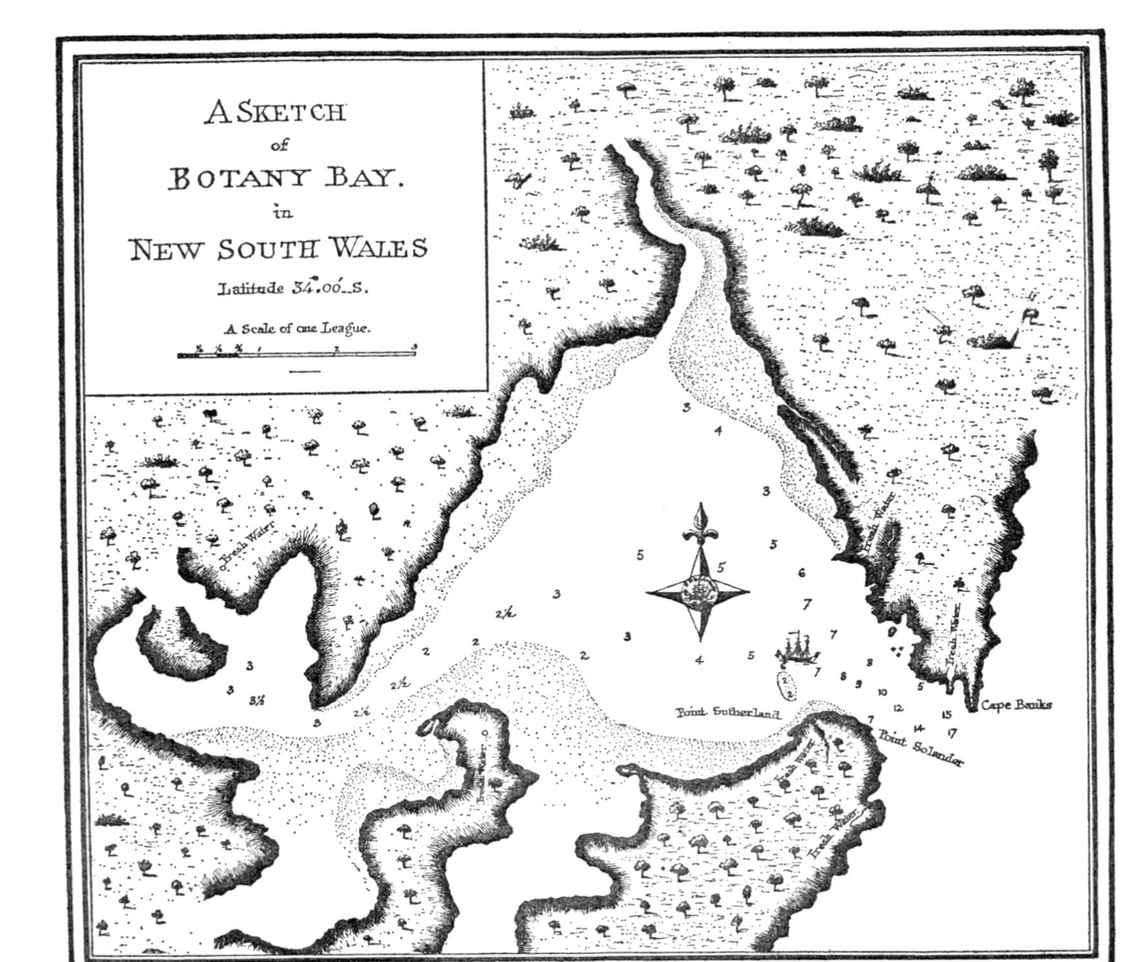
A Sketch
of
Botany Bay.
in
New South Wales
Latitude 34°.00′. S.
A Scale of one League.
Fresh Water
Point Sutherland
Point Solander
Cape Banks

Lignum Vitæ.[34] Another sort that grows tall and Strait something like Pines—the wood of this is hard and Ponderous, and something of the Nature of America live Oak. These 2 are all the Timber trees I met with; there are a few sorts of Shrubs and several Palm Trees and Mangroves about the Head of the Harbour. The Country is woody, low, and flat as far in as we could see, and I believe that the Soil is in general sandy. In the Wood are a variety of very beautiful birds, such as Cocatoos, Lorryquets, Parrots,[35] etc., and crows[36] Exactly like those we have in England. Water fowl[37] is no less plenty about the head of the Harbour, where there is large flats of sand and Mud, on which they seek their food; the most of these were unknown to us, one sort especially, which was black and white, and as large as a Goose, but most like a Pelican.[38] On the sand and Mud banks are Oysters, Muscles, Cockles, etc., which I believe are the Chief support of the inhabitants, who go into Shoald Water with their little Canoes and peck them out of the sand and Mud[39] with their hands, and sometimes roast and Eat them in the Canoe, having often a fire for that purpose, as I suppose, for I know no other it can be for. The Natives do not appear to be numerous, neither do they seem to live in large bodies, but dispers'd in small parties along by the Water side. Those I saw were about as tall as Europeans, of a very dark brown Colour, but not black, nor had they woolly, frizled hair, but black and lank like ours. No sort of Cloathing or Ornaments were ever seen by any of us upon any one of them, or in or about any of their Hutts; from which I conclude that they never wear any. Some that we saw had their faces and bodies painted with a sort of White Paint or Pigment. Altho' I have said that shell fish is their Chief support, yet they catch

34 Possibly *Casuarina glauca*, Swamp Oak (Mair).

35 These could be of several species. Black Cockatoos are mentioned in the Journal but the localities are not precisely stated. The Rainbow Lorikeet (*Trichoglossus moluccanus*) was described and figured as the "Blue-bellied Parrot" in Peter Brown's *New Illustrations of Zoology*, 1776, and stated to be "very numerous at Botany Bay". This is the earliest known published illustration of an Australian parrot (Hindwood).

36 The Australian Raven (*Corvus corvus coronoides*). It is the only species of the genus occurring near Sydney (Hindwood).

37 A number of species such as ducks could be covered by this entry (Hindwood).

38 Most probably the Black and White or Semipalmated Goose, now exterminated in these parts (Wharton). Doubtless the Australian Pelican (*Pelecanus conspicillatus*). Wharton's remark that the bird could be the Semipalmated Goose is but a guess. This species did occur near Sydney in the early days but generally in freshwater swamps, and not close to the coast. It is quite distinctive and does not resemble the pelican (Hindwood).

39 Botany Bay oysters are *Ostrea*. In general, cockles and mussels are unidentifiable to genus. Several kinds could have been referred to (McMichael). The so-called mud oysters were to be found on the coasts of New South Wales, Victoria, South Australia, Western Australia, and Tasmania, on a sandy bottom and in rock crevices. They are not as plentiful as rock oysters, and it has not proved possible to cultivate them commercially.

other sorts of fish, some of which we found roasting on the fire the first time we landed; some of these they strike with Gigs,[40] and others they catch with hook and line; we have seen them strike fish with gigs, and hooks and lines are found in their Hutts. Sting rays, I believe, they do not eat, because I never saw the least remains of one near any of their Hutts or fire places. However, we could know but very little of their Customs, as we never were able to form any Connections with them; they had not so much as touch'd the things we had left in their Hutts on purpose for them to take away. During our stay in this Harbour I caused the English Colours to be display'd ashore every day, and an inscription to be cut out upon one of the Trees near the Watering place, setting forth the Ship's Name, Date, etc. Having seen everything this place afforded, we, at daylight in the morning, weigh'd with a light breeze at N.W., and put to Sea, and the wind soon after coming to the Southward we steer'd along shore N.N.E., and at Noon we were by observation in the Latitude of 33° 50′ S., about 2 or 3 Miles from the Land, and abreast of a Bay, wherein there appear'd to be safe Anchorage, which I called Port Jackson.[41] It lies 3 leagues to the Northward of Botany Bay. I had almost forgot to mention that it is high water in this Bay at the full and change of the Moon about 8 o'Clock, and rises and falls upon a Perpendicular about 4 or 5 feet.

40 A fishing implement like a trident (Wharton).

41 Cook having completed his water at Botany Bay, and having many hundreds of miles of coast before him, did not examine Port Jackson, the magnificent harbour in which Sydney, the capital of New South Wales, now lies. His chart gives the shape of what he could see very accurately, but the main arm of the harbour is hidden from the sea. He named the bay after Mr (afterwards Sir George) Jackson, one of the Secretaries of the Admiralty. This fact is recorded on a tablet in the Bishop Stortford Church to the memory of Sir George Duckett, which name Sir George had assumed in later years. This interesting evidence was brought to light by Sir Alfred Stephen, Lieutenant-Governor of New South Wales, and puts an end to the legend which was long current, that Port Jackson was named after a sailor who first saw it. There was, moreover, no person of the name of Jackson on board (Wharton).

Jackson was Judge Advocate of the Fleet. His name was later changed to Duckett on account of a provision in the will of the uncle of his second wife. He followed Cook's career with interest, probably because as a boy the navigator had worked as a stable boy for Jackson's sister at Ayton, Yorkshire. The inscription in the Bishop Stortford Church reads:

> To the memory of Sir Geo. Jackson, Bart., afterwards Sir Geo. Duckett, Bart., who died Dec. 15, 1822, aged 97; for many years Secretary of the Admiralty and M.P. Capt Cook, of whom he was a zealous friend and early patron, named after him Port Jackson in N. Zealand and Port Jackson in N.S. Wales.

Jackson's name is also preserved in Port Jackson in the Coromandel Peninsula, New Zealand. In contrast to the harbour of the great metropolis of Sydney, Port Jackson in New Zealand has a population of about twenty.

When Botany Bay was found to be unsuitable for the establishment of a convict settlement, Governor Arthur Phillip entered the harbour on 21 January 1788 and decided to establish the settlement there.

Monday, 7th.—Little wind, Southerly, and Serene pleasant Weather. In the P.M. found the Variation by several Azimuths to be 8° E.; at sunset the Northermost land in sight bore N. 26° E.; and some broken land that appear'd to form a bay bore N. 40° W., distant 4 Leagues. This Bay I named Broken bay,[42] Lat. 33° 36′ S. We steer'd along shore N.N.E. all night at the distance of about 3 Leagues from the land, having from 32 to 36 fathoms, hard sandy bottom. A little after sunrise I took several Azimuths with 4 Needles belonging to the Azimuth Compass, the mean result of which gave the Variation of 7° 56′ E. At Noon we were by observation in the Lat. of 33° 22′ S., and about 3 Leagues from the land, the Northermost part of which in sight bore N. 19° E. Some pretty high land which projected out in 3 bluff Points, and occasioned my calling it Cape 3 Points (Lat. 33° 33′ S.), bore S.W., distant 5 Leagues; Long. made from Botany Bay 0° 19′ E.

Tuesday, 8th.—Variable Light Airs and Clear weather. In the P.M. saw some smooks upon the Shore, and in the Evening found the Variation to be 8° 25′ E.; at this time we were about 2 or 3 Miles from the land, and had 28 fathoms Water. Our situation at Noon was nearly the same as Yesterday, having advanced not one Step to the Northward.

Wednesday, 9th.—Winds northerly; most part a fresh breeze, with which we stood off Shore until 12 at Night. At the distance of 5 Leagues from the land had 70 fathoms, at the distance of 6 Leagues 80 fathoms, which is the Extent of the Soundings, for at the Distance of 10 Leagues off we had no ground with 150 fathoms. Stood in Shore until 8 o'Clock A.M., and hardly fetched Cape Three Points; having a little wind at N.W. by N., we tack'd, and stood off until Noon, at which Time we Tack'd with the wind at N.N.E., being then in the Lat. of 33° 37′ S., Cape Three Points bearing N.W. by W., distance 4 Leagues.

Thursday, 10th.—In the P.M., had the wind at N.E. by N., with which we stood in Shore until near 4 o'Clock, when we Tack'd in 23 fathoms Water, being about a Mile from the land, and as much to the Southward of Cape 3 Points. In the night the wind veer'd to N.W. and W., and in the morning to S.W. Having the advantage of a light Moon, we made the best of our way along shore to the North-

42 The Hawkesbury River, the largest on the east coast of Australia, runs into Broken Bay (Wharton). It is now a popular harbour for pleasure boats. The suburbs of Sydney extend as far as the southern shores. However, the bay to which Cook gave the name is several miles distant from present-day Broken Bay. See Beaglehole's note in Volume One, p. 313, of the Hakluyt edition of Cook's Journals.

ward. At Noon we were by observation in the Lat. of 32° 53′ S., and Long. 208° 0′ W., and about 2 Leagues from the land, which extended from N. 41° E. to S. 41° W. A small round rock or Island,[43] laying close under the land, bore S. 82° W., distance 3 or 4 Leagues. At sunrise in the Morning found the Variation to be 8° E. In the Lat. of 33° 2′ S., a little way inland, is a remarkable hill, that is shaped like the Crown of a Hatt, which we past about 9 o'Clock in the forenoon.

Friday, 11th.—Winds Southerly in the day, and in the night Westerly; a Gentle breeze and Clear weather. At 4 P.M. past, at the distance of one Mile, a low rocky point which I named Point Stephens (Lat. 32° 45′); on the N. side of this point is an inlet which I called Port Stephens[44] (Lat. 32° 40′; Long. 207° 51′), that appear'd to me from the Masthead to be shelter'd from all Winds. At the Entrance lay 3 Small Islands,[45] 2 of which are of a Tolerable height, and on the Main, near the shore, are some high round hills that make at a distance like Islands.[46] In passing this bay at the distance of 2 or 3 miles from the Shore our soundings were from 33 to 27 fathoms; from which I conjectured that there must be a sufficient depth of Water for Shipping in the bay. We saw several smokes a little way in the Country upon the flat land; by this I did suppose that there were Lagoons which afforded subsistance for the Natives, such as shell-fish, etc., for we as yet know nothing else they have to live upon. At ½ past 5, the Northermost land in sight bore N. 36° E., and Point Stephens S.W., distant 4 Leagues, at which time we took in our Steerings[47] and run under an Easey sail all night until 4 A.M., when we made all sail; our soundings in the night were from 48 to 62 fathoms, at the distance of between 3 and 4 Leagues from the land. At 8 we were abreast of a high point of Land, which made in 2 Hillocks;

[43] Nobby Head, at the entrance of Newcastle Harbour, formed by the Hunter River. Newcastle is the great coal port of New South Wales. It has a population of 20,000, and exports 1,500,000 tons of coal in the year (Wharton).

Nobby's Head, as it is now known, has had a varied history. Cook describes it as a round rock or island. It is now connected to the mainland by a breakwater which was built in the early part of the nineteenth century. Since Wharton edited the journals, Newcastle has become the second largest city in New South Wales, the population having increased ten-fold. Coal exports amount to nearly five million tons.

[44] Called after Mr Stephens, one of the Secretaries to the Admiralty. It is a large and fine harbour (Wharton). Later Sir Philip Stephens. Cook did not enter the harbour. The first ship to do so was the convict transport *Salamander* in 1791. It was explored by Governor Macquarie at the beginning of 1812, but was not thought suitable for settlement. A few years later a timber industry was established there. At various times bold plans for development have been put forward, including a proposal to establish a naval base, but Port Stephens is now primarily a holiday resort.

[45] Cabbage Tree Island, Boondelbah Island, and Little Island.

[46] Broughton Islands.

[47] Studding sails (Wharton).

this point I called Cape Hawke[48] (Lat. 32° 14′ S., Long. 207° 30′ W.). It bore from us at this time W. distant 8 Miles, and the same time the Northermost land in sight bore N. 6° E., and appear'd high and like an Island. At Noon this land bore N. 8° E., the Northermost land in sight N. 13° E., and Cape Hawke S. 37° W. Lat. in per Observation 32° 2′ S., which was 12 Miles to the Southward of that given by the Log, which I do suppose to be owing to a Current setting that way. Course and distance sail'd since Yesterday at Noon was first N.E. by E., 27 Miles, then N. 10° E., 37 Miles; Long. in 207° 20′ W.; Variation per morning Amplitude and Azimuth 9° 10′ E.

Saturday, 12th.—Winds Southerly, a Gentle breeze in the P.M. As we run along Shore we saw several smokes a little way in land from the Sea, and one upon the Top of a hill, which was the first we have seen upon elevated ground since we have been upon the Coast. At sunset we were in 23 fathoms, and about a League and a half from the land, the Northermost part of which we had in sight bore N. 13° E.; and 3 remarkable large high hills lying Contigious to each other, and not far from the shore, bore N.N.W. As these Hills bore some resemblance to each other we called them the 3 Brothers. We steer'd N.E. by N. all Night, having from 27 to 67 fathoms, from 2 to 5 and 6 Leagues from the Land, and at day light we steer'd N. for the Northermost land we had in sight. At noon we were 4 Leagues from the Land, and by observation in the Lat. of 31° 18′ S., which was 15 miles to the Southward of that given by the Log. Our Course and distance made good since Yesterday noon was N. 24° E., 48 miles. Long. 206° 58′ W.; several smokes seen a little way in land.

Sunday, 13th.—In the P.M. stood in shore with the Wind at N.E. until 6, at which time we Tack'd, being about 3 or 4 miles from the land, and in 24 fathoms. Stood off shore with a fresh breeze at N. and N.N.W. until midnight, then Tack'd, being in 118 fathoms and 8 Leagues from the Land. At 3 a.m. the wind veer'd to the Westward, and we Tack'd and stood to the Northward. At noon we were by Observation in the Lat. of 30° 43′ S., and Long. 206° 45′ W., and about 3 or 4 Leagues from the Land, the Northermost part of which bore from us N. 13° W.; and a point or head land, on which were fires that Caused a great Quantity of smoke, which occasioned my giving it the name of Smokey Cape,[49] bore S.W., distant 4 Leagues; it

[48] After Admiral Sir Edward Hawke, First Lord of the Admiralty (Wharton). The First Lord was also commemorated by Cook in Hawke Bay, which gives its name to the province of Hawke's Bay in New Zealand.

[49] A lighthouse has been erected on Smoky Cape. A hill about a mile north of the cape which rises to more than a thousand feet, was subsequently named Big Smoky.

is moderately high land. Over the pitch of the point is a round hillock; within it 2 others, much higher and larger, and within them very low land (Lat. 30° 51′, Long. 206° 5′ W.). Besides the smoke seen upon this Cape we saw more in several places along the Coast. The observed Lat. was only 5 Miles to the Southward of the Log.

Monday, 14th.—At the P.M. it fell Calm, and continued so about an hour, when a breeze sprung up at N.E., with which we stood in shore until 6 o'Clock, when, being in 30 fathoms and 3 or 4 Miles from the land, we Tack'd, having the wind at N.N.W. At this time Smoky Cape bore S. ¾° W., distant about 5 Leagues, and the Northermost land in sight N. ¼° E. At 8 we made a Trip in shore for an hour; after this the wind came off Shore, with which we stood along shore to the Northward, having from 30 to 21 fathoms, at the distance of 4 or 5 Miles from the Land. At 5 A.M. the Wind veer'd to N., and blow'd a fresh breeze, attended with Squalls and dark cloudy weather. At 8 it began to Thunder and Rain, which lasted about an Hour, and then fell Calm, which gave us an opportunity to sound, and found 86 fathoms, being about 4 or 5 Leagues from the Land; after this we got the wind Southerly, a fresh breeze and fair weather, and we Steer'd N. by W. for the Northermost land we had in sight. At noon we were about 4 Leagues from the land, and by observation in the Lat. of 30° 22′ S., which was 9 Miles to the Southward of that given by the Log. Long. in 206° 39′ W., and Course and distance made good since Yesterday Noon N. 16° E., 22 miles; some Tolerable high land near the Shore bore W. As I have not mentioned the Aspect of the Country since we left Botany Bay, I shall now describe it as it hath at different times appear'd to us. As we have advanced to the Northward the land hath increased in height, in so much that in this Latitude it may be called a hilly Country; but between this and Botany Bay it is diversified with an agreeable variety of Hills, Ridges, and Valleys, and large plains all Cloathed with wood, which to all appearance is the same as I have before mentioned, as we could discover no Visible alteration in the Soil. Near the shore the land is in general low and Sandy, except the points which are rocky, and over many of them are pretty high hills, which at first rising out of the Water appear like a Island.

Tuesday, 15th.—Fresh Gales at S.W., W.S.W., and S.S.W. In the P.M. had some heavy Squalls, attended with rain and hail, which obliged us to close reef our Topsails. Between 2 and 4 we had some small rocky Islands[50] between us and the land; the Southermost lies in the Lat. of 30° 10′, the Northermost in 29° 58′, and about 2 Leagues

[50] The Solitary Islands (Wharton). So named by Cook on his chart.

or more from the land; we sounded, and had 33 fathoms about 12 Miles without this last Island. At 8 we brought too until 10, at which time we made sail under our Topsails. Having the Advantage of the Moon we steer'd along shore N. and N. by E., keeping at the distance of about 3 Leagues from the land having from 30 to 25 fathoms. As soon as it was daylight we made all the sail we could, having the Advantage of a fresh Gale and fair weather.[51] At 9, being about a League from the Land, we saw upon it people and Smoke in Several places. At noon we were by observation in the Lat. of 28° 39′ S., and Long. 206° 27′ W.; Course and distance saild since Yesterday at Noon N. 6° 45′ E., 104 Miles. A Tolerable high point of land bore N.W. by W., distant 3 Miles; this point I named Cape Byron[52] (Lat. 28° 37′

A VIEW of CAPE BYRON and MOUNT WARNING

30″ S., Long. 206° 30′ W.). It may be known by a remarkable sharp peaked Mountain lying in land N.W. by W. from it. From this point the land Trends N. 13° W. Inland it is pretty high and hilly, but near the Shore it is low; to the Southward of the Point the land is low, and Tolerable level.

Wednesday, 16th.—Winds Southerly, a fresh Gale, with which we steer'd N. along shore until sunset, at which time we discover'd breakers ahead, and on our Larboard bow, being at this time in 20 fathoms, and about 5 miles from the land. Haul'd off E. until 8, at which time we had run 8 Miles, and had increased our Depth of Water to 44 fathoms. We then brought too with her head to the Eastward, and lay on this Tack until 10 o'Clock, when, having increased our Soundings to 78 fathoms, we wore and lay with her head in shore until 5 o'Clock a.m., when we made Sail. At daylight we were surprized by finding ourselves farther to the Southward than

51 During the night the entrance of the Clarence River, now the outlet for the produce of a large and rich agricultural district, was passed, and in the morning that of the Richmond River, which serves a similar purpose (Wharton).

52 Captain John Byron was one of Cook's predecessors in the exploration in the Pacific, having sailed round the world in H.M.S. *Dolphin*, in company with the *Tamar*, in 1764-66 (Wharton). Captain Byron was the grandfather of the poet Lord Byron. The cape is the most easterly point of the mainland.

we were in the evening, and yet it had blown strong all night Southerly. We now saw the breakers again within us, which we passed at the distance of about 1 League; they lay in the Lat. of 28° 8′ S., and stretch off E. 2 Leagues from a point under which is a small Island;[53] their situation may always be found by the peaked mountain before mentioned, which bears S.W. by W. from them, and on their account I have named it Mount Warning. It lies 7 or 8 Leagues in land in the Lat. of 28° 22′ S. The land is high and hilly about it, but it is Conspicuous enough to be distinguished from everything else. The point off which these shoals lay I have named Point Danger;[54] to the Northward of it the land, which is low, Trends N.W. by N.; but we soon found that it did not keep that direction long before it turn'd again to the Northward. At Noon we were about 2 Leagues from the land, and by observation in the Lat. of 27° 46′, which was 17 Miles to the Southward of the Log; Long. 206° 26′ W. Mount Warning bore S. 20° W., distant 14 Leagues; the Northermost land in sight bore N. Our Course and distance made good since yesterday N. 1° 45′ W., 53 miles.

Thursday, 17th.—Winds Southerly, mostly a fresh breeze, with which in the P.M. we steer'd along shore N. ¾ E., at the distance of about 2 Leagues off. Between 4 and 5 we discover'd breakers on our Larboard bow; our Depth of Water at this time was 37 fathoms. At sunset the Northermost land in sight bore N. by W., the breakers N.W. by W., distant 4 Miles, and the Northermost land set at Noon, which form'd a Point, I named Point Lookout, bore W., distant 5 or 6 Miles (Lat. 27° 6′).[55] On the North side of this point the shore forms a wide open bay, which I have named Morton's Bay,[56] in the Bottom of which the land is so low that I could but just see it from the Topmast head. The breakers I have just mentioned lies about 3 or 4 Miles from Point Lookout; at this time we had a great Sea from the Southward, which broke prodigious high upon them. Stood on N.N.E. until 8, when, being past the breakers, and having Deepned

53 Dr Beaglehole remarks that this island is doubtless Cook Island, which is off Fingal Head, some two miles south of Point Danger.

54 Point Danger is the boundary point on the coast between New South Wales and Queensland (Wharton).

55 There is some mistake in this latitude. It should be 27° 26′ (Wharton).

56 James, Earl of Morton, was President of the Royal Society in 1764, and one of the Commissioners of Longitude (Wharton).

A misspelling in Hawkesworth's edition of Cook's Journals has resulted in Cape Morton being perpetuated as Cape Moreton. Better known is Moreton Bay (for the suburbs of Brisbane now extend to the western shore) and Moreton Island, all of which should have preserved Cook's spelling. Moreton Island was named by Matthew Flinders seven years after the publication of the Hawkesworth edition. In doing so Flinders recorded that the island "would have received that name from Captain Cook had he known of its insularity".

our water to 52 fathoms, we brought too until 12 o'Clock, then made sail to the N.N.E. At 4 A.M. we sounded, and had 135 fathoms. At daylight I found that we had in the night got much farther to the Northward and from the Shore than I expected from the Course we steer'd, for we were at least 6 or 7 Leagues off, and therefore hauled in N.W. by W., having the Advantage of a Fresh Gale at S.S.W. The Northermost land seen last night bore from us at this time S.S.W., distant 6 Leagues. This land I named Cape Morton, it being the North point of the Bay of the same Name (Lat. 26° 56′ S., Long. 206° 28′). From C. Morton the Land Trends away W., further than we could see, for there is a small space where we could see no land; some on board where of opinion that there is a River there because the Sea looked paler than usual. Upon sounding we found 34 fathoms fine white sandy bottom, which alone is Sufficient change, the apparent Colour of Sea Water, without the Assistance of Rivers. The land need only to be low here, as it is in a Thousand other places upon the Coast, to have made it impossible for us to have seen it at the distance we were off. Be this as it may, it was a point that could not be clear'd up as we had the wind; but should any one be desirous of doing it that may come after me, this place may always be found by 3 Hills which lay to the Northward of it in the Lat. of 26° 53′ S. These hills lay but a little way inland, and not far from Each other; they are very remarkable on account of their Singular form of Elivation, which very much resembles Glass Houses,[57] which occasioned my giving them that Name. The Northermost of the 3 is the highest and largest. There are likewise several other peaked hills inland to the Northward of these, but they are not near so remarkable. At Noon we were by Observation in the Lat. of 26° 28′ S., which was 10 Miles to the Northward of the Log; a Circumstance that hath not hapned since we have been upon the Coast before. Our Course and distance run since Yesterday noon was N. by W. 80 Miles, which brought us into the Long. of 206° 46′. At this time we were about 2 or 3 Leagues from the land, and in 24 fathoms Water; a low bluff point, which was the Southern point of an open Sandy bay,[58] bore N. 52° W., distant 3 Leagues, and the Northermost point of land in sight bore N. ¼ E. Several Smokes seen to-day, and some pretty far inland.

57 The Glass Houses form a well-known sea mark on entering Moreton Bay, as the name is now written. Brisbane, the capital of Queensland, stands on the river of the same name, which falls into Moreton Bay (Wharton).

The "Glass Houses" to which Cook referred were the glass furnaces of his native Yorkshire. He remarked on only three of these remarkable peaks (though he noted other lesser ones), but in fact there are eleven main peaks, the highest of which is 1,823 feet. The Glasshouse Mountains are forty-five miles north of Brisbane.

58 Laguna Bay. The point is called Low Bluff (Wharton).

Friday, 18th.—In steering along shore at the distance of 2 Leagues off our Soundings was from 24 to 32 fathoms Sandy bottom. At 6 P.M. the N. point set at Noon bore N. ¼ W., distant 4 Leagues; at 10 it bore N.W. by W. ½ W., and as we had seen no land to the Northward of it we brought too, not knowing which way to steer, having at this time but little wind, and continued so for the most part of the night. At 2 P.M. we made sail with the wind at S.W., and at daylight saw the land extending as far as N. ¾ E. The point set last night bore S.W. by W., distant 3 or 4 Leagues; I have named it Double Island Point, on account of its figure (Lat. 25° 58′ S., Long. 206° 48′ W.). The land within this point is of a moderate and pretty equal height, but the point itself is of such an unequal Height that it looks like 2 Small Islands laying under the land; it likewise may be known by the white Clifts on the N. side of it. Here the land trends to the N.W., and forms a large open bay,[59] in the bottom of which the land appear'd to be very low, in so much that we could but just see it from the Deck. In crossing the mouth of this bay our Depth of Water was from 30 to 32 fathoms, a white sandy bottom. At Noon we were about 3 Leagues from the Land, and in the Lat. of 25° 34′ S., Long. 206° 45′ W.; Double Island Point bore S. ¾ W., and the Northermost land in sight N. ¾ E. The land hereabouts, which is of a moderate height, appears more barren than any we have yet seen on this Coast, and the Soil more sandy, there being several large places where nothing else is to be seen; in other places the woods look to be low and Shrubby, nor did we see many signs of inhabitants.

Saturday, 19th.—In the P.M. had Variable light Airs and Calms; in the night had a light breeze from the land, which in the A.M. veer'd to S.W. and S.S.W. In the evening found the Variation to be 8° 36′ E., and in the Morning 8° 20′; as we had but little wind we keept to the Northward all night, having from 23 to 27 fathoms fine sandy bottom, at the Distance of 2 or 3 Leagues from the Land. At Noon we were about 4 Miles from it, and by observation in the Lat. of 25° 4′, and in this situation had but 13 fathoms; the Northermost land in Sight bore N. 21° W., distant 8 Miles; our Course and distance saild since yesterday at Noon was N. 13° 15′ E., 31 Miles.

Sunday, 20th.—Winds Southerly, Gentle breezes. At 10 p.m. we passed, at the distance of 4 Miles, having 17 fathoms, a black bluff head or point of land, on which a number of the Natives were

59 Wide Bay (Wharton). It is now a heavily industrialised area with both primary and secondary industries.

Assembled, which occasioned my naming it Indian Head;[60] Lat. 25° 0'. N. by W., 4 Miles from this head, is another much like it. From this last the land Trends a little more to the Westward, and is low and Sandy next the Sea, for what may be behind it I know not; if land, it must be all low, for we could see no part of it from the Mast head. We saw people in other places besides the one I have mentioned; some Smokes in the day and fires in the Night. Having but little wind all Night, we keept on to the Northward, having from 17 to 34 fathoms, from 4 Miles to 4 Leagues from the Land, the Northermost part of which bore from us at daylight W.S.W., and seem'd to End in a point, from which we discover'd a Reef stretching out to the Northward as far as we could see, being, at this time, in 18 fathoms; for we had, before it was light, hauld our Wind to the Westward, and this course we continued until we had plainly discover'd breakers a long way upon our Lee Bow, which seem'd to Stretch quite home to the land. We then Edged away N.W. and N.N.W., along the E. side of the Shoal, from 2 to 1 Miles off, having regular, even Soundings, from 13 to 7 fathoms; fine sandy bottom. At Noon we were, by Observation, in the Lat. of 24° 26' S., which was 13 Miles to the Northward of that given by the Log. The extream point of the Shoal we judged to bear about N.W. of us; and the point of land abovementioned bore S. ¾ W., distant 20 Miles. This point I have named Sandy Cape,[61] on account of 2 very large white Patches of Sand upon it. It is of a height Sufficient to be seen 12 Leagues in Clear weather (Lat. 24° 46', Long. 206° 51' W.); from it the Land trends away W.S.W. and S.W. as far as we could see.

Monday, 21st.—In the P.M. we keept along the E. side of the Shoal until 2, when, judging there was water for us over, I sent a Boat a Head to sound, and upon her making the Signal for more than 5 fathoms we hauld our wind and stood over the Tail of it in 6 fathoms. At this time we were in the Lat. of 24° 22' S., and Sandy Cape bore S. ½ E., distant 8 Leagues; but the Direction of the Shoal is nearest N.N.W. and S.S.E. At this time we had 6 fathoms; the boat which was not above ¼ of a mile to the Southward of us had little more than 5 fathoms. From 6 fathoms we had the next Cast, 13, and then 20 immediately, as fast as the Man could heave the Lead; from

60 It was the custom of all the British explorers to call the native inhabitants of the South Seas Indians, a term which persisted for many years.

61 Sandy Cape is the northern point of Great Sandy Island. A long narrow channel separates the latter from the mainland, and opens at its northern end into Hervey Bay, a great sheet of water forty miles across. This channel is now much used by the coasting trade, as it avoids the long *détour* round Breaksea Spit, a most dangerous shoal (Wharton). The *Endeavour* skirted the east coast of Fraser or Great Sandy Island. Unknown to Cook, it was separated from the mainland by a narrow strait.

this I did suppose that the W. side of the Shoal is pretty steep too, whereas on the other side we had gradual Soundings from 13 to 7 fathoms. This Shoal I called Break Sea Spit, because now we had smooth water, whereas upon the whole Coast to the Southward of it we had always a high Sea or swell from the S.E. At 6, the Land of Sandy Cape extending from S. 17° E. to S. 27° E., distance 8 Leagues; Depth of Water, 23 fathoms, which depth we keept all Night, as we stood to the Westward with light Airs from the Southward; but between 12 and 4 A.M. we had it Calm, after which a Gentle breeze sprung up at S., with which we still keept on upon a Wind to the Westward. At 7 we Saw from the Masthead the Land of Sandy Cape bearing S.E. ½ E., distance 12 or 13 Leagues. At 9, we discover'd from the Mast head land to the Westward, and soon after saw smooke upon it. Our depth of Water was now decreased to 17 fathoms, and by Noon to 13, at which time we were by observation in the Lat. of 24° 28′ S., and about 7 Leagues from the Land, which extended from S. by W. to W.N.W. Long. made from Sandy Cape 0° 45′ W.[62]

A VIEW of SANDY CAPE bearing S. distant 5 Leagues

For these few days past we have seen at times a sort of Sea fowl we have no where seen before that I remember; they are of the sort called Boobies.[63] Before this day we seldom saw more than 2 or 3 at a time, and only when we were near the land. Last night a small flock of these birds passed the Ship and went away to the N.W., and this morning from ½ an hour before sun rise to half an hour after, flights of them were continually coming from the N.N.W., and flying to the S.S.E., and not one was seen to fly in any other direction. From this we did suppose that there was a Lagoon, River, or Inlet of Shallow Water to the Southward of us, where these birds resorted to in the day to feed, and that not very far to the Northward lay some Island, where they retir'd too in the night.

Tuesday, 22nd.—In the P.M. had a Gentle breeze at S.E., with which we stood in for the land S.W. until 4, when, being in the Lat.

[62] The large bay to the south-west of Breaksea Spit appears on Cook's chart as Hervey Bay, and was named for Captain Augustus John Hervey, who later became third Earl of Bristol, and was promoted to admiral.

[63] Possibly the Brown Gannet (*Sula leucogaster*) (Hindwood).

of 24° 36′ S., and about 2 Leagues from land, in 9 fathoms, we bore away along shore N.W. by W.; at the same time we could see the land extending to the S.S.E. about 8 Leagues. Near the Sea the land is very low, but inland are some moderately high hills, and the whole appeared to be thickly Cloathed with wood. In running along shore we shoaled our Water from 9 to 7 fathoms, and at one time had but 6 fathoms, which determined me to Anchor for the Night, and accordingly at 8 o'Clock we came too in 8 fathoms, fine gravelly bottom, about 5 miles from the land. This evening we saw a Water Snake, and 2 or 3 evenings ago one lay under the Ship's Stern some time; this was about 1½ Yards in length, and was the first we had seen. At 6 A.M. weighed with a Gentle breeze Southerly, and Steer'd N.W. ¼ W., edging in for the land until we got within 2 Miles of it, having from 7 to 11 fathoms; we then steer'd N.N.W. as the land laid. At Noon we were by Observation in the Lat. of 24° 19′ S.; Long. made from Sandy Cape 1° 14′ W.

Wednesday, 23rd.—Continued our Course alongshore at the distance of about 2 Miles off, having from 12 to 9, 8 and 7 fathoms, until 5 o'Clock, at which time we were abreast of the South point of a Large open Bay,[64] wherein I intended to Anchor. Accordingly we hauld in Close upon a Wind, and sent a boat ahead to sound; after making some Trips we Anchored at 8 o'Clock in 5 fathoms, a Sandy bottom. The South pt. of the bay bore E. ¾ S., distant 2 Miles; the North point N.W. ¼ N., about 2 Miles from the shore, in the bottom of the bay. Last night, some time in the Middle watch, a very extraordinary affair hapned to Mr. Orton, my Clerk. He having been drinking in the evening, some Malicious person or persons in the Ship took Advantage of his being Drunk, and cut off all the Cloaths from off his back; not being satisfied with this, they some time after went into his Cabin and cut off a part of both his Ears as he lay a Sleep in his Bed. The person whom he suspected to have done this was Mr. Magra, one of the Midshipmen; but this did not appear to me. Upon enquiry, however, as I had been told that Magra had once or twice before this in their drunken Frolicks cut off his cloaths, and had been heard to say (as I was told) that if it was not for the Law he would Murder him, these things consider'd, induced me to think that Magra was not Altogether innocent. I therefore for the present dismiss'd him the Quarter deck, and Suspended him from doing any duty in the Ship, he being one of those Gentlemen frequently found on board King's Ships that can very well be spared; besides, it was necessary in me to show my immediate resentment against the person on whom

[64] Bustard Bay (Wharton). See page 63. The name appears on Cook's chart, together with North Head and South Head.

the suspicion fell, least they should not have stop'd here. With respect to Mr. Orton, he is a man not without faults; yet from all the inquiry I could make, it evidently appear'd to me that so far from deserving such Treatment, he had not designed injuring any person in the Ship; so that I do–and shall always–look upon him as an injured man. Some reasons, however, might be given why this misfortune came upon him, in which he himself was in some measure to blame; but as this is only conjecture, and would tend to fix it upon some people in the Ship, whom I would fain believe would hardly be guilty of such an Action, I shall say nothing about it, unless I shall hereafter discover the Offenders, which I shall take every method in my power to do, for I look upon such proceedings as highly dangerous in such Voyages as this, and the greatest insult that could be offer'd to my Authority in this Ship, as I have always been ready to hear and redress every complaint that have been made against any Person in the Ship.[65]

In the A.M. I went ashore with a party of men in order to Examine the Country, accompanied by Mr. Banks and the other Gentlemen; we landed a little within the S. point of the Bay, where there is a Channel leading into a large Lagoon. The first thing that I did was to sound and examine the Channell, in which I found 3 fathoms, until I got about a Mile up it, where I met with a Shoal, whereon was little more than one fathom; being over this I had 3 fathoms again. The Entrance into this Channell lies close to the South point of this Bay, being form'd on the East by the Shore, and on the West by a large Spit of sand; it is about a ¼ of a Mile broad, and lies in S. by W.; here is room for a few Ships to lay very secure, and a small Stream of Fresh Water. After this I made a little excursion into the Woods while some hands made 3 or 4 hauls with the Sean, but caught not above a dozen very small fish. By this time the flood was made, and I imbarqued in the Boats in order to row up the Lagoon; but in this I was hindred by meeting everywhere with Shoal Water. As yet we had seen no people, but saw a great deal of Smook up and on the West side of the Lagoon, which was all too far off for us to go by land, excepting one; this we went to and found 10 Small fires in a very small Compass, and some Cockle Shells laying by them, but the people were gone. On the windward or S. side of one of the fires was stuck up a little Bark about a foot and a half high, and some few pieces lay about in other places; these we concluded were all the covering they had in the Night, and many of them, I firmly believe, have not this, but,

[65] This history of Mr Orton's misadventure is omitted from the Admiralty copy. It is an illustration of the times to note that the fact of Orton having got drunk does not seem to call for the Captain's severe censure. In these days, though the practical joker receives punishment, the drunkard would certainly come in for a large share also (Wharton).

naked as they are, sleep in the open air.[66] Tupia, who was with us, observed that they were Taata Eno's;[67] that is, bad or poor people. The Country is visibly worse than at the last place we were at; the soil is dry and Sandy, and the woods are free from underwoods of every kind; here are of the same sort of Trees as we found in Bottany Harbour, with a few other sorts. One sort, which is by far the most Numerous sort of any in the Woods, grow Something like birch; the Bark at first sight looks like birch bark, but upon examination I found it to be very different, and so I believe is the wood; but this I could not examine, as having no axe or anything with me to cut down a Tree.[68] About the Skirts of the Lagoon grows the true Mangrove,[69] such as are found in the West Indies, and which we have not seen during the Voyage before; here is likewise a sort of a palm Tree,[70] which grows on low, barren, sandy places in the So. Sea Islands. All, or most of the same sort, of Land and Water fowl as we saw at Botany Harbour we saw here; besides these we saw some Bustards,[71] such as we have in England, one of which we kill'd that weighed 17½ pounds, which occasioned my giving this place the Name of Bustard Bay[72] (Lat. 24° 4′, Long. 208° 22′ W.); we likewise saw some black and white Ducks. Here are plenty of small Oysters sticking to the Rocks, Stones, and Mangrove Trees, and some few other shell fish, such as large Muscles, Pearl Oysters, Cockels, etc.[73] I measured the perpendicular height of the last Tide, and found it to be 8 foot above low water mark, and from the time of low water to-day I found that it must be high Water at the full and Change of the Moon at 8 o'Clock.

66 It was a common practice for the Aborigines to construct windbreaks about 18 inches in height, usually of branches or brushwood or, as in this case, of sheets of bark. The members of a family huddled together for warmth in the shelter of the low wall, often with a fire at their feet or beside them, and these were replenished at intervals during the night.

67 Evil men. In the language of Tahiti "ino" means evil of any kind, "taata" is a man. Thus "E taata parau ino rahi roa ra" is "A man whose counsel is evil". In the Maori language "taata ino" becomes "tangata kino".

68 The "birch"-like species is uncertain. The *Eucalyptus* spp. here are not the same as those at Botany Bay (Mair).

69 *Rhizophora* sp. is probably meant by "true mangrove", but other mangroves would also be present, including *Bruguiera* and *Ceriops*, and these were collected. *Rhizophora* is the mangrove with stilt roots found on many tropical coasts (Mair).

70 Cannot be identified with certainty.

71 Australian Bustard (*Eupodotis australis*) (Hindwood).

72 The site of Cook's landing was north of Bundaberg, and as this is the first place on which he set foot in what later became the state of Queensland, a memorial has been erected to commemorate the first landing by a European.

73 *Crassostrea* (McMichael). Rock oysters occur plentifully on the eastern coast of Queensland and as far south as Victoria. They are delicate in flavour and have good keeping qualities. They are now cultivated successfully. It was found that black mangrove sticks were the ideal type of pole to use in the beds, for the oysters could readily be stripped from them, and the timber resisted boring organisms.

Thursday, 24th.—In the P.M. I was employ'd ashore in the Transactions before related; at 4 a.m. we weighed with a Gentle breeze at S., and made sail out of the Bay. In standing out our soundings were from 5 to 15 fathoms; when in this last Depth we were abreast of the North Point,[74] and being daylight we discover'd breakers stretching out from it about N.N.E., 2 or 3 miles; at the Outermost point of them is a Rock just above Water. In passing these rocks at the distance of ½ a mile we had from 15 to 20 fathoms; being past them, we hauld along shore W.N.W. for the farthest land we had in sight. At Noon we were by Observation in the Lat. of 23° 52′ S.; the North part of Bustard Bay bore S. 62° E., distance 10 miles, and the Northermost land in sight N. 60° W. Long. in 208° 37′ W., distance from the nearest shore 6 Miles; in this situation had 14 fathoms water.

Friday, 25th.—In the P.M. had it calm until 5, when a light breeze sprung up at S.E., and we steer'd N.W. as the land lay until 10, then brought too, having had all along 14 and 15 fathoms. At 5 A.M. we made sail; at daylight the Northermost point of the Main bore N. 70° W., and soon after we saw more land making like Islands, bearing N.W. by N.; at 9 we were abreast of the point, distant from it 1 mile; Depth of Water 14 fathoms. I found this point to lay directly under the Tropic of Capricorn, and for that reason call it by that Name.[75] Long. 209° 0′ W. It is of a Moderate height, and looks white and barren, and may be known by some Islands which lie to the N.W. of it, and some small Rocks one League S.E. from it; on the West side of the Cape there appeared to be a Lagoon. On the 2 Spits which form the Entrance were a great Number of Pelicans;[76] at least, so I call them. The most northermost land we could see bore from C. Capricorn N. 24° W., and appeared to be an Island;[77] but the Main land Trended W. by N. ½ N., which Course we steer'd, having from 15 to 16 fathoms and from 6 to 9, a hard sandy bottom. At Noon our Lat. by Observation was 23° 24′ S.; C. Capricorn bore S. 60° E., distance 2 Leagues; a small Island N. by E. 2 Miles.[78] In this Situation had 9 fathoms at the distance of 4 Miles from the Main land, which is here low and Sandy next the Sea, except the points which are moderately high and rocky; in land the Country is hilly, and affords but a very indifferent prospect.[79]

[74] Now known as Bustard Head.

[75] Cape Capricorn is at the northern end of Curtis Island. The islands some forty miles to the east are known as the Capricorn Group.

[76] Australian Pelican (*Pelecanus conspicillatus*) (Hindwood).

[77] Hummocky Island (Wharton).

[78] Dr Beaglehole conjectures that this may be North-west Island, one of the Capricorn Group.

[79] Between Bustard Bay and C. Capricorn is Port Curtis, in which stands the small town of Gladstone. C. Capricorn is the eastern point of Curtis Island, and to

Saturday, 26th.—In the P.M. light breezes at E.S.E., with which we stood to the N.W. until 4 o'Clock, when it fell calm, and soon after we Anchored in 12 fathoms. C. Capricorn bearing S. 54° E., distant 4 Leagues, having the Main land and Islands in a manner all around us. In the night we found the tide to rise and fall near 7 feet, and the flood to set to the Westward and Ebb to the Eastward; which is quite the reverse to what we found it when at Anchor to the Eastward of Bustard Bay. At 6 a.m. we weigh'd with the Wind at S., a Gentle breeze, and stood away to the N.W., between the Outermost range of Islands[80] and the Main land, leaving several small Islands between us and the Latter, which we passed Close by. Our soundings was a little irregular, from 12 to 4 fathoms, which caused me to send a Boat ahead to sound. At noon we were about 3 Miles from the Main, about the same distance from the Islands without us; our Lat. by Observation was 23° 7′ S., and Long. made from Cape Capricorn 18 Miles Wt. The Main land in this Lat. is tolerable high and Mountainious; and the Islands which lay off it are the most of them pretty high and of a Small Circuit, and have more the appearance of barrenness than fertility. We saw smookes a good way in land, which makes me think there must be a River, Lagoon, or Inlet,[81] into the Country, and we passed 2 places that had the Appearance of such this morning; but our Depth of Water at that Time was too little to haul in for them, where I might expect to meet with less.

Sunday, 27th.—We had not stood on to the Northward quite an hour before we fell into 3 fathoms, upon which I anchor'd, and Sent away the Master with 2 Boats to sound the Channell, which lay to Leeward of us between the Northermost Island and the Main Land, which appear'd to me to be pretty broad; but I suspected that it was Shoal, and so it was found, for the Master reported to me upon his return that he found in many places only 2½ fathoms, and where we lay at Anchor we had only 16 feet, which was not 2 feet more than the Ship drew.[82] In the Evening the wind veer'd to E.N.E., which gave us an opportunity to stretch 3 or 4 miles back the way we Came

---

the northward is Keppel Bay, into which falls the Fitzroy River. Up the latter, thirty-five miles from the sea, is Rockhampton, the second largest town of Queensland. All this coast is encumbered with shoals, outside of which Cook had so far prudently kept. To seaward begins the long chain of islands and reefs known as the Great Australian Barrier, which stretches up to Torres Strait. Cook was unaware of their existence, as they were out of sight, but he became painfully acquainted with them later, where the reefs approach the land, and make navigation along the coast anxious work; but he here began to get into difficulties with the shoals which stretch off the coast itself (Wharton).

80 The Keppel Islands (Wharton).

81 The Fitzroy River.

82 This was between Great Keppel Island and the Main. There is a mass of shoals here (Wharton).

before the Wind Shifted to S., and obliged us again to Anchor in 6 fathoms. At 5 o'Clock in the A.M. I sent away the Master with 2 Boats to search for a Passage out between the Islands, while the Ship got under sail. As soon as it was light the Signal was made by the boats of their having found a Passage, upon which we hoisted in the Boats, and made sail to the Northward as the land lay; soundings from 9 to 15 fathoms, having still Some small Islands without us.[83] At noon we were about 2 Leagues from the Main Land, and by observation in the Lat. of 22° 53′ S., Long. made from Cape Capricorn 0° 20′ W. At this time the Northermost point of Land we had in sight bore N.N.W., dist. 10 Miles; this point I named Cape Manyfold,[84] from the Number of high Hills over it; Lat. 22° 43′ S.; it lies N. 20° W., dist. 17 Leagues from C. Capricorn. Between them the shore forms a large Bay, which I call'd Keppel Bay, and the Islands which lay in and Off it are known by the same name; in this Bay is good Anchorage, where there is a sufficient depth of Water; what refreshment it may afford for Shipping I know not.[85] We caught no fish here, notwithstanding we were at Anchor; it can hardly be doubted but what it afforded fresh Water in several places, as both Mainland and Islands are inhabited. We saw smokes by day and fires in the night upon the Main, and people upon one of the Islands.

Monday, 28th.—Winds at S.S.E., a fresh breeze. At 3 o'Clock in the P.M. we passed Cape Manifold, from which the Land Trends N.N.W. The land of this Cape is tolerable high, and riseth in hills directly from the Sea; it may be known by 3 Islands laying off it, one near the Shore, and the other 2 Eight Miles out at Sea; the one of these is low and flat, and the other high and round.[86] At 6 o'Clock we shortnd sail and brought too; the Northermost part of the Main we had in sight bore N.W., and some Islands lying off it bore N. 31° W.; our soundings since Noon were from 20 to 25 fathoms, and in the Night 30 and 34 fathoms. At day light we made Sail, Cape Manifold bearing S. by E., distance 8 Leagues, and the Islands set last night in the same directions, distance from us 4 Miles. The farthest point of the Main bore N. 67° W., distant 22 Miles; but we could see several Islands to the Northward of this direction.[87] At 9 o'Clock we were

[83] The ship passed out between Great Keppel Island and North Keppel Island (Wharton).

[84] Now appearing on the map with the conventional spelling Cape Manifold.

[85] As before mentioned, the Fitzroy River falls into Keppel Bay, and forms a good harbour, though much encumbered with sand banks (Wharton). Keppel Bay and Keppel Islands were named after Viscount Keppel, a naval commander who later became First Lord of the Admiralty.

[86] Peak and Flat Islands (Wharton). So named by Matthew Flinders. The former is correctly "Peaked Island". They appear on Cook's chart as "The 2 Brothers".

[87] The easternmost of the Northumberland Islands (Wharton).

abreast of the above point, which I named Cape Townshend[88] (Lat. 22° 13′, Long. 209° 48′ W.); the land of this Cape is of a moderate and pretty even height, and is more barren than woody. Several Islands lay to the Northward of it, 4 or 5 Leagues out at Sea. 3 or 4 Leagues to the S.E. the Shore forms a bay,[89] in the bottom of which there appeared to be an inlet or Harbour to the Westward of the Coast, and Trends S.W. ½ S.; and these form a very large Bay, which turns away to the Eastward, and probably communicates with the Inlet above mentioned, and by that Means makes the land of the Cape an Island.[90] As soon as we got round the Cape we hauld our wind to the Westward in order to get within the Islands which lay scatter'd up and down in this bay in great number, and extend out to Sea as far as we could see from the Masthead; how much farther will hardly be in my power to determine; they are as Various in their height and Circuit as they are numerous.[91] We had not stood long upon a Wind before we meet with Shoal Water, and was obliged to Tack about to avoid it; after which I sent a boat ahead, and we

[88] Charles Townshend was Chancellor of the Exchequer 1767 (Wharton). Charles Townshend was the uncle of Thomas Townshend who later became first Viscount Sydney. Dr Beaglehole notes that the Charles Townshend who was honoured by Cook was not the Chancellor of the Exchequer who died in 1767 but his cousin who was known as "Spanish Charles" because of his diplomatic service in Spain. The cape is situated on an island to which Matthew Flinders extended the same name "to do honour to the noble family of Townshend". It is thought that Thomas Townshend believed that New South Wales would be "a very proper place" for a convict settlement. As Secretary of State for the Home Department, Thomas Townshend was responsible for arranging the dispatch of the first fleet and the appointment of Captain Phillip as leader of the expedition. In view of the fact that he reprimanded Phillip for seeking a new site when Botany Bay proved unsuitable, it is ironic that his name should be perpetuated in the largest city in Australia. Phillip gave the name to Sydney Cove in honour of Thomas Townshend, Viscount Sydney and the name was adopted for the settlement.

[89] Shoalwater Bay, a large inlet (Wharton). Dr Beaglehole has a valuable note on this portion of the text in the Hakluyt edition of *The Journals of Captain James Cook*, Volume One, page 329, in which he states that the text of the Journal is corrupt, for the words "Coast and" should read "Cape the land". Wharton had therefore misinterpreted the meaning, and in endeavouring to regularise the text by amending the punctuation, had distorted it. The complete sentence commencing "3 or 4 Leagues . . . Cape an Island" should read: "3 or 4 Leagues to the S.E. the Shore forms a bay in the bottom of which there appeared to be an inlet or Harbour. To the westward of the Cape the land trends SW½S° and there forms a very large bay which turns away to the Eastward, and probably communicates with the Inlet above mentioned, and by that means makes the land of the Cape an Island."

The first bay mentioned in the Journal, seen three or four leagues to the south-east, was doubtless Port Clinton, not Shoalwater Bay, as Beaglehole has noted; whereas the "very large Bay which turns away to the Eastward" is Shoalwater Bay.

[90] Cape Townshend is actually on Townshend Island at the head of Shoalwater Bay. The southern arm of the bay does not penetrate to the coast. The coastal area is therefore a peninsula, not an island as Cook suspected.

[91] The Northumberland Islands, a very extensive group (Wharton). Although not mentioned in the Journal, the name of this extensive group appears on Cook's chart, and was conferred in honour of Hugh Percy, first Duke of Northumberland.

bore away W. by N., leaving many small Islands, Rocks, and Shoals between us and the Main, and a number of Large Islands without us; soundings from 14 to 17 fathoms, Sandy Bottom. A little before noon the boat made the Signal for meeting with Shoal Water, upon which we hauld close upon a Wind to the Eastward, but suddenly fell into 3¼ fathoms water, upon which we immediately let go an Anchor, and brought the Ship up with all sails standing, and had then 4 fathoms Coarse sandy bottom. We found here a strong Tide setting to the N.W. by W. ½ W., at the rate of between 2 and 3 Miles an Hour, which was what Carried us so quickly upon the Shoal. Our Latitude by Observation was 22° 8′ S.; C. Townshend bore E. 16° S., distant 13 Miles, and the Westermost part of the Main Land in sight W. ¾ N., having a number of Islands in sight all round us.[92]

Tuesday, 29th.—Fresh gales between the S.S.E. and E.S.E., Hazey weather, with some showers of rain. In the P.M., having sounded about the Ship, and found that their was Sufficient Water for her over the Shoal, we at 3 o'Clock weigh'd and made Sail, and stood to the Westward as the Land lay, having first sent a boat ahead to sound. At 6 we Anchor'd in 10 fathoms, Sandy bottom, about 2 Miles from the Main Land, the Westermost part of which bore W.N.W., having still a Number of Islands in sight a long way without us. At 5 a.m. I sent away the Master with 2 Boats to sound the Entrance of an inlet, which bore from us W., distance about 1 League, into which I intended to go with the Ship to wait a few days, until the Moon increased, and in the meantime to examine the Country. By such time as we had got the Ship under Sail the Boats made the Signal for Anchorage, upon which we stood in with the Ship, and Anchor'd in 5 fathoms, about a League within the Entrance of the inlet, which we judged to be a River running a Good way inland, as I observed the Tides to flow and Ebb something considerable.[93] I had some thoughts of laying the Ship a Shore to Clean her bottom. With this view both the Master and I went to look for a Convenient place for that purpose, and at the same time to look for fresh Water, not one drop of which we could find, but met with several places where a Ship might be laid ashore with safety.

Wednesday, 30th.—In the P.M. I went again in search of Fresh Water, but had no better success than before; wherefore I gave over all thoughts of laying the Ship a Shore, being resolved to spend as little time as possible in a place that was likely to afford us no sort

[92] The ship was on the Donovan Shoal in Broad Sound Channel (Wharton).

[93] It is in reality a narrow channel which runs into Broad Sound (Wharton). The channel separates Quail Island and Long Island from the mainland.

of refreshment. But as I had observed from the Hills the inlet to run a good way in, I thought this a good time to penetrate into the Country to see a little of the inland parts. Accordingly I prepared for making that Excursion in the morning, but the first thing I did was to get upon a pretty high Hill,[94] which is at the N.W. entrance of the inlet, before Sunrise, in order to take a view of the Sea Coast and Islands, etc., that lay off it, and to take their bearings, having the Azimuth Compass with me for that purpose, the Needle of which differ'd from its True position something very considerable, even above 30 degrees, in some places more, and in other less, for I try'd it in several places. I found it differ in itself above 2 points in the space of about 14 feet. The loose stones which lay upon the Ground had no effect upon the Needle; I therefore concluded that it must be owing to Iron Ore upon the Hill, visible signs of which appeared not only here, but in several other places. As soon as I had done here I proceeded up the inlet. I set out with the first of the flood, and long before high water got about 8 Leagues up it; its breadth thus far was from 2 to 4 or 5 Miles upon a S.W. by S. direction; but here it spread every way, and formed a Large lake, which communicated with the Sea to the N.W. I not only saw the Sea in this direction, but found the tide of flood coming strong in from the N.W. I likewise observ'd an Arm of this Lake extending to the Eastward, and it is not at all improbable but what it Communicates with the Sea in the bottom of the bay, which lies to the Westward of Cape Townshend.[95] On the S. side of the Lake is a ridge of pretty high hills, which I was desirous of going upon; but as the day was far spent and high water, I was afraid of being bewilder'd among the Shoals in the night, which promised to be none of the best, being already rainy, dirty weather, and therefore I made the best of my way to the Ship. In this little Excursion I saw only 2 people, and those at a distance, and are all that we have seen in this place, but we have met with several fire places, and seen smokes at a distance. This inlet, which I have named Thirsty Sound, by reason we could find no fresh Water, lies in the Lat. of 22° 05′ S., and Long. 210° 24 W.; it may be known by a Group of small Islands Laying under the shore from 2 to 5 Leagues N.W. from it.[96] There is likewise another Group of Islands laying right before it between 3 and 4 Leagues out at Sea.[97] Over each of the Points that form the Entrance is a pretty high, round Hill; that on the N.W. is a Peninsula, surrounded by the Sea at high water; the distance from

94 Probably the summit of Quail Island.

95 This is exactly what it does (Wharton). Broad Sound does not communicate with Shoalwater Bay.

96 Barren Islands (Wharton).

97 Duke Islands (Wharton).

the one to the other is about 2 Miles bold to both Shores. Here is good Anchoring in 7, 6, 5, and 4 fathoms water, and very Convenient places for laying a Ship ashore, where at Spring Tides the tides doth not rise less than 16 or 18 feet, and flows at full and Change of the Moon about 11 o'Clock. We met with no fresh water, or any other kind of refreshments whatever; we saw 2 Turtle, but caught none, nor no sort of Fish or wild fowl, except a few small land birds. Here are the same sort of Water Fowl as we saw in Botany Bay, and like them, so shy that it is hardly possible to get within shott of them. No signs of Fertility is to be seen upon the Land; the Soil of the up lands is mostly a hard, redish Clay, and produceth several sorts of Trees, such as we have seen before, and some others, and clear of all underwoods. All the low lands are mostly overrun with Mangroves, and at Spring tides overflow'd by the Sea; and I believe in the rainy Seasons here are large land floods, as we saw in many places Gullies, which seem'd to have been made by torrents of Water coming from the Adjacent hills, besides other Visible signs of the Water having been a Considerable height above the Common Spring Tides. Dr. Solander and I was upon a rising Ground up the inlet, which we thought had at one time or another been overflow'd by the Sea, and if so great part of the Country must at that time been laid under Water. Up in the lakes, or lagoons, I suppose, are shell fish, on which the few Natives subsist. We found Oysters sticking to most of the Rocks upon the Shore, which were so small, as not to be worth the picking off.[98]

Thursday, 31st.—Winds Southerly and S.E.; Dark, Hazey weather, with rain. In the P.M., finding no one inducement to stay longer in this place, we at 6 a.m. Weighed and put to Sea, and stood to the N.W., having the Advantage of a fresh breeze at S.S.E. We keept without the Group of Islands which lay in Shore, and to the N.W. of Thirsty Sound, as there appear'd to be no safe passage between them and the Main; at the same time we had a number of Islands without us extending out to Sea as far as we could see; as we run in this direction our depth of Water was 10, 8 and 9 fathoms.[99] At Noon the N.W. point of Thirsty Sound, which I have named Pier head, bore S. 36° E., distant 5 Leagues; the E. point of the other inlet, which Communicates with the former, as I have before mentioned, bore S. by W., distance 2½ Leagues, the Group of Islands above mentioned laying between us and the point. The farthest part of the Main in sight, on

[98] *Crassostrea* (McMichael).

Cook was very unfortunate in his landing here. The channel is at the end of a long headland between two bays, Shoalwater Bay and Broad Sound, and was a very unlikely place either to find water or get any true idea of the country (Wharton).

[99] The ship passed between the Duke Islands and the maze of reefs and islands lying N.W. of Thirsty Sound (Wharton).

the other side of the inlet, bore N.W.; our Lat. by Observation was 21° 53′ S.

Friday, June 1st.—At ½ an hour After Noon, upon the Boat we had ahead sounding making the Signal for Shoal Water, we hauld our wind to the N.E., having at that time 7 fathoms; the Next cast 5, and then 3, upon which we let go an Anchor, and brought the Ship up. The N.W. point of Thirsty Sound, or Pier Head, bore S.E., distance 6 Leagues, being Midway between the Islands which lies off the E. point of the Western inlet and 3 Small Islands directly without them,[100] it being now the first of the flood which we found to set N.W. by W. ½ W. After having sounded about the Shoal, on which we found not quite 3 fathoms, but without it deep water, we got under Sail, and hauld round the 3 Islands just mentioned, and came to an Anchor under the Lee of them in 15 fathoms, having at this time dark, hazey, rainy weather, which continued until 7 o'Clock a.m., at which time we got again under sail, and stood to the N.W. with a fresh breeze at S.S.E. and fair weather, having the Main land in Sight and a Number of Islands all round us, some of which lay out at Sea as far as we could See. The Western Inlet before mentioned, known in the Chart by the Name of Broad Sound, we had now all open. It is at least 9 or 10 Leagues wide at the Entrance, with several Islands laying in and before, and I believe Shoals also, for we had very irregular Soundings, from 10 to 5 and 4 fathoms. At Noon we were by Observation in the Lat. of 21° 29′ S., and Long. made from Cape Townshend 59° W. A point of Land, which forms the N.W. Entrance into Broad Sound, bore from us at this Time W., distance 3 Leagues; this Cape I have named Cape Palmerston[101] (Lat. 21° 27′ S., Long. 210° 57′ W.). Between this Cape and Cape Townshend lies the Bay of Inlets, so named from the Number of Inlets, Creeks, etc., in it.[102]

Saturday, 2nd.—Winds at S.S.E. and S.E., a gentle breeze, with which we stood to the N.W. and N.W. by N., as the land lay, under an easey Sail. Having a boat ahead, found our Soundings at first were very irregular, from 9 to 4 fathoms; but afterwards regular, from 9 to 11 fathoms. At 8, being about 2 Leagues from the Main Land, we Anchor'd in 11 fathoms, Sandy bottom. Soon after this

100 The shoal is now known as Lake Shoal. The three Islands are the Bedwell Islands (Wharton).

101 Henry Viscount Palmerston was a Lord of the Admiralty, 1766-78 (Wharton).

102 The name Bay of Inlets has disappeared from the charts. Cook applied it to the whole mass of bays in this locality, covering over sixty miles. A look at a modern chart causes amazement that Cook managed to keep his ship off the ground, as the whole sea in his track is strewed with dangers (Wharton).

we found a Slow Motion of a Tide seting to the Eastward, and rode so until 6, at which time the tide had risen 11 feet; we now got under Sail, and Stood away N.N.W. as the land lay. From the Observations made on the tide last Night it is plain that the flood comes from the N.W.; whereas Yesterday and for Several days before we found it to come from the S.E. This is neither the first nor second time that we have observed the same thing, and in my Opinion easy accounted for; but this I shall do in another place. At sun rise we found the Variation to be 6° 45′ E. In steering along shore between the Island and the Main, at the Distance of 2 Leagues from the Latter, and 3 or 4 from the former, our soundings were Regular, from 12 to 9 fathoms; but about 11 o'Clock we were again ambarrassed with Shoal Water,[103] but got clear without letting go an Anchor; we had at one time not quite 3 fathoms. At Noon we were about 2 Leagues from the Main land, and about 4 from the Islands, without us; our Lat. by Observation was 20° 56′ S., Long. made from C. Palmerston 16° W.; a pretty high Promontory, which I named Cape Hillsborough,[104] bore W. ½ N., distant 7 Miles. The Main Land is here pretty much diversified with Mountains, Hills, plains, and Vallies, and seem'd to be tollerably Cloathed with Wood and Verdure. These Islands, which lay Parrallel with the Coast, and from 5 to 8 or 9 Leagues off, are of Various Extent, both for height and Circuit; hardly any Exceeds 5 Leagues in Circuit, and many again are very small.[105] Besides the Chain of Islands, which lay at a distance from the Coast, there are other Small Ones laying under the Land. Some few smokes were seen on the Main land.

Sunday, 3rd.—Winds between the S. by E. and S.E. A Gentle breeze and Clear weather. In the P.M. we steer'd along shore N.W. ½ W., at the distance of 2 Leagues from the Main, having 9 and 10 fathoms regular soundings. At sun set the furthest point of the Main Land that we could distinguish as such bore N. 48° W.; to the Northward of this lay some high land, which I took to be an Island, the N.W. point of which bore N. 41° W.; but as I was not sure that there was a passage this way, we at 8 came to an Anchor in 10 fathoms, muddy bottom. 2 hours after this we had a tide setting to the Northward, and at 2 o'clock it had fallen 9 Feet since the time we Anch'd. After this the Tide began to rise, and the flood came from the Northward, which was from the Islands out at Sea, and plainly indicated that there was no passage to the N.W.; but as this did not appear at day light when we got under Sail, and stood away to the

103 Blackwood Shoals (Wharton).

104 Earl of Hillsborough was the First Secretary of State for the Colonies, and President of the Board of Trade when the *Endeavour* sailed (Wharton).

105 The Cumberland Islands. They stretch along the coast for sixty miles (Wharton).

N.W. until 8, at this time we discover'd low land, quite a Cross what we took for an Opening between the Main and the Islands, which proved to be a Bay about 5 or 6 Leagues deep. Upon this we hauld our wind to the Eastward round the Northermost point of the Bay, which bore from us at this time N.E. by N., distance 4 Leagues. From this point we found the Main land trend away N. by W. ½ W., and a Strait or Passage between it and a Large Island[106] or Islands laying in a Parrallel direction with the Coast; this passage we Stood into, having the Tide of Ebb in our favour. At Noon we were just within the Entrance, and by observation in the Lat. of 20° 26′ S.; Cape Hillsborough bore S. by E., distant 10 Leagues, and the N. point of the Bay before mentioned bore S. 19° W., distance 4 Miles. This point I have named Cape Conway[107] (Lat. 20° 30′, Long. 211° 28′), and the bay, Repulse Bay,[108] which is formed by these 2 Capes. The greatest

A VIEW of PENTECOST ISLAND at the Southern entrance of WHITSUNDAYS PASSAGE

and least depth of Water we found in it was 13 and 8 fathoms; every where safe Anchoring, and I believe, was it properly examined, there would be found some good Harbour in it, especially on the N. Side within Cape Conway, for just within the Cape lay 2 or 3 Small Islands, which alone would shelter that side of the Bay from the S.E. and Southerly winds, which seem to be the prevailing or Trade Winds. Among the many Islands that lay upon this Coast there is one more Remarkable than the rest,[109] being of a Small circuit, very high and peaked, and lies E. by S., 10 Miles from Cape Conway at the S. end of the Passage above mention'd.

Monday, 4th.—Winds at S.S.E. and S.E., a Gentle breeze and Clear weather. In the P.M. Steerd thro' the passage,[110] which we found

106 Whitsunday Island (Wharton).

107 General H. S. Conway was the Secretary of State 1765-68 (Wharton).

108 According to the *Australian Encyclopaedia*, Volume 7, page 411, Cook probably gave the name because, in spite of the favourable aspect of the bay, he was unable to find a suitable place in which to careen the *Endeavour*. Dr Beaglehole, however, refers to the sentence: "low land, quite a Cross what we took for an opening between the Main and the Islands", this having "repulsed" Cook, forcing him to haul his wind to the eastward.

109 Probably Blacksmith Island (Wharton). Identified by Beaglehole as Pentecost Island.

110 Whitsunday Passage. The aspect of the shores is very pleasing (Wharton).

from 3 to 6 or 7 Miles broad, and 8 or 9 Leagues in length, N. by W. ½ W. and S. by E. ½ E. It is form'd by the Main on the W., and by Islands on the E., one of which is at least 5 Leagues in length.[111] Our Depth of Water in running thro' was between 25 and 20 fathoms; everywhere good Anchorage; indeed the whole passage is one Continued safe Harbour, besides a Number of small Bays and Coves on each side, where ships might lay as it where in a Bason; at least so it appear'd to me, for I did not wait to Examine it, as having been in Port so lately, and being unwilling to loose the benefit of a light Moon. The land, both on the Main and Islands, especially on the former, is Tolerably high, and distinguished by Hills and Vallies, which are diversified with Woods and Lawns that looked green and pleasant. On a Sandy beach upon one of the Islands we saw 2 people and a Canoe, with an outrigger,[112] which appeared to be both Larger and differently built to any we have seen upon the Coast. At 6 we were nearly the length of the N. end of the Passage; the N. Westermost point of the Main in sight bore N. 54° W., and the N. end of the Island N.N.E., having an open Sea between these 2 points. [This passage I have named Whitsundays Passage, as it was discover'd on the day the Church commemorates that Festival, and the Isles which form it Cumberland Isles, in honour of His Royal Highness the Duke of Cumberland.[113]] We keept under an Easey Sail and the Lead going all Night, having 21, 22, and 23 fathoms, at the distance of 3 Leagues from the land. At daylight A.M. we were abreast of the point above mentioned, which is a lofty promontory; that I named Cape Gloucester[114] (Lat. 19° 57′ S., Long. 211° 54′ W.). It may be known by an Island which lies out at Sea N. by W. ½ W., 5 or 6 Leagues from it; this I called Holbourn Isle.[115] There are also Islands laying under the Land between it and Whitsundays Passage. On the W. side of the Cape the Land Trends away S.W. and S.S.W., and forms a deep bay. The Sand in the bottom of this bay I could but just see from the Masthead; it is very low, and is a Continuation of the same

111 Whitsunday Island.

112 Outrigger canoes were most commonly used in the Cape York Peninsula region. Some of these were up to fifty feet in length. In *The World of the First Australians* R. M. and C. H. Berndt suggest that they were possibly the result of cultural diffusion from New Guinea by way of Torres Strait.

113 Henry Frederick, Duke of Cumberland, was a younger brother of George III (Wharton). The extensive chain of islands includes Hayman and Lindeman islands, which are now popular tourist resorts.

114 William Henry, Duke of Gloucester and Edinburgh, a younger brother of George III (Wharton). The name Gloucester has also been applied to the island at the entrance to Edgecumbe Bay and the channel that separates it from the mainland. Dr Beaglehole notes that the name Gloucester has been transferred to a high point on the mainland.

115 Admiral Francis Holbourne commanded the fleet in North America in which Cook served in 1757 (Wharton).

low land as is at the bottom of Repulse Bay. Without Waiting to look into this bay, which I called Edgcumbe Bay,[116] we continued our Course to the Westward for the Westermost land we had in sight which bore from us W. by N. ½ N., and appeared very high. At Noon we were about 3 Leagues from the Land, and by observation in the Lat. of 19° 47′ S., Cape Gloucester bearing S. 63° E., distant 7½ Leagues.

Tuesday, 5th.—Winds between the South and East, a Gentle breeze, and Serene weather. At 6 a.m. we were abreast of the Western point of Land above mentioned, distant from it 3 Miles, which I have named Cape Upstart, because being surrounded with low land it starts or rises up singley at the first making of it (Lat. 19° 39′ S., Long. 212° 32′ W.); it lies W.N.W. 14 Leagues from Cape Gloucester, and is of a height sufficient to be seen 12 Leagues; but it is not so much of a Promontory as it appears to be, because on each side of it near the Sea is very low land, which is not to be seen unless you are pretty well in with the Shore. Inland are some Tolerable high hills or mountains, which, like the Cape, affords but a very barren prospect. Having past this Cape, we continued standing to the W.N.W. as the land lay, under an easey Sail, having from 16 to 10 fathoms, until 2 o'Clock a.m., when we fell into 7 fathoms, upon which we hauled our wind to the Northward, judging ourselves to be very near the land; as so we found, for at daylight we were little more than 2 Leagues off. What deceived us was the Lowness of the land, which is but very little higher than the Surface of the Sea, but in the Country were some hills. At noon we were in 15 fathoms Water, and about 4 Leagues from the land. Our Lat. by Observation was 19° 12′ S; Cape Upstart bore 38° 30′ E., distant 12 Leagues. Course and distance sail'd since Yesterday noon N. 48° 45′, 53 Miles. At and before Noon some very large smokes were Seen rise up out of the low land. At sun rise I found the Variation to be 5° 35′ Easterly; at sun set last night the same Needle gave near 9°. This being Close under Cape Upstart, I judged that it was owing to Iron ore or other Magnetical Matter Lodged in the Earth.

Wednesday, 6th.—Light Airs at E.S.E., with which we Steer'd

116 In Port Denison, on the western side of Edgcumbe Bay, is the rising town of Bowen, the port of an agricultural district. There is good coal in the vicinity. Captain G. Edgcumbe commanded the *Lancaster* in the fleet in North America in 1758 in which Cook served. Afterwards Earl of Mount Edgcumbe (Wharton).

The bay was almost certainly named for Lord Edgcumbe who later became Earl of Mount Edgcumbe. There was a John Edgecumbe, sergeant of marines on the *Endeavour*, after whom Mount Edgecumbe in New Zealand was named; but as Cook has perpetuated the aristocracy of Great Britain in June 1770, there is little doubt that the noble lord was being honoured at this time.

W.N.W. as the Land now lay; Depth of Water 12 and 14 fathoms. At Noon we were by Observation in the Lat. of 19° 1′ S., Long. made from Cape Gloucester 1° 30′ W.; Course and distance saild since Yesterday noon W.N.W., 28 Miles. In this situation we had the Mouth of a Bay all open extending from S. ½ E. to S.W. ½ S., distance 2 Leagues. This bay, which I named Cleveland Bay,[117] appeared to be about 5 or 6 Miles in Extent every way. The East point I named Cape Cleveland, and the West, Magnetical Head[118] or Island, as it had much the appearance of an Island; and the Compass did not traverse well when near it. They are both Tolerable high, and so is the Main Land within them, and the whole appeared to have the most rugged, rocky, and barren Surface of any we have yet seen. However, it is not without inhabitants, as we saw smoke in several places in the bottom of the bay. The Northermost land we had in sight at this time bore N.W.; this we took to be an Island or Islands, for we could not trace the Main land farther than W. by N.

Thursday, 7th.–Light Airs between the S. and E., with which we steer'd W.N.W., keeping the Main land on board, the outermost part of which at sun set bore from us W. by N.; but without this lay high land, which we took to be Islands. At daylight A.M. we were the Length of the Eastern part of this Land, which we found to Consist of a Group of Islands[119] laying about 5 Leagues from the Main. We being at this time between the 2, we continued advancing Slowly to the N.W. until noon, at which time we were by observation in the Lat. of 18° 49′, and about 5 Leagues from the Main land, the N.W. part of which bore from us N. by W. ½ W., the Island extending from N. to E.; distance of the nearest 2 Miles. Cape Cleveland bore S. 50° E., distant 18 Leagues. Our Soundings in the Course of this day's Sail were from 14 to 11 fathoms.

Friday, 8th.–Winds at S.S.E. and S.; first part light Airs, the remainder a Gentle breeze. In the P.M. we saw several large smokes upon the Main, some people, Canoes, and, as we thought, Cocoa Nut

117 In Cleveland Bay is Townsville, the largest town in Northern Queensland. Population 12,000 (Wharton). Cleveland Bay was probably named for Henry, second Duke of Cleveland; or for John Cleveland, Secretary to the Admiralty from 1751 to 1763.

By 1968 the population of Townsville had grown to five times the number mentioned by Wharton, and of all the cities of Queensland was next to Brisbane in size.

118 Cook's conjecture that Magnetical Island (now known as Magnetic Island) had affected his compass was disproved by later navigators. The island is now a popular resort for the inhabitants of nearby Townsville.

119 Palm Islands (Wharton). The largest of the islands is called Great Palm Island.

Trees upon one of the Islands; and, as a few of these Nutts would have been very acceptable to us at this Time, I sent Lieut. Hicks ashore, with whom went Mr. Banks and Dr. Solander, to see what was to be got. In the Meantime we keept Standing in for the Island with the Ship. At 7 they returned on board, having met with Nothing worth Observing. The Trees we saw were a small kind of Cabbage Palms.[120] They heard some of the Natives as they were putting off from the Shore, but saw none. After the Boat was hoisted in we stood away N. by W. for the Northermost land we had in sight, which we were abreast of at 3 o'Clock in the Morning, having passed all the Islands 3 or 4 hours before. This point I have named Point Hillock,[121] on account of its Figure. The Land of this point is Tolerable high, and may be known by a round Hillock or rock that appears to be detached from the point, but I believe it joins to it. Between this Cape and Cape Cleveland the shore forms a Large bay, which I named Hallifax bay,[122] before it lay the Groups of Islands before mentioned, and some others nearer the Shore. These Islands shelter the Bay in a manner from all Winds, in which is good Anchorage. The land near the Shore in the bottom of the bay is very low and Woody; but a little way back in the Country is a continued ridge of high land, which appear'd to be barren and rocky. Having passed Point Hillock, we continued standing to the N.N.W. as the land Trended, having the Advantage of a light Moon. At 6 a.m. we were abreast of a point of Land which lies N. by W. ½ W., 11 Miles from Point Hillick; the Land between them is very high, and of a craggy, barren surface. This point I named Cape Sandwich;[123] it may not only be known by the high, craggy land over it, but by a small Island which lies E. one Mile from it, and some others about 2 Leagues to the Northward of it. From Cape Sandwich the Land trends W., and afterwards N., and forms a fine, Large Bay, which I called Rockingham Bay,[124] it is well Shelter'd, and affords good Anchorage; at least, so it appear'd to me, for having met with so little encouragement by going ashore that I would not wait to land or examine it farther, but continued to range

120 Identification uncertain.

121 Point Hillock is the east point of Hinchinbrook Island, which is separated from the main by a narrow and tortuous channel (Wharton).

122 The Earl of Halifax was Secretary of State 1763-65 (Wharton). It seems apparent that the present Halifax Bay was first named Rockingham Bay in the Journal, and that subsequently the position of the two names was reversed. Halifax Bay, Dunk Island, Mount Hinchinbrook, and Sandwich Bay in this vicinity were all named in honour of George Montagu Dunk, second Earl of Halifax, and John Montagu, fourth Earl of Sandwich, who was Cook's patron. His estate was named Hinchingbrooke. Cook did not realise that Mount Hinchinbrook was an island.

123 Earl of Sandwich was First Lord of the Admiralty 1763 (Wharton).

124 The Marquis of Rockingham was Prime Minister 1765-66 (Wharton).

along Shore to the Northward for a parcel of Small Islands[125] laying off the Northern point of the Bay, and, finding a Channel of a Mile broad between the 3 Outermost and those nearer the Shore, we pushed thro'. While we did this we saw on one of the nearest Islands a Number of the Natives collected together, who seem'd to look very attentively upon the Ship; they were quite naked, and of a very Dark Colour, with short hair. At noon we were by observation in the Lat. of 17° 59′, and abreast of the N. point of Rockingham Bay, which bore from us W. 2 Miles. This boundry of the Bay is form'd by a Tolerable high Island, known in the Chart by the Name of Dunk Isle; it lays so near the Shore as not to be distinguished from it unless you are well in with the Land. At this time we were in the Long. of 213° 57′. Cape Sandwich bore S. by E. ½ E., distant 19 Miles, and the northermost land in sight N. ½ W. Our depth of Water in the Course of this day's Sail was not more than 16, nor less than 7, fathoms.[126]

Saturday, 9th.—Winds between the S. and S.E., a Gentle breeze, and Clear weather, with which we steer'd N. by W. as the land lay, the northern extream of which at sunset bore N. 25° W. We keept on our Course under an Easey sail all night, having from 12 to 16 fathoms, at the distance of about 3 or 4 Leagues from the Land. At 6 a.m. we were abreast of Some small Islands, which we called Frankland Isles,[127] that lay about 2 Leagues from the Mainland, the Northern Point of which in sight bore N. by W. ½ W.; but this we afterwards found to be an Island,[128] tolerable high, and about 4 Miles in Circuit. It lies about 2 Miles from the Point on the Main between which we went with the ship, and were in the Middle of the Channell at Noon, and by observation in the Lat. of 16° 55′, where we had 20 fathoms of water. The point of land we were now abreast of I called Cape Grafton (Lat. 16° 55′ S., Long. 214° 11′ W.); it is Tolerable high, and so is the whole Coast for 20 Leagues to the southward, and hath a very rocky surface, which is thinly cover'd with wood. In the night we saw several fires along shore, and a little before noon some people.

Sunday, 10th.—After hauling round Cape Grafton we found the

125 The Family Islands (Wharton).

126 About here the Great Barrier Reefs begin to close in on the land. Cook kept so close to the latter that he was unconscious as yet of their existence; but he was soon to find them (Wharton).

127 Probably after Admiral Sir Thomas Frankland.

128 Fitzroy Island (Wharton). Augustus Henry Fitzroy was third Duke of Grafton and Prime Minister at the time of Cook's departure from England. The names of Fitzroy Island and Cape Grafton are therefore closely related.

land trend away N.W. by W.; 3 Miles to the Westward of the Cape is a Bay, wherein we Anchor'd, about 2 Miles from the Shore, in 4 fathoms, owsey bottom.[129] The E. point of the Bay bore S. 74° E., the West point S. 83° W., and a Low green woody Island laying in the Offing bore N. 35° E. The Island lies N. by E. ½ E., distance 3 or 4 Leagues from Cape Grafton, and is known in the Chart by the Name of Green Island.[130] As soon as the Ship was brought to an Anchor I went ashore, accompanied by Mr. Banks and Dr. Solander; the first thing I did was to look for fresh Water, and with that View rowed out towards the Cape, because in the bottom of the bay was low Mangrove land, and little probability of meeting with any there. But the way I went I found 2 Small streams, which were difficult to get at on account of the Surf and rocks upon the Shore. As we came round the Cape we saw, in a sandy Cove, a small stream of Water run over the beach; but here I did not go in the boat because I found that it would not be Easey to land. We hardly advanced anything into the Country, it being here hilly, which were steep and rocky, and we had not time to Visit the Low lands, and therefore met with nothing remarkable. My intention was to have stay'd here at least one day, to have looked into the Country had we met with fresh water convenient, or any other Refreshment; but as we did not, I thought it would be only spending of time, and loosing as much of a light Moon to little purpose, and therefore at 12 o'Clock at night we weighed and stood away to the N.W., having at this time but little wind, attended with Showers of rain.[131] At 4 the breeze freshned at S. by E., with fair weather; we continued steering N.N.W. ½ W. as the Land lay, having 10, 12, and 14 fathoms, at a distance of 3 Leagues from the Land. At 11 we hauld off N., in order to get without a Small Low Island[132] which lay about 2 Leagues from the Main; it being about high Water, about the time we passed it, great part of it lay under water. About 3 Leagues to the N. Westward of this Island, close under the Main land, is another Island,[133] Tolerable high, which bore from us at Noon N. 55° W., distant 7 or 8 Miles; we being at this time in the Lat. of 16° 20′ S., Cape Grafton bore S. 29° E., distant 40 Miles, and the Northermost point of Land in Sight N. 20° W., and in this Situation had 15 fathoms Water. The Shore between Cape Grafton and the above Northern point forms a large but not very deep Bay, which I named

129 Dr Beaglehole identifies this as Mission Bay.

130 This coral cay is now a notable holiday and tourist resort.

131 In the next bay west of where Cook anchored is Cairns, a small but rising town in the centre of a sugar-growing district (Wharton). Now a prosperous city and the centre of the northern Queensland tourist industry. The port of Cairns handles sugar, timber, and agricultural produce.

132 Low Isles. There is now a lighthouse on them (Wharton).

133 Snapper Island (Wharton).

Trinity Bay, after the day on which it was discover'd; the North point Cape Tribulation, because here began all our Troubles. Lat. 16° 6′ S., Long. 214° 39′ W.

Monday, 11th.—Wind at E.S.E., with which we steer'd along shore N. by W. at the distance of 3 or 4 Leagues off, having from 14 to 10 and 12 fathoms water. Saw 2 Small Islands in the Offing, which lay in the Lat. of 16° 0′ S., and about 6 or 7 Leagues from the Main. At 6 the Northermost land in sight bore N. by W. ½ W., and 2 low, woody Islands,[134] which some took to be rocks above Water, bore N. ½ W. At this time we shortened Sail, and hauld off shore E.N.E. and N.E. by E., close upon a Wind. My intention was to stretch off all Night as well to avoid the danger we saw ahead as to see if any Islands lay in the Offing, especially as we now begun to draw near the Lat. of those discover'd by Quiros, which some Geographers, for what reason I know not, have thought proper to Tack to this land.[135] Having the advantage of a fine breeze of wind, and a clear Moon light Night in standing off from 6 until near 9 o'Clock, we deepned our Water from 14 to 21 fathoms, when all at once we fell into 12, 10 and 8 fathoms. At this time I had everybody at their Stations to put about and come to an Anchor; but in this I was not so fortunate, for meeting again with Deep Water, I thought there could be no danger in standing on.[136] Before 10 o'Clock we had 20 and 21 fathoms, and Continued in that depth until a few minutes before 11, when we had 17, and before the Man at the Lead could heave another cast, the Ship Struck and stuck fast.[137] Immediately upon this we took in all our Sails, hoisted out the Boats and Sounded round the Ship, and found that we had got upon the S.E. Edge of a reef of Coral Rocks, having in some places round the Ship 3 and 4 fathoms Water, and in other places not quite as many feet, and about a Ship's length from us on the starboard side (the Ship laying with her Head to the N.E.) were 8, 10, and 12 fathoms. As soon as the Long boat was out we struck Yards and Topmast, and carried out the Stream Anchor on our Starboard bow, got the Coasting Anchor and Cable into the Boat, and were going to carry it out in the same way; but upon my sounding the 2nd time round the Ship I found the most water a Stern, and therefore had this Anchor carried out upon the Starboard Quarter, and hove upon

[134] Hope Islands (Wharton).

[135] In April 1606 Torres and Quiros sighted the island of Tikopia and sailed through the Banks Islands toward the northernmost island of the New Hebrides. It was called Austrialia del Espiritu Santo by Quiros, and was in approximately the same latitude as Cape Tribulation.

[136] The ship passed just northward of Pickersgill Reef (Wharton).

[137] The ship struck on Endeavour Reef.

it a very great Strain; which was to no purpose, the Ship being quite fast, upon which we went to work to lighten her as fast as possible, which seem'd to be the only means we had left to get her off. As we went ashore about the Top of High Water we not only started water, but threw overboard our Guns, Iron and Stone Ballast, Casks, Hoop Staves, Oil Jarrs, decay'd Stores, etc.; many of these last Articles lay in the way at coming at Heavier. All this time the Ship made little or no Water. At 11 a.m., being high Water as we thought, we try'd to heave her off without Success, she not being afloat by a foot or more, notwithstanding by this time we had thrown overboard 40 or 50 Tuns weight. As this was not found sufficient we continued to Lighten her by every method we could think off; as the Tide fell the ship began to make Water as much as two pumps could free: at Noon she lay with 3 or 4 Streakes heel to Starboard; Lat. observed 15° 45′ S.

Tuesday, 12th.—Fortunately we had little wind, fine weather, and a smooth Sea, all this 24 Hours, which in the P.M. gave us an Opportunity to carry out the 2 Bower Anchors, one on the Starboard Quarter, and the other right a Stern, got Blocks and Tackles upon the Cables, brought the falls in abaft and hove taught. By this time it was 5 o'Clock p.m.; the tide we observed now begun to rise, and the leak increased upon us, which obliged us to set the 3rd Pump to work, as we should have done the 4th also, but could not make it work. At 9 the Ship righted, and the Leak gain'd upon the Pumps considerably. This was an alarming and, I may say, terrible circumstance, and threatened immediate destruction to us. However, I resolv'd to risque all, and heave her off in case it was practical, and accordingly turn'd as many hands to the Capstan and Windlass as could be spared from the Pumps; and about 20 Minutes past 10 o'Clock the Ship floated, and we hove her into Deep Water, having at this time 3 feet 9 Inches Water in the hold. This done I sent the Long boat to take up the Stream Anchor, got the Anchor, but lost the Cable among the Rocks; after this turn'd all hands to the Pumps, the Leak increasing upon us.

A mistake soon after hapned, which for the first time caused fear to approach upon every man in the Ship. The man that attended the well took the Depth of water above the Ceiling; he, being relieved by another who did not know in what manner the former had sounded, took the Depth of water from the outside plank, the difference being 16 or 18 inches, and made it appear that the leak had gained this upon the pumps in a short time. This mistake was no sooner cleared up than it acted upon every man like a Charm; they redoubled their vigour, insomuch that before 8 o'clock in the morning they gained considerably upon the leak.[138] We now hove up the Best Bower, but found it impossible to save the small Bower, so cut it away at a whole Cable; got up the Fore topmast and Foreyard, warped the Ship to the S.E., and at 11 got under sail, and stood in for the land, with a light breeze at E.S.E. Some hands employ'd sewing Oakham, Wool, etc., into a Lower Steering sail to fother the Ship; others employ'd at the Pumps, which still gain'd upon the Leak.

Wednesday, 13th.—In the P.M. had light Airs at E.S.E., with which we keept edging in for the Land. Got up the Maintopmast and Mainyard, and having got the Sail ready for fothering of the Ship, we put it over under the Starboard Fore Chains, where we suspected the Ship had suffer'd most, and soon after the Leak decreased, so as to be keept clear with one Pump with ease; this fortunate circumstance gave new life to every one on board.

It is much easier to conceive than to discribe the satisfaction felt by everybody on this occasion. But a few minutes before our utmost Wishes were to get hold of some place upon the Main, or an island, to run the Ship ashore, where out of her Materials we might build a Vessel to carry us to the East Indies; no sooner were we made sencible that the outward application to the Ship's bottom had taken effect, than the field of every Man's hopes inlarged, so that we thought of nothing but ranging along Shore in search of a Harbour, when we could repair the Damages we had sustained.[139] In justice to the Ship's

[138] The circumstance related in this paragraph is from the Admiralty copy (Wharton).

[139] The foregoing paragraph is from the Admiralty copy. The situation was indeed sufficiently awkward. When it is considered that the coast was wholly unknown, the natives decidedly hostile, the land unproductive of any means of subsistence, and the distance to the nearest Dutch settlements, even if a passage should be found south of New Guinea, 1,500 miles, there was ample cause of apprehension if they could not save the ship. Knowing what we now know, that all off this coast is a continuous line of reefs and shoals, Cook's action in standing off might seem rash. But he knew nothing of this. There was a moon; he reduced sail to double reefed topsails with a light wind, as the log tells us, and with the cumbrous hempen cables of the day, and the imperfect means of heaving up the anchor, he was desirous of saving his men unnecessary labour. Cook was puzzled that the next tide did not, after lightening the ship, take him off; but it is now known that on this coast it is only every alternate tide that rises to a full height, and as he got ashore nearly at the top of the higher of the two waters he had to wait twenty-four hours until he got a similar rise. Lucky was it for them that the wind was light. Usually at this season the trade wind is strong, and raises a considerable sea, even inside the Barrier. Hawkesworth or Banks makes the proposition to fother the ship emanate from Mr Monkhouse; but it is scarcely to be supposed that such a perfect seaman as Cook was not familiar with this operation, and he merely says that as Mr Monkhouse had seen it done, he confided to him the superintendence of it, as of course the Captain had at such a time many other things to do than stand over the men preparing the sail. In 1886 the people of Cooktown were anxious to recover the brass guns of the *Endeavour* which were thrown overboard, in order to place them

Company, I must say that no men ever behaved better than they have done on this occasion; animated by the behaviour of every Gentleman on board, every man seem'd to have a just sence of the Danger we were in, and exerted himself to the very utmost. The Ledge of Rocks, or Shoal, we have been upon, lies in the Lat. of 15° 45′, and about 6 or 7 Leagues from the Main land; but this is not the only Shoal that lay upon this part of the Coast, especially to the Northward, and one which we saw to the Southward, the tail of which we passed over when we had the uneven Soundings 2 hours before we Struck. A part of this Shoal is always above Water, and looks to be white Sand; part of the one we were upon was dry at low Water, and in that place consists of Sand and stones, but every where else Coral Rocks. At 6 we Anch'd in 17 fathoms, about 5 or 6 Leagues from the land, and one from the Shoal. At this time the ship made about 15 Inches Water per hour. At 6 a.m. weigh'd and stood to the N.W., edging in for the land, having a Gentle breeze at S.S.E. At 9 we past close without 2 small low Islands, laying in the Lat. of 15° 41′, and about 4 Leagues from the Main; I have named them Hope Islands, because we were always in hopes of being able to reach these Islands. At Noon we were about 3 Leagues from the Land, and in the Lat. of 15° 37′ S.; the Northermost part of the Main in sight bore N. 30° W., and the above Islands extending from S. 30° E. to S. 40° E. In this situation had 12 fathoms water and several sandbanks without us. The Leak now decreaseth, but for fear it should break out again we got the Sail ready fill'd for fothering; the manner this is done is thus: We Mix Oacham and Wool together (but Oacham alone would do), and chop it up Small, and then stick it loosely by handfulls all over the Sail, and throw over it Sheep dung or other filth. Horse Dung for this purpose is the best. The Sail thus prepared is hauld under the Ship's bottom by ropes, and if the place of the Leak is uncertain, it must be hauld from one part of her bottom to another until one finds the place where it takes effect. While the Sail is under the Ship the Oacham, etc., is washed off, and part of it carried along with the water into the Leak, and in part stops up the hole. Mr. Monkhouse, one of my Midshipmen, was once in a Merchant Ship which Sprung a Leak, and made 48 Inches Water per hour; but by this means was brought home from Virginia to London with only her proper crew; to him I gave the direction of this, who executed it very much to my satisfaction.

Thursday, 14th.—P.M., had a Gentle breeze at S.E. by E. Sent the Master, with 2 Boats as well, to sound ahead of the Ship, as to look out for a Harbour where we could raise our defects, and put the

as a memento in their town; but they could not be found, which is not altogether surprising (Wharton).

Ship on a proper Trim, both of which she now very much wanted. At 3 saw an Opening that had the appearance of a Harbour;[140] stood off and on while the Boats were examining it, who found that there was not a sufficient depth of Water for the Ship. By this time it was almost sun set, and seeing many shoals about us we Anch'd in 4 fathoms about 2 miles from the Shore, the Main land extending from N. ½ E. to S. by E. ½ E. At 8 o'clock the Pinnace, in which was one of the Mates, return'd on board, and reported that they had found a good Harbour[141] about 2 Leagues to leeward. In consequence of this

information we, at 6 a.m., weigh'd and run down to it, first sending 2 Boats ahead to lay upon the Shoals that lay in our way; and notwithstanding this precaution, we were once in 3 fathoms with the Ship. Having pass'd these Shoals, the Boats were sent to lay in the Channell leading into the Harbour. By this time it begun to blow in so much that the Ship would not work, having missed stays Twice; and being entangled among Shoals, I was afraid of being drove to Leeward before the Boats could place themselves, and therefore Anch'd in 4 fathoms about a Mile from the Shore, and then made the Signal for the Boats to come on board, after which I went myself and Buoy'd the Channell, which I found very narrow, and the Harbour much smaller than I had been told, but very convenient for our Purpose. At Noon Lat. observed 15° 26′ S. [*Note.*—This day I restor'd Mr. Magra to his Duty, as I did not find him guilty of the crimes laid to his charge.]

Friday, 15th.—A fresh Gale at S.E. and Cloudy weather, attended with Showers of Rain. In the Night, as it blow'd too fresh to break the Ship loose to run into the Harbour, we got down the Topgallant yards, unbent the Mainsail, and some of the Small sails; got down the

140 Weary Bay. The name appears on the chart.

141 Cook Harbour, Endeavour River (Wharton). Cooktown, the town which became an important centre for the nearby Palmer goldfield a century later, is at the mouth of the Endeavour River. The town was of course named in honour of Captain Cook. Mount Cook, to the south of the town, was named by Phillip Parker King in 1819.

Although unnamed in the Journal and on the chart, the sketch that is reproduced above shows that Cook named this hill Gores Mount, doubtless after Lieutenant tenant Gore. See note on page 87.

Foretopgallant mast, and the Jibb Boom and Spritsailyard in, intending to lighten the Ship Forward as much as possible, in order to lay her ashore to come at the Leak.

Saturday, 16th.—Strong Gales at S.E., and Cloudy, hazey weather, with Showers of Rain. At 6 o'Clock in the A.M. it moderated a little, and we hove short, intending to get under sail, but was obliged to desist, and veer away again; some people were seen ashore to-day.

Sunday, 17th.—Most part strong Gales at S.E., with some heavy showers of rain in the P.M. At 6 a.m., being pretty moderate, we weigh'd and run into the Harbour, in doing of which we run the Ship ashore Twice. The first time she went off without much Trouble, but the Second time she Stuck fast; but this was of no consequence any farther than giving us a little trouble, and was no more than what I expected as we had the wind. While the Ship lay fast we got down the Foreyard, Foretopmast, booms, etc., overboard, and made a raft of them alongside.

Monday, 18th.—Fresh Gales and Cloudy, with Showers of Rain. At 1 p.m. the Ship floated, and we warped her into the Harbour, and moor'd her alongside of a Steep Beach on the S. side; got the Anchors, Cables, and all the Hawsers ashore.[142] In the A.M. made a Stage from

the Ship to the Shore, Erected 2 Tents, one for the Sick, and the other for the Stores and Provisions; Landed all the empty Casks and part of the Provisions, and sent a boat to haul the Sean, which return'd without Success.

Tuesday, 19th.—Fresh Gales at S.E. and Cloudy weather, with frequent showers of Rain. P.M., landed all the Provisions and Part of the Stores; got the Sick ashore, which amounted, at this time, to 8 or 9, afflicted with different disorders, but none very dangerously ill. This afternoon I went upon one of the highest Hills over the Harbour, from which I had a perfect View of the inlet or River, and adjacent

142 This was the future site of Cooktown. On 4 August Cook refers to his naming of the "Harbour, or River" as the Endeavour River.

country, which afforded but a very indifferent prospect. The Low lands near the River is all over run with Mangroves, among which the salt water flows every tide, and the high land appear'd to be barren and Stoney. A.M., got the 4 remaining Guns out of the hold, and mounted them on the Quarter Deck; got a spare Anchor and Stock ashore, and the remaining part of the Stores and ballast that were in the Hold; set up the Forge, and set the Armourer and his Mate to work to make Nails, etc., to repair the Ship.

Wednesday, 20th.—Winds at S.E., a fresh breeze, Fore and Middle parts rainy, the Latter fair. This day got out all the Officers' stores and the ground Tier of Water, having now nothing in the Fore and Main Hold But the Coals and a little Stone ballast.

Thursday, 21st.—P.M., landed the Powder, got out the stone ballast, wood, etc., which brought the Ship's Draught of water to 8 ft. 10 in. Forward, and 13 feet abaft. This I thought, by trimming the Coals aft, would be sufficient, as I find the Tides will rise and fall upon a Perpendicular 8 feet at Spring tides; but after the Coals was trimm'd away from over the Leak we Could hear the Water come Gushing in a little abaft the Foremast about 3 feet from her Keel. This determin'd me to clear the hold intirely; accordingly very early in the Morning we went to work to get out the Coals, which was Employment for all hands.

Friday, 22nd.—Winds at S.E., fair weather. At 4 p.m., having got out most of the Coals, cast loose the Ship's moorings, and warped her a little higher up the Harbour to a place I had pitched upon to lay her ashore to stop the Leak; draught of water Forward 7 ft. 9 in. and abaft 13 ft. 6 in. At 8, being high water, hauld her bow close ashore, but Keept her stern afloat, because I was afraid of Neaping her,[143] and yet it was necessary to lay the whole of her as near the ground as possible. At 2 a.m. the Tide left her, which gave us an Opportunity to Examine the Leak, which we found to be at her Floor Heads, a little before the Starboard Fore Chains; here the Rocks had made their way thro' 4 planks, quite to, and even into the Timbers, and wounded 3 more. The manner these planks were damaged—or cut out, as I may say—is hardly credible; scarce a Splinter was to be seen, but the whole was cut away as if it had been done by the Hands of Man with a blunt-edge Tool. Fortunately for us the Timbers in this place were very close; other wise it would have been impossible to have saved the Ship, and even as it was it appeared very extraordinary that she made

[143] I.e., having her so far on shore that they could not heave her off at Neap tide (Wharton).

no more water than what she did. A large peice of Coral rock was sticking in one Hole, and several peices of the Fothering, small stones, etc., had made its way in, and lodged between the Timbers, which had stopped the Water from forcing its way in in great Quantities. Part of the Sheathing was gone from under the Larboard bow, part of the False Kiel was gone, and the remainder in such a Shatter'd Condition that we should be much better off if it was gone also; her Forefoot and some part of her Main Kiel was also damaged, but not Materially. What damage she may have received abaft we could not see, but believe not much, as the Ship makes but little water, while the Tide Keeps below the Leak forward. At 9 the Carpenters went to work upon the Ship, while the Armourers were buisy making Bolts, Nails, etc.

Saturday, 23rd.—Winds S. Easterly, a fresh Gale and fair weather. Carpenters employed Shifting the Damaged planks as long as the tide would permit them to work. At low water P.M. we examined the Ship's bottom under the Starboard side, she being dry as far aft as the After-part of the Fore Chains; we could not find that she had received any other damage on this side but what has been mentioned. In the morning I sent 3 Men into the Country to shoot Pidgeons,[144] as some of these birds had been seen flying about; in the evening they return'd with about ½ a Dozen. One of the Men saw an Animal something less than a greyhound; it was of a Mouse Colour, very slender made, and swift of Foot.[145] A.M., I sent a Boat to haul the Sean, who return'd at noon, having made 3 Hauls and caught only 3 fish; and yet we see them in plenty Jumping about the harbour, but can find no method of catching them.

Sunday, 24th.—Winds and weather as Yesterday. P.M., the Carpenters finished the Starboard side, and at 9 heeld the Ship the other way, and hauld her off about 2 feet for fear of Neaping. In the A.M. they went to work repairing the Sheathing under the Larboard bow, where we found 2 planks cut about half thro'. Early in the morning I sent a party of Men into the Country under the direction of Lt. Gore[146] to seek for refreshments; they return'd about noon with a few Palm Cabbages and a Bunch or 2 of wild Plantains;[147] these last were

144 These could be of several species (Hindwood).

145 Kangaroo (Wharton).

146 Lieutenant Gore was the officer who had a dispute with Cook four months earlier while in the vicinity of Banks Peninsula. Gore was certain that he had seen land and Cook was equally certain that there was none there. The following day Cook altered the ship's course to prove his point. See *Captain Cook in New Zealand*, page 119.

147 Probably *Musa banksii*, a wild "plantain" or banana (Mair).

much Smaller than any I had ever seen, and the Pulp full of small Stones; otherwise they were well tasted. I saw myself this morning, a little way from the Ship, one of the Animals before spoke off; it was of a light mouse Colour and the full size of a Grey Hound, and shaped in every respect like one, with a long tail, which it carried like a Grey hound; in short, I should have taken it for a wild dog but for its walking or running, in which it jump'd like a Hare or Deer. Another of them was seen to-day by some of our people, who saw the first; they described them as having very small Legs, and the print of the Feet like that of a Goat; but this I could not see myself because the ground the one I saw was upon was too hard, and the length of the Grass hindered my seeing its legs.[148]

Monday, 25th.—At low water in the P.M. While the Carpenters were buisey in repairing the Sheathing and plank under the Larboard bow I got people to go under the Ship's bottom, to examine all her Larboard side, she only being dry Forward, but abaft were 9 feet water. They found part of the Sheathing off abreast of the Mainmast about her floor heads, and a part of one plank a little damaged. There were 3 people who went down, who all agreed in the same Story; the Master was one, who was positive that she had received no Material Damage besides the loss of the Sheathing. This alone will be sufficient to let the worm into her bottom, which may prove of bad consequence. However, we must run all risque, for I know of no method to remedy this but by heaving her down, which would be a work of Emence Labour and time, if not impractical in our present situation.

The Carpenters continued hard at work under her bottom until put off by the Tide in the evening, and the morning Tide did not Ebb out far enough to permit them to work upon her, for here we have

[148] In the considered opinion of Tom Iredale and Ellis Troughton this "Grey Hound"-like kangaroo could only have been the northern form of the Whiptail Wallaby, taking the name *Wallabia canguru.* The following paragraph appears in the ninth edition of *Furred Animals of Australia*, 1967, published by Angus and Robertson and reprinted by permission of the publishers: "The specific names *giganteus* (1790) and *major* (1800) were originally given to the Great Grey Kangaroo about the first settlement of Sydney. Both names have since been misapplied to Captain Cook's original species of wallaby. However, in order to 'fix' the priority of the name *giganteus* over *major* for the Great-Grey species, the International Commission on Zoological Nomenclature recently had recourse to the extreme (and illogical) measure of designating as 'neotype' of *giganteus*, a sub-adult specimen of Great-Grey from beyond the ecological environs of Cooktown [and range of Cook's party]! Unfortunately, to substantiate this finding, the Commission unhappily ruled for the suppression of the name *canguru.* With this latter ruling of the Commission I am personally in most categorical and emphatic disagreement."

Troughton writes further: "The description of the first 'kangaroo' shot, and described by Solander (not Cook) had among other features a naked or hairless muzzle or rhinarium, which absolutely eliminates the Great Grey which has an entirely hairy rhinarium." See also note for 14 July.

only one Tolerable low and high tide in 24 Hours. A.M., a party of Men were employ'd ashore filling water, while others were employ'd overhauling the rigging.

Tuesday, 26th.—Fair weather, a S.E. wind, and a fresh Gale; at low Water P.M. the Carpenters finished under the Larboard bow and every other place the tide would permit them to come at. Lashed some Casks under the Ship's bows in order to help to float her, and at high water in the Night attempted to heave her off, but could not, she not being afloat partly owing to some of the Casks not holding that were Lashed under her. A.M., employed getting more Casks ready for the same purpose; but I am much afraid that we shall not be able to float her now the Tides are Taking off.

Wednesday, 27th.—A fresh breeze of Wind at S.E. and Cloudy weather. P.M., lashed 38 empty Butts under the Ship's Bottom in order to float her off, which proved ineffectual, and therefore gave over all hopes of getting her off until the Next spring tides. At daylight we got a Considerable weight of sundry Articles from Aft forward to ease the Ship; the Armourer at work at the Forge repairing Iron work, etc., Carpenters caulking and Stocking one of the Spare Anchors, Seamen employ'd filling of Water and overhauling the rigging, and I went in the pinnace up the Harbour, and made several hauls with the Sean, but caught only between 20 and 30 lb. of fish, which were given to the sick and such as were weak and Ailing.

Thursday, 28th.—Fresh breezes and Cloudy. All hands employ'd as Yesterday.

Friday, 29th.—Wind and weather as Yesterday, and the employment of the People the same, Lieut. Gore having been 4 or 5 miles in the Country, where he met with nothing remarkable. He saw the footsteps of Men, and likewise those of 3 or 4 sorts of wild beasts, but saw neither Man nor beast. Some others of our people who were out Yesterday on the N. side of the River met with a place where the Natives have just been, as their fires was then burning; but they saw nobody, nor have we seen one since we have been in port. In these excursions we found some Wild Yamms or Cocos[149] growing in the Swampy grounds, and this Afternoon I sent a Party of Men to gather some. The Tops we found made good greens, and eat exceedingly well when Boil'd, but the roots were so bad that few besides myself could eat them. This night Mr. Green and I observ'd an Emersion of

[149] Possibly *Colocasia esculenta*, "taro", or perhaps the related *Alocasia macrorrhizos* (Mair).

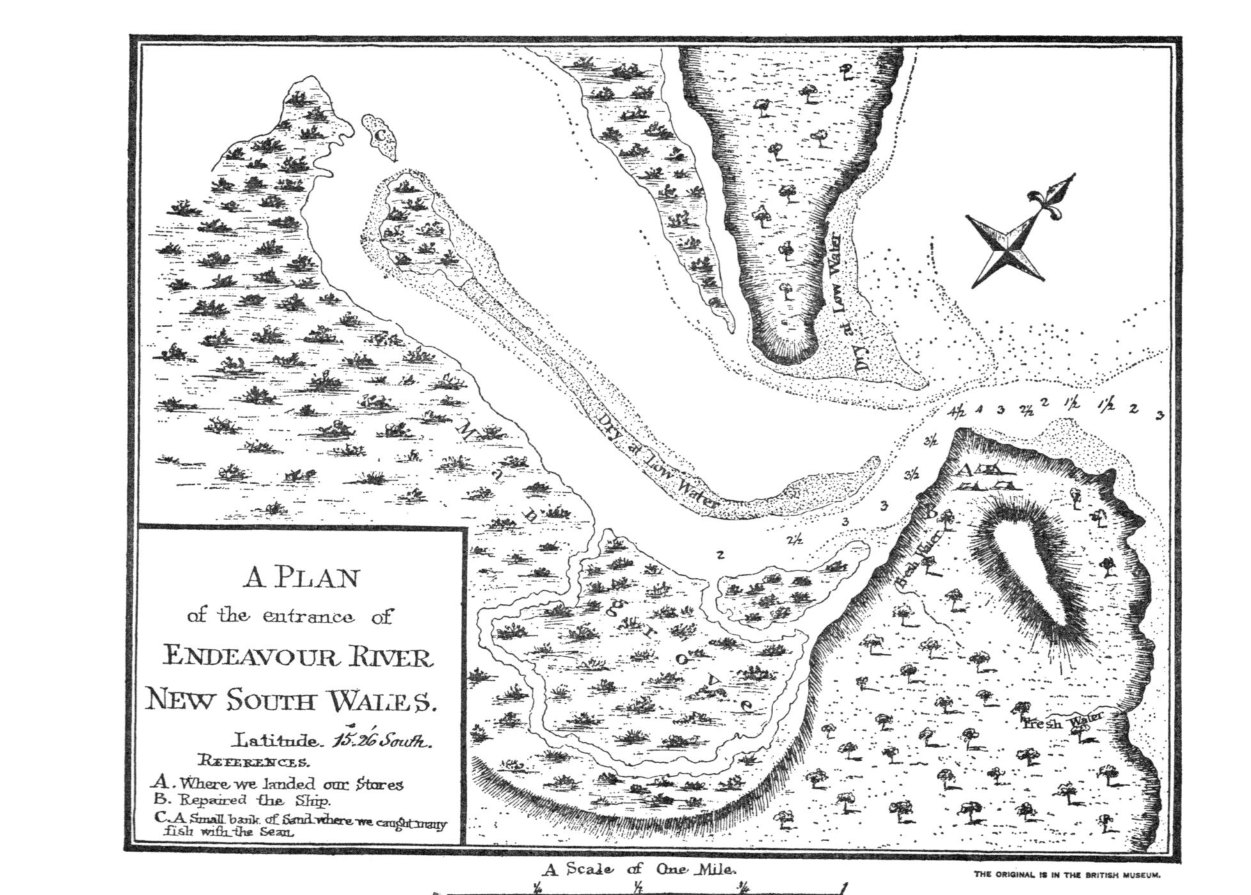

THE ORIGINAL IS IN THE BRITISH MUSEUM.

Jupiter's first Satellite, which hapned at 2 hrs. 58′ 53″ in the A.M.; the same Emersion hapnd at Greenwich, according to Calculation, on the 30th at 5 hrs. 17′ 43″ A.M. The differance is 14 hrs. 18′ 50″, equal to 214° 42′ 30″ of Long.,[150] which this place is West of Greenwich, and its Lat. 15° 26′ S. A.M., I sent some hands in a Boat up the River to haul the Sean, while the rest were employ'd about the rigging and sundry other Dutys.

Saturday, 30th.—Moderate breezes at S.E., and clear serene weather. P.M., the Boat returned from hauling the Sean, having caught as much fish as came to a pound and a half a Man. A.M., I sent her again to haul the Sean, and some hands to gather greens, while others were employ'd about the rigging, etc., etc. I likewise sent some of the Young Gentlemen to take a plan of the Harbour, and went myself upon the hill, which is near the South point to take a view of the Sea.[151] At this time it was now water, and I saw what gave me no small uneasiness, which were a Number of Sand Banks and Shoals laying all along the Coast; the innermost lay about 3 or 4 Miles from the Shore, and the outermost extended off to Sea as far as I could see without my glass, some just appeared above water.[152] The only hopes I have of getting clear of them is to the Northward, where there seems to be a Passage, for as the wind blows constantly from the S.E. we shall find it difficult, if not impractical, to return to the Southward.

Sunday, 1st July.—Gentle breezes at S.E., and Cloudy weather, with some Gentle Showers in the morning. P.M., the People return'd from hauling the Sean, having caught as much fish as came to 2½ pound per Man, no one on board having more than another. The few Greens we got I caused to be boil'd among the pease, and makes a very good Mess, which, together with the fish, is a great refreshment to the people. A.M., a party of Men, one from each Mess, went again a fishing, and all the rest I gave leave to go into the Country, knowing that there was no danger from the Natives. To-day at Noon the Thermometer in the Shade rose to 87°, which is 2 or 3 Degrees higher than it hath been on any day before in this place.

Monday, 2nd.—Do. weather. P.M., the fishing-party caught as much fish as came to 2 lbs. a Man. Those that were in the Country met with nothing New. Early in the A.M. I sent the Master in the pinnace out of the Harbour, to sound about the Shoals in the Offing and

150 This was an excellent observation. The true longitude is 214° 45′ (Wharton).
151 Grassy Hill (Wharton).
152 These were the innermost reefs of the Great Barrier. There is a tolerably clear passage about eight miles wide between them and the shore, though this has some small shoals in it (Wharton).

to look for a Channel to the Northward. At this time we had a breeze of wind from the land, which continued till about 9. What makes me mention this is, that it is the first Land breeze we have had since we have been in this River. At low water lashed empty Casks under the Ship's bows, being in some hopes of floating her the next high Water, and sent some hands a fishing, while others were employ'd in refitting the Ship.

Tuesday, 3rd.—Winds at S.E., Fore and Middle part gentle breeze, the remainder a fresh gale. In the evening the fishing Party return'd, having got as much fish as came to 2 lbs. a Man. At high water we attempted to heave the Ship off, but did not succeed. At Noon the Master return'd, and reported he had found a passage out to Sea between the Shoals, which passage lies out E.N.E. or E. by N. from the River mouth. He found these Shoals to Consist of Coral Rocks; he landed upon one, which drys at low Water, where he found very large cockles and a Variety of other Shell fish, a quantity of which he brought away with him. He told me that he was 5 Leagues out at Sea, having at that distance 21 fathoms water, and judg'd himself to be without all the Shoals, which I very much doubted.[153] After this he came in Shore, and Stood to the Northward, where he met with a Number of Shoals laying a little distance from the Shore. About 9 in the evening he landed in a Bay about 3 Leagues to the Northward of this Place, where he disturbed some of the Natives, whom he supposed to be at supper; they all fled upon his approach, and Left him some fresh Sea Eggs, and a fire ready lighted behind them; but there was neither House nor Hut near. Although these Shoals lay within sight of the Coast, and abound very much with Shell fish and other small fish, which are to be caught at Low water in holes in the Rocks, yet the Natives never visit them, for if they did we must have seen of these Large shells on shore about their fire places. The reason I do suppose is, that they have no Boats that they dare Venture so far out at Sea in.[154]

Wednesday, 4th.—Strong gales at S.E. and fair weather. P.M., the fishing party return'd with the usual success; at High water hove the ship Afloat. A.M., employ'd trimming her upon an even Kiel, intending to lay her ashore once more, to come at her bottom under the Larboard Main Chains.

Thursday, 5th.—Strong breezes at S.E. and fair weather. P.M.

[153] Cook was right. The shoals extend for four leagues farther (Wharton).

[154] Nevertheless the natives do get out to the islands which lie farther from the shore than these reefs, as Cook himself afterwards found (Wharton).

Warped the Ship over, and at high Water laid her ashore on the Sand-bank on the S. side of the River, for I was afraid to lay her broad side to the Shore where she lay before, because the ground lies upon too great a decent, and she hath already received some Damage by laying there these last Niep Tides, at least she still makes water.

Friday, 6th.—Do. weather. At low water in the P.M. had hardly 4 feet water under the Ship; yet could not repair the Sheathing that was beat off, the place being all under water. One of the Carpenter's crew, a Man I could trust, went down and Examin'd it, and found 3 Streakes of the Sheathing gone about 7 or 8 feet long, and the Main Plank a little rubbed; this account agrees with the report of the Master and others that were under her bottom before. The Carpenter, who I look upon to be well skill'd in his profession, and a good judge in these matters, was of Opinion that this was of little consequence; and as I found that it would be difficult, if not impractical, for us to get under her bottom to repair it, I resolved to spend no more time about it. Accordingly at high water hove her off, and moor'd her alongside the beach, where the Stores, etc., lay, and in the A.M. got everything in readiness for taking them on board, and at the same time got on board 8 Tuns of Water, and stow'd in the ground Tier in the after Hold. In the Morning Mr. Banks and Lt. Gore with 3 Men went in a small Boat up the Harbour, with a View to stay 2 or 3 days to try to Kill some of the Animals we have seen about this place.

Saturday, 7th.—Fresh breezes at S.E. and fair weather. Employ'd getting on board Coals, Ballast, etc., and caulking the Ship; a work that could not be done while she lay aground. The Armourer and his Mate are Still employ'd at the Forge making and repairing sundry Articles in the Iron way.

Sunday, 8th.—Gentle breeze and S.E., and clear weather. Early I sent the Master in a Boat out to Sea to sound again about the Shoals, because the account he had given of the Channell before mentioned was to me by no means Satisfactory; likewise sent some hands to haul the Sean, who caught near 80 lbs. of fish; the rest of the people I gave leave to go into the Country.

Monday, 9th.—In the Day Do. Winds, but in the night Calm. P.M., Mr. Gore and Mr. Banks return'd, having met with nothing remarkable; they were about 3 or 4 Leagues up in the Country without finding hardly any Variation either in the Soil or Produce. In the Evening the Master return'd, having been several Leagues out at Sea, and at that Distance off saw Shoals without him, and was of opinion there was no getting out to Sea that way. In his return he touched upon one of the Shoals, the same as he was upon the first time he was out; he here saw a great number of Turtle, 3 of which he Caught weighing 791 lbs. This occasion'd my sending him out again this morning provided with proper gear for Striking them, he having before nothing but a Boat Hook. Carpenters, Smiths, and Coopers at their respective Employments, and the Seamen employed getting on board stones, ballast, etc. This day all hands feasted upon Turtle for the First time.[155]

Tuesday, 10th.—Winds and weather as yesterday. Employ'd hoisting on board and stowing away the ground Tier of Water. P.M., saw 7 or 8 of the Natives on the S. side of the River, and 2 of them came down upon the Sandy point opposite the Ship; but as soon as I put off in a Boat in order to speak with them they run away as fast as they could. At 11 Mr. Banks, who had gone out to Sea with Mr. Molineux, the Master, return'd in his own Small Boat, and gave but a Very bad account of our Turtle-catchers. At the time he left them, which was about 6 o'Clock, they had not got one, nor were they likely to get any; and yet the Master was so obstinate that he would not return,[156] which obliged me to send Mr. Gore out in the Yawl this morning to order the Boat and People in, in Case they could not be employ'd there to some Advantage. In the A.M. 4 of the Natives came down to the Sandy point on the North side of the Harbour, having along with them a small wooden Canoe with Outriggers, in which they seem'd to be employed striking fish, etc. Some were for going over in a Boat to them; but this I would not suffer, but let them alone without seeming to take any Notice of them. At length 2 of them came in the Canoe so near the Ship as to take some things we throw'd them. After this they went away, and brought over the other 2, and came again alongside, nearer than they had done before, and took such Trifles as we gave them; after this they landed close to the Ship, and all 4 went ashore, carrying their Arms with them. But Tupia soon prevailed upon them to lay down their Arms, and come and set down by him, after which most of us went to them, made them again some presents, and stay'd by them until dinner time, when we made them understand that we were going to eat, and asked them by signals to go with us; but this they declined, and as soon as we left them they went away in their Canoe. One of these Men was something above the Middle Age, the other 3 were young;

[155] As they had had nothing fresh but a little fish for four months, and scarcely any meat since they left the Society Islands, eleven months before, we can imagine that this was a feast (Wharton).

[156] This seems rather hard upon the Master (Wharton).

none of them were above 5½ feet high, and all their Limbs proportionately small. They were wholy naked, their Skins the Colour of Wood soot, and this seem'd to be their Natural Colour. Their Hair was black, lank, and cropt short, and neither wooly nor Frizled; nor did they want any of their Fore Teeth,[157] as Dampier has mentioned those did he saw on the Western side of this Country. Some part of their Bodys had been painted with red, and one of them had his upper lip and breast painted with Streakes of white, which he called *Carbanda*.[158] Their features were far from being disagreeable; their Voices were soft and Tunable, and they could easily repeat any word after us, but neither us nor Tupia could understand one word they said.

Wednesday, 11th.—Gentle land and Sea breezes. Employed Airing the Bread, stowing away water, Stores, etc. In the night the Master and Mr. Gore returned with the Long Boat, and brought with them one Turtle and a few Shell fish; the Yawl Mr. Gore left upon the Shoal with 6 Men to endeavour to strike more Turtle. In the morning 4 of the Natives made us another Short Visit; 3 of them had been with us the preceeding day, the other was a stranger. One of these men had a hole through the Bridge[159] of his nose, in which he stuck a peice of Bone as thick as my finger. Seeing this we examin'd all their Noses, and found that they had all holes for the same purpose; they had likewise holes in their Ears,[160] but no Ornaments hanging to them; they had bracelets on their Arms made of hair, and like Hoops of small Cord. They sometimes may wear a kind of fillet about their Heads, for one of them had applied some part of an old shirt which I had given them to this use.

Thursday, 12th.—Winds and weather as Yesterday, and the Employment of the People the same. At 2 A.M. the Yawl came on board, and brought 3 Turtle and a large Skeat,[161] and as there was a proba-

157 Tooth evulsion was frequently an important element in initiation ceremonies amongst the Aborigines, though Spencer and Gillen have stated that in the Aranda tribe it is simply a fashionable practice designed "to produce in the face a resemblance to certain dark rain clouds". In New South Wales it was an obligatory sacred ceremony; in parts of Western Australia it was an ordeal to be endured before the more important rite of circumcision. Professor Elkin states that cicatrisation was the most prominent feature of the initiation ceremonies in eastern Queensland.

Dampier's observations in Western Australia were made in 1688 when he was one of the *Cygnet* buccaneers, and recorded in *A New Voyage Round the World*, published in 1697. When in command of H.M.S. *Roebuck* in 1699 he again made a brief contact with the Aborigines about fifty miles from Roebuck Bay.

158 "Evidently Cook's rendering of *kapan-da*, 'marks-with'" (Beaglehole).

159 The cartilage of the nostril (Wharton). It was a common practice to pierce the nasal septum, sometimes as part of the rites at puberty or initiation, sometimes apparently for decorative purposes.

160 Piercing of the lobe of the ear, according to Basedow, was practised only in the Cape York Peninsula region.

161 Unidentifiable.

bility of succeeding in this kind of fishery, I sent her out again after breakfast. About this time 5 of the Natives came over and stay'd with us all the Forenoon. There were 7 in all—5 Men, 1 Woman, and a Boy; these 2 last stay'd on the point of Land on the other side of the River about 200 Yards from us. We could very clearly see with our Glasses that the Woman was as naked as ever she was born; even those parts which I always before now thought Nature would have taught a woman to Conceal were uncovered.

Friday, 13th.—Gentle breezes from the S.E. in day, and Calm or light Airs from the Land in the Night. Employ'd taking on board water, Stores, etc. At Noon the Yawl return'd with one Turtle and a large Sting ray.

Saturday, 14th.—Gentle breezes at S.E. and Hazey weather. In the P.M. compleated our water; got on board all the Bread, and part of our Stores; in the evening sent the Turtlers out again. A.M., employ'd getting on board stone ballast and Airing the spare Sails. Mr. Gore, being in the Country, shott one of the Animals before spoke of; it was a small one of the sort, weighing only 28 pound clear of the entrails; its body was[162] long; the head, neck and Shoulders very Small in proportion to the other parts. It was hair lipt, and the Head and Ears were most like a Hare's of any Animal I know; the Tail was nearly as long as the body, thick next the Rump, and Tapering towards the End; the fore Legs were 8 Inches long, and the Hind 22. Its progression is by Hopping or Jumping 7 or 8 feet at each hop upon its hind Legs only, for in this it makes no use of the Fore, which seem to be only design'd for Scratching in the ground, etc. The Skin is cover'd with a Short, hairy furr of a dark Mouse or Grey Colour. It bears no sort of resemblance to any European animal I ever saw; it is said to bear much resemblance to the Jerboa, excepting in size, the Jerboa being no larger than a common rat.[163]

Sunday, 15th.—Gentle breezes at S.E. and E. P.M., got on board

162 Blank space in MS. (Wharton).

163 The following notes have been compiled from information supplied by Ellis Troughton. In a series of publications Iredale and Troughton have identified the original small kangaroo first shot, and described by Solander, as the northern form of the whiptail wallaby, subsequently named "*Mus*" *canguru* by Muller, as based on the description and figure in Hawkesworth. Correspondingly, the above authors' whiptail wallaby identification is based primarily on Solander's description, and the slender-formed, long-tailed and "Greyhound" type of kangaroo as depicted by line drawings by Parkinson. A number of authors in disagreement with the wallaby identification of Iredale and Troughton insisted that the first small kangaroo must have been a juvenile Great Grey Kangaroo, although this kangaroo has never been recorded from within the Cooktown vicinity, as bounded by the Endeavour River. See earlier notes for 24 June.

Painted by N. Dance Esq. R.A. Engraved by W. Holl.

CAPTAIN JAMES COOK.

Jam^s Cook

FISHER, SON, & Co LONDON, & PARIS.

New South Wales Department of Tourist Activities

Bateman's Bay

New South Wales Department of Tourist Activities

Bulli, where Cook attempted to land

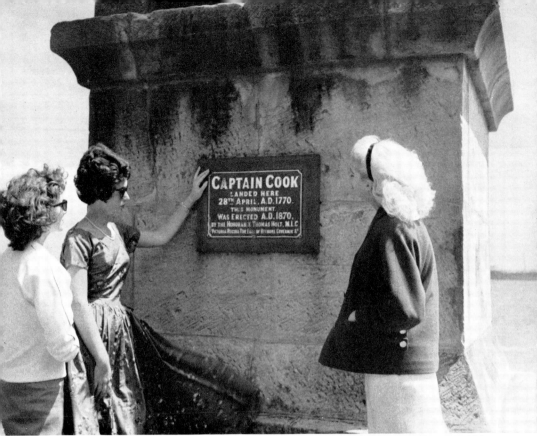

New South Wales Department of Tourist Activities

Monument at Kurnell in Botany Bay

South Head, at the entrance to Port Jackson

New South Wales Department of Tourist Activities

Newcastle

New South Wales Department of Tourist Activities

Port Stephens

State Public Relations Bureau, Queensland

Moreton Bay. An infra-red photograph of Moreton Bay looking north

State Public Relations Bureau, Queensland

Glasshouse Mountains

State Public Relations Bureau, Queensland

Fraser Island, or Great Sandy Island, looking south to Indian Head

State Public Relations Bureau, Queensland

Cape Capricorn Lighthouse on Curtis Island

State Public Relations Bureau, Queensland

Middle Island in the Northumberland Group

State Public Relations Bureau, Queensland

Pentecost Island and islands of the Cumberland Group

Qantas Photo

Whitsunday Passage from Hayman Island

State Public Relations Bureau, Queensland

The Lighthouse on Dent Island, Whitsunday Passage

State Public Relations Bureau, Queensland

Cape Edgecumbe, looking north from Flagstaff Hill

State Public Relations Bureau, Queensland

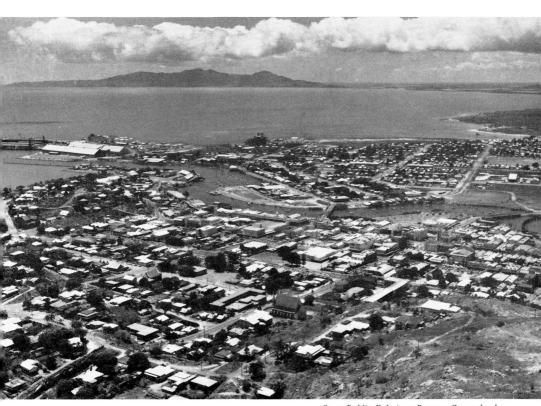

Townsville and Cleveland Bay, with Cape Cleveland in the distance

State Public Relations Bureau, Queensland

Magnetic Island, facing Cleveland Bay

State Public Relations Bureau, Queensland

Halifax Bay, north of Townsville

State Public Relations Bureau, Queensland

Hinchinbrook Island and the passage between the island and the mainland

State Public Relations Bureau, Queensland

Dunk Island and other islands in Rockingham Bay

State Public Relations Bureau, Queensland

Endeavour River

Model of the *Endeavour* in Cooktown Museum

Qantas Photo

State Public Relations Bureau, Queensland

Cook's Monument, Cooktown

State Public Relations Bureau, Queensland

The Plaque on Cook's Monument, Possession Island

State Public Relations Bureau, Queensland

Cape York

State Public Relations Bureau, Queensland

Prince of Wales Island from Thursday Island

Maatsuyker Island showing the lighthouse

Tasmanian Government Tourist and Immigration Department

Tasmanian Government Tourist and Immigration Department

D'Entrecasteaux Passage

Tasmanian Government Tourist and Immigration Department

Adventure Bay, Bruny Island

the Spare Sails and sundry other Articles. In the A.M., as the people did not work upon the Ship, one of the Petty Officers was desirous of going out to Catch Turtles. I let him have the Pinnace for that purpose, and sent the Long boat to haul the Sean, who caught about 60 fish.

Monday, 16th.—Fore and Latter parts gentle breezes at E.N.E.; in the night had light Airs and Calm. In the evening the Yawl came in with 4 Turtle and a Large Sting ray, and soon after went out again; but the Pinnace did not return as I expected. A.M., employ'd getting on board Cables; at the same time I went upon one of the high hills on the N. side of the River, from which I had an extensive view of the inland Country, which consisted of hills, Valleys, and Large plains, agreeably diversified with Woods and Lawns.

Tuesday, 17th.—Wind at S.E., a fresh breeze; people employed as yesterday setting up the rigging. In the evening the Pinnace returned with 3 Turtles, 2 of which the Yawl caught and sent in. At 7hrs. 41′ 17″ p.m. observ'd the first Satellite of Jupiter to Emerge, and the same Emersion hapned at Greenwich at 10hrs. 00′ 52″ in the a.m.; the difference is 14hrs. 19′ 35″ = to 214° 53′ 45″ of Long. The observation made on the 29th of last Month gave 214° 42′ 30″; the mean is 214° 48′ 7½″, which this place is W. of Greenwich.[164]

Wednesday, 18th.—Wind at E.S.E., a Gentle breeze. P.M., I sent the Master and one of the Mates in the Pinnace to the Northward to look for a Channell that way clear of the Shoal. Mr. Banks, Dr. Solander, and myself took a turn into the woods on the other side of the water, where we met with 5 of the Natives; and although we had not seen any of them before, they came to us without showing any signs of fear. 2 of these wore Necklaces made of Shells, which they seem'd to Value, as they would not part with them. In the evening the Yawl came in with 3 Turtle, and early in the A.M. she went out again. About 8 we were Visited by several of the Natives, who now became more familiar than ever. Soon after this Mr. Banks and I went over to the S.[165] side of the River, and Travel'd 6 or 8 miles along shore to the Northward, where we ascended a high hill,[166] from whence I had an extensive view of the Sea Coast; it afforded us a melancholy prospect of the difficulties we are to encounter, for in whatever direction we looked it was cover'd with Shoals as far as the Eye could see; after this we return'd to the Ship without meeting with anything

[164] As before mentioned, the true longitude is 214° 45′ (Wharton).

[165] This should be N (Wharton).

[166] Indian Head.

remarkable, and found several of the Natives on board. At this time we had 12 tortoise or Turtle upon our Decks, which they took more Notice of than anything Else in the Ship, as I was told by the officers, for their Curiosity was Satisfied before I got on board, and they went away soon after.

Thursday, 19th.—Gentle breezes and fair weather. Employ'd getting everything in readyness for Sea. A.M., we were Visited by 10 or 11 of the Natives; the most of them came from the other side of the Harbour, where we saw 6 or 7 more, the most of them Women, and, like the men, quite naked. Those that came on board were very desirous of having some of our Turtles, and took the liberty to haul 2 of them to the Gangway to put over the side; being disappointed in this, they grew a little Troublesome, and were for throwing every thing overboard they could lay their hands upon. As we had no Victuals dress'd at this time, I offer'd them some bread to Eat, which they rejected with Scorn, as I believe they would have done anything else excepting Turtle; soon after this they all went ashore, Mr. Banks, myself, and 5 or 6 of our people being their at same time. Immediately upon their Landing one of them took a Handful of dry grass and lighted it at a fire we had ashore, and before we well know'd what he was going about he made a larger Circuit round about us, and set fire to the grass in this way, and in an instant the whole place was in flames. Luckily at this time we had hardly anything ashore, besides the Forge and a Sow with a litter of young Pigs, one of which was scorched to Death in the fire. As soon as they had done this they all went to a place where some of our people were washing, and where all our nets and a good deal of linnen were laid out to dry; here with the greatest obstinacy they again set fire to the grass, which I and some others who were present could not prevent, until I was obliged to fire a Musquet load with small Shott at one of the Ring leaders, which sent them off. As we were apprised of this last Attempt of theirs we got the fire out before it got head, but the first spread like wild fire in the Woods and grass. Notwithstanding my firing, in which one must have been a little hurt, because we saw a few drops of blood on some of the linnen he had gone over, they did not go far from us; for we soon after heard their Voices in the woods, upon which Mr. Banks and I and 3 or 4 more went to look for them, and very soon met them coming toward us. As they had each 4 or 5 Darts, and not knowing their intention, we seized upon 6 or 7 of the first darts we met with. This alarm'd them so much that they all made off, and we follow'd them for near ½ a Mile, and then set down and called to them, and they stop'd also; after some little unintelligible conversation had passed they laid down their darts, and came to us in a very friendly manner. We now return'd the Darts we had taken from them, which reconcil'd everything. There were 4 Strangers among them that we had not seen before, and these were interduced to us by name by the others; the Man which we supposed to have been Struck with small Shott was gone off, but he could not be much hurt as he was at a great distance when I fir'd. They all came along with us abreast of the Ship, where they stay'd a short time, and then went away, and soon after set the woods on fire about a Mile and a half or two Miles from us.

Friday, 20th.—Fresh breezes at S.E. and Cloudy weather. P.M., got everything on board the Ship, new berth'd her, and let her swing with the tide. In the night the Master return'd with the pinnace, and reported that there was no safe Passage for the Ship to the Northward at low water. A.M., I went and Sounded and buoy'd the Bar, being now ready to put to sea the first opportunity.

Saturday, 21st.—Strong breezes at S.E. and Cloudy weather. P.M., sent a Boat to haul the Sean, which return'd with as much fish as came to 1¾lb. per Man; the Yawl return'd with only one Turtle, which was caught in the Net, for it blew too hard for the Boat to strike any. In the morning I sent her out again, but she was obliged to return, not being able to get to Windward. The Carpenters employ'd in repairing the Boats and overhauling the Pumps, and as the Wind would not permit us to sail, I sent the Boatswain with some hands ashore to make rope, and a petty Officer with 2 Men to gather Greens for the Ship's Company.

Sunday, 22nd.—Fresh breezes at S.E. and E.S.E. Employ'd as Yesterday. A.M., the weather would not permit us to Sail; sent the Turtlers out again. In opening of one to-day we found sticking thro' both Shoulder bones a wood Harpoon, or Turtle Peg,[167] 15 Inches long, bearded at the end, such as we have seen among the Natives; this proves to a Demonstration that they strike Turtle, I suppose at the Time they come ashore to lay their Eggs, for they certainly have no boat fit to do this at Sea, or that will carry a Turtle, and this Harpoon must have been a good while in, as the wound was quite heal'd up.

Monday, 23rd.—Fresh breezes in the S.E. quarter, which so long as it continues will confine us in Port. Yesterday, A.M., I sent some people in the Country to gather greens, one of which stragled from the rest, and met with 4 of the Natives by a fire, on which they

167 On the coasts of Cape York Peninsula and Arnhem Land, harpoons with detachable heads were used to catch dugong and turtles.

were broiling a Fowl, and the hind leg of one of the Animals before spoke of.[168] He had the presence of mind not to run from them (being unarm'd), least they should pursue him, but went and set down by them; and after he had set a little while, and they had felt his hands and other parts of his body, they suffer'd him to go away without offering the least insult, and perceiving that he did not go right for the Ship they directed him which way to go.

Tuesday, 24th.—Winds and weather continues. The Seamen employ'd making ropes, Caulking the Ship, Fishing, etc.

Wednesday, 25th.—Fresh gales at S.E. and fair weather. In the evening the Yawl came in, having not been able to Strike one Turtle on account of the blowing weather, nor can we catch much fish with the Sean in the Harbour.

Thursday, 26th.—Winds and weather as Yesterday. Such people as can be spared from the necessary Dutys of the Ship are employ'd fishing and gathering greens and other refreshments.

Friday, 27th.—Very fresh Gales at S.E. by S. and fair weather. A.M., caught as much fish as served ¾ lb. a man, and Mr. Gore shott one of the Animals before spoke of, which weighed 80 lbs. and 54 lbs., exclusive of the entrails, Skin, and head; this was as large as the most we have seen.[169]

Saturday, 28th.—Winds and weather as above, without the least Variation the whole of the 24 hours. The Carpenters finish'd caulking the Ship.

Sunday, 29th.—Winds at S.E., a fresh breeze until 5 a.m., at which time it fell calm, and soon after had a light breeze from the land. Upon this I sent a Boat to see what water was upon the bar (it being 2 hours Ebb), and hove up the Anchor in order to put to Sea; but upon the return of the Boat came too again, as there were only 13 feet water on the Bar, which was 6 Inches less water than what the Ship Draw'd. After this I sent the Yawl to look for Turtle, as those we had got before were nearly all expended. About 8 the Sea breeze set in again, which put an end to our Sailing this day; after which I sent the Pinnace to haul the Sean; she return'd with only 20 lbs. of Fish.

[168] The Aborigines made earth ovens to cook their food, but it was frequently singed and partially cooked on the embers of the fire, and eaten in a half-raw condition.

[169] This macropod is now generally accepted as being a northern form of Wallaroo (*Osphranter reginae* of Schwarz) (Troughton).

Monday, 30th.—Winds at S.E., a fresh Gale and fair weather in the P.M., the remainder Hazey, with rain, but the winds, tho more moderate, keept in the S.E. quarter.

Tuesday, 31st.—Fresh Gales at S.E., and hazey with rain all P.M. and most part of the Night. At 2 a.m. I had thoughts of trying to Warp the Ship out of the Harbour, but upon my going first out in a Boat I found it blow too fresh for such an Attempt.

Wednesday, 1st August.—Strong Gales from the S.E., with Squalls attended with Rain. P.M., the Yawl came in with 2 Rays, which together weighed 265 lbs.; it blow'd too hard all the time they were out for striking Turtle. Carpenters employ'd overhauling the Pumps, all of which we find in a state of decay; and this the Carpenter says is owing to the Sap having been left in, which in time has decay'd the sound wood. One of them is quite useless, and was so rotten when hoisted up as to drop to peices. However, I cannot complain of a Leaky Ship, for the most water She makes is not quite an Inch an Hour.

Thursday, 2nd.—Winds and weather as yesterday, or rather more Stormy; we have now no Success in the Sein fishing, hardly getting above 20 or 30 lbs. a day.

Friday, 3rd.—Strong breezes, and hazey until 6 a.m., when it moderated, and we unmoor'd, hove up the Anchor, and began to Warp out; but the Ship tailing upon the Sand on the N. side of the River, the Tide of Ebb making out, and a fresh breeze setting in, we were obliged to desist and moor the Ship again just within the Barr.

Saturday, 4th.—In the P.M., having pretty moderate weather, I order'd the Coasting Anchor and Cable to be laid without the barr, to be ready to warp out by, that we might not loose the least opportunity that might Offer; for laying in Port spends time to no purpose, consumes our Provisions, of which we are very Short in many Articles, and we have yet a long Passage to make to the E. Indies through an unknown and perhaps dangerous Sea; these Circumstances consider'd, make me very Anxious of getting to Sea. The wind continued moderate all night, and at 5 a.m. it fell calm; this gave us an opportunity to warp out. About 7 we got under sail, having a light Air from the Land, which soon died away, and was Succeeded by the Sea breezes from S.E. by S., with which we stood off to Sea E. by N., having the Pinnace ahead sounding. The Yawl I sent to the Turtle bank to take up the Net that was left there; but as the wind freshen'd we got out before her, and a little After Noon Anchor'd in 15 fathoms water, Sandy bottom, for I did not think it safe to run in among the Shoals until I had well view'd them at low Water from the Mast head, that I might be better Able to Judge which way to Steer; for as yet I had not resolved whether I should beat back to the Southward round all the Shoals, or seek a Passage to the Eastward or Northward, all of which appeared to be equally difficult and dangerous. When at Anchor the Harbour sail'd from bore S. 70° W., distant 4 or 5 Leagues; the Northermost point of the Main land we have in sight, which I named Cape Bedford[170] (Lat. 15° 17′ S., Long. 214° 45′ W.), bore N. 20° W., distant 3½ Leagues; but we could see land to the N.E. of this Cape, which made like 2 high Islands;[171] the Turtle banks bore E., distant one Mile. Lat. by Observation 15° 23′ S.; our depth of Water, in standing off from the land, was from 3½ to 15 fathoms.

I shall now give a Short description of the Harbour, or River,[172] we have been in, which I named after the Ship, Endeavour River. It is only a small Barr Harbour or Creek, which runs winding 3 or 4 Leagues in land, at the Head of which is a small fresh Water Brook, as I was told, for I was not so high myself; but there is not water for Shipping above a Mile within the barr, and this is on the N. side, where the bank is so steep for nearly a quarter of a Mile that ships may lay afloat at low water so near the Shore as to reach it with a stage, and is extreamly Convenient for heaving a Ship down. And this is all the River hath to recommend it, especially for large Shipping, for there is no more than 9 or 10 feet Water upon the Bar at low water, and 17 or 18 feet at high, the Tides rises and falling about 9 feet at spring Tide, and is high on the days of the New and full Moon, between 9 and 10 o'Clock. Besides, this part of the Coast is barrocaded with Shoals, as to make this Harbour more difficult of access; the safest way I know of to come at it is from the South, Keeping the Main land close on board all the way. Its situation may always be found by the Latitude, which hath been before mentioned. Over the S. point is some high Land, but the N. point is formed by a low sandy beach, which extends about 3 Miles to the Northward, then the land is again high.

The refreshments we got here were Chiefly Turtle, but as we had to go 5 Leagues out to Sea for them, and had much blowing weather, we were not over Stocked with this Article; however, what with these and the fish we caught with the Sean we had not much reason to

170 Probably after John, fourth Duke, who had been First Lord of the Admiralty, 1744-7 (Wharton).

171 Direction Islands (Wharton).

172 The only river in Australia named by Cook.

Complain, considering the Country we were in. Whatever refreshment we got that would bear a Division I caused to be equally divided among the whole Company, generally by weight; the meanest person in the Ship had an equal share with myself or any one on board, and this method every commander of a Ship on such a Voyage as this ought ever to Observe. We found in several places on the Sandy beaches and Sand Hills near the Sea, Purslain[173] and beans,[174] which

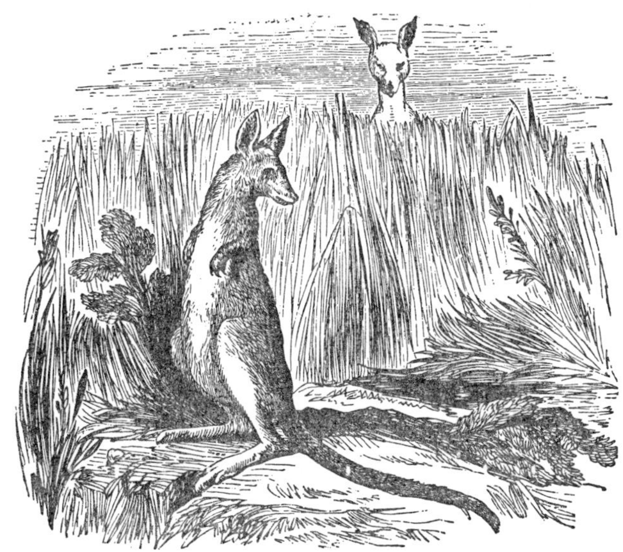

KANGUROO.

grows on a Creeping kind of a Vine. The first we found very good when boiled, and the latter not to be dispised, and were at first very serviceable to the Sick; but the best greens we found here was the Tarra, or Coco Tops, called in the West Indies Indian Kale,[175] which grows in most Boggy Places; these eat as well as, or better, than Spinnage. The roots, for want of being Transplanted and properly Cultivated, were not good, yet we could have dispensed with them could we have got them in any Tolerable plenty; but having a good way to go for them, it took up too much time and too many hands to gather both root and branch. The few Cabage Palms we found here were in General small, and yielded so little Cabage that they were not worth the Looking after, and this was the Case with most of the fruit, etc., we found in the woods.

173 Identification is uncertain, but may possibly have been *Sesuvium portulacastrum* (Mair).

174 Possibly *Canavalia* sp. (Mair).

175 *Alocasia macrorrhizos* (Mair).

Besides the Animals which I have before mentioned, called by the Natives Kangooroo, or Kanguru, here are Wolves,[176] Possums,[177] an Animal like a ratt, and snakes, both of the Venemous and other sorts. Tame Animals here are none except Dogs, and of these we never saw but one, who frequently came about our Tents to pick up bones, etc. The Kanguru are in the greatest number, for we seldom went into the Country without seeing some. The land Fowls we met here, which far from being numerous, were Crows, Kites, Hawkes, Cockadores of 2 Sorts, the one white, and the other brown, very beautiful Loryquets of 2 or 3 Sorts, Pidgeons, Doves, and a few other sorts of small Birds. The Sea or Water fowl are Herns, Whisling Ducks, which perch and, I believe, roost on Trees; Curlews, etc., and not many of these neither. Some of our Gentlemen who were in the Country heard and saw Wild Geese in the Night.[178]

The Country, as far as I could see, is diversified with Hills and plains, and these with woods and Lawns; the Soil of the Hills is hard, dry, and very Stoney; yet it produceth a thin Coarse grass, and some wood. The Soil of the Plains and Valleys are sandy, and in some places Clay, and in many Parts very Rocky and Stoney, as well as the Hills, but in general the Land is pretty well Cloathed with long grass, wood, Shrubs, etc. The whole Country abounds with an immense number of Ant Hills, some of which are 6 or 8 feet high, and more than twice that in Circuit. Here are but few sorts of Trees besides the Gum tree, which is the most numerous, and is the same that we found on the Southern Part of the Coast, only here they do not grow near so large. On each side of the River, all the way up it, are Mangroves, which Extend in some places a Mile from its banks; the Country in general is not badly water'd, there being several fine Rivulets at no very great distance from one another, but none near to the place where we lay;

[176] Dingoes.

[177] The possum would be a ringtail of the genus *Pseudocheirus*, possibly of the species *peregrinus*, though other species of closely related genera may be involved (Troughton).

[178] Crow (*Corvus cecilae*).

Kites. Probably the Fork-tailed Kite (*Milvus migrans*).

Hawks. These could be of several species.

Cockadores: White. The White Cockatoo (*Kakatoe galerita*).

Brown (?) The Red-tailed Black Cockatoo occurs in the area, but it is not brown.

Loryquets. The Rainbow Lorikeet and the Scaly-breasted Lorikeet occur in the area.

Herns. Several species occur in the area.

Whistling Ducks. Both the Whistling Tree-Duck (*Dendrocygna arcuata*) and Plumed Tree-Duck (*D. eytoni*) occur in the area.

Curlews. Possibly the Sea-Curlew or Eastern Curlew (*Numenius madagascariensis*), a common non-breeding migrant, from the northern hemisphere.

Wild Geese. Possibly Pied Geese (*Anseranas semipalmata*) (Hindwood).

at least not in the Dry season, which is at this time. However we were very well supply'd with water by springs which were not far off.[179]

Sunday, 5th.—In the P.M. had a Gentle breeze at S.E. and Clear weather. As I did not intend to weigh until the morning I sent all the Boats to the Reef to get what Turtle and Shell fish they could. At low water from the Mast head I took a view of the Shoals, and could see several laying a long way without this one, a part of several of them appearing above water; but as it appear'd pretty clear of Shoals to the N.E. of the Turtle Reef, I came to a Resolution to stretch out that way close upon a wind, because if we found no Passage we could always return back the way we went. In the Evening the Boats return'd with one Turtle, a sting ray, and as many large Clams as came to 1½ lbs. a Man; in each of these Clams were about 20 lbs. of Meat;[180] added to this we Caught in the night several Sharks. Early in the morning I sent the Pinnace and Yawl again to the Reef, as I did not intend to weigh until half Ebb, at which time the Shoals began to appear. Before 8 it came on to blow, and I made the Signal for the Boats to come on Board, which they did, and brought with them one Turtle. We afterwards began to heave, but the wind Freshening obliged us to bear away[181] again and lay fast.

Monday, 6th.—Winds at S.E. At 2 o'Clock p.m. it fell pretty Moderate, and we got under sail, and stood out upon a wind N.E. by E., leaving the Turtle Reef to windward, having the Pinnace ahead sounding. We had not stood out long before we discovered shoals ahead and on both bows. At half past 4 o'Clock, having run off 8 Miles, the Pinnace made the Signal for Shoal water in a place where we little Expected it; upon this we Tack'd and Stood on and off while the Pinnace stretched farther to the Eastward, but as night was approaching I thought it safest to Anchor, which we accordingly did in 20 fathoms water, a Muddy bottom. Endeavour River bore S. 52° W.; Cape Bedford W. by N. ½ N., distant 5 Leagues; the

179 Cooktown, which now stands on the Endeavour River, is a thriving place, and the northernmost town on this coast. It has some 2,000 inhabitants, and is the port for a goldmining district. A deeper channel has now been dredged over the bar that gave Cook so much trouble, but it is not a harbour that will admit large vessels (Wharton).

See note on page 84. In the days of the goldrush in the 1870s there was a population of several thousand, but since then Cooktown has declined and there are only a few hundred inhabitants.

180 *Tridacna* (McMichael). The giant clam of the northern part of the Great Barrier Reef is the world's largest shellfish. The shells of these enormous molluscs weigh up to 500 lb.

181 To veer cable, i.e., pay out more cable, in order to hold the ship with the freshening wind (Wharton).

Northermost land in sight, which made like an Island, N.; and a Shoal, a small, sandy part of which appear'd above water, N.E., distance 2 or 3 Miles. In standing off from this Turtle Reef to this place our soundings were from 14 to 20 fathoms, but where the Pinnace was, about a Mile farther to the E.N.E., were no more than 4 or 5 feet of water, rocky ground; and yet this did not appear to us in the Ship. In the morning we had a strong Gale from the S.E., that, instead of weighing as we intended, we were obliged to bear away more Cable, and to Strike Top Gallant yards.

Tuesday, 7th.–Strong Gales at S.E., S.E. by S., and S.S.E., with cloudy weather at Low water in the P.M. I and several of the Officers kept a look out at the Mast head to see for a Passage between the Shoals; but we could see nothing but breakers all the way from the South round by the East as far as N.W., extending out to Sea as far as we could see. It did not appear to be one continued Shoal, but several laying detached from each other. On the Eastermost that we could see the Sea broke very high, which made one judge it to be the outermost; for on many of those within the Sea did not break high at all, and from about ½ flood to ½ Ebb they are not to be seen, which makes the Sailing among them more dangerous, and requires great care and Circumspection, for, like all other Shoals, or Reefs of Coral Rocks, they are quite steep too. Altho' the most of these Shoals consist of Coral Rocks, yet a part of some of them is sand. The Turtle Reef and some others have a small Patch of Sand generally at the N. end, that is only cover'd at high water. These generally discover themselves before we come near them. Altho' I speak of this as the Turtle Reef, yet it is not to be doubted but what there are Turtle upon the most of them as well as this one. After having well viewed our situation from the Mast Head, I saw that we were surrounded on every side with Dangers, in so much that I was quite at a loss which way to steer when the weather will permit us to get under sail, for to beat back to the S.E. the way we came, as the Master would have had me done, would be an endless peice of work, as the winds blow constantly from that Quarter, and very Strong, without hardly any intermission;[182] on the other hand, if we do not find a passage to the Northward we shall have to come back at last. At 11 the Ship drove, and obliged us to bear away to a Cable and one third, which brought us up again; but in the morning the Gale increasing, she drove again. This made us let go the Small Bower Anchor, and bear away a whole

[182] The south-east trade wind blows home on this coast very strong from about June to October. Though the Barrier Reef prevents any great sea from getting up, the continuance of this wind is a great nuisance for a sailing ship from many points of view though from others it is an advantage (Wharton).

Cable on it and 2 on the other; and even after this she still kept driving slowly, until we had got down Top gallant Masts, struck Yards and Top masts close down, and made all snug; then she rid fast, C. Bedford bearing W.S.W., distant 3½ Leagues. In this situation we had Shoals to the Eastward of us extending from the S.E. by S. to the N.N.W., distant from the nearest part of them about 2 Miles.

Wednesday, 8th.—Strong gales at S.S.E. all this day, in so much that I durst not get up Yards and Topmasts.

Thursday, 9th.—In the P.M., the weather being something moderate, we got up the Top masts, but keept the Lower yards down. At 6 in the morning we began to heave in the Cable, thinking to get under sail; but it blow'd so fresh, together with a head sea, that we could hardly heave the ship a head, and at last was obliged to desist.

Friday, 10th.—Fresh Gales at S.S.E. and S.E. by S. P.M., the wind fell so that we got up the small Bower Anchor, and hove into a whole Cable on the Best Bower. At 3 in the morning we got up the Lower Yards, and at 7 weighed and stood in for the Land (intending to seek for a passage along Shore to the northward), having a Boat ahead sounding; depth of water as we run in from 19 to 12 fathoms. After standing in an hour we edged away for 3 Small Islands[183] that lay N.N.E. ½ E., 3 Leagues from C. Bedford. To these Islands the Master had been in the Pinnace when the Ship was in Port. At 9 we were abreast of them, and between them and the Main, having another low Island between us and the latter, which lies W.N.W., 4 Miles from the 3 Islands. In this Channell had 14 fathoms water; the Northermost point of the Main we had in sight bore from us N.N.W. ½ W., distant 2 Leagues. 4 or 5 Leagues to the N.E. of this head land appeared 3 high Islands,[184] with some smaller ones near them, and the Shoals and Reefs without, as we could see, extending to the Northward as far as these Islands. We directed our Course between them and the above headland, leaving a small Island[185] to the Eastward of us, which lies N. by E., 4 Miles from the 3 Islands, having all the while a boat ahead sounding. At Noon we were got between the head Land and the 3 high Islands, distant from the former 2, and from the latter 4 Leagues; our Lat. by observation was 14° 51′ S. We now judged ourselves to be clear of all Danger, having, as we thought, a Clear, open

183 The name appears on the chart as Three Isles.

184 The Direction Islands (Wharton). The chart renders the name Islands of Direction. See page 112.

185 The Two Isles. Cook had now got among the numerous islands and reefs that lie round Cape Flattery. There are good channels between them, but they are very confusing to a stranger. Cook's anxiety in his situation can well be imagined, especially with his recent disaster in his mind (Wharton).

Sea before us; but this we soon found otherwise, and occasioned my calling the Headland above mentioned Cape Flattery (Lat. 14° 55′ S., Long. 214° 43′ W.). It is a high Promontory, making in 2 Hills next the sea, and a third behind them, with low sandy land on each side; but it is better known by the 3 high Islands out at Sea, the Northermost of which is the Largest, and lies from the Cape N.N.E., distant 5 Leagues. From this Cape the Main land trends away N.W. and N.W. by W.

Saturday, 11th.—Fresh breezes at S.S.E. and S.E. by S., with which we steer'd along shore N.W. by W. until one o'Clock, when the Petty Officer at the Masthead called out that he saw land ahead, extending quite round to the Islands without, and a large reef between us and them; upon this I went to the Masthead myself. The reef I saw very plain, which was now so far to windward that we could not weather it, but what he took for Main land ahead were only small Islands, for such they appeared to me; but, before I had well got from the Mast head the Master and some others went up, who all asserted that it was a Continuation of the Main land, and, to make it still more alarming, they said they saw breakers in a Manner all round us. We immediately hauld upon a wind in for the Land, and made the Signal for the Boat, which was ahead sounding, to come on board; but as she was well to leeward, we were obliged to edge away to take her up, and soon after came to an Anchor under a point of the Main in ¼ less 5[186] fathoms, about a Mile from the Shore, Cape Flattery bearing S.E., distant 3½ Leagues. After this I landed, and went upon the point, which is pretty high, from which I had a View of the Sea Coast, which trended away N.W. by W., 8 or 10 Leagues, which was as far as I could see, the weather not being very clear. I likewise saw 9 or 10 Small, Low Islands and some Shoals laying off the Coast, and some large Shoals between the Main and the 3 high Islands, without which, I was now well assured, were Islands,[187] and not a part of the Mainland as some had taken them to be. Excepting C. Flattery and the point I am now upon, which I have named point Lookout, the Main land next the sea to the Northward of Cape Bedford is low, and Chequer'd with white sand and green Bushes, etc., for 10 or 12 Miles inland, beyond which is high land. To the northward of Point Lookout the shore appear'd to be shoal and flat some distance off, which was no good sign of meeting with a Channell in with the land, as we have hitherto done. We saw the foosteps of people upon the sand, and smoke and fire up in the Country, and in the evening return'd on board, where I came to a resolution to visit one of the high

186 The nautical manner of expressing four and three-quarters (Wharton).
187 The Howick Islands.

Islands in the Offing in my Boat, as they lay at least 5 Leagues out at Sea, and seem'd to be of such a height that from the Top of one of them I hoped to see and find a Passage out to sea clear of the Shoals. Accordingly in the Morning I set out in the Pinnace for the Northermost and largest of the 3, accompanied by Mr. Banks. At the same time I sent the Master in the Yawl to Leeward, to sound between the Low Islands and the Main. In my way to the Island I passed over a large reef of Coral Rocks and sand, which lies about 2 Leagues from the Island; I left another to leeward, which lays about 3 Miles from the Island. On the N. part of this is a low, sandy Isle, with Trees upon it; on the reef we pass'd over in the Boat we saw several Turtle, and Chased one or Two, but caught none, it blowing too hard, and I had no time to spare, being otherways employ'd. I did not reach the Island until half an hour after one o'Clock in the P.M. on.

Sunday, 12th, when I immediately went upon the highest hill on the Island,[188] where, to my Mortification, I discover'd a Reef of Rocks laying about 2 or 3 Leagues without the Island, extending in a line N.W. and S.E., farther than I could see, on which the sea broke very high.[189] This, however, gave one great hopes that they were the outermost shoals, as I did not doubt but what I should be able to get without them, for there appeared to be several breaks or Partitions in the Reef, and Deep Water between it and the Islands. I stay'd upon the Hill until near sun set, but the weather continued so Hazey all the time that I could not see above 4 or 5 Leagues round me, so that I came down much disappointed in the prospect I expected to have had, but being in hopes the morning might prove Clearer, and give me a better View of the Shoals. With this view I stay'd all night upon the Island, and at 3 in the Morning sent the Pinnace, with one of the Mates I had with me, to sound between the Island and the Reefs, and to Examine one of the breaks or Channels; and in the mean time I went again upon the Hill, where I arrived by Sun Rise, but found it much Hazier than in the Evening. About Noon the pinnace return'd, having been out as far as the Reef, and found from 15 to 28 fathoms water. It blow'd so hard that they durst not venture into one of the Channels, which, the Mate said, seem'd to him to be very narrow; but this did not discourage me, for I thought from the place he was at he must have seen it at disadvantage. Before I quit this Island I shall describe it. It lies, as I have before observed, about 5 Leagues from the

188 Lizard Island (Wharton). In addition to the importance of this island as the place where Cook sighted an opening in the Great Barrier Reef through which the *Endeavour* made its escape from the shoals, Lizard Island is also notable as the scene of the ordeal of Mrs Watson in 1881, and her escape from the Aborigines in an iron tank.

189 This was the outer edge of the Barrier Reef (Wharton).

Main; it is about 8 Miles in Circuit, and of a height sufficient to be seen 10 or 12 Leagues; it is mostly high land, very rocky and barren, except on the N.W. side, where there are some sandy bays and low land, which last is covered with thin, long grass, Trees, etc., the same as upon the Main. Here is also fresh Water in 2 places; the one is a running stream, the water a little brackish where I tasted it, which was close to the sea; the other is a standing pool, close behind the sandy beach, of good, sweet water, as I daresay the other is a little way from the Sea beach. The only land Animals we saw here were Lizards, and these seem'd to be pretty Plenty, which occasioned my naming the Island Lizard Island. The inhabitants of the Main visit this Island at some Seasons of the Year, for we saw the Ruins of Several of their Hutts and heaps of Shells, etc. S.E., 4 or 5 Miles from this Island, lay the other 2 high Islands, which are very small compared to this; and near them lay 3 others, yet smaller and lower Islands, and several Shoals or reefs, especially to the S.E. There is, however, a clear passage from Cape Flattery to those Islands, and even quite out to the outer Reefs, leaving the above Islands to the S.E. and Lizard Island to the N.W.

Monday, 13th.—At 2 P.M. I left Lizard Island in order to return to the Ship, and in my way landed upon the low sandy Isle mentioned in coming out. We found on this Island a pretty number of Birds, the most of them sea Fowl, except Eagles;[190] 2 of the Latter we shott and some of the others; we likewise saw some Turtles, but got none, for the reasons before mentioned. After leaving Eagle Isle I stood S.W. direct for the Ship, sounding all the way, and had not less than 8 fathoms, nor more than 14. I had the same depth of Water between Lizard and Eagle Isle. After I got on board the Master inform'd me he had been down to the Islands I had directed him to go too, which he judged to lay about 3 Leagues from the Main, and had sounded the Channel between the 2, found 7 fathoms; this was near the Islands, for in with the Main he had only 9 feet 3 Miles off, but without the Islands he found 10, 12, and 14 fathoms. He found upon the islands piles of turtle shells, and some finns that were so fresh that both he and the boats' crew eat of them. This showed that the natives must have been there lately. After well considering both what I had seen myself and the report of the Master's, I found by experience that by keeping in with the Mainland we should be in continued danger, besides the risk we should run in being lock'd in with Shoals and reefs by not finding a passage out to Leeward. In case we persever'd in keeping the Shore on board an accident of this kind, or any other that

[190] Eagle Island (Wharton). The Eagle was the Sea-Eagle (*Haliäeëtus leucogaster*) (Hindwood).

might happen to the ship, would infallibly loose our passage to the East India's this Season,[191] and might prove the ruin of both ourselves and the Voyage, as we have now little more than 3 Months' Provisions on board, and that at short allowance. Wherefore, after consulting with the Officers, I resolved to weigh in the morning, and Endeavour to quit the Coast altogether until such time as I found I could approach it with less danger. With this View we got under sail at daylight in the morning, and stood out N.E. for the N.W. end of Lizard Island, having Eagle Island to windward of us, having the pinnace ahead sounding; and here we found a good Channell, wherein we had from 9 to 14 fathoms. At Noon the N. end of Lizard Island bore E.S.E., distant one Mile; Lat. observed 14° 38′ S.; depth of water 14 fathoms. We now took the pinnace in tow, knowing that there were no dangers until we got out to the Reefs.[192]

Tuesday, 14th.—Winds at S.E., a steady gale. By 2 P.M. we got out to the outermost reefs, and just fetched to Windward of one of the openings I had discover'd from the Island; we tacked and Made a short trip to the S.W., while the Master went in the pinnace to examine the Channel, who soon made the signal for the Ship to follow, which we accordingly did, and in a short time got safe out. This Channel[193] lies N.E. ½ N., 3 Leagues from Lizard Island; it is about one-third of a Mile broad, and 25 or 30 fathoms deep or more. The moment we were without the breakers we had no ground with 100 fathoms of Line, and found a large Sea rowling in from the S.E. By this I was well assured we were got with out all the Shoals, which gave us no small joy, after having been intangled among Islands and Shoals, more or less, ever since the 26th of May, in which time we have sail'd above 360 Leagues by the Lead without ever having a Leadsman out of the Chains, when the ship was under sail; a Circumstance that perhaps never hapned to any ship before, and yet it was here absolutely necessary. I should have been very happy to have had it in my power to have keept in with the land, in order to have explor'd the Coast to the Northern extremity of the Country, which I think we were not far off, for I firmly believe this land doth not join to New Guinea. But this I hope soon either to prove or disprove, and the reasons I have before assign'd will, I presume, be thought sufficient

191 In November the wind changes to the N.W., which would have been a foul wind to Batavia (Wharton).

192 From the 13th to the 19th the language used in Mr Corner's copy of the Journal is quite different from that of the Admiralty and the Queen's, though the occurrences are the same. From internal evidences, it appears that Mr Corner's copy was at this period the first written up, and that Cook amended the phrases in other fair copies (Wharton).

193 Now known as Cook's Passage (Wharton).

for my leaving the Coast at this time; not but what I intend to get in with it again as soon as I can do it with safety. The passage or channel we now came out by, which I have named[194] lies in the Lat. of 14° 32′ S.; it may always be found and known by the 3 high Islands within it, which I have called the Islands of Direction, because by their means a safe passage may be found even by strangers in within the Main reef, and quite into the Main. Lizard Island, which is the Northermost and Largest of the 3, Affords snug Anchorage under the N.W. side of it, fresh water and wood for fuel; and the low Islands and Reefs which lay between it and the Main, abound with Turtle and other fish, which may be caught at all Seasons of the Year (except in such blowing weather as we have lately had). All these things considered there is, perhaps, not a better place on the whole Coast for a Ship to refresh at than this Island. I had forgot to mention in its proper place, that not only on this Island, but on Eagle Island, and on several places of the Sea beach in and about Endeavour River, we found Bamboos, Cocoa Nutts, the seeds of some few other plants, and Pummice-stones, which were not the produce of the Country. From what we have seen of it, it is reasonable to suppose that they are the produce of some lands or Islands laying in the Neighbourhood, most likely to the Eastward, and are brought hither by the Easterly trade winds. The Islands discover'd by Quiros[195] lies in this parrallel, but how far to the Eastward it's hard to say; for altho' we found in most Charts his discoveries placed as far to the West as this country yet from the account of his Voyage, compared with what we ourselves have seen, we are Morally certain that he never was upon any part of this Coast.[196] As soon as we had got without the Reefs we Shortened sail, and hoisted in the pinnace and Long boat, which last we had hung alongside, and then stretched off E.N.E., close upon a wind, as I did not care to stand to the Northward until we had a whole day before us, for which reason we keept making short boards all night. The large hollow sea we have now got into acquaints us with a Circumstance we did not before know, which is that the Ship hath received more Damage than we were aware of, or could perceive when in smooth Water; for now she makes as much water as one pump will free, kept constantly at work. However this was looked upon as trifling to the Danger we had lately made an Escape from. At day light in the morning Lizard Island bore S. by W., distant 10 Leagues. We now made all the sail we could, and stood away N.N.W. ½ W., but at 9 we

[194] Blank in MS. (Wharton).

[195] See page 80.

[196] The Island of Espiritu Santo, in the New Hebrides, which Quiros discovered, lies 1,200 miles to the eastward, and New Caledonia, from which these objects might equally have come, is 1,000 miles in the same direction (Wharton).

steer'd N.W. ½ N., having the advantage of a Fresh Gale at S.E.; at Noon we were by observation in the Lat. of 13° 46′ S., the Lizard Island bore S. 15° E., distant 58 Miles, but we had no land in sight.

Wednesday, 15th.—Fresh Trade at S.E. and Clear weather. At 6 in the evening shortened sail and brought too, with her head to the N.E. By this time we had run near 12 Leagues upon a N.W. ½ N. Course since Noon. At 4 a.m. wore and lay her head to the S.W., and at 6 made all Sail, and steer'd W., in order to make the land, being fearful of over shooting the passage, supposing there to be one, between this land and New Guinea. By noon we had run 10 Leagues upon this Course, but saw no land. Our Latitude by observation was 13° 2′ S., Long. 216° 00′ W., which was 1° 23′ to the W. of Lizard Island.

Thursday, 16th.—Moderate breezes at E.S.E. and fair weather. A little after Noon saw the Land from the Mast head bearing W.S.W., making high; at 2 saw more land to the N.W. of the former, making in hills like Islands; but we took it to be a Continuation of the Main land. An hour after this we saw a reef, between us and the land, extending away to the Southward, and, as we thought, terminated here to the Northward abreast of us; but this was only on op'ning, for soon after we saw it extend away to the Northward as far as we could distinguish anything. Upon this we hauld close upon a Wind, which was now at E.S.E., with all the sail we could set. We had hardly trimm'd our sails before the wind came to E. by N., which made our weathering the Reef very doubtful, the Northern point of which in sight at sun set still bore from us N. by W., distant about 2 Leagues. However, this being the best Tack to Clear it, we keept standing to the Northward, keeping a good look out until 12 at night, when, fearing to run too far upon one Course, we tack'd and stood to the southward, having run 6 Leagues N. or N. by E. since sun set; we had not stood above 2 Miles to the S.S.E. before it fell quite Calm. We both sounded now and several times before, but had not bottom with 140 fathoms of line.[197] A little after 4 o'clock the roaring of the surf was plainly heard, and at daybreak the Vast foaming breakers were too plainly to be seen not a mile from us, towards which we found the ship was carried by the Waves surprisingly fast. We had at this time not an air of Wind, and the depth of water was unfathomable, so that there was not a possibility of anchoring. In this distressed Situation we had nothing but Providence and the small Assistance the

[197] The description which follows, of the situation of the ship, and the occurrences until she was safely anchored inside the Barrier Reef, is from the Admiralty copy, as it is much fuller than that in Mr Corner's (Wharton).

Boats could give us to trust to; the Pinnace was under repair, and could not immediately be hoisted out. The Yawl was put in the Water, and the Longboat hoisted out, and both sent ahead to tow, which, together with the help of our sweeps abaft, got the Ship's head round to the Northward, which seemed to be the best way to keep her off the Reef, or at least to delay time. Before this was effected it was 6 o'clock, and we were not above 80 or 100 yards from the breakers. The same sea that washed the side of the ship rose in a breaker prodidgiously high the very next time it did rise, so that between us and destruction was only a dismal Valley, the breadth of one wave, and even now no ground could be felt with 120 fathom. The Pinnace was by this time patched up, and hoisted out and sent ahead to Tow. Still we had hardly any hopes of saving the ship, and full as little our lives, as we were full 10 Leagues from the nearest Land, and the boats not sufficient to carry the whole of us; yet in this Truly Terrible Situation not one man ceased to do his utmost, and that with as much Calmness as if no danger had been near. All the dangers we had escaped were little in comparison of being thrown upon this reef, where the Ship must be dashed to pieces in a Moment. A reef such as one speaks of here is Scarcely known in Europe. It is a Wall of Coral Rock rising almost perpendicular out of the unfathomable Ocean, always overflown at high Water generally 7 or 8 feet, and dry in places at Low Water. The Large Waves of the Vast Ocean meeting with so sudden a resistance makes a most Terrible Surf, breaking Mountains high, especially as in our case, when the General Trade Wind blows directly upon it. At this Critical juncture, when all our endeavours seemed too little, a Small Air of Wind sprung up, but so small that at any other Time in a Calm we should not have observed it. With this, and the Assistance of our Boats, we could observe the Ship to move off from the Reef in a Slanting direction; but in less than 10 Minutes we had as flat a Calm as ever, when our fears were again renewed, for as yet we were not above 200 Yards from the Breakers. Soon after our friendly Breeze visited us again, and lasted about as long as before. A Small Opening was now Seen in the Reef about a ¼ of a Mile from us, which I sent one of the Mates to Examine. Its breadth was not more than the Length of the Ship, but within was Smooth Water. Into this place it was resolved to Push her if Possible, having no other Probable Views to save her, for we were still in the very Jaws of distruction, and it was a doubt whether or no we could reach this Opening. However, we soon got off it, when to our Surprise we found the Tide of Ebb gushing out like a Mill Stream, so that it was impossible to get in. We however took all the Advantage Possible of it, and it Carried us out about a ¼ of a Mile from the breakers; but it was too Narrow for us to keep in long. However, what

Saturday, 18th.—Gentle breezes at E. and E.S.E. At 4 P.M. the Boats return'd from the Reef with about 240 lbs. of Shell-fish, being the Meat of large Cockles, exclusive of the Shells. Some of these Cockles are as large as 2 Men can move, and contain about 20 pounds of Meat, very good. At 6 in the morning we got under sail, and stood away to the N.W., as we could not expect a wind to get out to Sea by the same Channel as we came in without waiting perhaps a long time for it, nor was it advisable at this time to go without the Shoals, least we should by them be carried so far off the Coast as not to be able to determine wether or no New Guinea joins to or makes a part of this land.[201] This doubtful point I had from my first coming upon the Coast, determined, if Possible, to clear up; I now came to a fix'd resolution to keep the Main land on board, let the Consequence be what it will, and in this all the Officers concur'd. In standing to the N.W. we met with very irregular soundings, from 10 to 27 fathoms, varying 5 or 6 fathoms almost every Cast of the Lead. However, we keept on having a Boat ahead sounding. A little before noon we passed a low, small, sandy Isle, which we left on our Starboard side at the distance of 2 Miles. At the same time we saw others, being part of large Shoals above water, away to the N.E. and between us and the Main land. At Noon we were by observation in the Latitude of 12° 28′ S., and 4 or 5 Leagues from the Main, which extended from S. by W. to N. 71° W., and some Small Islands extending from N. 40° W. to N. 54° W., the Main or outer Reef seen from the Masthead away to the N.E.

Sunday, 19th.—Gentle breezes at S.E. by E. and Clear wether. At 2 P.M., as we were steering N.W. by N., saw a large shoal right ahead, extending 3 or 4 points on each bow, upon which we hauld up N.N.E. and N.E. by N., in order to get round to N. Point of it, which we reached by 4 o'clock, and then Edged away to the westward, and run between the N. end of this Shoal and another, which lays 2 miles to the Northward of it, having a Boat all the time ahead sounding. Our depth of Water was very irregular, from 22 to 8 fathoms. At ½ past 6 we Anchor'd in 13 fathoms; the Northermost of the Small Islands mentioned at Noon bore W. ½ S., distant 3 Miles. These Islands, which are known in the Chart by the name of Forbes's Isles,[202] lay about 5 Leagues from the Main, which here forms a mod-

201 Prado and Torres made the first passage of Torres Strait. In 1756 a map drawn by Robert de Vaugondy was included in Charles de Brosses's *Histoire des navigations aux Terres australes* and this was available to Cook. It clearly indicated some passage between New Holland and New Guinea, and Cook was determined at all cost to keep close to the mainland in order to verify or refute this information. See also page 117.

202 Admiral John Forbes was a Commissioner of Longitude in 1768, and had been a Lord of the Admiralty from 1756 to 1763 (Wharton).

erate high point, which we called Bolt head, from which the Land trends more westerly, and is all low, sandy Land, but to the Southward it is high and hilly, even near the Sea. At 6 A.M. we got under sail, and directed our Course for an Island which lay but a little way from the Main, and bore from us at this time N. 40° W., distant 5 Leagues; but we were soon interrupted in our Course by meeting with Shoals, but by the help of 2 Boats ahead and a good lookout at the Mast head we got at last into a fair Channel, which lead us down to the Island, having a very large Shoal on our Starboard side and several smaller ones betwixt us and the Main land. In this Channel we had from 20 to 30 fathoms. Between 11 and 12 o'Clock we hauld round the N.E. side of the Island, leaving it between us and the Main from which it is distant 7 or 8 Miles. This Island is about a League in Circuit and of a moderate height, and is inhabited; to the N.W. of it are several small, low Islands and Keys, which lay not far from the Main, and to the Northward and Eastward lay several other Islands and Shoals, so that we were now incompassed on every side by one or the other, but so much does a great danger Swallow up lesser ones, that these once so much dreaded spots were now looked at with less concern. The Boats being out of their Stations, we brought too to wait for them. At Noon our Latitude by observation was 12° 0′ S., Longitude in 217° 25′ W.; depth of Water 14 fathoms; Course and distance sail'd, reduced to a strait line, since yesterday Noon is N. 29° W., 32 Miles. The Main land within the above Islands forms a point which I call Cape Grenville[203] (Lat. 11° 58′, Long. 217° 38′); between this Cape and the Bolt head is a Bay, which I Named Temple Bay.[204] E. ½ N., 9 Leagues from Cape Grenville, lay some tolerable high Islands, which I called Sir Charles Hardy's Isles;[205] those which lay off the Cape I named Cockburn Isles.[206]

Monday, 20th.—Fresh breezes at E.S.E. About one P.M. the pinnace having got ahead, and the Yawl we took in Tow, we fill'd and Steer'd N. by W., for some small Islands we had in that direction.

[203] George Grenville was First Lord of the Admiralty for a few months in 1763, and afterwards Prime Minister for two years (Wharton).

[204] Richard Earl Temple, brother of George Grenville, was First Lord of the Admiralty in 1756 (Wharton). While admitting that Wharton's surmise is possible, Dr Beaglehole favours Henry Temple, second Viscount Palmerston, who was a Lord of the Admiralty from 1766 to 1777.

[205] Admiral Sir C. Hardy was second in command in Hawke's great action in Quiberon Bay, 1759 (Wharton). The name was given to the two islands which lie midway between Cape Grenville and the Great Barrier Reef.

[206] Admiral George Cockburn was a Commissioner of Longitude and Comptroller of the Navy when Cook left England.

Off C. Grenville the *Endeavour* again got into what is now the recognised channel along the land inside the reefs (Wharton).

After approaching them a little nearer we found them join'd or connected together by a large Reef; upon this we Edged away N.W., and left them on our Starboard hand, steering between them and the Island laying off the Main, having a fair and Clear Passage; Depth of Water from 15 to 23 fathoms. At 4 we discover'd some low Islands and Rocks bearing W.N.W., which we stood directly for. At half Past 6 we Anchor'd on the N.E. side of the Northermost, in 16 fathoms, distant from the Island one Mile. This Isle lay N.W. 4 Leagues from C. Grenville. On the Isles we saw a good many Birds, which occasioned my calling them Bird Isles. Before and at Sunset we could see the Main land, which appear'd all very low and sandy, Extends as far to the Northward as N.W. by N., and some Shoals, Keys, and low sandy Isles away to the N.E. of us. At 6 A.M. we got again under sail, with a fresh breeze at E., and stood away N.N.W. for some low Islands[207] we saw in that direction; but we had not stood long upon this Course before we were obliged to haul close upon a wind in Order to weather a Shoal which we discover'd on our Larboard bow, having at the same time others to the Eastward of us. By such time as we had weathered the Shoal to Leeward we had brought the Islands well upon our Leebow; but seeing some Shoals spit off from them, and some rocks on our Starboard bow, which we did not discover until we were very near them, made me afraid to go to windward of the Islands; wherefore we brought too, and made the signal for the pinnace, which was a head, to come on board, which done, I sent her to Leeward of the Islands, with Orders to keep along the Edge of the Shoal, which spitted off from the South side of the Southermost Island. The Yawl I sent to run over the Shoals to look for Turtle, and appointed them a Signal to make in case they saw many; if not, she was to meet us on the other side of the Island. As soon as the pinnace had got a proper distance from us we wore, and stood After her, and run to Leeward of the Islands, where we took the Yawl in Tow, she having seen only one small Turtle, and therefore made no Stay upon the Shoal. Upon this Island, which is only a Small Spott of Land, with some Trees upon it, we saw many Hutts and habitations of the Natives, which we supposed come over from the Main to these Islands (from which they are distant about 5 Leagues) to Catch Turtle at the time these Animals come ashore to lay their Eggs. Having got the Yawl in Tow, we stood away after the pinnace N.N.E. and N. by E. to 2 other low Islands, having 2 Shoals, which we could see without and one between us and the Main. At Noon we were about 4 Leagues from the Main land, which we could see Extending to the Northward as far as N.W. by N., all low, flat, and Sandy. Our Lat. by observation was 11° 23′ S., Long. in 217°

207 Boydong Keys (Wharton).

46′ W., and Course and distance sail'd since Yesterday at Noon N. 22° W., 40 Miles; soundings from 14 to 23 fathoms. But these are best seen upon the Chart, as likewise the Islands, Shoals, etc., which are too Numerous to be Mentioned singly.[208]

Tuesday, 21st.—Winds at E. by S. and E.S.E., fresh breeze. By one o'Clock we had run nearly the length of the Southermost of the 2 Islands before mentioned, and finding that we could not well go to windward of them without carrying us too far from the Main land, we bore up, and run to Leeward, where we found a fair open passage. This done, we steer'd N. by W., in a parallel direction with the Main land, leaving a small Island between us and it, and some low sandy Isles and Shoals without us, all of which we lost sight of by 4 o'Clock; neither did we see any more before the sun went down, at which time the farthest part of the Main in sight bore N.N.W. ½ W. Soon after this we Anchor'd in 13 fathoms, soft Ground, about five Leagues from the Land, where we lay until day light, when we got again under sail, having first sent the Yawl ahead to sound. We steer'd N.N.W. by Compass from the Northermost land in sight; Variation 3° 6′ E. Seeing no danger in our way we took the Yawl in Tow, and made all the Sail we could until 8 o'Clock, at which time we discover'd Shoals ahead and on our Larboard bow, and saw that the Northermost land, which we had taken to be a part of the Main, was an Island, or Islands,[209] between which and the Main their appeared to be a good Passage thro' which we might pass by running to Leeward of the Shoals on our Larboard bow, which was now pretty near us. Whereupon we wore and brought too, and sent away the Pinnace and Yawl to direct us clear of the Shoals, and then stood after them. Having got round the S.E. point of the Shoal we steer'd N.W. along the S.W., or inside of it, keeping a good lookout at the Masthead, having another Shoal on our Larboard side; but we found a good Channel of a Mile broad between them, wherein were from 10 to 14 fathoms. At 11 o'Clock, being nearly the length of the Islands above mentioned, and designing to pass between them and the Main, the Yawl, being thrown a stern by falling in upon a part of the Shoal, She could not get over. We brought the Ship too, and Sent away the Long boat (which we had a stern, and rigg'd) to keep in Shore upon our Larboard bow, and the Pinnace on our Starboard; for altho' there appear'd nothing in the Passage, yet I thought it necessary to take this method, because

208 It is very difficult to follow Cook's track after entering Providential Channel to this place. The shoals and islands were so confusing that their positions are very vaguely laid down on Cook's chart. It is easy to imagine how slow was his progress and tortuous his course, with a boat ahead all the time constantly signalling shallow water. Nothing is more trying to officers and men (Wharton).

209 Now called Mount Adolphus Islands (Wharton).

we had a strong flood, which carried us on end very fast, and it did not want much of high water. As soon as the Boats were ahead we stood after them, and got through by noon, at which time we were by observation in the Lat. of 10° 36′ 30″ S. The nearest part of the Main, and which we soon after found to be the Northermost,[210] bore W. southerly, distant 3 or 4 Miles; the Islands which form'd the passage before mentioned extending from N. to N. 75° E., distant 2 or 3 Miles. At the same time we saw Islands at a good distance off extending from N. by W. to W. N. W., and behind them another chain of high land, which we likewise judged to be Islands.[211] The Main land we thought extended as far as N. 71° W.; but this we found to be Islands. The point of the Main, which forms one side of the Passage before mentioned, and which is the Northern Promontory of this Country, I have named York Cape, in honour of his late Royal Highness, the Duke of York.[212] It lies in the Long. of 218° 24′ W., the N. point in the Lat. of 10° 37′ S., and the E. point in 10° 41′. The land over and to the Southward of this last point is rather low and very flatt as far inland as the Eye could reach, and looks barren. To the Southward of the Cape the Shore forms a large open bay, which I called Newcastle bay,[213] wherein are some small, low Islands and shoals, and the land all about it is very low, flatt, and sandy. The land on the Northern part of the Cape is rather more hilly, and the shore forms some small bays, wherein there appear'd to be good Anchorage, and the Vallies appear'd to be tolerably well Cloathed with wood. Close to the E. point of the Cape are 3 small Islands, and a small Ledge of rocks spitting off from one of them. There is also an Island laying close to the N. Point. The other Islands before spoke of lay about 4 Miles without these; only two of them are of any extent. The Southermost is the largest, and much higher than any part of the Main land. On the N. W. side of this Island seem'd to be good Anchorage, and Vallies that to all appearance would afford both wood and fresh Water. These Isles are known in the Chart by the name of York Isles.[214] To the Southward and S.E. of them, and even to the Eastward and Northward, are several low Islands, rocks, and Shoals. Our depth of Water in sailing between them and the Main was 12, 13, and 14 fathoms.[215]

210 Cape York, the northernmost point of Australia (Wharton).

211 The islands around Thursday Island (Wharton).

212 Edward Augustus, Duke of York and Albany, was a brother of George III (Wharton).

213 Dr Beaglehole suggests that the name was conferred in memory of Thomas Pelham-Hollis, Duke of Newcastle, who died in 1768.

214 Now called Mount Adolphus Islands (Wharton). The name York, given by Cook to the group, is now confined to one island.

215 In this channel is the dangerous rock on which the steamship *Quetta* was

Wednesday, 22nd.—Gentle breezes at E. by S. and clear weather. We had not steer'd above 3 or 4 Miles along shore to the westward before we discover'd the land ahead to be Islands detached by several Channels from the main land; upon this we brought too to Wait for the Yawl, and called the other Boats on board, and after giving them proper instructions, sent them away again to lead us thro' the Channell next the Main, and as soon as the Yawl was on board made sail after them with the Ship. Soon after we discover'd rocks and Shoals in this Channell, upon which I made the Signal for the boats to lead thro' the next Channel to the Northward[216] laying between the Islands, which they accordingly did, we following with the Ship, and had not less than 5 fathoms; and this in the narrowest part of the Channel, which was about a Mile and a ½ broad from Island to Island. At 4 o'Clock we Anchor'd about a Mile and a ½ or 2 Miles within the Entrance in 6½ fathoms, clear ground, distance from the Islands on each side of us one Mile, the Main land extending away to the S.W.; the farthest point of which we could see bore from us S. 48° W., and the Southermost point of the Islands, on the N.W. side of the Passage, bore S. 76° W. Between these 2 points we could see no land, so that we were in great hopes that we had at last found out a Passage into the Indian seas; but in order to be better informed I landed with a party of men, accompanied by Mr. Banks and Dr. Solander, upon the Islands which lies at the S.E. point of the Passage. Before and after we Anchor'd we saw a Number of People upon this Island, Arm'd in the same manner as all the others we have seen, Except one man, who had a bow and a bundle of Arrows, the first we have seen upon this Coast. From the appearance of the people we expected they would have opposed our landing; but as we approached the shore they all made off, and left us in peaceable possession of as much of the Island as served our purpose. After landing I went upon the highest hill, which, however, was of no great height, yet no less than twice or thrice the height of the Ship's Mastheads; but I could see from it no land between S.W. and W.S.W., so that I did not doubt but there was a passage. I could see plainly that the lands laying to the N.W. of this passage were compos'd of a number of Islands of Various extent, both for height and Circuit, ranged one behind another as far to the Northward and Westward as I could see, which could not be less than 12 or 14 Leagues.

Having satisfied myself of the great Probability of a passage, thro' which I intend going with the Ship, and therefore may land no more

---

wrecked, with such terrible loss of life, in 1890. By the *Endeavour's* track she must have passed very near it (Wharton).

[216] This lead to Endeavour Strait, but the recognised track is the channel farther north (Wharton).

upon this Eastern coast of New Holland, and on the Western side I can make no new discovery, the honour of which belongs to the Dutch Navigators, but the Eastern Coast from the Lat. of 38° S. down to this place, I am confident, was never seen or Visited by any European before us; and notwithstanding I had in the Name of his Majesty taken possession of several places upon this Coast, I now once More hoisted English Colours, and in the Name of His Majesty King George the Third took possession of the whole Eastern coast from the above Lat. down to this place by the Name of New Wales,[217] together with all the Bays, Harbours, Rivers, and Islands, situated upon the said Coast; after which we fired 3 Volleys of small Arms, which were answer'd by the like number from the Ship.

This done, we set out for the Ship, but were some time in getting on board on account of a very Rapid Ebb Tide, which set N.E. out of the Passage. Ever since we came in amongst the Shoals this last time we have found a Moderate Tide; the flood setting to the N.W. and Ebb to the S.E.; at this place is high water at full and change of the moon, about 1 or 2 o'Clock, and riseth and falleth upon a perpendicular about 10 or 12 feet. We saw upon all the Adjacent Lands and Islands a great number of smokes—a certain sign that they are inhabited—and we have daily seen smokes on every part of the Coast we have lately been upon. Between 7 and 8 o'Clock a.m. we saw several naked people, all or most of them Women, down upon the beach picking up Shells, etc.; they had not a single rag of any kind of Cloathing upon them, and both these and those we saw yesterday were in every respect the same sort of People we have seen everywhere upon the Coast. 2 or 3 of the Men we saw Yesterday had on pretty large breast plates, which we supposed were made of pearl Oyster Shells;[218] this was a thing, as well as the Bow and Arrows, we had not seen before. At low water, which hapned about 10 o'Clock, we got under sail, and stood to the S.W., with a light breeze at East,

217 The Admiralty copy, as well as that belonging to Her Majesty, calls it New South Wales. The island where the ceremony was performed was named on Cook's chart Possession Island, and is still so called (Wharton).

The highest point of the island is about 250 feet in height. The length of the island is about three miles. A memorial to commemorate Cook's act in taking formal possession of "New South Wales" was erected there in 1925.

It is to be noted that Cook took possession of "the whole Eastern coast", i.e. of the eastern regions of what are now the coasts of New South Wales and Queensland. Possession of the whole of the eastern part of the Australian continent and Van Diemen's Land was not taken until Governor Phillip read the proclamation to the members of the First Fleet on 7 February 1788. At that time New South Wales embraced the whole of the eastern half of Australia. Queensland was declared a separate state in 1859. The name Van Diemen's Land was changed to Tasmania in 1853.

218 Pearl shells threaded on a cord and suspended round the neck or from the waist were a favourite ornament amongst the tribes of the Cape York Peninsula.

which afterwards veer'd to N. by E., having the Pinnace ahead; depth of Water from 6 to 10 fathoms, except in one place, were we passed over a Bank of 5 fathoms. At Noon Possession Island, at the S.E. entrance of the Passage, bore N. 53° E., distant 4 Leagues; the Western extream of the Main land in sight S. 43° W., distant 4 or 5 Leagues, being all exceeding low. The S.W. point of the largest Island[219] on the N.W. side of the passage bore N. 71° W., distant 8 Miles; this point I named Cape Cornwall[220] (Lat. 10° 43′ S., Long. 218° 59′ W.),[221] and some low islands lying about the Middle of the Passage, which I called Wallace's Isles,[222] bore W. by S. ½ S., distance about 2 Leagues. Our Latitude by Observation was 10° 46′ S.

Thursday, 23rd.—In the P.M. had little wind and Variable, with which and the Tide of Flood we keept advancing to the W.N.W.; depth of Water 8, 7, and 5 fathoms. At ½ past 1 the pinnace, which was ahead, made the Signal for Shoal Water, upon which we Tackt and sent away the Yawl to sound also, and then Tack'd again, and stood after them with the Ship; 2 hours after this they both at once made the Signal for saving Shoal water. I was afraid to stand on for fear of running aground at that time of the Tide, and therefore came to an Anchor in ¼ less 7 fathoms, sandy ground. Wallice's Islands bore S. by W. ½ W., distant 5 or 6 Miles, the Islands to the Northward extending from N. 73° E. to N. 10° E., and a small Island[223] just in sight bearing N.W. ½ W. Here we found the flood Tide set to the Westward and Ebb to the Contrary. After we had come to Anchor I sent away the Master with the Long boat to sound, who, upon his return in the evening, reported that there was a bank stretching N. and S., upon which were 3 fathoms Water, and behind it 7 fathoms. We had it Calm all Night and until 9 in the morning, at which time we weigh'd, with a light breeze at S.S.E., and steer'd N.W. by W. for the Small Island above mentioned, having first sent the Boats ahead to sound; depth of Water 8, 7, 6, 5, 4, and 3 fathoms when upon the Bank,[224] it being now the last Quarter Ebb. At this time the most

219 Prince of Wales Island (Wharton).

220 Dr Beaglehole suggests that the name was chosen because it was the supplementary title borne by George Augustus Frederick, Prince of Wales.

221 This longitude is 70 minutes too far west, and one of the worst given in the Journal. There were no observations, and the dead reckoning among the shoals was difficult to keep (Wharton).

222 See note on page 127.

223 Booby Island (Wharton). The species of Booby found on this island is the Brown Booby (*Sula leucogaster*) (Hindwood).

224 The Endeavour Strait is now little used, on account of this great bank, which nearly bars its western part. There is, however, deeper water than Cook found, a few miles to the southward; but it is just the difficulty of finding this narrow pass, so far from land, and that fact that there is a deep though narrow channel north of Prince of Wales Island, that has caused it to be abandoned. The passage of Torres

Northermost Islands we had in sight bore N. 9° E.; the S.W. point of the largest Islands on the N.W. side of the Passage, which I named Cape Cornwall, bore E.; distant 3 Leagues. This bank, at least so much as we sounded, extends nearly N. and S., how far I cannot say; its breadth, however, is not more than ¼ or at most ½ a Mile. Being over the Bank, we deepned our water to a ¼ less 7 fathoms, which depth we carried all the way to the small Island ahead, which we reached by Noon, at which time it bore S., distant near ½ a Mile; depth of Water 5 fathoms. The most northermost land we had in sight (being part of the same Chain of Islands we have had to the Northward of us since we entered the Passage) bore N. 71° E.; Lat. in, by Observation, 10° 33′ S., Long. 219° 22′ W. In this situation we had no part of the Main land in sight. Being now near the Island, and having but little wind, Mr. Banks and I landed upon it, and found it to be mostly a barren rock frequented by Birds, such as Boobies, a few of which we shott, and occasioned by giving it the name of Booby Island.[225] I made but very short stay at this Island before I return'd to the Ship; in the meantime the wind had got to the S.W., and although it blow'd but very faint, yet it was accompanied with a Swell from the same quarter. This, together with other concuring Circumstances, left me no room to doubt but we had got to the westward of Carpentaria, or the Northern extremity of New Holland, and had now an open Sea to the Westward; which gave me no small satisfaction, not only because the danger and fatigues of the Voyage was drawing near to an end, but by being able to prove that New Holland and New Guinea are 2 separate Lands or Islands, which until this day hath been a doubtful point with Geographers.[226]

Strait is, however, still an anxious bit of navigation (Wharton).

Endeavour Strait, obviously named after the ship, is a channel lying between the tip of the Cape York Peninsula and Prince of Wales Island. There are reputedly nine channels through the strait, of which this is the most southerly.

225 Booby Island is now the great landmark for ships making Torres Strait from the westward. There is a light upon it (Wharton).

226 Luis Vaez de Torres, commanding a Spanish ship in company with Quiros in 1605, separated from his companion in the New Hebrides. He afterwards passed through the Strait separating New Guinea from Australia, which now bears his name. This fact, however, was little known, as the Spaniards suppressed all account of the voyage; and though it leaked out later, the report was so vague that it was very much doubted whether he had really passed this way. On most charts and maps of the period, New Guinea was shown joined to Australia, and to Cook the establishment of the Strait may fairly be given. Only the year before Bougainville, the French navigator, who preceded Cook across the Pacific, and who was steering across the Coral Sea on a course which would have led him to Lizard Island, abandoned his search in that direction, after falling in with two reefs to the eastward of the Barrier, because he feared falling amongst other shoals, and had no faith whatever in the reports of the existence of Torres Strait. Had he persevered, he would have snatched from Cook the honour of the complete exploration of Eastern Aus-

The N.E. entrance of this passage or Strait lies in the Latitude of 10° 27′ S., and in the Longitude of 218° 36′ W. from the Meridian of Greenwich.[227] It is form'd by the Main, or the northern extremity of New Holland, on the S.E., and by a Congeries of Islands to N.W., which I named Prince of Wales's Islands. It is very Probable that the Islands extend quite to New Guinea;[228] they are of Various Extent both for height and Circuit, and many of them seem'd to be indifferently well Cloath'd with wood, etc., and, from the smokes we saw, some, if not all of them, must be inhabited. It is also very probable that among these Islands are as good, if not better, passages than the one we have come thro', altho' one need hardly wish for a better, was the access to it from the Eastward less dangerous; but this difficulty will remain until some better way is found out than the one we came, which no doubt may be done was it ever to become an object to be

---

tralia, and of the verification of the passage between it and New Guinea. Bougainville paid dearly for his caution, as he found that retracing his steps against the trade wind, in order to pass eastward and northward of New Guinea, occupied such a weary time, that he and his people nearly starved before they reached a place of refreshment (Wharton).

In *The Discovery of Australia*, page 169, Andrew Sharp reminds us that the island to the north had been discovered by Jansz and Roossengin in 1606, but it was doubtful whether the members of Prado's and Torres's company had seen the mainland to the south in the same year. The following is the passage in which Torres describes his famous passage of the strait named after him. In the work mentioned above, Mr Sharp provides a careful examination of the evidence.

> Having gone 300 leagues of coast as I have said and decreased two degrees and a half so that we fetched up in nine, from here bgins a shallow of three fathoms to nine which runs along the coast a hundred and eighty and so many leagues: we went by it along the coast to seven degrees and a half, and the end of it is in five: we could not go ahead for the many shoals and great currents which are on all of it; so we had to go out in the direction of the south-west over the said bottom, to eleven degrees, and the shallow goes more shoal: there were very large islands, and they seemed more on the side of the south: they were inhabited by black people very stout naked: they have as weapons very thick long spears many arrows stone clubs very misshapen, none of their weapons could we use: I captured in all this land twenty persons of different peoples, in order with them to give a better account to Your Majesty they give much notifcation of ther peoples, although up to now they do not make themselves understood well: we went over this shallow two months, at the end of these we came into 25 fathoms of depth, and in five degrees of latitude, and ten leagues from the coast and having gone 480 leagues here the coast goes stretching back to the north-east: I did not get to it because the shallow got very shoal; thus I went running to the north and in 25 fathoms to four degrees so that we came on a coast which likewise extended from the east west, we did not make the end in the direction of the east, but from what we understand it is joined to that behind because the shallow goes to it, and because of the great calm that there is.

227 As before mentioned, this longitude is over a degree in error. The sun was not available for lunars until 24 August, and the first was observed on the 25th, when the ship was at Booby Island; but the result is not recorded in Mr Green's log. Mr Green was at this time ill. The latitude is a clerical error for 10.37, which Cook's chart shows, and is nearly correct (Wharton).

228 This conjecture was very near the truth. The whole of Torres Strait is obstructed by either islands or reefs that leave very little passage (Wharton).

looked for.[229] The northern Extent of the Main or outer reef, which limit or bounds the Shoals to the Eastward, seems to be the only thing wanting to Clear up this point; and this was a thing I had neither time nor inclination to go about, having been already sufficiently harrass'd with dangers without going to look for more.[230]

This passage, which I have named Endeavour Straits, after the Name of the Ship, is in length N.E. and S.W. 10 Leagues, and about 5 Leagues broad, except at the N.E. entrance, where it is only 2 Miles broad by reason of several small Islands which lay there, one of which, called Possession Island, is of a Moderate height and Circuit; this we left between us and the Main, passing between it and 2 Small round Islands, which lay N.W. 2 Miles from it. There are also 2 Small low Islands, called Wallice's Isles,[231] laying in the Middle of the S.W. entrance, which we left to the southward; the depth of Water we found in the Straits was from 4 to 9 fathoms. Every where good Anchorage, only about 2 Leagues to the Northward of Wallice's Islands is a Bank, whereon is not more than 3 fathoms at low Water, but probable there might be found more was it sought for. I have not been particular in describing this Strait, no more than I have been in pointing out the respective Situations of the Islands, Shoals, etc., on the Coast of New Wales; for these I refer to the Chart, where they are deliniated with all the accuracy that Circumstances would admit of.

With respect to the Shoals that lay upon this Coast I must observe, for the benefit of those who may come after me, that I do not believe the one ½ of them are laid down in my Chart; for it would be Absurd to suppose that we Could see or find them all. And the same thing may

[229] It is the western and not the eastern approach of Endeavour Strait that forms the difficulty, now the locality has been charted, for vessels of deeper draught than the *Endeavour*; though for small craft, as Cook says, you can hardly wish for a better (Wharton).

[230] The east coast of Australia, which Cook had now followed from end to end, is 2,000 miles in extent. He took four months over it, much less time than he had given to New Zealand; but this is easily accounted for. His people were getting worn out, and he was haunted by fears of not getting off the coast before the N.W. monsoon set in, which would have been a foul wind for him in getting from Torres Strait to Batavia, and his provisions were running short. Besides this, there was the grave doubt whether Australia and New Guinea were really separated. If this turned out to be false, there was a long round to make, back to the eastern extremity of the latter, and the voyage to Batavia would have been infinitely extended. Considering these circumstances, Cook's exploration of the coast was wonderful, and the charts attached to this book attest the skill and unwearied pains taken in mapping it from such a cursory glance. He only stopped at four places: Botany Bay, Bustard Bay, Thirsty Sound, and the Endeavour River; and from the neighbourhood of these, with the view obtained as he coasted along, he had to form his opinion of the country—an opinion, as we shall see, singularly correct (Wharton).

[231] These are probably called after Captain Wallis, who made a voyage across the Pacific in the *Dolphin* in 1767, and discovered Tahiti (Wharton). Captain Samuel Wallis. On the chart the name is rendered Wallais.

in some Measure be said of the Islands, especially between the Latitude of 20° and 22°, where we saw Islands out at Sea as far as we could distinguish any thing. However, take the Chart in general, and I believe it will be found to contain as few Errors as most Sea Charts which have not undergone a thorough correction.[232] The Latitude and Longitude of all, or most of, the principal head lands, Bays, etc., may be relied on, for we seldom fail'd of getting an Observation every day to correct our Latitude by, and the Observation for settling the Longitude were no less Numerous, and made as often as the Sun and Moon came in play; so that it was impossible for any Material error to creep into our reckoning in the intermediate times. In justice to Mr. Green,[233] I must say that he was indefatigable in making and calculating these observations, which otherwise must have taken up a great deal of my time, which I could not at all times very well spare; not only this, but by his instructions several of the petty Officers can make and calculate these observations almost as well as himself. It is only by such Means that this method of finding the Longitude at Sea can be put into universal practice; a Method that we have generally found may be depended upon within ½ a degree, which is a degree of Accuracy more than sufficient for all Nautical purposes. Would Sea Officers once apply themselves to the making and calculating these Observations they would not find them so very difficult as they at first imagine, especially with the Assistance of the Nautical Almanack and Astronomical Ephemeris, by the help of which the Calculation for finding the Longitude takes up but little more time than that of an Azimuth for finding the Variation of the Compass; but unless this Ephemeris is Published for some time to come, more than either one or 2 Years, it can never be of general use in long Voyages, and in short Voyages it's not so much wanted.[234] Without it the Calculations are Laborious and discouraging to beginners, and such as are not well vers'd in these kind of Calculations.

232 Cook's pride in his chart is well justified, as its general accuracy is marvellous, when one considers that he simply sailed along the coast. The great feature of this shore, however—the Barrier Reef—only appears on it at its northern end, where its approach to the land caused Cook to make such unpleasant acquaintance with it (Wharton).

233 From this phrase, and from various remarks in Mr Green's own log, it would appear that Mr Green was not very easy to get on with; but there is no doubt of his unwearied zeal in astronomical observations (Wharton).

234 The *Nautical Almanac* was first published in 1767. That for 1770 was not published until 1769; but it seems probable that Cook either had proof sheets, or the MS calculations (Wharton).

SOME ACCOUNT OF NEW WALES.[235]

In the Course of this Journal I have at different times made mention of the Appearance or Aspect of the face of the Country, the Nature of the Soil, its produce, etc. By the first it will appear that to the Southward of 33° or 34° the land in general is low and level, with very few Hills or Mountains; further to the Northward it may in some places be called a Hilly, but hardly anywhere can be called a Mountainous, Country, for the Hills and Mountains put together take up but a small part of the Surface in Comparison to what the Planes and Valleys do which intersect or divide these Hills and Mountains. It is indifferently well water'd, even in the dry Seasons, with small brooks and Springs, but no great Rivers, unless it be in the Wet Season, when the low lands and Vallies near the Sea, I do suppose, are mostly laid under Water. The Small Brooks may then become large Rivers; but this can only happen with the Tropick. It was only in Thirsty Sound that we could find no fresh Water, and that no doubt was owing to the Country being there very much intersected with Salt Creeks and Mangrove land.

The low land by the Sea, and even as far in land as we were, is for the most part friable, loose, sandy Soil yet indifferently fertile, and Cloathed with woods, long grass, shrubs, plants, etc. The Mountains or Hills are checquer'd with woods and Lawns; some of the Hills are wholy cover'd with Flourishing Trees; others but thinly, and the few that are upon them are small, and the spot of Lawns or Savannahs are rocky and barren, especially to the Northward, where the Country did not afford or produce near the Vegetation that it does to the Southward, nor were the Trees in the Woods half so tall and stout. The Woods do not produce any great variety of Trees; there are only 2 or 3 sorts that can be called Timber. The largest is the gum Tree, which grows all over the country; the wood of this Tree is too hard and ponderous for most common uses. The Tree which resembles our Pines I saw nowhere in perfection but in Botany Bay; this wood, as I have before observed, is something of the same Nature as American Live Oak;[236] in short, most of the large Trees in this Country are of a hard and ponderous nature, and could not be applied to many purposes. Here are several sorts of the Palm kind, Mangrove, and several other sorts of small Trees and Shrubs quite unknown to me, besides a very great number of Plants hitherto unknown; but these

[235] Called in the Admiralty and the Queen's copy New South Wales. It would appear that for this part of the voyage Mr Corner's copy was the first written, and that Cook's first idea was to christen the country New Wales (Wharton).

[236] *Casuarina glauca* (Mair).

things are wholy out of my way to describe,[237] nor will this be of any loss, since not only plants, but every thing that can be of use to the Learned World will be very accurately described by Mr. Banks and Dr. Solander. The Land naturally produces hardly anything fit for Man to eat, and the Natives know nothing of Cultivation. There are, indeed, growing wild in the wood a few sorts of Fruit[238] (the most of them unknown to us), which when ripe do not eat amiss, one sort especially, which we called Apples, being about the size of a Crab Apple; it is black and pulpey when ripe, and tastes like a Damson; it hath a large hard stone or Kernel, and grows on Trees or Shrubs.[239]

In the Northern parts of the Country, as about Endeavour River, and probably in many other places, the Boggy or watery Lands produce Taara or Cocos, which, when properly cultivated, are very good roots, without which they are hardly eatable; the Tops, however, make very good greens.

Land Animals are scarce, so far as we know confin'd to a very few species; all that we saw I have before mentioned. The sort which is in the greatest Plenty is the Kangooroo or Kanguru, so called by the Natives; we saw a good many of them about Endeavour River, but kill'd only 3, which we found very good Eating. Here are likewise Lizards, Snakes, Scorpions, Centapees, etc., but not in any plenty. Tame Animals they have none but Dogs, and of these we saw but one, and therefore must be very scarce, probably they eat them faster than they breed them; we should not have seen this one had he not made us frequent Visits while we lay in Endeavour River.

The land Fowls are Bustards, Eagles, Hawks, Crows, such as we have in England, Cockatoes of 2 sorts, White and Brown, very beautiful Birds of the Parrot kind, such as Lorryquets, etc., Pidgeons, Doves, Quails,[240] and several sorts of smaller birds. The Sea and Water Fowls are Herons, Boobies, Noddies,[241] Guls,[242] Curlews,

237 In the light of modern knowledge the account is quite incorrect, though understandable at the time. There are in fact many species of *Eucalypts*, and they include numerous useful timber trees. Cook, however, landed chiefly at points where the forest is poor and did not see the better stands of eucalypt timber (Mair).

238 The fruits are unidentifiable. *Plauchonella australis* (*Sapota australis* of the following note) may conceivably be among them, but there is no certainty of this (Mair).

239 The Black Apple or *Sapota australis* (Wharton).

240 Banks mentions quails in Botany Bay "much resembling the English ones". The species would be the Stubble Quail (*Coturnis pectoralis*) which is much like the English Quail, not the Brown Quail as suggested by Beaglehole (Vol. 2, page 59, footnote) (Hindwood). For other birds mentioned here, see earlier footnote.

241 Probably the Common Noddy (*Anous stolidus*). The White-capped Noddy (*A. minutus*) also occurs on the Barrier Reef Islands; it is tree-nested whereas the Common Noddy mostly nests either on the ground or in shrubs, and only occasionally in trees (Hindwood).

242 Probably Silver Gull (*Larus novaehollandiae*) (Hindwood).

Ducks, Pelicans, etc., and when Mr. Banks and Mr. Gore where in the Country, at the head of Endeavour River, they saw and heard in the Night great numbers of Geese. The Sea is indifferently well stocked with fish of Various sorts, such as Sharks, Dog-fish, Rock-fish, Mullets, Breams, Cavallies, Mack'rel, old wives, Leather Jackets, Five Fingers, Sting rays, Whip rays,[243] etc., all excellent in their kind. The Shell fish are Oysters of 3 or 4 sorts, viz., Rock Oysters and Mangrove Oysters, which are small, Pearl Oysters[244] and Mud Oysters; these last are the best and Largest I ever saw. Cockles and Clams of several sorts, many of those that are found upon the Reefs are of a prodigious size, Craw fish,[245] Crabs,[246] Muscles, and a variety of other sorts. Here are also upon the Shoals and Reefs great Numbers of the finest Green Turtle in the world, and in the River and Salt Creeks are some Aligators.[247]

The Natives of this Country are of a middle Stature, streight Bodies and Slender limb'd; their Skins the Colour of Wood soot, their Hair mostly black, some Lank and others curled; they all wear it Cropt Short; their Beards, which are generally black, they likewise crop short, or Singe off. There features are far from being disagreeable, and their Voices are soft and Tunable. They go quite Naked, both Men and Women, without any manner of Cloathing whatever;

243 *Old wives* are Enoploxus Armatus; *Leather jackets*, Monacanthus; *Five fingers*, Chilodactylus (Wharton).

It is impossible to give scientific names for all the fish mentioned. Mack'rel would have been *Pneumatophorus australasicus*, Old Wives *Enoplosus armatus*, Five Fingers *Nemadactylus macropterus* (of which Wharton's *Chilodactylus* is a synonym), and the Whip ray *Aetobatus australis* (Whitley).

244 *Pinetada* (McMichael).

245 The marine spring crayfish of tropical waters is of the genera *Panulirus*; those south of central New South Wales *Jasus* (Yaldwin).

246 *Portunus pelagicus* is the big "blue" swimming crab found on reefs, lagoons, and tidal inlets around much of Australia. *Scylla serrata* is the big greenish mud or mangrove crab found in mangrove swamps. Both are highly sought after for food today (Yaldwin).

247 In *Nature Walkabout* (A. H. & A. W. Reed, pages 92 and 93) Vincent Serventy describes the two species of crocodiles found in northern Australia:

> The freshwater crocodile, which ranges far in rivers and lakes, and the saltwater crocodile, found in rivers, estuaries, and the open sea.
>
> The freshwater species usually grows to about six feet in length though sometimes it may reach eight feet. It is harmless enough and feeds on tadpoles, water insects, and other small creatures; when larger it eats fish and is often called the fish crocodile. It has never been recorded as attacking humans and is very timid, so it is no easy matter to get a close look at one in the wild.
>
> The saltwater crocodile is much more dangerous. Lengths of thirty feet are now things of the past since hunters have destroyed most of the large animals. The speed of growth depends to a great extent on food and temperature. Not a great deal is known about this animal but judging by work done on the closely related Nile crocodile these reptiles might not be ready to breed until eighteen years of age. How long they live after this is anybody's guess, but there seems no reason why they should not live 100 years or more.

even the Women do not so much as cover their privities, altho' none of us was ever very near any of their Women, one Gentleman excepted, yet we are all of us as well satisfied of this as if we had lived among them. Notwithstanding we had several interviews with the Men while we lay in Endeavour River, yet, wether through Jealousy or disregard, they never brought any of their women along with them to the Ship, but always left them on the Opposite side of the River, where we had frequent Opportunities viewing them thro' our Glasses. They wear as Ornaments, Necklaces made of Shells, Bracelets, or Hoops, about their Arms, made mostly of Hair Twisted and made like a Cord Hoop; these they wear tight about the upper parts of their Arms,[248] and some have Girdles made in the same manner. The Men wear a bone, about 3 or 4 Inches long and a finger's thick, run thro' the Bridge[249] of their Nose; they likewise have holes in their Ears for

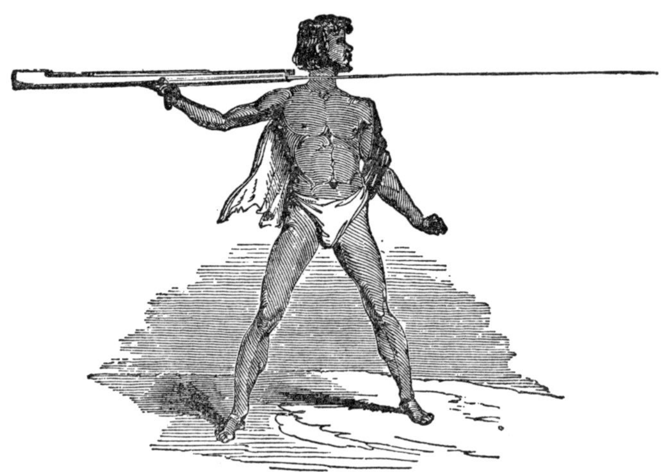

NEW HOLLANDER USING THE THROWING-STICK.

Ear Rings, but we never saw them wear any; neither are all the other Ornaments wore in Common, for we have seen as many without as with them. Some of these we saw on Possession Island wore breast plates, which we supposed were made of Mother of Pearl Shells. Many of them paint their Bodies and faces with a Sort of White paste or Pigment;[250] this they apply different ways, each according to his fancy.

[248] Girdles, head bands, and arm bands were frequently made of human hair, often that of deceased relatives. The practice varied in different parts of the country, animal fur, plant fibres, and cane also being used for this purpose.

[249] The cartilage of the nostril. Banks mentions that the bluejackets called this queer ornament the "Spritsail yard" (Wharton).

[250] Clay, gypsum, or lime was used as a white pigment, mixed with water to make a creamy paste.

Their offensive weapons are Darts; some are only pointed at one end, others are barb'd, some with wood, others with Stings of rays, and some with Sharks' Teeth, etc.; these last are stuck fast on with Gum.[251] They throw the Darts with only one hand, in the doing of which they make use of a piece of wood about 3 feet long, made thin like the blade of a Cutlass, with a little hook at one End to take hold of the End of the dart, and at the other end is fix'd a thin piece of bone about 3 or 4 Inches long; the use of this is, I believe, to keep the dart steady, and to make it quit the hand in a proper direction. By the helps of these throwing sticks, as we call them, they will hit a mark at the Distance of 40 or 50 yards, with almost, if not as much, Certainty as we can do with a Musquet, and much more so than with a ball. These throwing sticks we at first took for wooden swords, and perhaps on some occasions they may use them as such; that is, when all their darts are expended.[252] Be this as it may, they never Travel without both them and their Darts, not for fear of Enemies, but for killing of Game, etc., as I shall show hereafter. There defensive weapons are Targets, made of wood; but these we never saw used but once in Botany Bay.[253]

I do not look upon them to be a warlike people; on the contrary, I think them a Timerous and inoffensive race, no ways inclined to Cruelty, as appear'd from their behaviour to one of our people in Endeavour River, which I have before mentioned, neither are they very numerous. They live in small parties along by the Sea Coast, the banks of Lakes, Rivers, Creeks, etc. They seem to have no fixed habitation, but move about from place to place like wild beasts in search of Food, and, I believe, depend wholy upon the Success of the present day for their Subsistance. They have wooden fish Gigs, with 2, 3, or 4 prongs, each very ingeniously made, with which they strike fish. We have also seen them strike both fish and birds with their Darts.

251 The resin of the pine, gum, bloodwood and other trees or spinifex grass gum was used to make handles for stone knives and to secure the blades of axes, spears, and chisels to their shafts. Other uses of gum were the making of ornaments, repairing spear-throwers and coolamons, and sealing canoes. The spears with several prongs mentioned here would probably be fish spears.

252 An excellent description of the woomera or wommera. It had many purposes besides its primary function as an implement for launching a spear. The "little hook" at the end of the handle was a specially shaped chisel or pointed stone which was invaluable in making and decorating other implements and weapons. The woomera was also used as a lever to prise the bark from trees when searching for grubs, as a digging stick, a knife for cutting cooked meat, and as a fire-saw. As Cook conjectures, it might also be used as a weapon in an emergency.

253 Narrow shields designed to deflect spears were in use in south-eastern Australia as well as broader ones which were also found in most parts of the country. The largest ones were the fig-tree shields of north-eastern Queensland which Cook did not see. These were up to five feet in length and painted or engraved with decorative designs.

With these they likewise kill other Animals; they have also wooden Harpoons for striking Turtle, but of these I believe they get but few, except at the seasons they come ashore to lay. In short, these people live wholy by fishing and hunting, but mostly by the former, for we never saw one Inch of Cultivated land in the whole Country. They know, however, the use of Taara, and sometimes eat them; we do not know that they Eat anything raw, but roast or broil all they eat on slow small fires. Their Houses are mean, small Hovels, not much bigger than an Oven, made of Peices of Sticks, Bark, Grass, etc., and even these are seldom used but in the Wet seasons, for in the day-times we know they as often sleep in the Open Air as anywhere else. We have seen many of their Sleeping places, where there has been only some branches or peices of Bark, grass, etc., about a foot high on the Windward side.

Their Canoes are as mean as can be conceived, especially to the Southward, where all we saw were made of one peice of the Bark of Trees about 12 or 14 feet long, drawn or Tied together at one end. As I have before made mention, these Canoes will not Carry above 2 people, in general there is never more than one in them; but, bad as they are, they do very well for the purpose they apply them to, better than if they were larger, for as they draw but little water they go in them upon the Mud banks, and pick up Shell fish, etc., without going out of the Canoe. The few Canoes we saw to the Northward were made out of a Log of wood hollow'd out, about 14 feet long and very narrow, with outriggers; these will carry 4 people. During our whole stay in Endeavour River we saw but one Canoe, and had great reason to think that the few people that resided about that place had no more; this one served them to cross the River and to go a Fishing in, etc. They attend the Shoals, and flatts, one where or another, every day at low water to gather Shell fish, or whatever they can find to eat, and have each a little bag to put what they get in; this bag is made of net work.[254] They have not the least knowledge of Iron or any other Metal that we know of; their working Tools must be made of Stone, bone, and Shells; those made of the former are very bad, if I may judge from one of their Adzes I have seen.

Bad and mean as their Canoes are, they at Certain seasons of the Year (so far as we know) go in them to the most distant Islands which lay upon the Coast, for we never landed upon one but what we saw signs of People having been there before. We were surprized to find Houses, etc., upon Lizard Island, which lies 5 Leagues from

[254] The larger dilly bags used by women for carrying rushes, yams, shellfish and other foods were made of pandanus fibre and grass. Mostly they were loosely woven, but some were so closely knitted or plaited that they could be used for carrying honey and even as water bags.

the nearest part of the Main; a distance we before thought they could not have gone in their Canoes.

The Coast of this Country, at least so much of it as lays to the Northward of 25° of Latitude, abounds with a great Number of fine bays and Harbours, which are Shelter'd from all winds; but the Country itself, so far as we know, doth not produce any one thing that can become an Article in Trade to invite Europeans to fix a settlement upon it. However, this Eastern side is not that barren and miserable country that Dampier and others have described the Western side to be.[255] We are to consider that we see this country in the pure state of nature; the Industry of Man has had nothing to do with any part of it, and yet we find all such things as nature hath bestow'd upon it in a flourishing state. In this Extensive Country it can never be doubted but what most sorts of Grain, Fruit, roots, etc., of every kind would flourish here were they once brought hither, planted and Cultivated by the hands of Industry; and here are Provender for more Cattle, at all seasons of the Year, than ever can be brought into the Country.[256] When one considers the Proximity of this Country with New Guinea, New Britain, and several other Islands which produce Cocoa Nutts and many other fruits proper for the support of man, it seems strange that they should not long ago be Transplanted here; by its not being done it should seem that the Natives of this Country have no commerce with their Neighbours, the New Guineans.[257] It is very probable that they are a different people, and speak a different Language. For the advantage of such as want to Clear up this point I shall add a small Vocabulary of a few Words in the New Holland Language which we learnt when in Endeavour River.[258]

English	*New Holland*
The Head	Whageegee
„ Hair of the head	Morye or Moré
„ Eyes	Meul
„ Ears	Melea
„ Lips	Yembe or Jembi
„ Teeth	Mulere or Moile
„ Chinn	Jæal

255 See notes on Dampier's contact with the Aborigines, page 23.

256 It says a good deal for Cook's penetration that he wrote like this, for the coast of Australia is not promising, especially in the dry season; and coming as he did from the more apparently fertile countries of Tahiti and New Zealand, Australia must have appeared by a barren land (Wharton).

257 The climate is too dry for the coconut palm (Wharton).

258 The languages of the different tribes differ very much. This results from the continual state of war in which they live, as they have no communication the one with the other (Wharton).

Dr Beaglehole points out that the vocabulary is from the Koko-Yimidir language which was spoken from the Endeavour River to Cape Flattery. He refers to an informative comparison of Cook's and Banks's lists made by Walter E. Roth in 1901.

English	*New Holland*
The Beard	Waller
„ Tongue	Unjar
„ Nose	Bonjoo
„ Naval	Toolpoor or Julpur
„ Penis	Keveii or Kerrial
„ Scrotum	Coonal or Kunnol
„ Arms	Aw or Awl
„ Hand	Marigal
„ Thumb	Eboorbalga
„ Fore, Middle and Ring fingers	Egalbaiga
Little Finger	Nakil or Eboonakil
The Thighs	Coman
„ Knees	Ponga
„ Legs	Peegoorgo
„ Feet	Edamal
„ Nails	Kolke or Kulke
A Stone	Walba
Sand	Joo'wal, Yowall, or Joralba
A Rope or Line	Goorgo or Gurka
Fire	Maianang or Meanang
The Sun	Galan or Gallan
„ Sky	Kere or Kearre
A Father	Dunjo
„ Son	Jumurre
„ Man	Bamma or Bā ma
„ Dog	Cotta or Kota
„ Lorryquet	Perpere or Pier-pier
„ Cocatoo	Wanda
Male Turtle	Poonja or Poinja
Female	Mamingo
A great Cockle	Moenjo or Moingo
Cocos Yams	Maracotn
A Canoe	Maragan

From what I have said of the Natives of New Holland they may appear to some to be the most wretched People upon Earth; but in reality they are far more happier than we Europeans, being wholy unacquainted not only with the Superfluous, but with the necessary Conveniences so much sought after in Europe; they are happy in not knowing the use of them. They live in a Tranquility which is not disturbed by the Inequality of Condition. The earth and Sea of their own accord furnishes them with all things necessary for Life. They covet not Magnificient Houses, Household-stuff, etc.; they live in a Warm and fine Climate, and enjoy every wholesome Air, so that they have very little need of Cloathing; and this they seem to be fully sencible of, for many to whom we gave Cloth, etc., left it carelessly upon the Sea beach and in the Woods, as a thing they had no manner of use for; in short, they seem'd to set no Value upon anything we gave them, nor would they ever part with anything of their own for any one Article we could offer them. This, in my opinion, Argues that they think themselves provided with all the necessarys of Life, and that they have no Superfluities.[259]

I shall conclude the account of this Country with a few observations on the Currents and Tides upon the Coast, because I have mentioned in the Course of this Journal that the latter hath sometimes set one way and sometimes another, which I shall Endeavour to account for in the best manner I can. From the Lat. of 32°, or above downwards to Sandy Cape in the Lat. of 24° 46′, we constantly found a Current setting to the Sothward; at the rate of 10 or 15 Miles per Day, more or less, according to the distance we were from the land, for it runs stronger in shore than in the Offing. All this time I had not been able to satisfy myself whether the flood-tide came from the Southward, Eastward, or Northward, but judged it to come from the S.E.; but the first time we anchor'd upon the coast, which was in the Lat. of 24° 30′, and about 10 Leagues to the S.E. of Bustard Bay, we found there the flood to come from the N.W. On the Contrary, 30 Leagues further to the N.W., on the S. side of Keppel Bay, we found the Flood to come from the East, and at the Northern part of the said Bay we found it come from the Northward, but with a much Slower Motion than the Easterly Tide. Again, on the East side of the Bay of Inlets we found the flood to set strong to the Westward as far as the Op'ning of Broad sound, but on the N. side of that sound the flood come with a Slow motion from the N.W.; and when at Anchor before Repulse bay we found the flood to come from the northward. We need only admit the flood tide to come from the East or S.E., and then all these seeming Contradictions will be found to be conformable to reason and experience. It is well known that where there are deep Inlets, large Creeks, etc., into low lands, that it is not occasioned by fresh water Rivers; there is a very great indraught of the Flood Tide, the direction of which will be determin'd according to the possition or direction of the Coast which forms the Entrance into such Inlets; and this direction the Tide must follow, let it be ever so contrary to their general Course out at Sea, and where the Tides are weak, as they are in general upon this Coast, a large Inlet will, if I may so call it, attract the Flood tide for many Leagues. Any one need only cast an Eye over the Chart to be made sencible of what I have advanced. To the Northward of Whitsundays Passage there there are few or no large Inlets, and consequently the Flood sets to the Northward or N.W., according to the direction of the Coast, and Ebb the Contrary; but this is to be understood at a little distance from land,

259 Wharton has appended a footnote at this point on the Aborigines. It is omitted in this edition, as it provides critical and unfair comment. It is typical of the opinion held by many white settlers of the time it was written. Cook's own comments are much closer to the modern understanding of the Aboriginal people of Australia.

or where there is no Creeks or Inlets, for where such are, be they ever so small, they draw the flood from the Southward, Eastward, and Northward, and, as I found by experience, while we lay in Endeavour River.[260] Another thing I have observed upon the Tides which ought to be remarked, which is that there is only one high Tide in 24 Hours, and that is the night Tide. On the Spring Tides the difference between the perpendicular rise of the night and day Tides is not less than 3 feet, which is a great deal where the Tides are so inconsiderable, as they are here.[261] This inequality of the Tide I did not observe till we run ashore; perhaps it is much more so to the Northward than to the Southward. After we had got within the Reefs the second time we found the Tides more considerable than at any time before, except in the Bay of Inlets. It may be owing to the water being confin'd in Channels between the Shoals, but the flood always set to the N.W. to the extremity of New Wales, from thence W. and S.W. into the India Seas.

260 Cook's reasoning on the course of the flood stream is quite sound (Wharton).

261 This difference in the heights of consecutive tides is termed the diurnal inequality. It results from the tide wave being made up of a large number of undulations, some caused by the moon, some by the sun; some occurring twice a day, others only once. It occurs in all parts of the world, but is inconspicuous on the coasts of Europe. In Australia it is very marked, and occasions the night tides to be the highest at one time of the year, when the *Endeavour* was on the coast, and the day tides at the other. There are places on the east coast of Australia where the range of the tide is very great, but Cook did not anchor at any of them (Wharton).

A FURTHER ACCOUNT OF NEW SOUTH WALES[262]

Of this country, its products, and its people, many particulars have already been related in the course of the narrative, being so interwoven with the events as not to admit of a separation. I shall now give a more full and circumstantial description of each, in which, if some things should happen to be repeated, the greater part will be found new.

New Holland, or, as I have now called the eastern coast, New South Wales, is of a larger extent than any other country in the known world that does not bear the name of a continent: the length of coast along which we sailed, reduced to a straight line, is no less than twenty-seven degrees of latitude, amounting to near 2000 miles, so that its square surface must be much more than equal to all Europe. To the southward of 33 or 34, the land in general is low and level; farther northward it is hilly, but in no part can be called mountainous; and the hills and mountains, taken together, make but a small part of the surface, in comparison with the valleys and plains. It is, upon the whole, rather barren than fertile: yet the rising ground is chequered by woods and lawns, and the plains and valleys are in many places covered with herbage: the soil, however, is frequently sandy, and many of the lawns, or savannahs, are rocky and barren, especially to the northward, where, in the best spots, vegetation was less vigorous than in the southern part of the country; the trees were not so tall, nor was the herbage so rich. The grass in general is high, but thin, and the trees, where they are largest, are seldom less than forty feet asunder: nor is the country inland, as far as we could examine it, better clothed than the sea-coast. The banks of the bays are covered with mangroves, to the distance of a mile within the beach, under which the soil is a rank mud, that is always overflowed by a spring-tide; farther in the country we sometimes met with a bog, upon which the grass was very thick and luxuriant, and sometimes with a valley, that was clothed with underwood: the soil in some parts seemed to be capable of improvement, but the far greater part is such as can admit

262 Captain Cook's own account, which is appended to his Journal, appears on pages 129 to 138. This further account is taken from *The Voyages of Discovery of Captain James Cook*, published by Ward Lock and Bowden. The title page states that this account is "partly narrated by the great navigator himself, and partly compiled from his notes and journals by Dr Hawkesley". The account of New South Wales is an amalgam of observations made by Cook and Banks, and is included here because of the information recorded by the distinguished scientists who accompanied the expedition. Some observations on fire-making in other parts of the world, and a parallel vocabulary of Aboriginal words have been omitted.

of no cultivation. The coast, at least that part of it which lies to the northward of 25° S., abounds with fine bays and harbours, where vessels may lie in perfect security from all winds.

If we may judge by the appearance of the country while we were there, which was in the very height of the dry season, it is well watered: we found innumerable small brooks and springs, but no great rivers; these brooks, however, probably become large in the rainy season. Thirsty Sound was the only place where fresh water was not to be procured for the ship, and even there one or two small pools were found in the woods, though the face of the country was everywhere intersected by salt creeks and mangrove land.

MANGROVE TREE.

Of trees, there is no great variety. Of those that could be called timber, there are but two sorts: the largest is the gum-tree, which grows all over the country, and has been mentioned already: it has narrow leaves, not much unlike a willow; and the gum, or rather resin, which it yields, is of a deep red, and resembles the *sanguis draconis*; possibly it may be the same, for this substance is known to be the produce of more than one plant. It is mentioned by Dampier, and is perhaps the same that Tasman found upon Diemen's Land, where he says he saw "gum of the trees, and gum lac of the ground." The other timber tree is that which grows somewhat like our pines, and has been particularly mentioned in the account of Botany Bay. The wood of both these trees,[263] as I have before remarked, is extremely hard and heavy. Besides these, here are trees covered with a soft bark that is easily peeled off, and is the same that in the East Indies is used for the calking of ships.[264]

We found here the palm of three different sorts. The first,[265] which grows in great plenty to the southward, has leaves that are platted like a fan: the cabbage of these is small, but exquisitely sweet; and the nuts, which it bears in great abundance, are very good food for hogs. The second sort bore a much greater resemblance to the true cabbage-tree of the West Indies; its leaves were large and pinnated, like those of the cocoa-nut; and these also produced a cabbage, which, though not so sweet as the other, was much larger.[266] The third sort, which, like the second, was found only in the northern parts, was seldom more than ten feet high, with small pinnated leaves, resembling those of some kind of fern: it bore no cabbage, but a plentiful crop of nuts, about the size of a large chesnut, but rounder.[267] As we found the hulls of these scattered round the places where the Indians had made their fires, we took for granted that they were fit to eat; those, however, who made the experiment, paid dear for their knowledge of the contrary, for they operated both as an emetic and cathartic with great violence. Still, however, we made no doubt but that they were eaten by the Indians; and, judging that the constitution of the hogs might be as strong as theirs, though our own had proved to be so much inferior, we carried them to the sty; the hogs ate them, indeed, and for some time, we thought, without suffering any inconvenience; but in about a week they were so much disordered, that two of them died, and the rest were recovered with great difficulty. It is probable, however, that the poisonous quality of these nuts may lie in the juice, like that of the cassada of the West Indies; and that the pulp, when dried, may be not only wholesome, but nutritious.[268] Besides these species of the palm and mangroves, there were several small trees and shrubs altogether unknown in Europe, particularly one which produced a very poor kind of fig;[269] another that bore what we

263 Various species of *Eucalyptus* and *Agophora* (Mair).

264 Various species of *Melaleuca* Paper-bark Tea-trees (Mair).

265 *Livistona australis*, the Cabbage Palm or Cabbage Tree of the New South Wales coast (Mair).

266 Perhaps a species of *Archontophoenix* (Mair).

267 Probably *Cycas media*, which is a Cycad, not a true palm. The seeds are poisonous unless specially treated (Mair).

268 The Aborigines prepared the Macrozamia seeds (the cycad of the north) by shelling and slicing and pounding the kernel, and soaking in water (preferably running water) for twenty-four hours or more. The treated flour was fashioned into cakes and wrapped in paperbark to prevent burning when cooked on the embers of a fire.

269 Identity uncertain, except that it is some kind of native fig (*Ficus* sp.) (Mair).

called a plum, which it resembled in colour, but not in shape, being flat on the sides like a little cheese; and a third, that bore a kind of purple apple, which, after it had been kept a few days, became eatable, and tasted somewhat like a damson.

Here is a great variety of plants to enrich the collection of a botanist, but very few of them are of the esculent kind. A small plant, with long, narrow, grassy leaves, resembling that kind of bulrush which in England is called the Cat's-tail, yields a resin of a bright yellow colour, exactly resembling gamboge, except that it does not stain; it has a sweet smell, but its properties we had no opportunity to discover, any more than those of many others with which the natives appear to be acquainted, as they have distinguished them by names.[270]

I have already mentioned the root and leaves of a plant, resembling the cocco of the West Indies, and a kind of bean; to which may be added, a sort of parsley and purslain, and two kinds of yams, one shaped like a radish, and the other round, and covered with stringy fibres: both sorts are very small, but sweet; and we never could find the plants that produced them, though we often saw the places where they had been newly dug up; it is probable that the drought had destroyed the leaves, and we could not, like the Indians, discover them by the stalks.

Most of the fruits of this country such as they are, have been mentioned already. We found one in the southern part of the country resembling a cherry, except that the stone was soft; and another, not unlike a pine-apple in appearance, but of a very disagreeable taste, which is well known in the East Indies, and is called by the Dutch *Pyn Appel Boomen.*[271]

Of the quadrupeds, I have already mentioned the dog, and particularly described the kanguroo, and the animal of the opossum kind, resembling the phalanger of Buffon;[272] to which I can add only one more, resembling a polecat,[273] which the natives call *Quoll*; the back is brown, spotted with white, and the belly white unmixed. Several of our people said they had seen wolves; but, perhaps, if we had not seen tracks that favoured the account, we might have thought them little more worthy of credit than he who reported that he had seen the devil.

Of bats, which hold a middle place between the beasts and the

270 A species of *Xanthorrhoea*, the so-called grass-tree, though many have no trunk (Mair).

271 Identity uncertain. The pine-apple-like fruit may be that of *Pandanus* sp. (Mair).

272 This could be the ringtail possum, unless it was found on the far north-eastern coast where the true Phalanger or Cuscus occurs (Troughton).

273 The native cat, called "Quoll" by the Aborigines around Port Jackson and Botany Bay, takes the older name *Dasyurus viverrinus* Shaw, 1800 (Troughton).

birds, we saw many kinds, particularly one which, as I have observed already, was larger than a partridge; we were not fortunate enough to take one either alive or dead, but it was supposed to be the same as Buffon has described by the name of *Rouset* or *Rouget.*

The sea and other water-fowl of this country, are gulls, shaggs,[274] solan geese, or gannets, of two sorts; boobies, noddies, curlews, ducks, pelicans of an enormous size, and many others. The land-birds are crows, parrots, paroquets, cockatoos, and other birds of the same kind, of exquisite beauty; pigeons, doves, quails, bustards, herons, cranes, hawks and eagles. The pigeons flew in numerous flocks, so that, notwithstanding their extreme shyness, our people frequently killed ten or twelve of them in a day: these birds are very beautiful, and crested very differently from any we had seen before.[275]

Among other reptiles, here are serpents of various kinds, some noxious, and some harmless; scorpions, centipedes, and lizards. The insects are but few. The principal are the mosquito and the ant. Of the ant there are several sorts; some are as green as a leaf,[276] and live upon trees, where they build their nests of various sizes, between that of a man's head and his fist. These nests are of a very curious structure: they are formed by bending down several of the leaves, each of which is as broad as a man's hand, and gluing the points of them together, so as to form a purse; the viscus used for this purpose, is an animal juice, which nature has enabled them to elaborate. Their method of first bending down the leaves, we had not an opportunity to observe; but we saw thousands uniting all their strength to hold them in this position, while other busy multitudes were employed within, in applying the gluten that was to prevent their returning back. To satisfy ourselves that the leaves were bent, and held down by the effort of these diminutive artificers, we disturbed them in their work, and as soon as they were driven from their station, the leaves on which they were employed, sprung up with a force much greater than we could have thought them able to conquer by any combination of their strength. But, though we gratified our curiosity at their expense, the injury did not go unrevenged; for thousands immediately threw themselves upon us, and gave us intolerable pain with their stings, especially those who took possession of our necks and our hair, from whence they were not easily driven: the sting was scarcely less painful than that of a bee; but, except it was repeated, the pain did not last more than a minute.

274 Cormorants. Four species have been noted in the area, Black, Little Black, Pied and Little Pied (Hindwood).

275 Possibly the Topknot Pigeon (*Lopholaimus antarcticus*) (Hindwood). See earlier notes on the other birds mentioned in this paragraph.

276 The Green Tree-ant, *Oecophylla smaragdina virescens* (Hindwood).

Another sort are quite black, and their operations and manner of life are not less extraordinary. Their habitations are the inside of the branches of a tree, which they contrive to excavate by working out the pith almost to the extremity of the slenderest twig; the tree at the same time flourishing, as if it had no such inmate. When we first found the tree we gathered some of the branches, and were scarcely less astonished than we should have been to find that we had profaned a consecrated grove, where every tree, upon being wounded, gave signs of life; for we were instantly covered with legions of these animals, swarming from every broken bough, and inflicting their stings with incessant violence. They are mentioned by Rumphius in his *Herbarium Amboinense*, vol. ii. p. 257; but the tree in which he saw their dwelling is very different from that in which we found them.[277]

A third kind we found nested in the root of a plant, which grows on the bark of trees in the manner of mistletoe, and which they had perforated for that use. This root is commonly as big as a large turnip, and sometimes much bigger: when we cut it we found it intersected by innumerable winding passages, all filled with these animals, by which, however, the vegetation of the plant did not appear to have suffered any injury. We never cut one of these roots that was not inhabited, though some were not bigger than a hazel-nut. The animals themselves are very small, not more than half as big as the common red ant in England. They had stings, but scarcely force enough to make them felt; they had, however, a power of tormenting us in an equal, if not a greater degree; for the moment we handled the root, they swarmed from innumerable holes, and running about those parts of the body that were uncovered, produced a titillation more intolerable than pain, except it is increased to great violence. Rumphius has also given an account of this bulb and its inhabitants, vol. vi. p. 120, where he mentions another sort that are black.

We found a fourth kind, which are perfectly harmless, and almost exactly resemble the white ants of the East Indies; the architecture of these is still more curious than that of the others.[278] They have houses of two sorts; one is suspended on the branches of trees, and the other erected upon the ground: those upon the trees are about three or four times as big as a man's head, and are built of a brittle substance, which seems to consist of small parts of vegetables kneaded together with a glutinous matter, which their bodies probably supply; upon breaking this crust, innumerable cells, swarming with inhabitants, appear in a great variety of winding directions, all communicating with each other, and with several apertures that lead to other nests upon the same tree; they have also one large avenue, or covered way, leading

277 The ants are not identifiable from this description (Hindwood).
278 A species of Termite (Hindwood).

to the ground, and carried on under it to the other nest or house that is constructed there. This house is generally at the root of a tree, but not of that upon which their other dwellings are constructed: it is formed like an irregularly sided cone, and sometimes is more than six feet high, and nearly as much in diameter. Some are smaller; and these are generally flat-sided, and very much resemble in figure the stones which are seen in many parts of England, and supposed to be the remains of druidical antiquity. The outside of these is of well-tempered clay, about two inches thick; and within are the cells, which have no opening outwards, but communicate only with the subterranean way to the houses on the tree, and to the tree near which they are constructed, where they ascend up the root, and so up the trunk and branches, under covered ways of the same kind as those by which they descended from their other dwellings. To these structures on the ground they probably retire in the winter, or rainy seasons, as they are proof against any wet that can fall; which those in the tree, though generally constructed under some overhanging branch, from the nature and thinness of their crust or wall, cannot be.[279]

The sea in this country is much more liberal of food to the inhabitants than the land; and though fish is not quite so plenty here as they generally are in higher latitudes, yet we seldom hauled the seine without taking from fifty to two hundred weight. They are of various sorts; but except the mullet, and some of the shellfish, none of them are known in Europe: most of them are palatable, and some are very delicious. Upon the shoals and reef there are incredible numbers of the finest green turtle in the world, and oysters of various kinds, particularly the rock-oyster and the pearl-oyster. The gigantic cockles have been mentioned already; besides which there are sea-crayfish, or lobsters, and crabs; of these, however, we saw only the shells. In the rivers and salt creeks there are alligators.[280]

The only person who has hitherto given any account of this country or its inhabitants is Dampier; and though he is, in general, a writer of credit, yet in many particulars he is mistaken. The people whom he saw were indeed inhabitants of a part of the coast very distant from that which we visited; but we also saw inhabitants upon parts of the coast very distant from each other; and there being a perfect uniformity in person and customs among them all, it is reasonable to conclude that distance in another direction has not considerably broken it.

The number of inhabitants in this country appears to be very small in proportion to its extent. We never saw so many as thirty of

[279] Many of the insects brought back by Cook were named by Fabricius. For full details of the specimens described see A. Musgrave, *A Bibliography of Australian Entomology*, Sydney, 1932, page 86 *et seq.*

[280] See notes on page 131.

them together but once, and that was at Botany Bay, when men, women, and children, assembled upon a rock to see the ship pass by: when they manifestly formed a resolution to engage us, they never could muster above fourteen or fifteen fighting men, and we never saw a number of their sheds or houses together that could accommodate a larger party. It is true, indeed, that we saw only the sea-coast on the eastern side; and that, between this and the western shore, there is an immense tract of country wholly unexplored: but there is great reason to believe that this immense tract is either wholly desolate, or at least still more thinly inhabited than the parts we visited. It is impossible that the inland country should subsist inhabitants at all seasons without cultivation: it is extremely improbable that the inhabitants of the coast should be totally ignorant of arts of cultivation, which were practised inland; and it is equally improbable that, if they knew such arts, there should be no traces of them among them. It is certain that we did not see one foot of ground in a state of cultivation in the whole country, and therefore it may well be concluded, that where the sea does not contribute to feed the inhabitants, the country is not inhabited.

The only tribe with which we had any intercourse we found where the ship was careened: it consisted of one-and-twenty persons, twelve men, seven women, one boy, and one girl: the women we never saw but at a distance, for when the men came over the river they were always left behind. The men, here and in other places, were of a middle size, and in general well made, clean-limbed, and remarkably vigorous, active, and nimble: their countenances were not altogether without expression, and their voices were remarkably soft and effeminate.

Their skins were so uniformly covered with dirt, that it was very difficult to ascertain their true colour: we made several attempts, by wetting our fingers and rubbing it, to remove the incrustations, but with very little effect. With the dirt, they appear nearly as black as a negro, and according to our best discoveries, the skin itself is of the colour of wood soot, or what is commonly called a chocolate colour. Their features are far from being disagreeable; their noses are not flat, nor are their lips thick; their teeth are white and even, and their hair naturally long and black, it is, however, universally cropped short; in general, it is straight, but sometimes it has a slight curl; we saw none that was not matted and filthy, though without oil or grease, and to our great astonishment free from lice. Their beards were of the same colour with their hair, and bushy and thick; they are not, however, suffered to grow long. A man, whom we had seen one day with his beard somewhat longer than his companions, we saw the next with it somewhat shorter, and upon examination found the ends of the hairs burnt; from this incident, and our having never seen any sharp instrument among them, we concluded that both the hair and the beard were kept short by singeing them.

Both sexes, as I have already observed, go stark naked, and seem to have no more sense of indecency in discovering the whole body, than we have in discovering our hands and face. Their principal ornament is the bone, which they thrust through the cartilage that divides the nostrils from each other. What perversion of taste could make them think this a decoration, or what could prompt them, before they had worn it or seen it worn, to suffer the pain and inconvenience that must of necessity attend it, is perhaps beyond the power of human sagacity to determine. As this bone is as thick as a man's finger, and

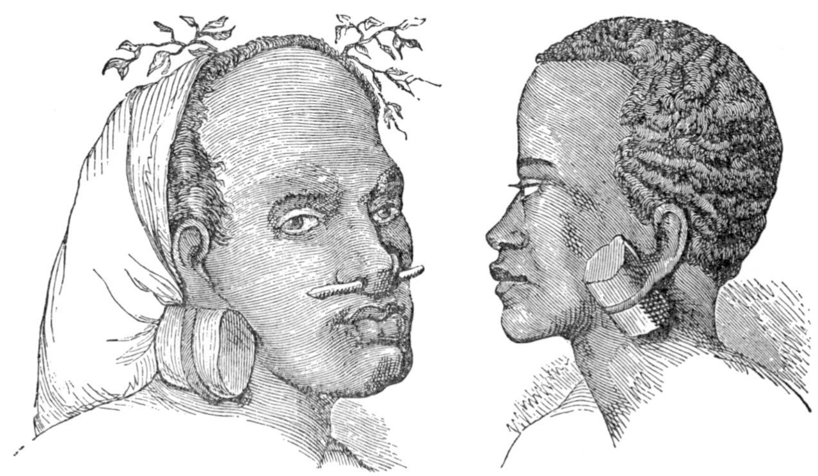

HEADS OF NEW HOLLANDERS, NATIVES OF MANEVAI, MALE AND FEMALE.

(The Man wears the Nose Ornament described in the Text.)

between five and six inches long, it reaches quite across the face, and so effectually stops up both the nostrils, that they are forced to keep their mouths wide open for breath, and snuffle so when they attempt to speak, that they are scarcely intelligible even to each other. Our seamen, with some humour, called it their spritsail-yard; and, indeed, it had so ludicrous an appearance, that till we were used to it, we found it difficult to refrain from laughter. Beside this nose jewel, they had necklaces made of shells, very neatly cut and strung together; bracelets of small cord, wound two or three times about the upper part of their arm, and a string of plaited human hair about as thick as a thread of yarn, tied round the waist. Besides these, some of them had gorgets of shells hanging round the neck, so as to reach across the breast. But though these people wear no clothes, their bodies have a covering besides the dirt, for they paint them both white and red: the red is commonly laid on in broad patches upon the shoulders and breast, and the white in stripes, some narrow, and some broad: the narrow were drawn over the limbs, and the broad over the body, not without some degree of taste. The white was also laid on in small patches upon the face, and drawn in a circle round each eye. The red seemed to be ochre, but what the white was we could not discover: it was close-grained, saponaceous to the touch, and almost as heavy as white lead; possibly it might be a kind of *Stealites*, but to our great regret we could not procure a bit of it to examine.[281] They have holes in their ears, but we never saw any thing worn in them. Upon such ornaments as they had, they set so great a value, that they would never part with the least article for anything we could offer; which was the more extraordinary, as our beads and ribbons were ornaments of the same kind, but of a more regular form and more showy materials. They had, indeed, no idea of traffic,[282] nor could we communicate any to them: they received the things that we gave them, but never appeared to understand our signs when we required a return. The same indifference which prevented them from buying what we had, prevented them also from attempting to steal: if they had coveted more, they would have been less honest; for when we refused to give them a turtle, they were enraged, and attempted to take it by force, and we had nothing else upon which they seemed to set the least value; for, as I have before observed, many of the things that we had given them we found left negligently about in the woods, like the playthings of children, which please only while they are new. Upon their bodies we saw no marks of disease or sores, but large scars in irregular line, which appeared to be the remains of wounds which they had inflicted upon themselves with some blunt instrument, and which we understood by signs to have been memorials of grief for the dead.[283]

They appeared to have no fixed habitations, for we saw nothing like a town or village in the whole country. Their houses, if houses they may be called, seemed to be formed with less art and industry than any we had seen, except the wretched hovels at Terra del Fuego,

[281] White ochre, see note on page 132. Iron oxide provided a red pigment; in some places yellow hydrated oxide of iron was heated to drive off the water and thus produce red ochre. In initiation ceremonies blood was used to provide the red colouring.

[282] While this statement is true of their contacts with Cook and his men, barter was practised throughout the continent. Prized objects and materials were "traded" along recognised routes. The red ochre mentioned in the previous note was one of the objects of widespread trade.

[283] Cicatrisation took many forms and was practised for several different reasons. Amongst some tribes it was simply an ornament; in others it was an important part of the rites of initiation, the pattern and number of scars indicating the grade that had been reached. The flesh was cut with sharp stones. Ashes were rubbed into the wounds to heal them and to raise scars that were universally admired.

and in some respects they are inferior even to them. At Botany Bay, where they were best, they were just high enough for a man to sit upright in, but not large enough for him to extend himself in his whole length in any direction: they are built with pliable rods about as thick as a man's finger, in the form of an oven, by sticking the two ends into the ground, and then covering them with palm-leaves and broad pieces of bark: the door is nothing but a large hole at one end, opposite to which the fire is made, as we perceived by the ashes. Under these houses, or sheds, they sleep, coiled up with their heels to their head, and in this position one of them will hold three or four persons. As we advanced northward, and the climate became warmer, we found these sheds still more slight: they were built, like the others, of twigs, and covered with bark; but none of them were more than four feet deep, and one side was entirely open: the close side was always opposed to the course of the prevailing wind, and opposite to the open side was the fire, probably more as a defence from the mosquitoes than the cold. Under these hovels it is probable that they thrust only their heads and the upper part of their bodies, extending their feet towards the fire. They were set up occasionally by a wandering horde in any place that would furnish them for a time with subsistence, and left behind them when, after it was exhausted, they went away; but in places where they remained only for a night or two, they slept without any shelter, except the bushes or grass, which is here near two feet high. We observed, however, that though the sleeping huts, which we found upon the main, were always turned from the prevailing wind, those upon the islands were turned towards it; which seems to be a proof that they have a mild season here, during which the sea is calm, and that the same weather which enables them to visit the islands makes the air welcome even while they sleep.

The only furniture belonging to these houses that fell under our observation is a kind of oblong vessel made of bark, by the simple contrivance of tying up the two ends with a withy, which not being cut off serves for a handle; these we imagined were used as buckets to fetch water from the spring, which may be supposed sometimes to be at a considerable distance. They have, however, a small bag, about the size of a moderate cabbage-net, which is made by laying threads loop within loop, somewhat in the manner of knitting used by our ladies to make purses. This bag the man carries loose upon his back by a small string which passes over his head; it generally contains a lump or two of paint and resin, some fish-hooks and lines, a shell or two, out which their hooks are made, a few points of darts, and their usual ornaments, which includes the whole worldly treasure of the richest man among them.

Their fish-hooks are very neatly made, and some of them are exceedingly small. For striking turtle they have a peg of wood which is about a foot long, and very well bearded; this fits into a socket at the end of a staff of light wood, about as thick as a man's wrist, and about seven or eight feet long: to the staff is tied one end of a loose line about three or four fathom long, the other end of which is fastened to the peg. To strike the turtle, the peg is fixed into the socket, and when it has entered his body, and is retained there by the barb, the staff flies off, and serves for a float to trace their victim in the water; it assists also to tire him, till they can overtake him with their canoes, and haul him ashore. One of these pegs, as I have mentioned already, we found buried in the body of a turtle, which had healed up over it. Their lines are from the thickness of a half-inch rope to the fineness of a hair, and are made of some vegetable substance, but what in particular we had no opportunity to learn.[284]

Their food is chiefly fish, though they sometimes contrive to kill the kanguroo, and even birds of various kinds; notwithstanding, they are so shy that we found it difficult to get within reach of them with a fowling-piece. The only vegetable that can be considered as an article of food is the yam; yet doubtless they eat the several fruits which have been mentioned among other productions of the country; and indeed we saw the shells and hulls of several of them lying about the places where they had kindled their fire.

They do not appear to eat any animal food raw; but having no vessel in which water can be boiled, they either broil it upon the coals, or bake it in a hole by the help of hot stones, in the same manner as is practised by the inhabitants of the islands in the South Seas.

Whether they are acquainted with any plant that has an intoxicating quality, we do not know; but we observed that several of them held leaves of some sort constantly in their mouths, as a European does tobacco, and an East Indian betel: we never saw the plant, but when they took it from their mouths at our request; possibly it might be a species of the betel, but whatever it was, it had no effect upon the teeth or the lips.[285]

As they have no nets, they catch fish only by striking, or with a hook and line, except such as they find in the hollows of the rocks and shoals, which are dry at half ebb.[286]

[284] Twine and heavier cord were made from human hair, animal fur, strips of pandanus and other leaves, the fibres of many kinds of grass, and bark. The fibres were led from one hand to another, rolled on the thigh, and wound on to a spindle. Twine made in this way was usually two-ply.

[285] Pituri, a plant growing in south-west Queensland, was traded over a wide area, and keenly sought after as a stimulant. The dried stems and leaves were broken up and chewed.

[286] Though nets were not seen by the explorers they were used in most parts of the continent both for fishing and hunting.

Their manner of hunting we had no opportunity to see; but we conjectured by the notches which they had everywhere cut in large trees in order to climb them, that they took their station near the tops of them, and there watched for such animals as might happen to pass near enough to be reached by their lances: it is possible, also, that in this situation they might take birds when they came to roost.

I have observed that when they went from our tents upon the banks of Endeavour River, we could trace them by the fires which they kindled in their way; and we imagined that these fires were intended some way for the taking the kanguroo, which we observed to be so much afraid of fire, that our dogs could scarcely force it over places which had been newly burnt, though the fire was extinguished.

They produce fire with great facility, and spread it in a wonderful manner. To produce it they take two pieces of dry soft wood, one is a stick about eight or nine inches long, the other piece is flat: the stick they shape into an obtuse point at one end, and pressing it upon the other, turn it nimbly by holding it between both their hands as we do a chocolate mill, often shifting their hands up, and then moving them down upon it, to increase the pressure as much as possible. By this method they get fire in less than two minutes, and from the smallest spark, they increase it with great speed and dexterity. We have often seen one of them run along the shore, to all appearance with nothing in his hand, who stooping down for a moment, at the distance of every fifty or hundred yards, left fire behind him, as we could see first by the smoke, and then by the flame among the drift wood, and other litter which was scattered along the place. We had the curiosity to examine one of these planters of fire, when he set off, and we saw him wrap up a small spark in dry grass, which, when he had run a little way, having been fanned by the air that his motion produced, began to blaze; he then laid it down in a place convenient for his purpose, inclosing a spark of it in another quantity of grass, and so continued his course.

The weapons of these people are spears or lances, and these are of different kinds: some that we saw upon the southern part of the coast had four prongs, pointed with bone, and barbed; the points were also smeared with a hard resin, which gave them a polish, and made them enter deeper into what they struck. To the northward, the lance has but one point: the shaft is made of cane, or the stalk of a plant somewhat resembling a bulrush, very straight and light, and from eight to fourteen feet long, consisting of several joints, where the pieces are let into each other, and bound together; to this are fitted points of different kinds; some are of hard heavy wood, and some are the bones of fish: we saw several that were pointed with the stings of the sting-ray, the largest that they could procure, and barbed with several that were smaller, fastened on in a contrary direction; the points of wood were also sometimes armed with sharp pieces of broken shells, which were stuck in, and at the junctures covered with resin: the lances that are thus barbed are indeed dreadful weapons; for when once they have taken place, they can never be drawn back without tearing away the flesh, or leaving the sharp ragged splinters of the bone or shell which forms the beard behind them in the wound. These weapons are thrown with great force and dexterity: if intended to wound at a short distance, between ten and twenty yards, simply with the hand; but if at the distance of forty or fifty, with an instrument which we called a throwing stick. This is a plain smooth piece of a hard reddish wood, very highly polished, about two inches broad, half an inch

NEW HOLLAND SHIELD.

thick, and three feet long, with a small knob, or hook at one end, and a cross piece about three or four inches long at the other: the knob at one end is received in a small dent or hollow, which is made for that purpose in the shaft of the lance near the point, but from which it easily slips, upon being impelled forward: when the lance is laid along upon this machine, and secured in a proper position by the knob, the person that is to throw it holds it over his shoulder, and after shaking it, delivers both the throwing-stick and lance with all his force; but the stick being stopped by the cross piece which comes against the shoulder, with a sudden jerk, the lance flies forward with incredible swiftness and with so good an aim, that at the distance of fifty yards these Indians were more sure of their mark than we could be with a single bullet. Besides these lances, we saw no offensive weapon upon this coast, except when we took our last view of it with our glasses, and then we thought we saw a man with a bow and arrows, in which it is possible we might be mistaken.[287] We saw, however, at Botany Bay, a shield or target of an oblong shape about three feet long and eighteen inches broad, which was made of the bark of a tree: this was fetched out of a hut by one of the men that opposed our landing, who, when he ran away, left it behind him, and upon taking it up, we found that it had been pierced through with a single pointed lance near the centre. These shields are certainly in frequent use among the people here; for though this was the only one that we saw in their possession, we frequently found trees from which they appeared manifestly to have been cut, the marks being easily distinguished from those that were made by cutting buckets: sometimes also we found the shields cut out, but not yet taken off from the tree, the edges of the bark only being a little raised by wedges, so that these people appear to have discovered that the bark of a tree becomes thicker and stronger by being suffered to remain upon the trunk after it has been cut round.[288]

The canoes of New Holland are as mean and rude as the houses. Those on the southern part of the coast are nothing more than a piece of bark, about twelve feet long, tied together at the ends, and kept open in the middle by small bows of wood: yet in a vessel of this construction we once saw three people. In shallow water they are set forward by a pole, and in deeper by paddles, about eighteen inches long, one of which the boatman holds in each hand; mean as they are, they have many conveniences, they draw but little water, and they are very light, so that they go upon mud banks to pick up shellfish, the most important use to which they can be applied, better perhaps than vessels of any other construction. We observed, that in the middle of these canoes there was a heap of sea-weed, and upon that a small fire; probably that the fish may be broiled and eaten the moment it is caught.

The canoes that we saw when we advanced farther to the northward, are not made of bark, but of the trunk of a tree hollowed, perhaps by fire. They are about fourteen feet long, and, being very narrow, are fitted with an outrigger to prevent their oversetting. These are worked with paddles, that are so large as to require both hands to manage one of them: the outside is wholly unmarked by any tool, but at each end the wood is left longer at the top than at the bottom, so that there is a projection beyond the hollow part resembling the end of a plank; the sides are tolerably thin, but how the tree is felled and fashioned, we had no opportunity to learn. The only tools that we saw among them are an adze, wretchedly made of stone,

287 The bow and arrow were not an Aboriginal invention. The reference may be to the boomerangs or woomeras seen at Botany Bay. See note on page 42.

288 Coolamons were also sometimes made by this method.

some small pieces of the same substance in form of a wedge, a wooden mallet, and some shells and fragments of coral. For polishing their throwing-sticks, and the points of their lances, they use the leaves of a kind of wild fig-tree, which bites upon wood almost as keenly as the shave-grass of Europe, which is used by our joiners: with such tools, the making even such a canoe as I have described must be a most difficult and tedious labour: to those who have been accustomed to the use of metal, it appears altogether impracticable; but there are few difficulties that will not yield to patient perseverance; and he who does all he can will certainly produce effects that greatly exceed his apparent power.

The utmost freight of these canoes is four people; and if more at any time wanted to come over the river, one of those who came first was obliged to go back for the rest: from this circumstance, we conjectured that the boat we saw, when we were lying in Endeavour River, was the only one in the neighbourhood, we have however some reason to believe that the bark canoes are also used where the wooden ones are constructed; for upon one of the small islands where the natives had been fishing for turtle, we found one of the little paddles which had belonged to such a boat, and would have been useless on board any other.

By what means the inhabitants of this country are reduced to such a number as it can subsist, is not perhaps very easy to guess; whether, like the inhabitants of New Zealand, they are destroyed by the hands of each other in contests for food; whether they are swept off by accidental famine, or whether there is any cause which prevents the increase of the species, must be left for future adventurers to determine. That they have wars, appears by their weapons; for supposing the lances to serve merely for the striking of fish, the shield could be intended for nothing but a defence against men; the only mark of hostility, however, which we saw among them, was the perforation of the shield by a spear, which has been just mentioned, for none of them appeared to have been wounded by an enemy. Neither can we determine whether they are pusillanimous or brave; the resolution with which two of them attempted to prevent our landing, when we had two boats full of men, in Botany Bay, even after one of them was wounded with small shot, gave us reason to conclude that they were not only naturally courageous, but that they had acquired a familiarity with the dangers of hostility, and were, by habit as well as nature, a daring and warlike people; but their precipitate flight from every other place that we approached, without even a menace, while they were out of our reach, was an indication of uncommon tameness and timidity, such as those who had only been occasionally warriors must be supposed to have shaken off, whatever might have been their natural disposition. I have faithfully related facts, the reader must judge of the people for himself.

From the account that has been given of our commerce with them, it cannot be supposed that we should know much of their language; yet as this is an object of great curiosity, especially to the learned, and of great importance in their researches into the origin of the various nations that have been discovered, we took some pains to bring away such a specimen of it as might, in a certain degree, answer the purpose, and I shall now give an account how it was procured. If we wanted to know the name of a stone, we took a stone up into our hands, and as well as we could, intimated by signs, that we wished they should name it: the word that they pronounced upon the occasion we immediately wrote down. This method, though it was the best we could contrive, might certainly lead us into many mistakes; for if an Indian[289] was to take up a stone, and ask us the name of it, we might answer a pebble or a flint; so when we took up a stone, and asked an Indian the name of it, he might pronounce a word that distinguished the species and not the genus, or that, instead of signifying stone simply, might signify a rough stone, or a smooth stone; however, as much as possible to avoid mistakes of this kind, several of us contrived, at different times, to get from them as many words as we could, and having noted them down, compared our lists: those which were the same in all, and which, according to every one's account, signified the same thing, we ventured to record, with a very few others, which, from the simplicity of the subject, and the ease of expressing our question with plainness and precision by a sign, have acquired equal authority.

289 Early explorers usually referred to all native people of the Pacific as Indians.

[On leaving Australia Cook sailed along the south coast of New Guinea, called at Batavia and Cape of Good Hope, and reached England in 1771.]

SECOND VOYAGE

MADE IN H.M. BARKS *RESOLUTION* AND *ADVENTURE*

1772-75

This voyage was made with the purpose of discovering the great southern continent. The search proving unavailing, Cook turned northwards in March 1773, reaching New Zealand later the same month. On 8 February the two vessels had lost sight of each other. The Adventure, *commanded by Captain Tobias Furneaux, sailed northwards to Tasmania. His visit was brief. It is recorded here.*

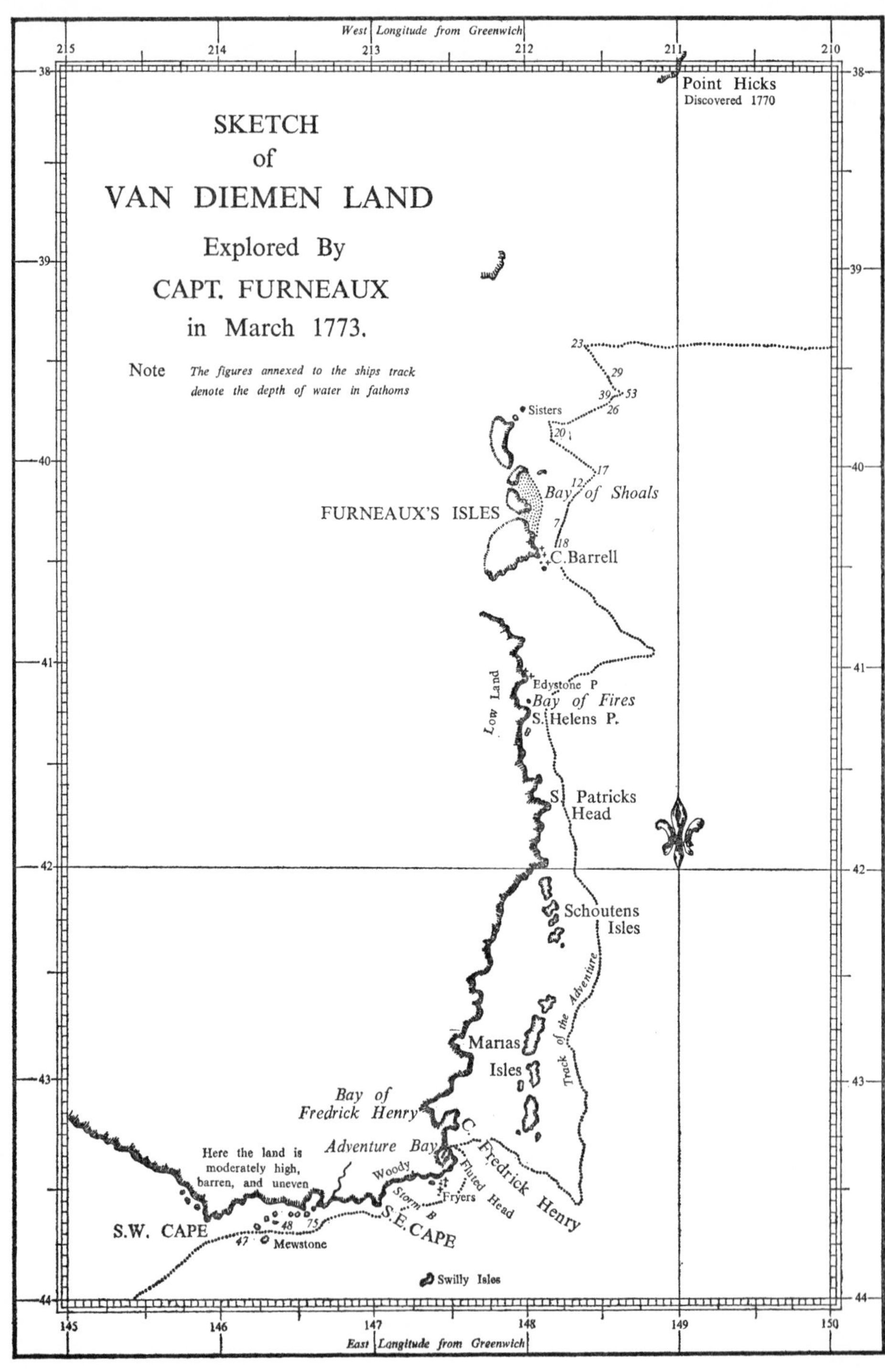
West Longitude from Greenwich
215
214
213
212
211
210
38
39
40
41
42
43
44
Point Hicks
Discovered 1770
SKETCH
of
VAN DIEMEN LAND
Explored By
CAPT. FURNEAUX
in March 1773.
Note The figures annexed to the ships track denote the depth of water in fathoms
23
29
39
53
26
Sisters
20
17
12
Bay of Shoals
FURNEAUX'S ISLES
7
18
C. Barrell
Edystone P
Bay of Fires
S. Helens P.
Low Land
S. Patricks Head
Schoutens Isles
Track of the Adventure
Marias Isles
Bay of Fredrick Henry
Adventure Bay
C. Fredrick Henry
Fluted Head
Fryers
Woody
Storm B
S.E. CAPE
Here the land is moderately high, barren, and uneven
S.W. CAPE
48
75
47
Mewstone
Swilly Isles
145
146
147
148
149
150
East Longitude from Greenwich

CAPTAIN FURNEAUX'S NARRATIVE OF A BRIEF VISIT TO VAN DIEMEN'S LAND[290]

9 March 1773 - 19 March 1773

On the first of March we were alarmed with the cry of land by the man at the mast-head, on the larboard beam; which gave us great joy. We immediately hauled our wind and stood for it, but to our mortification were disappointed in a few hours; for what we took to be land, proved no more than clouds, which disappeared as we sailed towards them. We then bore away and directed our course toward the land laid down in the charts by the name of Van Diemen's Land, discovered by Tasman in 1642, and laid down in the latitude 44° south, and longitude 140° east, and supposed to join to New Holland.[291]

On the 9th of March, having little wind and pleasant weather, about nine A.M., being then in the latitude 43° 37′ south longitude, by lunar observation, 145° 36′ east, and by account, 143° 10′ east, from Greenwich, we saw the land bearing N.N.E. about eight or nine leagues distance. It appeared moderately high, and uneven near the sea; the hills further back formed a double land and much higher.

290 Captain Tobias Furneaux was appointed to the command of the *Adventure*. After sailing for the south, the *Resolution* and the *Adventure* accidentally parted company. Furneaux sailed to Tasmania and later rejoined Cook at Queen Charlotte Sound in New Zealand.

291 The first men to enter the strait that separates Tasmania from the mainland were fourteen escaped convicts who stole a boat at Port Jackson and sailed southward in the hope of finding the *Sydney Cove*, which had been wrecked on Preservation Island in the Furneaux group. They sailed as far as a small island on the western side of Wilson Promontory, thus penetrating a considerable way into the strait. Seven of them took possession of the boat and returned to Port Jackson, leaving the remainder of the party stranded on the island.

On 3 December of the same year, 1797, the surgeon George Bass left Port Jackson in a whaleboat with a crew of six on a voyage of expedition. The furthest extent of his journey was Westernport. Having reached this point he was still not certain that the strait existed, but seemed reasonably sure that there was a passage, for he wrote in his Journal: "Whenever it shall be decided that the opening between this and Van Dieman's Land is a strait, this rapidity of tide, and that long S.W. swell that seems to be continually rolling in upon the coast to the westward, will then be accounted for." Bass discovered the marooned convicts. As there was no room for them all in the boat he took two of them back to Sydney, sending the others overland, but they were never heard of again.

Bass's conjectures were confirmed later in 1798 when he accompanied Matthew Flinders in the *Norfolk* and circumnavigated the island. Governor Hunter named the strait after him in honour of his exploits and discoveries.

There seemed to be several islands, or broken land, to the N.W. as the shore trended; but by reason of clouds that hung over them, we could not be certain whether they did not join to the main. We hauled immediately up for it, and by noon were within three or four leagues of it. A point, much like the Ramhead, off Plymouth, which I take to be the same that Tasman calls South Cape,[292] bore north four leagues off us. The land from this cape runs directly to the eastward; about four leagues alongshore are three islands about two miles long, and several rocks, resembling the Mewstone[293] (particularly one which we so named) about four or five leagues E.S.E. ½ E. off the above Cape, which Tasman has not mentioned, or laid down in his drafts.[294] After you pass these islands the land lies E. by N. and W. by S. by the compass nearly. It is a bold shore, and seems to afford several bays or anchoring places, but believe deep water. From the S.W. cape, which is in the latitude of 43° 39′ south, and longitude 145° 50′ east, to the S.E. cape, in the latitude 43° 36′ south, longitude 147° east, is nearly sixteen leagues, and sounding from forty-eight to seventy fathoms, sand and broken shells, three or four leagues off shore. Here the country is hilly and full of trees, the shore rocky and difficult landing, occasioned by the wind blowing here continually from the westward, which occasions such a surf that the sand cannot lie on the shore. We saw no inhabitants here.

The morning on the 10th of March being calm, the ship then about four miles from the land, sent the great cutter on shore with the second lieutenant, to find if there was any harbour or good bay. Soon after, it beginning to blow very hard, made the signal for the boat to return several times, but they did not see or hear anything of it; the ship then three or four leagues off, that we could not see anything of the boat, which gave us great uneasiness, as there was a very great sea. At half-past one P.M. to our great satisfaction, the boat returned on board safe. They landed, but with much difficulty, and saw several places where the Indians had been, and one they lately had left, where they had a fire, with a great number of pearl scallop shells round it, which shells they brought on board, with some burnt sticks and green boughs. There was a path from this place, through the woods, which in all probability leads to their habitations; but, by reason of the weather, had not time to pursue it. The soil seems to be very rich; the country well clothed with wood, particularly on the lee side of the hills; plenty of water, which falls from the rocks in beautiful cascades

292 Actually South-west Cape.

293 Another distant group of islands to the south Furneaux named Swilly Islands after his birthplace near Portsmouth.

294 The Maatsuyker Islands, named by Tasman in 1642. The lighthouse which now stands on Maatsuyker Island is the most southerly in Australia. Mewstone is an island in this group.

for two or three hundred feet perpendicular into the sea; but they did not see the least sign of any place to anchor in with safety. Hoisted in the boat, and made sail for Frederick Henry Bay. From noon to three P.M. running along-shore E. by N. at which time we were abreast of the westernmost point of a very deep bay, called by Tasman, Stormy Bay.[295] From the west to the east point of this bay, there are several small islands, and black rocks which we called the Fryars. While crossing this bay we had very heavy squalls and thick weather; at times, when it cleared up, I saw several fires in the bottom of the bay, which is near two or three leagues deep, and has, I doubt not, good places for anchoring, but the weather being so bad, did not think it safe to stand into it. From the Fryars the land trenches away about N. by E. four leagues. We had smooth water, and kept in-shore, having regular soundings from twenty to fifteen fathoms water. At half-past six we hauled round a high bluff point, the rocks whereof were like so many fluted pillars,[296] and had ten fathoms water, fine sand, within half a mile of the shore. At seven, being abreast of a fine bay, and having little wind, we came to, with the small bower, in twenty-four fathoms, sandy bottom.[297] Just after we anchored, being a fine clear evening, had a good observation of the star Antares and the moon, which gave the longitude of 147° 34′ east, being in the latitude of 43° 20′ south. We first took this bay to be that which Tasman called Frederic Henry Bay; but afterwards found that his is laid down five leagues to the northward of this.

At day-break the next morning, I sent the master in-shore to sound the bay, and to find out a watering-place; at eight he returned, having found a most excellent harbour, clear ground from side to side, from eighteen to five fathom water all over the bay, gradually decreasing as you go in-shore. We weighed and turned up into the bay; the wind being westerly, and very little of it, which baffled us much in getting in. At seven o'clock in the evening, we anchored in seven fathoms water, with the small bower, and moored with the coasting anchor to

295 Furneaux was in fact sailing across the southern entrance of D'Entrecasteaux Channel which separates Bruny Island from the mainland. Tasman's Storm Bay was further north. This mistaken identification led to further misconceptions which were accepted by Captain Cook four years later. A detailed survey of the subject is found in Dr Beaglehole's notes in *The Journals of Captain James Cook*, Volume Two, pages 163-4.

296 The cape at the southern end of Adventure Bay is called Fluted Cape, after Furneaux's Fluted Head.

297 Adventure Bay, so named subsequently after Furneaux's vessel. In 1642 Tasman tried to enter the bay but was driven away by the wind. In 1777 Cook entered the bay and remained there for two days. In 1788 Bligh anchored the *Bounty* there, and again in 1792. D'Entrecasteaux visited the bay in the same year. Adventure Bay, on the eastern shore of Bruny Island, is thus closely linked with several notable early explorers. Furneaux was not aware that the bay was on an island.

the westward, the north point of the bay N.N.E. ½ E., (which we take to be Tasman's Head,)[298] and the easternmost point (which we named Penguin Island, from a curious one we caught there)[299] N.E. by E. ¾ E. the watering-place W. ½ N. about one mile from the shore on each side; Maria's Island, which is about five or six leagues off, shut in with both points; so that you are quite land-locked in a most spacious harbour.

We lay here five days, which time was employed in wooding and watering (which is easily got), and overhauling the rigging. We found the country very pleasant; the soil a black, rich, though thin one; the sides of the hills covered with large trees,[300] and very thick, growing to a great height before they branch off. They are, all of them, of the evergreen kind, different from any I ever saw; the wood is very brittle and easily split; there is very little variety of sorts, having seen but two. The leaves of one are long and narrow; and the seed (of which I got a few) is in the shape of a button, and has a very agreeable smell. The leaves of the other are like the bay, and it has a seed like the whitehorn, with an agreeable spicy taste and smell. Out of the trees we cut down for fire-wood, there issued some gum, which the surgeon called gumlac. The trees are mostly burnt, or scorched near the ground, occasioned by the natives setting fire to the underwood in the most frequented places; and by these means they have rendered it easy walking. The land birds we saw, are a bird like a raven; some of the crow kind, black, with the tips of the feathers of the tail and wings white, their bill long and very sharp; some parroquets; and several kinds of small birds. The sea-fowl are ducks, teal, and the sheldrake. I forgot to mention a large white bird, that one of the gentlemen shot, about the size of a large kite, of the eagle kind.[301] As for beasts, we saw but one, which was an *opossum*: but we observed the dung of some, which we judged to be of the deer kind. The fish in the bay are scarce; those we caught were mostly sharks, dog-fish,[302] and a fish called by the seamen nurses, like the dog-fish, only full of small white spots; and some small fish not unlike sprats. The lagoons (which are brackish) abound with trout, and several other sorts of

298 Tasman Head is actually at the southern end of Bruny Island.

299 This penguin is the Rockhopper Penguin (*Eudyptes crestatus*), earlier listed under the specific name of *chrysocome*, a name based on more than one species of penguin (Hindwood).

300 Various *Eucalyptus* spp. (Mair).

301 Raven. *Corvus coronoides.*

"Crow kind". Black Currawong (*Strepera fuliginosa*).

Teal. Either the Grey Teal or the Chestnut Teal.

Sheldrake. Mountain Duck.

"Kite of the eagle kind". White Goshawk (*Accipiter novaehollandiae*) (Hindwood).

302 *Flakeus megalops.* The other fishes are mentioned in such general terms that they cannot be scientifically identified (Whitley).

fish, of which we caught a few with lines, but being much encumbered with stumps of trees, we could not haul the seine.

While we lay here, we saw several smokes and large fires, about eight or ten miles in-shore to the northward, but did not see any of the natives; though they frequently come into this bay, as there were several wigwams or huts, where we found some bags and nets made of grass, in which I imagine they carry their provisions and other necessaries. In one of them there was the stone they strike fire with, and tinder made of bark, but of what tree could not be distinguished. We found, in one of their huts, one of their spears, which was made sharp at one end, I suppose with a shell or stone. Those things we brought away, leaving in the room of them, medals, gun-flints, a few nails, and an old empty barrel with the iron hoops on it. They seem to be quite ignorant of every sort of metal. The boughs of which their huts are made, are either broken or split, and tied together with grass in a circular form, the largest end stuck in the ground, and the smaller parts meeting in a point at the top, and covered with fern and bark; so poorly done, that they will hardly keep out a shower of rain. In the middle is the fire-place, surrounded with heaps of muscle, pearl scallop, and cray-fish shells; which I believe to be their chief food, though we could not find any of them. They lie on the ground, on dried grass, round the fire; and, I believe, they have no settled place of habitation (as their houses seemed built only for a few days), but wander about in small parties from place to place in search of food, and are actuated by no other motive. We never found more than three or four huts in a place, capable of containing three or four persons each only; and what is remarkable, we never saw the least marks either of canoe or boat, and it is generally thought they have none; being altogether, from what we could judge, a very ignorant and wretched set of people, though natives of a country capable of producing every necessary of life, and a climate the finest in the world. We found not the least signs of any minerals or metals.

Having completed our wood and water, we sailed from Adventure Bay, intending to coast it up alongshore, till we should fall in with the land seen by Captain Cook, and discover whether Van Diemen's Land joins with New Holland. On the 16th we passed Maria's Islands,[303] so named by Tasman; they appear to be the same as the mainland. On the 17th, having passed Schouten's Islands,[304] we hauled in for the mainland, and stood alongshore at the distance of two or three leagues off. The country here appears to be very thickly inhabited, as there was a continual fire along-shore as we sailed. The

303 The name Maria Island has been retained.

304 So named by Tasman.

land hereabouts is much pleasanter, low and even; but no signs of a harbour or bay, where a ship might anchor with safety. The weather being bad, and blowing hard at S.S.E., we could not send a boat on shore to have any intercourse with the inhabitants. In the latitude of 40° 50′ south, the land trenches away to the westward, which I believe forms a deep bay,[305] as we saw from the deck several smokes arising a-back of the islands that lay before it, when we could not see the least signs of land from the mast-head.

From the latitude of 40° 50′ south, to the latitude of 39° 50′ south, is nothing but islands and shoals; the land high, rocky, and barren. On the 19th, in the latitude of 40° 30′ south, observing breakers about half a mile within-shore of us, we sounded, and finding but eight fathoms, immediately hauled off, deepened our water to fifteen fathoms, then bore away, and kept along-shore again. From the latitude of 39° 50′ to 39° S. we saw no land, but had regular soundings from fifteen to thirty fathoms. As we stood on to the northward, we made land again in about 39°; after which we discontinued our northerly course, as we found the ground very uneven, and shoal water some distance off. I think it a very dangerous shore to fall in with.

The coast, from Adventure Bay to the place where we stood away for New Zealand,[306] lies in the direction S. ½ W. and N. ½ E. about seventy-five leagues; and it is my opinion that there is no strait between New Holland and Van Diemen's Land, but a very deep bay.[307] I should have stood farther to the northward, but the wind blowing strong at S.S.E., and looking likely to haul round to the eastward, which would have blown right on the land, I therefore thought it more proper to leave the coast, and steer for New Zealand.

[*After leaving Tasmania, Furneaux proceeded to New Zealand and made his rendezvous with Cook in Queen Charlotte Sound in the South Island of New Zealand. The two vessels then sailed northwards to Tahiti.*]

305 Named the Bay of Fires by Furneaux who also named Eddystone Point at the northern end of the bay. On his last voyage Cook gave the same name to a rock off South-east Cape (see page 167).

306 Having traversed the eastern coast of Tasmania, Furneaux discovered the group of islands later named after him by Captain Cook, and then sailed eastward to New Zealand.

307 After Furneaux's rendezvous with Cook in Queen Charlotte Sound in the South Island of New Zealand a few weeks later, the commander of the expedition intended to set sail for New Holland to determine once and for all whether or not Van Diemen's Land was part of the continent; but Furneaux was so certain that the westward trend of the land was no more than a deep bay that Cook accepted his opinion.

THIRD VOYAGE

MADE IN H.M. BARKS *RESOLUTION* AND *DISCOVERY*

1776-80

On his last voyage Cook attempted the discovery of the North-west Passage in the Arctic regions. He left England in July 1776. After calling at Cape Town and Kerguelen Island, Cook appointed Adventure Bay in Van Diemen's Land as a place of rendezvous, in the event of the Resolution *and* Discovery *being separated.*

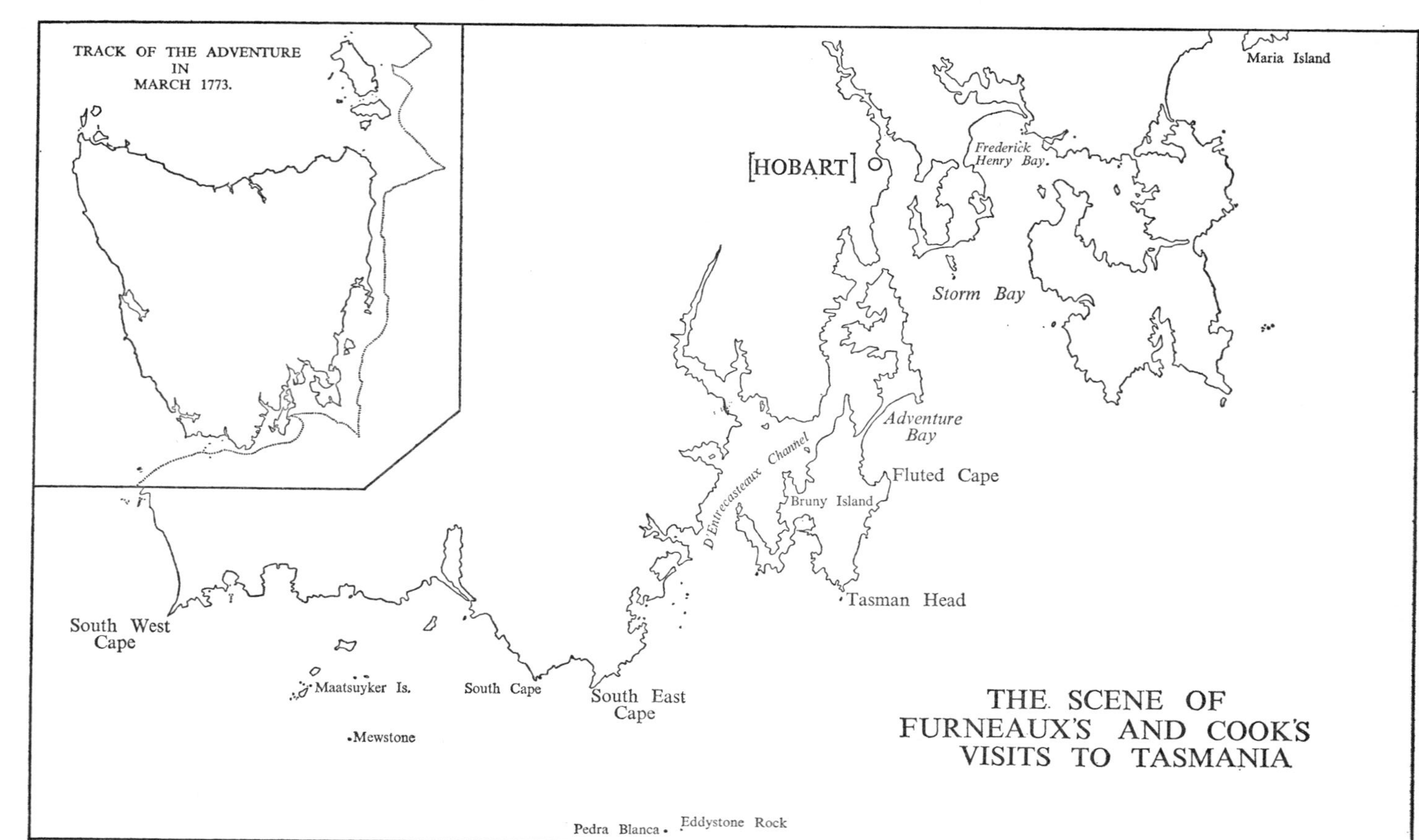

THE SCENE OF FURNEAUX'S AND COOK'S VISITS TO TASMANIA

THIRD VOYAGE

MADE IN H.M. BARKS *RESOLUTION* AND *DISCOVERY*

1776-80

24 January 1777 - 10 February 1777

On the 24th [January, 1777], at three o'clock in the morning, we discovered the coast of Van Diemen's Land, bearing N. ½ W. At four o'clock, the south-west Cape bore N.N.W. ½ W.; and the Mewstone, N.E. by E. three leagues distant. There are several islands and high rocks lying scattered along this part of the coast, the southernmost of which is the Mewstone.[308] It is a round, elevated rock, five or six leagues distant from the south-west Cape, in the direction of S. 55° E. At noon, our latitude was 43° 47′ S., longitude 147° E.; and the situation of the lands round us, as follows: An elevated round-topped hill[309] bore N. 17° W.; the south-west Cape, N. 74° W.; the Mewstone, W. ½ N.; Swilly Isle or Rock,[310] S. 49° E.; and the south-east or South Cape, N. 40° E., distant near three leagues. The land between the south-west and the south capes is broken and hilly, the coast winding, with points shooting out from it; but we were too far off to be able to judge whether the bays formed by these points were sheltered from the sea-winds. The bay, which appeared to be the largest and deepest, lies to the westward of the peaked hill above mentioned. The variation of the compass here was 5° 15′ E.

At six o'clock in the afternoon we sounded, and found sixty fathoms water, over a bottom of broken coral and shells. The South Cape then bore N. 75° W., two or three leagues distant; Tasman's Head, N.E.; and Swilly Rock, S. by W. ½ W. About a league to the eastward of Swilly is another elevated rock, that is not taken notice of by Captain Furneaux. I called it the Eddystone, from its very great resemblance to that lighthouse. Nature seems to have left these two rocks here for the same purpose that the Eddystone lighthouse was built by man, viz., to give navigators notice of the dangers around

308 Named by Furneaux in 1773. See page 160.

309 Mount La Perouse.

310 Swilly Isles also appear on Furneaux's chart. "Swilly Isle or Rock" was described by Tasman in November 1642 as "like Pedra Branca", the White Rock off the coast of China. The name persists to the present day as Pedra Blanca. It is sixteen miles south of the Tasmanian coast and the most southerly point in Australia.

them: for they are the conspicuous summits of a ledge of rocks under water, on which the sea in many places breaks very high. Their surface is white with the dung of sea-fowls, so that they may be seen at some distance, even in the night. On the north-east side of Storm Bay,[311] which lies between the South Cape and Tasman's Head, there are some coves or creeks, that seemed to be sheltered from the sea-winds; and I am of opinion, that were this coast examined, there would be found some good harbours.

Soon after we had sight of land, the westerly winds left us, and were succeeded by variable light airs and alternate calms till the 26th at noon. At that time a breeze sprung up and freshened at south-east, which put it in my power to carry into execution the design I had, upon due consideration, formed, of carrying the ships into Adventure Bay, where I might expect to get a supply of wood, and of grass for the cattle; of both which articles we should, as I now found, have been in great want, if I had waited till our arrival in New Zealand. We therefore stood for the bay, and anchored in it at four o'clock in the afternoon, in twelve fathoms water, over a bottom of sand and ooze. Penguin Island, which lies close to the east point of the bay, bore N. 84° E.; the southernmost point of Maria's Islands[312] bore N. 76° ½ E.; and Cape Frederic Henry, or the north point of the bay, bore N. 33° E. Our distance from the nearest shore was about three quarters of a mile.

As soon as we had anchored, I ordered the boats to be hoisted out. In one of them I went myself, to look for the most commodious place for furnishing ourselves with the necessary supplies; and Captain Clerke went in his boat upon the same service. Wood and water we found in plenty, and in situations convenient enough, especially the first: but grass, of which we stood most in need, was scarce, and also very coarse. Necessity, however, obliged us to take such as we could get.

Next morning early, I sent Lieutenant King[313] to the east side of the bay, with two parties, one to cut wood, and the other to cut grass, under the protection of the marines, whom I judged it prudent to land as a guard. For although, as yet, none of the natives had appeared, there could be no doubt that some were in our neighbour-

311 Like Furneaux, Cook mistook D'Entrecasteaux Channel which separates Bruny Island from the mainland, for Tasman's Storm Bay. See fuller note on page 161.

312 Maria Island is not visible from Adventure Bay. "The southernmost point of Maria's Islands" must be identified as the southerly cape of the Tasman Peninsula.

313 Lieutenant James King, second lieutenant on the *Resolution*, had some scientific training. He was invaluable to Cook as an observer, and was largely responsible for making astronomical observations. After the death of Captain Cook, Charles Clerke, captain of the *Discovery*, who became Cook's successor, placed Lieutenant King in command of the *Resolution*.

hood, as we had seen columns of smoke from the time of our approaching the coast, and some now was observed at no great distance up in the woods. I also sent the launch for water, and afterwards visited all the parties myself. In the evening we drew the seine at the head of the bay, and, at one haul, caught a great quantity of fish. We should have got many more, had not the net broken in drawing it ashore: most of them were of that sort known to seamen by the name of elephant fish. After this, every one repaired on board with what wood and grass we had cut, that we might be ready to sail whenever the wind should serve. This not happening next morning, the people were sent on shore again, on the same duty as the day before. I also employed the carpenter, with part of his crew, to cut some spars for the use of the ship; and despatched Mr. Roberts, one of the mates, in a small boat, to survey the bay.

In the afternoon, we were agreeably surprised, at the place where we were cutting wood, with a visit from some of the natives; eight men and a boy. They approached us from the woods, without betraying any marks of fear, or rather with the greatest confidence imaginable; for none of them had any weapons, except one, who held in his hand a stick about two feet long, and pointed at one end. They were quite naked, and wore no ornaments; unless we consider as such, and as a proof of their love of finery, some large punctures or ridges raised on different parts of their bodies, some in straight, and others in curved lines. They were of the common stature, but rather slender. Their skin was black, and also their hair, which was as woolly as that of any native of Guinea; but they were not distinguished by remarkably thick lips nor flat noses. On the contrary, their features were far from being disagreeable. They had pretty good eyes; and their teeth were tolerably even, but very dirty. Most of them had their hair and beards smeared with a red ointment; and some had their faces also painted with the same composition.

They received every present we made to them without the least appearance of satisfaction. When some bread was given, as soon as they understood that it was to be eaten, they either returned it, or threw it away, without even tasting it. They also refused some elephant fish, both raw and dressed, which we offered to them. But upon giving some birds to them, they did not return these, and easily made us comprehend that they were fond of such food. I had brought two pigs ashore, with a view to leave them in the woods. The instant these came within their reach, they seized them, as a dog would have done, by the ears, and were for carrying them off immediately; with no other intention, as we could perceive, but to kill them. Being desirous of knowing the use of the stick which one of our visitors carried in his hand, I made signs to them to show me; and so far succeeded, that one of them set up a piece of wood as a mark, and threw at it, at the distance of about twenty yards. But we had little reason to commend his dexterity; for after repeated trials, he was still very wide from the object.[314] Omai, to show them how much superior our weapons were to theirs, then fired his musket at it; which alarmed them so much, that notwithstanding all we could do or say, they ran instantly into the woods. One of them was so frightened, that he let drop an axe and two knives, that had been given to him. From us, however, they went

HEAD OF MAN OF VAN DIEMEN'S LAND.

to the place where some of the Discovery's people were employed in taking water into their boat. The officer of that party, not knowing that they had paid us so friendly a visit, nor what their intent might be, fired a musket in the air, which sent them off with the greatest precipitation.

Thus ended our first interview with the natives. Immediately after their final retreat, judging that their fears would prevent their remaining near enough to observe what was passing, I ordered the two pigs, being a boar and sow, to be carried about a mile within the woods, at the head of the bay. I saw them left there by the side of a fresh-water brook. A young bull and a cow, and some sheep and goats, were also, at first, intended to have been left by me as an additional

314 The Aborigines were normally dexterous in the use of throwing sticks. The throwing stick was the precursor of the boomerang which was not used in all parts of the continent. It was hurled with considerable force, turning over and over in its flight, creating a wide path of destruction.

present to Van Diemen's Land. But I soon laid aside all thoughts of this, from a persuasion that the natives, incapable of entering into my views of improving their country, would destroy them. If ever they should meet with the pigs, I have no doubt this will be their fate. But as that race of animals soon becomes wild, and is fond of the thickest cover of the woods, there is great probability of their being preserved. An open place must have been chosen for the accommodation of the other cattle; and in such a situation, they could not possibly have remained concealed many days.

The morning of the 29th was ushered in with a dead calm, which continued all day, and effectually prevented our sailing. I therefore sent a party over to the east point of the bay to cut grass; having been informed that some of a superior quality grew there. Another party, to cut wood, was ordered to go to the usual place, and I accompanied them myself. We had observed several of the natives this morning sauntering along the shore, which assured us, that though their consternation had made them leave us so abruptly the day before, they were convinced that we intended them no mischief, and were desirous of renewing the intercourse. It was natural that I should wish to be present on the occasion. We had not been long landed, before about twenty of them, men and boys, joined us, without expressing the least sign of fear or distrust. There was one of this company conspicuously deformed; and who was not more distinguishable by the hump upon his back, than by the drollery of his gestures, and the seeming humour of his speeches; which he was very fond of exhibiting, as we supposed, for our entertainment. But, unfortunately, we could not understand him; the language spoken here being wholly unintelligible to us. It appeared to me to be different from that spoken by the inhabitants of the more northern parts of this country, whom I met with in my first voyage; which is not extraordinary, since those we now saw, and those we then visited, differ in many other respects.[315] Nor did they seem to be such miserable wretches as the natives whom Dampier mentions to have seen on its western coast.

Some of our present group wore loose round their necks three or four folds of small cord, made of the fur of some animal; and others of

[315] The original inhabitants of Tasmania, now extinct, exhibited differences from those of the mainland and are supposed to be of a Papuan-Melanesian type. One theory is that they may have come to Tasmania by canoe from the New Hebrides or New Caledonia. Professor Elkin (*The Australian Aborigines*, fourth edition, Angus & Robertson Ltd) refers to "their spirally, tufty hair, dark skins and short stature". In *The Australian Encyclopaedia* they are described as having "woolly hair, flat noses, wide nostrils, full fleshy lips and big ears with large lobes".

There was a pronounced difference between the language spoken (probably in four separate dialects) in different parts of Tasmania and on the continent. The basic structure was probably similar, and a few words had been borrowed from Victorian tribes, but otherwise there was little similarity.

them had a narrow slip of the *kangooroo* skin tied round their ankles. I gave to each of them a string of beads and a medal; which I thought they received with some satisfaction. They seemed to set no value on iron, or on iron tools. They were even ignorant of the use of fish-hooks, if we might judge from their manner of looking at some of ours which we showed to them. We cannot, however, suppose it to be possible that a people who inhabit a sea-coast, and who seem to derive no part of their sustenance from the productions of the ground; should not be acquainted with some mode of catching fish, although we did not happen to see any of them thus employed; nor observe any canoe or vessel in which they could go upon the water. Though they absolutely rejected the sort of fish that we offered to them, it was evident that shell-fish, at least, made a part of their food, from the many heaps of muscle-shells we saw in different parts near the shore, and about some deserted habitations near the head of the bay.[316] These

OPOSSUM RAT AND TASMANIAN WOLF.

were little sheds or hovels built of sticks, and covered with bark. We could also perceive evident signs of their sometimes taking up their abode in the trunks of large trees, which had been hollowed out by fire, most probably for this very purpose. In or near all these habitations, and wherever there was a heap of shells, there remained the marks of fire; an indubitable proof that they do not eat their food raw.

After staying about an hour with the wooding party and the

[316] Cook's observation was correct, but for once his deduction may have been at fault. Shellfish, crustaceans, and large sea mammals were sought for food, but apparently the Tasmanians had an aversion to scale fish.

natives, as I could now be pretty confident that the latter were not likely to give the former any disturbance, I left them, and went over to the grass-cutters on the east point of the bay, and found that they had met with a fine patch. Having seen the boats loaded, I left that party, and returned on board to dinner; where, some time after, Lieutenant King arrived. From him I learned that I had but just left the shore, when several women and children made their appearance, and were introduced to him by some of the men who attended them. He gave presents to all of them, of such trifles as he had about him. These females wore a *kangooroo* skin (in the same shape as it came from the animal) tied over the shoulders and round the waist. But its only use seemed to be, to support their children when carried on their backs; for it did not cover those parts which most nations conceal; being in all other respects as naked as the men, and as black, and their bodies marked with scars in the same manner. But in this they differed from the men, that though their hair was of the same colour and texture, some of them had their heads completely shorn or shaved; in others this operation had been performed only on one side, while the rest of them had all the upper part of the head shorn close, leaving a circle of hair all round, somewhat like the tonsure of the Romish ecclesiastics. Many of the children had fine features, and were thought pretty; but of the persons of the women, especially those advanced in years, a less favourable report was made.

In the afternoon I went again to the grass-cutters, to forward their work. I found them then upon Penguin Island, where they had met with a plentiful crop of excellent grass. We laboured hard till sunset, and then repaired on board, satisfied with the quantity we had collected, and which I judged sufficient to last till our arrival in New Zealand.

During our whole stay, we had either calms or light airs from the eastward. Little or no time, therefore, was lost by my putting in at this place. For if I had kept the sea, we should not have been twenty leagues advanced farther on our voyage. And, short as our continuance was here, it has enabled me to add somewhat to the imperfect acquaintance that hath hitherto been acquired with this part of the globe. Van Diemen's Land has been twice visited before. It was so named by Tasman, who discovered it in November 1642. From that time it had escaped all farther notice by European navigators, till Captain Furneaux touched at it in March 1773.[317] I hardly need say, that it is the southern point of New Holland, which, if it doth not deserve the name of a continent, is by far the largest island in the world.

The land is, for the most part, of a good height, diversified with

317 A brief passing visit was made in 1772 when Marion du Fresne anchored in Marion Bay between capes Frederick Hendrick and Bernier on the east coast.

hills and valleys, and everywhere of a greenish hue. It is well wooded; and if one may judge from appearances, and from what we met with in Adventure Bay, is not ill supplied with water. We found plenty of it in three or four places in this bay. The best, or what is most convenient for ships that touch here, is a rivulet, which is one of several that fall into a pond that lies behind the beach at the head of the bay. It there mixes with the sea-water; so that it must be taken up above this pond, which may be done without any great trouble. Firewood is to be got with great ease in several places. The only wind to which this bay is exposed, is the N.E. But as this wind blows from Maria's Islands, it can bring no very great sea along with it; and, therefore, upon the whole, this may be accounted a very safe road. The bottom is clean, good holding-ground, and the depth of water from twelve to five and four fathoms.

Captain Furneaux's sketch of Van Diemen's Land, published with the Narrative of my last Voyage, appears to me to be without any material error, except with regard to Maria's Islands, which have a different situation from what is there represented. What my idea of them is, will be seen in the sketch of that coast here inserted;[318] and I insert it, not as the result of a more faithful, but merely of a second examination. The longitude was determined by a great number of lunar observations which we had before we made the land, while we were in sight of it, and after we had left it; and reduced to Adventure Bay, and the several principal points, by the time-keeper. The following Table will exhibit both the longitude and latitude at one view:—

	Latitude south			*Longitude east*		
Adventure Bay	43°	21′	20″	147°	29′	0″
Tasman's Head	43	33	0	147	28	0
South Cape	43	42	0	146	56	0
South-west Cape	43	37	0	146	7	0
Swilly Isle	43	55	0	147	6	0

Adventure Bay { Variation of the compass 5° 15′ east.
Dip of the south end of the needle 70° 15½′.

We had high-water on the 29th, being two days before the last quarter of the moon, at nine in the morning. The perpendicular rise then was eighteen inches; and there was no appearance of its having ever exceeded two feet and a half. These are all the memorials useful to navigation, which my short stay has enabled me to preserve, with respect to Van Diemen's Land.

Mr. Anderson, my surgeon, with his usual diligence, spent the few days we remained in Adventure Bay, in examining the country. His account of its natural productions, with which he favoured me, will more than compensate for my silence about them: some of his remarks

318 This sketch has not been discovered, so far as is known at present.

on the inhabitants will supply what I may have omitted or represented imperfectly; and his specimen of their language, however short, will be thought worth attending to, by those who wish to collect materials for tracing the origin of nations. I shall only premise, that the tall straight forest-trees which Mr. Anderson describes in the following account, are of a different sort from those which are found in the more northern parts of this coast.[319] The wood is very long and close-grained; extremely tough; fit for spars, oars, and many other uses; and would, on occasion, make good masts (perhaps none better), if a method could be found to lighten it.

At eight o'clock in the morning of the 30th of January, a light breeze springing up at W., we weighed anchor, and put to sea from Adventure Bay. Soon after, the wind veered to the southward, and increased to a perfect storm. Its fury abated in the evening, when it veered to the E. and N.E. This gale was indicated by the barometer, for the wind no sooner began to blow than the mercury in the tube began to fail. Another remarkable thing attended the coming on of this wind, which was very faint at first. It brought with it a degree of heat that was almost intolerable. The mercury in the thermometer rose, as it were, instantaneously, from about 70° to near 90°. This heat was of so short a continuance, that it seemed to be wafted away before the breeze that brought it; so that some on board did not perceive it.

We pursued our course to the eastward, without meeting with anything worthy of note till the night between the 6th and 7th of February, when a marine belonging to the Discovery fell overboard, and was never seen afterward. This was the second misfortune of the kind that had happened to Captain Clerke since he left England. On the 10th, at four in the afternoon, we discovered the land of New Zealand.

319 As Cook states, the *Eucalypts* found in Tasmania are different from those in the north (Mair).

MR. ANDERSON'S REMARKS ON VAN DIEMEN'S LAND[320]

At the bottom of Adventure Bay is a beautiful sandy beach, which seems to be wholly formed by the particles washed by the sea from a very fine white sandstone, that in many places bounds the shore, and of which Fluted Cape, in the neighbourhood, from its appearance, seems to be composed. This beach is about two miles long, and is excellently adapted for hauling a seine, which both ships did repeatedly with success. Behind this, is a plain or flat, with a salt, or rather brackish lake (running in length parallel with the beach), out of which we caught, with angling rods, many whitish bream, and some small trout. The other parts of the country adjoining the bay are quite hilly; and both those and the flat are an entire forest of very tall trees, rendered almost impassible by shrubs, brakes of fern, and fallen trees; except on the sides of some of the hills, where the trees are but thin, and a coarse grass is the only interruption. To the northward of the bay, there is low land, stretching farther than the eye can reach, which is only covered with wood in certain spots; but we had no opportunity to examine in what respects it differed from the hilly country. The soil on the flat land is either sandy, or consists of a yellowish mould, and, in some places, of a reddish clay. The same is found on the lower part of the hills; but farther up, especially where there are few trees, it is of a grey tough cast, to appearance very poor.

In the valleys between the hills, the water drains down from their sides; and at last, in some places, forms small brooks; such indeed as were sufficient to supply us with water, but by no means of that size we might expect in so extensive a country, especially as it is both hilly and well wooded. Upon the whole, it has many marks of being naturally a very dry country; and perhaps might (independent of its wood) be compared to Africa, about the Cape of Good Hope, though that lies ten degrees farther northward, rather than to New Zealand, on its other side, in the same latitude, where we find every valley, however small, furnished with a considerable stream of water. The heat too appears to be great, as the thermometer stood at 64, 70, and once at 74. And it was remarked, that birds were seldom killed an hour or two, before they were almost covered with small maggots, which I would rather attribute merely to the heat; as we had not any reason to suppose there is a peculiar disposition in the climate to

[320] William Anderson, a man of considerable gifts and a keen observer, was surgeon on the *Resolution* on this voyage. His Journal makes a valuable supplement to Cook's own records.

render substances soon putrid. No mineral bodies, nor indeed stones of any other sort, but the white sand one already mentioned, were observed.

Amongst the vegetable productions, there is not one, that we could find, which afforded the smallest subsistence for man. The forest-trees are all of one sort, growing to a great height, and in general quite straight, branching but little, till towards the top. The bark is white, which makes them appear, at a distance, as if they had been peeled; it is also thick; and within it are sometimes collected pieces of a reddish transparent gum or resin, which has an astringent taste. The leaves of this tree are long, narrow, and pointed; and it bears clusters of small white flowers, whose cups were, at this time, plentifully scattered about the ground, with another sort resembling them somewhat in shape, but much larger; which makes it probable that there are two *species* of this tree.[321] The bark of the smaller branches, the fruit, and leaves, have an agreeable pungent taste, and aromatic smell, not unlike peppermint; and in its nature, it has some affinity to the *myrtus* of botanists. The most common tree, next to this, is a small one about ten feet high, branching pretty much, with narrow leaves, and a large, yellow, cylindrical flower, consisting only of a vast number of filaments; which, being shed, leave a fruit like a pine-top.[322] Both the above-mentioned trees are unknown in Europe. The underwood consists chiefly of a shrub somewhat resembling a myrtle, and which seems to be the *Leptospermum scoparium*, mentioned in Dr. Forster's *Char. Gen. Plant.*; and, in some places, of another, rather smaller, which is a new species of the *Melaleuca* of Linnæus.[323] Of other plants, which are by no means numerous, there is a species of *Gladiolus*, rush, bell-flower, samphire, a small sort of wood-sorrel, milkwort, cudweed, and Job's tears; with a few others, peculiar to the place. There are several kinds of fern, as polypody, spleenwort, female fern, and some mosses; but the species are either common, or at least found in some other countries, especially New Zealand.[324]

321 There are of course many more than two species (Mair).

322 Probably *Banksia marginata*, a common species in Tasmania (Mair).

323 Some species of *Leptospermum* and *Melaleuca* (tea-trees). These do, in fact, belong to the myrtle family, as does *Eucalyptus* (Mair).

324 Gladiolus. Some member of the Iridaceae but not *Gladiolus*.

Rush. Could be *Juncus* spp., true rushes, but not necessarily so.

Bell-flower. Perhaps *Wahlenbergia* spp.

Samphire. *Salicornia quinqueflora.*

Wood sorrel. *Oxalis* sp.

Milkwort. Perhaps a species of *Comesperma* which belongs to the same family as the "milkwort" (*Polygala*).

Cudweed. Some member of the Compositae, not necessarily a true cudweed (*Gnaphalium*).

Job's tears. Probably *Gahnia psittacorum*, a tall sedge with pendulous nutlets, cer-

The only animal of the quadruped kind we got, was a sort of *opossum*, about twice the size of a large rat; and is, most probably, the male of that species found at Endeavour River, as mentioned in Hawkesworth's Collection of Voyages. It is of a dusky colour above, tinged with a brown or rusty cast, and whitish below. About a third of the tail, towards its tip, is white, and bare underneath; by which it probably hangs on the branches of trees, as it climbs these, and lives on berries. The *kangooroo*, another animal found farther northward in New Holland, as described in the same voyage, without all doubt also inhabits here, as the natives we met with had some pieces of their skins; and we several times saw animals, though indistinctly, run from the thickets when we walked in the woods, which, from the size, could be no other. It should seem also, that they are in considerable numbers, from the dung we saw almost everywhere, and from the narrow tracks or paths they have made amongst the shrubbery.

There are several sorts of birds, but all so scarce and shy, that they are evidently harassed by the natives, who, perhaps, drew much of their subsistence from them. In the woods, the principal sorts are large brown hawks or eagles;[325] crows nearly the same as ours in England; yellowish parroquets,[326] and large pigeons.[327] There are also three or four small birds, one of which is of the thrush kind;[328] and another small one, with a pretty long tail, has part of the head and neck of a most beautiful azure colour; from whence we named it *Motacilla cyanea*.[329] On the shore were several common and sea gulls;[330] a few black oyster-catchers, or sea-pies;[331] and a pretty plover of a stone colour, with a black hood.[332] About the pond or lake behind the beach, a few wild ducks were seen; and some shags used to perch upon the high leafless trees near the shore. Some pretty large blackish snakes[333] were seen in the woods; and we killed a large,

---

tainly not the true "Job's Tears" (*Coix lacrymi-jobi*), which is a tropical grass. The ferns are too vaguely indicated; some species do occur in other countries, others do not, but they would appear quite similar to the botanical collector of the eighteenth century (Mair).

325 Possibly the Wedge-tailed Eagle, though the smaller Brown Hawk and Swamp Hawk are possibilities (Hindwood).

326 Almost certainly the Green Rosella (*Platycercus caledonicus*) (Hindwood).

327 Either the Common Bronzewing (*Phaps chalcoptera*) or the Brush Bronzewing (*P. elegans*) (Hindwood).

328 Probably the Grey Thrush (*Colluricincla harmonica*) (Hindwood).

329 Blue Wren (*Malarus cyaneus*) (Hindwood).

330 The "common" gull is probably the Pacific gull (*Larus pacificus*), while the sea gulls are doubtless silver gulls (*L. novaehollandiae*) (Hindwood).

331 As the birds are stated to be black they would be the Sooty Oystercatcher (*Haematopus unicolor*). The "sea pies" applied to the same black bird, is usually given to the Pied Oystercatcher (*H. ostralegus*), which also occurs in Tasmania (Hindwood).

332 Hooded Dotterel (*Charadrius cucullatus*) (Hindwood).

333 Probably the Copperhead Snake (*Denisonia superba*) (Hindwood).

hitherto unknown, lizard, fifteen inches long and six round, elegantly clouded with black and yellow;[334] besides a small sort, of a brown gilded colour above, and rusty below.[335]

The sea affords a much greater plenty, and at least as great a variety as the land. Of these the elephant fish,[336] or *pejegallo*, mentioned in Frezier's Voyage, are the most numerous; and though inferior to many other fish, were very palatable food. Several large rays, nurses, and small leather-jackets, were caught; with some small white bream, which were firmer and better than those caught in the lake. We likewise got a few soles and flounders; two sorts of gurnards, one of them a new species; some small spotted mullet;[337] and, very unexpectedly, the small fish with a silver band on its side, called *Atherina hepsetus* by Hasselquist.[338] But that next in number, and superior in goodness, to the elephant fish, was a sort none of us recollected to have seen before. It partakes of the nature both of a round and of a flat fish,[339] having the eyes placed very near each other; the fore-part of the body much flattened or depressed, and the rest rounded. It is of a brownish sandy colour, with rusty spots on the upper part, and whitish below. From the quantity of slime it was always covered with, it seems to live after the manner of flat fish, at the bottom.

Upon the rocks are plenty of muscles, and some other small shellfish. There are also great numbers of sea-stars; some small limpets; and large quantities of sponge; one sort of which, that is thrown on shore by the sea, but not very common, has a most delicate texture; and another, is the *Spongia dichotoma*. Many pretty *Medusa's heads* were found upon the beach; and the stinking *Laplysia*, or sea-hare, which, as mentioned by some authors, has the property of taking off the hair by the acrimony of its juice; but this sort was deficient in this respect.[340]

Insects, though not numerous, are here in considerable variety. Amongst them are grasshoppers, butterflies, and several sorts of small moths, finely variegated. There are two sorts of dragon-flies, gad-flies, camel-flies; several sorts of spiders; and some scorpions; but the last

334 The Southern Blue-tongued Lizard (*Tiliqua nigrolutea*) (Hindwood).

335 White's Skink (*Egernia whitii*) (Hindwood).

336 The Elephant fish or *pejegallo* is *Callorynchus milii* (Whitley).

337 *Mugii dobula* (Whitley).

338 The other fishes mentioned here could have belonged to any of several genera and species (Whitley).

339 A Flathead (*Platycephalus* sp.). This is the first recorded description of the Australian Flathead (Whitley).

340 Sea-hares are soft molluscs with tentacles, and have been given the name because of a fancied resemblance to hares. The genus *Aplysia* has a shell protected by lobes which are used in swimming. Angas's sea-hare (*Aplysia angasi*) is a large-lobed, true swimming type with black rings on a green body, and is widely distributed in the western Pacific waters.

are rather rare. The most troublesome, though not very numerous tribe of insects, are the musquitoes; and a large black ant,[341] the pain of whose bite is almost intolerable, during the short time it lasts. The musquitoes, also, make up the deficiency of their number, by the severity of their venomous proboscis.

The inhabitants whom we met with here had little of that fierce or wild appearance common to people in their situation: but, on the contrary, seemed mild and cheerful, without reserve or jealousy of strangers. This, however, may arise from their having little to lose or care for. With respect to personal activity or genius, we can say but little of either. They do not seem to possess the first in any remarkable degree; and as for the last, they have, to appearance, less than even the half-animated inhabitants of Terra del Fuego, who have not invention sufficient to make clothing for defending themselves from the rigour of their climate, though furnished with the materials. The small stick, rudely pointed, which one of them carried in his hand, was the only thing we saw that required any mechanical exertion, if we except the fixing on the feet of some of them pieces of kangaroo skin, tied with thongs; though it could not be learned whether these were in use as shoes, or only to defend some sore. It must be owned, however, they are masters of some contrivance, in the manner of cutting their arms and bodies in lines of different lengths and directions, which are raised considerably above the surface of the skin, so that it is difficult to guess the method they use in executing this embroidery of their persons.[342] Their not expressing that surprise which one might have expected from their seeing men so much unlike themselves, and things to which, we were well assured, they had been hitherto utter strangers—their indifference for our presents, and their general inattention, were sufficient proofs of their not possessing any acuteness of understanding.

Their colour is a dull black, and not quite so deep as that of the African Negroes. It should seem, also, that they sometimes heightened their black colour, by smutting their bodies; as a mark was left behind on any clean substance, such as white paper, when they handled it. Their hair, however, is perfectly woolly, and it is clotted or divided into small parcels, like that of the Hottentots, with the use of some sort of grass, mixed with a red paint or ochre, which they smear in great abundance over their heads. This practice, as some might imagine, has not the effect of changing their hair into the frizzling texture we observed; for, on examining the head of a boy, which appeared never to have been smeared, I found the hair to be of the same kind. Their noses, though not flat, are broad and full. The lower

341 Probably the Black Bull-dog Ant (*Myrmecia pyriformis*) (Hindwood).
342 See note on page 148.

part of the face projects a good deal, as is the case of most Indians I have seen; so that a line let fall from the forehead, would cut off a much larger portion than it would in Europeans. Their eyes are of a middling size, with the white less clear than in us; and though not remarkably quick or piercing, such as give a frank, cheerful cast to the whole countenance. Their teeth are broad, but not equal, nor well set; and either from nature or from dirt, not of so true a white as is usual among people of a black colour. Their mouths are rather wide; but this appearance seems heightened by wearing their beards long, and clotted with paint, in the same manner as the hair on their heads. In other respects, they are well-proportioned; though the belly seems rather projecting. This may be owing to the want of compression there, which few nations do not use, more or less. The posture of which they seem fondest, is to stand with one side forward, or the upper part of the body gently reclined, and one hand grasping (across the back) the oposite arm, which hangs down by the projecting side.

What the ancient poets tell us of Fauns and Satyrs living in hollow trees, is here realised. Some wretched constructions of sticks, covered with bark, which do not even deserve the name of huts, were indeed found near the shore in the bay; but these seemed only to have been erected for temporary purposes; and many of their largest trees were converted into more comfortable habitations. These had their trunks hollowed out by fire, to the height of six or seven feet; and that they take up their abode in them sometimes, was evident from the hearths, made of clay, to contain the fire in the middle, leaving room for four or five persons to sit round it. At the same time, these places of shelter are durable; for they take care to leave one side of the tree sound, which is sufficient to keep it growing as luxuriantly as those which remain untouched.

The inhabitants of this place are, doubtless, from the same stock with those of the northern parts of New Holland. Though some of the circumstances mentioned by Dampier, relative to those he met with on the western coast of this country, such as their defective sight, and want of fore-teeth, are not found here; and though Hawkesworth's account of those met with by Captain Cook of the east side shows also that they differ in many respects, yet still, upon the whole, I am persuaded that distance of place, entire separation, diversity of climate, and length of time, all concurring to operate, will account for greater differences, both as to their persons and as to their customs, than really exist between our Van Diemen's Land natives, and those described by Dampier, and in Captain Cook's first Voyage. This is certain, that the figure of one of those seen in Endeavour River, and represented in Sidney Parkinson's Journal of that voyage, very much resembles our visitors in Adventure Bay. That there is not the like resemblance in their language, is a circumstance that need not create any difficulty. For though the agreement of the languages of people living distant from each other may be assumed as a strong argument for their having sprung from one common source, disagreement of language is by no means a proof of the contrary.

However, we must have a far more intimate acquaintance with the languages spoken here and in the more northern parts of New Holland, before we can be warranted to pronounce that they are

IMMENSE TREE OF VAN DIEMAN'S LAND.

totally different. Nay, we have good grounds for the opposite opinion; for we found that the animal called kangooroo at Endeavour River was known under the same name here; and I need not observe that it is scarcely possible to suppose that this was not transmitted from one another, but accidentally adopted by two nations, differing in language and extraction. Besides, as it seems very improbable that the Van Diemen's Land inhabitants should have ever lost the use of canoes or sailing vessels if they had been originally conveyed thither by sea, we must necessarily admit that they, as well as the kangooroo itself, have been stragglers by land from the more northern parts of the country. And if there be any force in this observation, while it traces the origin of the people, it will, at the same time, serve to fix another point, if Captain Cook and Captain Furneaux have not already decided it, that New Holland is nowhere totally divided by the sea into islands, as some have imagined.

As the New Hollanders seem all to be of the same extraction, so neither do I think there is anything peculiar in them. On the contrary, they much resemble many of the inhabitants whom I have seen at the islands Tanna and Manicola. Nay, there is even some foundation for hazarding a supposition that they may have originally come from the same place with all the inhabitants of the South Sea. For, of only about ten words which we could get from them, that which expresses *cold* differs little from that of New Zealand and Otaheite; the first being *Mallareede*, the second *Makka'reede*, and the third *Ma'reede.*[343] The rest of our very scanty Van Diemen's Land Vocabulary is as follows:—

Quadne,	A woman.
Eve'rai,	The eye.
Muidje,	The nose.
Lae'renne,	A small bird, a native of the woods here.
Ka'my,	The teeth, mouth, or tongue.
Koy'gee,	The ear.
No'onga,	Elevated scars on the body.
Teegera,	To eat.
Toga'rago,	I must be gone, or I will go.

Their pronunciation is not disagreeable, but rather quick, though not more so than is that of the other nations of the South Sea; and if we may depend upon the affinity of languages as a clue to guide us in discovering the origin of nations, I have no doubt but we shall find, on a diligent inquiry, and when opportunities offer to collect accurately a sufficient number of these words, and to compare them, that all the people from New Holland, eastward to Easter Island, have been derived from the same common root.[344]

[343] Hawaiian: maaelele (to be cold); Maori: makariri (cold, frost).

[344] As noted on page 171, it has not yet been determined whether the Tasmanians came from the mainland or from Melanesia, or yet again whether they were Melanesian negroids who migrated southwards along the eastern coast of Australia crossing Bass Strait, which was once much narrower than at present, until they came to Tasmania. There is adequate evidence to show that the physical characteristics and language were pronouncedly different to those of the Aborigines in other parts of Australia.

[On leaving Tasmania Cook sailed to New Zealand, and then to the far north, discovering the Sandwich Islands (Hawaii). He penetrated "Cook's Inlet" but was forced to turn back, as he met a wall of ice. He returned to Hawaii and on Sunday, 14 February 1779, was killed by the natives. The vessels continued their voyage to Kamchatka, where further search was made for the North-west Passage, but without success. The homeward journey was made by way of Japan and China, and Cape of Good Hope. The Nore was reached on 4 October 1780.]

INDEX

Books on the Theatre by George Jean Nathan

Mr. Nathan, who is the authority on the American theatre and drama for the *Encyclopædia Britannica* and the *Britannica Book of the Year,* has published the following books on the subjects:

Testament of a Critic
Art of the Night
The House of Satan
The Autobiography of an Attitude
Since Ibsen
Land of the Pilgrims' Pride
Materia Critica
Comedians All
The Popular Theatre
The Critic and the Drama
The Theatre, the Drama, the Girls
The World in Falseface
Mr. George Jean Nathan Presents
Another Book on the Theatre
The Avon Flows
Passing Judgments
The Intimate Notebooks of George Jean Nathan
The Theatre of the Moment
The Morning After the First Night
Encyclopædia of the Theatre
The Entertainment of a Nation
The Theatre Book of the Year, 1942–43
The Theatre Book of the Year, 1943–44

Books on Mr. Nathan

The Dramatic Criticism of George Jean Nathan, by Constance Frick, M.A.

The Theatre of George Jean Nathan, by Professor Isaac Goldberg, Ph.D.

The Quintessence of Nathanism, by Vladimar Kozlenko.

Three Prejudices: A Study of the Nathan Critical Credo, by Isabel Barclay Dobell (in preparation).

The Theatre Book of the Year

1944 ~ 1945

The THEATRE Book
OF THE YEAR
1944 ✧ 1945

A Record and an Interpretation

B Y

GEORGE JEAN NATHAN

ALFRED  A. KNOPF

NEW YORK : 1946

PUBLISHED OCTOBER 18, 1945

SECOND PRINTING, JANUARY 1946

Foreword

THE SEASON was notable, first, for an unparalleled box-office prosperity; secondly, for the continued poverty in drama of authentic quality; and, thirdly, for a persisting emphasis upon the lighter entertainment fare. The public response to this last was such that, in one winter week alone, the combined intake of the musical shows on view amounted to more than 436,000 dollars. And many of the plays that catered to the amusement taste were relatively quite as successful.

It was thus that, while the theatre offered the serious drama critic very little over which to exercise his talents, it nevertheless periodically afforded him a good time, which was embarrassing. A serious critic, by the dictates of tradition, is not supposed to have any such good time, that is, save in the presence of drama of deep merit, which frequently has a lamentable way of being very tragical and which, while it auspiciously purges his soul in the higher directions, is not calculated to make him especially jolly about the immediate world and his comfort in it.

I am not defending the kind of plays which, on the other hand, entertained him considerably. They no more call for defense, at least in this critical opinion, than a very pretty girl who happens to be a little dumb, or a good Limburger sandwich, or even a traveling salesman story which succeeds in making one laugh. I may wish for plays of greater repute and I may wish for them heartily, as I do; but mere entertainment, as it is condescendingly designated by the pundits, has something to recommend it too, just as occasionally the cup that cheers has or, under certain circumstances, a nocturnal hansom cab ride through the Park, or playing with one's pet dog.

Take, for example, some such play as Mary Chase's *Harvey*. The critic, however scholastically solemn, who would say that he does not hugely enjoy it is, presuming him to exist, a liar, a fraud, and a menace to the body politic. It may be perfectly true that it is many levels below the high shelf occupied by drama of lasting worth and importance, but it nonetheless provides an evening that is definitely gustful and diverting. What is more, it does not lack intelligent observation and the humor derived from such observation. Treating, as you will subsequently be reminded, of a tosspot who meets up in alcoholized imagination with a large rabbit named Harvey and who thereafter embraces him as a boon crony, and of his concerned relatives who would lodge him in a sanitarium by way of exorcising the rabbit and restoring their brother to normal, it is now and again touched with a worldly wit and wisdom not always encountered in plays of greater critical size. "Nobody," philosophically allows the tosspot, "ever brings anything little into a bar." "You have to be very intelligent in this world — or very pleasant," meditates his elderly sister. And, in further instance, thus finally to the latter the taxi driver who has brought the toper out to the sanitarium: "Listen, lady, I've been drivin' this route fifteen years. I've brought 'em out here to get that stuff and drove 'em back after they had it. It changes 'em. On the way out here they sit back and enjoy the ride. They talk to me. Sometimes we stop and watch the sunsets and look at the birds flyin'. Sometimes we stop and watch the birds when there ain't no birds and look at the sunsets when it's rainin'. We have a swell time and I always get a big tip. But afterward — whew! They crab, crab, crab. They yell at me to watch the brakes, watch the intersections. They got no faith — in me or my buggy — yet it's the same cab, the same driver, and we're goin' back over the very same road. . . . Lady, after this, he'll be a perfectly normal human being, and you know what bastards *they* are!"

And the tosspot and his Harvey are wisely allowed to go on their former mellifluous way.

The Late George Apley, dramatized from the J. P. Marquand novel by Mr. Marquand and George S. Kaufman, was another small benefaction. It may have its critical defects, even on its own light terms, but it similarly tendered the professor a pleasant holiday from the classroom.

Here, as you will be further reminded, is the theme of the relentless austerity of the old Boston Brahmin tradition in conflict with the younger generation. The play emphasizes this theme out of proportion to the novel and enters into certain jocosities which are somewhat foreign to the book, but on the whole, for all the liberties, it amounts to highly acceptable "mere entertainment" that marks a welcome escape from things like Piscator's production of *King Lear,* Margaret Webster's of *The Cherry Orchard* and *The Tempest,* and similar papier-mâché knife stabs at dramatic art.

There was a measure of relieving amusement to be had, also, in even so synthetic an exhibit as the Norman Krasna-Moss Hart *Dear Ruth,* albeit it was properly to be waved aside the next morning as a sheer Broadway box-office concoction. But deliberate Broadway box-office concoction or not, it nevertheless at intervals stubbornly assaulted the midriff. No stuff for Schlegel, perhaps, but even Schlegel, recall, sank to the depths of defending that comical atrocity, the play upon words. "Those who cry out against the play upon words as an unnatural and affected invention," he declared, "only betray their own ignorance of original nature."

And these were not all that recalled the great man who once said, "He who is ashamed of his laughter makes others ashamed of his poverty of intelligence." There is a place for everything in this world — and a good, loud, healthy, ceiling-rattling laugh never hurt anyone, even a critic.

In the way of serious dramatic quality, the season had to content itself in the matter of new plays mainly and relatively with the Messrs. Richardson's and Berney's *Dark of the Moon,* a treatment of the Barbara Allen folk legend at times racily imaginative and intermittently sprayed with some verbal radiance, though there were many who esteemed Tennessee Williams' *The Glass Menagerie* more highly.

Among the disappointments of the year was the municipally controlled City Center Theatre. The founded intention of the enterprise, as everyone knows, was to bring fine drama and fine musical exhibits to the masses at prices within their means and so encourage and develop in them a growing love for the theatre, to the latter's potential great prosperity. That the plan was a worthy one and promised the enterprise a future place among the angels of Heaven was to be admitted, and with cheers. But that, whether in the case of drama or musical shows, it up to date has panned out, is more than dubious.

Just how an incipient profound attachment for the theatre may be instilled in the City Center's customers by the great majority of the second-hand dramatic dispensations and shabby musical presentations which it thus far has offered them is difficult to figure. Aside from a meritorious revival of the familiar *Little Women,* its season's dramatic program delivered only a run-down showing of the feeble *Harriet,* brought in from the 1942–1943 Broadway season; the sorely defective LeGallienne-Webster revival of Chekhov's *The Cherry Orchard,* brought in in turn for a week's run after a road engagement, from the 1943–1944 Broadway season; and a very poor revival, with a company headed by Fred Stone, of *You Can't Take It With You,* from the 1936–1937 Broadway season. There was nothing else.

Since it hopefully threw open its doors to capture audiences which hitherto had been strangers to the theatre and which had necessarily confined themselves, because of high admission charges, to the low-priced moving pictures, the City Center has further proffered six musical items. Of the six, only one, a revival of *Porgy and Bess,* has been sufficiently professional and impressive to promote in the audiences any respect for the theatre and to induce in them any warm inclination to forsake the screen parlors.

Consider the rest from the viewpoint of proficiency. *The New Moon* was shown in so slipshod a production that City Center audiences who had heard of its previous big success in the theatre could not even vaguely understand the reason for it, and speculated that, if this was the kind of thing the theatre esteemed, the theatre could be hardly what it had been cracked up to be. The revival of *The Merry Widow,* which had enjoyed a record run of 321 performances at the Majestic Theatre, in its City Center manifestation suffered such a let-down and was generally so unsatisfactory that the customers again scratched their heads and again were besieged by skepticism as to the touted grandeur of the theatre.

With the appearance of *The Gypsy Baron* in a production so tawdry that even an old-time Cincinnati beer-garden would have gagged at it, their doubts over the much heralded glories of the theatre increased by leaps and bounds. And when *La Vie Parisienne* came along in a production that for the most part was approximately as gaily Parisian as Tolstoi, the doubts resolved themselves into something closely approaching complete conviction. Nor were the doubts materially lessened when, finally, the originally excellent *Carmen Jones* appeared in cut-down road production shape, and at prices only slightly lower than those charged for the Broadway production.

The Broadway theatre is not, true enough, invariably superior to the City Center in respect to musical exhibits. One has only to observe the productions of things like *A Lady Says Yes* to appreciate the fact. But four times out of five, even at its poorest, it is so considerably superior in the way of productions that to compare the City Center with it is like comparing a meal at Sloppy Moe's to one at the Colony.

Censorship again reared its feared head when License Commissioner Paul Moss brought about the closing of the play *Trio* by refusing an extension of the license of the theatre in which it was showing unless the play were withdrawn. Mr. Moss announced that he had received complaints against the exhibit from many persons and was therefore constrained to act as he did. These many persons boiled down, by his own admission, to exactly sixteen. In other words, the objection of sixteen people out of all the six or seven millions in New York City was sufficient to bring about his explosion. It further remains that, of the sixteen, six were not residents of New York City but of towns in New Jersey and on Long Island. If sixteen complaints were enough to induce Mr. Moss to cause a play to be withdrawn, one might have offered him seventeen apiece against *School For Brides* and *A Lady Says Yes,* to say nothing of sixty-three contending that, as one of those responsible for Mayor LaGuardia's City Center, he should promptly have been haled into court to stand trial for presenting in that theatre the ballet, *Frankie and Johnny,* which not only touched, like *Trio,* upon Lesbianism, but which was declared morally shocking in general by the various newspaper reviewers who attended it.

The License Commissioner concurred in the complainants' statement that *Trio* was offensive "because it deals primarily with an abnormal perversion and therefore is especially dangerous to the public morals and specifically in the case of the young." While it is true that *Trio* did deal with such a perversion, he, along with the complainants, overlooked the clear fact that it dealt with it in terms of acute disgust, led one of the parties thereto violently to condemn the other, and led this other in turn to suicide as the only way out. Just how, accordingly, it could have been especially dangerous in encouraging immorality in the public, young or old, was not easy to determine. If the subject had been handled sympathetically, things conceivably might have been different, but it was handled in such a way as to make it thoroughly odious and contemptible.

If we are to have censorship, individual or by vote of court, we may properly ask that it be consistent. If perversion of any kind is to be arbitrarily taboo, let us know about it. In that event we may resign ourselves never again to see on the New York stage such classics as *Electra* and *Œdipus,* or many such modern and hitherto undisturbed plays as *The Green Bay Tree, Oscar Wilde, The Children's Hour,* and *Mourning Becomes Electra.* On the index, too, must go plays by dramatists like Wedekind, Stephen Phillips, Donnay, Lenormand, *et al.*

When it comes to public morals, how could anyone believe that a play like *Trio,* which treated of abnormality and which hence could not be particularly alluring to the overwhelming majority of congenitally normal persons, was one-tenth so conducive to immorality as a play like, say, *The Voice Of The Turtle,* which treats very alluringly of the pleasures of promiscuous normal sex intercourse? Yet there remain people like Mr. Moss who are apparently convinced that the average person who goes to the theatre is dangerously susceptible to what he may see on the stage, and that if what he sees there is morally or even conventionally oblique it may start him on the road to ruin. If this were even remotely true, there would be danger of countless women in the audiences of *Anna Lucasta* forthwith becoming prostitutes and of innumerable men in the audiences of *I Remember Mama* rushing out and acquiring mistresses, since in both cases the moral aberrations are presented in a far from disagreeable light. Were the stage to exercise any such influence, the romantic *Raffles* would have made us, even in far more innocent days, a nation of thieves; *Way Down East* would have populated the country with so many illegitimate babies that we would have had to go to war for *Lebensraum;* and in more recent years *You Can't Take It With You* would have set into motion such an inflation that it would cost Mr. Moss all of two hundred and fifty dollars to buy a cardboard frame for his affectionately inscribed photograph of John S. Sumner.

I do not believe that Mr. Moss has a dirty mind. It did not take a dirty mind, for example, to object, as he did, to the song, "My Bunny," in *Star And Garter,* because "My Bunny" was a dirty song even to anyone with a perfectly clean mind, and the management of the show knew it. But I do believe that he has a small boy's mind and that that small boy's mind, like many small boys' minds, instilled in him an urge to be the neighborhood show-off and tough guy, to set himself up as the leader of the gang, and to bully it over others. He is, in short, constitutionally a little man and his office of license commissioner with censorship powers was his pair of elevator shoes.

In connection with *Trio,* this Moss declared, "There are various other plays and musicals which border on the line of indecency and the managers are warned that this must not continue. There is a war going on and every effort must be made to prevent the letting down of the bars to indecent performances. The reputation of New York City is at stake, especially since we have here the greatest aggregation of theatres in the world." One such theatre in New York City is the municipally operated City Center, with which he is associated in an official capacity. If the reputation of New York City is at stake, as he says, let him be reminded that the stage of that theatre with which he is connected has offered in various plays and musicals a sufficiency of illicit sexual relationships, profane language, and highly suggestive dances. It might have been a good idea for him to look to his own nest.

It seems, however, that Mr. Moss did not and does not know real smut when it appears, and hence, when it came to censorship, could not be trusted even by Mayor La Guardia and others who were his champions. The scene in Mae West's *Catherine Was Great* involving Mae and one of the actors in a bed was one of the dirtiest scenes shown on the New York stage in years, yet he did nothing about it. *School For Brides* was chock full of smut, yet again he did nothing about it. In *Laffing Room Only!* there was a homosexual episode that should properly have been offensive to him, yet still again he did nothing about it. What he did was rather to bring about the suppression of a play which he termed "lewd and lascivious" and which contained not one single word or scene that was anywhere nearly so objectionable.

Something, in conclusion, is rotten not only in Denmark when a Postmaster General has been able to hold up the mailing privileges of a reputable national magazine simply because it contained the kid word "backside" and when a minor political appointee in New York City has been able single-handed to censor off the stage a play with a theme that down the centuries has figured in illustrious poetry, literature, and drama.

Widespread indignation over the *Trio* episode resulted, however, in plans to set into motion legal measures curbing Moss' future independent censorship activities and the giving over to the consideration of the courts and juries the matter of supressions of plays following reputable complaints against their infractions of morals.

It is, finally, a favorite outcry of non-New Yorkers that New York does not theatrically represent the nation, that its taste is not necessarily that of the rest of the nation and that, inferentially, the taste of the rest of the nation is immeasurably superior, indeed so closely identified with the dramatic classics that the occasional view of a Broadway company performing some low commercial item like, say, *Boy Meets Girl* is enough to induce a comprehensive nausea, accompanied by fainting spells. So definitive is the mortification that even some New Yorkers have themselves come to believe it and have lent their sympathetic voices to a plea for a national theatre which might truly represent the country and thus relegate Broadway to its proper place, somewhere down the end of the line near the sewer.

It is a pert notion and one to fascinate the attention, like a flea circus. But though, like a flea circus, it has its diverting points, it further like a flea circus does not make much sense.

That New York has its faults of taste along with the other American communities is fully to be granted. But when it comes to comparative values it still stands generally, despite such episodes as *Trio,* as the most liberal, the most hospitable, and the most endorsable theatrical center in the nation, and its taste, all things duly considered and weighed, as in the aggregate relatively the best in the nation. No other city has in the last twenty years or more corrected New York when New York has now and again ignorantly dismissed a play of quality. No other city, proportionate to its population, has so fully endorsed estimable plays. And no other city, for all New York's occasional deplorable coldness, has encouraged creditable new, young playwrights so often.

The idea, dispensed by various profound thinkers in the

hinterland and by their counterparts in New York, that the New York theatre is a purely commercial one and that it both in other years and in these has been and is hostile to any and all experiment does not meet the facts. It has been this alleged commercial theatre that has provided the means for experiment in the last forty-odd years to a striking variety of drama ranging all the distance from Moody's *The Great Divide* to Wilder's *The Skin Of Our Teeth.* It has been this alleged commercial theatre that has ventured such productions as the modern dress *Hamlet,* the early experimental William Butler Yeats, the first so-called streamlined Shakespeare (forty-one years ago), the first attempt at real American comic opera, the first local multiple stage drama, the earliest Shaw as well as the earliest revolutionary plays of many other Europeans, the daring verse drama of Stephen Phillips, and recent plays like *Our Town, The Time Of Your Life, Dark of The Moon,* and *The Glass Menagerie.*

The list might be prolonged to the point of reader impatience. It would include innumerable items like *Peter Pan,* which was received so frigidly upon its tryout in Washington, D. C., that only the determination of Charles Frohman saved it for the "commercial" New York stage, the first farcical treatments of venerated American institutions, the musical satire *Of Thee I Sing,* the Chinese paraphrase *The Yellow Jacket, Carmen Jones, Peer Gynt, Chicago* (which had been condemned in an advance reading of the script as too risky by a Yale University dramatic solon), and the dramatic treatise on yellow fever called *Yellow Jack.* To say nothing of *Lady Precious Stream,* the played-backwards *On Trial,* the first drama of Robert Browning, the sixteenth century Japanese play *The Flower of Yamato,* T. S. Eliot's *Murder In The Cathedral,* and the first miniature-cast play. And further to say nothing of *The Insect Comedy, The Green Pastures,* O'Neill's first full-length play, *Beyond The Horizon,* O'Neill's five-hour *Strange Interlude,* the dramaturgically inventive *Seven Keys To Baldpate,* the outspoken *What Price Glory?,* the poetic melodrama *Winterset,* the classic Greek paraphrase *Daughters*

Of Atreus, the first combination of drama and motion pictures, the first comedy in the Restoration tradition, the first identification of an audience with the stage action, the first employment of a sound track in conjunction with drama, the first dramatization of lights and colors, the first American one-character play, the first American play to treat of animals in terms of human beings, the first sternly realistic Catholic play, the first truthful play about the newspaper business and the first realistic play about fashionable American society (all three in part the contribution of Joseph Medill Patterson, presently publisher of the New York *Daily News*), the burlesque show, the minstrel show, the cartoon show, and the form of girl show subsequently copied by the European theatre.

Passing from the New York professional theatre to the New York group and guild theatres, it was the latter and not similar groups and guilds in other cities that provided the American stage with the first native expressionist play, the first American poetic modern chronicle, the first American historical travesty, the first authentic American one-act plays, the first American attempt at real psychological drama, the first modern treatment of seventeenth century farce, the first experiments with the imported impressionist drama, the first reputable American folk drama, the first ditto American Negro drama, the first driving American labor drama, the first realistic American poetic tragedy, and the first American cubist play.

So, again all things considered, if we are going to have a national theatre it might be well to build it right on Broadway, or on one of the streets just off Broadway.

May 20, 1945

Contents

Honor List

THE BEST NEW DRAMATIC PLAY:
DARK OF THE MOON, by Howard Richardson and William Berney

THE BEST NEW COMEDY:
HARVEY, by Mary Chase

THE BEST NEW MUSICAL:
CAROUSEL, by Oscar Hammerstein II and Richard Rodgers

THE BEST MALE ACTING PERFORMANCE:
LEO G. CARROLL, in *The Late George Apley*

THE BEST FEMALE ACTING PERFORMANCE:
LAURETTE TAYLOR, in *The Glass Menagerie*

THE BEST ENSEMBLE PERFORMANCE:
THE COMPANY in *The Glass Menagerie*

THE BEST STAGE DIRECTOR:
JOHN VAN DRUTEN, in *I Remember Mama*

THE BEST SCENE DESIGNER:
JO MIELZINER, in *The Glass Menagerie*

THE BEST COSTUME DESIGNER, DRAMATIC:
LUCINDA BALLARD, in *I Remember Mama*

THE BEST COSTUME DESIGNER, MUSICAL:
MILES WHITE, in *Bloomer Girl*

THE BEST STAGE LIGHTING:
JO MIELZINER, in *The Glass Menagerie*

The Theatre Book of the Year

1944 ~ 1945

The Year's Productions

DREAM WITH MUSIC. May 18, 1944

A musical fantasy, book by Sidney Sheldon, Dorothy Kilgallen and Ben Roberts, lyrics by Edward Eager, music by Clay Warnick. Produced by Richard Kollmar for 28 performances in the Majestic Theatre.

PROGRAM

(In Reality)

Ella	*Betty Allen*	Western Union Boy	*Alex Rotov*
Marian	*Joy Hodges*	Michael	*Ronald Graham*
Dinah	*Vera Zorina*	Robert	*Robert Brink*

(In the Dream)

Scheherazade	*Vera Zorina*	Perfume Merchant	*Robert Beam*
Jasmin	*Joy Hodges*	Fakir	*Michael Kozak*
Sultan	*Robert Brink*	Candy Salesman	*Bill Jones*
Wazier	*Alex Rotov*	Musical Instrument Merchant	*John Panter*
Mispah	*Marcella Howard*	Snake Charmer	*Byron Milligan*
Hispah	*Janie Janvier*	Sand Diviner	*Ralph Bunker*
Rispah	*Lois Barnes*	Sinbad	*Leonard Elliott*
Tispah	*Lucille Barnes*	Mrs. Sinbad	*Betty Allen*
Fispah	*Jane Hetherington*	Genie	*Dave Ballard*
Kispah	*Donna Devel*		
Aladdin	*Ronald Graham*		
Rug Merchant	*Ray Cook*		

SYNOPSIS: Act I. Scene 1. *Dinah's apartment.* Scene 2. *The palace of Shariar, King of the Indies.* Scene 3. *A street in the bazaars of Bagdad.* Scene 4. *Sinbad's garden.* Scene 5. *A corridor in Sinbad's house.* Scene 6. *The magic carpet.* Scene 7. *In the clouds.* Act II. Scene 1. *Aladdin's forest — China.* Scene 2. *Aladdin's game preserve.* Scene 3. *The corridor — Sinbad's.* Scene 4. *Aladdin's palace.* Scene 5. *The corridor — Sinbad's.* Scene 6. *The palace of Shariar.* Scene 7. *Dinah's apartment.*

This was the first of the summer interregnum dispensations and once again reflected our producers' conviction that, the moment the warm weather sets in, theatregoers who previously have enjoyed themselves at such plays as *Hamlet* and *Othello* and such musical exhibits as those of Strauss, Offenbach and Lehár are instantaneously transformed into half-wits who can stand only the kind of drama in which someone, preferably a grandmother, falls downstairs and lands in the goldfish bowl and the kind of musicals in which someone foots someone else at least six times in the buttocks, preferably to tunes stolen from some established previous kleptomaniac. Now and again there may conceivably come a play or a show that falls into a slightly loftier slot, but for the most part what is produced are the sort of plays that, if put on during the chilly months, would freeze to death during the road try-out period, vaudeville shows whose masters of ceremonies make killing cracks about the theatre's cooling system being so proficient that all one has to do to get a mint julep is to suck a peppermint lozenge, and musical shows whose imaginative triumph, like the one here under consideration, consists in bringing on the perspiring chorus girls in furs.

In justification of their esoteric philosophy that the public is deliriously partial to such summer exhibits, the producers customarily offer four points. The first, in their words, is "What's so odd about it? You wouldn't think of putting on other kind of stuff in a season when people are in a holiday mood, would you?" It is futile to ask them to explain why it is then that they put on what they term that other kind of stuff during the Christmas and New Year season when people are equally in a holiday mood. The second is that "people don't like to think in hot weather," to which it might be replied that the sales statistics nevertheless generally indicate that serious books are among the best sellers in the warm months and that the box-office statistics of the period show a continued big trade for such hardly frothy plays as *The Searching Wind, Jacobowsky And The Colonel, Angel Street,* and *Othello.*

The third point is that the critics become lazy when summer sets in and prefer casual shows which they may review with little effort and, further, that they would never be in the mood for serious things and would clearly indicate their displeasure in their notices. It would be of no benefit to ask the producers why it is that the kind of things they do put on usually get condemnatory reviews or why they believe that something like a new O'Neill drama, were it to be put on instead, would inevitably get even worse ones. And the fourth is that the public is never so choosey in hot weather and that one can accordingly get away with plays and shows which it would never accept in cold weather. A sufficient answer to this is that, in the ten years preceding the present season, out of a grand total of forty-three new plays produced during the warm weather months from May first on only a single one scored a success with the public, that the great majority, as a matter of record, were dispatched to the storehouse in quick order, and that out of a grand total of twenty-two new musical shows, including the military exhibit, *This Is The Army,* all of seventeen were failures and only five, including *This Is The Army,* were successes.

That something therefore appears to be slightly askew with the ipsedixits' ideology is obvious. And equally obvious is the dubiety of their meteorological calculations. Their idea in this direction seems to be that there is never a single even relatively cool interlude during the warm spell, that it never rains a chill rain, that the nights are invariably hellish, and that it is all one can do from early May until late August to keep from floating down to the sea on the tide of one's own sweat. New York in summer, true enough, isn't always like living inside a gin rickey, but it seems to be the long experience of the rest of us that it isn't on the other hand exactly like living inside a blast furnace. There are many days and nights quite as comfortable for theatregoing as during some of the sleet, slush and snow months — and it is a deal easier to get taxicabs.

The notion that it is much simpler to please audiences in summer than in winter has been responsible over the years for losing the producers many hundreds of thousands of dollars. If anything, it is harder. Far from being in a holiday mood, the average person who finds himself in the city during the summer achieves a certain crankiness and impatience. That it is generally unwarranted is neither here nor there but, as any observer of human nature will agree, it is nonetheless a pretty well established fact. And when that person goes to the theatre he dosn't go in his more carefree and receptive winter mood but in a determined mood to be shown and to get his money's worth. And as for the vacation visitors to the city, the producers' theory that they are easy prey for any new claptrap that may be put on calls for considerable overhauling. What those visitors in the main go to are not any such summer makeshifts but the big successes of the earlier year about which they have heard and have for some time been eager to see.

Surely neither they nor the town folk gave any encouragement to the theatrical hot weather philosophy of Mr. Kollmar who saw fit to produce this *Dream With Music,* which suffered their absence to a loss of 240,000 dollars and was driven to the storehouse after only twenty-eight performances. Dealing with a female writer of soap operas who dreams she is Scheherazade, it disclosed itself to be a paraphrase of *The Arabian Nights* which sought to merchant the rich flavor of the delightful tales chiefly in terms of overworked stage trapdoors and uphill jokes about the sexual relation. Mr. Kollmar's education does not seem to have included a distaste for such dull, soiled quips. His antecedent production, *Early To Bed,* like his collaborative production before that, *By Jupiter,* contained a copious dose of them and, though it appeared for some eleven months on Broadway, did not in that period make a cent for its backers. He might accordingly well have studied such prosperous shows as *Carmen Jones, Mexican Hayride* and the like and learned that while cleanliness may not exactly be next to godliness it is often in these days pretty close to the box-office.

In the preparation of *Dream With Music,* Mr. Kollmar originally sought the services of two witty men who know something about writing: Wolcott Gibbs and Franklin P. Adams. Both were amenable, in the early stages of negotiation. But Mr. Gibbs blanched when the producer looked askance at any of his humor that was slightly more elevated than such subsequently incorporated jocosities as "He's so influential he could get Errol Flynn a room at the Y.W. C.A." and "I'd hate to lose my head; I'm attached to it." And Mr. Adams went equally pale when he proposed a lyric line containing the word "preface" and was firmly apprised that it was altogether too highbrow and would not be understood by the public.

Small wonder, therefore, that the 240,000 dollars were thrown to the winds and blew the talents of Vera Zorina along with them. The first curtain had not been up ten minutes when all around one heard the groans of the customers. For in that ten minutes the imagination of the producer and his corps of Broadway gilberts had vouchsafed as a token of things to come the above-noted Errol Flynn line, a radio hideously screeching a soap opera, a maid stretched out saucily on a divan and ordering her mistress to answer the door-bell, one of the more decrepit sardonic allusions to a husband, and Zorina herself, that fair creature, strutting brashly about in the role of a concocter of radio commercials.

Among the things that all this betokened and that duly and subsequently put in an appearance was — and one illustration suffices to describe the whole — an episode in which a dwarf tried elaborately to seduce the leading lady.

CAREER ANGEL. May 23, 1944

A professional production of the Gerard M. Murray comedy originally shown in the antecedent season in the Blackfriars' Guild Theatre. Produced by the Messrs. Billings, Dicks and Shay to 15 sparse audiences in the National Theatre.

PROGRAM

Brother Gregory	*Donald Foster*
Donnie McAdams	*Allen Rich*
Willie Garvey	*Charles Nevil*
Brother Fidelis	*Ronald Telfer*
Kurt Rheinhold	*Tony Miller*
Brother Seraphim	*Whitford Kane*
Angel Guardian	*Glenn Anders*
Hurdles	*Alvin Allen*
Glinsky	*Robert Ramsen*
Thompson	*Robert Lee*
Rinn	*Charleton Carpenter*
Bruno Chevoski	*Michael Dreyfuss*
Barr	*Wendell Whitten*
Brother Ubaldus	*Mason Adams*
Duval Devois	*Dorn Alexander*
Al Fuller	*Gerald Matthews*
Billy	*David Kelly*

SYNOPSIS: Act I. *Late afternoon.* Act II. Scene 1. *Three weeks later.* Scene 2. *Midnight of the same day.* Scene 3. *The following morning. Act III. One week later.*

The entire action takes place in the Superior's office of the Bosco Institute, somewhere in Georgia.

The time is spring—prior to Pearl Harbor.

It most often in these days is a grievous mistake to bring to Broadway a play which has made a favorable impression when first shown in an amateur theatre. What looks very attractive in such a quarter frequently loses much of its attractiveness, even if recast with professional actors, when it is moved into more sophisticated surroundings. In this respect the play resembles a pretty girl in a small town who captures one's fancy and whom one invites to visit New York. In the small town, where the competition is negligible and where the metropolitan eye is disposed to suspend judgment, the girl in her simple country dress looks like a dream. But, as many men in their day have appreciated, when that same girl in that same dress appears in the big city not only she and the dress look considerably out of place but what seemed her prettiness in the rural regions doesn't now look half so pretty.

Thus, last season, *Only The Heart,* which may have seemed engaging to some when shown down in the little Provincetown Playhouse, seemed relatively less so to the same persons when it was brought to Forty-fifth Street. And thus again *Career Angel,* for all its much better performance, now didn't look like the same girl it was in its little Blackfriars' Guild home. It remained an amiable play for all its numerous stark deficiencies, but somehow not nearly so amiable as it was in its simple habitat.

A description and criticism of the play appears in *The Theatre Book of the Year, 1943–1944.*

A STRANGE PLAY. JUNE 1, 1944

A nonesuch by Patti Spears, preceded by a curtain-raiser, According To Law, *by Noel Houston. Produced by Eugene Endrey for one performance in the Mansfield Theatre.*

PROGRAM

ACCORDING TO LAW

JIM NAILEY	*Gregory Robbins*
HENRY TERRY	*Robert Harrison*
HENRY YANCEY	*Windsor Bryan*
LUKE	*Burton Mallory*
SENATOR LAWRENCE	*Dayton Lummis*
CHARLIE TEAGUE	*Wardell Saunders*
GEORGE RANDALL	*Henry Wilson*
BEN STAGGS	*Don Appell*
MRS. HARKNESS	*Lorraine MacMartin*
HARVEY	*Harvey Marlowe*

Scene. *A courtroom. A county seat.*
Time. *The present. A gray morning.*

A STRANGE PLAY

DR. STEPHEN DURYEA	*Richard Gordon*
CLAIRE	*Alicia Parnahay*
PAUL CARTWRIGHT	*Herbert Heyes*
WILLIAM DOUGLAS	*Ralph Clanton*
JAMES	*Byron Russell*

Time. *Today.*

THE BILL EARNED the proud distinction of being the first production in two years to close after a single performance. The first half, a one-act play designed seriously to picture the cruelty of Southern courts to the Negro, was so confusedly and badly written that it induced an hilarity akin to that of the famous old burlesque courtroom skit, *Irish Justice,* revived in the previous season by Bobby Clark in *Star and Garter.*

The second half, a two-act play, was unintentionally even more hilarious. Confected by a lady radio vocalist and with its scene laid on Long Island, it was as swell as a tidal wave. Nothing quite so touchingly high-toned had been seen hereabout since Sam T. Jack, the burlesque entrepreneur, some forty-odd years ago first introduced the idea of clothing the Chinamen in a Bowery opium dive skit in full evening dress, with chrysanthemums in their lapels.

The rise of the curtain started things off. Elegantly adorned with immaculately pressed white dinner suits and shirts that evidently hadn't been introduced to a laundry, the gentlemanly actors were beheld lounging luxuriously on Macy divans and Louis Quatorze chairs, the while the sole actress, clad in a pale blue gauze evening gown as ruffled as the show's backer, bade the butler, in turn as tony as a biddle, to pass around the brandy bottle. Not one but four rounds did the butler make, prefacing each pour with the confidential information that what he was putting into the glasses was real, genuine, aged Napoleon brandy, sir.

"Ah, Napoleon brandy!" successively exclaimed each of the recipients, smacking his lips. "Good, rare, old, aged Napoleon brandy!" "Have a care it does not signify your Waterloo!" wittily cautioned the actress, poising her own glass fashionably and with connoisseur finesse at her right ear.

"The night breathes romance and passion," thereupon observed an actor who was described as a great dramatist. "The sky billows with dream clouds, the stars are translucent diamonds flirting with the golden moon, and the scent of flowers in the garden carries with it the message of youth and love and desire. But" — after a profound pause — "I am worried. I seem to be unable to evolve an epic idea for my next play. But wait (*sotto voce*), I think I have it! I shall observe these people, my hosts, and dramatize what I shall discern."

What he discerned was his hostess betraying his dear friend, her husband, with a young man. "Aha!" he mused, "my theme shall be shall I tell my dear friend, her husband, or shall I not?" Noting that the wife, husband and lover had now seated themselves at a card table, he eavesdropped their conversation. "I hold the ace," said the lover. "I hold two hearts," said the wife. "Who holds the knave?" inquired the great dramatist with a meaningful inflection

— and, lapsing shudderingly for the moment into proletarian speech, added, "Will the knave cop the queen?"

The rest of the evening was occupied by the great dramatist's imaginings — acted out by the cast — of what would happen, first, if he did not tell the husband; secondly, if he did tell; and, thirdly, if the butler were to tell, necessitating a triple duplication of much the same stage action, God forbid.

The idea, which has seen service in one form or another for years, was so amateurishly handled, what with such lines as the impassioned, romantic lover's "Darling, how could you ever forget Atlantic City!", that the one and only audience howled in derision. The stage direction was by the producer, Mr. Endrey, identified in the program as an Hungarian genius who "had begun producing in Europe, one of his most successful offerings being the novel combination of stage plays with screen continuity, an idea that brought him to America." Although Mr. Endrey did not quite invent what he considers a novel idea, since the combination of a stage play with screen continuity was originally devised in this country by Augustus Thomas and Robert H. Davis in their dramatization of Frank L. Packard's *The Battle Cry,* shown at the old Astor Theatre some thirty-seven years ago, he did on this occasion invent some of the worst direction ever beheld on the local professional stage. And his instruments, the actors, were just as bad.

THAT OLD DEVIL. June 5, 1944

A comedy by J. C. Nugent. Produced by Lodewick Vroom for an impecunious 2 weeks' run in the Playhouse.

Program

Hester	*Ruth Gilbert*	Wilbur Blime	*J. Colvil Dunn*
Officer Williamson	*David S. Jordan*	Lila Merrill	*Agnes Doyle*
		Martha Blair	*Luella Gear*
John Woodruff	*Matt Briggs*	Mrs. Woodruff	*Ruth Gates*
Jim Blair	*J. C. Nugent*	Mrs. Blime	*Lou McGuire*
Doctor Davis	*Matthew Smith*	Mrs. Robinson	*Mary Dickson*
Harry Robinson	*Warren Lyons*	Jerry Swift	*Michael Ames*

SYNOPSIS: Act I. *The living-room of Jim Blair's home, Beechville, Conn. Evening.* Act II. *Same. Next morning.* Act III. *Same. That evening.*

Time. *Early September.*

Mr. Nugent, the records show, is now over seventy years of age. He has written many plays in his lifetime, all of them of a pious innocence and in the main virtuously eschewing sex. In this, his latest, however, he privileged himself a long deferred fling, as is not uncommon with old boys who previously have led a pure literary life.

For extra measure Mr. Nugent treated himself to the leading role in his spree, just as George M. Cohan did in his own belated spree called *Dear Old Darling*. And did he have himself a time! No more of that bygone nonsense of sitting paternally in front of the fireplace in slippers. No more of that playing hide-and-seek with small grandchildren. No more of that Scriptures reading to the family. Avaunt such gingerless spongecake! Heigh-ho, and on to the fleshpots with the roustabouts, and a beaker of French sauce on the house!

Our venerable friend kicked off the traces, and good. As the hero of his own imagination he presented himself to the customers, who unfortunately for him were few, as a hot dog of the first karat. Though his lifelong morality stubbornly imposed its qualms upon him and brought him periodically to reassure the audience that he was only spoofing and that he was at bottom the same old chaste Nugent, he didn't fool anybody. He loved himself in his vicarious role. I haven't seen an actor enjoy himself so enormously in years.

There was no stopping his picnic. He made all the other actors on the stage look upon him as the father of the ingénue's illegal baby. He necked the pert young household maid and gleefully confided to the rest of the cast that he had basked in the favors of the maid's beautiful younger sister. He had himself anatomically sought after by the wives of all the neighbors, and sighed over as a combination Casanova and Nat Goodwin, with a little De Wolf Hopper and Lou Tellegen thrown in to flavor. He reinspired his young wife with amorous dreams, issued cracks so blue that they made his previous self blush, put down enough gay booze to flood a Johnstown suburb, ogled everything in skirts and permitted himself to be ogled back with a trenchant significance, and conducted himself generally like a Sacha Guitry born in Niles, Ohio. It was wonderful to contemplate, and pathetic.

To see a pleasant and engaging old actor making such a spectacle of himself to what he fruitlessly imagined might be box-office ends wasn't easy on the critical spirit. If his ability as a playwright had been more substantial, it would not have been so bad. But, on this occasion at least, it suggested nothing quite so much as Wilson Collison, author of such creams as *Up In Mabel's Room* and *Getting Gertie's Garter,* collaborating with the Harold Orlob of *Hairpin Harmony.* In other words, Mr. Nugent was smutty without being funny.

The tragedy of theatrical age is that it often tries to battle itself into line with what it imagines to be contemporary taste and prejudice. Nugent, sweet soul, doubtless imagined that the present, newfangled demand was for naughty sex comedy and, like a lovable old grandpa valiantly trying to dance a jig and impress the youngsters that he is still fit as a fiddle, set himself to write one. But his every effort to be up-to-date refractorily retained the scent of long-ago camphor balls, and his every attempt to be one of the boys betrayed his mental discomfort. The thing simply wasn't in him, and he offered himself in the light of a Denman Thompson trying to sell the Old Homestead by hanging a red light in the vestibule.

To make bad matters worse, he directed what was essentially a farce in terms of comedy, pacing the action so slowly that the audience was given altogether too much time to meditate the gaping holes. In the central role, furthermore, he allowed himself so much of his established hesitational acting technique that the play frequently had to skirt around him to maintain a semblance of life. As his wife, Luella Gear, that competent comédienne, gave a satisfactory account of herself despite the direction; and as the ingénue Agnes Doyle acted a praiseworthy conviction into a part that in other hands might have seemed a mere roll of wet pink ribbon. For the rest, the company closely resembled one of the lesser pre-war summer barn aggregations.

BROKEN HEARTS OF BROADWAY
June 12, 1944

A travesty of old-fashioned melodrama by Ralph Matson. Produced and withdrawn after 14 performances by Selected Artists, Inc., in association with Alan Corelli, atop the Central Opera House.

Program

Sal, a Frivolous Sort of a Gal — *Bibi Osterwald*
Captain Fairaday, an Old Salt with Blue Blood — *George Spelvin*
Peter Coverly, a Rich Man's Noble Son — *Derrick Lynn-Thomas*
Daisy Blowhard, a Rich Man's Un-noble Daughter — *Natalie Hammond Core*
Twinkle Fleetfoot, a Man of the Moment — *Brian O'Mara*
Mrs. Fairaday, the Captain's Spouse — *Louise Kelley*
Prudence Fairaday, almost a Broken Heart — *Margaret Linskie*
Osmund Blowhard, a Wall Street Scorpion — *Steven Cochran*
Spider Gideon, Blowhard's Cruel Accomplice — *Max Leavitt*

The action takes place in New York during the great panic of 1895.

Periodically in the last dozen or so years someone, usually a tyro in the producing profession, has concluded that it would be a great idea to ridicule an old-time melodrama to the accompaniment of beer and pretzels. Supplementary to the great idea has been the even greater one to put on the show in some disused, remote church building, hall or ginmill accessible only to the more intrepid explorers. The present producers, somewhat tardy in the acquisition of the great idea, put on their exhibit on the roof of a disused, remote opera house. Otherwise they offered nothing in the way of novelty.

The playbill as usual bore a chromo of the darksome villain browbeating the tearfully beseeching heroine, invited the audience to hiss the scoundrel and, between the acts, to join in the "songs of the horse and buggy days." And the stage as heretofore presented a troupe of actors, to uncoin a word, going through the old business of overplaying, with a self-conscious ferocity or coyness, the clichés of the drama of peanut-gallery memory.

It is apparently the persistent theory of the producers of such doings that after a person has had two beers he will have the gay time of his life at almost anything, even something like this *Broken Hearts of Broadway*. Far from me to argue contrarily, considering that all kinds of people seem to enjoy themselves hugely over such parodies of the serious drama as *The Searching Wind* without even a single beer. But when it comes specifically to your recorder it takes a little more than two beers — say maybe a case of Scotch — to loosen up his hilarity at this late theatrical date with any such stale melodramatic travesty.

When the business first began, there was a certain humor in the idea, and hitherto sedate citizens appeared to delight in filling themselves with hops to the point of making derogatory noises at the villain and, in the intermissions, in filling themselves with more hops and singing old Charles K. Harris ballads at the tops of their lungs. But gradually, what with the repetition of the shows, the sport lost its allure and roaring with mirth over some such line as "I have you in me power at last, me proud beauty!" and booing the actor who spoke it, beer or no beer, pretzels or no pretzels, didn't longer seem to constitute a particularly rich and gala time.

The gentlemen responsible for this latest exhibit were consequently a bit too late. Too much beer has passed under the bridge in the intervening years. The only thing that might likely have reinspired their customers' old-time reaction would have been free vodka, by the seidel.

SLIGHTLY SCANDALOUS. June 13, 1944

A comedy by Frederick Jackson. Produced by Charles Leonard in association with Thomas McQuillan for 7 performances in the National Theatre.

PROGRAM

David Stuart	*Nino Pipitone, Jr.*
Walter Stuart	*William Berens*
Jane	*Dorothy Vaughan*
Connie	*Elizabeth Burt*
James Willoughby	*Paul McVey*
Frances Stuart	*Janet Beecher*
Millicent Stuart	*Anne Henderson*
Edward Morrow, Jr.	*Michael Meehan*
Archie Campbell	*Barry Macollum*
Wareef of Farak	*Ben Shaw*
General Georges Rigaud	*Jean De Briac*
Jan Letzaretzsko	*Gene Gary*
Sir Michael Norman	*Boyd Davis*
Mrs. Henry J. Crewe	*Francis Carson*
Daphne Crewe	*Brooke Shane*

SYNOPSIS: Act I. *Drawing-room of Frances Stuart's home. Westchester, New York. Morning.* Act II. *Late Friday afternoon. Two weeks later.* Act III. *The following Sunday evening.*

BASED UPON an idea in a play by Roland Bottomley called *Olivia Bows To Mrs. Grundy,* produced in 1932 for a road tryout and never brought into New York, Mr. Jackson's comedy amounts further to a paraphrase, with emphasis upon the sex angle, of the idea in the late John Barrymore's final vehicle, *My Dear Children,* shown locally in 1940. In that play, an aging father entertains three children, each born of a different mother, who have now grown up and seeks to resolve the difficulties they are experiencing with their several romances. In *Slightly Scandalous,* as in *My Dear Children* and as in the earlier Bottomley play, an aging mother entertains three children, each illegitimately born of a different father, who have now grown up and seeks to resolve the difficulties two of them in turn are experiencing with their romances.

The idea, despite overuse, is possibly still a workable one, but the present manipulator has failed it completely, as might not be unanticipated from one who displayed the kind of imagination that originally called his play by such titles as *Are Fathers Necessary?* and *Love And Learn* and could finally achieve nothing more fecund than yet another turn on such already tried and slightly enervating Broadway ones as *Slightly Delirious, Slightly Married, et al.* Designating the exhibit a play is, indeed, in the nature of flattery, since what Mr. Jackson has negotiated is rather merely a succession of monologues for his leading actress periodically interrupted by his other characters. Of action in almost any sense there is scarcely a trace. The theme obviously also calls for a light wit and a light pace, and the author has omitted the wit save for two or three lines, and his pace is that of a tortoise afflicted with infantile paralysis. His humor, such as it is, furthermore rests largely in such business as a mother's injunction to her small son not to eat any candy lest it spoil his lunch and then seizing the box from him and eating some herself. Which may be allowed to be hardly appropriate to a comedy which strives for the airy Noel Coward sort of thing.

The sedentary direction, in addition, was such that one had the feeling that, if anyone had stolen the stage's couch and chairs, the actors would have found themselves reading their lines lying on the floor.

In a previous section, it has been pointed out that of forty-three plays produced during the warm weather period in the ten previous seasons only one was successful. In the present warm season this production marked the fourth successive failure, bringing the total to forty-six. *Slightly Scandalous,* further, marks still another New York disaster for plays that have been produced with success on the West Coast. *Cry Havoc, Slightly Married, "—But Not Goodbye," That Old Devil* and many such others which have attracted favorable attention out there have uniformly failed to attract a like attention on Broadway.

FOR KEEPS. June 14, 1944

A comedy by F. Hugh Herbert. Produced by Gilbert Miller for 30 performances in the Henry Miller Theatre.

PROGRAM

Miss Maxwell	*Zolya Talma*	Jimmy McCarey	*Donald Murphy*
Anna	*Ellen Mahar*	Nancy Vanda	*Patricia Kirkland*
Paul Vanda	*Frank Conroy*	Charlie	*Joseph R. Garry*
Mr. Reamer	*Geoffrey Lumb*	Frank	*Grover Burgess*
Pamela Vanda	*Julie Warren*	Norma	*Joan Wetmore*
June	*Norma Clerc*	Terry	*George Baxter*

SYNOPSIS: Act I. *Paul Vanda's studio apartment, New York City.* Act II. Scene 1. *The same. Ten days later.* Scene 2. *Later that night.* Act III. Scene 1. *The same. Two weeks later.* Scene 2. *A few hours later.*

The warm weather catastrophies, with this production, added up, with but a single break in eleven seasons, to forty-seven and indicated once again that the credo of producers which holds that anything will go with audiences if only their collars are wilting has need of a sizeable and very blue pencil.

Gilbert Miller is fond of telling the story about an encounter with his late, illustrious father, Henry, upon achieving his own first theatrical presentation. "Well, dad," observed Gilbert proudly, "a chip of the old block, eh?" To which his father replied wryly, "Say rather a slice of the old ham." In relation to the production of *For Keeps,* however, papa was wrong, in a way. With it, Gilbert discloses himself to be a chip of the old block, at least in one direction. Henry Miller was particularly fetched by the kind of plays in which a young daughter or ward unwelcomely came back to a not altogether circumspect household and in the end proved herself a happy reforming influence. Gilbert now appears to be following in his footsteps, since *For Keeps* is fundamentally in the line of such of daddy longlegs' favorites as *The Rainbow,* etc. The chief difference, however, is that daddy's selections had something to recommend them in the way of agreeable entertainment whereas the chip's selection is as dully talkative and uninspired a concoction as the stage has uncovered in quite a time.

When the evening was over, indeed, the only recollection one had of it was of young Patricia Kirkland occupying the stage for two steady hours and chattering away for dear life, about nothing. At two points during the session one of the other characters impatiently proclaimed, "You talk too much!", thus usurping to himself the province of the reviewers, which if it keeps up isn't going to be particularly comfortable for the latter, who rely on being paid for such things. Miss Kirkland battled with her difficult assignment valiantly, and came off moderately well as an actress, if unavoidably as something of a bore. But someone should tell her that eyes made up like indigo billiard balls do not lend themselves to attractive facial expression. A number of the company, in fact, had so much sickly blue makeup smeared on their lids that the spectacle was less that of human beings indulging in oral intercourse than of so many decayed meatballs animated by Walt Disney.

TAKE A BOW. June 15, 1944

A variety show, originally called Slap Happy. *Produced for 14 performanecs by Lou Walters in the Broadhurst Theatre.*

Principals

Jay C. Flippen, Chico Marx, Cross and Dunn, Raye and Naldi, Gene Sheldon, the Murtah Sisters, Pat Rooney, Think-a-Drink Hoffman, the Whitson Brothers, Johnny Mack, and Loretta Fischer.

Mr. Walters' attempt to revive vaudeville took the following form:

8:40 p.m. — Some chorus girls came on and nasalized a song called "Take A Bow," the lyric having to do with the grand performers who were to follow and who would surely have to take bows for their wonderful talents.

8:45 — Jay C. Flippen, the master of ceremonies, appeared and exchanged some badinage with Chico Marx, seated in a box, as to what they should do to make the show amusing. They allowed, with a skittish facetiousness, that they didn't know.

8:55 — Gene Sheldon, assisted by Loretta Fischer, did his old, familiar banjo and pantomime act.

9:10 — Flippen reappeared in a different suit, cracked an old smoking-car joke, and wound up with a supposedly comical song.

9:18 — A tap dancer named Johnny Mack, backed by the girls, went through his routine.

9:25 — Chico Marx and Sheldon merchanted the old poker game business from *The Cocoanuts*.

9:30 — Flippen reappeared in another suit and cracked another old blue joke.

9:34 — Cross and Dunn harmonized after their established twenty-year-old pattern.

9:44 — Flippen again in another suit. Observing one of the showgirls, he cracked, "A She Grows In Brooklyn."

9:48 — White-haired old Pat Rooney, celebrating his fiftieth year on the vaudeville stage, executed a jitterbug dance with one of the chorus girls, and almost collapsed.

9:55 — Flippen, in another suit, cracked another mildewed joke and introduced Think-a-Drink Hoffman.

9:57 — Hoffman did his familiar turn producing various drinks from an apparently empty pitcher and a pair of cocktail shakers, spilling most of them on his assistants and on the members of the audience who were seated down front.

10:05 — Flippen, in yet another suit, walked on and announced, "Now we'll have a short intermission so the ladies can go to the ladies' room."

Intermission.

10:15 — The chorus girls again came on and performed a dance number called "The Hollywood Jump," consisting of leaps into the air and a wild waving of arms.

10:20 — Flippen in another suit and with another maizey joke.

10:22 — Gene Sheldon reappeared and burlesqued a classical dance. He followed this with his old act of listening with mock rapture to a woman making a speech about him.

10:33 — A pair of ballroom dancers, Raye and Naldi, tossed each other around.

10:45 — A sister act, the Murtahs, "in a cycle of their inimitable songs," harmonized like a trio of darling coyotes.

10:52 — Flippen in another creation and with another joke that Abe Lincoln didn't laugh at.

10:55 — Chico Marx and his twenty-year-old piano act.

11:08 — The Whitson Brothers, acrobats.

11:15 — Flippen again in another choice sartorial confection: "Now goodnight, ladies and gentlemen, and come again soon."

ANNA LUCASTA. June 16, 1944

A play by Philip Yordan, adapted by Abram Hill and Harry Wagstaff Gribble. Produced by the American Negro Theatre group for 19 performances in the 135th Street Library Theatre.

PROGRAM

Noah	*Lionel Monagus*	Stanley	*John Proctor*
Joe	*Alvin Childress*	Anna	*Hilda Simms*
Rudolph	*Earle Hyman*	Blanche	*Alice Childress*
Catherine	*Letitia Toole*	Eddie	*Martin Slade*
Theresa	*Alberta Perkins*	Danny	*Billy Cumberbatch*
Frank	*Frederick O'Neal*	Lester	*Buddy Holmes*
Stella	*Betty Haynes*		

SYNOPSIS: Act I. Scene 1. *The Lucasta living-room, Pennsylvania, early 1941.* Scene 2. *Noah's bar, Brooklyn, the same night.* Act II. *The Lucasta living-room, evening, four days later.* Act III. Scene 1. *The Lucasta living-room, three days later.* Scene 2. *Noah's bar, Brooklyn, a week later.*

This fifth production by the American Negro Theatre group over a five year span, put on in a Harlem cellar, deals with a young prostitute who tries to abandon the life of sin and settle down to married respectability. The shadow of her past pursues her and in the end again envelops her in its shade. The fifth production is accordingly hardly noteworthy for any great thematic originality. The assisted author, a former Chicago lawyer, writes, however, with intermittent force and, while a greasepaint heaviness deadens sections of the play, several portions have a measure of dramatic drive. And for all the familiarity of the subject matter it exercises a share of theatrical interest.

There is something about a Negro company that often peculiarly makes a play seem a little better than it actually is, at least to the generality of reviewers, who on occasion ooze an unaccustomed good will and sympathy. Expecting little — without warrant or logic — they permit themselves to expand over playwriting and acting which would make a relatively small impression upon them in the white theatre. It is another and more impulsive form of the good will and sympathy which found and finds demonstration when an eighty-year-old actress like the late Mrs. Whiffen appears on the stage; or when a blues singer like Jane Froman, injured in an airplane crash, is wheeled out in a chair to do her numbers; or when the late Sarah Bernhardt appeared in her declining years with a wooden leg; or when in the final days of her career it was rumored that Duse was suffering from tuberculosis. Or even when the late Lowell Sherman once cleverly showed up with a heavy bandage wound about a perfectly intact head. It matters little whether the performances are critically worthy or not; the reviewing hearts give out.

The Negroes under immediate discussion are far, very far, from being unworthy, but they are, save in the cases of Hilda Simms and Frederick O'Neal, hardly less far from being quite the extraordinary blooms which in some overly impressible quarters they have been made out to be.

The exhibit was brought downtown into the Mansfield Theatre, on August 30, by John Wildberg for a run that lasted beyond the season. A few changes were made in the cast, notably Canada Lee in the small role of Danny, and several changes in the script, notably a greater emphasis upon humor and the tacking on of a ridiculously bogus happy ending.

LOVE ON LEAVE. June 20, 1944

A comedy by A. B. Shiffrin, originally called Spare The Rod. *Produced by Charles Stewart and Martin Goodman for 7 performances in the Hudson Theatre.*

Program

Sam Wilson	*Millard Mitchell*	Hoagy	*Bert Freed*
Mary	*Mary Sargent*	Nick Hardy	*John Conway*
Paula	*June Wilson*	Slim	*Ramsay Williams*
Lucy	*Rosemary Rice*	Dr. Graham	*Ross Matthew*
Larry Draper	*James Dobson*	Mrs. Lewis	*Eleanor Gordon*
Robert Lewis	*Stanley Bell*	A Policeman	*Roderick Maybee*
Flo	*Joann Dolan*	Sergeant	*John Farrell*

A Group of Teen-Age Girls and Boys.

SYNOPSIS: Act I. Scene 1. *The studio-living-room of the Wilsons.* Scene 2. *Approach to the Times Square subway station.* Scene 3. *Same as Scene 1.* Act II. Scene 1. *A room in Hotel Esquire.* Scene 2. *Same as Act I, Scene 1.* Act III. *Same as Act I, Scene 1.*

The entire action takes place within a few hours of a summer evening in 1944.

Mr. Shiffrin, not content with the obviousness of the sailors on the loose among the girlfolk theme, has added for good measure a dose of the equally obvious juvenile delinquency theme and further has not neglected such even staler ingredients as alleged pregnancy on the part of a female youngster. His exhibit accordingly and duly brought the failures in the perspiration period of the previous ten seasons and this one to the handsome total of forty-eight.

Mr. Shiffrin's general observation is of a piece with his noted originality. He is apparently convinced, for instance, that when anyone has a first article accepted by the *Saturday Evening Post* he is instantly besieged by fancy offers from lecture bureaus, book publishers, and the radio. He also seemingly believes that national fame promptly follows the publication of any such article, and that if the *Reader's Digest* reprints it tremendous wealth lies just around the corner. He thinks that a violation of the Sullivan law gets precisely the same police treatment as an unleashed dog and that the Times Square subway station was built by Thompson and Dundy. And he appears to have the notion that a hack writer may handily support a wife and two daughters, one of them full-grown, on an occasional little essay that brings three cents a word.

His humor and dramaturgical invention are not less piquant. "That awful word!" horrifiedly exclaims the wife when her husband uses a mild damn. "Oh!" surprisedly ejaculates the young daughter who enters the room and after several minutes observes her father loudly pounding at a typewriter a few feet away, "I didn't see you!" The father looks up and inquires what the daughter is reciting. "I am going to play in *Lady Windowmere's Fan,*" the latter proudly tells him. "I'd rather you played in a band," he wittily retorts. Not allowing the audience to recover from its rib-cracking mirth, the daughter then asks her mother, "Was Oscar Wilde a fairy?", to which the mother answers modestly, "Well, he was a homosensual." The father shudders over his daughter's question. "She's your daughter!" he proclaims to his wife. "She's yours too!" excruciatingly comes back the latter.

HATS OFF TO ICE. June 22, 1944

A musical "icetravaganza," with songs by James Littlefield and John Fortis. Produced by Sonja Henie and Arthur M. Wirtz for a beyond the season run in the Center Theatre.

PRINCIPALS

Carol Lynne, Freddie Trenkler, the Caley Sisters, the Brandt Sisters, Helen Carter, the Four Sailors, Lucille Page, Geoffrey Stevens, Elouise Christine, James Caesar, Rudy Richards, Pat Marshall, and Don Rogers.

THE NATION-WIDE SUCCESS of the ice-skating shows, now running big into their seventh year, is undoubtedly due to the American admiration of monotony. The average American will, of course, indignantly deny any such thing, but the facts nevertheless seem to indicate its general plausibility. In the field of entertainment, for example, he not only relishes the inherent monotony of these ice-skating, to say nothing of roller-skating, exhibits but over the long years that of countless pairs of so-called ballroom dancers who perform almost exactly the same routines, acrobats who haven't varied their doings since the days of Tony Pastor, and trick dog acts that are as alike as so many sister singing acts, Indian club jugglers, tap dancers, and trained seals, in all of which he similarly since childhood has delighted.

There is little, furthermore, that fetches our average fellow-citizen more fully than blues singers, nine-tenths of them completely indistinguishable from one another; or radio quiz programs, which with minor exception vary as little as Hollywood horror movies, which he steadily attends with gusto; or the literature of Lloyd C. Douglas, which for some years now he has constituted among the best of the best-sellers. Willie Howard, who has been doing the same thing for almost twenty-five years, is close to his fancy, and until Charlie Chaplin gave up his art for love our fellow-countryman couldn't get enough of him, though

Charlie purveyed much the identical antics throughout his career.

It is needless to extend the catalogue; the few illustrations suffice to suggest the panorama's sweep. And the same worship of monotony obtains in other directions. The Italian restaurant table d'hôte business has luxuriated for more than half a century and, if anyone has ever discovered one such table d'hôte that has differed to a single damp anchovy from all the rest, he is cousin to Amerigo Vespucci. Yet our brother hasn't stopped gourmandizing them, just as he hasn't changed the color of his suits, which are invariably blue or gray or brown; or the nonsensical habit of carrying his handkerchief in the difficultly accessible upper left, instead of right, pocket; or the place in which he spends his annual vacations.

It is thus that some such ice-skating show as this *Hats Off To Ice,* the latest in the series, was pretty certain once again to appeal to him. It offered him the same old two and one-half hour monotonous entertainment and he accordingly had the night of his life at it. For two and one-half satisfying hours he could richly pleasure himself with the skaters executing the familiar twirls and whirls and racing for dear life hell-bent for nowhere. For two and one-half hours he could enchant himself with the spectacle of skating comedians landing on their netherparts, and ballet numbers which, save for a mere change of their titles, were fundamentally like the ballet numbers in the previous shows, and all the rest of the items that he had seen time and again.

For those of his fellow-countrymen who get a little fed up on scaloppini Marsala and trained seals, the show, however, may be allowed to have lacked an alleviating variety. Watching the clown Trenkler skating furiously toward a bench as if to sit down upon it and then whimsically bypassing it, no longer, after watching the same thing over a period of years, constituted the food of stintless humor. Surveying a series of ballets called "Isle Of The Midnight Rainbow," "Persian Legend," "Slavic Rhapsody," etc., which in view of the identity of the skating maneuvers might just as well, save for the costumes, have been called by the same name, and that borrowed from the ice ballets of the previous shows, hardly constituted in turn an overly refreshing visual holiday. And the remaining acts, such as skaters jumping over obstacles, skating contortionists, knock-about comedy skaters in sailor suits, the female skater with bow and arrow clad as Diana and performing as "Goddess Of The Hunt," boogie-woogie skaters, and Russian kick-out and half-sit skaters, though all perfectly competent as of yore, only induced the feeling that Ouspensky's theory of spiral time was something of an establishd theatrical fact and that one was viewing the same ice show back in the year 1940.

TEN LITTLE INDIANS. June 27, 1944

A murder mystery play by Agatha Christie. Produced for a beyond the season run by the Shuberts and Albert de Courville in, initially, the Broadhurst Theatre.

PROGRAM

Rogers	*Neil Fitzgerald*
Mrs. Rogers	*Georgia Harvey*
Fred Narracott	*Patrick O'Connor*
Vera Claythorne	*Claudia Morgan*
Philip Lombard	*Michael Whalen*
Anthony Marston	*Anthony Kemble Cooper*
William Blore	*J. Pat O'Malley*
General Mackenzie	*Nicholas Joy*
Emily Brent	*Estelle Winwood*
Sir Lawrence Wargrave	*Halliwell Hobbes*
Dr. Armstrong	*Harry Worth*

SYNOPSIS: Act I. *A summer evening in August.* Act II. Scene 1. *The following morning.* Scene 2. *The same day — afternoon.* Act III. Scene 1. *The same day — evening.* Scene 2. *The following afternoon.*

The scene of the play is in the living-room of a house on Indian Island, off the coast of Devon, England.

THIS IS ANOTHER in the line of mystery plays in which an assortment of persons gathered in quarters from which they cannot escape receive warning that they are about to meet their deaths and in which the successive demises drive the temporary survivors, and theoretically the audience, crazy with suspense. The theatre never rests very long without a refurbishing of the plot. It was already fully familiar all of fifteen years ago when Owen Davis again figged it out in *The Ninth Guest,* and since then various paraphrases have popped up at intervals to keep us from becoming unduly famished.

The exhibits are usually confined to one of two localities. They are laid either in the living-room of a town residence or mountain retreat or in the living-room of a house on a remote and rugged little island, with the sea running threateningly high. Miss Christie's is laid in the living-room of a house on a remote and rugged little island, with the sea running threateningly high.

Miss Christie is also not too original in other directions. Who their mysterious host is, her characters are at a loss to know. Her butler comports himself with such touching innocence that the early betting, she hopes, will be twenty to one that he is the murderer, though obviously, as usual, he is not. One by one, as in *A Study In Scarlet,* diminishing numbers, in this instance ten small Indian figures, count off doom. And divers other such long favored devices are not missing, as might be anticipated from a confector of popular mystery tales invariably given to such stereotypes as "With a devastating ear-splitting blast on the horn an enormous Super Sports Dalmain car rushed past him at eighty miles an hour. Dr. Armstrong nearly went into the hedge. One of these young fools who tore around the country. He hated them. That had been a near shave, too. Damned young fool!"

A literata who is fond of descriptions like "an arrogant, almost cruel mouth," "the thick lips of Mr. Isaac Morris," and "his six feet of well-proportioned body, his crisp hair, tanned face, and intensely blue eyes" is furthermore hardly likely to emerge suddenly as an expert hand at dramatic character delineation. Nor is one given to such stuff as "Queer business when you came to think of it — the whole thing was queer — very queer . . . ," "But he felt uneasy; damned odd sort of place," and "I'm all right now; it just — gave me a turn" likely to emerge any more quickly as more than a mediocre writer of mystery drama. Miss Christie is the literata in point.

The only way to inject renewed vitality into the time-worn plot which Miss Christie has selected for her play and which she has borrowed for the purpose from her novel, *The Nursery Rhyme Murders,* published a half dozen or so years ago, is to invent means for the successive murders that may interest by virtue of their refreshing cunning and novelty. But in this direction she also fails signally. She has been able to think up nothing newer than the poison dropped into a drinking glass, the overdose of sleeping medicine, the push over a high cliff, and the like. And as a playwright of any critical merit she has, in addition and worse, not stopped to consider that the dramatic repetition implicit in the numerous successive deaths must be wearying when it is not waywardly comical, and that to avoid any such impression and result it is necessary to exercise considerable dramaturgic ingenuity, which is apparently beyond her.

The one and only trace of relative ingenuity which Miss Christie has indicated in her novel lies in the manner in which she has her culprit dispose of himself. And even that is not altogether unfamiliar to addicts to mystery fiction. Yet she is handicapped by not being able to employ it on her stage, and so loses theatrically the single touch of approximate invention.

What is more, she is not wholly honest and above-board. A close observer of her stage may readily detect at least three instances wherein she, unquestionably agreeing with her play's director, deliberately misleads her audience and cheats her last act solution by causing her murderer to conduct himself otherwise than she subsequently apprises us he conducted himself. To specify only one, he does not covertly drop the potassium cyanide into Marston's glass, as it is later explained he did. The best mystery plays, of which *The Bat* is an example, deceive their audiences with strict legitimacy. The poorer ones, of which Miss Christie's is an example, intermittently are guilty of bogus deception.

It is popularly supposed that mystery plays are as close to the fancy of theatregoers as mystery stories are to the generality of readers. The supposition, if the records count for anything, is seemingly without basis in fact. So-called psychological thrillers aside, of the fifty-nine straight out-and-out mystery plays produced in the Broadway theatre during the previous dozen years fifty-three were failures and only six were real successes. Furthermore, among the sixty-five plays that have achieved the longest runs in the theatre — again, the psychological thriller, *Angel Street,* not counting — only one, the before-mentioned *The Bat,* was a straight mystery play.

The particular, damaging critical weakness of the specimen under consideration is this: when one goes to a murder play one wants to see the murders in action, and Miss Christie in considerable part simply talks about them, and not very convincingly. Her murders are too often committed off-stage and merely announced to the audience. Except for the sight of young Marston clutching at his throat and tumbling over the furniture, the other corpses achieve their corpsedom either in the wings or apparently meet death, it seems, from sitting tranquilly too long in a chair. To observe a character like her General Mackenzie amble out to a terrace and deposit himself peacefully in a chair and then be informed some minutes later that he is dead from a knife thrust, when one plainly has seen not the slightest suspicion of any knife thrust, scarcely makes for exciting melodrama. General Mackenzie might every bit as well have been announced to have died from pernicious anemia.

The exhibit nevertheless was a box-office success, making the score seven hits out of sixty tries.

SCHOOL FOR BRIDES, August 1, 1944

A farce by Frank Gill, Jr., and George Carleton Brown. Produced, initially, in the Royale Theatre for a beyond the season run by Howard Lang.

PROGRAM

Charlie	*John Sheehan*	Stephanie	*Lucia Carroll*
Stephen Garrett	*Charles Gary*	Ronnie	*Joan Webster*
Julie	*Yolande Donlan*	Suzan	*Kay Lawrence*
Diane	*Frances Charles*	Vicki	*Shirley Whitney*
Alice	*Mary Best*	Frederick M. Hasty	*Roscoe Karns*
Joanne	*Olivia Russell*	Dean Baxter (Constance King)	*Bernadene Hayes*
Leslie	*Elizabeth Worthington*	Mary	*Ann Turner*
Grace	*Darby Moore*		
Jeff Connors	*Warren Ashe*		

SYNOPSIS: Act I. Scene 1. *Drawing-room of Stephen Garrett's summer home on Long Island Sound.* Time. *Morning.* Scene 2. *The same, seven weeks later.* Time. *Afternoon.* Act II. Scene 1. *Upstairs bedroom of Garrett's home. Next morning.* Scene 2. *The same—midnight.* Act III. *Same as Act I. Early next morning.*

HAVING AS CO-PRODUCER made a sack of money on a revision of the old Charlton Andrews-Avery Hopwood farce, *Ladies' Night In A Turkish Bath,* retitled *Good-Night Ladies,* which had established a record run of one hundred weeks in Chicago, Mr. Lang bethought him that he might further enrich his bank balance with a farce considerably louder and much dirtier. *School For Brides* was the result. Following a rewarding engagement in Chicago, where apparently anything can happen, including great prosperity for an allotment of cheap smut called *Maid In The Ozarks,* Mr. Lang brought his article to Broadway and, though critically apprised of his error in terms usually reserved to defective sewers and Southern politics, managed to harvest a considerable share of the public's dollars, thereby proving that apparently anything can also happen in New York, including equal prosperity for an allotment of cheap smut called *School For Brides.*

This *School For Brides* was disclosed to be a herring paraphrase of the idea in numerous plays like *School For Husbands, The Charm School, School For Princesses,* etc. For two hours and a quarter a stage full of females, successively unadorned with scant bathing suits, sweaters that gave free play to their mammary glands, transparent negligées and adhesive pajamas and supposedly being coached in the arts of amour, occupied themselves in sniffing an eligible millionaire, jumping into and out of beds, and seizing every opportunity to reply to anything addressed to them, however innocent, in double or more often single entendre.

Every twenty minutes or so, by way of momentary relief from the lavatory dialogue, the humor was permitted to take a more immaculate turn and resolved itself into such rich forms as a woman's remark, "I'm going to complain to Ickes," with the query, "What are Ickes?" But the dominating motif of the evening consisted in edging as closely as possible to the word "fornication" without articulating it. Embroidering the script in the way of wit were such further biological jocosities as "What a student body! What a body!", such choice epigrams as "A peccadillo is sex in low gear," and such bits of business as a young woman spreading wide her legs over the side of a chair and, upon being reprimanded by the dean of the school, tartly observing that none of the men she knew had ever complained about it.

The cameo, in short, enjoyed all the attributes of a garbage-can save only the latter's somewhat less overpowering stench.

CATHERINE WAS GREAT. AUGUST 2, 1944

A play by Mae West for Mae West. Produced, initially, in the Shubert Theatre for 191 performances by Michael Todd.

PROGRAM

(In the Prologue)

JIM	*Hubert Long*
MIKE	*Robert Strauss*
GREG	*Philip Huston*
ROY	*Mischa Tonken*
CORPORAL JOE	*Joel Ashley*

(In the Play)

COUNT NIKOLAI MIROVICH	*Coburn Goodwin*
CAPTAIN DRONSKY	*Philip Cary Jones*
ENGLISH AMBASSADOR	*Henry Vincent*
AMBASSADOR CHOISEUL	*Owen Coll*
AMBASSADOR MURAD PASHA	*Don de Leo*
CAPTAIN DANILOV	*Don Gibson*
ALEXIS ORLOFF	*Hubert Long*
COUNT PANIN	*Charles Gerrard*
CHIEF CHAMBERLAIN	*John Stephen*
GREGORY ORLOFF	*Philip Huston*
CATHERINE II	*Mae West*
PRINCE POTEMKIN	*Joel Ashley*
VARVARA	*Elinor Counts*
FLORIAN	*Ray Bourbon*
LIEUTENANT BUNIN	*Gene Barry*
MARSHAL SUVOROV	*John Parrish*
IVAN VI	*Michael Bey*
PUGACHEFF	*Bernard Hoffman*
INNKEEPER	*Harry Bodin*
MAURICE	*Leon Hamilton*
SEMYONEV	*Victor Finney*
VANYA	*Frank Baxter*
CHIMNEYSWEEP	*Lester ("Red") Towne*
CHECHKOFSKI	*Dayton Lummis*

SYNOPSIS: Prologue. *A USO Recreation Room in the United States of America.* Time. *The present.* Act I. Scene 1. *a council chamber in the Winter Palace, St. Petersburg, Russia.* Time. *1762.* Scene 2. *The royal suite of the Empress Catherine II. A half-hour later.* Scene 3. *The council chamber. A few months later.* Act II. Scene 1. *The royal suite. That night.* Act II. Scene 1. *An inn several miles outside St. Petersburg. Later that night.* Scene 3. *A court-martial room in the Winter Palace. The next morning.* Scene 4. *The royal suite. Night.* Act III. Scene 1. *The royal suite. The following morning.* Scene 2. *The fireplace in the room of Count Mirovich. Night.* Scene 3. *The royal suite. A few minutes later.* Scene 4. *The secret room of Ivan VI. A short time later.* Scene 5. *The council chamber. Later that night.*

THE HISTORY OF the American stage includes a ripe number of performers who have achieved eminence through relatively the same means as have served champion pie eaters, flagpole sitters, and long distance spitters. This should not, however, be regarded as given to too much aspersion, since say what you will it also takes talent, of a sort, to negotiate several gross of pies, especially such as are inoculated with aniseed and cocoanut; to squat atop a wooden pole for a month, when everyone appreciates the discomfort of sitting on baseball bleachers for a mere hour without getting up to stretch; or to master the art of expectoration to the point where one can hit a spittoon or Prohibition candidate for Congress in the next lot.

The fact albeit remains that, talent aside, the players in question have acquired for themselves a species of enduring, if peculiar, fame which has been withheld from any number of their colleagues admittedly far more gifted and that they probably will be remembered, particularly in the barrooms and other such haunts of mankind *in nubibus,* long after their aforesaid colleagues are forgotten.

Even old-timers who today can not for the life of them remember such actresses as, say, Nellie McHenry, Kate McLaurin and Effie Germon, haven't the slightest difficulty in recalling, for example, the Cherry Sisters. And if either talent or beauty were the issue, the offspring of M. and Mme. Cherry, in comparison with even the actresses named would be something of a piece with not overly burnished battleaxes. But nonetheless, though they were so bad in every way that parents used to take their more delinquent children to see them by way of punishment, they are recollected with a wayward relish, to such a degree, indeed, that they have become one of the apparently deathless legends of our theatre.

There perhaps never was allowed at large a more caseous star Shakespearean actor than John McCullough, who flourished back in the days before most of us still living were born. Yet though his roar and rant were of such proportions that, when he was in good form, audiences had to strap themselves into their seats lest they be knocked out of them and projected against the auditorium's walls and though at times the more refined taste made it incumbent upon the poor fellow to play behind a net, he is vividly remembered at this late day even by men and women otherwise so feeble that they can no longer climb into bed and have to sleep on the floor.

Anna Held, at a somewhat later period, was another curio. With negligible genius beyond the ability to make what in the lingo of her time were known as bedroom eyes and to wink seductively through a pair of ditties called "Won't You Come And Play Wiz Me" and "I Joost Can't Make My Eyes Behave," she contrived nevertheless to establish herself not only as a diseuse of considerable artistic bulk but as the meridian of Gallic sex appeal. And it wasn't long before the Archie Gunn chromos of her displaying her come-hither look and a timid segment of undraped fundament swept the adoring countryside and she became the favorite pin-up girl of the Teddy Roosevelt era.

Then there was Henry E. Dixey, who rose to a celebrity that endures to this hour hardly on the strength of his acting, which was of the species presently encountered in the small sidestreet theatres with wooden benches, but rather solely on the score of a shapely figure. When that figure was first disclosed to the public in tights in a show called *Adonis,* Henry's niche was carved out for him, and for many years he occupied the place in the affections of the ladies and their serving maids that was later to be occupied on the part of the latter alone by Chauncey Olcott and Andrew Mack. And the memory of Henry as a matinée idol *par excellence* persists, even in the case of countless persons who never saw him.

It similarly takes a theatre-lover stricken with amnesia not to recognize the name of Rose Melville, who in her time enchanted the nation in the role of Sis Hopkins. She was one of the biggest sensations of her period, though her acting ability consisted for the most part in wearing pigtails, standing with her feet wide apart, and pulling furiously at a white stocking that was ever on the point of falling down, always with her mouth idiotically open. Just what it was that constituted Rose such a furore isn't easy for the historian to deduce, unless it was the open-and-shut hokum nature of the Sis Hopkins character. But even that seemingly obvious explanation doesn't entirely hold water, since her personal pull was so great that theatregoers flocked to see her dozens of times, collected her photographs (and she was not overly blessed with looks) as they later collected those of the stage's prime beauties, and rushed to read everything printed about her, especially in the road towns.

Cléo de Mérode and the girls known as Polaire and Corinne are further testimonials to our thesis. None had the slightest endowment, although Corinne could occasionally sing a song on key and, if provided with enough frou-frou petticoats, could give the effect of dancing, yet all made an impression which is still imbedded in recollection. Both Cléo and Polaire were purely the offspring of shrewd press-agentry. The former was a fairly good-looking woman with deep, dark eyes who wore her hair plastered down over her ears and who was elevated into the public's thirst through a cagy dissemination of the fable that she wore it that way because both her ears had been cut off by a jealous lover, of whom the tale went on to say that she had at least fifty.

Polaire, on the other hand, while she shared the Mlle. Mérode's deficiency in any discernible theatre gifts, hardly shared in her hypothetical abundance of frenzied anatomical admirers, but was contrariwise promoted into the public's rapt interest through the communiqué that she was the homeliest woman in the world, albeit one possessed of the smallest waist. The communiqué, while faulty on both counts, was swallowed whole by the proletariat, who in the oblique idiosyncrasy native to it substituted a paradoxical admiration for what more naturally might have been expected to be a ribald unconcern. Polaire was in reality not any homelier than two dozen women on the stage at the time; as a matter of fact, she was perceptibly better-looking than a number of such actresses as, say, Lorena Atwood

Sadie Harris, Belle Blanche, May Vokes, and Ida Hawley. And while her waist was factually very small, it was no smaller than those of several other stage girls of the era, if we are to trust such able research students of her day as the late Jim Huneker, Charles Frederic Nirdlinger, and Larry Elkins.

As for Corinne, whose full name, restricted to family use, was Corinne Belle De Briou, she enjoyed, for all her limitations, the hearty favor of the public for many years, winning its enthusiastic applause in everything from operetta to musical comedy and revue. She had no beauty to sell; she had nothing of what is known as sex attraction; and her stage qualifications were minute. Yet she, too, has left her slipper prints in the sands of time.

There were many others. Long before, the celebrated Adah Isaacs Menken, a distinctly minor actress, became the rage and lasted as the rage for years for having appeared, in a melodrama called *Mazeppa,* in what at the time was regarded as scant clothing but in what today would be looked upon, in the phrase of a lesser Franco-American scholar of my acquaintance, as the "whole *tout ensemble.*" Books have been written about her. Maggie Mitchell, a likable but indifferent actress of the persistent ingénue type whose histrionic virtuosity consisted largely in comporting herself as if she had just got up from sitting on an electric fan, became a public pet of such proportions that the stage-doors of the theatres in which she appeared took on the aspect of the Homestead riots. And Charlotte Crabtree, famous to the theatre as Lotta, with a talent not materially much more handsome, remains to this day and hour a symbol of her own period's pride and joy.

Sadie Martinot, who was not a French importation as most persons believed and still believe but who was born in New York in the second year of the Civil War, Mrs. James Brown Potter (Cora Urquhart) and Mrs. Leslie Carter were three other ewes who achieved high recognition for reasons that baffle critical inquiry. Sadie, who appeared on both the musical and the dramatic stages, was at one time the toast of the town, though she was assuredly no glamour girl, had a figure that the late William Winter could look at with no danger to his puritanical conscience and libido, and purveyed a species of singing and acting that may generously be described as so-so. Mrs. Potter, the description of whose acting calls for an even greater generosity mixed perhaps with the politesse of a head-waiter, was, however, something of a beauty, had a wardrobe of uncommon elegance, and was married to the scion of a socially prominent and wealthy metropolitan family. These latter attributes in combination lifted her high into the American audience esteem and even into some critical regard both here and in England, and for years the pictures of her, her long autumnal hair tumbled down over her shoulders and her eyes as full of soulfulness as a hungry Sealyham's, adorned the temples of dramatic art at home and abroad, next to those of Duse and Bernhardt. She is another who remains a legend.

Mrs. Carter, whose acting probably needs no description since it has been experienced by many who compose the present day audience, was an amateur propelled into the public consciousness through the combined agency of a sensational divorce case and that canny showman, David Belasco. By means of such hocus-pocus as made even Hermann the Great blush, Belasco contrived not only to put the lady over on the public but to have her accepted as an artiste of such virtuosity as had seldom been excelled within the memory of the oldest Greek. And to this moment there are many who still accept his coggery at its face value.

What all this leads up to is, as you have anticipated, the later-day phenomenon, Miss Mae West, the Valeska Suratt of the Walter Lippmann era. Valeska, you will recall, since she bloomed not so very long ago as the cock crows, was one who got where she did by following the principle that masculine nitwits will inevitably mistake affectedly half-closed eyes, provided only they be accompanied by the wriggle of a hip encased in a tightly fitting gown, for overwhelming sex appeal, and their chauffeuse for a delightfully naughty baby. Mae has followed Valeska right down the alley. She has, in point of fact, whether in the theatre or the moving pictures, followed Valeska down the alley ever since she showed up on the New York stage in the April of 1926 in a stint also of her own authorship called *Sex,* which was something.

Mae's acting technique is patterned after that of the chatelaine of an old-time *maison de joie,* which is to say the presentation of alumna sex elaborately pretending, with a measure of aberrant self-conviction, to be still one of the girls. And, despite its long employment, it is almost as effective today as it was when first she executed it. Mae West, in short, has made a name for herself largely through combining the Anna Held ocular technique with the bustle undulations of Corinne, adding to them a drawling nasal speech that suggests an Elsie Janis imitation of Ethel Barrymore, and fitting them all into the aloof indifference of the aforesaid Suratt. And that name has become as familiar to the masses as the names of Sherlock Holmes, Charlie Chaplin, and Elsie the Cow.

The great lady has, however, now made what seems to be the mistake of her life and it may conceivably in the long run cost her her previous large favor with the public. Aspiring to higher things, she has sought to establish herself as a more or less serious actress and has been rewarded with sighs of deep concern on the part of many in her erstwhile devout congregation. Her *Catherine Was Great* amounts to nothing more than a dirty-minded little school-girl's essay on the celebrated Russian empress, and her performance of the stellar role to little more than the kind of thing that used to be merchanted by third-rate road actresses in such overstuffed junk as *In The Palace Of The King, The Helmet of Navarre, The Sword Of The King* and *Under The Red Robe,* plus only a lot of hip-tossings, anal oscillations, and assorted leers. Our Mae has done herself and us wrong. And that way, for all the temporary traces of recalcitrantly remaining interest, lies eventual forgetfulness, and the graveyard.

Like *School For Brides,* Mae's play sticks resolutely to a single sex joke and might accordingly have saved her producer a lot of money had he skipped the redundant expensive sets, costumes and large cast and simply played it on a phonograph record. After Mae has rolled her hips for the two-hundredth time and nasally droned her glandular intentions in respect to most of the males in the troupe, even the staunchest West disciple feels faintly surfeited and would settle, with loud cheers, for Cornelia Otis Skinner in Bible readings.

Miss West is an all-right girl on her own account and her leers and drawls can still be amusing, but on this occasion she provided nothing to serve them. Her script amounts only to a painfully dull and wearisome French bedroom farce periodically interrupted by even duller and more wearisome excerpts from the history books, all already long familiar even to her Hollywood neighbors' school-children. And her attempts at humor, except in rare cases, are no better than confusing the Seven Deadly Sins with the Ten Commandments, allowing that the enemy guilty of murder, pillage and rape will be punished for the murder and pillage, and shovelling double entendre in freight loads in remarks about going to bed with Voltaire or Rabelais, making sure that the more backward customers will be spared undue embarrassment by carrying a book in her hand.

Miss Mae's entrances, of which there are ten or twelve, are further something to behold. Clad in a succession of gowns and head-dresses that might easily be mistaken for the Philadelphia Sesquicentennial lit up for a celebration of Benjamin Franklin's birthday, Miss Mae, to the accompaniment of a thunderous recording of Tschaikowski mixed with a little Harry Von Tilzer, emerges from time to time with such grandeur as hasn't been witnessed on the local stage since De Wolf Hopper knocked down half the cast and scenery of *Wang* by coming on atop an elephant.

Miss Mae is apparently the species of actress who deems it inexpedient and even slightly demeaning to make an entrance after the manner of some tramp like, say, Réjane or Bernhardt. Her epiphany must needs be heralded by a dozen court criers, must be preceded by a parade of guards with drawn sabres, must be orchestrated to a symphony of ecstatic oh's and ah's, and must be followed, lest the stunning moment prove too evanescent, by a bespangled satin train so long that it consumes another two minutes for its own entrance. Or, if the scene be laid indoors, she must effect a grand entry by holding up the action for a space of time almost long enough to permit the playing of the second act of *Strange Interlude,* by then appearing in a statuesque pose behind slowly parted velour curtains and, after a properly extended pause wherein to suffer the breathless admiration of the audience, by moving imperiously down a flight of steps, like Sousa's brass band in *El Capitan.*

It is a pity. Mae has in her the stuff for a gay evening. But, so far as Catherine of Russia is concerned, East is East and West is West and never the twain shall meet.

GOOD MORNING, CORPORAL
AUGUST 8, 1944

A comedy by Milton Herbert Gropper and Joseph Shalleck. Produced by William B. Friedlander for 13 performances in the Playhouse.

PROGRAM

CORPORAL ROURKE	*Joel Marston*	A MAN	*Donald Foster*
DOTTIE CARSON	*Charita Bauer*	ALVIN STACEY	*Lionel Wilson*
HELEN MOORE	*Frances Tannehill*		
O'BANION BRODERICK	*Russell Hardie*		

SYNOPSIS: Act I. *Morning.* Act II. *That night.* Act III. *Immediately following.*

The scene is Dottie Carson's apartment, New York City. Time. *The present.*

LIKE THE two antecedent offerings, this also fatigues itself with a single sex joke, in this case concerned with which one of three males will be the first to master the virginity of the heroine. The latter is a feather-brain who deems it her patriotic duty to marry men in the armed services in order that they may have something sentimentally to remember and fight for. Her resolve brings her a trio of husbands, since two who were thought to have been killed in action are found to be still alive. It also brings her what was hoped to be an hilarious comedy but what proves to be an importunate turkey.

The business opens with the antique situation of the young soldier and the heroine in bed, the former suffering from an acute hangover and, upon his dizzy awakening and surprised sight of his *vis-à-vis,* not aware that he has married her the night before. When finally he digests the news, he promptly and loudly claims his connubial rights, for twenty minutes. Presently the marine, whom the girl had married and thought dead, appears on the scene and in turn loudly claims his connubial privileges, for forty minutes. Then the sailor, whom she had married and thought defunct, shows up and loudly repeats the demand, for fifty-five minutes. The few minutes that are left of the evening are consumed by all three voicing the demand simultaneously and eventually leaving the great privilege to the soldier. At intervals throughout, everyone undresses down to undershirts, underdrawers, silk slips, pajamas and nightgowns, and thereupon instantaneously dresses again. And the bed is worked overtime for hypothetical comedy purposes.

The humor, when momentarily it departs sexual intercourse, takes the following forms:

1. Heroine: "I'm Dotty." Soldier: "You sure are!"
2. Soldier: "In civilian life, I'm a pedalogist." Marine: "A pedwhatagist?" Soldier: "I am a foot doctor, and Dotty's my wife!" Marine: "Humph, you couldn't support an arch!"
3. Marine (*surveying a full-busted woman in a tight sweater*): "If a sheep only knew where it's gonna end up!"
4. Soldier: "Why didn't you go to sleep at the Y.M.C.A.?" Marine: "I don't play handball."
5. Soldier: "She makes sense if you don't listen to the words."
6. Soldier: "You give me a pain in the neck." Marine: "You give me a pain when I sit down."
7. Soldier: "I'm a pedalogist." Girl: "Well, why not? Religion is free in this country."
8. Marine: "I was in a prison camp." Girl: "But not long enough."

Samples of the less direct sexual intercourse humor:

1. Marine: "That baby maybe can't find her way around in the daytime but, oh boy, does she know her way around when the lights are turned out!"
2. Girl (*advising Marine*): "I wouldn't sleep with Dotty." Marine: "What's the use of two women sleeping with each other?"

Samples of the direct sexual intercourse humor:

1–100: Consult the works of John Cleland.

The presenting company was of a piece with the play. The leading lady contented herself in acting her role largely with her eyes and nose, popping the former wide open to register interest and half-closing them in turn to register disinterest, and alternately elevating and dejecting the latter to indicate, respectively, hauteur and humility. The soldier hero didn't bother to go to all that trouble and composed his art for the greater part of the evening in simply popping his eyes wide open to register everything, including what he apparently imagined was infectious charm. The actress in the role of the leading lady's girl-friend relied, on the contrary, upon a variety of techniques, the techniques being, seriatim, a toss of the rear to convey lofty indifference and a double toss of the rear to indicate lofty contempt. And the actor who played the hardboiled Marine confined his role, save for the occasional making of a fist, to the back of his throat.

Warm weather failure No. 49.

SONG OF NORWAY. August 21, 1944

An operetta, book by Milton Lazarus based upon a play by Homer Curran, music by Edvard Grieg adapted by Robert Wright and George Forrest, with lyrics by same. Produced for a far beyond the season run by Edwin Lester in the Imperial Theatre.

Program

Sigrid	*Janet Hamer*
Einar	*Kent Edwards*
Eric	*Robert Antoine*
Gunnar	*William Carroll*
Grima	*Patti Brady*
Helga	*Jackie Lee*
Rikard Nordraak	*Robert Shafer*
Nina Hagerup	*Helena Bliss*
Edvard Grieg	*Lawrence Brooks*
Father Grieg	*Walter Kingsford*
Father Nordraak	*Philip White*
Mother Grieg	*Ivy Scott*
Freddy	*Frederic Franklin*
Count Peppi le Loup	*Sig Arno*
Louisa Giovanni	*Irra Petina*
Frau Professor Norden	*Doreen Wilson*
Elvera	*Sharon Randall*
Hedwig	*Karen Lund*
Greta	*Gwen Jones*
Margahreta	*Ann Andre*
Hilda	*Elizabeth Bockoven*
Miss Anders	*Sonia Orlova*
Henrik Ibsen	*Dudley Clements*
Tito	*Frederic Franklin*
Maestro Pisoni	*Robert Bernard*
Butler	*Cameron Grant*
Adelina	*Alexandra Danilova*
Maid	*Nora White*
Signora Eleanora	*Barbara Boudwin*
Children	*Sylvia Allen, Grace Carroll*

SYNOPSIS: Act I. Scene 1. *Troldhaugen (Hill of the Trolls) — just outside the town of Bergen, Norway. Midsummer's Eve — in the 1860's.* Scene 2. *A square on the outskirts of Bergen.* Act II. Scene 1. *Copenhagen — reception room of the Royal Conservatory. One year later.* Scene 2. *Rome — Tito's chocolate shop. One year later.* Scene 3. *Rome — ballroom of Villa Pincio.* Scene 4. *Troldhaugen — interior of the Grieg home. Some time later.* Scene 5. *The Song of Norway.*

This is still another in the line of theatrical presentations dealing with a noted composer and making use of his compositions. In this case the composer is Edvard Hagerup Grieg, whom Hans von Bülow dubbed the Norwegian Chopin.

Most of these exhibits follow a more or less familiar stage

pattern. In the beginning, we see the composer as a poor and struggling figure, his genius unrecognized save by a character actor who quaveringly admonishes, "Just you wait and see; just you wait and see!," and by the ingénue whose knowledge of music, if any, is scarcely indicated in her vocal interpretations of his melodies but who loves him, despite his whiskers.

Next, we engage him in a state of affluence and acclaim, his masterpiece finished and himself a lion, sought after by duchesses and barmaids alike. But he is not happy. What induces his misery commonly takes one of two forms. Either the lady of his heart, which is usually depicted as being inordinately timid, misunderstands his reserve and announces in a pique that she is to be the betrothed of some one else, or her parents, who opposed him in his days of poverty and neglect, alienate her from him by whispering to her that he has a mistress, the Baroness Ludmilla von Heishosen, who has been responsible for his pecuniary and social success. One or the other of these contretemps so disconcerts him that he either tears up his masterpiece or, if the librettist considers that going a bit too far in view of the historical record, vows he is done with composition forevermore.

In the final stanza, all is usually again set to rights and, to a fortissimo rendering by the entire company of whichever of the composer's melodies has been selected as the theme song, we behold him, now in talcumed hair or a gray wig, in contentful proximity to his lady love, with an emissary of the Emperor standing by with an invitation to spend the weekend at the palace.

In the movies, I am told, there have been a lot of two-reelers devoted similarly to lives of the great composers, interlarded in each case with those of their compositions that are familiar to the movie public from phonograph records. In that medium, I am further apprised, the business invariably follows much the same track, except that the composer never under any circumstances gets the inspiration for his masterpiece in surroundings other than an arbor constituted of obviously artificial flowers and never performs it on a piano or violin save the latter and himself are illuminated by a shaft of moonlight streaming through the window.

While the music in both the stage and screen exhibits is naturally more than satisfactory, the books in both cases may be said to leave something to be desired. The basic stories, adhering in sufficient degree to biography, may here and there not be too painful. But the persistent conviction of the authors that the box-office willy-nilly demands a leaven of comedy generally leads to grim disaster. To attend, say, an operetta treating of the life and works of Franz Schubert and to hear his lovely "Heidenröslein" followed by some small-time vaudeville joke like "'Marriage is an institution, but who wants to live in an institution?" is to induce the feeling in the judicious that the management has doubtless confused Schubert with Raymond Hubbell. Nor is there materially more comfort when one goes to a treatise on Johann Strauss, as one periodically has gone, and hears one of his beautiful waltzes interrupted by a pair of theoretical comedians exchanging banter on the altitude of Herbert Hoover's collars.

For one exhibit like Guitry's delicately charming *Mozart,* it seems to be our theatrical portion to get at least three or four which, except for the music, are in essence little more than old Harry B. Smith and Stanislaus Stange musical comedies, with only the latter's heroes given a maroon velvet house coat, wig, and accent. The plot procedure is generally identical: faith and hope, disillusion and despair, triumph and beatification. Substitute for the composer's music tunes by some Tin-Pan Alley illuminatus and one would not be able to differentiate between what is going on on the stage and what went on years ago when Helen Bertram left Ritchie Ling standing forlorn in the purple moonlight or vice versa, the while Gus Weinburg kicked Josie Sadler in the petticoat.

Though *Song Of Norway* does not depart signally from formula, its book enjoys at least one considerable virtue. Aside from a comedian's observation, upon grimacingly downing a cup of aquavit, that the toast should not be "skol" but "scald," there is a gratifying absence of the two-a-day jocosities which invariably go a long way toward wrecking such operettas. This alone is enough to recommend the evening to previous customers of exhibits of a piece who have been driven to bite their neighbors upon hearing something like "Roses From The Southland" accompanied by such facetiæ as "I am starved for love" — "Well, then, you'll have to go hungry for some time, kid."

Point No. 2 in the evening's favor is a company that not only can sing but that contains several players new to the Broadway theatre blessed with highly attractive personalities. In Helena Bliss, absurdly condemned in a couple of earlier shows to almost invisible roles and, in addition, to stand behind a potted palm where the audience couldn't see her without falling half-way out of its seats, the local operetta stage has acquired one of its most engaging young women and one who, to boot, both in the matter of voice and acting comportment is a delight and satisfaction. Irra Petina, formerly a member of the Metropolitan opera company, supplements her vocal talents with a surprising comedy equipment and maneuvers a role which in other hands might be torpid into a genuinely droll creation. As Grieg, Lawrence Brooks, an erstwhile night club singer, succeeds nicely in avoiding the suggestion of prosciutto usually encountered in the delineation of composer roles, and Sig Arno, a Hitler refugee, proves himself a welcome comic in the grand old bogus-elegance manner of Nineties.

The weakness of the exhibit, aside from the dialogue, lies in the dance and ballet department. George Balanchine, who in the past has sometimes acquitted himself rather handsomely, has been able to provide the present occasion with little more than stereotyped peasant dances, an obvious waltz ballet and, worse, a symbolic ballet concluding the evening that for supreme silliness has not been matched in some years. If the management had been wise, it would have eliminated that final choreographic nonsense, since not only does it unduly prolong the evening but minimizes the agreeable impression of what has preceded it. Had it let Grieg play his paean to Norway and let off-stage voices gradually take it up, the operetta would have achieved its right and proper curtain.

The Grieg compositions from which the songs have been derived include, among others, the A-minor concerto, waltz Op. 12, No. 2, the violin sonata No. 2 in G major, the nocturne and "Wedding in Troldhaugen," " 'Twas a Lovely Eve in June," "To Spring," "Water Lily," "The Brook" of the Haugtusse cycle, "Albumblatt," "Poème Erotique," "Springtide," "Waltz Caprice," "Ich Liebe Dich," "Woodland Wanderings" and "Peer Gynt."

LOWER NORTH. August 25, 1944

A comedy-drama, so-termed, by Martin Bidwell. Produced by Max J. Jelin for 11 performances in the Belasco Theatre.

Program

Hank	*Jerry Rand*
Peterson	*Frank Bradley*
Sobieschyk	*David Graham*
Cochran	*Dort Clark*
Heath	*Douglas Jones*
Johnson	*Dean King*
Curley	*Arthur Hunnicutt*
Bruce	*Robert Brenton*
Karnes	*Eddie Waglin*
Spadoni	*Robert Myers*
Jim	*Kim Spalding*
Pratzell	*Rusty Lane*
Phillips	*Bob Lackaye*
Barton	*Charles Clancy*
Mary	*Sara Anderson*
Johnny	*John Farrell*
Marine (Dress Blues)	*Royal Rompel*
Andy	*Don Grusso*
Frank	*Phil Pine*
Ruby	*Blanche Faye*
Pearl	*Blanche Gladstone*
Burks	*Paul Ford*
The Marine Sergeant	*John Conway*
Mr. Hines (Travelling Salesman)	*Watson White*
Phyllis	*Cora Smith*
Dorothy	*Flora Knight*
Messenger	*Mitchell Ahrons*

SYNOPSIS: Act I. *Upper deck of Group I. School building in a naval training station. Saturday morning.* Act II. *The Rendezvous Bar. That evening. Act III. The next morning — Sunday — in the cubicle called Lower North.*

The play derives its title from that quarter of a ship in which the sailors bunk. As drama, the play itself derives from the verb. The author, a Hollywood scenario writer, is reported to have gained his material at first hand but, in gaining it, he seems to have snooped around with a box of Max Factor movie makeup in his hand and a locket containing a photograph of Samuel Goldwyn around his neck. Purporting to depict the life of gobs at a naval training station, his exhibit resolves itself into a dramaless succession of episodes overblown with declamation which probably need only a few moving picture lot pretty boys and several so-called starlets with shapely figures to convert them into a Roxy stampede. Employing assorted types of young men from various sections of the United States and indicating their reactions to the new and strange existence into which the war emergency has thrust them, he is able to develop nothing from his characters but the old theatrical business of bringing them ultimately, after the usual doubts, bewilderments and disaffections, to the conclusion that "there are things in this world more important than we are and that must be fought for so that the future may be made safe for all the little people and that right may again prevail over wrong."

The embellishments include the stereotyped monologue by a marine returned from Guadalcanal, accompanied by the stereotyped recollection of its terrors, the conventional dormitory antics, the usual roadside saloon jive, the rubber-stamp business of magnanimously covering up one of the boys who has been away without leave, the sensitive lad whose brother is at the fighting front, the lanky youth from the corn-belt who drawls his philosophies about war, the officer who hides a tender heart under his gruff exterior, and, among other such stock characters and stock appurtenances, of course the never-omitted floozies. And collaterally, of course, the usual blanket talk about women and sex.

The author shares fundamentally in this last respect much of the juvenility of the majority of playwrights who concoct plays about sailors and men of the sea generally. Almost to a nose they adhere to the credo that sailors as a class are as overpowered by their sexual instincts as *Lepus cuniculus,* whereas foot soldiers, the cavalry, artillery, the air forces and all other branches of the armed services are relatively as chill and moral as an equal number of polar bears. Like the notion that all Frenchmen are such lovers that the female population of France hasn't had a good night's sleep since most of them went away on the first Crusade under Godfrey of Bouillon, the idea that American sailors in the mass are even more copiously glandular pops up in the theatre almost every time an actor comes on in pants that flare at the bottom.

That there are sailors given to miscellaneous sexual activity is unquestionably something of a fact, just as there are bookkeepers, cab drivers, and Senators. But that every last single sailor the moment he hits land, even the Congo, can not restrain his libido and comports himself like a combination Petronius, Cellini and Hollywood movie director is a little hard to believe. The basis of the hypothesis is a bit shaky as well, involving as it does the invigorating nature of the salt air which the sailor constantly breathes, his long periods of forced abstinence, the plain and hearty food he eats at sea, the stimulating regular hours, the enforced exercise, etc. Analysis finds most of such theoretical reasons for the tar's virility open to some skepticism.

The larger portion of the life of a sailor at sea isn't exactly like lounging in the breeze-swept palm court of the old *Berengaria*. For the small time he spends on the open deck there are many hours when he is somewhere down in the ship's innards, where the air isn't perceptibly more invigorating than in a Hoboken ginmill. Far from acquiring sexual desire, he instead finds it diminished by the exhausting routine of physical activities. The food which he eats aboard ship, while substantial, is not of the kind that contributes to anatomical incalescence and, in such cases as it is feared it may, is customarily dosed up with a depressant in the form of saltpeter. He often sleeps in a small hammock or hard cubicle which has a tendency to make an anchorite for days afterward of almost any man, even a movie actor. Long abstinence, in its paradoxical fashion, tends sometimes to minimize his sexual urge. And so on. The idea, incidentally, that long abstinence in itself is conducive to such amorous activity as would shame the heroes of all the plays that Tristan Bernard ever wrote would, if true, make any sailor look like an amateur in comparison with any Arctic explorer, jailbird, or smallpox victim. If the general conception of sailors is true, moreover, every highly respected admiral has a lot retroactively to answer for to his pastor, which is, of course, unthinkable.

Warm weather failure No. 50.

SLEEP NO MORE. AUGUST 31, 1944

A farce by Lee Loeb and Arthur Strawn. Produced by Clyde Elliott for 7 performances in the Cort Theatre.

PROGRAM

GEORGE SLATER	*Raymond Bramley*
SMITHERS	*John "Skins" Miller*
HARRY FOSTER	*John Kane*
DIANA CLARK	*Patricia Ryan*
MILLIE JENKINS	*Louise Larabee*
H. CLIFFORD GATES	*Robert Armstrong*
MR. RILEY	*Len Hollister*
WILLIAM JENNINGS BROWN	*George Offerman, Jr.*
DETECTIVE SERGEANT KRUMP	*G. Swayne Gordon*
MRS. RIDGEWAY	*Doris Underwood*
OSCAR RIDGEWAY	*Gerard Martin*
MR. MCCLELLAN	*Horace Cooper*
JOHN B. TIMMONS	*Ed Latimer*

SYNOPSIS: Act I. *George's barber shop. Morning.* Act II. *The "new" offices of H. Clifford Gates and Associates. Several days later.* Act III. *Same as Act II. Next morning.*

A THROWBACK TO the period of George M. Cohan's *Get-Rich-Quick-Wallingford,* Roi Cooper Megrue's *It Pays To Advertise* and their various imitations and paraphrases, the farce indulges in much the same plot shenanigan and much all the old other stuff. The present writers, however, haven't an iota of the skill of the earlier playwrights, nor an iota of their ingenuity and humor. Their effort, accordingly, is an arthritic zombie.

The plot deals again with the slicker who tries to capitalize on phony inventions, among them a mechanical hair restorer, a contrivance for persuading hens to lay more eggs, and a laundry machine that operates without soap and water. Just as things look black for him he comes upon a young man who has experimented with a pill that precludes the necessity for sleep. Seizing upon the idea, the slicker runs up orders to the tune of 3,000,000 dollars only to be stymied at the height of his success by the pill's discoverer himself falling a victim to Morpheus. The rest of the evening is occupied by his frantic efforts to get himself out of a hole. Although he extricates himself, he fails to extricate the play.

The first curtain isn't up one minute before an allusion to toilet paper and another to Yom Kippur firmly establish the witty virtuosity of the authors. The rest of the evening doesn't disappoint. A character dashing excitedly about the stage steps into a wire wastebasket, gets his foot caught in it, and can't get it out. Everybody rushes to hand a prospective customer a cigar and, when he puts one in his mouth, solicitously crowds around to light it for him. When a character whose wife has left him appears to be worried, another asks him if he fears she will not come back, whereat he replies that he is afraid she will. The mechanical contrivance for growing hair is adjusted to a customer's head and explodes. The male characters allude to the females as canaries, and dollars are called clams. And whenever a deal seems about to be closed, the three partners rush at one another and frantically shake hands. The only restraint indicated during these last or any other moments of the turbulent evening, and the only trace of originality, is in the authors' abstinence from the usually concomitant ejaculation, "Oh, boy!"

Final warm weather failure No. 51.

LAST STOP. SEPTEMBER 5, 1944

A play by Irving Kaye Davis. Produced by Victor Hugo-Vidal for 23 forced performances in the Ethel Barrymore Theatre.

PROGRAM

MRS. SHEPPARD	*Frederica Going*
MRS. CHUBB	*Enid Markey*
REV. MR. CUMMINGS	*William Hughes*
MRS. MANNING	*Mary Gildea*
MRS. HOLLISTER	*Nell Harrison*
MRS. MILLER	*Daisy Belmore*
MRS. SMITH	*Laurie McVicker*
MRS. DINGMAN	*Mary Perry*
MRS. FITZPATRICK	*Grace Valentine*
MRS. BALDWIN	*Augusta French*
MRS. MABLEDOOR	*Eda Heineman*
WALTER	*Seth Arnold*
CATHERINE CHANDLER	*Catharine Doucet*
MR. COOK	*Gregory Robins*
MRS. ANNA HAINES	*Minnie Dupree*
HOWARD HAINES	*Raymond Bailey*
ISABEL HAINES	*Mavis Freeman*
MARY STEVENS	*Effi Afton*
MR. WHITE	*Robert Stewart*
STATE TROOPER	*Clark Poth*
REPORTER	*Alan Brock*

SYNOPSIS: The action takes place in the parlor of an Old Ladies Home. Act I. Scene 1. *One Saturday noon. Early October.* Scene 2. *Later that afternoon.* Act II. Scene 1. *Evening. The next day.* (*Sunday.*) Scene 2. *The next day, about five o'clock in the afternoon.*

THAT THE WORST was to be feared on this occasion was clear to anyone familiar with Mr. Davis' antecedent bequests to the theatre. There are playwrights like that. It is, of course, not mannerly for a reviewer to stamp them in advance of each actual production, but there is nothing in the critical by-laws to prevent him from smelling them from afar, and smelling them from afar is the easiest thing he does. He knows — and long experience has proved him right — that any playwright who has indicated no slightest merit in the past and whose output has invariably consisted of zeros is not very likely to metamorphose himself suddenly into something of a dramatic genius, or even a moderately succulent fellow. There may be times when he miraculously turns out a play that is not quite so entirely bad as his previous plays, but not within the memory of the oldest theatregoer has he turned out one which has been much better than that and which has made his critics eat their earlier distasteful words.

Last Stop accordingly disappointed no one. It was just as dowdy as clairvoyant instinct had predicted. The idea of a home for aged females might possibly be developed by an adept playwright into a combination of sentiment and humor that would make for some theatrical entertainment. But Mr. Davis' conception of sentiment seemingly does not go much beyond having an inmate of such an institution elaborately fondle a doll and indulge in moist elocution about the aching need of motherly arms. And his humor resolves itself largely into such things as a faded inmate's insistence that when she was young she was a pretty saucy package so far as the men were concerned.

Mr. Davis, in short, has no imagination, no invention, and writes like one of the lesser contributors to the pulp magazines. One of his old, frayed women is thus presented as the coy, fluttery type who seeks laughter through her use of a perfume called "Lovely Forever." Another follows suit with an intimate allusion to Gypsy Rose Lee. Still another is made the low-comedy Irish type and goes in for remarks about toilet rooms. Another still is the typical deaf character who garbles the names of persons to whom she is introduced. And so on.

The dialogue is equally fertile. A male visitor to the home allows that he has seven children and observes that since seven is a lucky number he has decided to have no more, whereupon one of the old ladies admonishes him that eleven is also a lucky number. A woman quavers that she is ninety-two years old and another whimsically confides to the others that the woman is ninety-five if she is a day. There is badinage over the dropping of cigarette butts into the lavatory bowl. An aged inmate says that her birthday is three days hence and is asked what she intends to do with the three days, whereas another interrupts that she would want the three days to change her mind. An aged actress character reading a large book is asked what it is, replies that it is her press book, and is asked what she presses in it. It goes on as merrily as that.

The evening was further agonized by a double ear-strain. Not only did Catharine Doucet, upon whom fell the burden of outlining the plot, speak her lines so *pianissimo* that the audience had to guess what the plot was (which wasn't, however, too hard), but the air-cooling apparatus throughout the proceedings emitted a steady, loud whistling sound that drowned out even the guessing. Add to all this stage direction by Erwin Piscator which permitted the actors to dash madly hither and thither as if the old home were superintended by Sonja Henie; a son, daughter and daughter-in-law who could not afford to support an old mother yet who were allowed to dress in the height of fashion and to wear enough jewelry to stock Tiffany's window; and the poor old mother herself in a modish pink frock topped by a Lilly Daché flowered bonnet; and you get not only a picture of the whole but probably the jitters.

There is further reason to doubt whether an audience's reaction to a play about a lot of destitute women is materially assisted when it observes in the program that the paupers' shoes, stockings and hats are the creations of very soigné artisans.

Although, along with butlers and policemen, old women's roles are relatively easy to play and are generally certain of audience acceptance, the performances by the actresses on this occasion were mostly so poor that they provided an exception to the hokum rule.

THE DAY WILL COME. SEPTEMBER 7, 1944

A play by Leo Birinski. Produced by Harry Green with Harry Green in the leading role for 20 performances in the National Theatre.

PROGRAM

BARANOVA	*D. J. Thompson*	FRANZ	*Richard Bolton*
SHURA	*James Dobson*	GENERAL VON BRUCK	*Arthur Vinton*
ARTAMON	*Bruce Halsey*	CAPTAIN BIRKENBACH	*Ronald Alexander*
FYODOR SEMIONITCH	*John Paul*	SERGEANT	*William Forrest*
MARPHA	*Jan Sherwood*	GENERAL GENSLER	*Stephen Roberts*
PARASHA	*Camila Ashland*	GENERAL ZIEMSEN	*Bernard Pate*
NIKITA	*John F. Hamilton*	GENERAL VON HOFF	*William Pringle*
MOSHKO	*Sterling Mace*	ADOLF HITLER	*Brandon Peters*
KOLYA	*Ronnie Jacoby*		
ANUSHKA	*Lenore Thomas*		
AVRUM DOVID	*Harry Green*		
KARL	*Frederick Coe*		

SYNOPSIS: The action of the play takes place in a Russian Isba. Act I. *Afternoon.* Act II. *Two days later.* Act III. *Four days later.*

THIS IS STILL another paraphrase of the Wandering Jew theme by a playwright who in the years before the war contributed at times to the pleasure of the lighter Central European stage. In this serious essay he has not, however, contributed to the satisfaction of the American. Mixing realism with symbolism and fantasy, he has tried to picture a meeting between Adolf Hitler and a patriarchal Jew on the steppes of Russia during the march on Moscow and has succeeded only in doing very badly by a basic theme that has been handled with immeasurably more skill and persuasion by the authors of *Jacobowsky And The Colonel.*

The fundamental difficulty with the play, as with the majority of others of a kidney, is that, like a set piece of fireworks, one knows more or less exactly what will ensue even before the match is applied. The theme of Jews and their persecutors, especially when treated by the persecuted themselves, is bound to follow the single, familiar track; the setup of the characters is inevitably obvious; and the philosophies expressed are fully those anticipated.

That sincerity and passionate conviction are the portion of the authors of such exhibits is plain. Yet sincerity and passionate conviction, though conventionally praised by the generality of reviewers as if they were *desiderata par excellence,* are frequently responsible for some very bad plays. An intense belief in a theme may conceivably help a playwright, but it may just as conceivably debilitate him, since it obscures those facets of vagrant imagination, critical selection, and humor which might greatly improve his work. Sincerity is as often the attribute of hacks as of geniuses. Passionate conviction is as frequently the mark of amateur intelligences as of great poets. Shaw's early sincerity and conviction produced only such an inferior play as *Widowers' Houses;* some of his finest plays, like *Caesar And Cleopatra,* were the result of subsequent tongue in cheek. Brieux's passionate assurance contrived such claptrap as *Damaged Goods;* when he left off indignation and smiled sardonically at himself he turned out something like *Les Hannetons,* one of the best and most intelligent comedies of our time. The same with Maugham. His one play doubtless profoundly felt by him, *For Services Rendered,* does not compare with the best of his light comedies, written, he once confided to his friends, simply to get the money to buy some good real estate properties in London. I have known Eugene O'Neill long and intimately. Of all the plays he has written, *Days Without End* is, I believe, closest to his inner self, and it is one of his very weakest. Sincerity and passionate conviction, in our American drama, have given birth chiefly to the stage stuffs of such second- and third-raters as Augustus Thomas, Charles Rann Kennedy, George Broadhurst, and Charles Klein. Birinski's share of the qualities has blinded him in the writing of drama of merit.

That *The Day Will Come* is high-minded may be allowed. That it is at the same time tedious to an equally high degree is the demonstrated fact. After less than an act of it the interest evaporates, and all that is left to the auditor is the reflection that these refugee authors had far better revert to the kind of plays they wrote before the war and apply their indignation, righteous and wholly to be sympathized with, to the book rather than to the dramatic stage form.

As if conscious of his lack of humor in the face of his theme and as if appreciating from experience the necessity arbitrarily to incorporate a little on behalf of the box-office, Birinski has recourse to such infirmities as "There isn't a worse headache in the world than a wife who is a headache," which further enfeeble his already feeble play. And even further enfeebling it in production was a stage set supposedly representing the interior of a small Russian peasant cottage which more closely resembled the Maisonette Russe in the St. Regis Hotel; peasants in the grip of muddy war as spick and span as the chorus in Rimsky-Korsakov's *The Girl From Pskov;* makeup on Harry Green as the Wandering Jew that suggested Monty Wooley even further disguised as Santa Claus; a Hitler in the person of Brandon Peters who looked disconcertingly like Franklin P. Adams and acted like Willie Howard; and stage direction by Lee Elmore that treated the script simultaneously like Simonov's *The Russian People* and Jerome K. Jerome's *The Passing Of The Third Floor Back,* with faint overtones of *Uncle Tom's Cabin.*

DOWN TO MIAMI. September 11, 1944

A comedy by Conrad Westervelt. Produced by Edgar MacGregor for 8 performances in the Ambassador Theatre.

Program

Torrence Applegate	*Herbert Heyes*
Mrs. Applegate	*Merle Maddern*
Rufus Applegate	*Charles Lang*
Helen Gunston	*Lyn Logan*
Stella	*Anna Franklin*
Morris Mandel	*Robert Leonard*
Mrs. Mandel	*Dora Weissman*
Harry Katz	*John Gould*
Gloria Mandel	*Elaine Ellis*
Lois	*Robert Strauss*
Waiter	*Zac Caully*
Michael O'Hara	*Brian O'Mara*

SYNOPSIS: The entire action of the play takes place in and around the Rooney Square Hotel in Miami Beach. Act I. *The Terrace breakfast room, late morning.* Act II. *The lounging room of a private bathing suite, that afternoon.* Act III. *The Mandel suite, the following afternoon.*

Here, beyond much doubt, is the worst play shown on the New York stage in the last quarter-century, surpassing in complete hopelessness such past triumphant horrors as *Love's Call, The House Of Doom, Reprise,* and even, impossible as it seems, this very season's *A Strange Play.* A paraphrase of *The Cohens And The Kellys, Abie's Irish Rose* and other such conspiracies wherein the stroke of eleven p.m. proves to be an irresistible catalyzer of Jews and Gentiles who fifteen minutes earlier have not been able to stand the sight of each other, it achieves signal eminence by virtue of the fact that its author apparently knows nothing of playwriting and supplements his virtuosity in that direction with a total lack of originality, humor, taste, and acquaintance with the dramatic elements of the English language. He fashions his entire goose-egg around a single point, to wit, that a Gentile girl and a Jewish boy can not swim, whereas the Jewish boy's sister and the Gentile girl's brother can, thus making both couples inevitably preordained for the marriage altar. And he hits this single note for the entire two and one-half hours without deviation of any kind, save possibly for a few moments when the Jewish father discourses on the high prices of food at Miami hotels and an extraneous Irish policeman sings "Mother Machree" for no other reason than that the producer seemingly discovered that the actor engaged for the role had once been in a musical comedy troupe.

The occasion was further enriched by stagehands who could not manage the setting up of the elaborate scenery and who conducted their grievances so volubly and audibly when the several curtains were down that the audience in turn found it impossible to conduct its own grievances on the odor of the play itself.

Speculation on how any such verjuice ever came to be produced was partly explained away by a newspaper interview by Edgar MacGregor, the impresario, several days before the opening. In it, Mr. MacGregor, who announced that the play "had cost 46,000 dollars in actual money and will show it," indicated, despite some experience in the theatre, that he knew less about plays than even about audiences and critics. *Down To Miami,* he emphatically affirmed, was an audience play not a critics' play and its appeal, which he trusted would be great, would be rather to the countless people who relished the formula species of drama. He then nevertheless promptly dispatched reviewing seats to all the critics, which under the circumstances appeared to be in the nature of a gratuitous invitation to smallpox.

The play, as noted, is an incontrovertibly bad play, yet where, notwithstanding, did Mr. MacGregor get the idea that the critics invariably dislike bad plays? He should get around more. Looking over the records, it seems that the critics, or at least an appreciable number of them, have liked a lot of bad plays which audiences, to whom Mr. MacGregor was much too condescending, would subsequently have nothing to do with. In evidence whereof, let Mr. MacGregor analyze *Variety's* annual critics' box scores.

Conversely, where did Mr. MacGregor get the further idea that critics and audiences do not often like exactly the same kind of plays, irrespective of quality? Study the catalogue of plays that have achieved the longest runs in our later-day theatre and, from the years of *The Bat* down to *Life With Father,* it will be found that nine times out of ten the tastes of the critics and audiences have coincided. If, furthermore, it be argued that the long runs were simply a consequence of the critics' good notices and hence no exact proof of the identity of tastes, reflect that many plays in the same long period which received equally good, if not much better, notices achieved runs hardly visible to the eye.

Since Mr. MacGregor's offering, as observed, vaguely resembled *Abie's Irish Rose,* it is likely that he had that nonesuch in mind when he indulged in his interview. *Abie's Irish Rose,* true enough, was not what Mr. MacGregor elects to describe as a critics' play and, though most of the critics didn't like it, it still turned out to be an audience play of hefty proportions. But what does that prove? It proves nothing and only confuses the MacGregor logic thrice over. The critics, to come closer to the moment, didn't like nine out of the thirteen plays produced just prior to *Down To Miami* and neither did the audiences, with the result that the plays either closed in quick order or continued desperately at a financial loss.

Some years ago, the late Edgar Selwyn paved the way for Mr. MacGregor and his interview. He also gave out that a play of his, *Anything Can Happen,* was not a critics' play but an audience play and that the critics wouldn't care for it. They didn't. The audience didn't either, and the play shut down instanter.

Mr. MacGregor observed yet further that *Down To Miami* would appeal only to people who like the old formula sort of thing. How, to pursue the argument, did that in his mind eliminate the critics? If ever there was an instance of the old formula sort of thing in drama we have had it in *Anna Lucasta,* and the great majority of the critics have loved it.

The only sliver of intelligence indicated by Mr. MacGregor was in his statement that the critics wouldn't like *Down To Miami.* He certainly had something there. But he goes down to the end of the class for his belief that audiences would. On the opening night there weren't enough people left in the house after the second act to fill a telephone booth. On the second night the intake was fifty-five dollars. On the third night it was forty-five. Thereafter, the show played only to the ushers.

STAR TIME. September 12, 1944

A variety show. Produced by Paul Small at $2.50 a head for 120 performances in the Majestic Theatre.

Principals

Lou Holtz, Benny Fields, the De Marcos, the Berry Brothers, Shirley Dennis, the Mulcays, the Whitson Brothers, Armand Cortez, Francine Bordeau, and George Prospery.

Aside from Lou Holtz, who resembles a bored non-Aryan Noel Coward, acts like a bored Aryan Willie Howard and was as comically juicy as ever, and the De Marcos, who never danced more attractively, one might just as well, so far as vaudeville was concerned, have gone up to Central Park, looked at the seal, and saved money. It is possible that vaudeville may not yet be dead but Mr. Small, the present entrepreneur, had need of a lot better sulfa drugs, aside from the two specified, to persuade his critics of the fact.

Even when acrobats are good I, for one, will give you all of them for a single joke like Holtz's about Honeysuckle Epstein and his automobile that went so fast a pursuing cop thought his motorcycle had stopped and got off. And when, like the Whitson Brothers, they indulge in what they imagine to be humorous conversation while performing their tricks, I'll give them to you for not even the joke. You may also have for a cent male crooners like Benny Fields who, resplendent in Broadway tuxedos, vocalize like blast factories into microphones, accompany themselves by tapping their left feet, and emphasize the final notes by sweeping their opera hats off their heads. And for the same cent, or one like it, I'll present you with all the super-blondes like Shirley Dennis who evidently admire Betty Hutton out of all proportion and scream their songs into a microphone, the meanwhile vibrating their torsos and throwing italic fists at the audience. And when, like Miss Dennis, they conclude their handsome bequests by making exits beaming and bowing like so many Flagstads at the height of latter's careers, I'll let you owe me the cent.

I further am not overly enchanted by harmonica players, aside maybe from Larry Adler, and then not much. So far as the Mulcays plus microphone go, I do not consider that a charge of two cents would be unduly swindling you. As for the Berry Brothers and their Negro strutting and cane-twirling, I have seen them do the same routine for so many years now that the only variety they impart to any so-called variety show lies in their color. And the sketch performed by the Messrs. Cortez and Prospery and Mlle. Bordeau was stale stuff even before a Lambs Club Gambol some years ago cabbaged the idea from one shown in the Paris revue theatre at least twenty-five years before.

Previous to the opening, Mr. Small issued a statement saying that rather than waste money on expensive scenery he preferred to give the customers entertaining performers. To accomplish this, he stated that it would cost him 13,500 dollars a week to operate the show, the chief expense item being Holtz's weekly honorarium of 3,000 dollars. If Mr. Small had raised Holtz's reward to 4,000 dollars, had allowed the 750 dollars for the De Marcos, and had booted the rest of the performers, he might have saved 8,750 dollars and would still have had a very much better show.

WHILE THE SUN SHINES
September 19, 1944

A comedy by Terence Rattigan. Produced by Max Gordon for 39 performances in the Lyceum Theatre.

Program

Horton *J. P. Wilson*	The Duke of Ayr and Stirling *Melville Cooper*
The Earl of Harpenden *Stanley Bell*	Lieutenant Colbert *Alexander Ivo*
Lieutenant Mulvaney *Lewis Howard*	Mabel Crum *Cathleen Cordell*
Lady Elizabeth Randall *Anne Burr*	

SYNOPSIS: The action passes in the sitting-room of Lord Harpenden's chambers in the Albany, London. Act I. *Morning.* Act II. Scene 1. *Eleven o'clock at night.* Scene 2. *Four hours later.* Act III. *Morning.*

THE INCREASING general decline of the English theatre is to be appreciated in no more rueful manner than by contemplating what has happened, for instance, to its comedy writing, once and long its boast and joy. With John van Druten having renounced his British citizenship and now sometime since in the American fold, there remains no younger writer of any even remotely sound quality in that field, and the older men are either on the retired list or have indicated a calamitous ebb. Noel Coward still occasionally tosses off one of his powdered baubles, which in the prevailing drought is slavered out of all degree to its merits, and once in a while some other middle-aged youth or less pubescent writer contrives a specimen that gets by with the no longer particular London audience, but not since Ashley Dukes delivered *The Man With A Load Of Mischief* has a single comedy of authentic style made an appearance. Mr. Rattigan, the author of the present importation, provides a first-rate example of the besetting condition.

In *French Without Tears,* Mr. Rattigan's directly previous comedy, three men make a play for a provocative young woman who keeps them on emotional pins and needles. In this *While The Sun Shines,* his latest, three men make a play for a provocative young woman who keeps them on emotional pins and needles. Mr. Rattigan may not be said to be a man of boundless imagination.

There is nevertheless something that may be said for him. Unlike so many other young English playwrights, he deals with the emotions of normal people, which comes as a relief. For some years now we have been treated in English imports to so much degeneracy, perversion, and psychopathic aberration that the mere sight of a character putting his arms around a woman and kissing her is in the nature of a sensational dramatic event.

Review these British benefactions in the later seasons. In one, *Night Must Fall,* we were regaled with a pervert whose pleasure consisted in murdering females, cutting them up, and treasuring their severed heads in hat-boxes. In *Love From A Stranger,* we were invited to attend a diseased intellect whose passion was marrying for the delight it provided him in strangling his successive wives. In both *Wise Tomorrow* and *Love Of Women,* on the other hand, we were bidden to relish the spectacle of Lesbian amour. And in a number of plays like *Oscar Wilde* we were requested in turn to observe additional manifestations of homosexuality. *They Walk Alone* attempted to enchant us with a female pervert whose sensual gratification was achieved through letting the mortal blood out of any male corpus with which she came into contact, and *Murder Without Crime* sought to elevate us with not one but two male degenerates, one a sadist and the other a blighted neurotic who couldn't control his homicidal eccentricities. *Design For Living* offered us a pretty picture of impertinent effeminacy, and *Point Valaine* a male whose reaction to females was to spit into their faces. *Black Limelight* promoted a nyctalopian curio who, whenever darkness fell, could not resist the impulse to make away with any female he encountered; *Guest In The House* gifted us with a woman whose taint took the form of insinuating foul thoughts into the minds of other women; and further exhibits like *Ladies In Retirement, Angel Street, Hand In Glove, The Stranger, et al.,* have bespoken our notice with an increased variety of morbid, depraved, and rotten fruits.

Under such circumstances an occasional London importation, whatever its lack of quality, which deals with people one might possibly encounter this side of a clinic has something, albeit slight, to recommend it to an American theatregoer who, while not in the least concerned with morality, has nevertheless been surfeited with endless amateur treatments of its opposite.

Mr. Rattigan, whose play amounts to little more than a machine-made box-office tool, rusted, has gone down deep into the old wastebasket for his observations and his characters. His young Earl who talks about class distinctions in reverse is a quotation from John Drinkwater's *Bird In Hand* of sixteen years ago. His cadging, reprobate old Lordship is out of French comedy of the remote Caillavet-Flers era. His whimsical prostitute of the ingratiating manner stems from Frederick Lonsdale's *Spring Cleaning* and two dozen plays before and since. His amorous Frenchman is the rubber-stamp amorous stage Frenchman of the last sixty years. His manservant with the impeccable manner is an alumnus of more English plays than one can remember. His American with his "wows," his slapping of women on their rears, and his general "homely charm" is the recognizable character out of English and Continental exhibits without number. And his young woman of the aristocracy who succumbs to the attractions of a commoner has in one form or another already appeared in so many plays on both sides of the Atlantic that it would take an adding machine to arrive at the figure.

His devices are not less familiar. The woman who tries to hide a tear professes to have got a cinder in her eye, although George S. Kaufman's otherwise passable direction permitted so ceaseless an eye-blinking on the part of most of the other actors, notably Anne Burr and Lewis Howard, that at times it seemed almost everybody in the cast had suffered cinders. The lovers who play their sentimental scene back to back is the same old childish invention that we got regularly in the plays of the De Mille *The Lost Paradise* era, which was some fifty years ago. The exhausted butler who tries vainly to get a needed wink of sleep on the drawing-room couch is recalled from the period of R. C. Carton, which was some forty years ago. The scene in which Lady Elizabeth becomes intoxicated and warms up to a stranger is a paraphrase of one of the frequently used scenes in plays of the *The Man From Blankley's* epoch, which was also some forty years ago. The lady of position who enters the house unexpectedly and is mistaken for the lady of loose morals who was expected has been in evidence in one shape or another since the days of the Elizabethans, which was some centuries ago. And so on.

I do not know the play in its original form but, though the program failed to note the fact, it is clear that Mr. Kaufman has toyed with any number of the lines. The allusions to the OWI and to the whiskey being of the pre-Roosevelt period; the reference to an apartment being known in England as chambers, with the duly anticipated joke about chambers; the American woman who married a title and is now working at Woolworth's; such slang as wise-guy; the whimsy about Mistinguette — these and other garnishes have an unmistakable Kaufman ring to them.

The play, in short, has a few amusing moments, among them his Lordship's idiotic telephone conversation with a crony who seems to be still at the racetrack at midnight and his Lordship's speculation as to whether the horses haven't probably gone home, but it gradually peters out into nothingness and ends on a curtain that might profitably in view of patent padding have been lowered at least fifteen minutes earlier. Like the remark about a negligible man of whom one can't think to say anything better than that "he has a nice face," it may also charitably be allowed that the play has a nice face. Its externals are fairly acceptable. But its internals do not make the slightest impression.

Melville Cooper, acting his Lordship in broad musical comedy style, was personally a humorous delight, despite the obtruding scent of his materials. As the American bombardier, Lewis Howard looked like a younger Wendell Willkie and acted like a Lennie out of a *Of Mice And Men* directed by Helena Rubinstein. Alexander Ivo, as the Frenchman, comported himself elaborately like the usual stage Frenchman; Stanley Bell, as the young Earl with Adam's apple, evidently admires Noel Coward as a pin-up boy and patterned his acting accordingly; Cathleen Cordell, as the good-natured trollop, was savoury; and Anne Burr, as Lady Elizabeth, confused her larynx with her nose.

KORB'N. September 20, 1944

A melodrama by David Blum. Produced by Modern Play Productions, Inc., for 24 performances in the Provincetown Playhouse.

Program

Sally Klein	*Josephine Lombardo*
Abraham Cohen	*John Francis*
Sammy Cohen	*Robert Feyti*
Harry Shulman	*Noah Jason*
Joe Berkowitz	*James Gale*
Mr. Caplan	*Cae Johnston*
Mr. Mandelbaum	*Peter Zube*
Jake Goldberg	*Ralph Arnold*
Agnes Ryan	*Sally Hughes*
Isidore Shulman	*Joseph Di Stefano*
Harold Stern	*Melvin Davis*
Mrs. Blumenthal	*Blanche Rohmier*
District Attorney	*Norman Danneman*
Rabbi James Goldstein	*Cornelius T. Frizell*
Joe Snyder	*Raymond Lehrer*

The scenes are laid in the Cohen apartment, the pressing-room of a dress factory, a slum street, and a courtroom. Place. *New York City.* Time. *1935.*

THE AUTHOR ATTEMPTS a saga of a young labor union agitator which begins with his desertion of his fiancée that he may give his all to the cause and ends with his arrest as the killer of a scab workman. The writing is at once intense, like jungle fever, and unrelievedly amateurish. Mr. Blum is evidently a life subscriber to the *New Masses;* he might better have invested some of the money in plays like Hauptmann's *The Weavers* and Galsworthy's *Strife.* Like many another novice who looks to the small alley theatres for an outlet to his sociological indignations, his dramatic competence is hardly of a piece with his passion to show the world what is wrong with it.

The presentation in its entirety, including the acting, was on the minor apprentice side, and the Provincetown Playhouse once again lived down to its later-day reputation.

THE ODDS ON MRS. OAKLEY

October 2, 1944

A farce, originally and successively called It Runs In The Family, Fanny *and* Our Fanny, *by Harry Segall. Produced by Robert Reud for 24 performances in the Cort Theatre.*

Program

Oliver Oakley	*John Archer*
Susan Oakley	*Joy Hodges*
The Professor	*Morton L. Stevens*
Eddie	*Ben Laughlin*
Dennie	*Hildegarde Halliday*
Gladys	*Virginia Reed*
Sam	*Allen Kearns*
Louie	*John Effrat*
La Verne	*Betty E. Haynes*
Jim	*Don Darcy*
Jim's Wife	*Sally Gabler*
Howard Stickney	*Bruce MacFarlane*

SYNOPSIS: Act I. Scene 1. *Private booth in safe deposit vault of bank. Noon.* Scene 2. *Turf Club cocktail lounge at race track. A year later.* Scene 3. *Susan's apartment. Three months later.* Act II. Scene 1. *Turf Club cocktail lounge. Three months later.* Scene 2. *Susan's apartment. Two weeks later.* Scene 3. *Same. Evening. Ten days later.*

The Present Time. *New York City.*

The chances in these later years that any kind of play dealing with a race horse will be of popular entertainment value are small, and the contribution in immediate question proved to be no exception. Half a century ago, even a quarter of a century ago, things were different and a host of melodramas and comedies concerned with such animals caught the fancy of the public. They ranged all the way from melodramas like *In Old Kentucky* and *The Whip* and comedies like *Checkers* to melodramas like *Blue Grass* and *The Derby Winner* and comedies like *The County Fair* and, with minor variation, usually promoted either the spectacle of a horse being affectionately kissed on the nose by the heroine, for whom the winning of the race meant life or death, with the words, "Go in and win, Rosebud, go in and win, and God bless you, darling!", and then being led offstage for a race subsequently described by the wide-eyed and breathless heroine to the audience, or the spectacle of the race itself on a treadmill which made so much noise that the audience generally thought the winning jockey must be General Phil Sheridan.

These plays were shortly followed by others, mainly comedies like *Wildfire,* which while abandoning the treadmill still did not forego the kiss on the horse's nose, and farces like *If I Had Money,* in which the horse was kept offstage and its track activities again frantically reported on by several male characters whose fortunes rested on its superior speed. But it was not long thereafter that the public taste, which even then had given unmistakable signs of surfeit, resolved the signs into fact, and salads of the species soon went into the discard, at least temporarily. After a proper lapse of time, however, they began intermittently, though in negligible number, to reappear but, with one exception, without the success which they formerly enjoyed. That exception was *Three Men On A Horse,* shown in 1934. Other exhibits like, for example, *Horse Fever* quickly expired from lack of public interest.

The approach to the subject in the more recent years has uniformly altered. Whereas in the earlier periods the theme was, as noted, handled in terms of melodrama or comedy, it now became primarily the material for farce. No longer, apparently, were audiences willing to expend their emotions trembling in their seats over the ritual of two or three nags exerting themselves on a rotary apparatus on behalf of a mortgage on the heroine's old home or the salvation of the hero's economic future from a knave who had thought cunningly to insert a splinter in the favorite's foot. And no longer, it seemed, were they to be cajoled by the relatively milder form of entertainment wherein it was difficult to determine whether the genial little hero, often either a track clocker or a young man of reputable antecedents whom the fates had made a bookie, was in love with a woman or a mare. With the endless repetitions, the whole business had become laughable — and farce was arbitrarily the only way out. Thus the horse itself disappeared permanently from the stage, and the only time one has been viewed by an audience in many years was in the beforementioned farce, *Horse Fever,* in which the poor beast was arbitrarily brought on for a few moments solely for burlesque purposes.

The horse farces, such as they have been when they have showed up at all, have confined the performances of the animals to the wings and have visited what racing the audiences have been permitted to see upon the actors. These latter have most frequently been directed into such speed contests against the scripts as have made the old treadmill chases seem sedentary. Matters came to the point, indeed, where members of an audience who were racetrack devotees would willingly have backed a director like George Abbott against War Admiral, and would have laid liberal odds. And it again wasn't long before evidence presented itself that the customers of such entertainment had begun to lose their enthusiasm for selling-plater farce maneuvered into a semblance of the thoroughbred species, nor was it longer that it became clear that if farce dealing with racing were to survive at all someone would have to write one that had something to recommend it aside from the old-time basic plot mechanics and the new-time directorial confusion of the actors with the horses.

Mr. Segall's attempt was simply another in the line of corpses. It revolved about a race horse, the divided property of a divorced couple that won only when in the custody of the woman, which throughout the evening was kept off-stage and never appeared. Mr. Segall made a big mistake. If he had brought the horse on and kept his actors off his farce might have gained some of the velocity that it lacked and sorely needed. Furthermore, not only pace but humor, which is widely rumored to be a desirable element of farce, was similarly concealed in the wings. In its stead the author trotted out the oldest joke in racing play history, "Don't you believe in reciprocity?" with the query, "What race is he in?" and followed it up with such beauties as "My ears burn" with the retort, "If you're wrong, something else about you will burn!"; "What'll you drink?" with the answer, "Just plain soda — with Bourbon"; "You can have a pair of my nylons" with the husband's reply, "Thanks, but they're not my size"; and divers simultaneous plays on the horse's name, Fanny, and the posteriors of the ladies in the company. Things continued in that tempo until toward the end of the evening, when the author's invention achieved a grand climax in the report of the race over a radio.

The stable of actors included, among other spavined histrios, a choice leading woman who alluded to one of the male characters as a "congeneral idiot" and, whenever the script demanded that one character or another proclaim, "Gosh, you're beautiful!", acquiescently screwed up her features like a corduroy sponge, the meanwhile furiously opening and shutting her eyes, painted a rich Navy blue, like the doors in an 1890 French farce. And the stage direction had the company indulge in so ceaseless a walking around tables, chairs, sofas, and floor lamps in the belief that it constituted dramatic action that by ten o'clock the actors were almost as exhausted as the audience.

Mr. Reud, the producer, is reported to rely upon astrology for guidance in his theatrical activities. On this occasion he might better have consulted a book on theatrical statistics and saved himself a deal of money. He might have learned what astrology apparently didn't reveal; to wit, that, along with plays about baseball, plays about horse racing haven't with the single exception previously noted made a nickel in the last twenty years.

MEN TO THE SEA. October 3, 1944

A play by Herbert Kubly. Produced by Dave Wolper for 23 performances in the National Theatre.

Program

Hazel	*Maggie Gould*	Reuben	*Maurice Ellis*
Christabel	*Toni Gilman*	Howard Moore	*James Alexander*
Nic	*Joe Verdi*	Hyacinth	*Mildred Smith*
Madame Mosh	*Grace Mills*	French Sailor	*James Elliott*
Julie	*Joyce Mathews*	Dick Graham	*Frank Etherton*
Bonnie	*Susana Garnett*	Hughes	*Bill Hunt*
Joe Foster	*Tom Noonan*	Tall Girl	*Mary Jean Copeland*
Duckworth	*Randolph Echols*	Red	*Marguerite Clifton*
Brophy	*Richard Camp*	Harry	*Paul Crabtree*
Chauncey	*Michael Strong*		

SYNOPSIS: Act I. Scene 1. *Christabel's room on the first floor of a rooming house in Brooklyn, late afternoon of September of a war year.* Scene 2. *Christabel's room the next afternoon.* Scene 3. *Hazel's room, late that night.* Scene 4. *Christabel's room, an evening ten days later.* Act II. Scene 1. *Hazel's room on Christmas Eve, four months later.* Scene 2. *A gun tub on the deck of the destroyer Christabel, on Christmas Eve.* Act III. Scene 1. *Christabel's room on an evening in the first week of the following June.* Scene 2. *Christabel's room at twilight two days later.*

The chief interest provided by the play was in the moral alarms it set into motion. Its theme, the infidelity of the wives of sailors in the armed forces, so aroused the indignation, patriotic and otherwise, of various people and was so denounced out of hand during the New Haven and Boston try-out period that the gravely disturbed management was driven, previous to the New York engagement, to call its publicity agents into the breach with excerpts from two sources attesting to the theme's substantiality. The first was from an article in *Time* which allowed, among other things, that an Army chaplain had said, "American women have failed their fighting men. The men come in and tell me that they are going to divorce their wives. After a man has flown seventy or ninety missions over Europe, laying his life on the block to protect his home and then finds his home has been wrecked by infidelity, there is little I can tell him to convince him he should forgive and forget. I know of one G.I. married ten years who got a letter in Kiska from his wife asking him for a divorce. A pilot in the Thirteenth Air Force on Guadalcanal, also married for a long time, got a letter from his wife whom he hadn't seen for eighteen months saying, 'I'm pregnant. I'll explain when I see you.' "

Fearing that this single testimonial might not be sufficiently convincing, a second was hurled at the skeptics by way of a devastating climactic punch. It was from no less authoritative a source than Dorothy Dix's syndicated newspaper column and was signed "Five Desperate Girls." It read: "We are five girls who are very close friends and now we all face the same difficulty. Just before Pearl Harbor we met five Army officers with whom we fell in love and married. Because of parental objection we kept this a secret. Now our husbands are insisting that we reveal our marriages and come to them, but the trouble is that one of our group is going to have a baby who is not the child of her husband, and if we go back to our husbands it will expose our double lives to our parents. Also, our husbands will know that we have been untrue to them. We had planned to go to a distant city and get work. There the baby would be born and could be given for adoption and neither our parents or the husbands would be the wiser. And if we refuse to go to our husbands, they will suspect that we have been untrue and demand to know why we did not come to them. What would be the best thing to do?"

That the umbrage of the moral objectors to the play was not materially lessened by the document was perhaps to be explained in their pardonable suspicion that it was the sly work of the play's management, since the play was found also to deal with five wives, one of whom was also going to have a baby not an issue of her husband, and with the others in the main also untrue to their lawful mates.

Although objection to the play on grounds of patriotic

morale was understandable, objection to it on factual grounds, despite such touching evidence as provided by Miss Dix, was open to some question. And assuredly there could be no sound condemnation of it on dramatic grounds, since the theme of a wife's infidelity to a husband long away has without improbation served the drama for innumerable years, even the drama in uniform. What entertained the critic was rather the moralists' apparently tacit, if under the circumstances somewhat puzzling, acceptance of infidelity on the part of the husbands. Things would seem to be looking up in moral quarters.

In both New Haven and Boston virtuous indignation reached such a pitch that further performances were possible only after all kinds of excisions were made in the script and all kinds of changes made in the staging. In New Haven, for example, a figure of the Virgin was peremptorily ordered out on the ground that the characters were indulging in sex talk, though the idea of substituting for it a figure of Christ was genially endorsed.

In both cities the authorities forbade a slight jazzing up of the hymn "Silent Night" and nothing could persuade them to alter their stand. "You can't do that with a song that's religious!" they affirmed. It is apparent that the education of the authorities in question has not embraced religious music in any of its phases. "Onward, Christian Soldiers" is, in the words of a late Harvard professor and able critic, "set to the militant religiosity of Baring Gould's un-Christ-like words," and has been frequently used as a football song. The "Good Friday" music from *Parsifal* is, as everyone else knows, of sexuality all compact and follows a puzzled wonder over the gayety of Nature on the Day of Agony. Honneger's "King David" oratorio is not without its jazz passages, and "Yes, We Have No Bananas" is derived in part from Handel's "Hallelujah Chorus." There are points in common between "Nearer, My God, To Thee" and that old booze party favorite, "Goodbye, My Bluebell." And the variations upon "Silent Night" to which the authorities wrathfully objected were foreshadowed years before in a ragtime parody called "Silent Newt," which never got a complaining peep in Boston when sung by the visiting minstrel show troupes.

Men To The Sea is a poor play but it is not a dirty or a blasphemous play and the Boston censure of it was only a further sign of that city's psychosomatic morality. I do not like dirt whether in ears, steamed clams or the drama, but if the bedroom scene in Kubly's play is dirty, as Boston insisted it was and ordered deleted, then the bedroom scene in *The Voice Of The Turtle,* which Boston passed and which isn't dirty either, nevertheless is or should be twice as dirty from the Boston viewpoint. As for New Haven and its attitude toward religious music, matters are probably to be forgiven, since it is obvious that its moral cops' musical experience does not extend much beyond "Boola Boola."

Kubly's effort to mix religion and sex has been far from fortunate in the eyes of drama criticism, but no one may contend that he has not been perfectly honest in his effort or that he has been deliberately and calculatingly smutty. His play, muddled and amateurish though it be, is as a matter of fact a lot cleaner than any number of plays with similar themes which have been welcomed by church and lay authorities.

This whole business of plays that touch on religion calls for a going-over in the interests of censorship clarification. If *Men To The Sea* is censorable, what, for example, of some of the early Passion Plays — the *Passion Of Revello* for one, or of the early Festival Plays — *The Feast Of The Ass* and *Feast Of Fools* for two, or of the early Mystery Plays — *The Baptism Of The Virgin* for one? And when it comes to what in the moralists' eyes is sacrilegious, why not go the whole hog and consider, yes consider even today, at least in New Haven and Boston, the treatment of the cloth in Sudermann's *The Fires Of St. John,* Synge's *The Tinker's Wedding* and Henry Arthur Jones's *The Crusaders* and *The Hypocrites*? To say nothing of in the plays of Ibsen, Hauptmann, Björnson, and others? If we must have censorship, let us, to repeat, at least try to get a little logic into it.

It is a far cry from the wives of absent Army flyers as

depicted by Moss Hart in *Winged Victory* to those of absent sailors as depicted by Kubly. Whereas Hart saw his girls entirely in terms of such tutti-frutti dialogue as "Oh God, if they don't come back I don't think I can bear it!", Kubly sees his for the most part in terms of such as "Jeez, if they do come back they'll catch us, damn it, with our boyfriends!" Since my social life, such as it is, hasn't brought me into contact with the lonely wives of either flyers or sailors, I am not one to say which of the two pictures is the more accurate. But since my critical life brings me into contact with all sorts of plays, I can say that, poor as it is, Kubly's is at least the better of the two, which isn't saying much, or in fact anything at all.

It is often the mark of a novice playwright — this is Kubly's first effort — either to oversensationalize sex or to view it dreamily as a kind of Swedenborgian deep-breathing exercise. Kubly does both at one and the same time. It is also often the mark of a novice to accompany the latter treatment with quotations and parallels from the Scriptures, interlarded with little touches of one or another of the romantic poets. Kubly duly indulges not only in the parallel of Jesus and the Magdalen but of Hosea and Gomer, and quotes François Villon, somewhat copiously, on the side. When the sex gets particularly hot, he even has recourse to Chaucer. Good plays, alas, are not written that way.

The heavy mixture of realism and symbolism, the latter involving the old business of falling autumn leaves and altar lights that hint at death by suddenly going out, would be a difficult hurdle for any director and it was to Eddie Dowling's credit that he managed to jump it theatrically with a measure of his old-time skill. Here and there the ingredients of the play led him into a strained and false ecclesiastical pattern, but in the main he succeeded in bringing some stage life to what was essentially merely a dummy upon which a valid playwright might have draped the materials of sound drama.

SOLDIER'S WIFE. OCTOBER 4, 1944

A play by Rose Franken. Produced by William Brown Meloney for 252 performances in the Golden Theatre.

PROGRAM

KATHERINE ROGERS	*Martha Scott*	ALEXANDER CRAIG	*Glenn Anders*
FLORENCE LANE	*Frieda Inescort*	PETER GRAY	*Lili Darvas*
JOHN ROGERS	*Myron McCormick*		

SYNOPSIS: Act I. *An evening in late summer.* Act II. *An afternoon in early fall.* Act III. *Several days later.*

The action of the play takes place in the Rogers' apartment in Manhattan.

The time is the present.

FOR ONE ACT the author has tried to write a play about the readjustment of the married life of a young wife and her returned soldier husband, has then given it up as a bad job and for the two following acts has turned it into a kind of parlor vaudeville that has next to nothing to do with her initial theme but that, while maybe not quite so amusing as Lou Holtz, is nevertheless not without its moments of entertainment. As a play the evening, considering some of Miss Franken's previous work, is a dark disappointment, but as a variety show in masquerade it is periodically diverting in its later stretches.

When the author, at the outset of the proceedings, sets herself to consider the problem of marital equilibration she discloses herself to be of a starkly superficial mind. When she throws the problem out of the window that same superficiality stands her in good stead, since nothing obviously would be so damaging to vaudeville as a suggestion of mentality, which was sufficiently proved last season in the depressing *Chauve-Souris.* As a fabricator of theatrical confetti she is superior to a philosophical wit, as may be appreciated from such of her attempts in the latter direction as "People who have gone through things are never sentimental." Her observations, too, are essentially out of the old mothbag as, for example, "There's nothing that makes you feel sadder than hearing a train whistle at night," along with things like "the mystic look in soldiers' eyes." And her dramatic writing, involving such hoary lines as "I don't know whether to laugh or cry," actually resorts to such even hoarier devices as "You say he's due here at 4:30; why, it's almost that now!" As a playwright of critical merit, Miss Franken is here with small standing in the community.

It is rather as a parlor entertainer that she earns, as the French say, her beefsteak. In that capacity, she occasionally gets off some fairish nifties and rewards the light in mind and heart with a pleasant triviality. Even if one be not given to uncontrollable spasms over jokes about new antique furniture and corned beef and cabbage there are probably others to serve as a periodic anodyne.

What the consignment in the aggregate amounts to is, however, little more than a paraphrase of its author's *Claudia* commercially designed for devotees of the art of trained seals and ZaSu Pitts. It is only intermittently, as noted, that some humor derived from character and palatable to the more particular taste emerges. Miss Franken has talent and even when she deliberately sacrifices it to the box-office, as in this case, it can not entirely resist her. But it is to be regretted, since she doesn't need the money, that she does not continue to apply her gifts to the more reputable drama as represented by her last season's *Outrageous Fortune*.

She is also surely above the brand of much of the humor which she peddles on this occasion. When, in addition to the samples before mentioned, she places in the mouth of her pro-tem bachelor character such stuff as "The nearest I'll ever get to a baby is the Stork Club"; when she goes in for such Hollywood jokes as the one about people having two big houses with swimming pools and living in hotels; when she follows them up with the wife's whimsy that her husband is acting so sweetly one would think he wasn't married to her; and when, not content with the other stale jocosities about Hollywood, she indulges in the one about it making no difference whether a writer for the movies can write — when she vouchsafes such frayed and faded minstrelsy, one is to be forgiven for wishing to spank her apparent passion for easy mazuma. After all, there is such a thing as pride, or should be.

She even goes to the extent, in general cheap writing, of merchanting lines like "How would I know what's going on in that foolish little head of yours?" As the author of the before-noted *Outrageous Fortune* she must shudder while she pockets the box-office intake.

In the role of the young wife, Martha Scott once again confused the business of gazing intently with set, open eyes with the business of convincing "listening." Myron McCormick indicated some development as a comedian in the part of the soldier husband, though his pink makeup was a bit confounding in view of the wife's remark, upon his return from the battle front, that he was so awfully brown. Glenn Anders, as the much married bachelor, handled what occasional humor was provided him with droll effect; Lili Darvas, as the editor of a woman's page, was quite charming for all one's speculation as to what an Hungarian was doing on the *Herald Tribune;* and Frieda Inescourt had little to do, and did it, in a sister-in-law role that was mainly seated on a couch and instructed to be sedate.

BLOOMER GIRL. October 5, 1944

A musical show, music by Harold Arlen, lyrics by E. Y. Harburg, and book by Sig Herzig and Fred Saidy from an unproduced play by Lilith and Dan James. Produced by John C. Wilson in association with Nat Goldstone for a far beyond the season run in the Shubert Theatre.

PROGRAM

Serena	*Mabel Taliaferro*	Hiram Crump	*Dan Gallagher*
Octavia	*Pamela Randell*	Dolly	*Margaret Douglass*
Lydia	*Claudia Jordan*	Jeff Calhoun	*David Brooks*
Julia	*Toni Hart*	Paula	*Lee Barrie*
Phoebe	*Carol MacFarlane*	Prudence	*Eleanor Jones*
Delia	*Nancy Douglass*	Hetty	*Arlene Anderson*
Daisy	*Joan McCracken*	Betty	*Eleanor Winter*
Horatio	*Matt Briggs*	Hamilton Calhoun	*Blaine Cordner*
Gus	*John Call*	Pompey	*Dooley Wilson*
Evelina	*Celeste Holm*	Sheriff Quimby	*Charles Howard*
Joshua Dingle	*Robert Lyons*	Augustus	*Hubert Dilworth*
Herman Brasher	*William Bender*	Alexander	*Richard Huey*
Ebenezer Mimms	*Joe E. Marks*	State Official	*John Byrd*
Wilfred Thrush	*Vaughn Trinnier*	Governor Newton	*Butler Hixon*

The action takes place in Cicero Falls, a small Eastern manufacturing town, in the spring of 1861.

THE GREAT SUCCESS of the show suggested that audiences were beginning to be *gobemouches* for almost anything in the old Americana line. With *Oklahoma!* pointing the way and with this contribution following suit there was promise of similar baits invoking a lucrative nostalgic response from souls born long years after the particular periods dealt with but vicariously permitting themselves knowing and expansive sighs over times and places which they never experienced and could accordingly hardly either recall or miss. When next they disclose a show about, say, the tender, simple, innocent life in the Chicago of 1886 and I observe the audience wistfully basking in its pathos-of-distance I am going to get the more venerable members of it to join my venerable self in putting on forthwith a revival of the Haymarket riots, which somehow inconsiderately horned into the picture in the same year.

Aside from some handsome sets and costumes by Lemuel Ayres and Miles White, the exhibit, though hailed by most of the reviewers with adjectives that made the Ringling Brothers' press agents seem like mutes, with writer's cramp, escapes my powers of appreciation. So torpid are the proceedings that even a pair of Agnes de Mille ballets augment its pace. The book, despite a valid enough idea in aligning an orthodox manufacturer of hoopskirts against a female champion of bloomers, is heavily overblown and dreary. There is so much talk in the first of the two acts that I began to feel that I had perhaps got into the wrong place and was at a party over at Dorothy Thompson's, with George Sokolsky. And when it comes to humor, I find it very easy to restrain any excessive mirth over such lines as "I want bosom companions, not just bosoms" or over a confusion of the word "posterity" with "posterior." I am not awfully particular; I have even laughed once at Zero Mostel; but if stuff like that constitutes the height of wit, as some of my colleagues imply, I am too weak to scale it.

There was also a deal of enthusiasm over Mr. Arlen's score. Just how anyone with the slightest appreciation of music could persuade himself that a juke-box tune like "Evelina" was nigh Mozartian in its compositional beauty or that any of the rest of Mr. Arlen's songs were enough to make Victor Herbert turn green with envy in his grave and drive Jerome Kern and Richard Rodgers into shamed hiding remains something of a puzzle. And no less a puzzle were the tributes to the striking originality of Mr. Harburg's lyrics having to do with "It Was Good Enough For Grandma," "Rakish Young Man With The Whiskers," "Farmer's Daughter," and "When The Boys Come Home."

The presence of a Negro male singer was similarly the occasion for considerable rapture on the part of most of the reviewers and all of the public. However, it generally is. Bringing a Negro male singer into a show these days has taken the place of bringing on the Marines in those of other days. It saves the situation when things do not look too good. Let a show give signs of sagging and all one seemingly has to do to restimulate the customers is to introduce a colored man, preferably a deep bass or baritone, and dress him in a blue shirt and ragged trousers. It seldom misses. Whether he has talent or not doesn't especially matter; the customers are sure to applaud him by way of handsome indication of their lack of race prejudice and their admirable, democratic openmindedness. It is accordingly next to impossible for a Negro to fail on the stage nowadays. I certainly do not mean to reflect on Negroes in the slightest; I am all for them. But just the same they have a big edge in the theatre over their white brothers and sisters. If you don't believe it, consult the records. Not one colored actor and but one colored actress in the drama or on the musical stage has in the last half dozen years got the bad break that many of the whites occasionally have.

Returning to the matter of the show's book which, as noted, enjoys a substantial basic idea and one possible of amusing treatment, the Hollywood Messrs. Herzig and Saidy have made nothing of it. The feud between the rich hoopskirt manufacturer and his sister-in-law patroness of pantalettes, with his daughter rebelliously siding with her aunt, is resolved into little more than an obvious paraphrase of some such time-dishonored musical show plot as the objection of a father to his daughter's marriage to the man of her heart, with the main theme itself confined largely to the period costumes. In addition, the twain have seen fit, by way of posing themselves as possessors of an acute if somewhat belated social consciousness, to overload their story with so considerable a to-do about women's rights, abolition of slavery and such that about the only thing which they seem to have neglected is a consideration of Stephen A. Douglas' advocacy of squatter sovereignty in terms of the New Deal. And when they are not intruding such questions into their book they are introducing so much news about the firing on Fort Sumter, the early production of the controversial *Uncle Tom's Cabin* and like cullings from the *Encyclopædia Britannica* that one waits momentarily for the Pony Express, the first visit to America of the Prince of Wales, the appearance of Jefferson Davis, and a courier, covered with paper snowflakes, bearing the tidings of Queen Victoria's proclamation of neutrality.

The theory that musical show books must generally and necessarily be that bad, to which one or two of the acquiescently enthusiastic reviewers in this case have committed themselves, has been blown up so often in the past that one would think it long discarded. Any number of books from the days of Harry B. Smith and Henry Blossom, and before, to the more recent time of *Show Boat* and *Music In The Air* and a half-dozen others have been eminently acceptable. The book of *Bloomer Girl,* too, might easily have been bettered with a little imagination. The scene in the former bordello which now serves simply as the headquarters of a journal published by Dolly Bloomer and her aides, for example, might have been made genuinely amusing by introducing some of the girls who were formerly quartered therein, who have been on their uppers ever since the women's emancipation crusade got under successful way, and who protest heatedly against the ruinous new order of things. The eventual triumph of the campaign for bloomers as opposed to hoopskirts might similarly have been made satirically amusing by a rebellion of the men against the hideous habiliments, their determined neglect of the women made ugly by them, their pursuit of the first girl to show up again in lace panties, and the women's realization that, while emancipation in other directions may be meet, they can not emancipate themselves from feminine apparel and at the same time retain any sex appeal and hold their men. It would be simple to indicate various other such changes that would give the present routine book a little flavor.

The lyrics might also prosper from a bit of invention. The obviousness of Topsy's song "I Never Was Born" is implicit in its title. A lyric proudly attesting to her possible illegitimacy and specifying by name all her famous historical illegitimate relatives might have helped, as might such an improvement on the emancipated women lyric as a doubtful speculation on just how much better a time after all such emancipated old girls as Susan B. Anthony, Carrie Chapman Catt, Frances Willard, Lucretia Mott, and Elizabeth Cady Stanton were going to enjoy in the world.

As for the Arlen music, it might have been ameliorating simply to have Walter Donaldson's old "Carolina In The Morning" in place of its paraphrase "Evelina," which is hailed as the show's masterpiece, or the old time "Ida" of blessed saloon memory instead of a gratuitous revamping.

Among the members of the troupe singled out for encomiums were Celeste Holm and Joan McCracken, both of whom had appeared previously in *Oklahoma!* Miss Holm is a prepossessing young woman but hasn't sufficient voice or a sufficiently strong personality to carry the leading role in a musical show which is essentially so passive that a scene on a doubly passive small town Sunday morning becomes the most exciting item in it. And Miss McCracken, who received such notices as in the past were customarily reserved for Ada Rehan, again merchanted a performance that for riotous cuteness probably has not been matched since the human doll act last appeared in the vaudeville halls. Someone should speak paternally to Miss McCracken and confide to her that making with the eyes, arching her posticous bulge, girlishly tossing her head about like a badminton quill, and comporting herself assiduously like a coy lambkin does not quite contribute to the impression that she is another Yvonne Printemps.

THE MERRY WIDOW. October 7, 1944

A return engagement of the Franz Lehár-Victor Leon-Leo Stein operetta, with a revised book by Sidney Sheldon and Ben Roberts and with lyrics by Adrian Ross. Produced by the New Opera Company for a 4 weeks' engagement in the City Center Theatre.

Program

The King	*John Harrold*
Popoff	*Karl Farkas*
Jolidon	*Nils Landin*
Natalie	*Xenia Bank*
Olga Bardini	*Lucy Hillary*
General Bardini	*Gordon Dilworth*
Novakovich	*Alan Vaughan*
Cascada	*Dennis Dengate*
Khadja	*Alfred Porter*
Nish	*Norman Budd*
Sonia Sadoya	*Marta Eggerth*
Prince Danilo	*Jan Kiepura*
Clo-Clo	*Lisette Verea*
Lo-Lo	*Annette Norman*
Frou-Frou	*Mary Broussard*
Do-Do	*Babs Heath*
Margot	*Alice Borbus*
Jou-Jou	*Annette Norman*
Premiere Danseuses	*Babs Heath, Nina Popova*
Premier Dancer	*Jack Gansert*
Gaston	*John Harrold*

SYNOPSIS: Act I. 1. *Prologue.* 2. *The Marsovian embassy in Paris. A summer evening in the year 1906.* Act II. *Grounds of Sonia's house, near Paris: the following evening.* Act III. *Maxim's restaurant, Paris, later that same evening.*

Following a return engagement of eleven performances, beginning on September 27, of Helen Hayes in the shabby Ryerson-Clements treatise on Harriet Beecher Stowe called *Harriet,* the City Center pursued its theatrical activities with a return showing of the Lehár operetta in a performance which was a withering come-down from that offered in the Broadway production in the previous season. The two occasions gave still further dubious pause in the consideration of the basic merits of the municipality's theatrical scheme which up to this point had still resolved itself into a mere second-hand showshop, and for the major part a very poor second-hand one at that.

It has been argued that one of our contemporary theatre's greatest ills is the poverty in new playwriting talent and that the only hope of developing it lies in the establishment of professional community theatres and municipal theatres like this City Center. That the poverty exists there is little disputing, but that such theatres as are prayed for would quickly remedy the situation and give miraculous birth to a carload of whiteheaded young playwrights calls, I fear, for disputing of somewhat larger bulk.

The independent smaller theatres in the communities and colleges which have been in existence for some time now have not noticeably produced any considerable number of new, young gifted writers. In point of fact, with the exception of the Messrs. Richardson and Berney, authors of *Dark Of The Moon,* they have given birth to little or nothing. And even in such exceptional cases as they have uncovered some traces of talent they have rarely furthered them and have left the job to the impeached Broadway theatre. And as for other experimental theatres, they have not produced anything of any real merit in years.

In this last connection, the monitors are ever pointing back to Eugene O'Neill. It is true that the little Provincetown group gave O'Neill his first hearing, but only because O'Neill wanted it to be the first to give him a hearing. And it gave him a first hearing only with one-act plays. His initial full-length play was seized by the so-called commercial theatre immediately it got wind that there was such a manuscript. You may take my word for it, since I myself sent it along to a producer, the first to see it, who read it overnight and put it on as soon as he could. And if that same producer, John D. Williams, had been able to get hold of the one-act plays ahead of the Provincetowners he would gladly have produced them just as quickly.

It took the Broadway theatre and its collateral guilds and groups to give a hearing to Saroyan's best work, whereas the provincial little theatres have in the main contented themselves with his minor efforts, some of them very bad. Broadway and these contributory groups, not the theatres dreamed of by the visionaries, gave the early Lillian Hellman, S. N. Behrman, John Steinbeck, Ernest Hemingway, Rose Franken, Maxwell Anderson, Laurence Stallings, Robert Sherwood and Sidney Kingsley their first chances, as they did Clifford Odets, George Kaufman, Moss Hart, Marc Connelly, Elmer Rice, George Kelly, Sidney Howard, Robert Ardrey and almost every other playwright of any subsequent consequence of whom one can think. The non-Broadway theatre, on the other hand, rests its case wholly on Paul Green, Susan Glaspell, Arnold Sundgaard and several such others, of whom only Green has critically later amounted to anything.

Broadway gave the Maurine Watkins of *Chicago* a chance when no one else would. It gave the Hatcher Hughes of even *Hell-Bent Fer Heaven* a chance, and the Zona Gale of *Miss Lulu Bett,* and the Robert Turney of *Daughters of Atreus.* Damned for its commercialism and for its apathy to ambitious playwrights, it nevertheless has gambled its money over the years on such poets, often impracticable, as Lynn Riggs, Stanley Young, T. S. Eliot, Brian Hooker, and others. And it has been the Broadway theatre or its allied interests, not the hinterland art centers, that have brought to light all the more recent hopeful novices like William Bowers, Alexander Greendale and Margaret Curtis.

The idea, furthermore, that civic theatres would be the answer to a maiden playwright's prayer is on the doubtful side. Look at this New York venture in that direction, for just one weathervane. Thus far in its life it has confined itself simply to reproductions, mainly defective, of established Broadway plays and musical shows, and the only new talent it has given a chance are the ushers. To believe that the institution of a professional community theatre or a municipal theatre in, say, Toledo, Ohio, or Scranton, Pennsylvania, would result markedly otherwise and uncover such local dramaturgical genius as has not been heard of in the world since Molière showed up in the French provinces on the back of a wagon takes some rather heroic believing.

The pre-war German municipal theatres, which were

always pointed out in other countries, including our own, as being all that such theatres should be, were not the cradles of dramatic talent. That talent for the greater part first saw the light in other German theatres, as the records attest.

However, blaming Broadway for every misservice in the catalogue has become a habit and one can no more change it than one can get a waiter, for all one's prayers and injunctions otherwise, to serve one iced tea without the habitual slice of lemon. Broadway, true enough, is not without its faults — I could, if urged, nominate maybe two or three thousand — but its faults are hardly those almost always nominated in turn by its critics.

Another of the latter's indignations, for example, is Broadway's indifference to the classics. It is true that Broadway is not particularly noted for any steady enthusiasm in the way of revivals of the finer drama of the past, but neither for that matter, so far as I am able to make out, are the remote-from-Broadway theatres which are customarily whispered to be hotbeds of culture. The otherwise meritorious Pasadena, California, Playhouse, for one such, has indicated a much more consistent interest in revivals of Kaufman and Hart, George M. Cohan, Maxwell Anderson and Sidney Howard than in revivals of Sophocles, Aristophanes, Corneille, and Shakespeare. And the other admired theatres of a kidney have not to my knowledge concerned themselves unduly with the classics. But Broadway at its worst has at least given us productions in the last dozen years of no less than sixty-six of the classics, ancient and modern, and included have been the works of Sophocles, Shakespeare, Strindberg, Ibsen, Sheridan, Wycherley, Molière, Shaw, Rostand, Chekhov, Wilde, Gogol, Yeats, Synge, *et al.* Which isn't too terribly bad.

Urging as a cure for Broadway's grim malaise the further launching of theatres by municipalities, Arthur Hopkins, who is one of the current leading Thersites, has had this to say over the radio: "When cities take as great pride in their theatres as they do in their baseball teams, America will be growing up culturally and spiritually. That day is coming.

It is my hope that this radio program (*Arthur Hopkins Presents*) will accelerate its arrival."

Just how a radio program featuring such Broadway box-office plays as *The Late Christopher Bean, The Male Animal, Mr. Pim Passes By,* and *The Philadelphia Story* will assist in the cultural and spiritual growth of the nation appears to be Mr. Hopkins' secret.

Mr. Hopkins is a fine and upstanding fellow, and in his day served the theatre dutifully, but like so many complainants does not, one suspects, always ring the bell. "The economic burdens of the commercial theatre make venturesome production prohibitive," he says. He is right only to a degree. The economic burdens of the Broadway commercial theatre are certainly heavy, but they nevertheless have not made venturesome production prohibitive. All kinds of such venturesome productions have not only been made but have turned out to be financially successful. The trouble is that there simply are not enough venturers.

Among these venturesome productions that have succeeded in more recent years for all the alleged prohibitive cost have been *The Skin Of Our Teeth, The Time Of Your Life, Shadow And Substance, The Children's Hour, Abraham Lincoln, Juno And The Paycock, Winterset, Of Mice And Men, Death Takes A Holiday, The Glass Menagerie, The Last Mile, The Green Pastures, Uncle Vanya,* and *The Cherry Orchard.* Also *The Barretts Of Wimpole Street* (after 27 producers had refused to be venturesome), *Mourning Becomes Electra, Tobacco Road, Russet Mantle, Family Portrait, Ethan Frome, Lady Precious Stream, Our Town, Oscar Wilde,* and *The White Steed.* Also, and if you want further examples of venturesomeness, *Arsenic And Old Lace* and *Carmen Jones.* And that is only a small part of the story.

Mr. Hopkins' final, devastating criticism is as follows: "I believe the day is gone when America can look to Broadway for dramatic sustenance. More each year it becomes exclusively an amusement center."

Where, aside from the classics, one may ask, is this dramatic sustenance of which the good gentleman speaks?

Broadway can not be expected to produce what does not exist, and if the dramatic sustenance is lying around unnoticed, I, for one, would like to learn just where it is lying. If it is around, why, furthermore, doesn't Mr. Hopkins himself produce it? The answer is plain. There is a tragic shortage of worthy dramatic scripts these days, both American and European, and Mr. Hopkins himself well knows it, since he has for some time now bemoaned his inability to find anything to which he might give proud production.

Another thing. What is so dreadful about amusement? I leave the answer to that one to Mr. Hopkins and the reader.

THE MIRACLE OF THE WARSAW GHETTO
OCTOBER 10, 1944

A play by Harry Levick, with incidental music by Sholem Secunda. Produced by Joseph Green and Jacob Ben-Ami for 9 weeks' performances in the New Jewish Folk Theatre.

PROGRAM

LONE MAN	*Solomon Krause*
SEXTON	*Moishe Belawsky*
REB ARYE	*Morris Strassberg*
LEIBUSH	*Isaac Rothblurn*
EISAK	*Michael Gibson*
YIDDEL	*Ben-Zion Katz*
COURTYARD EMISSARY	*Jacob Mestel*
BLACKSMITH	*Misha Fishsohn*
FRIGHTENED MAN	*Max Rosen*
YOUNG WORKER	*Gene Benton*
COURTYARD EMISSARY	*Goldie Lubritzky*
GRANNIE GITTA	*Dora Weissman*
ISRAEL	*Jacob Ben-Ami*
REB YITZHOK	*Menachem Rubin*
YECHIEL	*Isidor Casher*
JOSEPH	*Michael Goldstein*
WANGURSKY	*Abraham Teitelbaum*
WANDA	*Dina Halpern*
ESTHER	*Berta Gersten*
RACHEL	*Muriel Gruber*
DAVID	*Mark Topel*
VICTOR	*Maurice Doner*
REPRESENTATIVE OF POLISH UNDERGROUND	*Morris Strassberg*

LAID IN the Warsaw ghetto in the April of 1943, the play has to do with a devout Jew who, returning from Lublin, learns that his family has been annihilated by the Nazis but in whom the ethics of race are so deeply rooted that he protests the vengeance of force. "That is not the eternal Jewish way — with a knife in one's hand," he philosophizes. As doom darkens, however, he slowly comes to understand the true significance of the uprising of his racial brothers and, convinced that he must battle "not only for the Name of God, Kiddush Ha-Shem, but also for the dignity of man and the dignity of his people," goes forth to do his share.

The play, so far as I could gather from the printed synopsis and from the pantomime of the actors, is an overemotionalized melodrama adorned with rituals of the Hebrew faith and, while seemingly stirring to its lay audience, is rather too much in the "In the name of God, do not despair" spirit, one fears, to satisfy any critic versed in its language and competent thoroughly to understand and appraise it. Some of it, even to one alien to any real comprehension of it, appears to have a certain folk quality and a measure of vitality. But that remains largely guess-work.

Preceding the play on October 7, a bi-lingual show by Isadore Friedman called *Good News* was offered for 205 performances in the Second Avenue Theatre. A mixture of musical comedy and war-background romantic drama, it offered Menasha Skulnik, the pet clown of the Yiddish stage, in stale vaudeville give-and-take with Yetta Zwerling, clad in a wardrobe resembling a riot in a paint factory, and Miriam Kressyn and Max Kletter in a succession of moist love ditties. The chorus and ballet were hardly in the Ziegfeld tradition. I may safely report that much, since eyes are eyes in any language. My animadversions on the stale vaudeville give-and-take are also open to small question, since it was as wholly recognizable in the alien tongue as it long has been in the English. And the same holds for the songs with their accompanying profuse sentimental eye-blinking and the general stage business.

At approximately the same time a musical comedy, *They All Want To Get Married,* with a book by Julie Berns and tunes by Al Olshanetsky, was displayed in the Public Theatre, also very successfully. The cast included Max Wilner, Lucy Gehrman, Aaron Lebedeff, Diana Goldberg, Nina Rochelle, and Irving Grossman. The plot, as obligingly related to the uninitiated by the friendly press agent, "opens with a novelty chorus seeking mates and a dummy bride and groom in a store window coming to life and telling them that marriage isn't all it's said to be. The tale tells of a match-maker who, attempting to escape from would-be brides, hies to the Catskills. The dramatic interlude deals with a refugee, fleeing from Europe after killing a couple of Nazis, who later finds her mother in America." The press agent obliged further by confiding that the story was "very light, yet sincere and often funny," and added that the exhibit "will, I believe, do more to erase racial prejudice than any single medium."

Make up your own minds.

The New Jewish Folk Theatre followed its production of *The Miracle Of The Warsaw Ghetto* with, on December 19, a drama by David Bergelson called *We Will Live,* dealing with "the invasion of a Ukrainian town and the attempt of the Nazi commander to extract the secret of a formula conceived in a Jewish scientist's laboratory." The play was condemned by various reviewers acquainted with its language as "hackneyed," "over-long," and "generally dull." It nevertheless enjoyed a fair run.

MEET A BODY—. October 16, 1944

A murder mystery play by Jane Hinton. Produced by H. Clay Blaney for 24 performances in the Forrest Theatre.

PROGRAM

Margaret MacGregor	Ruth McDevitt
Officer McVey	John Boyd
John MacGregor	Whitford Kane
Manny Siegelmann	Al Shean
Everett T. George	Le Roi Operti
Tim MacGregor	Paul Potter
Norman Clark	John McQuade
Horace Craig	Forrest Orr
Ellen Thorne	Nan Butler
Carla Thorne	Helene Ambrose
Doctor Hester	Dann Malloy
Detective Sergeant Corey	Harry Gribbon
The Dancer	Stephen Morrow

SYNOPSIS: Scene. *The living-room of MacGregor's mortuary on the lower east side of New York.* Act I. *Late Saturday afternoon.* Act II. Scene 1. *One hour later.* Scene 2. *Shortly before midnight.* (*Lights will be extinguished during the scene to denote the passing of several minutes.*) Act III. *Three hours later.*

Miss Hinton is a Hollywood literata and her play is a Hollywood movie of the species commonly shown in the Rialto Theatre, where weekly the screen public is regaled with mystery and horror films involving Frankenstein monsters in pursuit of blonde starlets, zombies in pursuit of brunette starlets, murderers in pursuit of red-haired starlets, and escaped lunatics in pursuit of platinum starlets, with in all cases marked-down Ronald Colmans with little mustaches in pursuit of the villains. Nothing is missing for a bad Grade-C picture. The multiple murders, the corpses tumbling out of suddenly opened doors, the eerie green lights, the off-stage playing of "Danse Macabre" on a phonograph record, the shadows on the wall, the sinister poisons, the sword canes, the clutching hands — all these and more are in constant operation. The evening notwithstanding remains rebelliously unmysterious. "Why are you so curious?" blandly inquires one character of another when the third or fourth murder occurs. "I wouldn't be curious if

I weren't a woman," loudly retorts the other, waking up all the women in the audience who had fallen peacefully asleep some time since.

In the *Theatre Book Of The Year, 1942–1943* I observed in reviewing a mystery play called *The Cat Screams,* which turned out to be merely a meow, that the majority of such tocsins with their disappointing last-minute dénouements are like sitting nervously around for two hours waiting for a telephone call from one's best girl and then at long length suddenly hearing the bell ring, jumping up eagerly to answer it, and finding that it is her mother. I also took occasion to point out that the reviewers' adherence to the irrational punctilio imposed upon them by the authors and producers which restrains them from telling the solutions of the mysteries very often assists in swindling the public by concealing the plays' rank lack of imagination and gross silliness. Just why the writers of mystery plays should be granted any such charity above the writers of all other kinds of plays, I could not digest.

I am gratified to note that Edmund Wilson, that very able literary critic, has since got in some extra-good licks. After reading a heap of poor mystery stories he allows that he felt he was unpacking large crates by swallowing the excelsior in order to find at the bottom a few bent and rusty nails. He repeats that the stories in general profit by the aforesaid unfair advantage in the code which forbids the reviewer to give away the secret to the public and hides the pointlessness of many of the stories. "It is not difficult to create suspense by making people await a revelation, but it demands a certain originality to come through with a criminal device which is ingenious or picturesque or amusing enough to make the reader feel the waiting has been worth while," he continues and concludes that the real secret which this or that author had been screening was "a meagreness of imagination of which one only came to realize the full horror when the last chapter had left one blank."

In the case of a good mystery play I am perfectly willing to oblige the author and producer by keeping the play's secret and so adding to the interest of possible audiences.

But in the case of one so thoroughly bad as this of Miss Hinton's, I decline to be a party to the public cheating. Therefore, out with the punctilio, and know ye, should her dud ever be produced anywhere else, that her murders are accomplished, seriatim, by one of Conan Doyle's old *Sign Of The Four* poisoned darts, by Doyle's old instantaneous aconite, by the old Borgia poisoned ring, by the old electrical contrivance, here hidden in a death mask, and by the old escaped lunatic.

However charitable you may happen to be in the other directions, you still surely can't forgive that escaped lunatic.

THE VISITOR. October 17, 1944

A "psychological" melodrama by Kenneth White, based on a novel of the same name by Leane Zugsmith and Carl Randau. Produced by Herman Shumlin for 23 performances in the Henry Miller Theatre.

PROGRAM

ELIZABETH	*Dorrit Kelton*	DAVID CUNNINGHAM	*Walter N. Greaza*
WALTER DAWSON	*Ralph Forbes*	MACK BURRELL	*Thomas Chalmers*
JUDITH CUNNINGHAM	*Frances Carson*	BUD OWEN	*Richard Hylton*
ELLEN WOOD	*Anna Minot*	JOE WILLARD	*Will Hare*

SYNOPSIS: Act I. *Early evening. Mid-July.* Act II. Scene 1. *Morning. Five days later.* Scene 2. *Mid-afternoon. Three days later.* Act III. Scene 1. *Evening. The following day.* Scene 2. *An hour and a half later.*

The play takes place in the living-room of David Cunningham's house. The time is the present.

THE RECORDS SEEM to indicate that there generally has been no surer dramatic box-office device than that of mistaken and puzzling identity. Of the many modern plays in which it has figured, very few have failed to captivate the public. For the most part the plays have taken one of four forms.

In the first, as in such exhibits as *The Servant In The House* and *The Passing Of The Third Floor Back,* a gentle and philanthropic stranger who is mistaken in the earlier portions of the evening for someone like Bernie Baruch turns out, though cautiously not specified in so many words, to be the Saviour. In the second, as in such as *The Lodger* and *At Mrs. Beam's,* an almost equally gentle and solicitous stranger who is guessed to be Frank Crowninshield turns out to be either Jack-the-Ripper or a notorious thief. In the third, as in boons like *The Masquerader* and *In The Fog,* a protean actor is employed to play two different men, one the soul of honor and the other an ignominious bum, who look exactly alike and who bewilder the spectators no end when the wife's bedroom scene comes around and one of the indeterminable twain makes his entrance into it, eventually betraying his foul identity through wearing a red instead of a pink boutonnière and revealing, as he is about to unbutton his shirt, a missing third finger. And, in the fourth, a variation of the Enoch Arden theme, a man thought to be the one who disappeared from his home and family long years before returns to the scene and gradually arouses the suspicion and doubt of the audience when in the course of the action he seems peculiarly not to remember precisely where all of two decades ago he left his pipe.

Mr. White's play falls into the last named slot, like a lead nickel. For all the traditional sure-fire quality of its general scheme, it takes its place among the several failures, and for reasons that are plain. Asking an audience to believe that a mother even momentarily would have doubts about her young son's identity and regard him as a possible impostor after he had been away from her for only three years hardly leads to even faintly rational and acceptable suspense. And staging any such strainful nonsense as solemnly as if the mother were Medea and the son Hamlet only serves to make the nonsense more nonsensical.

It is customary, of course, in these hand-outs known to the Broadway lingo as psychological melodramas for a director to cause the actors to depict their soul aches by making such faces as are more usually associated with aches rather lower down, to walk fearfully around the stage as if imminently anticipating paralytic strokes, and to speak their lines as if the playwright had left out every other word, which, as I have recorded on certain similar occasions in the past, would be an improvement. Herman Shumlin, the present director, here not only did not vary the pattern but, having seen service in Hollywood, further staged the play as if for a slow-motion film camera, with the actors frequently conveying the impression that they were posing for closeups. Perhaps he was simply bent upon killing two birds with one stone, since the Warner Brothers' company had already bought the motion picture rights to the play before it opened and since it seemed likely that he might also be offered the direction of the screen version.

This Mr. Shumlin, who several times in the past has proved himself able in the business of stage direction, seems to be on the way toward constituting himself a bobby-sox Stanislavsky. Whatever the nature of the dramatic materials in hand, he appears to be unable to resist visiting upon them a considerable measure of portentously grave Russian shading and pacing them as if they were part and parcel of a memorial service for Dostoievski.

Returning briefly to the play itself, it may be described impressionistically as the kind wherein the mother, a plain, small-town woman, indulges in such soigné locutions as "Aren't I?" and wherein she indicates her unquenchable maternal love for her son by ceaselessly pursuing his corpus about the stage with devouring eyes. It may be further described, if additional description be deemed necessary, as the species in which suspense is hoped for by inducing the characters to act and speak exactly opposite to the manner in which they would act and speak if they were rational human beings.

The acting performances under Mr. Shumlin's guiding wand were in line for a curio cabinet. Frances Carson, as the mother, registered her tortured psyche wholly in terms of an unremitting, violent trigeminal neuralgia complicated with a ruptured appendix; Walter Greaza, as the suspicious stepfather, sniffed gloweringly about the stage as if shadowed by a crate of Liederkranz cheese; Ralph Forbes, as the drunken, cadging brother-in-law, performed like Pawnee Bill playing Falstaff; and most of the rest seemed to have confused dramatic character interpretation with a kind of facial Delsarte.

Under the circumstances, the mother might have been forgiven for suspecting her son to be King Lear.

I REMEMBER MAMA. October 19, 1944

A stage adaptation by John van Druten of Kathryn Forbes' book, Mama's Bank Account. *Produced by Richard Rodgers and Oscar Hammerstein II for a far beyond the season run in the Music Box.*

PROGRAM

Katrin	*Joan Tetzel*	Mr. Thorkelson	*Bruno Wick*
Mama	*Mady Christians*	Dr. Johnson	*William Pringle*
Papa	*Richard Bishop*	Arne	*Robert Antoine*
Dagmar	*Carolyn Hummel*	A Nurse	*Marie Gale*
Christine	*Francis Heflin*	Another Nurse	*Dorothy Elder*
Nels	*Marlon Brando*	Soda Clerk	*Frank Babcock*
Mr. Hyde	*Oswald Marshall*	Madeline	*Cora Smith*
Aunt Trina	*Adrienne Gessner*	Dorothy Schiller	*Ottilie Kruger*
Aunt Sigrid	*Ellen Mahar*	Florence Dana Moorhead	
Aunt Jenny	*Ruth Gates*		*Josephine Brown*
Uncle Chris	*Oscar Homolka*	Bellboy	*Herbert Kenwith*
A Woman	*Louise Lorimer*		

The action passes in and around San Francisco some years ago.

Professorial criticism would be horrified by the play, which to its strict mind is hardly a play at all and which violates most of the rules and regulations in the class-room books. It has no plot; its action is static; its dramaturgy, such as it is, is lacking in steady progression; it offers no conflict, no crises, no climaxes; it is, in short, merely a series of sketches loosely gathered together and more in the line of a family picture album than drama. But, like several other things frowned upon by the ipsojures, it confounds their wisdom by turning out to be not only in large part an intelligently enjoyable theatrical evening but a striking popular success. And this for all the fact that even the less professorial and more catholic criticism may also readily find plenty the matter with it.

This latter criticism, speaking as one of its merchants, finds me wishing, for example, that the playwright might have refrained from incorporating into his play a narrator in the form of a young daughter of the Norwegian-American household whom he seats to one side of the stage and bathes in a spotlight's glow and whose periodic contribution to the proceedings consists in introducing the various episodes with lines like "I well remember how Mama, etc.," "Then, one day, Papa and Mama, etc.," and "I still can't forget the time Uncle Chris, etc." The device is not only altogether too worn with theatrical wear but, more to the point, is here entirely unnecessary, since it detracts from rather than adds to the story's movement. It further betrays the playwright as one perhaps commercially dubious about the play's turn of the century period and intent upon giving it at least a small, safe measure of contemporary flavor by constituting his narrator, initially in the current dress, a tie between the past and present. Moreover, when he keeps his narrator quite as young as she was during the much earlier period of the exhibit his device seems all the more hollow, and when he makes her the later biographer of her family and introduces such a routine literary homily as, in effect, "A person shouldn't try to write of things he doesn't actually know about but, if he would be successful, only about what he actually knows and has experienced" — when he conducts himself in such wise he lays himself open not only to professorial but to any other kind of criticism.

There is also the matter of his use of so-called fadeouts, or short episodes played on small revolving platforms at either side of the stage, which often have about them the air of cinema flashbacks. The narrator business is only one of these. There is always something about the use of such fadeouts and flashbacks that implies a playwright is not as competent in the dramaturgical craft as he should be. The best dramatists, past and present, have hardly had need of them; they have been able to incorporate their essence directly into their dramatic fabrics. While on this occasion they have been manipulated with mechanical smoothness and hence are not as disturbing as they usually are, they nevertheless take their place in critical disfavor.

The flashback as we all too often get it is, even on purely

theatrical grounds, far from satisfactory and generally a little ridiculous. We observe a character wrinkledly ruminating that he or she recalls a night twenty or more years ago and then wait patiently for several blank minutes while the stagehands noisily shift the scene (even slide or revolving stages sometimes have a way of not sliding or revolving as velvetly as they should) and presently behold a number of actors trying to regain their balance on the slowly settling platforms and go ahead with their lines. The effect is less the convincing flowing of one period into another than of a sardonic contest between the actors and scene shifters, and the more important consequence is a violation of the mood which the playwright has sought to establish in his audience. Even when handled as adroitly as in the present case, the business seems intermittently to be unnecessarily distracting and it is only by virtue of that dexterous handling that the audience is halfway persuaded to suspend critical judgment and swallow the rigmarole.

The impression which the play, above such considerations, makes is wrought by Mr. van Druten's honest simplicity, his avoidance of any slightest strain to give his innocent dramatic materials more importance than they possess, his similar avoidance of extrinsic humors, and his uncommon talent in casting and stage direction. There is no better man in these respects in our theatre, as he proved sufficiently in the instance of his last year's *The Voice Of The Turtle*. Episode after episode in the life of the Norwegian-American family is dramatically manipulated in its own artless terms and never once is there resort to an overemphasis which would play havoc with its simple internals. The result amounts to an easy turning of the pages in the family's album which presents more tellingly than any repeated showy moistening of a playwright's thumb the panorama of all those big and little comedies and tragedies that go to make up the life of a household.

The settings by George Jenkins are first-rate and the acting company, notably Oscar Homolka as the spuriously gruff old uncle with a bottle in one hand and a mistress in the other, is for the greater part endorsable.

A final note slightly apart. The performances as in other theatres were prefaced, as customary, by the playing of "The Star Spangled Banner." Not only is little more discouraging to the proper patriotic spirit than the national anthem as rendered by three-fourths of these theatre orchestras but little is more positively discouraging to any anticipatory theatre mood. In the case of the larger orchestras in the musical show houses, things are not so bad. But when it comes to the smaller ones, usually quartettes, in the dramatic theatres, the stimulation provided is approximately equal to that of "Rock-a-bye Baby." Standing up to the national anthem ventilated by the average quartette composed of a piano that apparently has not been tuned since the heyday of Mayme Gehrue, a squealy violin, a hock-shop 'cello and a clarinet or, God wot, an accordion is hardly likely to inflame the standee, albeit a direct descendant of half a dozen of the Founding Fathers, with a great pride of country so much as with a feeling that it will be swell to sit down again and go to sleep. This feeling overwhelms him in particular when the union gets to the slow movement, which is usually interpreted in the lugubrious tempo of "Japanese Sandman" as dispensed by a female crooner giving out in a military hospital ward. What is needed to make the anthem what it should be are some good loud brasses and, certainly, at least one good loud drum. As a public-spirited theatregoer, I herewith offer to supply such a drum to any house manager who alleges that he can not afford the extra expense. What is more, I promise to get Major de Seversky, the long-distance bomber, to sit in the pit and at the proper moment give it the works.

VIOLET. October 24, 1944

A comedy by Whitfield Cook, based on his series of popular magazine stories. Produced by Albert Margolies for 23 performances in the Belasco Theatre.

Program

Clarence	*John Cherry*	Sidney Watrous	*Carlo Robinson*
Pete Granden	*Harvey Stephens*	Walter Meeker	*Mason Adams*
Mrs. Elfie Tunison	*Doro Merande*	Crystal	*Fay Baker*
Elisha Bly	*Len Hollister*	Charlotte Watrous	*Joan Vitez*
Lily Foster	*Helen Claire*	Henry Watrous	*Leslie Litomy*
Esther	*Paula Trueman*	W. W. Upthegrove	*Russell Gaige*
Bruce (Batch 1)	*Billy Nevard*		
Violet (Batch 1)	*Pat Hitchcock*		
Evelyn (Batch 2)	*Fuzzy McQuade*		
Arthur (Batch 2)	*Martin David*		
Susie (Batch 2)	*Jimsey Somers*		

SYNOPSIS: Act I. *Late evening, December 31st.* Act II. *Noon the next day.* Act III. *Morning two days later.*

The action takes place in the living-room of Pete Granden's remodeled farmhouse in Vermont.

LIKE THE PLAYS dealing with mistaken and puzzling identity (*vide The Visitor*), the plays dealing with adolescents also fall roughly into four catalogues. In the first, as in exhibits like Wedekind's *Awakening Of Spring* and Schönherr's *The Children's Tragedy,* the adolescents are viewed sombrely as being either beset by an incipient and baleful sex urge or doomed to misery by the acts of their parents, with suicide in one case or the other occasionally the only way out. In the second, as in Hauptmann's *Hannele* and the sort, they are treated to the gentle embroideries of fantasy and are frequently bequeathed scenes in which, during a serious illness, they entertain visions of one kind or another (customarily given stage interpretation in terms of considerable gilt tinsel and fancy lighting effects) wherein they see themselves either in Heaven or its equivalent in some such shape as an enormous candy store with barrels of sweets theirs for the asking.

In the third, as in O'Neill's *Ah, Wilderness!* and van Druten's *Young Woodley,* they are provided with a comedy treatment and either have adventures with loose girls in back rooms of saloons or in juke joints (involving their first heroic attempts at alcoholic liquor and smoking tobacco) or wistfully fall in love with women (usually experienced in the ways of the world or school-teachers) who are considerably older than themselves and hence embarrassed by their calf-like overtures. In this third group, too, are the lesser specimens like *Junior Miss, Janie,* and *Kiss And Tell* which resort to the device of making the adult characters act more or less like adolescents and the adolescents more or less like adults, thus guaranteeing the gratification of the youthful matinée trade and no less the manifold older souls in the nocturnal audiences who flatter themselves that the authors are only fooling, for comedy purposes. And in the fourth, as in *Brother Rat* and *What A Life!,* the youngsters are farcically presented as so many white Topsys, male and female, who comport themselves for the most part as if they were the progeny of Harry Thaw and Charley's Aunt.

Violet is one of the very worst of these diaper dramas. Its general classification comes under the comedies which give to the leading brat all the sagacity that the older characters lack. It is so wretchedly written, however, that even children who might otherwise be tickled by the idea would be exhausted by the supreme dulness of its execution.

Telling basically the same story as F. Hugh Herbert's *For Keeps* (*q.v.*), Mr. Cook's play only makes suffering worse by introducing five obstreperous children instead of one and again causing their leader, whilst the others are messing about the stage, to go through the old motions of untangling her much-marrying father's love life in order finally to find a comfortable home for herself. Sample humors concern a speculation as to whether a painting of trees represents a boat, a hypothetical teetotaler who shows up drunk, a brat's lordly appearance in one of her mother's elaborate evening gowns, impromptu excursions on the part of the youngsters to the bathroom and, last but not least, a romantic heroine who indulges in such starlit locutions as "Get it off your chest." In the drama, save when ably written, as in life, one child may be amusing, two tolerable, but three or more in congress assembled, as in this case, enough to drive one to the bottle.

The Metro-Goldwyn-Mayer film company was responsible for this particular spit into the theatre's face. It financed the play with a deposit of 100,000 dollars to apply against a maximum of 250,000, the difference to come from weekly payments based on a percentage of the box-office receipts. Since the exhibit was unanimously denounced as rubbish by the reviewers and played to no audiences and a heavy loss, the Metro-Goldwyn-Mayer film company got nothing for its investment except possibly a movie that will be proclaimed an epic and make a million or more dollars.

SNAFU. October 25, 1944

A farce-comedy by Louis Solomon and Harold Buchman. Produced by George Abbott for 157 performances, initially in the Hudson Theatre.

Program

Josephina	*Eugenia Delarova*
Madge Stevens	*Elspeth Eric*
Laura Jessup	*Patricia Kirkland*
Ben Stevens	*Russell Hardie*
Mr. Taylor	*John Souther*
Kate Hereford	*Bethel Leslie*
Aunt Emily	*Enid Markey*
Senator Phil Ford	*Ralph W. Chambers*
1st Legionnaire	*Edwin Cooper*
2nd Legionnaire	*Ernest Rowan*
3rd Legionnaire	*Stephen Gierasch*
Ronald Stevens	*Billy Redfield*
Pfc. Danny Baker	*Dort Clark*
Mrs. Garrett	*Ann Dere*
Detective	*Cliff Dunstan*
Martha	*Eve McVeagh*
Col. West	*Winfield Smith*

SYNOPSIS: Act I. Scene 1. *About noon, of an inevitably sunny day in spring.* Scene 2. *The next morning, about 5:30.* Act II. *The following day — late morning.* Act III. *Several hours later.*

The entire action of the play takes place in the living-room of the Stevens home in southern California.

Like both the plays about mistaken identity and adolescents, the later-day plays dealing with soldiers similarly for the major part register themselves under four headings. In the first, the soldiers are presented as young men full of idealism and Bartlett poetry quotations who meet their ends on the field of battle, with their mothers and sweethearts back home pausing only long enough in their pursuit of the household culinary arts stoically to observe that man's noblest duty is self-sacrifice that the world may live forevermore in tranquillity, good will and peace. In the second, they are constituted ghosts who, visible only to their mothers, return from the grave and persuade everyone but their uncles who have made millions out of the munitions business that wars are futile and that, if the future happiness of mankind is to be preserved, nations should content themselves, if they feel the need of letting off steam, in playing cowboys-and-Indians in the back yard.

In the third, the soldiers are vouchsafed a comedy treatment which in turn takes three forms. First, we have them jovially boozing and wenching whilst the property man in the wings works himself into a lather making loud sounds indicative of a war going on, the soldiers meanwhile working themselves into an even greater lather in trying to drown out the sounds with louder cuss words and jocund slaps on one another's pantaloons. Secondly, we have them home either honorably discharged or invalided out of the service or on furlough and endeavoring to readjust themselves to their wives, who have become independent in their absence or perhaps amorously interested in someone else, usually depicted as a loafer, or to their old surroundings, which seem humdrum after the experiences they have gone through. And, thirdly, we have them on leave and passing their holiday either in light sexual diversions which are subsequently moralized into holy matrimony or in light sexual diversions which aren't.

In the fourth, the boys are given the farcical treatment and either wake up the next morning with a severe hangover in strange beds adjacent to those occupied by wide-eyed cuties, who professedly are scared out of their wits, or spend all the time they can spare from their families in dancing jig steps upon the sight of the gluteal prominence of a shapely female and exclaiming "Oh, boy!"

The Messrs. Solomon's and Buchman's *Snafu* is a combination of the honorably discharged soldier who tries to readapt himself to the old surroundings and the soldier who dances the amatory jig steps whenever a personable young woman crosses the scene. And naturally added to the combination for extra measure, since George Abbott had a hand in the fabrication, are not only such before-mentioned slices of the short pants drama as constitute adolescents the intellectual superiors of their parents and the latter the inferiors of the adolescents but also the suggestion that the youngsters are not the parents' offspring but rather those of Wild Bill Hickok and Babe Didrickson. Further stirred into the chowder are the business of mistaken identity, the scene in which a parent begins apprehensively to give his offspring some esoteric advice and presently finds the latter giving it to him (recognizable from S. N. Behrman's *The Talley Method, et al.*), the comical servant girl, the dumb detective, the pompous Senator, and other such strips of theatrical bacon.

Out of the familiar and long over-worked materials the authors, materially aided by Mr. Abbott, have, however, managed a farce-comedy periodically not without some amusement. It takes much too long to get into motion and the third act up to within ten minutes of the final curtain slows down considerably, but in between there are funny moments.

The play brought to twelve the number of exhibits thus far in the season that have included characters in uniform. It also brought to twelve the number of reviewers' complaints about authors and directors who permit the use of somewhat over-active telephones. While I agree that over-active telephones may be depressing from the audience point of view, I doubt whether any reviewer or other person with the slightest experience of the cursed instrument may legitimately complain that from a dramatic point of view their ardor is not entirely within the realistic fact and critically legitimate.

The title of the play stems, in the definition of the *Encyclopædia Britannica* quoted in the program, from military slang and means "in a mess, haywire, and derives from the first letters of the words 'situation normal all fouled up.' " The eminent *Encyclopædia Britannica* should be taken gently in hand and told about the birds and the flowers. The first letter of the fourth word may be all right, but the word itself, as any soldier may inform it, is hardly "fouled."

THE PERFECT MARRIAGE
October 26, 1944

A play by Samson Raphaelson. Produced by Cheryl Crawford for 92 performances in the Ethel Barrymore Theatre.

PROGRAM

Rosa	*Evelyn Davis*	Addison Manning	*James Todd*
Dale Williams	*Victor Jory*	Gloria Endicott	*Martha Sleeper*
Jenny Williams	*Miriam Hopkins*	Helen Williams	*Joyce Van Patten*
Mabel Manning	*Helen Flint*		

SYNOPSIS: Act I. Scene 1. *A Saturday evening in early October, about 10:30.* Scene 2. *Ten minutes later.* Act II. Scene 1. *The next morning, about noon.* Scene 2. *Five o'clock in the afternoon, the same day.* Act III. *That evening, 10:30.*

The entire play is set in the upstairs sitting-room and bedroom of the home of Mr. and Mrs. Dale Williams in New York City.

For more than half a century French playwrights, and occasionally Italians like Bracco and Austrians like Schnitzler, have been writing about the sexual coolness that often develops after years of otherwise happy marriage. To enumerate the plays in which the idea has figured, beginning with Sardou and not ending with the Bernstein of *The Thief,* would fill pages. Various playwrights of other nations, including our own as in the instance of Vincent Lawrence, have also considered the theme, which in all cases is customarily resolved either in a satisfactory reunion through the agency of jealousy, peek-a-boo lingerie, or champagne and epigrams, or, if the vein be more solemn, in a decision of the mates thereafter to go their separate ways. Any number of the plays, when handled in terms of comedy, have been amusing and several of the more serious nature have amounted to sound drama.

Not so, however, with Mr. Raphaelson's tardy effort, a hybrid of comedy and drama, and equally bad on both counts. Devoid of wit and avid of every stereotype imaginable, it reduces the theme to a mere endlessly wordy skirmish between a couple of suspiciously impotent alley cats. Neither his husband nor wife, who have been married for ten years and have a sizeable daughter, are redeemed by the faintest suggestion of charm or intelligence and their anatomical disputations accordingly take on the flavor of a debate between two authors of such tomes as *Secrets Of Sex In Marriage,* with the four-letter words hesitantly left out. The result is, I suppose, what passes for a clean and moral play, but it remains an essentially dirty and disgusting one.

When Mr. Raphaelson's pair of characters are not getting into fancy boudoir habiliments in the hope of stimulating each other's libidos and vainly horsing around on a bed, situated conspicuously throughout the evening at stage right, they are propounding their author's theories of sex and matrimony, all venerable with age and periodically taking such matinée contours as "After two people have been in love and then one day they decide to settle for friendship — that's a bad day." And at such widely separated moments as they are spared from shouting their glandular philosophies at each other they are given the stage business of pretending to search for matches wherewith to light their cigarettes, presumably indicative of their need for a few minutes' profound reflection. The net impression is of a phonograph on a bed screeching over and over again a single scene from a play written by Mae West at the age of twelve.

One of Mr. Raphaelson's troubles, hinted at in certain of his past efforts, is his apparent conviction that he is something of a savant in matters pertaining to the amatory arts and sciences. What he is, rather, is simply a writer for the stage who unknowingly repeats the most hackneyed observations of countless playwrights before him, and repeats even those that once may have had some humor with a perfectly straight and very grave face. And his writing still further betrays his posturing worldliness in such bus-boy locutions as "We'll tell them we've got a nice cold bottle of champagne on ice", in such stale greasepaint beliefs as the superior efficacy of a violent quarrel in bringing two lovers together again, and in such meditations as have to do with the sexual desirability of young girls as against old women of thirty.

Both the casting of the leading roles and Mr. Raphaelson's stage direction were lamentable. If, in place of Miss Hopkins and Mr. Jory, players somewhat gifted in smooth comedy had been hired, the play, for all its inner leaden quality, might at least superficially have seemed less leaden than it did. Miss Hopkins purveyed in the main only poor imitations of Tallulah Bankhead and Gertrude Lawrence when she was not exploding dramatically in Hollywood fashion, and Mr. Jory rested his histrionic art largely in grim frowns when erect and in dejecting his head and allowing the audience to admire his oiled black curly hair when seated.

As for the staging, in a pamphlet dealing with the history of theatrical entertainment in Seattle and published by the University of Washington I find, among others, these reflections on acting and direction quoted from an article by the critic for *Every Sunday* of Tacoma and dated December 26, 1891:

> "When a child actress has something particular to confide to her papa or mamma, it would be the height of ill manners did she not crouch down on the floor by the side of her parent."
>
> "When an actor enters into confidential conversation with another actor, it is the proper thing for him to hang his leg over the back of a chair (or couch), with his foot resting on its seat."

Since the same devices were visible under Mr. Raphaelson's direction, it becomes evident that either the stage of Tacoma, for all the irony of the critic quoted, was fifty-three years ahead of its time or Mr. Raphaelson's stage is fifty-three years behind its.

NO WAY OUT. October 30, 1944

A play by Owen Davis. Produced by Robert Keith for 8 performances in the Cort Theatre.

PROGRAM

Cora Hilliard	*Viola Frayne*	Dr. Walter Levenseller	*Donald Foster*
Dr. Enid Karley	*Irene Hervey*	Hesther Darrow	*Jean Casto*
Bob Karley	*Jerome P. Thor*	Dr. Niles Hilliard	*Robert Keith*
Barbara Trent	*Nancy Marquand*	Jim Slade	*Maurice Burke*
Napoleon	*John Marriott*		
Molly Levenseller	*Viola Roache*		

SYNOPSIS: Act I. *A September afternoon.* Act II. *The day following.* Act III. *That night.*

The Scene. *The living-room of "the old Trent mansion" in a large city in northern New York.*

Mr. Davis, who is now in his seventies, has written more than three hundred plays, the great majority of them utterly worthless. This latest is no exception. Treating of medical ethics which in the case of an unscrupulous physician may conceivably be utilized to criminal ends, the exhibit, which attempts to conceal its superficiality in the stridors of melodrama, is of the species that in the early years of the present century was known as a problem play. As in most such problem plays of that period the chief problem is largely the playwright's and consists in his painstaking effort to avoid its more or less obvious and simple solution until a few minutes before the final curtain is due to fall.

The pseudo-problem in the instance of this particular specimen proceeds from a plot involving the aforesaid knavish medico and a step-daughter who stands in the way of his acquiring his wife's fortune. The step-daughter, a victim of Addison's disease, is mortally ill and, though he knows the nature of her ailment, the medico works for her death through a deliberately false diagnosis. A woman doctor, who is a visitor in the house, privately diagnoses the girl's true condition and, her suspicions of the medico aroused by an old Negro retainer of the family who informs her that the latter had got rid of his wife's first husband through a similar villainy, demands that she be brought into consultation. The medico refuses and the woman doctor can do nothing under the circumstances because of professional ethics.

For two long hours the theme is assiduously belabored by the playwright with the gratuitous philosophical despair of a blacksmith striking an anvil with a lollipop, all under the apparent impression that the problem involved will stimulate an audience with its perplexity. Unfortunately for the playwright, however, it doesn't, since the audience, long used to the dramatic subterfuge of arbitrary deferment of a transparent solution, simply wonders before the play is half through why the woman doctor does not solve her difficulty very readily by persuading the faithful Negro retainer, who is close to the step-daughter, to tell her what her scoundrelly step-father is up to.

The play, in short, is much the kind of bogus profundity that might have been concocted by Augustus Thomas or some young local admirer of Eugene Brieux thirty-five years ago. What it essentially is, in the more immediate description, is a seedy Owen Davis paraphrase of Rose Franken's seedy *Doctors Disagree* of the previous season, which was in turn a poor Rose Franken paraphrase of Rachel Crothers' seedy *A Man's World* and Dorothy Brandon's hardly less seedy *The Outsider.*

It begins to look as if the possible mark of an inferior playwright is to be found in his recourse to a Negro character in Caucasian surroundings as the symbol of uprightness and decency. In Herbert Kubly's *Men To The Sea* a Negro and his wife were presented as the only really pure characters among a group of sexually miscellaneous whites. In Samson Raphaelson's *The Perfect Marriage* a Negress was guaranteed to be the only decently minded character in a group of vulgar-minded whites. In Edward Chodorov's last season's *Decision* a Negro and Negress were offered as relative paragons in a white group composed in considerable part of rats. And in this *No Way Out* the Negro retainer is one of the two characters amidst all the whites who has any visible intelligence and concept of honor.

EMBEZZLED HEAVEN. October 31, 1944

A play by Ladislaus Bush-Fekete and Mary Helen Fay, derived from the novel by Franz Werfel. Produced by the Theatre Guild for 52 performances in the National Theatre.

PROGRAM

TETA	*Ethel Barrymore*
BICHLER	*Sanford Meisner*
COUNTESS ARGAN	*Bettina Cerf*
MOJMIR (THE CHILD)	*Edward Fernandez*
MILA	*Wauna Paul*
ZDENKA	*Madeline Lee*
GEORGE	*Val Witherill*
JARMILA	*Peggy Meredith*
FRANZISKA	*Augusta Roeland*
MAIL CARRIER	*Don Valentine*
MRS. SCHULTZ	*Else Basserman*
PASTOR	*Martin Blaine*
KOVALSKY	*Frank Richards*
PROSSNITZER	*Wolfe Barzell*
MOJMIR	*Eduard Franz*
MASHA	*Sheila Trent*
SOTTOMAESTRO	*Marcel Dill*
KOMPERT	*Harry Neville*
MONSIGNORE	*John McKee*
POPE	*Albert Basserman*
MAESTRO DI CAMERA	*Edward Kilcullen*
PAPAL VALET	*Julian Benjamin*
SWISS GUARDS	*Paige Edwards, Robert Fletcher*
SEDIARIS	*David Barnaby, Robert O'Brien*
PHYSICIAN	*Graham Velsey*

Pilgrims, Papal Retinue

SYNOPSIS: Prologue. *Teta's room. The Argan Castle, near Prague, 1913.* Act I. *The kitchen, Argan Castle, 1938.* Act II. *The church garden, Detva, Moravia. The next day.* Act III. *Reception hall. The Vatican. A few weeks later.*

WITH MOST of the romantic figures of our theatre gone to their Maker and with our contemporary stage so largely bare of players who have about them the old brilliant air, it is always at least a sentimental satisfaction when Ethel Barrymore reappears on the scene. For she retains that quality of person, whatever the merit of her vehicles, which singles her out from a current parade constituted in considerable part of actresses, however talented, for whom no connoisseur horse of other days would have abandoned his carriage in favor of undiscriminating admirers.

This latest vehicle of Miss Barrymore's, however, needs not a horse but a sizeable cavalry to lend it any movement. Alleged to be a dramatization of the Werfel novel about a poor Czech woman's attempt to bribe her way after life into God's grace through the praying offices of a nephew whom she supports on the way to the priesthood only to find that he has used her funds to other ends, it is nothing of the kind, for no play emerges. What it is, rather, is merely a succession of dramaless episodes, heavily repetitious, snipped out of the novel with a sickle and placed upon a stage. Only a section of its last act has the faintest trace of theatrical life, and that life proceeds less from any drama than from the pictorial quality of the Vatican setting and costumes. For the rest, the evening consists chiefly in the spectacle of Miss Barrymore seated in a chair or lounging at one side of the stage and ruminating on her chances eventually of getting into Heaven. She sits beautifully and she lounges gracefully and she ruminates artfully with that melodious voice of hers, but that, unless I am seriously mistaken, hardly constitutes a play.

The language in which the quasi-play is couched is furthermore for the most part surprisingly commonplace, does not suggest the hitherto gifted Werfel save at widely spaced intervals, and draws the exhibit in with a check-rein rather than releases it. It is to be submitted that, Werfel or not, such old Stanley J. Weyman lingo as, for example, "You tried to buy a mediator with earthly coin — and you failed; now you have the purchase price: love!" is scarcely conducive to the inoculation of the more sensitive auditor with any great exaltation of the spirit. It is only in the noted last act that any slightest sense of the spiritual stimulation vital to the prosperity of the theme creeps into the proceedings, and it creeps into them less for what is spoken than for what the eye sees. There is something about the spectacle of a Pope of Rome on the stage that arbitrarily exercises an impressive effect upon an audience whatever the value of a play, and it here exercised it again for all the circumstance that the actor chosen for the role, Basserman, had a thick, beery Teutonic accent worthy of an old North German Lloyd smoking-room steward.

Iden Payne's direction of the play, save in the final act, gave the production the aspect of having taken a sleeping pill. His materials, true enough, challenged him with their lifelessness but even so his manipulation of the stage doubled their lethargy. On such occasions as he was desperately determined to inject a little vitality into the exhibit at any cost he furthermore committed the mistake of confusing a bogus acting effervescence with dynamic character interpretation, with the result that two of the play's characters, the gardener turned footman and the swindler nephew, conducted themselves almost exactly alike and gave the effect of the two Dromios having wandered out of *The Comedy Of Errors* and finding themselves in Czechoslovakia.

We return to Miss Barrymore and to the place which she, with a few others, occupies in the fancy of theatre audiences.

In Hollywood, what is known as a glamour girl is uniformly a chick of tender years. Talent generally plays no, or at best very small, part in the quality attributed to her. The glamour consists mainly in a press agent's imagination, which various hired hands around the studio set about converting into an approximation to reality.

This approximation is maneuvered in devious ways, behind all of them the press agent master-mind and entrepreneur. First, a dentist goes to work on the girl, very often one whose sole assets are youth, a good figure, and a ferocious ambition some day to achieve the high artistic eminence of a ringside seat at a recherché Hollywood night club, and converts the little one's teeth, which may resemble the stubs in a November corn field, into so many unbelievably symmetrical pearls. Secondly, a hair-doer is drafted to exercise his virtuosity on the little one's locks and, whatever they be like, forthwith to change them. Only in the rarest instances is their color sacred. If black, they must be altered to yellow; if yellow, to black; if brown to red; if red to something else. Too, they must be arranged in a coiffure that mama back home in Texas or jail would never recognize and, if she did, would faint. Thirdly, if the little one's figure is not exactly what it should be, a physical culture expert is summoned to pummel and roll the little one out of what lumps and bumps are in the malapropos places.

Next comes the makeup professor who goes to work on the little one's face. The erstwhile thick eyebrows are shaved into the contours of slender crescent moons. False eyelashes, in some cases approximating Gauguin's paint brushes, are glued to the patient's lids, lending her the appearance of a whiskbroom wistfully enamoured of itself. An exotic compound of belladonna and possibly crème de cacao is dropped into her eyes to lend them a beam and glisten that would frighten the average seacoast lighthouse out of its wits. And miladi's face itself is shellacked, powdered, pencilled and painted into a spectacle so different from what it originally was that aghast mama, fainting after a look at the coiffure, upon squinting it falls into a mortal coma.

The metamorphosed little one is now ready for the couturier, and presently emerges from the atelier looking like what the third assistant press agent who gets sixty dollars a week raptly calls a million dollars.

Our beauty is thereupon placed in the hands of a photographer. This genius, manipulating countless lights, draperies, screens and gauzes and adjusting our beauty in a series of poses and postures calculated best to reveal the puissant splendors of her bosoms and limbs, confects views of her theoretically capable of sending normal men into spasms of ecstasy. And then at length re-enters upon the scene the master press agent.

That worthy now gets busy with a vengeance. The pictures are dispatched far and wide to work their subtle will upon the movie public. Stories relating the heart-breaking powers of the beauty, the manifold heroes of the screen who have succumbed to her devastating allure, and the scions of wealth and high society who have cast themselves into the Gowanus Canal in despair of achieving her hand in marriage enrich the film magazines and Sunday newspaper supplements. Photographs of the paragon arriving orchid-laden at the LaGuardia airport or Grand Central station, or both simultaneously, further embellish the prints. And other pictures showing our heroine in an invisible swim suit beside her visible private two-hundred-by-four-hundred pool, with her seven Russian wolf hounds, in her modest little 20,000 dollar flower garden, and in her simple little bed that looks like a combination of Billy Rose's *Diamond Horseshoe* and the late Everleigh Club vie with the news at breakfast, lunch and dinner tables throughout the countryside. And another Hollywood glamour girl has been born — and made.

There are, as you need not be reinformed, scores of such synthetic wonderbabies in the film capital, and almost all of them are much of a youthful piece. How do they compare with the glamour girls of Broadway and the theatre?

These glamour girls of Broadway are, to put it mildly, a somewhat different sort. Far from being if not exactly wet, still slightly moist behind the ears, only one of the five authentic glamourousæ of today's stage is still in her thirties and the others, three of them, are in their forties, and the fifth actually in her sixties. When it is recorded that these women achieve in the world of the theatre the romantic response achieved in the world of the movies by the cuties aforesaid, it is the established fact and not, as some may sardonically elect to believe, mere senescent sentimental nonsense or a commentator's strain to put an arbitrarily different slant on the matter. For the impersonal truth is that at the present time there is not a single young actress in the theatre — and there are a number of them who are remarkably pretty, charming and animating — who is publicly accepted as being as romantically inveigling as any of the five women alluded to and who, with the one exception noted, are old enough to be the girls' mothers.

Who are these five?

First, there is Katharine Hepburn, the youngest of the lot, who is thirty-eight. Second, there are Gertrude Lawrence, who is forty-seven; Katharine Cornell, who is also forty-seven; and Tallulah Bankhead, who is forty-three. And, finally, there is the perennial Miss Barrymore, who proudly confesses to being all of sixty-six. Of this quintette only Miss Hepburn approaches even remotely to the Hollywood concept of glamour and its concomitant, sex appeal. And even she, who has been in pictures, sometime since surrendered her glamour standing in Hollywood to such very much younger items as Veronica Lake, Rita Hayworth, Lauren Bacall, and the like. Furthermore, in the sheer matter of looks, as looks are popularly regarded, she alone of the quintette satisfies the popular sentimental, pictorial demand. Yet the other four exercise an invocation not only equal to hers, but here and there immeasurably superior.

None of these women, Hepburn included, has gone through a beauty mill. All of them are more or less as nature originally fashioned them. Perhaps, in some cases, the hair has been touched up a little; perhaps a tooth has here and there been prettied up a bit; but no Hollywood brand of metamorphosis has been visited upon any of them. It is not, moreover, as it is in England, any arbitrary loyalty to favorite actresses on the part of the theatre public that accounts for that public's romantic esteem. When these actresses have appeared in bad plays their public in two cases out of three has remained away. Nor is it, in some cases, a matter of loftier talent. Judith Anderson, to name but one, has a talent far exceeding that of several of them, and so, to name but another, has Helen Hayes. But neither of these and none of the gifted rest has exactly the species of peculiar personal appeal that the five in question have.

It has not been expert press-agentry, or fancy photography, or swimming pools and Russian wolf hounds, or cantaloupe sweaters, or views of delirious silken boudoirs, or even always shrewdly chosen vehicles that have made these actresses what they are in the public's imagination. Nor, surely, has it been the tantalizing species of corporeal embellishment that Hollywood relies upon. Hepburn in her careless slacks, Bankhead in her two-year-old velvet gowns, Lawrence in her humdrum street outfits, Cornell in her chill tailor-mades, and Barrymore usually dressed as if clothes were the last thing in the world to interest her — certainly there is nothing in this quarter to make men or women turn around on the street to look. It is, rather, that these women as individuals seem to have something in them, whatever it is, that catches and holds the theatre public's personal fancy as no five or ten or fifty Hollywood blossoms could conceivably hope to.

The quality which is the personality of Ethel Barrymore has persisted for all of forty-odd theatrical years. In her youthful day the belle of New York, with more avid swains in pursuit than one could crowd into the Brown Derby, she has come through the changes of the long years with the loss of little more than that dark, slim young beauty which brooded from photographs on end tacked to college boys' walls in the early Nineties. The voice that crawled into the heart of a nation, that voice with the sound of a blues song addressed to a muffled drum, hasn't changed, nor has the gentleness of stage person, nor have the unstudiedly graceful gestures, nor has that physical suggestion of being always half-absent.

Katharine Cornell, who in her earliest theatrical appearances vaguely suggested the Katharine Hepburn who was yet to come, is now, in her late forties, a woman of sable dignity, of impressive reserve, of implied intelligence, and with a voice that, while it has only a measure of the cajolery of Miss Barrymore's, deftly combines Béchamel sauce with Worcestershire and is dramatically palatable.

Tallulah Bankhead is no more like either of these than the late lamented Jeanne Eagels was like Elita Proctor Otis. Tallulah, whose Dixie looks might easily be mistaken for English, is the archebiotic, the to-hell-with-you-and-you sort, who drives at one like a brakeless tally-ho and whose voice always suggests that she has smoked seventy cigarettes too many. Her mouth seems ever poised to put the bouncer in his place. Her flowing hair she tosses to and fro about her head as if it were an irksome basketball. Her appearance she doesn't give a hoot about. The take-it-or-leave-it type, she may come in for the moment like a lamb, but she stays and goes out like a circus lion. She is a nitroglycerine sandwich, three-decker with mustard.

Gertrude Lawrence came to America first from her native England as a singing and dancing girl in a Charlot revue. Her figure is still as slender and full of grace as it was then; her spirit is quite as lively — on occasion even disturbingly livelier; and the only thing about her that has materially changed is her talent, which has developed so astonishingly that she is perhaps the most versatile actress on the contemporary American stage. She can play a dramatic scene forcefully; she can sing a song drolly; she can dance and shake a naughty hip with the best of them; she can do, it would seem, pretty nearly everything. She isn't beautiful; she isn't the kind movie magazines spread in six-color grandeur on their covers; she would never get an Oscar for being the most popular girl in Hollywood; and Cesar Romero probably never heard of her. But she, like the others named, is one of the theatre's own real glamour girls.

In short and in general, when a beautiful young screen actress ages there are only two roads open to her: either retirement, forced or voluntary, or more or less low-comedy roles which are insulting to her persistent adorable picture of herself. When, on the other hand, a beautiful young stage actress grows older, the loss of her beauty means little and her career may continue on its path without change. There is not, I believe, a single former great film beauty now in her middle forties who, if she has a job at all, isn't condemned to roles designed to make movie audiences laugh. On the other hand, there are any number of formerly lovely ladies of forty, fifty and even sixty on the stage today who are far from being cruelly peddled to the trade as clowns.

HARVEY. November 1, 1944

A fantastic farce-comedy by Mary Chase. Produced by Brock Pemberton for a far beyond the season run in the 48th Street Theatre. Awarded the Pulitzer prize.

PROGRAM

Myrtle Mae Simmons — *Jane Van Duser*	Marvin Wilson — *Jesse White*
Veta Louise Simmons — *Josephine Hull*	Lyman Sanderson, M.D. — *Tom Seidel*
Elwood P. Dowd — *Frank Fay*	William R. Chumley, M.D. — *Fred Irving Lewis*
Miss Johnson — *Eloise Sheldon*	Betty Chumley — *Dora Clement*
Mrs. Ethel Chauvenet — *Frederica Going*	Mr. Peeples — *Lawrence Hayes*
Ruth Kelly, R.N. — *Janet Tyler*	Judge Omar Gaffney — *John Kirk*
	E. J. Lofgren — *Robert Gist*

SYNOPSIS: Act I. Scene 1. *The library, afternoon.* Scene 2. *Chumley's Rest, an hour later.* Act II. Scene 1. *The library, an hour later.* Scene 2. *Chumley's Rest, four hours later.* Act III. *Chumley's Rest, a few minutes later.*

The action of the play takes place in a city in the Far West in the library of the old Dowd family mansion and the reception room of Chumley's Rest.

Time. *The present.*

Some thirty-odd years ago H. L. Mencken composed a philosophy to the effect that the Creator had overlooked an idea in not surcharging the atmosphere about us with ethyl alcohol. Had He done so, pondered Mencken, the world would be infinitely happier and more contented than it is or has been; its inhabitants, breathing in the salubrious air, would be constantly maintained in a glowing, expansive, and beneficent state; peace and good will would reign on earth; and heroes would be born, in their own grandiose estimation, by the hour. Much this same philosophy is the core of Miss Chase's play, which, for all its several lapses, constitutes a generally delightful theatrical evening.

A mixture of fantasy, comedy and farce, that evening concerns a gentleman given to spirituous liqours who, while in a blissful condition, meets up in alcoholic fancy with a rabbit six feet one and one-half inches tall and who enjoys him thereafter as a steady, understanding, and sympathetic companion. So enviable a companion is the rabbit, indeed, that others who have been wont to look askance at the cupful gentleman engage him as well, and find him all that his first discoverer has found him. The latter's family, however, like most unthinking families, presently deem it expedient that their blood-brother rid himself of the beast and to that end have him consigned to a sanitarium. But just as he is about to receive the treatment that will banish the rabbit forevermore they acquire wisdom from a passing taxi driver long versed in the way of humans — the wisdom, to wit, that teetotalers and other such theoretically normal fowl are quarrelsome, grasping, querulous, and miserable — and decide to allow their blood-brother to go on being as kindly, generous, happy, and sans souci as he has been.

As you may gather, what you have here is an extended paraphrase of the familiar skit in the burlesque shows wherein the inebriated low comedian is told that he is sitting opposite a great big beautiful luscious blonde and drinking champagne wine and wherein he thereupon for the next fifteen minutes accepts the delusion as fact and has himself a wonderful time, embroidered with the Pirandello and Synge (*The Well Of The Saints*) theory of the superiority of illusion to reality. In short, what the play dramaturgically is is the character of Joe, the gentle alcoholic out of Saroyan's *The Time Of Your Life,* provided with a rabbit variation of the burlesque blonde. But Miss Chase has added so much of her own and has played over the whole a fantasy at once so paradoxically realistic and basically so in keeping with life that her exhibit, despite an overly long induction and a third act that suffers a bad twelve-minute let-down, amounts in sum to excellent entertainment. Saroyan might on the whole have written a critically much better play on the theme, one touched with considerably more poetic imagination than Miss Chase's, but, in Saroyan's absence, Miss Chase's will do, and very nicely. What is more, nine people out of every ten (and that includes certain of the professional reviewers) have liked and will like it better than what Saroyan might have made of it. Which is the American theatre's reward, in a manner of speaking, for keeping fancy closer to ground.

Some of Miss Chase's humor is exceptionally fertile. Her account of the barfly's first meeting with Harvey, which is the rabbit's name, after he had solicitously put a brother tosspot to bed is an example. "I saw him leaning against a lamp post when I came out and he called me by name," the lush tells an inquiring psychiatrist. "Didn't you think that rather peculiar?" asks the latter, significantly narrowing his eyes. "No," easily replies Elwood P. Dowd, the lush; "you know how it is in a small town; everybody knows everybody else."

Harvey, according to Elwood, has some extraordinary virtues. He can stop clocks and you can go wherever you wish and do anything you please and when you come back you find that not so much as one minute has passed. And he does away with time and space and is better than Einstein, for he does away with time and space — and objections.

In the leading role, Frank Fay, the old vaudeville headliner, is capital. His drunk is not the more usual actor drunk who moves unsteadily about the stage or accompanies his speech with an obbligato of hiccups or engages in any other such ritualistic business, but one in whom a sincere absorption of alcohol has left only a benign fogginess and whose physical deportment and locutions are not materially different from those of the average abstemious member of society. Fay underplays as any long experienced lush always underplays, whereas the usual stage lush overplays like an amateur affected by two drinks. And as his sister who, though deeply concerned about him on one occasion also sees Harvey, Josephine Hull is an admirable comic foil.

Mr. Pemberton's physical production, designed by John Root, looks, however, as if it cost all of ten dollars.

SLEEP, MY PRETTY ONE
November 2, 1944

A play by Charlcie and Oliver H. P. Garrett. Produced by Richard W. Krakaur, in association with Roger Clark, for 4 performances in the Playhouse.

PROGRAM

EDWARD *J. Colville Dunn*
KATHRYN STURDEVANT *Norma Chambers*
EMILY GROAT *Theresa Dale*
ELEANOR COATES *Audrey Ridgewell*
WINIFRED AGATE *Julie Stevens*
DONALD STURDEVANT *Harry Ellerbe*
MRS. ALICIA STURDEVANT *Pauline Lord*
LT. ("HANK") WILLIAMS *Don Gibson*
DR. OGDEN POMFRET *Ivan Simpson*

SYNOPSIS: Act I. *The living-room late Saturday afternoon.* Act II. *The same. Sunday morning.* Act III. Scene 1. *A sitting-room at the top of the house. Late Sunday afternoon.* Scene 2. *The same, after dinner, Sunday night.*

The action of the play takes place in a house on Gramercy Park during a week-end in the spring of 1944.

THE POSSESSIVE MOTHER theme is so familiar to the local stage that, save an exceptionally able playwright pitch his imaginative talent against it, it is pretty certain to result in a barbiturate evening. The Garretts are far from being exceptionally able playwrights and their imaginative talent is invisible. Their variation is consequently without the slightest critical merit, as were such last season's plays on the theme by equally inexpert writers as *The House In Paris, Only The Heart,* and *Pretty Little Parlor,* all of which similarly were box-office failures.

The mother in the Garretts' job is determined to hold on to her son at all costs and to that end resorts to everything from malicious gossip to murder by way of keeping him from marrying. She gets rid of his first fiancée by pushing her to her death out of a high window. She gets rid of the second by scaring the wits out of the poor girl with gruesome family secrets. And she plots against the third with hints to her son that the girl is sexually miscellaneous, with — when that does not seem to work — poisoned drinks, and with — when that in turn does not work — an attempt at murder via the same high window that figured in the demise of fiancée No. 1, which, though it too does not work, succeeds in driving the terrified young woman out of the house. Finally, she swallows the poisoned drink herself and dies, happy in the realization that her son is still hers.

The balderdash, which is neither dramatic fish, psychological flesh nor good melodramatic fowl but greasepaint herring, is retailed in dialogue that bears only a remote resemblance to normal human speech and is dramatized generally in such terms as the butler who, while alternately arranging the flowers, setting the tea table and stirring the grate fire, acquaints the audience with facts about the family; the mother who addresses her Machiavellian plottings from a wheel-chair; the son who, upon being told of his fiancée's alleged sexual indiscretions, indulges in such Pineroisms as his determination to stand by her for all the dictates of morality; the sister with the acidulous tongue who sits to one side and intermittently comments on what is going on; the fiancée who skips breezily up and down the stairs, tosses her hair about, and makes darling little *moués* at her intended; and the old family doctor in the black coat, wing collar and Ascot tie who butters the old mother by telling her that she is still as beautiful as when he first saw her thirty or forty years ago.

Pauline Lord acted the role of the mother half-heartedly, which was fifty percent in excess of its deserts. The rest of the company, excepting Julie Stevens as the third fiancée and Don Gibson as the young naval lieutenant who eventually gets her, performed like an old-time Priscilla Knowles stock company.

The direction by Roy Hargrave kept the members of the family moving so ceaselessly about the stage that the Gramercy Park house resembled the Harlem Savoy dance hall.

DON'T, GEORGE! November 2, 1944

A comedy by Katherine Laure. Produced by the Blackfriars' Guild for 21 performances in the Blackfriars' Theatre.

Program

Adelaide Averson	*Carol Dunning*
George Averson	*Hal Hershey*
Laura Carwood	*Romola Robb*
Paul Leland	*Arthur Allen*
David Averson	*Jack O'Neil*
Edythe Averson	*Eleanor Stafford*

SYNOPSIS: *The entire action of the play takes place in the living-room of the Averson family. Act I. Early evening of a day in October, 1929.* Act II. Scene 1. *Early morning in April, 1941.* Scene 2. *Late afternoon of the same day.* Act III. Scene 1. *An evening several days later.* Scene 2. *Midnight the same day.*

The Blackfriars' Guild has devoted itself for the most part to the experimental drama. On this occasion its experiment lay in an apparent effort to duplicate the kind of play that shows up on Broadway at regular intervals and is dispatched forthwith to the storehouse. The experiment was successful.

Miss Laure is an apprentice in dramaturgy and her play sufficiently proves it to anyone conceivably unaware of the statistic. Dealing with a mother who tries to steal her sister's fiancé on behalf of her daughter and whose husband sets himself to undo her plans, her dramatic construction is such that her main characters are waved aside in midstream and her focus thereafter directed upon others considerably less material. She further mixes the moods of farce and drama and has a penchant for rather odious puns.

The Blackfriars' name this time was Gustav Blum.

ROBIN HOOD. November 7, 1944

Revival of the comic opera by Reginald De Koven and Harry B. Smith. Produced by R. H. Burnside for 15 performances in the Adelphi Theatre.

PROGRAM

Robert of Huntington (afterwards Robin Hood)	*Robert Field*	Friar Tuck	*Jerry Robbins*
Sheriff of Nottingham	*George Lipton*	Alan-a-Dale	*Edith Herlick*
Sir Guy of Gisborne	*Frank Farrell*	Lady Marian Fitzwalter (A Ward of the Crown, afterwards Maid Marian)	*Barbara Scully*
Little John	*Harold Patrick*	Dame Durden	*Zamah Cunningham*
Will Scarlett	*Wilfred Glenn*	Annabel	*Margaret Spencer*

Milkmaids, Sheriff's Men, King's Men, Villagers, Archers, and Outlaws.

SYNOPSIS: Act I. *A market place in Nottingham.* Act II. *Sherwood Forest.* Act III. *Courtyard of the Sheriff's castle.*

The scene is laid in England at the time of Richard I.

Whenever one of these old comic operas is revived, members of the younger generation who have long heard their elders bask warmly in recollection of it are often to be observed scratching their noses, if polite, or fingering them, if not, and grunting to the effect that, if that is what the old days were like, good riddance to them and thank the gods for even *Bloomer Girl.*

The attitude of the younger folk is, however, contrary to the general idea not entirely the result of changed tastes. Tastes have changed much less than is commonly supposed, as the persistent success of operettas of years ago like those of Gilbert and Sullivan and like *Die Fledermaus* (*Rosalinda*) and *The Merry Widow* indicates. The theory that the younger generation is composed in its entirety of addicts to juke boxes and the Messrs. Sinatra and Crosby is hardly true. The adolescents who are addicted to them seldom go to the theatre and hence do not figure in the argument. The young ones who do attend the theatre are of a relatively superior cut and are not wholly the ignorami their elders sometimes believe them to be.

There is, accordingly, something to be said for their attitude. Time and again a show that in its original incarnation was all that their elders' memories recall it to have been is, in revival, so lacking in its original brilliance that the elders themselves are tempted to adopt the youngsters' nose exercises. Time and again the principals figuring in the revival are so abjectly inferior to those in the bygone productions, the scenery and costumes so inexpedient, and the atmosphere of the whole so damp in comparison that the oldsters may be pardoned for doubting the merit of their former enthusiasm. The younger generation's attitude is thus like that of the little girl who saw Lillian Russell late in life when avoirdupois had overtaken her and who wondered audibly about the sanity of her old man who had told her that Lillian was the most gorgeous creature he had ever seen on the stage and boasted loudly that he had once quaffed champagne from her tiny slipper.

This latest revival of the De Koven operetta is a case in illuminating point. Produced originally in 1890 by that outgrowth of the Boston Ideal Opera Company which became famous under the name of the Bostonians, it caught the fancy of the public largely by virtue of its score and the exceptional aggregation that sang it. Not only did the De Koven music become a household piano word but its stage merchants soon figured among the pin-up favorites of theatregoers far and wide. The roster of the company, including such celebrated names as Henry Clay Barnabee, George B. Frothingham, William H. MacDonald, Jessie Bartlett Davis, *et al.*, was equalled by no other local comic opera troupe of the era.

Smith's romantic book, too, found favor with a public that welcomed a little relief from the many musical show books based upon stale French farces about the peccadillos of various Gastons and Fifis, or devised solely to exhibit Frank Daniels as an Ameer, Caliph, Grand Vizier or whatnot trying to trick the adventurous baritone out of stealing the idol's ruby eye, or concerned with fairy tales which seemed to center their legendary charm largely in trapdoors that didn't work. And though criticism here and there condescended to the exhibit as being "a comic opera with a monocle: one eye seeing English, the other American," it took its place as the first relatively authentic American item of its genre in the esteem of the theatre trade.

I did not see that opening production, but I did see it later on its road travels, and I saw the New York revivals in 1900 and 1902 with much the same principals, and I have seen, I think, almost every revival with other companies in the following years. And that is the reason why, within limits, I can sympathize with the youngsters who, now beholding the show for the first time, are skeptical as to what all the fever was for.

The voices in the present revival are generally unequal to the score, and not one of the principals has about him or her any faintest trace of the talent or stage splendor of the originals. In place of the Bostonians we have, eheu, the Burnsideans. And where once the stage offered a scenic and costume picture at least notable in its day, it now offers something not materially superior to Mr. Burnside's last season's Gilbert and Sullivan stage, which came near to hitting a new low. And the direction, which in earlier presentations of the comic opera aptly fused the score and book into a flowing entity, is of the slipshod species which lends to the evening the air of a succession of turns in which the performers come on, do their acts, and then either stand to one side looking over the house or walk off. So do not speak too harshly to the younger generation.

That generation's theory that we older folk are always inclined sentimentally to recall virtues in plays and shows of the past which probably were non-existent somehow occasionally has some sense in it. I say occasionally, for though I think it on the whole without merit in the instance of the Bostonians' version of this *Robin Hood,* I grant it considerable merit in the instance of certain subsequent revivals. To believe that all these revivals were deserving of deep nostalgic sighs is worse than foolish. I have seen a revival or two that were no whit better than the poor one here considered. And I have seen at least one that was actually not quite so good.

But it is not the revivals, it is the Bostonians' performance that chiefly occupies us. And even in that case the younger generation may be tickled to know that not everything as a matter of fact was, in the phrase of their French governesses, *sans tache.* In its earliest stages, the show was found suddenly to go lifeless at one point and it was not until the subsequently famous "O Promise Me," derived from an old Italian song called "Forbidden Music," was incorporated that the dead spot was got rid of. (In later years and in other directions it was "Poor Butterfly" that was rushed in to save a big Hippodrome show and "They Wouldn't Believe Me" belatedly hurried into the breach from *The Girl From Utah* to fill a blank spot in, of all things, *The Dollar Princess.*)

The celebrated "Brown October Ale," furthermore, had to be staged in three different ways before its final full effect was realized. The stage lighting, in addition, at times seriously disturbed the equanimity of the historians, since the repertoire of the company operated to confuse the gentleman at the switchboard, with the result that Sherwood Forest now and again fitfully dazzled forth like the old Waldorf's ballroom and the market place took on the sombre gloom of the forest. And, finally, the internal jealousies of the company, which were to bring about its end in 1905, were haplessly not always too well concealed from the audiences. But the *Robin Hood* of the Bostonians was nonetheless, kids, a far, a very far cry — say about 10,000 miles — from the *Robin Hood* of the Burnsideans.

What inevitably ages in the old comic operas, including this one, is, naturally, some of the humor. Certainly such jocosities as "I dote on you" — "What I want is an antidote" hardly remain the source of any mirth. Nor do such bits of stage business as involve a male holding another male's hand under the impression that it is that of a woman who has slyly absented herself, or the two characters who stealthily tiptoe on backward from opposite sides of the stage, bump into each other and thereupon give vent to frightened shrieks, or the inebriated character who in trying to make an exit bumps into a door, staggers back and then extends his forefinger as a guide and follows it through the door. But at their worst they are not any flatter and any staler than a lot of the jokes and byplay which infect the many musical shows of today and which seem greatly to entertain audiences. And, furthermore, there was all the difference in the world between the manner in which they were handled by such expert comics of the past as Barnabee and are handled by such inexpert ones of the present as George Lipton. There is, for example, nothing particularly funny about, say, the expression, "I'm mortified!"; a dozen minor comedians may proclaim it and leave an audience's features undisturbed; but let a proficient comedian like Jimmy Durante get his hands on it and it makes an audience howl for years on end.

IN BED WE CRY. NOVEMBER 14, 1944

A play by Ilka Chase, derived from her novel of the same title. Produced by John C. Wilson for 47 forced performances in the Belasco Theatre.

PROGRAM

JASPER DOOLITTLE	*Paul McGrath*	NICK VAN ALSTON	*Maury Tuckerman*
BRUCE MORELY	*John Kane*	DICK HADLEY	*Douglas Gregory*
DEVON ELLIOTT WAINWRIGHT	*Ilka Chase*	JENNIE MOORE	*Ruth Matteson*
SUZANNE	*Virginia Kaye*	CLAIRE DANGERFIELD	*Eleanor Audley*
TIM WAINWRIGHT	*Francis DeSales*	FAIRWEATHER	*Harold Crane*
HILDA	*Gynia Gray*	KURT FABRI	*Frederic Tozere*
MIRIAM DOYLE	*Claudia Walden*	DELIVERY BOY	*Milton Spelvin*
BARBARA HORLICK	*Helen Marcy*	MARIA SELLNER	*Elena Karam*

SYNOPSIS: Act I. Scene 1. *Devon Elliott's office in Devonshire House, evening, January, 1941.* Scene 2. *Devon's drawing-room. About six weeks later. Late February.* Act II. Scene 1. *The same. March, three weeks later.* Scene 2. *Kurt's apartment. November evening.* Scene 3. *The drawing-room, December evening, three days before Christmas.* Act III. Scene 1. *The office, April morning.* Scene 2. *The same, ten days later.*

THE EXHIBIT is what is customarily described as a "smart" play, chiefly by the kind of fashionables whose vocabularies do not permit "smart" and "intelligent" as synonyms. A smart play, we have come to learn from them, is rather one in which a poverty in mentality is concealed in a wealth of external personal adornment, in which the characters perseveringly employ conversation to evade thought, and in which sex is an act negotiated on the part of the males not biologically but linguistically and on the part of the females in the miscellaneous manner of their canine prototypes.

There are other attributes common to the smart play. The manners are for the most part consistently bad; the morals are worse; and worldliness and sophistication are hopefully sought for through what is essentially only an impertinent parochialism. Insult is esteemed to be the mark of a superior mind, and gentility, tenderness, sympathy, and normal decency are regarded as qualities impossibly demoded. The characters in the average smart play, in short, represent persons who in life would be denied entrance into any house of the slightest self-respect and who would be able to get into the other kind only on the score of their clothes and money.

An adroit playwright gifted with a satiric wit may of course lay hold of such materials and contrive an entertaining and very acceptable play out of them, as Maugham has attested on a number of occasions and as other writers for the stage, English, French and American, have similarly indicated. But given a playwright without such dramatic talent and without such wit and humor and what is most often likely to result is the sort of exhibit which oppositely reminds one of Kin Hubbard's explanation of the good, clean country air in the fact that the farmers keep their windows closed. Miss Chase's contribution, based on her novel of the same title, unfortunately leaves its windows open. And since she is deficient in any relieving wit or humor her play gives the nasal impression, usual under the circumstances, of a lot of very wet, soiled underclothes pinned up on a line to dry. The perfume is hardly edifying.

The lady's intense efforts to mold her materials into the pseudo-smart pattern only go to make her exhibit the more trying. Posing as a woman of the world, her dialogue indulges in such small town epigrams as "A woman too often mistakes a man's attention for intention" and in such marked-down cynicisms as "You surely don't mean to say that you are going to bed with your husband." Essaying to give her heroine's sexual excursions the desired smart offhand air, her shortcomings as a writer succeed only in making the air off-color. And relying upon a modish couturier to make externally attractive what in internal character is repulsive she haplessly for her purposes brings down the house when in the role of her heroine she comes on in a white satin circus-horse creation with what appears to be a window-box of red geraniums attached to its rear and causes a lover upon beholding her in it raptly to exclaim,

"That gown, I take it, is calculated to reduce resistance!," thereupon promptly indicating his own unconditional surrender by fingering aside the bodice and imprinting a couple of loud labial smacks upon its wearer's bosoms.

It thus certainly can not be said that Miss Chase, like certain other actresses who have composed plays in their own honor, hasn't had herself a time, usurping it from her audience. That she has mistaken vulgarity for smartness in any genuine sense and that she has confused dialogic brittleness with crispness, leading to lines that crack rather than crackle, doesn't seem to interfere with her personal pleasure in the least. She treats herself to enough entrances in fancy frocks to serve a pre-war Ambassadeurs revue; she causes herself to be addressed as "one of the most successful women in America" and to be greased by the other characters on her charm, intelligence, and powerful physical allure; she provides herself with three different men who are crazy about her and who can hardly live without her; she sends herself huge baskets of flowers; she gratifies herself with two or three scenes in which an actor-lover kisses her so long and passionately that she emerges from the picnic completely breathless; she allows herself an episode in which to display her bare legs; she presents herself as the superior of all the other characters on the stage in the matter of repartee; and she brings down the act curtains with herself invariably in the pitcher's box, and going strong.

As for her acting performance, it passed muster only when she called upon herself to discharge acidulous remarks. When she demanded of herself that she indicate any depth of emotion the result was a series of facial contortions which suggested a deeply troubled spirit infinitely less than an imminent very bad nose cold.

The most peculiar thing among the many peculiar things in a peculiar evening was the author's strange conviction that she had fashioned a highly sympathetic role for herself in the character of a woman who can not understand, simply because she has a former lover living in the same house with her and because she is indulging in an extensive affair with still another, why her husband sees fit to leave her.

SADIE THOMPSON. November 16, 1944

A musical version, by Rouben Mamoulian and Howard Dietz, of the play Rain *by John Colton and Clemence Randolph, which was in turn a dramatization of W. S. Maugham's story,* Miss Thompson; *music by Vernon Duke, lyrics by Howard Dietz. Produced by A. P. Waxman for 60 performances and a loss of 180,000 dollars in the Alvin Theatre.*

PROGRAM

JOE HORN	*Ralph Dumke*	CICELY ST. CLAIR	*Doris Patston*
CORPORAL HODGSON	*Daniel Cobb*	LAO LAO	*Remington Olmsted*
PRIVATE GRIGGS	*Norman Lawrence*	SADIE THOMPSON	*June Havoc*
SERGEANT TIM O'HARA	*James Newill*	QUARTERMASTER BATES	*William Lynn*
AMEENA	*Grazia Narciso*	REVEREND ALFRED DAVIDSON	*Lansing Hatfield*
HONEYPIE	*Beatrice Kraft*	PREMIERE DANSEUSE	*Milada Mladova*
MRS. ALFRED DAVIDSON	*Zolya Talma*	PREMIER DANCER	*Chris Volkoff*

Marines, Natives and Children

SYNOPSIS: Act I. Scene 1. *Trader Joe Horn's hotel-store in Pago Pago, on the island of Tutuila, in the South Seas.* Scene 2. *The jungle.* Act II. *Same as Act I, Scene 1.*

THE GENERAL DISAPPOINTMENT in the presentation seemed to be predicated on three or four reasons, all of them wrong. It was contended, first, that *Rain* is essentially too serious a play to lend itself to musical treatment of any kind. The play *Porgy* is hardly less serious, yet it lent itself satisfactorily in the case of *Porgy and Bess.* It was argued, secondly, that there is something a little ridiculous in having a man of the church like the Rev. Davidson burst periodically into song. Yet it has never been thought ridiculous in the case of *Nanon, The Colleen Bawn,* etc. Thirdly, it was ventured that a musical exhibit which ends with death in shark-infested waters is hardly in proper key with the medium. But one like *Norma* which ends with death on a funeral pyre has been perfectly acceptable. And, fourthly, there was complaint that the prostitute Sadie is not a sufficiently romantic character for a heroine in the musical form. Yet it is difficult to see why Sadie isn't a character quite as romantic as, say, the prostitute Panama Hattie in the successful show of that name. And the further contention that a harlot character is altogether too stale anyway for the current stage doesn't seem to hold in the case of the enormously successful *Anna Lucasta.*

If *Sadie Thompson* is a disappointment, it is not, surely, on any such counts. There is no reason in the world why it might not have been a good musical play. It isn't one simply because, while the play element is competent, the musical element is not, and because the whole enterprise has been damaged by the application to it of too much of what Broadway is pleased to regard as imagination.

This so-called imagination in the present instance goes a long way toward throwing a wrench into the show. Instead of leaving well enough alone, the producer has invested the proceedings with so much unnecessary embroidery in the way of arty choreography and choral numbers that the net impression is considerably less of the stimulating Thompson of the original Maugham fancy than of a depressing imitation of the Thompson of the old Hippodrome firm of Thompson and Dundy.

It is this embroidery that frequently interferes with the flow and flavor of the show and diminishes what might be its pleasure, much as the pleasure of a dinner is inevitably diminished by a similar too elaborate and intrusive service. If the enterprise had been allowed a greater measure of directness and simplicity, the result would have been, I daresay, considerably more prosperous. As it is, the show gives the effect of a play vitiated by ballet, of ballet vitiated by choral singing, of choral singing vitiated by incidental pantomime, and of the whole intermittently invaded by colorless tunes set to malapropos lyrics. Surely such things as a paraphrase of Raymond Hitchcock's old ditty, "Life's A Funny Proposition," called "Life's A Funny Present" are scarcely suitable to the character of Sadie Thompson in a serious moment. And such lyrics as "Poor As A Church Mouse" are considerably less fitting to the character in her lighter moments than such as "I Lived In A House With A Piano" and "I'm A Stayin'-in Girl For A Stayin'-out Man," which for some inscrutable reason were deleted during the rehearsal period. What the show all in all amounts to, in brief, is a hybrid composed of one-third *Rain,* one-third *Run, Little Chillun,* and one-third run-down juke box. Out of it emerges only a Sadie in the person of June Havoc who is pictorially perfect and dramatically often believable.

The "imagination" with which Mr. Mamoulian, the director, has invested the show, and wrecked it, is part and parcel of the current campaign in certain quarters to rid the stage of realism at all costs, however sound and in keeping with its particular medium it may happen to be. As one of the outstanding campaigners we have Mr. Mamoulian's hand-brother, Mr. Robert Edmond Jones, the well-known scene designer and himself also an occasional stage director. Performing in the public prints, this Mr. Jones issues with a somewhat more copious spray of indignation than several hundred other past joneses the aforesaid peremptory demand for less realism and more fancy. While it is far from me to disagree with him and his several hundred antecedents on the basic principle involved, I think that he, even more than the others, is guilty of something closely approaching a tin-horn snobbishness, which is no way to win arguments on behalf of the theatre or anything else.

"The other day at a cocktail party," he observes, "I found myself discussing the current theatre with a very charming and intelligent young woman. In the course of our conversation she said to me, 'I haven't seen many plays lately; they don't seem so interesting this season, somehow; do you think so? But I did see one good play last week. You know the one I mean — I never can remember names — the one that has the icebox in it. Do you know, that was a real icebox and those were real ice cubes. Now, that's the kind of a play I like.' "

Whereat Mr. Jones, his æsthetic soul revolted, shudderingly exclaims, "Ice cubes!," as if they were the effluvium of a skunk.

Partly regaining his equilibrium, Mr. Jones then proceeds agonizedly to reflect on "the Childs restaurant which David Belasco set bodily on the stage of his theatre in the third act of *The Governor's Lady,* complete with real coffee urns and real waiters and real butter cakes." His tortured conclusion is that "here we are, after thirty years, face to face again with the old conflict between realism and imagination in the theatre, the same preoccupation with externalities."

It is something of a pity that Mr. Jones' experience and critical faculties are not so developed as his exasperation. The Belasco play of which he speaks was rubbish and would not have been any better in the way of imagination if the Childs restaurant scene had been omitted or even painted by Mr. Jones, in his most imaginative manner, on the backdrop. Furthermore, when he singles out the absurd Belasco realism as typical of the theatre in its year, which was 1912, he indicates a very poor acquaintance with the period. On that stage in the same year were such hardly realistic plays as Louis N. Parker's *At Versailles, 1780,* James Bernard Fagan's *Bella Donna,* Pierre Loti's *The Daughter Of Heaven,* Charles Rann Kennedy's adaptation of *The Flower Of The Palace Of Han,* Edward Sheldon's *The High Road,* Lady Gregory's *The Image,* and Edward Knoblauch's *Kismet.* Also Richard Walton Tully's *The Bird Of Paradise,* Compton Mackenzie's *Carnival,* Bernard Shaw's *Fanny's First Play,* Rostand's *The Lady Of Dreams,* the Hazelton-Benrimo *The Yellow Jacket,* Rudolf Besier's *Lady Patricia,* and Booth Tarkington's *Monsieur Beaucaire.* And in addition numerous such others as Galsworthy's *The Pigeon,* Synge's *Riders To The Sea,* the fairy tale play, *Snow White And The Seven Dwarfs,* and Freksa's highly fanciful *Sumurun.*

Unlike the trashy *The Governor's Lady* with its real coffee urns, real waiters and real butter cakes, the current play upon which Mr. Jones heaps his scorn for its real icebox and real ice cubes (*The Voice Of The Turtle*) is a charming lyric comedy, imaginative, adroitly written, and altogether commendable. To sneer at it simply because it contains a few realistic properties, which, incidentally, are necessary to the play, is a childish business and quite as silly as it would be to scoff at Hauptmann's *The Weavers* for its real looms, real winding wheels and real cook-stove, at Shaw's *Man And Superman* for its real automobile, at O'Neill's *The Straw* for its real weighing machine, or at Sean O'Casey's *Purple Dust* for its real farm roller. Or, for that matter, at the production of Shakespeare's *Richard III,* in which Mr. Jones himself had a big hand, for its real horse.

That Mr. Jones and the brother joneses should either relinquish cocktail parties with their brain-confounding gins or select only those attended, God forbid, by professional critics, becomes further evident from his additionally derived indignations.

"I thought," he says, "of all the artists in other fields who have done and are doing so much to crystallize the increasingly dynamic point of view of our time." Whereupon he illustrates with, among others, the names of Virgil Thomson, James Joyce, Gertrude Stein, E. E. Cummings, John Dos Passos, Ruth and Paul Draper, Angna Enters, George Balanchine, and Martha Graham. "And then," he rushes on, "I thought of the output of the Broadway theatre of 1944, contemporary, so far as its approach to life is concerned, with the Rogers Group and with Landseer's *Dignity And Impudence* and with the barroom nudes of Bougereau. Why is it, I asked myself, that the theatre so persistently avoids the possibilty of any contagion from the other arts?"

Since I do not cultivate cocktail parties and hence preserve myself in a measure from mist, I answer the question which raddles Mr. Jones. The theatre does not persistently avoid the contagion of which he speaks. What is more, it doesn't seem to profit greatly from it when it exposes itself to it. Consider some of the very names which our friend stipulates, at the top of his voice. Virgil Thomson and Gertrude Stein collaborated on *Four Saints In Three Acts* which the theatre produced to no sound critical end. Mr. Thomson's so-called ballet-document, *Filling Station,* similarly didn't help much. Miss Stein has written a number of plays, all of them so bad that to produce them on the stage would be to suffer richly deserved ridicule. James Joyce has seen production with a play called *Exiles,* which was mediocre drama, and his *Finnegans Wake* constituted the body of *The Skin Of Our Teeth,* which I am prepared to give to Mr. Jones as a present, gratis. John Dos Passos has been represented in the theatre by *The Moon Is A Gong* and *Airways, Inc.,* neither of which disclosed anything beyond an arbitrary desire to "experiment"; both were wholly negligible contributions to the drama. And E. E. Cummings, if memory serves, had his chance with a play called *Him,* which explored nothing in the vein of dramatic merit.

As for the others Mr. Jones sighs over, George Balanchine has already served the theatre, and well, in connection with a number of musical shows and operettas, and Eugene Loring, whom Mr. Jones forgets to name, is responsible for a lot of the delight in *Carmen Jones.* Paul Draper has displayed his dancing art on the stage, and Ruth Draper her mimetic art, and Angna Enters her pantomimic art, and Martha Graham her choreographic art, and one or two of them have further had a hand, if I am not mistaken, in certain productions. But, with all their talent, just how the drama can profitably catch anything contagious from Paul Draper's tap dance steps or from Ruth Draper's imitations, I, for one, must doubtless go to a cocktail party to learn. (It didn't catch anything, save a very bad headache, from Miss Draper's colleague, Cornelia Otis Skinner, when she invaded it with *Edna, His Wife.*) Nor can I see, teetotaler that I am at the fleeting moment, just how Miss Enters' pantomimes might be instrumental in injecting more imagination into the drama than was injected many years ago by the plays *Sumurun, L'Enfant Prodigue, Puppet-Play, et al.,* or how Miss Graham has anything that might influence to their prosperity the imaginations of a herd of new young Eugene O'Neills or even Saroyans, presuming their birth or existence.

Apparently still inflamed by his Martini, Mr. Jones' dudgeon thereupon takes the form of a denunciation of the later plays. "They are not," he cries out, "plays so much as animated photographs, candid camera shots of life, living movies with a few exciting 'personal appearances' thrown in from time to time for good measure. They do not, properly speaking, belong to the theatre at all."

When Mr. Jones goes on the waterwagon again, we may venture to ask him how the following more recent plays fit his definitions of mere "animated photographs, candid camera shots and living movies": *A Highland Fling, The Innocent Voyage, Harvey, The Pirate, Lady In The Dark, Outrageous Fortune, Career Angel, Dark Of The Moon, The Glass Menagerie,* etc., etc.

Melancholiously negotiating the olive, Mr. Jones, summing up his laments, thuswise finally composes his misery: "I tried to communicate some of these thoughts to my companion ['the very charming and intelligent young woman' who had made the initial remark about ice cubes] who looked at me with an expression of growing bewilderment from under her dizzy little hat with the hortensias on it. As I turned away to say goodbye to my hostess her voice followed me: 'Well, I don't care what he said, I liked that play!' "

As Mr. Jones turned away, my voice, had I been at the party, would have followed him along with that of the young woman's.

Mr. Jones and all the other joneses who have resolved themselves into an Imagination Salvation Army commit, I believe, the same error in logic. That they are to be commended for praying for a drama that will more often fly aloft to the stars is surely open to no question, and I hereby add my own pat on the back to that of everyone else who has any affection and respect for the theatre. It is, however, their conception of what constitutes imagination in drama that transforms that pat on the back into a more emphatic manual application to a somewhat lower section of the anatomy.

It seems to be their idea, promulgated either directly or

by implication, that true imagination is necessarily and inevitably linked with experiment and that, inferentially, it does not and can not flower in the more conventional dramaturgical patterns. Among his other cocktail meditations, Mr. Jones, for example, nominated directly in this connection plays like *The Green Pastures, Mourning Becomes Electra* and *The Great God Brown.* Now, while there is no gainsaying that these plays were invested simultaneously with imagination and experiment, it nevertheless stands gainsaying that such non-experimental (in the jonesian sense) plays as, say, the same authors' *The Wisdom Tooth, Anna Christie* and *Desire Under The Elms* were, for that reason, devoid of imagination. Imagination, surely, is not necessarily confined to skeletonized scenery, masks, four-hour plays or sets manipulated, as in *The Skin Of Our Teeth,* which Mr. Jones also names, by ropes in the hands of the actors. One might even argue that such things and others like them proudly hinted at by the joneses do not even constitute experiment, since most of them, far from falling under that head, have seen previous use in the theatre.

The so-called realistic drama, further, has often shown an imagination far superior to what the joneses endorse as the drama of fancy, romance, and imagination. There is infinitely greater imagination, in any sound critical appraisal, in Hauptmann's *Drayman Henschel* than in something like Maeterlinck's *Alladine and Palomides.* There is much more true imagination in a play like Strindberg's *The Dance Of Death* than in one like Rostand's *The Romancers.* And I'll give Mr. Jones all the imagination he seems to be able to find in the aforesaid *The Skin Of Our Teeth* for the imagination in even a single act of a purely realistic play like *Of Mice And Men.*

But while the joneses, along with myself, may, whatever our respective definitions, demand imagination in the theatre, it seems to be doubtful that we aren't pretty much alone in the demand. Nine out of every ten imaginative plays — and I here submit to the Jones definition — which have been produced in our theatre in the recent years have, whatever their quality, proved to be commercial failures. On the side of quality the failures have ranged all the way from *The Beautiful People, A Highland Fling, My Heart's In The Highlands, Magic,* and *Murder In The Cathedral* to, on the other side, *Lily Of The Valley, Mr. Sycamore, Talking To You, Achilles Had A Heel,* and *Kindred.* Dozens of plays, relative quality or little, like *Thunder Rock, Time And The Conways, I Have Been Here Before, Heavenly Express, Love's Old Sweet Song, Across The Board On Tomorrow Morning, On Stage,* and *How Beautiful With Shoes,* which at their poorest at least ventured some imagination, may here and there have gratified the joneses, and here and there the nathans, but apparently they gratified no one else.

What the theatre most often evidently prefers is *The Two Mrs. Carrolls* and *Kiss And Tell.*

THE STREETS ARE GUARDED

November 20, 1944

A play by Laurence Stallings. Produced by John C. Wilson for 24 performances in the Henry Miller Theatre.

PROGRAM

ADMIRAL OVERHOLD, U.S.N. — *Len Doyle*
COLONEL WHITE, U.S.M.C. — *Gordon Nelson*
HOSPITAL CORPSMAN, U.S.N. — *David Lewis*
TOM JELKS, CH. PHAR. MATE, U.S.N. — *Morton L. Stevens*
THE MARINE — *Phil Brown*
MEMPHIS JONES, CH. BOSUN'S MATE, U.S.N. — *George Matthews*
MASTER SERGEANT WINTERS, U.S.A.A.F. — *Robertson White*
CORPORAL BEASELEY, U.S.A.A.F. — *Paul Crabtree*
CORPORAL CROFTON, U.S.A.A.F. — *Joel Marston*
CHOPPY, MUSICIAN 2ND CLASS, U.S.N. — *Jack Manning*
ANGELIKA — *Jeanne Cagney*
NAVAL AIDE, LIEUT. COMDR., U.S.N. — *John Effrat*
SEAMAN, U.S.N. — *Byron Griffith*
SEAMAN, U.S.N. — *Terry Little*
HANSON, CH. YEOMAN, U.S.N. — *Lewis Charles*
A COLONEL OF MARINES — *Roderick Maybee*

The time is the immediate past, the action taking place at the U. S. Naval Hospital at Washington, and on an island in the Pacific.

MR. STALLINGS' chief stock in dramatic trade has been the kind of lustiness associated with either the drinking cup or the pursuit of the female of the species. His merchants of it have been either twentieth-century Gambrini in military uniforms or seventeenth-century Casanovas in buccaneer regalia. With such characters and their detonating vocabularies he has been most at home. When he has briefly departed from them and joined up with those somewhat more punctilious, he has been a fish out of water. His stamping-ground has been where men are men and where words of more than four letters, aside from a certain lengthier genealogical phrase, are socially ostracized. He has been, in short, a tough guy.

Though hard-boiled, he has been, however, no egg. A bit of ham, possibly, but no egg. He has known how to write; he has had a proper feel for drama; and his subject matter has usually been close to his knowledge and in some degree to his experience. If on occasion he has seemed to bluff, it was to be allowed that he generally had at least two good cards out of five. Which, say what you would, as the game went was something.

In this, his latest effort, he is again where he belongs, among the robust men of the armed forces in World War II. But something has happened to him. Here and there are still traces of his old salty dialogue and his old round oaths and his old ribald swing. Yet a new, strange and badly muddled mysticism has crept into his writing like a dank mist and has cast a pallor over most of it. And his play, as a consequence, gives one the impression of his rare old Quirt and Flagg out of the worthy *What Price Glory?*, which he wrote in collaboration with Maxwell Anderson twenty-one years ago, dreamily confusing their gay booze companion Charmaine with the Angel of the Marne and all three sanctimoniously climbing on the waterwagon.

Nor is that the only impression left by the play. An even deeper and more general one is of a patchy paraphrase of *The Passing Of The Third Floor Back* with the Stranger in a Marine's uniform. There is no reason why an amalgam of realism and mysticism might not have served the play as Stallings initially visualized it, but while his imagination has automatically encompassed the realism it has failed him completely in the instance of the mysticism, and the result of his attempt to create an analogy between the Saviour and a mysterious Marine operating on the South Pacific front is confusion twice confounded.

The play is further weakened by the author's conviction, shared by most of his war-play contemporaries, that the incorporation of a female element is necessary, however at odds it may possibly be with the immediate dramatic materials. This element, while occasionally justifiable, is more often, as in the present case, simply so much decorative parsley, pretty to look at and sometimes vaguely appetizing but of no value whatever to the dramatic meat itself. The wide success of a poor war play like the English *Journey's End* may possibly have been credited to the novelty of its womanless cast of characters, although there was some skepticism on that distaff score on the part of a few saucy American critics. Most of the war plays that failed in the period of and following the first World War as well as those that have failed in the period of the second have been little other than Henry Arthur Jones and his lady friends in uniform. For one *Lifeline* minus the ladies, which, however, was otherwise so faulty it could not have succeeded even had it included a *Follies* chorus, all that the majority of other recent war play failures have needed to convert them into successes were a few good tunes by Jerome Kern or Richard Rodgers, along with maybe costumes by Raoul Pene Du Bois.

A second reflection. Among the many later war plays, including this, which thus far have emerged from America, England and Russia there has been none with a theatrically romantic hero. Whereas the plays dealing not only with the first World War but with wars from the beginning of dramatic time have here and there offered in their central figures magnificos to warm the cockles of the romantic heart, the more recent exhibits have purveyed protagonists sympathetic, pitiable, admirable, valiant, efficient and what not else, but in no case that I recall one of the rose-wreathed and imagination-bouncing fellows of other days.

The more war becomes a matter steadily less of brilliant plumes and shining swords and dazzling uniforms and is increasingly resolved into politics, mathematics and machines this is perhaps bound to be. The picturesqueness of past wars has gone with the wind, and with it inevitably the picturesqueness of its heroes. And thus it is that we presently have protagonists little different from so many business men in olive drab suits, and making the same kind of speeches, the same kind of gestures, and even the same kind of love.

Since it would require altogether too much space to give a complete catalogue in illustrative proof, run your eye quickly over some of the specimens factually disclosed in the last three or four seasons:

Elderly sea captains viewing the war as just another prosaic job; Cockney barge owners belatedly waking up to danger only when their shacks have been bombed by the enemy; surgeons going about their business as impersonally as veterinarians; Russian officers comporting themselves like Dun and Bradstreet bookkeepers; wearied soldiers trapped in cellars with Nazis and struggling for two stage hours against fatal drowziness; and American farm youths sentimentally resigning themselves to the cause and, after kissing their girls a brief goodbye, making off and subsequently conducting their action with letters to the girls and to their parents. All thoroughly commendable, surely, but hardly romantic by the theatre of yesterday's star-woven and emotionally stimulating standards.

Go on. Civilians converting themselves into saboteurs and going about their jobs like so many union plumbers; aviators losing their flying nerve because their wives are philandering with movie actors; other aviators who, after announcing that they have just shot down an enemy plane, spend the rest of the evening miscellaneously fondling the wenches in a barroom; profound college professors exerting themselves to persuade twelve-year-old Nazi children that they have been on the wrong track; and Mayors of small invaded towns philosophizing: "I am afraid, I am terribly afraid, and I thought of all the things I might do to save my own life, and then" — and then scholastically quoting Socrates.

Go on further. Soldiers held by the enemy and leaning weakly on Helen Hayes to liberate them; English secret service agents made fools of by a Nazi masquerading as the British Chief of Staff; clergymen in Scottish bomb cellars trying to beat Hitler with prayers; young American soldiers in camp fluctuating between their love for burlesque stripteasers and their duty; Norwegian barbers' sons shoveling Nazi corpses down cellar doors; privates spouting war economics for two and one-half hours; young English soldiers billeted in rich homes and insulting their hosts with belligerent reflections on class distinctions; young Russians betraying their Chinese allies and learning their lesson from female dipsomaniacs; and now, in this *The Streets Are Guarded,* an American Marine wandering about the stage like a Sunday school teacher and, worse, talking like one.

The romantic heroes of war drama from the time of ancient Greece to William Gillette must be turning over in their tombs.

Mr. Stallings noted in the program his thanks for assistance in details of his play to the various personnel of the Offices of Public Relations of the United States Army, United States Navy, United States Marine Corps, and the Armed Guard Center at Mitchell Field. He somehow neglected to include the late Ed Howe from whom he liberally borrowed various lines as, for just one example, "Keep your mouth shut and your bowels open."

THE LATE GEORGE APLEY
November 21, 1944

A play by John P. Marquand and George S. Kaufman, based on the Marquand novel of the same name. Produced by Max Gordon for a beyond the season run in the Lyceum Theatre.

PROGRAM

Margaret	*Mrs. Priestly Morrison*	Horatio Willing	*Reynolds Evans*
George Apley	*Leo G. Carroll*	Jane Willing	*Catherine Proctor*
Catherine Apley	*Janet Beecher*	Agnes Willing	*Margaret Phillips*
John Apley	*David McKay*	Howard Boulder	*John Conway*
Eleanor Apley	*Joan Chandler*	Lydia Leyton	*Ivy Troutman*
Wilson	*Byron Russell*	Emily Southworth	*Mabel Acker*
Amelia Newcombe	*Margaret Dale*	Julian H. Dole	*Howard St. John*
Roger Newcombe	*Percy Waram*	Henry	*Sayre Crawley*

SYNOPSIS: Act I. *George Apley's house in Beacon Street, Boston. Thanksgiving Day, 1912.* Act II. *A week later.* Act III. *The following morning.* Epilogue. *A corner of the Berkeley Club, 1924.*

A NOVEL FREQUENTLY loses some of its inner dimension on its way into play form just as a play invariably loses even more of its on its way into cinema form. Marquand's esteemed novel is no exception, yet enough of its savour remains to constitute the dramatization a generally sufficient job and one which provides a very genial theatrical evening. What critical faults the play has are not, in view of the skill of the presentation, likely to concern the spectator while he is engaging it but will assail him only the next morning, like a minor hangover.

Admirably staged by Mr. Kaufman save for some cannonball exits which periodically suggest that George Abbott must be a secret guest in the otherwise sedate Apley house and for an oversight in allowing several younger members of the company an application of so much facial makeup that they seem to be less part of the austere Boston scene than of a four-color magazine advertisement of Campbell's Tomato Soup; beautifully cast and acted, with but two exceptions, by a troupe headed by Leo Carroll; and handsomely set and costumed by Stewart Chaney, the sheer theatrical proficiency of the exhibit, quite apart from any consideration of the play itself, is gratifying in a day of so many productions that look as if they had been thrown together over a weekend.

As for the play, it offers again a family study in the general basic line, become so popular in late seasons, of *Life With Father* and *I Remember Mama,* but with an undertone measurably more significant. And once more we have the story told not in terms of closely knit drama but in a succession of stray episodes. The effect, again, is of glimpses into a household and of overheard snatches of family confidences rather than of cautiously planned dramaturgy, and that effect, for all possible objection by the formalists, is unstrainedly pleasant, as much in life is that is relievingly casual. There are several damp spots, notably an incorporated hokum scene in which the father confides to his son that he loved another than his wife on the eve of their marriage and an extended episode in which an old crony of Apley's wistfully lectures him on the need for making other people happy. And some of Kaufman's gags have the air of having wandered into the wrong house. But on the whole an educated humor envelops the evening and one departs the theatre with the mind feeling that it has had a few swigs of Apley's own treasured Madeira.

There are several scenes that are particularly fetching: the overstuffed family slowly emerging from Thanksgiving dinner; the girl hearing from her cousin whom she has expected to marry that his heart is elsewhere; the scene in the epilogue between the heir to the Apley traditions and the worldly old friend of his deceased father wherein the latter expounds his formula for never forgetting a wedding anniversary in having always taken a drink to indicate each married year and at the moment negotiating his successive fortieth. In brief, the kind of play that hardly sets the critical conscience on fire but one that is nonetheless sufficiently warming.

The Boston Brahmin whose character the novel developed gradually is presented in his stage incarnation in full later development yet loses little that is essential because of the dramatic constriction. The main atmosphere of the book, with its mixture of sentiment, light cynicism and humor applied to the tradition-bound Apley family and the rebellion of its young son and daughter, the former's short-lived and the latter's successful, loses even less in the stage version. And certain liberties taken by the box-office-wise Mr. Kaufman in his role of collaborator, while critically anything but endorsable, still somehow, except for the before-mentioned mushy scene between Apley and his brother-in-law, serve their intended practical purposes, however deplorable, to repeat, they may be in analytical consideration. For example, when Apley and his wife are made to discuss Freud and Apley remarks, "It seems to be Dr. Freud's idea that sex largely governs the lives of the people — in other parts of the country," a feeling that one is listening to the Doughgirls rather than to the Apleys properly overcomes one, but laughter makes the pill not too hard to swallow. And so with a number of other such Broadway intrusions. It is only when Kaufman — with Marquand's obvious, strange concurrence — heaves into the fabric such vaudeville as a remark that the Apley family dentist is so old that he can't see the cavities, with the rejoinder, "No, but he is very good if you find your own," and such as involves repeated snorts of an intrinsic Kalamazoo-Oshkosh flavor at the expense of Worcester, Kansas City, Detroit, etc., that an absence of laughter leaves the pill lodged uncomfortably in the throat.

In recapitulation, a play which, for all its foreign elements, captures a recognizable slice of Americana, which has a sparkling mind hovering over it, and which, aside from those musical comedy jokes and the earlier noted scenes that smack much more of Channing Pollock than Marquand or even Kaufman, constitutes a cultured and generally entertaining comedy.

RHAPSODY. NOVEMBER 22, 1944

An operetta by Fritz Kreisler, book by Leonard Levinson and Arnold Sundgaard, based on a story by A. N. Nagler; lyrics by John LaTouche. Produced by Blevins Davis and Lorraine Manville Dresselhuys for 14 performances in the Century Theatre.

PROGRAM

LOTZI HUGENHAUGEN	*John Cherry*
LILI HUGENHAUGEN	*Gloria Storey*
CHARLES ECKERT	*John Hamill*
FRAU TINA HUGENHAUGEN	*Bertha Belmore*
ILSE BONEN	*Patricia Bowman*
GRETA	*Mildred Jocelyn*
CASANOVA	*Eddie Mayehoff*
MADAME BOTICINI	*Rosemarie Brancato*
DEMI-TASSE	*Mister Johnson*
IVAN	*George Zoritch*
SONYA	*Alexandra Denisova*
EMPEROR FRANCIS I	*George Young*
EMPRESS MARIA THERESA	*Annamary Dickey*
CAPTAIN OF THE PALACE GUARD	*Randolph Symonette*
JAILER	*Gar Moore*
SPECIALTY DANCER	*Jerry Ross*

SYNOPSIS: Act I. Scene 1. *Music room of the Hugenhaugen home.* Scene 2. *Gardens at Schoenbrunn Palace.* Scene 3. *A room in the palace.* Scene 4. *Maywine Pavilion outside Vienna.* Act II. Scene 1. *The jail.* Scene 2. *Anteroom of the Empress' chambers.* Scene 3. *Apartment of Casanova in the palace.* Scene 4. *A hall in the palace.* Scene 5. *The ballroom of Schoenbrunn Palace.*

Time. *Reign of Maria Theresa.*

Place. *Vienna.*

THE NOVICE PRODUCERS of this venture, having observed that seven out of the twelve new musical exhibits put on last season had failed to a total tune of more than one million dollars and having scrutinized the reasons therefor, sought to avoid their forebears' errors but in the avoiding committed some worse ones of their own.

Figuratively taking their hapless forebears by the hand, they seemed to address them as follows:

In the first place, gentlemen, you apparently had not

learned that the public is dead sick of your smutty jokes. If perchance you here and there did learn it, you put your learning to use long after the cow was out of the stable, as in some such case as *Jackpot,* from which you deleted the smut a week after the show opened and when it already had been stamped as an irrevocable failure. The trouble with these dirty jokes by and large is not so much that they are dirty as that they aren't jokes. They are for the preponderant part not the least funny, and they hit an audience in the ear like so many mudballs. If in the future you can find a first-rate such joke or even a good second-rate one, go ahead and use it. We will promise to laugh with the rest of the house, only louder. But let us meanwhile stop this peddling of dull muck. *We* certainly shall.

Secondly, there is the matter of your topical songs, particularly those like "New York Is Like That," "What's New In New York," and the sort. The public has had enough of them. If you thought, as in the instance of your 100,000 dollar failure called *Allah Be Praised!,* that it would still experience a sublime treat in such lyrics as "You don't see Mrs. Vanderbilt at Lindy's, and Lindy doesn't hang out at the Ritz," you now know that you were badly mistaken. Yet let one of you still get hold of a number including some such schmalz as "If you want to be sardonic about Sardi's, eat your sardines at the Auto-mat," and you will persist in being as high-spirited as a baby with the hives. And if one of you then gets hold of a lyric writer who is a really great genius and who wittily inserts "mit onions" after the Automat, and you have it sung by a woman who delivers it with such beaming self-assurance as suggests it surpasses anything ever written by Samuel Butler, you will begin dreaming of the crowds storming McBride's and Tyson's. The next morning you will duly wake up and begin wondering where you are going to be able to borrow a quarter. *We* certainly shall not commit that mistake.

In the third place, when one of you goes into a huddle at "21" with the book writer for that show you are contemplating, pause and reflect on the big success in the last two seasons of the revivals of musical comedies and operettas out of the past. Reflect, in short, on the fact that the books of these older shows have all of them that air of romance which is so valuable to the musical stage but which nevertheless is generally neglected in the kind of shows you put on nowadays. After all, when one goes to a musical show one goes in something of a moonlight and champagne mood and that mood isn't exactly promoted into any high estate by books dealing with a band of female horn blowers trying to land a radio contract on a program boosting a cathartic, as in *Hairpin Harmony;* or with a squad of aviators quartered in the dormitory of a girls' school and jumping up and down like kangaroos and yelling "Oh, boy!" on finding a pair of ladies' lace drawers, as in *What's Up;* or with a female whose husband is in the zipper business and whose orchid delicacy is indicated in periodic complaints that the trouble with him is that he is all zippers and no zip, as in *My Dear Public. We* certainly shall not be guilty of any such error.

We don't say that what the public should be given instead is necessarily the kind of book in which the beautiful Princess falls in love with Rudolf, the commoner, and learns later at the big Autumn ball in the castle that he is really a Duke in disguise. Such books can be pretty bad, too. But we do believe that the public is surfeited with the other kind, usually concocted by someone like George Marion, Jr., in which the Princess is converted into a hot blues singer in love with a Rudolf converted into a traveling salesman of gents' suspenders and ending up in a castle converted into a red light establishment. It might not be so hard on the public, awful as it is, if things were allowed to rest there, but when it turns out that Rudolf is a Yale man and proves it by coming on in the second act in a red and green blazer and singing something about Dorothy Lamour to the tune of "Old Nassau" in swing time — when such bootleg poison is served to the public it seems to be a little too much. *We* certainly have learned that lesson.

Then, fourthly, there is the routine matter of the showgirls. Whereas in such older musicals as *The Merry Widow* and *Rosalinda* they are incorporated with some sense of value into a gala at Maxim's or a ball in Orlofsky's palace, in the later day shows they are dragged onto the stage without rhyme or reason and are simply stood around like dummies suffering from a suffusion of chilblains. Looking at stage after stage and seeing always the same lines of altitudinous clothes-horses doing nothing but seemingly waiting around for Shipwreck Kelly to sit on them is not, we believe, the average man's idea of a particularly gay evening. And when on occasion one or more of the icicle-covered skyscrapers is given a line to speak and speaks it in a voice resembling a fingernail scratching a slate the gayety isn't noticeably augmented. We herewith accordingly set about proposing the organization of a Society For the Prevention of Show-Girls, and announce our candidacy for the board of governors.

In the fifth place, let something further be done about the leading female singers. For one acceptable one like Ethel Merman we usually get two or three who are apparently of the conviction that all it takes to be a Merman is to strut down to the footlights, put on a fixed plumber's smile, and accompany a number with a lot of shadow-boxing in the direction of the audience. The next time we go to a show and see one of these steam-boilers trying to get a song over by throwing her fists at the customers we are going to get up and go around to Madison Square Garden where such pugilism is considerably more relevant.

We come to Item 6, in other words, to the gag writers. Finding that his book hasn't enough comedy, the producer, instead of persuading the author to apply himself to thinking it up in key with the rest of his book, calls in one or more jokesters of the species who concoct wheezes for radio programs, night club masters of ceremonies, and the like. These wits duly hurry into the breach with wonderful lines like "I grew up in Brooklyn" — "You don't look like a tree to me" and the delighted producer incorporates them into that scene in the book wherein the fashionable Palm Beach hostess is giving a musicale for Abyssinian royalty. The result is not, we believe, exactly what might be termed colossal.

Now and then, by one of those rare accidents that no one can account for, one of the extraneous gags may turn out to be funny. But more often in their grimness they only emphasize the lack of the book's comedy which otherwise might not be quite so depressing. And, funny or not, they invalidate the flow of the book by being arbitrarily inserted at the wrong points. It isn't entirely conducive to comfort to have a scene in which the hero is making love to the heroine in a rose-bower interrupted by a lackey who drops a tray on his foot and thereupon howlingly pulls the one about wishing it had been a deuce.

In the seventh place, how about a little rest from the notion that the comedian must inevitably be given a song to sing in the last act? Maybe it is part of a comedian's regular contract. If it is, we don't suppose anything can be done about it. But if it isn't, let's have an end to it. It wouldn't be so bad if the songs were amusing, but the average producer somehow inscrutably seems to think that even the dullest lyric imaginable becomes a riot if only the comedian of the show delivers it.

Some of us have been going to the theatre now for more years than Lee Shubert can remember. We have in those years laughed fit to kill at any number of comedians. But in all those years laughter has generally deserted us when the otherwise grand boys have felt it incumbent upon them to come down to the front of the stage around 10:30 and demonstrate their comic prowess in song. In all that long time we have heard not more than half a dozen such songs out of hundreds that had anything comical about them. One was "Who Paid The Rent For Mrs. Rip Van Winkle When Rip Van Winkle Was Away?" Another was "Mister Dooley." And the other four were those serio-comic numbers, we forget their names, that Raymond Hitchcock used to croak toward the end of his several performances. Most of the others have only succeeded in spoiling what impression the comedians have made before they ventured them.

We will not fall into any such traps with our own venture. We will go back to the romantic operetta form uncorrupted by the Yale man in the red and green blazer; we will have no smutty jokes; we will have no icicle show-girls; we will permit no Lindy and Automat lyrics; our female singers will refrain from engaging in fisticuffs with the audience; and our comedian will not be allowed to come down to the footlights around 10:30 and gratify his vanity with a vocal burst. And the public, we believe, will be duly grateful and make our venture a huge success.

The novice producers kept their promises. They eliminated the dirty jokes and substituted for them such as "He's a perpetual emotion machine"; "You ought to be thankful you're in jail because you couldn't get a room anywhere else these days"; and "This drink will pick you up" — "I hope it won't lay me down." They eliminated the show-girls and substituted for them a quota of toe-dancers who came on at regular intervals and, with set grins instead of the polar expressions, each and every time went through exactly the same toe routines. They eliminated the lyrics about Lindy's and the Automat and offered in place of them lyrics about how young the world is when one is in love and about the determination of men to be free in the world. They eliminated the lackey who drops a tray on his foot and such bourgeois humor as involves arboreal life in Brooklyn and substituted such refined humor as concerns cheeses, bedbugs, and warts. And, finally, they set themselves to present a book with all the desired old-time moonlight and champagne flavor.

In this last connection their procedure suggested the children's game wherein the youngsters apprise one another what they would do if they had a million dollars and, after all kinds of transcendent dreams, find themselves compromising with the same old five-cent lollipop at the corner drugstore. With the million dollars or a reasonable percentage thereof actually at their command they ended up at the same drugstore but came out without even the nickel lollipop. With bundles of money at their beck — their show represented an investment of 365,000 dollars — and with a Fritz Kreisler score safe in the bank, they huddled in the back yard over a libretto that would richly satisfy the occasion and got back to the house with one of those Alt Wien court intrigue numbers that have gathered so much dust that only an Okie could grope his way through them.

Their belated, gloomy and defeated conclusion that such poor books are perhaps unavoidable and that a really good one is almost impossible to find remains the facile delusion of producers whose imagination is confined to their purses. One can hardly get a well-fitting suit at the grocer's and one can hardly get a well-fitting musical book by patronizing the grocer's literary equivalents. One of these days operetta producers like those under immediate consideration are going to startle the theatre by passing up the spinach merchants and hiring writers who got tired of Alt Wien the day Johann Strauss died, who are content to leave the humors of the Nishes, Pishes and fat court chamberlains to bygone generations, and whose flights of fancy do not end in white satin ball gowns, mastodonic crystal chandeliers, and scenes in which an emperor, prince or baritone lover has to hide in a wardrobe.

Rhapsody in due and quick course dropped the novice producers' 365,000 dollars.

THE MAN WHO HAD ALL THE LUCK

November 23, 1944

A play by Arthur Miller. Produced by Herbert H. Harris for 4 performances in the Forrest Theatre.

PROGRAM

Shory	*Grover Burgess*
J. B. Feller	*Forrest Orr*
Hester Falk	*Eugenia Rawls*
David Beeves	*Karl Swenson*
Aunt Belle	*Agnes Scott Yost*
Patterson Beeves	*Jack Sheehan*
Amos Beeves	*Dudley Sadler*
Dan Dibble	*Sydney Grant*
Gustav Eberson	*Herbert Berghof*
Harry Bucks	*James MacDonald*
Augie Belfast	*Lawrence Fletcher*

SYNOPSIS: A small Mid-Western town, not so long ago. Act I. Scene 1. *David Beeves' repair shop. An evening in early April.* Scene 2. *The same. Three days later, near dawn.* Scene 3. *The same. Several hours later.* Act II. Scene 1. *The living-room of David's house. July. About two years later. Early afternoon.* Scene 2. *A spare bedroom in David's house. Later that evening.* Act III. Scene 1. *David's living-room. A night the following January.* Scene 2. *The same. An evening one month later.*

THE AUTHOR'S THEME was the venerable one relating to whether man's fate is preordained or whether it rests in his own hands. His treatment of it was so diffuse, disorderly and opaque that it was often impossible to decipher just what he was driving at. As is sometimes the eccentricity in such circumstances, this difficulty in understanding clearly what he had in mind however led some people to mistake the fog for the veil of a prophet and the author himself for one very possibly gifted with an enormous esoteric profundity. What he seemed to others, including the present recorder, was simply a very bad tyro playwright with but a single thought in his head, and that the entirely obvious one above noted. Moreover, it remained in his head, since no trace of it beyond a dim shadow made its appearance in his play and since that shadow was produced in the pervading mist by the tiniest ray of illumination imaginable. What the exhibit on the whole seemed to be was an amateurish paraphrase and extension of the kind of one-act vaudeville play written twenty-five or thirty years ago by Aaron Hoffman and covered with the species of quasi-philosophical sauce which intermittently was smeared over such other old vaudeville dramatic playlets as those in which Robert Hilliard was wont proudly to display himself.

That is about as near to any inner description of the bisque as I can come, since much of it, as I have said, baffled my attempts to make head or tail of it, though two of my colleagues professed to find the job very simple indeed, albeit each seemed peculiarly to arrive at a totally different conception of it. It was easy enough to follow the physical actions of the playwright's protagonist and also of the protagonist's brother, the one a garage mechanic whose luck never ran out on him and the other an ambitious baseball player with whom luck declined to flirt. It was also easy enough to follow the upward progress of the former and the downward progress of the latter. But the author's reflections on the fate of both and the means whereby each, the former in particular, embraced it were either so cloudy or so distorted that the play took on the aspect of a tin mirror. And his apparent ultimate conclusion that it was hard work and a nimble mind that alone were responsible for what seemed to be mere luck was so undemonstrated by his central character that most of the audience confidently expected the final curtain to come down upon the spectacle of everyone on the stage squirting seltzer siphons at one another and with the central character thereupon stepping to the footlights and confiding to the house that the whole enterprise had been conceived as burlesque — and that money would be refunded at the box-office to anyone who had not duly appreciated it early in the evening and was conceivably disappointed.

That the play was at least an unintentional burlesque of its theme was, however, the one thing that a liberal share of the audience, the two reviewers alluded to among the few exceptions, could clearly understand about it. For just how hard work and mind could otherwise figure in the luck of a character predicated on the fortuitous arrival in his garage of an Austrian refugee who explained to him the intricacies of automobile machinery which before he could not comprehend, on the death by accident of the man who stood in the way of his marriage, on the fact that he wished for a male offspring and that his wife presently delivered it to him, and on other such phenomena would have been something a bit difficult of satisfactory digestion.

WALK HARD. NOVEMBER 30, 1944

A play by Abram Hill, based on the novel Walk Hard—Talk Loud *by Len Zinberg. Produced by the American Negro Theatre for 42 performances in the 135th Street Library Theatre.*

PROGRAM

ANDY WHITMAN	*Roy Allen*	LOU FOSTER	*Joseph Kamm*
MACK WHITFIELD	*Leonard Yorr*	LARRY BATCHELO	*Ray Marlowe*
BOBBY	*John Hickton*	THE BARTENDER	*Morris Singer*
BENTLEY	*Joe Nathan*	DOROTHY	*Dale Shell*
RUTH	*Ruby Dee*	SADIE	*Aida Marlowe*
MR. BERRY	*Fred Carter*	THE BELLHOP	*Bob Wilkes*
CHARLIE WHITMAN	*Maurice Lisby*	THE HOTEL CLERK	*Bentley Edmonds*
BECKY	*Jacqueline Andre*	LADY FRIEND	*Cathy Parsons*
HAPPY	*Howard Augusta*	A REPORTER	*Samuel Stone*
MICKEY	*Milton Gordon*		

THE STORY OF the play is of a young Negro prize-fighter who simultaneously battles race prejudice on his fighting way toward the ring championship. Some of the detail is vivid and theatrically whetting, as in the case of the seamy side of professional pugilism with its assortment of cheap hangers-on, brash palookas, crooks, and general fungi. But the play itself often wanders aimlessly out of focus and dawdles into a spurious happy ending which corrupts the whole. Upon a basis of authentic realism the playwright has also superimposed a measure of symbolism about the evil of physical force which corrupts that whole twice over and diminishes doubly what power the play might possibly have enjoyed had he told his story with directness and simplicity.

As a sample of the experimental theatre's wares, the exhibit is hardly encouraging, though its central idea at least has a greater vitality than the routine thematic fare which so often spreads itself over the professional stage. The performances of the mixed company of Negroes and whites were for the larger share to be identified more closely with purely physical activity than with considered histrionism; and the direction by the playwright, which was responsible, added further to the presentation's vitiating stridor by italicizing even its passive verbs.

HAND IN GLOVE. December 4, 1944

A play by Charles K. Freeman and Gerald Savory, based on the latter's novel, Hughie Roddis. *Produced by Arthur Edison for 40 performances in the Playhouse.*

Program

Jenny	*Jean Bellows*	Purple Cap	*Almon Bruce*
Mr. Ramskill	*George Lloyd*	Bowler Hat	*Todd Stanton*
Auntie B.	*Isobel Elsom*	Sergeant	*Robin Craven*
Hughie	*Skelton Knaggs*	Chief Constable	*Wallace Widdecombe*
Mr. Forsythe	*St. Clair Bayfield*	Man from London	*Aubrey Mather*
Mrs. Willis	*Viola Roache*		
Lily Willis	*Islay Benson*		
Curly Latham	*Victor Beecroft*		

SYNOPSIS: Prologue. *A deserted narrow street near the Old Queens Dock, Halsey, Yorkshire, England. Winter, 1944.* Act I. *The kitchen in Auntie B.'s house. Early the following morning.* Act II. *The same. Sunday night, ten days later. (Curtain will be lowered briefly to denote the passing of two hours.)* Act III. *The same. The following evening.*

The divisions of the thriller crime drama are, again, four: the detective mystery thriller, the detective thriller minus the mystery, the mystery thriller minus the detective, and the thriller — to use the word in all cases tentatively — minus both the detective and the mystery. The Messrs. Freeman's and Savory's contribution falls into the groove of the detective thriller minus the mystery, which most often is the weakest of the four forms. If what might be the mystery is revealed to an audience in a prologue, as in this case, there seldom remains much to agitate the nervous system, unless the playwright is more than usually dexterous, which the present twain unfortunately are not. After all, if you are told that the rabbit is concealed in the silk hat's false bottom, you can not be expected to open your mouth wide in speculation and awe when the prestidigitator goes in for a lot of mumbo-jumbo and finally with a profound flourish pulls it out. That is, save the prestidigitator be a low comedian and confine himself to burlesque, or save you be in your cups.

Furthermore, English or English-derived plays like this one which are steeped in abnormal psychology and perversion have been unloaded on our stages so often that the startle they once may have possessed has vanished, and all that remains is the impression of indifferent melodrama attemptedly concealed in some hitherto theatrically unstated species of emotional kink or degeneracy. In this instance we have already had the species stated or implied on at least two previous occasions, so little is left but the indifferent melodrama.

What the stage discloses on this Krafft-Ebing occasion is a young Cockney who is short on the amorous end and whose mental torture induced by his impotence drives him to seek sexual relief and satisfaction in murdering and slicing up the women whom he can not negotiate. In order to divert suspicion, the young man concocts evidence against an idiot youth in the house in which he is boarding, but eventually is trapped by an agent of Scotland Yard. The writing is of the conventional detective story cut, and the acting, except in the case of Aubrey Mather as the sleuth, poor as it was and downright dreadful in the particular case of one Skelton Knaggs as the idiot who resembled a cross between all the old Lon Chaney moving picture roles and a high-school dramatic society Oswald, was even further mangled by James Whale, the director, who now and then had apparently been thinking of an entirely different play manuscript.

Perhaps the only distinction I enjoy in the world of my distinguished fellows is that I am one of the very few men who do not achieve an enormous pleasure out of murder mystery and detective stories. But, like many another luminary in his own land, I have yet to be properly honored for the fact. Rather am I taken to task, albeit indirectly, by such eminent literati as W. Somerset Maugham, *et al.,* who lately have spread their enthusiasm for the tales in the public prints and have argued that their authors embrace merits which the authors of other forms of fictional literature too often lack. All right, but I'll still take Gide, Mann and Co., including Maugham himself.

It isn't that I can't in a way understand the attraction for many men of the mystery-detective yarns, as I can similarly understand in a way the attraction for them of golf, cards, the flattery of uncritical women, and other such time-killers and anodynes. But time seems personally to be so fast-moving and immensely valuable and so fertile in other possibilities that to dissipate it on the literary or dramatic equivalents of tick-tack-toe is something that skips my comprehension.

Nor can I appreciate the alleged exceptional escape attributes of the general run of mystery stories and plays. The escape they offer is on an amateur par with that of a jail with licorice candy window bars. They call upon and gratify not the imagination, which is the only real avenue of intelligent escape, but merely the guessing faculties. And they amount at bottom only to a repetition of one's father's old game of asking one to guess which hand he was holding something in, a sport designed for the diversion and rapt interest of very young children and dogs. The end sum of the stories and plays, it seems to me, is a non-alcoholic Harvey.

Hand In Glove marked the fifty-sixth failure out of sixty-three detective or mystery exhibits produced in the period hereinbefore noted.

A BELL FOR ADANO. December 6, 1944

A dramatization of the John Hersey novel by Paul Osborn. Produced by Leland Hayward for a beyond the season's run in the Cort Theatre.

Program

Major Victor Joppolo	*Fredric March*
Sergeant Leonard Borth, M.P.	*Everett Sloane*
Giovanni Zito	*Gilbert Mack*
Guiseppe Ribaudo	*Tito Vuolo*
Cacopardo	*Silvio Minciotti*
Craxi	*Joe Verdi*
Father Pensovecchio	*Leon Rothier*
Margherita	*Miriam Goldine*
Carmelina	*Alma Ross*
Laura Sofia	*Florence Aquino*
Gargano	*Harold J. Stone*
Tina	*Margo*
Captain Purvis	*Bruce MacFarlane*
Sergeant Frank Trapani, M.P.	*Jack Arnold*
Corporal Chuck Schultz, M.P.	*Fred Barton*
Colonel George Middleton	*Harry Selby*
Bellanco	*Michael Vallon*
D'Arpa	*Mario Badolati*
Spinnato	*Doreen McLean*
Pietro Afronti	*Albert Raymo*
Carlo Erba	*Charles Mayer*
Giovanni Basile	*J. Scott Smart*
Mayor Nasta	*Rolfe Sedan*
Joe Pollock, M.P.	*Clark Poth*
Tomasino	*Alexander Granach*
Lt. Livingston, U. S. Navy	*Phil Arthur*
Bill Munroe, M.P.	*Rex King*

SYNOPSIS: Act I. Scene 1. *July, 1943. Midday.* Scene 2. *Five days later.* Scene 3. *Two days later.* Act II. Scene 1. *A few days later. Late afternoon.* Scene 2. *A week later. Early morning.* Act III. Scene 1. *A few days later. Morning.* Scene 2. *Some hours later. Late afternoon.*

It has been rare that the dramatization of a novel has not been accompanied by the familiar complaint that the restrictions of the stage have operated to its disadvantage, and that the play was therefore less satisfactory than the book from which it was derived. Not only the critics but often the playwrights themselves have indulged in the lament. Mr. Osborn still remains no exception. In an article published in the New York *Times* before his play opened, he wistfully indicated what he had been driven to leave out of it and resigned himself to the necessity allegedly imposed upon him. It is true that he omitted from his dramatization a number of the elements of the novel, but it is happily not true that the omissions have materially damaged his play. He has done a very satisfactory job. It is also and furthermore hardly true that, capable as he is, he might not, had he wished, incorporated some of the omissions if his capability as a dramatist had been greater.

There is altogether too much apology for the stage in matters like this. The stage has certain restrictions, granted; but they are in no wise so severe as the lesser dramatists elect for their personal comfort and self-protection to make out. The novel has seldom given us a more complete picture of character and episode than *Hamlet* or *Macbeth,* or than *The Cherry Orchard* or *The Three Sisters,* or than *Strange Interlude* or *Mourning Becomes Electra.* The authors of at least three of these successfully waved aside the alleged stage restriction of time, as other dramatists of eminence have successfully waved aside all kinds of other hypothetical restrictions. The promiscuous allegation of such restrictions proves, when analyzed and closely investigated, to be generally hollow; and no better way to appreciate the fact is to scrutinize the motion pictures, whose advocates constantly champion for their ability to do things that the stage can not.

Sitting some time ago over the cheese rabbits with the accomplished film director, Mr. Rouben Mamoulian, the conversation turned, surprisingly enough, to these motion pictures, commonly designated by physicians of culture as the venereal disease of the arts. I say surprisingly enough because Mr. Mamoulian is also, despite *Sadie Thompson,* an at times accomplished stage director who admires and respects the theatre, so naturally I did not expect it. "The stage," he nevertheless began, "has limitations that the pictures readily conquer. For one example, the stage could not possibly show anything like the sweep of distance, the expanse of scene, that the pictures can."

"No?" I ventured. "Did you ever happen to see or hear of a spectacle called *The Magic Doll,* produced in the theatre years before the movies were invented? It showed a child lost in an impenetrable forest. Gradually, as the child gropingly moved through it, the trees parted, closed in again, parted and closed in again endlessly, tier upon tier. The effect was of trees, trees, trees for miles. Have the pictures, with the factual outdoors at their disposal, ever surpassed that?"

"I guess no," allowed Mr. Mamoulian.

"But what about coloring?" he presently asked. "Can the stage equal the brilliant coloring made possible by the invention of the Technicolor process?"

"It can not only equal it but, to any sensitive eye, outdo it," I replied, in a suitably modulated voice lest the rabbits be blown off the table.

"How come?" bade my guest, in his best drawing-room Armenian.

"Technicolor has never so far approached the duplication of beauty that has been offered by the dazzling Alma Tadema scenic designs painted by the Harkers, or by the sets Joseph Urban did for the old Ziegfeld *Follies,* or by the brilliant *Hamlet* setting of Gordon Craig, or by the costumes done by Miles White for *The Pirate* and *Early To Bed,* or by a score of other such stage eye-tonics."

"I think, rabbit or no rabbit, I'll turn from beer to Scotch," said Mr. Mamoulian.

"Me, too," said I, not to be outdone by my guest's drawing-room Armenian, in my best drawing-room Scotch.

"But don't you think that the brilliant coloring made possible by Technicolor has added to the artistic progress of the screen?" bade my friend.

"I have seen a Madonna on the screen who, under the brilliantly artistic Technicolor process which you mention, looked for all the world as if she were on her way to a Mardi Gras ball. Incidentally — and forgive me for talking so much, but I can smell good material for *The Theatre Book Of The Year, 1944–45* in all this, or maybe it's only the rabbits — incidentally, in all the great Madonnas in history's greatest paintings have you ever seen *one* done in similar brilliant hues?"

"No," said Mr. Mamoulian, "and another Scotch please, double."

"But what of outdoor scenes?" my friend continued. "And where is that lazy waiter?"

"The trouble with Nature," I remarked, "is that it is sometimes too much like Nature," meanwhile fearing that I had probably cabbaged the profundity from Wilde, Whistler, or some other such fancy talker. "Technicolor, except in very rare instances, duplicates Nature so closely that it paradoxically doesn't seem real, just as the wax fruit on the mantel in a Victorian house never because of its too-realness seemed real."

"But," at length protested my patient friend, "you can't deny that the screen can show things in general that the stage can not."

"For example, *mon cher?*" I inquired. "And, captain, tell that snail-paced baboon of a waiter to hurry up or we'll both die of thirst!"

"For example," responded *mon cher,* "can the stage show such things as a railroad locomotive rushing headlong at the audience, or a raging forest fire, or a realistic wreck at sea, or a fire engine galloping to a fire, or an automobile racing at top speed, or anything else like that?"

"Certainly," vouchsafed your mastermind. "The stage has showed everything you speak of, and much more. Furthermore, it has showed it with a very high degree of realism. Langdon McCormick showed a railroad locomotive rushing headlong toward the audience in *The Ninety and Nine,* a raging forest fire in *The Storm,* and a wreck at sea in *Shipwrecked.* A fire engine on the gallop was the big feature of Lee Arthur's *The Still Alarm,* and Lincoln J. Carter's *Bedford's Hope* which, incidentally, was the first play I ever reviewed, had an automobile racing at top speed that would have knocked your eye out."

"All right," allowed my still patient friend, "but aside from such purely spectacular things, what of the other virtues of the screen in being able to show details that are beyond the scope of the dramatic stage? Take, for instance, some such play as *Life With Father.* The screen, when it eventually gets there, can embroider it with countless details that the stage can't: Father in full regalia parading Fifth Avenue, the scene in the church, the horses and carriages of the period, shots of the New York of the time, etc., etc."

"The very virtue of the stage is that it doesn't show such details," observed your elocutionist. "The drama wisely dismisses all such items as irrelevant and immaterial. The screen simply clutters itself up with them by way of supplying to the audience what the film people think it can not sufficiently imagine, like a child drawing a picture of a cow and labeling it a cow for extra safe measure. The drama is a process of selection. The screen is a process of over-embellishment. More Scotch, waiter."

"Yet the screen, whether they are important or not, has, you will admit, devised various camera tricks that are most amusing and that contribute to original entertainment," pursued the amiable Mr. Mamoulian.

"Go on, please," pursued the amiable Mr. Nathan.

"Well, for a couple of pointed illustrations, the trick of making a person invisible or of making a man disappear suddenly into space, as in the *Topper* pictures."

"That was done, and most effectively, years before in, respectively, Roland West's melodrama, *The Unknown Purple,* and, years still before that, in Charles H. Yale's famous old spectacle, *The Devil's Auction.*"

The eye of my friend achieved a determined gleam. "Now don't try to tell me," he said, "that the screen can't provide a much more beautiful, actual view of, say, Venice, or the Orient, or the countries of the Caribbean than the artificial scenery of the stage!"

"I fear," said I, "that once again I shall have to spoil the taste of your Scotch for you. Venice was never half so beautiful as the Venice that Erik Charell showed on the stage of *Casanova*. The Orient was never one-third so fascinating as it was on the stage of either *Kismet* or *Mecca*. And Martinique, for example, never in actuality approached even distantly the beauty of Martinique in George Jenkins' lovely backgrounds for *Early To Bed*. Besides, anyone who has ever been to Venice, the Orient or Martinique knows they smell like hell, and you can't smell them on the stage."

"Nor on the screen!" triumphantly exclaimed my friend.

"Point one-half of one for the defence," magnanimously allowed his friend.

"In a picture about Queen Christina which I did some years ago with Greta Garbo," Mr. M. continued, "I think I managed something that the stage would find rather difficult. At the very end of the picture, when Christina has lost her love and all, you may recall that I showed Garbo standing alone in the prow of a vessel. The only thing visible about her was her face and that pale face, which the lights were centered upon and the sad features of which remained immobile, wrought a spell on audiences that they could not forget."

"The stage," answered this persistent bore, "long before managed many such things quite as effectively. Whoever that saw the pale face of Bernhardt immobile on the pillow of Camille's death-bed at the play's end has been able to forget it? Or the pale, immobile face of Eleonora Duse, with the lights similarly playing upon it, at the end of not only that same play but also — surely also — of *Cosi Sia*? Or the face of any actress who ever played Flavia in *The Prisoner Of Zenda,* illuminated by the moonlight on the terrace of the castle and finding surcease in her loneliness with the cry, 'If love were all!' And, besides, do you honestly believe, my friend, that the spell you speak of in the picture you mention would have been wrought upon movie audiences if, instead of it being Garbo's face they saw, it had been Edna May Oliver's or ZaSu Pitts'?"

"This Scotch seems a little weak," said my friend. "I think I need some brandy."

"With soda?" I inquired.

"Without soda!" he yelled.

"But the screen in its time," Mr. M. presently resumed, "has surely produced some cinema masterpieces: *The Birth of a Nation, Intolerance, Hearts of the World, The Cabinet of Dr. Caligari* in its earlier years; such pictures as *The Informer* in its more recent."

"Even movie audiences who in later years have seen those earlier masterpieces, Griffith's *The Birth of a Nation, Intolerance* and *Hearts of the World,* along with the European *The Cabinet of Dr. Caligari,* have derisively laughed themselves sick at them. I know, because I was there. As for *The Informer,* it is certainly better than the great majority of pictures but there are any number of things in it that would make theatre audiences laugh themselves sick in turn. For a single example, the women in the bordello scene all wearing hats. In addition, even at its best it amounted to little more than the obvious kind of melodrama that occupies an inferior place on the dramatic stage."

"If movie audiences now laugh at the old Griffith pictures," objected our friend, "it doesn't prove that they weren't once good, does it?"

"Did you ever," your Nuisance Value asked, "hear any theatre audiences laugh loudly at the centuries-old *Hamlet* or *Macbeth* or, let's say, a play of much the same Griffith period like Shaw's *Saint Joan* when it has been subsequently reshown, even badly?"

"I may simply reply," said Mr. M., "that the screen, unlike the drama, is a young art, still in its infancy."

"The drama was also once in its infancy," I reminded, "and don't forget that while in that infancy it produced, long years before the birth of Christ, some of the world's still enduring masterpieces."

"But," howled my friend, "can't the screen do *anything*?"

"Yes," I was happy to reply, "there are some things it can do, and do handsomely. It can in its news-reels show remarkable happenings that the stage can't. It can show pie-throwing slapstick comedy very efficiently, often almost as efficiently as the stage. It can make women seem infinitely more attractive than they are with the aid of stand-ins' legs, hands, feet and whatnot cleverly substituted for the women's defective own. It can show scenes of battle more fully and realistically than the stage. It can, by virtue of film cutting and other tricks, make an actor or actress of a man or woman who can't act. It can at times make a million dollars when the theatre can make only fifty thousand or less. It can bring fame, such as it is, to persons who in the theatre couldn't possibly rise higher than stage extras, one-performance playwrights, or assistant box-office treasurers. It can transport countless morons, whom the theatre would only depress, to another and to them glorious sphere. It can make clerks and shopgirls dress better. It can show an octopus on the sea's bottom winding its tentacles around Buster Crabbe, which the stage can't and certainly wouldn't if it could. It can do a lot of such things, and more."

"Waiter!" screamed Mr. Mamoulian; "if you don't throw this man out, he'll drive me crazy! And, meanwhile, half a dozen aspirins, if you please."

In the specific case of the dramatized novel, the self-imposed duty of the dramatic critic in expatiating at length on what the playwright has left out and in lamenting the omissions more or less extendedly, while occasionally justified, is at times as gratuitous as would be a literary critic's lament, on reviewing the novel, that it did not contain photographs of Ethel Barrymore, Mady Christians and Leo G. Carroll, several colored drawings by Stewart Chaney giving an idea of the setting, and a phonograph recording of the speaking voices of the central characters.

The old notion that any novel which was dramatized was something of a sacred masterpiece is now, however, gradually disappearing from the critical credo. And it is thus that we here welcomely have had Osborn's play taken largely on its own and without the previous sobs and wails that a few things have been deleted from the book. That they have been deleted and that in the book they were effective is true. But that the deletion, except in one particular, weakens and damages his play is not, as almost everyone has agreed.

Hersey's theme of an AMG major who brings the tenets of American democracy to a small Fascist town in Italy has been transferred to the stage with quite as much force and eloquence as Hersey himself managed, and the play, while here and there on its own terms somewhat over-melodramatized, provides a theatrical evening of considerable vitality. That it is in essence and in execution of hokum all compact is in this instance not greatly to be held against it. You either have the hokum or you have no play or, for that matter, no novel. Moreover, the sure-fire of both book and play is not all arbitrary; it is often honest and deep in the materials.

There may be moments in the exhibit when the constriction of the action to one setting, the former office of the mayor in the town's City Hall, operates toward a crowding of Yankee Doodle episode that heightens the effect of the little town having been taken over and being supervised by George M. Cohan, with an American flag in his hand. Yet for many more moments the novelist's probity, echoed by the playwright, rescues the stage from what in other days might have been mere grand food for the gallery gods. And the final moment with the bell of democracy ringing out in the theatre, though also paraphrased hokum as would have delighted the souls of the author and producer of *The Heart Of Maryland,* is, when one comes right down to theatrical fact, genuinely galvanizing.

Although Fredric March's Major Joppolo left something to be desired, most of the rest of the company were first-rate. And the direction by H. C. Potter and the Motley physical production were equally so.

THE SEVEN LIVELY ARTS
December 7, 1944

A revue with songs and lyrics by Cole Porter and sketches by Moss Hart, George S. Kaufman, Charles Sherman, and Joseph Schrank. Produced by Billy Rose for 182 performances in the Ziegfeld Theatre.

Principals

Beatrice Lillie, Bert Lahr, Benny Goodman, Alicia Markova, Anton Dolin, Doc Rockwell, Albert Carroll, William Tabbert, Nan Wynn, Dolores Gray, Mary Roche, Jere McMahon, and Dennie Moore.

To say that Billy Rose is the foremost showman in the present American theatre isn't entirely fair to him. There has come to be something about the word "showman" that is not especially complimentary. Too often it is used to describe a man who successfully puts over on the public an oversized, mild monkey out of some South American public park zoo as a ferocious, man-eating orang-outang that in its day has dined off at least two dozen Ecuadorian vice-presidents. Or one who has produced a show that, if there were any justice in the world, would go to the storehouse by Saturday night but which he manipulates into a big box-office success by means closely identified in other days with the sale of the Brooklyn Bridge.

Rose is a showman of different stripe. He does not practise his virtuosity on hypothetical orang-outangs or the selling of theatrical bridges. His showmanship consists rather in giving the people something considerably bigger and better in its particular line than most other producers give them, and then going to the wholly unnecessary trouble and expense of selling it to them with an advertising ballyhoo that puts Barnum and even Darryl Zanuck to shame. If he has a show that calls, even before it opens, for several extra men in the box-office to handle the crowds stampeding to buy tickets, does he beamingly retire to his arm-chair and let things go at that? Not Billy. He forthwith enters upon a publicity campaign more relevant to an abject failure and, by the time he is through, there is nothing left for those who have been woefully disappointed in not being able to get seats but craftily induced hara-kiri.

This latest of the Rose ventures was a post-Ziegfeld show housed in the remodeled and handsome Ziegfeld Theatre, which Billy bought for himself as an extra trinket for a minor outlay of some 700,000 dollars. As if the show, which in large part was a dandy, and the theatre, which is wholly a dandy, were not enough for the first-night audience, he moreover for double measure installed a Salvador Dali art gallery, which was made available to all subsequent customers, and free vintage champagne served by twenty-eight white-gloved bartenders and butlers, which was not. But the show no more needed champagne for its appreciation than his *Carmen Jones* needed gin or marijuana.

Handsomely staged and lighted by Hassard Short and no less handsomely set and costumed by, respectively, Norman Bel Geddes and Valentina and Mary Grant, the exhibit's highlights were the following:

Item. A hilarious sketch by Moss Hart in which Beatrice Lillie, the show's outstanding feature, played an English lady of title trying to make American doughboys in an English canteen feel at home by speaking to them in what she believed to be the current American lingo, most of it startling the boys out of their wits with its sexual double entendre.

Item. Nan Wynn and Mary Roche, two girls who would have pleased Ziegfeld's eye and who sang fetchingly.

Item. Beatrice Lillie in another Hart sketch standing in line at a box-office to buy a seat for a ballet the name of which she could not remember but thought was "S. Hurok."

Item. Bert Lahr, dressed as an English Admiral on the deck of an old battleship, singing a drinking song which made such a realistic impression upon him that he wound up dead drunk.

Item. Beatrice Lillie's several wittily risqué ditties.

Item. A derisive finale to the first act, titled "Billy Rose Buys The Metropolitan Opera House," which showed what might befall that institution if Billy were to get hold of it.

Item. A ballet number by Alicia Markova and Anton Dolin.

Item. A jam session led by Benny Goodman.

Item. A jocund sketch, "Local Boy Makes Good," by George S. Kaufman, based on the lofty independence of stage-hands.

Item. The most beautiful girls seen on the local stage in some time.

Among the relatively few lowlights were these:

Item. Doc Rockwell's stale physiology lecture, which should never have been exhumed.

Item. A sketch by Hart lampooning the drama critics, including the present commentator, which was too strainedly polite and which accordingly went to pieces at the finish, whereas a more hearty impudence and vulgarity might have made it amusing.

Item. A poor sketch, "The Great Man Speaks," by Charles Sherman, dealing with the vanity of the actor, Orson Welles.

Item. Rockwell's running commentary on the show, written by Ben Hecht, which was both obvious and sub-juvenile.

SPOOK SCANDALS. December 8, 1944

A bill of 3 one-act plays plus song and dance, the music and lyrics by Sergio De Karlo. Produced by the Michael Todd Midnight Players for 2 performances in the President Theatre.

Players

Paul Haakon, Raul and Eva Reyes, Jerry Sylvon, Sergio De Karlo, Al Henderson, Don De Leo, Gedda Perry, Dean Myles, Mila Niemi, Kendal Bryson, Arthur Gondra, John Conray, Janet Gaylord, John Robinson, and Eddy Grove.

The plays, of the so-called horror species, were *Gobi Curse,* by Arthur Gondra, *The Coffin Room,* by Al Henderson, and *The Blind Monster,* by Jerry Sylvon, who organized the show, which sought cutely to fit the over-all *Spook Scandals* title by being produced at midnight. The Paris Grand Guignol, which achieved its reputation over many years through such horror exhibits, presented its bills at 8:45 in the evening, which for the assimilation of spectacles involving the pouring of carbolic acid on a woman's face and the inoculation of a man with cholera morbus germs was not only a considerably less horrible hour but which commodiously permitted the sufferers thereafter to acquire an antidote at the Bal Tabarin and like clinics.

The plays in this amateurish imitation of the little theatre in the Rue Chaptal were, save in one of the three cases, horrible only in their total lack of fresh imagination and dramatic competence, the exception being an appropriation of the Guignol's well-known vitriol vignette, *Kiss In The Dark,* produced locally years ago by the Holbrook Blinn players in the old Princess Theatre, and even that was spoiled in the rewriting. The one really frightening thing on the bill was the show's song and dance business, which rivalled in horror anything ever displayed at the Guignol.

Scrutinizing the exhibit on the opening night, Michael Todd, who put up the money for the acting group, shuddered in appropriate terror, requested the reviewers "to forget the whole thing," and withdrew the infliction from the stage on the following night.

DARK HAMMOCK. December 11, 1944

A melodrama by Mary Orr and Reginald Denham. Produced by Meyer Davis and Sam H. Grisman for 2 performances in the Forrest Theatre.

Program

Coral Platt	*Mary Orr*	Goldie	*Alonzo Bosan*
Marvin Platt	*Charles McClelland*	Andrew Jackson Sparks	*Arthur Hunnicutt*
Doc Bunnell	*Scott Moore*	Florence McDavid	*Elissa Landi*
Carlos Antuna	*James Ganon*	Amelia Coop	*Mary Wickes*
Belle	*Mabel D. Bergen*	Butch Smith	*Alan Dreeben*

SYNOPSIS: Act I. *June, early evening.* Act II. Scene 1. *Noon, the following day.* Scene 2. *Evening, three days later.* Act III. Scene 1. *Late afternoon, one month later.* Scene 2. *That night.*

Scene. *Marvin Platt's farmstead, known as "Dark Hammock" on the Kissimee Prairie, Florida.*

Time. *1910.*

The authors' horticultural pursuits, which got under way last season with *Wallflower,* progressed with misfortune to this peculiar little jimson, or stinkweed. The weed in question is a growth dramatically indigenous to English moors and the American bayou country, as well as to any other soil and climate which the leading female character, brought up in a less darksome milieu, can not tolerate. Her antipathy to her surroundings, augmented by the presence of her husband who exercises upon her much the same effect as the soil and climate, along with the incidental circumstance that she is amorously inclined toward a younger man, usually with black curly hair, located elsewhere, contrives in all cases to induce in her thoughts of murder, and to induce in the audience thoughts of exactly the same kind.

The Orr-Denham plant differs from most of the other specimens of its genre in only one particular: it is much worse. Not only does it have recourse to the old business of the slowly administered poison and the eventual switching of the glasses that does the would-be murderer in, but it presents in its female sleuth a character so slow-witted and dumb that, in view of the play's snail-pace movement, it is evident that she believes the word "clue" is spelled with a *g*.

The dramaturgy, to boot, is as palsied as the package's materials. The sleuth, for example, at one point in the proceedings exclaims, "I can always remember things better when I put them down," and thereupon seats herself at a table, takes out a notebook and pencil and writes down at great length, while repeating aloud what she writes, everything with which the audience is already perfectly familiar, and profoundly bored. Whenever, furthermore, the sleuth and her woman assistant peer at or move a piece of furniture the guilty heroine lets out a shriek of protest lest they discover a trapdoor underneath or the hidden poison, with the consequent feeling that the Hawkshaw and her assistant will momentarily remove their metaphorical whiskers and proclaim themselves to be Olsen and Johnson.

But even that is not the worst of it. Discovering the jug of liquid phosphorus with which the husband-poisoning is being negotiated, the lady sleuth bids her auxiliary to put out all the lights and thus allows the jug to betray its greenish-blue hue, whereupon she triumphantly exclaims, "See!" The audience, unfortunately, has anticipated her triumph fully an hour before, since the guilty heroine has been whittling off enough sulphur from matches to start a couple of new white springs in West Virginia. And the laborious manner in which the sleuth leaves the evidence of her suspicion lying about for its due discovery by the guilty party is worthy of the old musical comedy book in which the Sherlock went around confidentially whispering to all the suspects, "I'm a detective!"

Things were hardly improved by casting the role of the mortally ill husband with a ruddy, powerful, two-hundred-pound actor who had previously played cowboy roles, by an actress in the sleuth's role who frequently mumbled her lines as if she were rehearsing the part to herself, and by the routine waddling, fat colored actress in the role of a servant who laughed up and down the scale after each of her speeches.

The untoward incident opened on Monday night and closed on Tuesday night, and registered the fifty-seventh failure out of sixty-four such presentations.

LITTLE WOMEN. December 12, 1944

A revival of Marian De Forest's dramatization of the Louisa May Alcott novel. Produced by Eddie Dowling for a limited engagement of 23 performances at the City Center Theatre.

Program

Jo	*Mary Welch*	Laurie	*John Ruth*
Meg	*Margot Stevenson*	Mr. Laurence	*Harrison Dowd*
Amy	*Susana Garnett*	Aunt March	*Grace Mills*
Beth	*Frances Reid*	Mr. March	*David Lewis*
Mrs. March	*Velma Royton*	Professor Bhaer	*Herbert Berghof*
Hannah	*Valerie Valaire*		
John Brooke	*Clark Williams*		

SYNOPSIS: Act I. *The sitting room of the March home in Concord, Mass. An afternoon in December, 1863.* Act II. Scene 1. *The same, three months later. Morning, March, 1864.* Scene 2. *The same, six months later. Late afternoon, September, 1864.* Act III. Scene 1. *The same, two and one-half years later.* Scene 2. *The same, eighteen months later. An afternoon in October, 1868.*

First shown locally thirty-three years ago and last seen thirteen ago, the dramatization marked yet still another in the series of reproductions and revivals to which Mayor La Guardia's theatrical project seems to be ferociously committed. If the policy, which is to be viewed with increasingly narrowed eyes, is to be continued, the City Center could, however, hardly do better than to leave the revivals in the hands of Mr. Dowling and Jessie Royce Landis, his present director, at least judging from this example of their work. It was the most efficient job that the house has displayed. By virtue of its proficiency the venerable minor American classic took on a surprising freshness and a measure of unaccustomed life and provided an amiable theatrical evening. Miss Landis deftly directed the play out of much of its former too thick sentiment and by intelligent cutting lent to its writing a needed lift. Here and there her

George Abbott training caused her to overspeed the action, but by and large she did wonders in blowing off the play's shelf-dust and in giving it a semblance of stage modernity.

As the tom-boy Jo, a newcomer named Mary Welch was excellent, and both Margot Stevenson and Susana Garnett served the roles of Meg and Amy nicely, albeit the latter occasionally betrayed the fact that someone had told her she looked like a young Billie Burke and was inclined to pattern herself after her idol. Frances Reid was haplessly not the actress for the role of the delicate Beth, and her fixed broad grin was less appropriate to the dying daughter of the March household than to a healthy chorus girl angling for a prospect sitting down front. The others, notably Velma Royton as the mother and Herbert Berghof as the professor, were, however, very good.

Little Women, believe it or not, is, in short, still serviceable theatre, and a felicitous journey out of the hard-boiled present into the lace-valentine yesterday. The argument that it is overly sentimental is true. But it could not well be otherwise, since it happens to deal with overly sentimental people. As soundly argue that *The Lower Depths* is overly cynical.

There are some people, critics among them, who insist upon a villain in even something like *Ode To A Nightingale.*

DEAR RUTH. December 13, 1944

A farce-comedy by Norman Krasna. Produced by Joseph M. Hyman and Bernard Hart for a far beyond the season run in the Henry Miller Theatre.

PROGRAM

Dora	*Pauline Myers*
Mrs. Edith Wilkins	*Phyllis Povah*
Miriam Wilkins	*Lenore Lonergan*
Judge Harry Wilkins	*Howard Smith*
Ruth Wilkins	*Virginia Gilmore*
Lt. William Seawright	*John Dall*
Albert Kummer	*Bartlett Robinson*
Martha Seawright	*Kay Coulter*
Sgt. Chuck Vincent	*Richard McCracken*
Harold Kobbermeyer	*Peter Dunn*

SYNOPSIS: Act I. Scene 1. *Saturday morning.* Scene 2. *Same day. 5:30 p.m.* Scene 3. *Sunday morning. 1:30 a.m.* Act II. Scene 1. *Sunday morning. 10:00 a.m.* Scene 2. *Same day. Noon.* Scene 3. *Same day. 4:00 p.m.*

The setting is the living-room of the Wilkins home, New York City, in the late summer of 1944.

This is a synthetic farce-comedy compounded of long familiar materials, including some of the jokes, which by virtue of some initiated editing and staging on the part of Moss Hart amounts in the aggregate to amusing Broadway theatrical fare. It is not often that something which in its original form must have been little more than a Hollywood motion picture script is made into a good show, but Hart has managed, at least for a share of the evening, to turn the trick.

Consider the plot scheme which, in story form, magazine editors have been turning down for the last thirty years: the young girl who sends loving letters to a strange man signed with her older sister's name and the eventual appearance of the recipient, in this case put into an Army flier's uniform, to claim his hypothetical admirer. There is surely little in that to bounce one out of one's seat. Turn to some of the humor: radio cracks about Frank Sinatra, Felix Frankfurter, *et al.,* lines like " I poured my heart out " — "Who's going to pour it back?", and, among other items, the dropping of a plate of spaghetti on someone's clothes, the drinking of a big glass of whiskey by a female stripling, and the blowing of tobacco smoke into a character's face followed by the latter's choking. There is certainly also little there to split anyone's sides. Turn then to some of the characters: the precocious brat out of *Junior Miss,* etc., etc., the patient paterfamilias, the solicitous, fluttery materfamilias, the heroic young aviator, the stodgy fiancé of the heroine, and so on. Nothing there either to convulse the consumer. And turn finally to a number of other such ingredients as, once again, the colored servant girl who laughs uproariously on her every exit, the character who elaborately insists she is sober and then imagines that an inanimate object is talking to her, and the dimwit who has to have jokes explained to him. Hardly the sort of materials to galvanize the interest. Yet it remains that the commodity on the whole has been finagled by Hart into one of those jobs that the popular theatre of Broadway knows so well how to do and one which is periodically gagged up so artfully, sentimentalized so professionally, maneuvered in its physical aspects so ably, and cast so intelligently that it amounts in sufficient part to lively entertainment. As anything critically reputable it is nil. But as vaudeville with some foxy observation of character it passes nicely.

Its first-night audience, operating on its own, would in all possibility have gone a long way toward making even something like *Down To Miami* a stunning box-office success. Made up in ample part of friends of the author, director and producers, and including many people from the author's and other Hollywood movie lots, its enthusiasm went into action even before the show started. And when at length the curtain rose and disclosed a perfectly conventional set of scenery on an empty stage the enthusiasm was expressed in such thunderous applause as has not been heard in a theatre — if history is correct — since the opening of Aristophanes' *The Frogs.*

Nothing thereafter could stem the audience's frantic admiration. The mere mention of Henry Stimson's name drove it crazy with mirth, and the menu phrase "eggs lilac" had it rolling in the aisles. A line like "How did you sleep?" followed by "Like a top; spun around all night" caused a veritable explosion. A sentimental description of the young aviator hero as the sweet kind of fellow who loves to ride in the Subway and on the tops of Fifth Avenue buses and wants to eat at the Automat induced a flood of wistful tears and nose-blowings. And a scene in which the maid delivered an oversized package of Crackerjack into the living room literally brought down the house.

To repeat, there is, however, enough of another kind of humor to make one laugh without feeling too ashamed of one's self.

LAFFING ROOM ONLY! December 23, 1944

A show with book by Olsen and Johnson and Eugene Conrad, music and lyrics by Burton Lane. Produced by the Shuberts and Olsen and Johnson for a beyond the season run in the Winter Garden.

Principals

Olsen and Johnson, Frank Libuse, Betty Garrett, Mata and Hari, Willie West and McGinty, Ethel Owen, William Archibald, Kathryn Lee, Pat Brewster, Ida James, Margot Brander, Penny Edwards, Frances Henderson, and Lou Wills, Jr.

The latest in the series of Olsen-Johnson rumpuses, like its predecessors *Hellzapoppin* and *Sons o' Fun,* successfully pursues the theory that there is money in catering to the many people who confuse personal embarrassment and physical discomfort with pleasure. George C. Tilyou discovered the fact many years ago and made a fortune out of his Steeplechase Parks, which endlessly gratified their customers by upsetting them in revolving barrels, splitting their trousers on bumpy slides, blowing their skirts up over their heads, and spinning them off turntables onto the hard floor. By way of playing doubly safe, the Messrs. Olsen and Johnson have augmented the Tilyou technique with an amount of noise which is guaranteed to further the customers' delight by cracking their eardrums and which lends to the show in general the aspect of Hallowe'en in a cannon works. And to play triply safe they have borrowed from the Frankie Hyers-Pat Harrington night club in West Fifty-second Street that institution's basic philosophy, to wit, that customers seem not only to relish having full soup plates dumped upon their heads but to be inordinately tickled by being verbally insulted while the aforesaid dumping is in operation.

That there may be no delay in pleasing their customers, the Messrs. O. and J. set things into motion twenty minutes before their first curtain rises. Actors rush up and down the aisles shooting off pistols, leaky beer bottles are passed around and spilled upon laps, large bologna sausages are tossed about the auditorium, women stooges crawl over one's legs and yell at the tops of their lungs, extras parade in the aisles and suddenly let out indignant howls alleging that members of the audience have, as the vulgarity goes, "goosed" them, blinding spotlights are focused upon the customers' eyes, exploding cameras are poked at their noses, and candy filled with sawdust is dispensed right and left. When at length the audience is thus made happy beyond all bounds, the overture gets under way, with the conductor periodically turning around and loudly ordering the happy folk to "shut their traps" and behave themselves. And the rest of the evening consists largely in overjoying them no end by throwing bricks at them from the stage, causing objects to be dropped upon them from the balcony, having actors wander up and down the aisles and fall over them, and otherwise treating them as if they were up for membership in a leper colony.

During the few relatively quieter moments, magnanimously inserted into the show to allow the audience to catch its breath, the stage and auditorium are given over to such business as a boy choir rendering "Silent Night" and at its conclusion firing off revolvers, such jokes as "It is very eerie on this train" with the witty rejoinder, "But this is the Union Pacific," such burlesque mementos as the act in which a man indignant at someone else chokes an innocent bystander, such screams as a strip-teaser finally revealing herself in long woolen underwear, such refined topical humor as a woman made up to resemble Eleanor Roosevelt and crossing the stage at ten-minute intervals with her teeth flashed at the audience, and such piquant invention as a man in one of the boxes proclaiming in the darkened theatre that he is going to shoot the rat who invaded his home and who, when the lights go up again after a pistol shot, is beheld holding aloft a stuffed rodent.

There is no end to the delicate drollery. A man beplastered as a piece of living statuary in the pose of Rodin's

"Thinker" and displayed in the early part of the evening seated at the right side of the stage is shown later on seated on a privy. Shortly afterward the Willie West and McGinty carpenter act offers as its climax the spectacle of Mr. West hurrying into another privy. A sailor and soldier then rush around the auditorium in brassières, ladies' pants and girdles. Mr. Olsen meanwhile orders a whiskey and soda over a telephone and the instrument squirts it into his face. He then orders coffee and the instrument squirts it into his face. Follows a scene in which three men garbed as Russian soldiers and preparing to shoot a spy find their rubber rifle barrels drooping, only to observe them rising stiffly when a scantily dressed woman interposes herself between them and her spy lover. An actor appears in the aisle holding several rabbits and shouts that he is looking for Harvey. "Who'll take these rabbits off my hands?" he yells. From the balcony comes the yell, "I will!" "And who are you?" yells the first man. "I. J. Fox" yells back the voice in the balcony. A girl is brought on seated in a bubble bath. Mr. Johnson inquires, "Who blows your bubbles for you?," whereupon a man sticks his head out of the tub and grimaces, "Busy little bee, ain't I?" Mr. Olsen then chases a fat actor mimicking a homosexual off the stage with the remark, "Not you for me!" Mr. Olsen exits and reappears clad in his underdrawers. A man says that he wants to buy a bed. Mr. Olsen says that he will show him one, opens a large slot in the scenery, and hauls out a bed containing a man and woman cuddling. An actor made up as Herbert Hoover sits under a sign lettered "The Forgotten Man." Another actor made up as Thomas Dewey comes on and sits next to him. A Scot enters a door bearing the sign "Ladies' Room." He is kicked out. "I thought it said 'Laddies' Room'," he protests.

At the conclusion of the performance a midget scurries around the rear promenade biting people in the legs.

SOPHIE. December 25, 1944

A comedy by George Ross and Rose C. Feld, based upon the latter's Sophie Halenczik, American *stories. Produced by Meyer Davis and George Ross for 9 performances in the Playhouse.*

Program

Annie Halenczik	*Ann Shepherd*	Irene Halenczik	*Donna Keath*
Ernest Hopkins	*Will Geer*	Mrs. Scudder	*Doris Rich*
Tom Blanchard	*Richard Deane*	Capt. Thornton Scudder	*Ronald Alexander*
Chet Blanchard	*John McGovern*	Marge Nelson	*Marguerite Clifton*
Frankie Halenczik	*Donald Buka*	Anton Halenczik	*Louis Sorin*
Sophie Halenczik	*Katina Paxinou*	Elsie	*Eda Reiss Merin*
George Odanos	*John Harmon*	Joey	*Jerry Boyar*
Mr. Parker	*Kurt Richards*		

SYNOPSIS: The home of Sophie Halenczik, R.F.D. 4, Ridgetown, Conn. Act I. Scene 1. *Mid-June.* Scene 2. *Ten days later.* Act II. Scene 1. *A month later.* Scene 2. *The following Saturday.* Act III. *The next morning.*

FALLING INTO the catalogue of so-called folk plays — this one dealing with a family of Czechs quartered in Connecticut — the exhibit is even less successful in its purpose than other such folk plays, disclosed locally in recent seasons, as *Papa Is All,* which treated of the Pennsylvania Dutch, *The First Crocus,* which had to do with Scandinavian-Americans, *The Great Big Doorstep,* which dealt with the Cajuns, and *The First Million,* which was concerned with Kentucky hillbillys. It is without the slightest suggestion of dramatic action, whether physical or verbal; its characters, embracing the brash brat, the parasite son-in-law, the girl with illegitimate child, the indolent old sponging uncle, the all-wise mother, the daughter separated from the boy she loves, *et al.,* are entirely the effigies out of past plays on end; the humor takes such forms as "I think you've got something up your sleeve" with the retort "Yes, my arm," to say nothing of Olsen and Johnson witticisms about toilet seats and the human posterior, the latter here provided with a folk flavor by being referred to as a "heinie"; and the acting, with minor exception, was of the species more usually encountered in the one-floor-up little theatres.

To make matters worse, the authors have incorporated into their play a solemn message which under the circumstances assumes a low-comedy mask. The message in point is a plea for the understanding kind of Americanism that will be tolerant of foreigners in our midst, which, since it is put into words by a female Czech who experiences intolerance solely and singly at the hands of an idiotic prig who appears to be equally intolerant of his American neighbors and whom the American community in which the Czech woman lives thoroughly detests, may be said to possess a force akin to that of a plea for American tolerance of Porterhouse steaks.

The star of the occasion was Madame Katina Paxinou, a Greek actress who had appeared in New York briefly a few seasons before as Hedda Gabler in one of the poorest performances of the role within the memory of the oldest living critic and who subsequently and perhaps conformably won the Motion Picture Academy's award for a performance in a film. The Madame, despite the tribute paid to her by Hollywood, remains every bit as bad an actress as she was before she went West. Her performance as the Czech heroine was simply a pitched-battle between physical contortions and face-makings; in it there was no trace of inner feeling, or of emotional command, or of anything that was not wholly on the surface, like a splashing goldfish.

The direction by one Michael Gordon of Hollywood involved so much mad galloping about the stage and so much noise that the audience momentarily expected the actors to come down into the aisles as in the Olsen and Johnson show and dance with it.

SING OUT, SWEET LAND! December 27, 1944

A "salute to American folk and popular music," book by Walter Kerr, music arranged and especially composed by Elie Siegmeister. Produced by the Theatre Guild for 101 performances in the International Theatre.

Principals

Alfred Drake, Burl Ives, Bibi Osterwald, Alma Kaye, Philip Coolidge, Jack McCauley, Robert Penn, James Westerfield, Peter Hamilton, Irene Hawthorne, and Ethel Mann.

Mr. Kerr, abetted by the Theatre Guild, has badly fumbled a scheme which might have been developed into excellent theatre. His purpose was to present a combination Johnny Appleseed and Paul Bunyan banished for levity from old Puritan New England who, resolved into a timeless minstrel, wanders in the long, following years throughout a growing America and seeks through its common song to bring to its peoples neighborliness, mutual understanding, happiness, and unity. Imaginatively treated, the theme's possibilities are plain. But so coquettish is much of the writing that has been visited upon it, so childish, when it is not downright cheap, is the humor, and so lacking in sound fancy is the general approach that the result in the aggregate is little more than a poorly extended paraphrase of such an exhibit of the late Labor Stage as the pageant called *Labor Sings,* in a program which embraced the Walt Whitman derived *I Hear America Singing.*

Furthermore, not only is the theme written out of its potentialities but its proud essence waywardly gets out of the playwright's hands. The American people among whom his hero roams down the years are for the greater part a worthless and criminal lot: river-boat gamblers and swindlers, gangsters, crooked police, speakeasy operators, harlots, cadging tramps, seducers, street-walkers, drunks, and the like. And where they are not of that general species they are so silly, as in the instance of old Oregon trail pioneers who enter into a copious burlesque show weeping upon the sound of a melancholy ditty, that the presentation's basic sentimental but heroic idea takes on an equal coating of the ridiculous.

The attempts at humor contribute additionally to the theme's deterioration, as does such character nomenclature as Barnaby Goodchild, Parson Killjoy, Charity Wouldlove, etc. For example, the songs "While Strolling Through The Park" and "Heaven Will Protect The Working Girl" are made to serve a travesty ten-twenty-thirty melodrama in which the dark, moustache-curling villain pursues the virtuous maiden and which is not only staler than stale but which is more suited to a side-street beer hall of the 1920's than to any such historical pageant as Mr. Kerr may originally have had in mind. Nor are less invalidating such humors as lie in a man's violently colored underwear, the old business of a man's holding another man's hand under the impression that it is that of a woman who has stealthily made her exit, the further business of the man who observes resolutely that women can not boss him and who a moment later subserviently obeys one's command, the old Weber-Fields card game, such lines as a disreputable tramp's remark that he will be unable to get to the reunion of his class at Harvard, the baby-talk gangster's moll, and unremitting jokes about marriage.

How the author hoped to realize his intention of inducing a nostalgic affection in his audience with any such materials is difficult to determine. And not less difficult is how he hoped to induce in it pride in America's past, present, and future. Under the circumstances, the main impression an audience gets is merely that of a vaudeville performer singing a program of folk and popular songs before backdrops representing various periods in American history and being interrupted by the lesser comedians and dancers on the same bill.

The exhibit's songs include, among others, Puritan hymns, "Way Down The Ohio," "Foggy, Foggy Dew," "Little Mohee," "The Devil And The Farmer's Wife,"

"Oh, Susannah," "Oregon Trail," "Watermelon Cry," "Didn't My Lord Deliver Daniel," "Frankie and Johnny," "The Roving Gambler," "Polly Wolly Doodle," "Blue Tail Fly," "Casey Jones," "Rock Candy Mountain," "Wanderin'," "Hallelujah, I'm A Bum," "A Bicycle Built For Two," "A Hot Time In The Old Town Tonight," "Basement Blues," "I Got Rhythm," "At Sundown," "My Blue Heaven," "Yes, Sir, That's My Baby," etc. Why some of these popular later tunes by Gershwin and Donaldson were chosen in preference to such considerably more popular tunes as Berlin's "Alexander's Ragtime Band" and Burnet's "Melancholy Baby" is no less puzzling than the use of W. C. Handy's little known "Basement Blues" in preference to either his famous "Beale Street Blues" or "St. Louis Blues." And certainly, when it comes to popular songs, more popular and more widely sung in America than some of those incorporated into the show were "After The Ball," "The Bowery," "Do, Do, My Huckleberry, Do," "And The Band Played On," "Hiawatha," "I'm A Yankee Doodle Dandy," "Go Way Back And Sit Down," "I'd Leave My Happy Home For You,' "In The Good Old Summertime," "Tramp, Tramp, Tramp, The Boys Are Marching," "Just Before The Battle, Mother," "The Battle Cry Of Freedom," "My Gal's A Highborn Lady," "My Old Kentucky Home," "The Sidewalks Of New York," "On The Banks Of The Wabash," and a dozen or two such obvious others.

Any so-called cavalcade of American song, folk and popular, as this *Sing Out, Sweet Land!* purports to be would seem to call for a good orchestra in the pit and some superior voices. The Theatre Guild's failure to provide them has resulted in a presentation more appropriate to the platform of Town Hall than to the professional stage. When done originally by the Catholic University of Washington, D. C., which by and large offers one of the most frequently inventive and progressive amateur theatre groups in the country, the show must have managed a much better impression, since where little in the way of financial outlay is possible or expected an audience hospitably remits judgment and is pleased by results within the means at hand.

But any critical audience in the present professional theatre is not so inclined to remit judgment; it has been spoiled by productions that spend every last cent to constitute them what they should be; and managerial scrimping upsets it and tends to make it hostile. What any such folk song panorama, even at its poorest, theatrically demands is by no means a necessarily lavish treatment but at least a sufficient professional treatment, and, to repeat, the Guild has neglected to supply it. Since considerable motion picture money is reported to have been invested in the enterprise, it is hard to determine the reason for the Guild's scrimping in the directions noted. Perhaps it is a case less of scrimping than of poor judgment and weak theatrical taste. Whatever it may be, things are not right. For all the show's intrinsic feebleness it might have been fabricated into an at least superficially more lively evening had its casting been more expert and its staging more expansive.

As it is, only Burl Ives, the popular balladist, emerges with any measure of credit.

ON THE TOWN. DECEMBER 28, 1944

A musical show with book and lyrics by Betty Comden and Adolph Green, music by Leonard Bernstein. Produced by Oliver Smith and Paul Feigay for a beyond the season run in, initially, the Adelphi Theatre.

PROGRAM

WORKMAN	*Marten Sameth*
2ND WORKMAN	*Frank Milton*
3RD WORKMAN	*Herbert Greene*
OZZIE	*Adolph Green*
CHIP	*Cris Alexander*
SAILOR	*Lyle Clark*
GABEY	*John Battles*
ANDY	*Frank Westbrook*
TOM	*Richard D'Arcy*
FLOSSIE	*Florence MacMichael*
FLOSSIE'S FRIEND	*Marion Kohler*
BILL POSTER	*Larry Bolton*
LITTLE OLD LADY	*Maxine Arnold*
POLICEMAN	*Lonny Jackson*
S. UPERMAN	*Milton Taubman*
HILDY	*Nancy Walker*
POLICEMAN	*Roger Treat*
FIGMENT	*Remo Bufano*
CLAIRE	*Betty Comden*
HIGH SCHOOL GIRL	*Nellie Fisher*
SAILOR IN BLUE	*Richard D'Arcy*
MAUDE P. DILLY	*Susan Steell*
IVY	*Sono Osato*
LUCY SCHMEELER	*Alice Pearce*
PITKIN	*Robert Chisholm*
MASTER OF CEREMONIES	*Frank Milton*
SINGER	*Frances Cassard*
WAITER	*Herbert Greene*
SPANISH SINGER	*Jeanne Gordon*
THE GREAT LOVER	*Ray Harrison*
CONDUCTOR	*Herbert Greene*
BIMMY	*Robert Lorenz*

SYNOPSIS: Act I. Scene 1. *Brooklyn Navy Yard.* Scene 2. *Subway.* Scene 3. *Street.* Scene 4. *Miss Turnstiles.* Scene 5. *A taxi.* Scene 6. *Museum.* Scene 7. *Outside the park.* Scene 8. *Corridor of Carnegie Hall.* Scene 9. *Carnegie Hall (Madame Dilly's studio).* Scene 10. *Claire's apartment.* Scene 11. *Hildy's apartment.* Scene 12. *Times Square.* Act II. Scene 1. *Night clubs* (a) *Diamond Eddie's,* (b) *Congacabana,* (c) *Slam-Bang.* Scene 2. *Gabey in the playground of the rich.* Scene 3. *The subway.* Scene 4. *Coney Island.* Scene 5. *Navy Yard.*

THE POPULAR SUCCESS of the show re-emphasizes the later day predilection of theatregoers for stages given over to plays and musicals devoted to the young of the species. The predilection is apparently a reflection of John Mason Brown's acute lecture observation that the American passionate eagerness to keep young amounts almost to a genius for arrested development. I should think, however, that if anything could help to discourage that eagerness it would be the many shows, let alone plays, like this one which pursue the theory that anyone, male or female, under twenty-one years of age invariably comports himself, both mentally and physically, like a combination Arab vaudeville tumbler and congenital imbecile. Yet any such discouragement is far from the fact, and youth thus presented continues to be thought both refreshing and lovable, and the exhibits which merchant it are generally pretty certain of box-office prosperity.

That youth, whether on the stage or off, is frequently attractive and charming there is no debating, save in the case of elderly cynics who hope to conceal their Faustian disappointments in Mephistophelian epigrams, however here and there fraught with the wisdom of experience. But to be attractive and charming on the stage, particularly the stage of musical shows, it is hardly too much to ask that its chosen representatives possess faces and figures that one may look at without æsthetic alarm, which is scarcely the case in the show under immediate scrutiny and in most of the young women in that show in particular. It is not easy to dream of vernal beauty in the presence of a stage replete with physiognomy that is downright frightening, figures that disclose a heavy deficit, and legs become so knobby and knees so bruised from protracted terpsichorean gymnastics that ballets and dance numbers take on the appearance of alumni Rugby football games.

The show itself is an elaboration of the Ballet Theatre's *Fancy Free,* which dealt with three sailors on shore leave and their girls and the choreography, music and scenery of which were respectively by the same Jerome Robbins, Leonard Bernstein and Oliver Smith who are responsible for a considerable portion of it. Robbins' ballet theme, which sufficed for something like half an hour, is here stretched strainfully like a small rubber band to embrace fivefold that length of time and, while now and again providing some fair amusement, too often abruptly snaps back into its pullers' faces.

Involved in the pull are Betty Comden and Adolph Green, night club entertainers whom the trio named have summoned to their aid. Their contribution to the pull is hardly powerful. It is evident that their humors, properly to be enjoyed, require an obbligato of alcoholic liquor. Without any such stimulant, dialogue like a sailor's "Will you show me the road to the Museum of Natural History?" and a female's retort, "I'll show you the road to ruin!" is not likely to get any enthusiastic reaction. Nor are witticisms like "Now that I'm done with *Tobacco Road,* I'm going to wash my feet" — "And live on *Angel Street,* I suppose." Lyrics having to do with a loose girl's assurance to a man that she can nevertheless cook and with the loneliness of a stranger in New York are further scarcely calculated to over-impress the cold sober. And such stage business as a woman's measuring a male's skull to determine his affinity with an ape, the struggle for an empty seat in a Subway train, and a burlesque of a cabaret floor show (negotiated some seasons ago in *Pal Joey* with infinitely more wit) are additionally remiss as substitutes for the cup.

The ballet phases of the show, contrived by Mr. Robbins, in one or two instances display symptoms of imagination, but the stage is overburdened with them and before the evening is done one is sorry one ever made remarks about the Tiller girls. Moreover, just one such ballet that didn't conclude with the men holding the principal female dancer aloft would be a welcome novelty.

The staging of the other portions of the exhibit by George Abbott, who is always fetched by these exercises in stage youth, is in his best jumping-jack, scooter tradition and contributes prosperously to the previously noted affectionate legend that young folk never under any circumstances enjoy a moment of repose but spend their days as if every twenty-four hours were a steeple-chase. So given to an admiration of mere movement for movement's sake is Mr. Abbott that he has even resorted at six different periods to something that one had thought had happily disappeared from the stage years ago, to wit, what is known in theatrical parlance as the lobster-box, that flickering contrivance which gives actors in slow motion the appearance of being hell-bent for one destination or another.

Bernstein's music, while occasionally not without some intrinsic merit, more frequently strains with patent discomfort for popularity. Smith's sets, picturing various metropolitan localities, are nicely in key with the show's intention, though one may be forgiven for wishing that scene designers will soon abandon the dated idea that lopsided buildings, simply by virtue of the fact that they are not painted in an upright position, become scenic art worthy of the French modernists at their best. Among the performers, Nancy Walker with her tough girl antics and Sono Osato, when she dances and does not speak, are the most acceptable. Miss Comden and Mr. Green, the collaborators on the show who also act in it, respectively content their histrionism with two-hour imitations of Miss Ilka Chase and the Ringling Brothers' Toto.

TRIO. DECEMBER 29, 1944

A play by Dorothy and Howard Baker, based upon the former's novel of the same title. Produced by Lee Sabinson for 67 performances in the Belasco Theatre.

PROGRAM

JANET LOGAN	*Lois Wheeler*	RALPH HACKETT	*Ken Tower*
PAULINE MAURY	*Lydia St. Clair*	MRS. GIRARD	*Sara Perry*
RAY MACKENZIE	*Richard Widmark*	DEAN HARRY KENNEDY	*Harry Irvine*
TED GORDON	*Kenneth Williams*	HOUSE BOY	*Henry Goon*
MISS HAWLEY	*Mary Alan Hokanson*		

SYNOPSIS: Act. I. Scene 1. *Pauline Maury's apartment.* A Thursday *afternoon.* Scene 2. *The same. One hour later.* Act II. *Ray Mackenzie's apartment. An evening three weeks later.* Act III. *Same as Act I. Later that evening.*

LEE SHUBERT refused the play a booking in any of his New York theatres on the ground that its Lesbian theme might possibly bring about a padlocking under the Wales law. Having suffered a year's such shutting down of his Ambassador Theatre in the case of *Wine, Women And Song* several seasons before, he declared that he was unwilling to risk another chance and was roundly denounced for his action by persons who, having nothing to lose, constituted themselves bravely vociferous champions of the play's authors and producer. Mr. Shubert nevertheless had a great deal on his side. Though the play is perfectly decent, had played without interference for several weeks in Boston and Philadelphia, and is rightly uncensorable, there was no way for him to foretell what official reaction to it in New York might be. The moralists had once raided *The Captive,* Bourdet's fine treatment of the Lesbian theme and, though both *Love Of Women* and *Wise Tomorrow* subsequently dealt with the same theme and went free, no one could insure against a reversion to their earlier idiosyncrasy. *Wine,*

Women And Song was no whit dirtier than half a dozen other shows that have been allowed to run their courses, and it was far less dirty than *Hairpin Harmony,* which expired on its own without any outside protest against it, or than *Catherine Was Great, School For Brides,* and numerous other such smutty plays that have been given official *carte blanche.* It is all very well for one ducally to fight for a free stage, but it becomes an academic matter in the face of the realistic fact that irresponsible and ignorant censorship, though it may not cost one a cent, may cause a theatre owner not only to lose possession of his theatre for an entire year at great expense to himself but may also cause him to be thrown summarily into jail. That Mr. Shubert's precautions were not ill-founded was demonstrated when, after the play had been running for two months, censorship in the person of License Commissioner Moss pounced upon the Belasco Theatre and declared its license forfeited save the play be immediately withdrawn, which it was.

Trio is a completely honest play dealing with an older woman's sexual and mental control over a young girl and the latter's eventual break from perversion through the intervention of a young man whom she has come to love. It is without sensationalism, and without any deliberate intent to catch the ear of prurient groundlings. Compared with Bourdet's excellent play it is third-rate; it out-talks its subject matter, it engages at two points in extrinsic melodrama, and it in one instance, that of the young man's character, neglects to support his stubborn blindness to the young girl's sexual abnormality with any such hintful psychological explanation as, say, Schnitzler employed in the case of his Anatol and Hilda, or Cora as she is known in the Granville-Barker translation. But it nonetheless otherwise contains some sharp appreciation of character and some intermittently sound writing, and as drama is superior to the average run. The long scene in the second act wherein the boy and girl vainly struggle with themselves and each other toward an understanding is in particular ably written and projects itself with no little force.

Bretaigne Windust's direction, except for the melodramatic crockery-smashing at the end of the second act and the handling of the play's conclusion in the suicide of the older woman, was first-rate. Lydia St. Clair, a French actress, while occasionally given to the trick exhibitionism common to many European actresses, managed the role of the prehensile Lesbian for the most part satisfactorily; Richard Widmark, who was so very bad in the previous season's *Get Away, Old Man,* was surprisingly right, doubtless because of intelligent direction, as the young man; and Lois Wheeler, practically a novice in the theatre, gave in the role of the sexual victim one of the most remarkable performances on the part of a new, young actress that we have seen on the local stage in several years. Her occasional awkwardness, criticized by some, was wisely not coached out of her by Mr. Windust and added materially to the portrayal of a character that, if devoid of such occasional awkwardness, would have taken on in artificially induced smooth manner a sense of sophistication which would have utterly ruined it.

THE HASTY HEART. January 3, 1945

A play by John Patrick. Produced by Howard Lindsay and Russel Crouse for a beyond the season run in the Hudson Theatre.

PROGRAM

ORDERLY	*Francis Neilsen*	TOMMY	*Douglas Chandler*
YANK	*John Lund*	MARGARET	*Anne Burr*
DIGGER	*John Campbell*	COLONEL	*Edward Cooper*
KIWI	*Victor Chapin*	LACHLEN	*Richard Basehart*
BLOSSOM	*Earl Jones*		

SYNOPSIS: Act I. *Early morning.* Act II. Scene 1. *Two weeks later.* Scene 2. *A few nights later.* Act III. Scene 1. *The next day.* Scene 2. *The following morning.*

The entire action takes place in a convalescent ward of a British general hospital behind the Assam-Burma front.

MR. PATRICK believes properly that emotion is the keystone of drama. Though this, his latest play, indicates a greater critical reticence in that direction than his two previous efforts, it still suggests, however, that given any single emotion he has difficulty in allowing it to pursue its natural course but must needs seize it in his theatrical teeth and fling it this way and that long after the life in it has expired. In *Hell Freezes Over,* produced for twenty-five performances a decade ago, he tortured the theme of a group of explorers caught in the icy wastes of the South Pole into a super-Grand Guignolism which involved excruciating deaths from exposure, from vengeful bullets fired by betrayed husbands and vindictive lovers, from poison administered both to a cripple and to himself by a doctor attached to the expedition, and from starvation induced in a man sadistically handcuffed to the wreck of a dirigible. In *The Willow And I,* produced for twenty-eight performances three seasons ago, he permitted himself a slightly greater emotional restraint in the case of two sisters ferociously in love with the same man, one of whom was determined to shoot herself if she lost him to the other and the first of whom, in fighting for possession of the gun, was shot. Believing that she had killed her, the other sister went crazy and for the ensuing thirty years purveyed enough extravagant emotionalism to stock the entire Sardou drama, all to the accompaniment of detonating thunder and lightning stage effects. In *The Hasty Heart,* Mr. Patrick's economy has progressed to the point where the restraint embraces the spectacle of a single stubborn, introspective, selfish and suspicious Scot soldier's violent reaction to sympathetic proffers of friendship on the part of military colleagues who know, though he does not, that he is doomed soon to die, of his gradual reluctant if overly verbose surrender to the proffers, of his shocked discovery of their motivation and his copious indignation at being made an object of pity, and of his final truce with the good offices. Mr. Patrick seemingly is making some headway against melodrama.

Though his theme, while more or less familiar, is still functionable, he however so insistently strikes the same emotional chord, he so continuously grinds his heel into ground already furrowed, and he writes in so commonplace and unillumined a manner that it loses much of its pregnancy. Two or three scenes manage briefly to capture some eloquence, but for the most part a play that should honorably emotionalize an audience succeeds only in emotionalizing its actors. Throughout its course I could not resist the feeling that it should have been written by an Irishman. That feeling was induced by a recollection of Synge's idea of style: "In a good play, every speech should be as fully flavored as a nut or apple, and such speeches can not be written by any one who works among people who have shut their lips on poetry. In Ireland for a few years more we have a popular imagination that is fiery and magnificent and tender, so that those of us who wish to write start with a chance that is not given to writers in places where the springtime of the local life has been forgotten, and the harvest is a memory only, and the straw has been turned into bricks." And that recollection was brought about in turn, and doubtless waywardly, by a speech in the play having to do with the protagonist's proud declaration, after his metamorphosis, that he had psychically enjoyed the experience of a king. "Did you see an old woman going down the path?" asks the mother of her son in Yeats' *Cathleen ni Houlihan,* after Cathleen, the personification of Ireland, has left their peasant hut. "I did not," the boy answers, "but I saw a young girl, and she had the walk of a queen!"

Mr. Patrick's speeches, far from being as fully flavored as a nut or apple, are prune-dried, and all the soaring fire that should be in such a one as that alluding to a king is diminished to a minor flicker.

The attempts humorously to lighten the whole, furthermore, often contribute to an additional weakening of the theme. "I had a terrible dream last night — I dreamt I was working," is one example. Hearing a sleeping soldier's loud snoring, another soldier observes, "It sounds like a rhinoceros calling his mate," which is a second. A nurse's plunging of a clinical thermometer into a garrulous soldier's mouth to make him shut up is still another. A soldier's repeated facetiæ about having been shot in the posterior; a soldier's indignant denial that he is fat but, according to the hospital report, only obese; another's remark that he is going to write to his Congressman whose name is probably Mabel; yet another's that the only reason for playing a bagpipe is to get away from the sound; and such business as the thrifty Scot's careful preservation of the butt of a cigarette are other examples, one and all calling for the ministrations of a chiropodist. And, if not a chiropodist, surely the application of a sizeable Blue-jay plaster would be beneficial as well to such humors as involve a couple of men belaboring each other with fly swatters or distributing themselves on the floor in order to determine what, if anything, a Scot wears under his kilt.

The dramaturgical enterprise which Mr. Patrick undertook was not an easy one. Any play laid throughout in the convalescent ward of a hospital offers a serious challenge to dramatic movement. And when, in addition, what movement the theme may conceivably possess is lodged largely in a single character's mouth, with the other characters serving as mere sounding-boards, the challenge is increased. That is, save the writing, as noted, have bloom, which Mr. Patrick's has not. Now and again a sprig of green fights its way through the frozen soil, but too often, for all the applaudable effort to thaw the ground, the plant remains only a promise.

The favorable public response to the play means only that what might possibly have been a dignified contribution to drama has been willy-nilly written down to the box-office and popularized out of its dignity. Sentimentality, which in this case is simply sentiment filtered through poor writing, takes its toll of an intrinsically upright theme, and the net dramatic impression is of John Shand paraphrased by the author of *The Wookey*.

Bretaigne Windust's direction was once again as expert as the obstinate materials permitted, and the male members of the company, especially John Lund as a tough Yankee ambulance driver and Richard Basehart (there is an old 10–20–30 melodrama name for you!) as the Scot protagonist, were endorsable. Miss Burr, however, once again brought to the nurse's role that abundance of rapid eye-blinking to indicate everything from tender affection to acute indignation and that tendency to articulate her speeches through the nasal septum which in combination heretofore have disabled her performances.

MANY HAPPY RETURNS. January 5, 1945

A comedy by Clare Kummer. Produced by Harry Bloomfield for 3 performances in the Playhouse.

PROGRAM

ETHEL	*Nan Butler*	CHARLES BARROWS	*Rex O'Malley*
JO BARNETT	*Michael Dreyfuss*	JANE	*Jayne Cotter*
HENRY BURTON	*Neil Hamilton*	CYNTHIA LACEBY	*Mary Astor*
ALBERT	*Leonard Carey*	TOM CARRUTHERS	*Vincent Gardner*
FAY	*Nell O'Day*		
EDDIE	*Don Gibson*		

SYNOPSIS: Act I. Scene 1. *Living-room of Henry Burton's house in New York City.* Scene 2. *The same. After dinner.* Act II. *Mrs. Laceby's apartment. A little later.* Act III. *Same as Act I. Later still.*

Time. *The present.*

Place. *New York City.*

WHAT MRS. KUMMER's play was like in its original form, I have no exact means of knowing. But, knowing her previous plays well and learning further that she had lodged a protest with the Dramatists' Guild over the alterations which had been made in her script by the management, it may safely be ventured that, even at its poorest, it was nevertheless in general far superior to the exhibit offered. Even as offered, a comedy not without some sly remaining wit and intrinsic charm was to be detected through the thick, wet cloud of wholly unsuitable casting, dismal acting, miserable stage direction, and rankly gratuitous manuscript revisions.

It has always been the Kummer dramaturgical technique to eliminate from any theme she may select what meat there may be in it and to serve only the distilled gravy, as it has ever been her writing device to avoid direct dialogic statement in so far as possible and to suggest its content elliptically. This has been true of all her playwriting from *Good Gracious, Annabelle* to *A Successful Calamity* and from *Rollo's Wild Oat* to *Be Calm, Camilla* and *The Lights Of*

Duxbury. She is, in a way, a kind of American Sacha Guitry minus the Guitry sex element and her light, fragile comedies demand much the same stage treatment as Guitry's. Save they be cast with precisely the right actors and directed into the airy abandon of a toy balloon they go to pieces. A moment of overly studied action, a moment of serious pause, and they are lost.

In the present instance Mrs. Kummer has taken the recognizable theme of a middle-aged father who, finding his son's marriage threatened by the boy's infatuation for another woman, goes through the old Nat Goodwin motions of seeking out the woman with the intention of buying her off and of being himself fascinated by her. The story, however, is as usual in her case of no particular moment; she employs it simply as something with which to hit off droll little facets of character and to sneak away from with polite badinage. The badinage as we get it in the presented version of the comedy is sometimes, however, so remote from the previous Kummer quality ("We were all fish once" — "Some of us are still fish" is a horrible example) that it is obviously the insertion of other hands. Such other hands, indeed, are clearly visible throughout the play, and where they have not made heavy pudding of what was soufflé, the before-mentioned casting, acting and direction contrived to throw the author's original plan completely out of focus and to weigh down what should have been nimble froth with performances and stage manipulation more aptly suited to a bad specimen of the problem drama of the 1890's.

What the comedy demanded was the sort of acting and production which Arthur Hopkins visited upon the author's early plays. What it got was the motion picture actress, Miss Astor, in a role that called for someone like Ina Claire or a similarly experienced polite comédienne who would not, among other things, intrude such pronunciations as "repertore" and "iridiscent" into a portrayal of elegant savoir faire; the motion picture actor, Neil Hamilton, in a role that cried for the dry suavity of the William Gillette who served *A Successful Calamity* and that received instead acting which suggested that its occupant was reading his lines from a blackboard held aloft behind a film camera; and stage direction by three or four persons under the blanket name of Peter Berneis which consisted largely of pouring out sherry at five-minute intervals, causing those characters who drank it to smack their lips elaborately for three minutes afterward, and making those who didn't want it exit for no other discernible reason.

A single moving picture actor has frequently helped to devastate a play, and this one suffered two. The unanimous condemnation of the play itself by the reviewers was therefore, it seems to me, while in a way understandable under the circumstances, the old visual issue of the woods and the trees.

Mrs. Kummer was thoroughly justified in entering the blanket protest with the Dramatists' Guild, even though a court decision denied her the award of five thousand dollars for the damage done to her play. While playwrights have often prospered through revisions and handling of their work by intelligent producers, there have been plenty of others who, falling into unintelligent hands, have helplessly seen their work botched out of all recognition and have suffered blame from the reviewers through no fault of their own and which, to anyone acquainted with the facts, was richly undeserved.

Several seasons ago, for example, a play called *The Walking Gentleman* was shown in New York. By a strange coincidence a play of exactly the same name by Fulton Oursler and Grace Perkins was advertised to open on the same night. By an even stranger coincidence the names of Fulton Oursler and Grace Perkins appeared as authors of the play that did open. But by an even still stranger coincidence the play that opened was no more like the play that didn't than mush is like mushrooms. The play that opened closed after just six performances. The play that did not might conceivably have achieved some success.

The play that didn't open was frankly designed as a thrill murder melodrama; the play that did turned out to be a kind of French sex-problem play, and about as bernsteinish as they come. The responsible party was, to a large extent, a

French movie actor named Victor Francen, who had been engaged to play the leading role. This Francen, who apparently esteems himself a lady-killer of irresistible beauty, fascination, and charm, instantly took charge of things. An exciting scene in the original script wherein he was called upon to choke to death a serving maid whom he suspected of having eavesdropped a dangerous admission on his part and who was subsequently revealed to him as being deaf and dumb, he peremptorily declared out. "It would make me unsympathetic to the audience," was his firm explanation. A Jekyll-Hyde transformation scene found him adamant on two points: either the Hyde mask which he would wear must be hardly less comely than his own face when disclosed as Jekyll or the whole business would have to be eliminated, which it was. The scene in which he got his wife alone in her apartment preparatory to strangling her must not, he insisted, be played menacingly but with a Palais Royal farcical touch, which is the way he played it. And just before sneaking up threateningly behind his intended victim, he must, for the effect it would have on the ladies out front, execute a droll *pas seul* and then hand her, with a low bow, a rose!

These are only a few of the reasons for the current insanity of the play's authors. And speaking of insanity, there naturally comes to mind Saroyan. If Saroyan is crazy, as some maintain, the causes are similarly not far to seek. I nominate just one out of many. When his *Love's Old Sweet Song* was in the process of Philadelphia try-out, Walter Huston, the leading actor, professed to find the touching curtain to the second act, showing a small child deserted on the steps of the burning house and calling through its tears for its parents, quite unsatisfactory. It was his opinion grounded on long experience, he averred, that, as he was the star of the play, the audience would be sorely disappointed if he were not on the stage at the fall of the curtain, and hence on the stage he should and must be. So out went the scene over Saroyan's dead or at least despairingly alcoholized body, and Huston was there, like a troop of pleased Marines, to the child's rescue.

The preliminary stages of Saroyan's lunacy came into evidence at the try-out, some time before, of *The Time Of Your Life* in New Haven, Connecticut. Arriving from Fresno, he hurried to the theatre and there laid eyes upon something that caused him to exclaim My God! so loudly and so consecutively that the Yale students on the campus a mile away concluded that the Ouachita Baptist College basketball team must have just pulled into the station and was rehearsing its college yell. What he laid eyes on was his low saloon on the San Francisco waterfront transformed under director Robert Lewis' inspiration into a setting that looked like a lovely oriental version of little Hannele's bedroom, with in a far corner a bar just big enough for the service of a single cocktail and with enough purple, green, amber, peachbloom and vermilion lights playing upon it to equip Grauman's Chinese movie palace for the world première of a two million dollar class-F picture. What he further laid eyes on was, under the ingenious spell of the same director, a company of actors who had been coached to play his ragtag and bobtail characters as if they were participants in a Japanese *Nō* play written by Frederick Lonsdale in collaboration with Maurice Maeterlinck. And what he still further saw, before they carried him out on a stretcher frothing at the mouth and wildly calling out the names of Ruby Foo, Sessue Hayakawa and Warden Lawes, was a play dealing with the riff-raff in an Embarcadero gin-and-beer dump which was directorially indistinguishable in its main features from the Russian ballet's *Petrouchka*.

For countless years before and since the late Louis Mann sent the author of the play, *The Consul*, to Matteawan by suddenly incorporating into it on the opening night a secretly long-treasured sentimental fifteen-minute homily on the beauties of home life, which wrecked the play, producers, actors and directors have conspired against the sanity of those negligibilities whose sole contribution to the drama is drama. Like my otherwise good friend Walter Wanger, who one day some years ago happened to glimpse the actor Walter Pidgeon walk into his Hollywood studio office in a becoming uniform and promptly got on six telephones and commanded as many scenario writers to get busy at once on a movie in which he could wear it, theatrical producers, directors and almost everybody else associated with them view writers much as wives view husbands, necessary evils not exactly always to be murdered on the spot but maybe to be contemptuously tolerated and endured only on the chance that they may turn in a little money on Saturday night.

When Edward Sheldon and Charles MacArthur wrote *Lulu Belle,* it was their intention that the play, broadly speaking, be a Negro paraphrase of the *Carmen* theme. David Belasco, the producer, had other ideas however. And gradually as rehearsals progressed their play, to their loud outcries and agonies, resolved itself into a Negro *Camille.* Tearing his hair, MacArthur indignantly argued with his collaborator that they should immediately remove their names from the abortion, to which Sheldon, as they led him out violently protesting that he was Williams and Walker and quite sane, issued the parting sigh that they should at least both be satisfied that Belasco had not turned it into a Negro *Ben Hur.*

More recently, a brace of Irish playwrights were released from the sanitarium, whence productions of their plays had sent them, only after several months' observation and treatment. The two were Paul Vincent Carroll and St. John Ervine. Carroll was not in America when his *The Old Foolishness* opened and soon thereafter closed, but when the notices and communiqués reached him he threw himself to the floor and, before they could stop him, had frantically nibbled seven square feet of carpet. What destroyed his reason was the news that the play's director, Rachel Crothers, dissatisfied with some of his Celtic dialogue, had written some of her Bloomington, Illinois, own to take its place and had thus brought the reviewers to flay the hide off him for his peculiar, sudden literary collapse. And not only that. Pursuing some personal whim, this Miss Crothers had further, he learned, not only so staged the play that the emphasis fell heavily upon a character it was not intended to, thereby throwing the theme wholly out of kilter, but had cut out the long final speech, the one really beautiful bit of writing in the script, and thus destroyed what little was left of the mess.

At length recovering from the shock sufficiently to be allowed at large, Carroll was again promptly returned to the sanitarium upon his receipt of news of the casting of his *The Strings, My Lord, Are False.* The threatened deletion of the phrase *My Lord* from his fine title derived from *Julius Caesar,* which met the clerical nature of the play perfectly, he managed to survive with the aid of a couple of cases of Scotch. But when he heard that in the role of his parish priest, whom he had pictured as a gentle cross between Cedric Hardwicke and Al Shean, the producer had cast that grim Phi Beta Kappa emotionalist Walter Hampden, celebrated earlier in the season for his conversion of Sir Anthony Absolute into a walking case of whooping cough complicated with hay fever, he got down eight more square feet of the carpet — to say nothing of an extra square foot on the casting of the coloratura comédienne Ruth Gordon as the tragic young heroine — before the ambulance arrived.

St. John Ervine, our other Irish guest-playwright, was perfectly normal until he discovered what they had done to his play, *Boyd's Shop.* As with Carroll, the change of the title to *Boyd's Daughter* by way of foolish hope more greatly to fascinate the box-office did not too seriously exercise him. But when he learned that one of the actors in the play was coming before the curtain at the end of each of the acts and delivering a facetious monologue about the play, the players and even the audience, to the complete demolition of any interest his play might possibly have had, his appetite for what remained of Carroll's carpet may naturally be understood.

Upon observing what the Theatre Guild had done to his play, *Dynamo,* including among other things the casting in a highly dramatic role of the then fair cutie, Claudette Colbert, who placed her beautiful legs on distracting display whenever the going became serious, Eugene O'Neill vowed he would never again permit a work of his to be produced unless he himself could be present to safeguard its interests. The vow was well taken, even though a subsequent play, which chivalrously shall be nameless, went largely to pot in the second act when the rugged looking young actor who had been cast in a forthright masculine role tardily and dismayingly revealed himself to be *Viola tricolor,* and with a falsetto that would have put the late Florence Mills to shame. But the vow was assuredly well taken in the instance of *Days Without End* when, a few days before the play was to open, O'Neill appeared at rehearsal and to his horror found that the Guild for reasons of economy had substituted for the all-important crucifix in the old church, described by O'Neill as "a great cross with a life-size figure of Christ, and an exceptionally fine piece of wood carving," a miniature plaster of paris crucifix of the kind sold in the Sixth Avenue novelty shops for peanuts.

What the immediate state of S. N. Behrman's health is, I do not know. But if he is still convalescing from the pains of *The Talley Method,* I can comprehend and sympathize. When the play first went into rehearsal, the direction was entrusted to Elmer Rice, a fellow-member with Behrman in the Playwrights' Company. After due process of trial and error, which ran into long weeks, Rice was voted out and Herman Shumlin brought in. Shumlin did what he could, but when the play opened in New York the actors, utterly confused by the two totally different methods and styles of direction, found themselves playing according to both at one and the same time, thus projecting a performance that was as peculiar a mixture as if the understudies of a company playing *Dear Ruth* were called in at the last moment to substitute for a company playing *Anna Lucasta.*

It is easy for us critics to criticize playwrights, but the remarkable thing, considering all the circumstances, is that they retain enough sanity to write even the kind of plays they lately have been writing. In testimony thereto, consider Robert Turney's *Daughters Of Atreus,* a formal paraphrase of classic Greek drama cast with such a variety of German, Russian, Polish, Boston and what not other foreign accents that it sounded like a Weber and Fields show put on by the Moscow Art Theatre in Chinese. Think, too, of John Barrymore's miscellaneous low asides to his fellow actors and saucy remarks to the audience which drove at least one author to drink and another and more celebrated one, long dead, to grave acrobatics. Recollect further Richard Bennett's and Lowell Sherman's periodic denunciations of audiences who didn't seem sufficiently to be relishing their performances and what happened to the poor authors' plays. And while you are about it, meditate the star actress who got herself so full of strong waters on the opening night of a certain well-known dramatist's play that, in its most important scene, she walked haughtily into a bookcase under the impression that it was a door; of another who also under the influence got herself so tangled up in her voluminous boudoir negligée that she fell plumb on her nates, with the play following suit; of still another, cold sober, who more recently came on the stage wearing tiny bells on her slippers, which she tinkled merrily whenever another actress in the company whom she didn't like threatened to divert the audience's attention from her; and — still speaking of the ladies — of the fairly venerable one who not so long ago, under the impression that she was being youthfully cute, kept jumping over the seated leading man's extended legs and thus turned the playwright's intended character of a woman of aristocratic bearing into a vaudeville kangaroo.

Poor Mrs. Kummer.

A LADY SAYS YES. JANUARY 10, 1945

A musical comedy originally titled A Lady Of ?, *book by Clayton Ashley, music by Fred Spielman and Arthur Gershwin, lyrics by Stanley Adams. Produced by J. J. Shubert in association with Clayton Ashley for 87 performances in the Broadhurst Theatre.*

PROGRAM

CAPTAIN DESIRI	*Pittman Corry*	CHRISTINE	*Christine Ayres*
FRANCESCA	*Helene Le Berthon*	HILDEGARDE	*Jacqueline Susann*
ROSA	*Blanche Grady*	LICETTA	*Sue Ryan*
CARMELA	*Jackson Jordan*	GASPARE	*Earl McDonald*
DR. BARTOLI	*Jack Albertson*	KILLER PEPOLI	*Fred Catania*
ISABELLA	*Martha King*	SECOND	*Al Klein*
SCAPINO	*Bobby Morris*	PANTALOON	*Steve Mills*
ANTHONY GASPARE	*Arthur Maxwell*	GHISELLA	*Carole Landis*
		PAGE BOY	*Francelia Schmidt*

SYNOPSIS: Prologue. *Time 1945.* Scene 1. *Waiting room of a hospital.* Scene 2. *The operating room.* Act I. *Time 1545.* Scene 1. *A street in Venice.* Scene 2. *Ghisella's bedroom.* Act II. *Time 1545.* Scene 1. *Street in Venice.* Scene 2. *Garden of the Emperor of China.* Scene 3. *Hospital laboratory — Time 1945.* Scene 4. *A garden party, Washington, D. C.*

CLAYTON ASHLEY is the pseudonym of Dr. Maxwell Maltz, a New York plastic surgeon whose performances in that branch of surgery, judging from his book, have included an unsuccessful operation to remove the *Sch* from his born surname. The doctor's writing kit is greasy with lard, and the lard is frequently mixed with dirt, and both are very hard on even a hokum stomach.

For his basic scheme the doctor, who incidentally supplied most of the money for the production of the show, has resorted to the rococo dream device of transporting modern characters back into a past century, which happily always allows any producer of an economical tendency to retrieve a lot of fancy old costumes from his theatrical warehouse, to say nothing of sparing him the necessity of finding a quorum of chorus and show-girls with symmetrical legs. Superimposed upon the ancient scheme is the equally ancient superstition that a male's sexual virtuosity is predicated upon the size of his nose, which affords the doctor an opportunity to indulge in leers of pretended misunderstanding whenever a character utters such a word as "function."

The doctor's general idea of humor is, forsooth, something that should interest a colleague in the profession of taxidermy. "What is that you have on?" inquires a man of a woman clad in a filmy negligée. "A negligée," replies the latter. The man takes a long, hard look. "Negli-gee!" he exclaims. "I've been asked to get married many times," confides a woman. "So have I," replies another, "by the same people — my mother and father." A man hails a show-girl with "Oh, señorita!" "I am not a señorita, I am a señora," loftily allows the show-girl. "Who cares how you sleep?" retorts the man.

The fecundity of the doctor's wit takes such further forms as confusing Marco Polo with a game played on horses with sticks, alluding to the hair on a comedian's chest as tobacco and specifying it as Chesterfield, observing of a weakling who describes himself as Don Juan that he is Don Two, and replying to a query as to a taste for Kipling, "I don't know — I've never kippled." Let alone such forms as confounding Sir Walter Raleigh with a brand of cigarettes, observing of a woman's raucous voice that it is the Voice of the Turtle and of another's inappreciable rear that it is the Lost Weekend, stating that still another is not only medieval but evil, noting that yet still another whose job is a receptionist had not been known to be so receptive, and a female comic's reply to a description of her hair as being chestnut, her eyes hazel, and her complexion walnut, that she is the nuts.

The music of the show obviously derives its name solely from the circumstance that its sounds have been arbitrarily entrusted to a pit orchestra, and the lyrics have to do with such subjects as the dulness of life without caresses, the galvanizing effect of vitamins, the fact that it is the girl everytime who counts, and the eccentricities of Brooklyn. And the costumes and scenery are strictly in the R. H. Burnside tradition.

If I have omitted anything, think up any derogatory descriptive adjectives you can, and you will be right.

The production marked the third stage appearance within ten days of a moving picture star in an important role, which did neither any of them nor the roles any good. The three were the Mary Astor and Neil Hamilton of the preceding chapter and here Carole Landis. Both Miss Astor and Miss Landis are visually attractive young women, the latter especially so; and Mr. Hamilton is also attractive in the characterless way that so many motion picture actors and actresses are. But it is to be feared, as earlier hinted, that when it comes to the business of acting, whether on the dramatic or musical stage, such screen favorites are far beyond their depth.

Miss Astor, for example, has a pleasant manner and conceivably with prolonged experience might develop into a serviceable actress, but as things stand she simply substitutes a likable screen personality for the somewhat more complicated craft of acting. A gay smile, however winning, is hardly a deceptive camouflage for a lack of inner comedic spirit; an air of savoir faire is not to be captured merely in nonchalant shoulder shruggings; and there must be more to a satisfactory projection of charm than speaking lines with a soft chuckle and the ability to play the piano.

Mr. Hamilton, to recapitulate and without further ado, is, as a stage actor, non-existent. Judging from his performance in the Kummer play, he apparently believes that dramatic acting is identical with the screen species and so contents himself with presenting his handsome profile to the audience, scrupulously following imaginary chalk marks about the stage, and reading his lines in a bleak monotone which a Hollywood "mixer," if present, might be relied upon to resolve into tones of a rich pear shape, worthy of Beerbohm Tree.

Miss Landis contributes to the musical show stage the considerable good looks noted and a figure not to be sneered at, which, say what the solemn will, are something. But fears as to her other competences assail one. Her delivery of lines is agreeable enough, but her singing and motions toward dancing, it grieves one to report, since any such pretty creature invokes an uncritical chivalry, hardly constitute further stimulants to a stage already adorned by a number of such girls as Helena Bliss, Mary Martin, June Havoc, and the like.

The truth seems to be that the girls who have come on from Hollywood to try their luck in the theatre in the last few seasons have not been very fortunate. Of them all — and there has been a goodly freight of them — only Arleen Whelan, Virginia Gilmore, and K. T. Stevens among the younger ones have made any critical impression on the dramatic stage, and only Jan Clayton on the musical. Gwen Anderson, Wendy Barrie, Dolly Haas, Nancy Kelly, Florence Rice, Ilona Massey, Margaret Lindsay, Jeanne Cagney, Pert Kelton, Julie Warren, Marjorie Lord, Annabella, Patricia Morison, Margaret Hayes, and at least half a dozen others have come and gone without causing a ripple. A few of the older Hollywood women like Geraldine Fitzgerald who are generically stage actresses have critically fared somewhat better, but such as Joan Blondell, Glenda Farrell, and Miriam Hopkins have lost much of whatever share of earlier interest both criticism and their theatre public may have had in them. Even Mae West, though still showing some box-office life, appears doomed to the down-grade. And the simon-pure Hollywood ZaSu Pitts, after her little day in court, should keep her fingers crossed.

While actresses like Margaret Sullavan, Katharine Hepburn, Betty Field and Martha Scott, all primarily of the theatre rather than the screen, have held the theatre's affection, the last three seasons, along with the two that preceded them, have demonstrated rather clearly that the distance between Hollywood and the stage is far, and the road rocky. Phyllis Brooks, Elaine Shepard, Margaret Tallichet, Sally O'Neil, Helen Twelvetrees, Elsa Lanchester and Betty Furness have tried to cover it, and have dropped by the wayside. And so, too, have many otherwise nice girls like

Lila Lee, Heather Angel, Helene Reynolds, Mary Healy, Louise Stanley, Fay Wray, Rosemary Lane, Beverly Tyler, Lillian Bond, June Clyde, Irene Hervey, Mary Anderson, Luise Rainer, Elissa Landi, and Gloria Swanson. Where a single Jane Wyatt, Margo or, above all, Mary Martin has survived, a dozen have gone under. And in these exceptional cases it is usually the actress who has had stage training who is numbered among the survivors.

The reason for the failure of so many of the Hollywood actresses is hardly at this late date the basis of a particularly big news story. Some of them are blessed with all the desired physical attributes; some of them have good speaking voices; and some of them are not without the valuable quality that goes by the stereotyped term personality. But, while the camera has made them, the stage unmakes them. The two mediums, at least reading from right to left, are strangers. A stage actress thus has a much easier time in succeeding on the screen than a screen actress has on the stage, which has been sufficiently proved in the cases of many of them. The cinema is largely a process of external photography; the drama a process of inner. The stage actress so brings to the cinema that extra something, gained from dramatic experience, which adds just a little bit more to the cinema than it customarily enjoys and that, like an oversized tip to a cafeteria waiter, comes as an agreeable surprise, even if the waiter, or picture audience, can not quite understand the reason for it. The screen actress, on the other hand, most often brings to the stage only the outward characteristics and shadow of acting, and one will usually find that where occasionally a screen actress brings more than that she is essentially not really a screen actress at all but a stage actress who has wandered into the wrong medium, and has not, to boot, been overly successful in it.

LA VIE PARISIENNE. JANUARY 12, 1945

A new English version of the Jacques Offenbach operetta (first heard in Paris in 1866) by Felix Brentano and Louis Verneuil, with lyrics by Marian Farquhar. Produced by Yolanda Mero-Irion for the New Opera Company for 37 performances in the City Center Theatre.

PROGRAM

STATIONMASTER	*Phillip George*
POLICEMAN	*Roy Ballard*
NEWSBOY	*Irene E. Sherrock*
FLOWER GIRL	*Loretta Schere*
COMTE RAOUL DE GARDEFEU	*Brian Lawrence*
BARON BOBINET	*Edward Roecker*
METELLA	*Marion Carter*
GONTRAN	*Lee Edwards*
JACKSON	*David Morris*
EVELYN	*Lillian Andersen*
MR. HUTCHINSON	*Arthur Newman*
PREMIERES DANSEUSES	*Anna Istomina* *Elena Kramarr*
PREMIER DANCER	*James Lyons*
CUSTOMS INSPECTORS	*Nicholas J. Insardi* *Sylvan Evans*
GABRIELLE	*Frances Watkins*
ALPHONSE	*Lee Edwards*

SYNOPSIS: The action takes place in Paris in spring, between 1880 and 1890. Act I. *A railway station, in the evening.* Act II. Scene 1. *Three days later — salon at Gardefeu's house, in the late afternoon.* Scene 2. *The following evening — the famous private banquet room at the fashionable Cafe Anglais.* Act III. *Later the same night at Gardefeu's salon.*

ON NOVEMBER 28, 1944, the City Center offered for an engagement of three weeks Johann Strauss' *The Gypsy Baron*. Through mental processes not difficult to penetrate, it offered it to the attention of music critics rather than theatre critics, since while the music of *The Gypsy Baron* is charming the book hardly exercises enough charm to fascinate even the least of what the late Percy Hammond described as contented rattlesnakes. Through mental processes rather more difficult to penetrate, the City Center offered this revival of the Offenbach operetta to theatre critics rather than their music brothers. Since the book, while not entirely so dismal as that of *The Gypsy Baron,* was even in its first incarnation pretty bad and since it was in this reincarnation still less virtuous and since, further, the music remains the one asset the exhibit enjoys, the aforesaid difficulty may be appreciated.

The production of *The Gypsy Baron* was in all respects shabby; the production of *La Vie Parisienne,* with which the New Opera Company had toyed before, was somewhat better. But, though relatively better, it still left much to be prayed for by those persons who had seen the operetta in some of its presentations in Europe. The new version of the book, which always has needed liberal cutting, suffered from witless hands; its attempts at humorous modernization went even to the absurd extent of allusions to Oshkosh and the Republican party. The staging by Ralph Herbert, fairly expert in the first act, thereafter descended to concluding a duet number by having the male singers deject themselves with merry exhaustion upon a couch, to having the members of a comical quartette alternately step forward out of the line and coyly beam the lyrics at the audience, to converting the famous Can-Can number into a hybrid ballet, and to serving the champagne in the Café Anglais scene out of what very evidently were beer bottles. Several of the actors and actresses whose English speech was of a distinctly suburban timbre became suddenly such purists when called upon to enunciate a French word and delivered themselves so elegantly of "frah" for "franc" and "cawh" for "compte" that the effect was hilarious sub-Berlitz. And the musical arrangements by Antal Dorati, which too frequently by senseless way of trying to liven up an already lively enough score determinedly recast some of the music into a monotonously overworked *allegrissimo,* depressed the proceedings further. Offenbach, though in this operetta himself not always free from monotony, does not need help from Mr. Dorati.

The most interesting person on the stage was the relative newcomer, Lillian Andersen, in the role of the daughter of the American millionaire. Miss Andersen has both beauty and voice, though her studiously elaborate labial formations in the delivery of higher notes occasionally detract from the former.

One of the music critics, under the spell of several of the Offenbach compositions, delivered himself of an extensive testimonial to the power of music generally over the mental faculties of mankind and to its stimulation of the higher cerebral centers. This is one of the theories that it has always entertained me to scrutinize. That music inspires one to profound and lofty thoughts, many of them of competitive rank with Hegel, Kant and Herbert Spencer, is a theory assuaging to æsthetics, but I fear that it is prettier than true. Great music may instil in one an awe and respect for its composer but, beyond that, the meditations it gives birth to are generally less transcendent and metaphysical than mundane, and of a philosophical, ethical, and even romantic bulk not materially greater than those generated by a half-pint of good Scotch whiskey. As for inferior music, which constitutes about nine-tenths of the tonal art, if one doesn't dance one either goes to sleep and dreams dreams far beyond the imaginations of its artificers or loudly demands more alcohol to drown out the aural and mental torture.

Music in the aggregate, in point of mathematical fact, does not, aside from a great critical satisfaction and pleasure in the best of it, provide the imaginaton with half the blooms and fertile fields vouchsafed by malt and the grape; and what cerebral exercises it induces, compared with those of the latter, are both in essence and expansiveness relatively puny. Its gifts to the cerebrum are mainly those of rememoration or wistful speculation on the present and future. In its spell one thinks of such sentimental trivia as a woman loved and lost, some beautiful creature whom one knows damned well one will never achieve, or the theoretically happy days that are gone and the theoretically happy ones to come. On rare occasions the mind may be inspired to take a slightly more trenchant flight, but in the main all that music contributes to the psyche is a philosophical sedative which comfortably reassures idiots of the virtue of their idiocy and reconciles wiser men to their lack of emotional pragmatism.

The effect of music, even great music, upon the human

brain is in no better way to be appreciated than by observing the results in the instance of most musicians and orchestra conductors. With probably not more than three exceptions at most, no conspicuous musician or maestro has ever given the slightest evidence that his art had inculcated in him thoughts above those of a twelve-year-old child or has ever made a single remark which indicated that his imagination had been inspired beyond the capacity of that of a bass drummer. Consider, on the other hand, the mere mint julep. After the first, the mind proceeds to dredge up from nowhere any number of piquant ideas: choice epigrams, hitherto unanswered telephone numbers that offer a challenge to realistic romance, sidelights on the political philosophies of such old Southern colonels as Thomas Jefferson, James Madison, and James Monroe, the influence upon their illustrious husbands of such Dixie belles as Martha Custis, Martha Skelton, Rachel Robarts, and Letitia Christian, the psychological impulses in the philosophy of Benedetto Croce, and the part valuably played by alcoholic spirits in the campaigns of Octavius Caesar, William of Orange, and General Jacob S. Coxey.

After the second, and after a continued resolute assault on the telephone numbers, comes a period of rosy tranquillity wherein the mind gives life to a repertoire of sauceful considerations: that America, for all its cultural progress, still refuses to accept at his full value any critic like the late James Huneker simply because he looked upon the wine when it was red and the women when they were pink and reserves its fullest approval for inferior critics like the late Stuart Sherman who in ex-officio life were immaculate stuffed-shirts; that in the happiest period of his life Beethoven wrote *Fidelio,* one of his poorest jobs, whereas in the most troubled he produced the great *Ninth Symphony;* that the lowbrow who wrote such flubdub as "Walter Scott is a great genius," "The Chinese think, act and feel almost exactly like ourselves," and "Hugo's *Notre Dame de Paris* is the most abominable book that was ever written" was none other than Goethe; and that most of the greatest loves in history, contrary to the established philosophy of amour, involved little or no respect on the part of either of the principals.

After the third julep, one is besieged by ideas like the one which constitutes this meditation, which at its worst may possibly be granted to be at least slightly more tinctorial than any six ideas generated by anything that Mendelssohn ever wrote.

HEDGEROW THEATRE REPERTOIRE
JANUARY 16, 1945

A month's program of plays from the repertoire of the Moylan, Pennsylvania, little theatre group. Produced in the Cherry Lane Theatre.

PRINCIPALS

Jasper Deeter, Miriam Phillips, Arthur Rich, Catherine Rieser, Mahlon Naill, Elsie Winocour, Rose Schulman, Thomas Meigs, Arthur Hanson, Audrey Ward, Helen Alexander, Dan Christman, Joseph Leberman, Kenneth Carter.

THE HEDGEROW THEATRE was founded twenty-two years ago by Jasper Deeter and in that period has produced one hundred and fifty-five plays, thirty-nine of them new and presented by the organization for the first time. With the Pennsylvania countryside roads closed by the heavy winter snows and with sufficient gasoline unavailable even when they were open, the worthy little band of players emigrated to New York to display their wares in more commodious surroundings and opened in the remote Greenwich Village section of the city on a night that for snow-choked roads and stalled cars was as defeating as any they had experienced in their native Rose Valley.

The opening production was Eugene O'Neill's *The Emperor Jones,* first produced in New York a quarter-century ago. This was followed by a new play by Jack Kinnard called *Tomorrow's Yesterday,* another new play by the young Mexican, Ramon Naya, called *Quintin Quintana,* and by Jean Black's dramatization of the Christopher Morley novel, *Thunder On The Left,* originally produced by the Hedgerow players in 1929 and subsequently seen in the New York theatre in 1933. The O'Neill play, one of his best, is too well known to need further comment. The Kinnard play, its 22-year-old author's first produced work, purports to be a study of typical, everyday American life and is so overly verbose and badly muddled a mixture of realism and symbolism that it constantly trips over itself. The Naya exhibit is described by its sponsors as dealing with "a young and vital Mexico invaded and exploited by predatory pseudo-sophistication from the States," and further showing "old Mexico's new youth and vitality attacked by the cancer of a dying culture which bores from within." The author, whose *Mexican Mural* was produced in New York in 1942, here again indicates a measure of descriptive talent but also once again the lack of a sufficient dramaturgical knowledge to convert it into valid theatre. He is also given unnecessarily to obscenity. The Black-Morley fantasy, a child's-eye view of adults, offers some humorous observation and a measure of originality that constitute it often likable pastime.

All the productions were largely of an amateur quality, yet the fundamental spirit and the enterprise of Mr. Deeter's organization can not but call upon one's respect. With negligible means at his disposal, he has steadfastly carried on in what he believes to be the better interests of an American theatre for more than two decades and, if his achievements have not always been able to compete with the professional stage, they at least have occasionally been worth-while and deserving of a hospitable suspension of too critical judgment.

GOOD NIGHT LADIES. JANUARY 17, 1945

An adaptation by Cyrus Wood of the Avery Hopwood-Charlton Andrews farce, Ladies' Night In A Turkish Bath, *presented by A. H. Woods 25 years ago. Produced by Howard Lang and Al Rosen for 78 performances in the Royale Theatre.*

PROGRAM

MARIE	*Rosemary Bertrand*
DODIE TARLETON	*Randee Sanford*
KITTIE BONNER	*Sunnie O'Dea*
MIKE BONNER	*Skeets Gallagher*
MRS. THERESA TARLETON	*Kathryn Givney*
ALICIA BLAKE	*Marlo Dwyer*
FRED BLAKE	*Max Hofmann, Jr.*
PROF. JOHN MATTHEWS	*James Ellison*
MRS. BLANCHE O'BRIEN	*Ann Fortney*
ANNA	*Lucille Benson*
MYRTLE SHEA	*Louise Jarvis*
EVE LA BOUCHE	*Lana Holmes*
POLICEWOMAN	*Beatrice Newport*
FIREMAN	*Wendell Ates*

SYNOPSIS: Act I. *The Bonner apartment. Early evening.* Act II. *The Cosmetarium. Several hours later.* Act III. *Same as Act I, 2:30 a.m.* Time. *Present.*

PERCEIVING that his cargo of minsky, *School For Brides* (*q.v.*), was to the taste of the New York box-office, Mr. Lang, assisted in this instance by one Rosen, reconsidered his qualms as to that other cargo of the same called *Good Night Ladies,* which had prospered inordinately in Chicago and other thitherward communities, and brought it into the metropolis as soon as he could persuade its author to play safe by adding to it a few more bad jokes. While not as smutty as the earlier *coup,* it is even duller, if that be possible, relying for its humor as it does upon the antiquated theme of a pair of men lying themselves into a gay night off from their wives, being caught in a raid upon the scene of their frolic, and thereafter exerting themselves in one fashion or another to avoid detection by their mates. The theme was such a favorite in the theatre of France and Germany seventy-five years ago that it was a rare season that did not merchant several treatments of it. And it was not many years after that that it began to appear on the American stage almost annually either in adaptations of the French and German farces or in paraphrases of them, sometimes from the hand of Leo Ditrichstein, sometimes from that of George Broadhurst, and now and then from that of some less well known theatrical artisan of the period.

The present version has been culled from the Hopwood-Andrews farce noted, which in turn had been culled basically from such farces as *It Happened To Jones,* which in double turn had been culled from numerous French and German predecessors. It has been vulgarized into the worst kind of drivel imaginable; it has no single moment of genuine humor; and its presented spectacle of semi-nude females comporting themselves like bootleg burlesque queens is less than edifying. The whole has been patently designed to gratify that portion of the theatrical trade which believes that a woman is not an actress unless she takes her clothes off on the stage and that humor is not humor unless it involves a male dressed up as a female. If the male thus garbed then smears some cold cream on his face and to his horror is apprised by the woman thus ungarbed that it is a depilatory, the trade in point prepares to have the time of its life. And if a moment later he is laid out on a massage slab and a whizzing dimpling needle applied to his behind, to its anguished contortions, the trade can not contain itself.

As further samples of the author's wit there are such lines as "I have adored you from afar" — "Oh, I see; remote control"; "Women are a closed book to me" — "All you need is a paper-cutter"; "I'm afraid I'm old-fashioned" — "Yes, just one Old-fashioned after another"; and, upon a woman's saucy remark, the admonition, "Remember, there are men present!"

The speech of the acting personnel took such contours as "Saracuse" for Syracuse, "genius" for genus, and the cultured like.

REBECCA. January 18, 1945

A dramatization by Daphne Du Maurier of her novel of the same title. Produced by Victor Payne-Jennings for 20 performances in the Ethel Barrymore Theatre.

PROGRAM

Frith *Richard Temple*	Mrs. de Winter *Diana Barrymore*
Beatrice Lacy *Margaret Bannerman*	Maid *Jacqueline Max*
Major Giles Lacy *Franklyn Fox*	Robert *Kenneth Treseder*
Frank Crawley *Claude Horton*	Mrs. Danvers *Florence Reed*
Maxim de Winter *Bramwell Fletcher*	Jack Favell *George Baxter*
	Col. Julyan *Reginald Mason*
	William Tabb *Edgar Kent*

SYNOPSIS: The action of the play takes place in the southern end of the hall at Manderley, the home of Maxim de Winter, in Cornwall, England, some years before the present war. Act I. Scene 1. *Early evening in May.* Scene 2. *Morning, six weeks later.* Act II. Scene 1. *Evening, the same day.* Scene 2. *4 a.m. the following morning.* Act III. Scene 1. *Afternoon, the same day.* Scene 2. *Early evening, two days later.*

The play suggests nothing quite so much as Laura Jean Libbey bound in half-Morocco. All the fancy stage trappings can not conceal the essential Libbey materials: the faithless first wife, the young second wife brought to the grand manor house, the sinister housekeeper, the drowning of the first wife and the suspicions of murder, the scoundrelly blackmailer, etc., etc. The novel succeeded in concealing them to a degree, but in the play manufactured from it the pseudo-psychological elements have been reduced to a miscellaneous melodramatic furrowing of brows, the spectre of the defunct first wife that haunts the second becomes merely a kind of Harvey with a villainous false black mustache, the sinister housekeeper, Mrs. Danvers, at least as acted by Florence Reed, is Mother Goddam directly out of *The Shanghai Gesture,* and the exhibit as a whole has an aspect of something out of the remote *East Lynne-Jane Eyre* stock company period.

The plot is doubtless familiar to you from the novel or, if you are given to the cinema, from the picture made from it. Charles Garvice brings to his great house in Cornwall a second wife in the person of a young girl named Bertha M. Clay. The house, like Garvice's mind, is haunted by the memory of the deceased first wife, whose name was Augusta J. Evans. Garvice's obsession slowly tortures Bertha out of her wits, her profound discomfort not being lessened by the acts of Augusta's vicious and still loyal old housekeeper, Mrs. Alex McVeigh Miller. It presently develops that Garvice murdered Augusta because she had been unfaithful to him and that it is hate not love that envelops his memory of her. A knave named E. Phillips Oppenheim who was Augusta's lover and who is aware of Garvice's guilt now seeks to extract funds from him and, rebuffed, tells all. But in the end Garvice goes free, Bertha is released from her prolonged agony, and a jolly neighbor named Mary J. Holmes helps to celebrate the occasion with the happily reunited couple. The manor house is not burned to the ground in the play as it was in the novel, probably because it would have taken an extra 3,000 dollars to buy the rights to Langdon McCormick's old stage fire effect.

As Garvice, Bramwell Fletcher indicated his overpowering mental perturbation mainly by pacing the stage with a slouched right shoulder and by keeping his eyes glued to his succession of faultlessly creased trousers. As Bertha M. Clay, Miss Barrymore was tortured not only by the spectre of Garvice's first wife but by some very poor playwriting and by direction that kept her for a large share of the evening simply standing around with an air of injured innocence and watching the other actors, which was not exactly a treat.

The play, despite its failure in New York because of bad casting and acting, was a great box-office success on the road and seemed to indicate once again that little perhaps remains more satisfying to the American theatre public at large, and to the metropolitan at least nine times out of ten, than what the pure in soul deem to be deplorable, highly immoral, or worse. Maxim de Winter, completely unsympathetic to audiences in the earlier portion of *Rebecca,* promptly became an object of the deepest sympathy upon his statement that he had murdered his first wife, and audiences, including New York's, were furthermore wholeheartedly on his side against the forces of the law that sought to trap him. The enormous popular success of *Harvey* is due in no small degree to its warm defense of alcoholic indulgence. The prosperity of *I Remember Mama* is predicated to an almost equal degree upon the character of an old boozer with a mistress. The trash, *School For Brides,* achieved a long run on the score of its sexual misdemeanors, and Mae West's *Catherine Was Great* was kept going for many months by the spectacle of its heroine's miscellaneous gay affairs.

The one and only scene in the claptrap, *The Perfect Marriage,* which garnered the audiences' sympathy was that wherein the husband tried to negotiate another woman upon whom he had lodged an illicit eye. The dubious *The Searching Wind* humanizes its icy stuffed-shirt of a protagonist for the audience only when it becomes known that some years before he had allowed love to take its biological course. Without its character of the philandering Alexander Craig, *Soldier's Wife* could hardly have gained the popular trade that it did. And the anatomically suppressed but mink-eyed Emily in *Snafu* went a long way toward guaranteeing the box-office in the case of that play.

The sympathetic heroine of the great hit, *Anna Lucasta,* is a prostitute, and the ditto of that even greater hit, *The Voice Of The Turtle,* takes love where she finds it. *Chicken Every Sunday* is a riot with the public largely because of its unquenchable nymphomaniac and other glandularly effervescent characters. *Arsenic And Old Lace,* that gold-mine, makes murder lovable, and I don't have to tell you about that other gold-mine, *Tobacco Road. Lovers And Friends,* dreadful rubbish, managed a considerable run on the score of its husband's and wife's extra-marital peccadillos, and *Wallflower's* heroine was a girl who learned that the way to be popular with the boys was, well, to be popular with them —and who put her lesson into practise. The delinquent little heroine of *Pick-Up Girl* had audiences weeping copious tears for her. And many of the hit musical shows' most successful elements have been and are situations and songs that would cause a pious bartender to fear for his soul.

But this is no new development in the theatre. The theatre provides an escape and a holiday for people ordinarily circumspect, and when people, however punctilious, go on a picnic they do not want to be given the day in and day out family oatmeal. An appetite-stimulating dill pickle, a sandwich spiced with anchovy paste, a swig out of a flask is more to their taste, and plays and shows that cater cleverly to their wayward palates reap the reward. The average person who goes to the theatre sniffs a little mental cocaine and sticks a carnation into his heart on the way. It is so now as it has been so for time on end.

It is thus that Marguerite Gautier and Get-Rich-Quick Wallingford, Iris Bellamy and Arsène Lupin, Don Juan, Du Barry, Peck's Bad Boy and all the other sinners big and little have held an attraction for audiences that in most instances has been irresistible, even when the plays that have included them have been nothing to brag about. The Cinderellas and Peg o' My Hearts, the Little Lord Fauntleroys and Rudolf Rassendylls have held and still hold their places too, but when all is said and done they can not for a moment oust from the affectionate admiration of the body politic the knaves and the rascals, the heart-loose ladies, and the flouters of conventional morality in general.

Of the fifty-odd plays that have achieved the longest stage runs in our more modern American theatre, the greater proportion, by way of evidence, have fascinated audiences with themes and characters that would be spanked, to say the very least, in the audiences' homes. They have dealt sympathetically with everything from miscegenation to murder, untrammeled sex to criminal enterprise, and moral revolt to delirium tremens, or its equivalent. They have made a virtue of shiftlessness, as in *Lightnin'*, of lack of thrift, as in *You Can't Take It With You,* of acid meanness, as in *The Women,* and of wantonness, as in *Rain.* They have made entrancing the characters of crooks and thieves and killers, as in *The Bat, Within The Law, Broadway,* and

Angel Street; they have made sinful love romantic, as in *White Cargo* and *Strictly Dishonorable;* they have made mock of sexual morality, as in *Boy Meets Girl, The Doughgirls,* and *Separate Rooms;* and they have broken most of the Commandments in the combined cases of *Tobacco Road, My Sister Eileen, The Children's Hour, Dead End, Street Scene, Kiki, Personal Appearance, Sailor, Beware!,* and a dozen others.

And the bulk of our thoroughly respectable fellow-citizens has loved them.

It is to be gravely feared, accordingly, that the great body of our theatregoers is not always on the side of the gods. A grievous and depressing thought, but true, alas, nonetheless. The great body of our theatregoers would seem, in point of fact, to be something of a heel. In its eyes the representatives of moral order and decency are frequently objects to be scoffed at, ridiculed, and profoundly disliked. The character of the young man in *Dear Ruth,* for example, who stands for the conventions, who believes that a man's fiancée should not go about necking with strangers, and who hopes to build a home and family is looked upon as an odious ass. And the father in *Anna Lucasta,* for another, who doesn't relish the idea of his daughter being a waterfront whore and tells his family that he doesn't like to have her around his orderly house is regarded as an objectional person and as even something of a villain.

As in days gone by, it is the girl with illegitimate child or her equivalent who is simultaneously driven out into the snow and into the hearts of the audience.

It isn't, as may be thought, that human nature is generally for the underdog; in the theatre it is not only for the underdog but for any kind of dog, particularly mutt. The dramatic gallery of rakes, scoundrels, and jades who have captivated audiences would fill a book. It has embraced crooks like Jim the Penman, Raffles and Jimmy Valentine; strumpets like Laura Murdock, Lulu Belle and Anna Christie; libertines like Chevrial and the gay Lord Quex; drunks like Falstaff, Joxer and Fluther Good; vixens like Hedda and Regina Giddens; loose fish like Magda, Rose Bernd and

Paula Tanqueray; murderers like Killer Mears, and wastrels like Rip, and cadgers like Haji the beggar of Bagdad, and a thousand other such sports and sinners. And the public, to repeat, has adored them.

And, incidentally, much of the time I have been part of that lamentable public.

HOME IS THE HERO. January 18, 1945

A play by Courtenay Savage. Produced by the Blackfriars' Guild for 23 performances in the Blackfriars' Guild Theatre.

PROGRAM

Tillie Baylis	*Ella Playwin*	Ivy Woodman	*Dorothy Buquo*
Joy Harris	*Kate Gibbons*	Jerry Merrill	*Harold Heagy*
Joe Kelly	*David Bell*	Mary Fisher	*Beth Shea*
Joan Scott	*Laura McClure*	Ray Kelly	*Richard Corby*
Ann Gardner	*Miriam Galley*	Fred Kelly	*Robert Echlin*
Frances Merrill	*Virginia Dwyer*		

SYNOPSIS: The action takes place in the living-hall of a Los Angeles mansion which has been converted into a war-time rooming house. Act I. *Late afternoon.* Act II. Scene 1. *Two weeks later; early evening.* Scene 2. *Two weeks later; the dinner hour.* Act III. *A week later* (*Sunday morning*).

It is not easy to determine why the Blackfriars' Guild, which is dedicated to the experimental drama, for the second successive time in a season resorted to the kind of play to which lesser Broadway producers so often in turn dedicate themselves, and to no profit. Mr. Savage in the past has been a big source of supply to such producers with hapless trade goods like *Don't Bother Mother, Virtue's Bed, The Buzzard, The Queen At Home,* and *Loose Moments,* all routine fare and scarcely contributing to any noticeable elevation of either the drama or the box-office. This, his latest effort, is hardly more propitious.

For his theme, Mr. Savage has not too originally had recourse to the problems of the returned married soldier, involving, as usual, his difficulties in readjusting himself to family life, his wife's determination to pursue the working career she has entered upon in his long absence, and so on. Though he has set himself to view the subject more seriously than, for example, Rose Franken in *Soldier's Wife* (*q.v.*), he has succeeded in getting no appreciable distance and a tidal wave of garrulity overwhelms and drowns what drama the topic may conceivably possess. Instead of dramatizing his materials, he simply reduces them to endless colloquies between the soldier and his mate, which leave his other characters in the position of supers idly standing around, without spears. The colloquies, moreover, consist of the fully anticipated ingredients and the attempt to lend them an air of importance by pitching them in an indignant key only converts them into so many audience bivouacs.

A GOOSE FOR THE GANDER

January 23, 1945

A comedy by Harold J. Kennedy. Produced by Jules J. Leventhal and Frank McCoy for 15 performances in the Playhouse.

Program

David	*Conrad Nagel*	Katherine	*Gloria Swanson*
Suzy	*Maxine Stuart*	Jonathan	*John Clubley*
Lorraine	*Choo Choo Johnson*	Chauffeur	*George Margolis*
Benson	*Joyce Sirola*	Wally	*David Tyrrell*
Tony	*Harold J. Kennedy*		

SYNOPSIS: Entire action of the play takes place in the living-room of David Richardson's home in Greenwich, Conn. Time is the present. Act I. Scene 1. *Noon.* Scene 2. *Late that afternoon.* Act II. Scene 1. *After dinner, the same evening.* Scene 2. *Three hours later.* Act III. *Late the same evening.*

The Playhouse holds eight hundred and sixty-five people. On the opening night eight hundred and sixty-five people duly filled the house but only two people had a good time and they, unfortunately, were not members of the audience. They were on the stage and their names were Gloria Swanson and Harold J. Kennedy. There were also seven other people on the stage, but they didn't seem to be having any better time than the eight hundred and sixty-five on the other side of the footlights.

Miss Swanson, still another and the latest movie actress to challenge the drama, was apparently in clover, though scarcely in the direction of anything that might be said even remotely to have approached acting. She occupied a role, especially manufactured for her, which had four different men so crazy about her intellectual qualities, beauty, and sex appeal that they could hardly stand it. She privileged herself a succession of costumes by Valentina that were calculated, she felt sure, to drive the women in the audience even crazier than the aforesaid four men. She had herself a held-up grand first entrance, preceded by servants carrying on enough expensive luggage to serve an operatic version of Joseph Schildkraut, which was designed to make the audience even still crazier with anticipation than either the four men or the aforesaid women. And so on. She had herself, in short, one hell of a time.

Mr. Kennedy, who not only wrote the play but bequeathed himself a choice role in it, was not far behind Miss Swanson in a consuming happiness. He gave himself all the so-to-speak best gags; he pictured himself as a boyish lover bursting with ineffable charm; he insinuated himself elaborately into the action with the subtlety of a freight locomotive; and so on. He swam in self-delight.

For everybody else the evening was something pretty grisly.

The play was a dreary paraphrase of the kind of comedies in which Grace George used frequently to appear years ago which, when they weren't *Divorçons,* were such dreary paraphrases of it as *Sauce For The Gander* and the like. You can always tell what you are in for in these cases when you look at the cover on the program showing a husband and wife at a breakfast table with the wife about to pour the coffee and the husband kissing her hand. You know that the husband has been fooling around with another woman, that the wife will pretend to fool around with another man by way of bringing him around again, and that the coffee will duly be poured at eleven o'clock, indicating mutual understanding and happy reconciliation. You also know that, among other things, the dialogue will embrace such reflections on marriage as "Once the fish is caught, why bother about the bait?"; that there will be a scene in which the wife gets pleasantly tipsy on champagne; that she will at one point in the proceedings demonstrate that she can play the piano; and that in the end the husband will prove to her satisfaction that his affair with the other woman was purely platonic. So why wait for the coffee?

THE TEMPEST. JANUARY 25, 1945

A Margaret Webster staging of the fantasy by William Shakespeare, with music by David Diamond. Produced by Cheryl Crawford for 100 performances in, initially, the Alvin Theatre.

PROGRAM

SHIP-MASTER	*Joseph Hardy*
BOATSWAIN	*Steven Elliott*
ALONZO, KING OF NAPLES	*Philip Huston*
GONZALO	*Paul Leyssac*
ANTONIO	*Berry Kroeger*
SEBASTIAN	*Eugene Stuckmann*
PROSPERO	*Arnold Moss*
MIRANDA	*Frances Heflin*
ARIEL	*Vera Zorina*
CALIBAN	*Canada Lee*
FERDINAND, PRINCE OF NAPLES	*Vito Christi*
ADRIAN	*Jack Bostick*
TRINCULO	*George Voskovec*
STEPHANO	*Jan Werich*
MASTER OF CEREMONIES	*Larry Evers*
DANCER	*Diana Sinclair*

The Prologue. *On a ship at sea.*
The Play. *On an island.*

MISS WEBSTER's production was to be strongly recommended as a valuable education in what, at least partly, a production of *The Tempest* should not be. That it impressed and even enchanted the groundlings was, however, obvious, since it offered the novelty of a beautiful ballerina in the role of Ariel and a well-known Negro ex-prize-fighter in that of Caliban, and since it made use of a Joe Cook revolving stage which as always guaranteed a rapt fascination on the part of those more innocent theatregoers who are never so interested as when such mechanical stage trickery substitutes for drama played on a floor which remains disappointingly quiescent. That it further impressed audiences who had appreciated the play chiefly from hearsay was also clear, since Miss Webster had on at least two previous occasions demonstrated herself to be an expert in deception in the case of the numerous people who believe that, whether in drama or vaudeville, you can actually saw a woman in half even if not long afterward she jumps out of the box *in toto* and laughs them off for a lot of come-ons. What was still more, her exhibit fetched even some who knew the play well but who remain so overly susceptible to any gestures toward eccentric staging and unconventional casting that they mistake them for a vital and indeed very intellectual interpretation of the play itself.

Miss Webster knows her Shakespeare and is generally a woman of uncommon intelligence. But it is this uncommon intelligence that is now and then her undoing. Like many another cerebrally gifted person, her very intelligence induces in her a restlessness and impatience which arbitrarily impel her to be discontented with any conventional and perfectly sound interpretation of the play in hand and which drive her through sheer, though understandable, perversity to satisfy her ego in an interpretation somewhat more capricious and less recognizable, and not always, alas, above suspicion.

That perversity doubtless caused her in the present instance to stage the Shakespearean classic not in the manner which her calm intelligence convinced her it should be staged, but rather in a manner that might profitably persuade others of less intelligence that she was intellectually independent, inventive and very progressive, at which she herself, at least on this occasion, must have permitted herself a private smile. She is fundamentally much too wise not to appreciate that the less stage hocus-pocus one visits upon any such fantasy, the fuller the play upon the imagination that fantasy, so richly worded, will exercise. That she indulged in such hocus-pocus was therefore surely a concession to the uncritical box-office and to those many persons who want, above everything else, what they call a show.

It is perfectly true that such a show has been made of *The Tempest* in the past. Furthermore, there are arguments of a sort for making it one. But those arguments are certainly not the kind that would ever really persuade Miss Webster or anyone else with her Shakespearean critical sense. The fact accordingly remains that she sacrificed that good critical sense in this case to the business of Broadway showmanship.

Even if we give her the benefit of the doubt, her position in the matter was debatable. She contended in the public prints that not only are fancy stage garnishes traditional in the presentation of *The Tempest,* but that they are valuable in furthering the spirit of the fantasy. Well, let us grant for the sake of argument that they are. Granting that they are, it must then nevertheless be allowed that they must be as fancifully beautiful and as poetically persuasive as Shakespeare's fantasy itself. And that is just where Miss Webster, among other things, fell down, though perhaps through no direct fault of her own.

You can not properly adorn and embellish *The Tempest* as it should be adorned and embellished — still granting that it calls for any such carpentered ornamentation — for a mere 50,000 dollars, which was reported to be the amount of the present investment. To do it as well and as richly as it should be done — again assuming that it should be done at all — would require at least twice that amount, if not more. It costs from 30,000 to 40,000 dollars these days to put on even a simple one-set play in any fully reputable manner. To put on *The Tempest* as a real show for 50,000 is therefore in the current situation the dream of a producer and director living back in 1920 or thereabout. It can not be done.

It would consequently have been much better had Miss Webster permitted her intelligence as to the fantasy to function normally and to have staged it as unmechanically as well she knows for its finer effect it should be staged. As it was, those 50,000 dollars took at least a 35,000 toll of what should have been and is the play's intrinsic magic and loveliness.

Miss Webster, oddly enough, was praised in various quarters for the "simplicity" of her staging. The praise was difficult to understand, since, while she abandoned a lot of painted settings and some of the old accessories, the completely bogus nature of that simplicity was to be appreciated in her affected employment of a rotary stage built up to several levels and carrying a succession of enough stairs to serve the Maxim's scenes in half a dozen *The Merry Widows* and enough bizarre architectures, ostensibly indicating various localities on the enchanted island but looking more like bombed French cathedrals, Aztec ruins and Arizona florists' cacti displays, to constitute a year-book of the Schurz Evening Junior College's classes in design. Her so-called simplicity thus took the form of substituting an intricate and distracting mechanical device for the more conventional much less intricate and entirely less distracting canvas backgrounds.

"The poetry of *The Tempest* is so magical that it would make the scenery of a modern theatre ridiculous," once wrote Shaw. The poetry of *The Tempest* is so magical that it makes the imposition upon it of the mechanical contraptions of the yet more modern theatre even more ridiculous. The Bard and a merry-go-round, particularly any such Rube Goldberg merry-go-round as Miss Webster made use of, do not jell. To the poet, as Shaw said, should be left the work of conjuring up the isle "full of noises, sounds and sweet airs." The noises and sounds made by a heavily bedizened revolving stage are hardly conducive to sweet airs. "The reason is," concluded Shaw, "not that a man can *always* imagine things more vividly than art can present them to him, but that it takes an altogether extraordinary degree of art to compete with the pictures which the imagination makes when it is stimulated by such potent forces as the maternal instinct, superstitious awe, or the poetry of Shakespeare."

Miss Webster eliminated the old transformation scenes with their scrims and wires and other properties, but in their place gave us something quite as destructive to the poetic atmosphere of the play in the shape of whirligigs elaborately wound 'round with stairways down which one momentarily expected to behold a parade of Earl Carroll show-girls, at least.

It is time that modern stage producers let Shakespeare well enough alone. What with Reinhardt having converted his *A Midsummer Night's Dream* into a cross between the Vendome's show-windows and the Hanlon Brothers' *Fantasma,* what with Piscator having turned his *King Lear* into an acrobatic exhibition atop what resembled one of the loftier Swiss Alps, and what with other such producers both dead and alive having been and being still intent less upon staging him than themselves, the poor fellow, viewing the results from the grave, must wonder if his plays must not, after all, have been the work of Bacon.

The acting performances varied from the Shakespearean of Arnold Moss as Prospero, Philip Huston as Alonso and Paul Leyssac as Gonzalo to the George Abbott of a number of the others, and in the case of the clowns, Trinculo and Stephano, save for the absence of pistols and blank cartridges, to the Olsen and Johnson. Vera Zorina's Ariel remained a professional ballet dancer imitating an airy spirit; airy spirits are not in our imaginations so studiously concerned with making every little physical movement, in the language of the song, have a meaning of its own. Canada Lee's Caliban was in part effectively projected, though his ceaseless heavy nasal breathing, presumably intended to indicate savage perturbation, occasionally lent to the portrayal the suggestion of his having swallowed a toy steam engine.

What, in short, emerged from the Webster *The Tempest* with its surplusage of noisy mechanical appurtenances amid which the poetry, like a dreaming child forlornly wandered astray in a nut and bolt factory, was lost was less the impression of William Shakespeare than of Henry J. Kaiser, let alone the impression of a nocturne staged and largely played like a jazzed dirge.

UP IN CENTRAL PARK. January 27, 1945

A musical comedy, book by Herbert and Dorothy Fields, music by Sigmund Romberg. Produced by Michael Todd for a far beyond the season run in the Century Theatre.

PROGRAM

A Laborer	*Bruce Lord*
Danny O'Cahane	*Walter Burke*
Timothy Moore	*Charles Irwin*
Bessie O'Cahane	*Betty Bruce*
Rosie Moore	*Maureen Cannon*
John Matthews	*Wilbur Evans*
Thomas Nast	*Maurice Burke*
William Dutton	*John Quigg*
Andrew Monroe	*Robert Field*
Vincent Peters	*Paul Reed*
Mayor A. Oakey Hall	*Rowan Tudor*
Richard Connolly	*George Lane*
Peter Sweeney	*Harry Meehan*
William Marcey Tweed	*Noah Beery, Sr.*
Butler	*Herman Glazer*
Mildred Wincor	*Lydia Fredericks*
Joe Stewart	*Fred Barry*
Porter	*Harry Matlock*
Lotta Stevens	*Delma Byron*
Fanny Morris	*Kay Griffith*
Clara Manning	*Martha Burnett*
James Fisk, Jr.	*Watson White*
Daniel	*Daniel Nagrin*
Governess	*Louise Holden*
1st Child	*Ann Hermann*
2d Child	*Joan Lally*
3d Child	*Janet Lally*
4th Child	*Mary Alice Evans*
Page Boy	*Henry Capri*
Arthur Finch	*Wally Coyle*
Ellen Lawrence	*Elaine Barry*
Bicycle Rider	*Stanley Schimmel*
George Jones	*Guy Standing, Jr.*

SYNOPSIS: Act I. Scene 1. *A site in Central Park (June, 1870).* Scene 2. *The Park Commissioner's temporary office in Central Park (July, 1870).* Scene 3. *The lounge of the Stetson Hotel (formerly McGown's Pass Tavern), (Christmas Eve, 1870).* Scene 4. *The bird house in the Central Park Zoo.* Scene 5. *The Central Park Gardens (February, 1871).* Act II. Scene 1. *The annual Tammany Hall outing (July, 1871).* Scene 2. *Office of George Jones (owner of "The New York Times"), (later that day).* Scene 3. *Central Part West (next day at noon).* Scene 4. *The Stetson Hotel (the same afternoon).* Scene 5. *The Mall in Central Park (July 4, 1872).* Scene 6. *The bandstand in the Mall (that evening).*

THOUGH FREQUENTLY PITCHED in much too slow a tempo and here and there tediously inclined to plot tautology, the show on the whole amounts to a pleasant evening. Its book, with Central Park as its background and treating of the

Tweed ring's machinations in connection with it back in the 1870's, has an inner juice considerably superior to the more usual book about sailors rabbiting after girls, modern characters dreaming themselves back into another century, and Counts mistaking saucy midinettes for celebrated opera singers. It is true that it is not given to much comedy, but then neither is the book of the otherwise admirable *Show Boat,* with which, however, this *Up In Central Park* does not in any remotest sense compare. Though a major share of Romberg's music once again suggests that he is gifted with an ear of elephant-like virtuosity—one may hum part of a Planquette song from *The Chimes Of Normandy,* part of another from Strauss' *The Gypsy Baron* and much of a third in the form of *Upsadaisy* along with three of his without noticeably disturbing the singers or the orchestra—there are several that fondle the emotions and one or two, while also hardly unfamiliar, that evoke a contentful aural response. And some of the dances staged by Helen Tamiris, notably an ice skating ballet in the Currier and Ives snow, are both novel and attractive. The concluding scene, furthermore, with its band-stand in the Mall etched by the amber Park lights and with its scarlet-coated fiddlers, tooters and drummers banging out the martial *The Big Back Yard* is great showshop stuff and guaranteed to tickle all those of us who still recall the grand old shows in which such brass bands as John Philip Sousa's were wont to parade onto the stage at the finish and send us out of the theatre on a wave of such sound as makes any bell for Adano in comparison a pitiable little tinkle.

That the show conduces to nostalgia, as many have averred, strikes me as an error. I for one can not see just how any pathos of distance is conjured up by the most corrupt gang of swindling politicians that New York ever knew. The mood stimulated is rather one of disgust that such a gang could ever have existed and prospered. But even that is a relief from the bogusly nostalgic shows which seek to induce in us a sentimental tear over the gone yesterdays with storehouse rose arbors, insistent purple lights, and waltzes danced by sopranos and tenors in polka rhythm.

The fact remains, too, that you can not hope to work up any honest audience nostalgia, assuming that that was the producer's intent, with female principals, albeit as talented as those in this show, who lack the kind of looks and personalities that set the eyes and mind to dreaming of fragrant rosemary.

Nevertheless, to repeat, the show over-all has considerable refreshment in it: its settings by Howard Bay have all the nostalgia which the book misses; its music, while often an old and tried friend, is at least not too Tin Pan Alley; and, if humor is largely absent, it is better that it be so than that the book-writers depress us further with such attempts as, for example, "Those parlor curtains made a very nice dress."

Directly after the curtain fell on the opening night, Mr. Todd, the producer, invited the reviewers to what I was told was a very fancy champagne supper dance in the Tavern-On-The-Green. Moreover, in order to spare them any inconvenience with taxicabs, he antecedently provided them with stylish conveyances at their various places of dining to fetch them to the theatre. Just why Mr. Todd, whose show was a sufficiently good and sure-fire one, should have deemed it necessary thus to ingratiate himself with the reviewers, I can not understand. But it remains that in this respect he was not and is not alone. A number of his fellow-producers, themselves also with good shows, have done much the same thing.

Mr. Pemberton, for example, producer of the extremely enjoyable and successful *Harvey,* gave not one party for the critics but two or three, including a gala at the Copacabana which included in turn a beautiful Powers model hostess who saw to it that they were supplied with other beautiful models as table companions. Mr. Rose, whose *The Seven Lively Arts* handsomely adorned his handsome new Ziegfeld Theatre, purveyed vintage Bollinger, Veuve Cliquot, Krug, and Moët and Chandon to the fraternity not only before his first-night curtain went up but in the intermission and after the show. Mr. Lester, producer of the highly prosperous *Song Of Norway,* gave the reviewers a midnight feast at the Astor, which, I am further informed, ran the gamut from Beluga caviar to Beluga crêpes Suzette and lasted nigh unto dawn. And other producers with similarly successful shows have not only partied the critical gentry to within an inch of their lives but have even seen to it that their jobs have been made doubly easy for them by supplying special Pullmans, properly stocked with Scotch, to allow them previews of their shows in the outlying cities.

The paradox is that the majority of these solicitous producers had and have exhibits which are so meritorious that they can perfectly well stand on their own feet and have no need of ethyl alcohol, tournedos Louis XV, and beautiful models to induce the desired assimilation and hospitable critical mood. Beyond a couple of glasses of entr'acte champagne at *The Seven Lively Arts,* I personally, following the well-known old Indian philosophy, have abstained from all these social activities, since, among other reasons, cocktails and late supper parties and Powers models do not agree with me and since I consider a good show to be a wholly sufficient pleasure and reward in itself.

In the case of poor shows, the situation is, of course, materially different and it might not be such a bad idea if the producers of them took over this party business from their gratuitously over-generous colleagues. Certainly the critics should be given at least a grand ball by the producer of anything like *Good Night Ladies,* and the very least the producer of something like *A Goose For The Gander* could do would be to give them a special train, outfitted with gallons of Martinis, a first-rate chef, and maybe twenty or thirty Conover models, to take them to French Lick to recuperate.

To return to the show and Mr. Romberg, say what you will about him he nevertheless seems to know the trick of concocting the kind of sentimental songs that transport the public, like other such mechanical contrivances as the Subway and trolley cars. For years, in exhibits like *The Student Prince, The New Moon,* the Schubert paraphrased *Blossom Time,* etc., he has managed the manufacture of often synthetic melodies, patterned more or less not only after the work of past composers but on occasion after his own previous popular compositions, which have auspiciously put a wistful gulp in the throats of his customers and set them to dreaming of whatever people with Romberg gulps in their throats wistfully dream of under such circumstances. And in the present show, notably in songs like "Close As Pages In A Book," he turns the trick again.

Pinero's old recommendation that a playwright tell an audience a thing seven times in order that it may safely assimilate it has been taken to heart musically by Mr. Romberg. If, as in the well-known clinical sound experiments that determine which musical note or chord will make a dog howl, Mr. Romberg discovers a note or chord that is successful in evoking a sentimental response from his auditors, he never lets go of it, like the dog tenaciously hanging on to a bone. And not only doesn't he let go of it but he gives it, in composition after composition over the seasons, the Pinero works. The result has been that the public at large year after year has come almost automatically to swallow the à la Newburg bait, much like an undiscriminating fish might swallow a worm smeared with molasses. And Mr. Romberg has become a rich man, able to play pinochle with Rudolf Friml.

ALICE IN ARMS. January 31, 1945

A comedy, originally known as Star In The Window, *by Ladislas Bush-Fekete, Mary Helen Fay and Sidney Sheldon. Produced by Edward Choate and Marie Louise Elkins for 5 performances in the National Theatre.*

Program

Mike	*Johnnie Venn*	Collins	*Tom McElhany*
Willis	*James O'Neil*	1st Private	*Jerry Vincent*
Daisy	*Florence Shirley*	2nd Private	*Richard Coogan*
Alice	*Peggy Conklin*	Steve	*Kirk Douglas*
Helen	*Judith Abbott*	Beeker	*George Ives*
Florence	*Darthy Hinkley*	Henry	*Mickey Stewart*
Walter	*Roger Clark*	Colonel Benson	*G. Albert Smith*

SYNOPSIS: Act I. *Evening.* Act II. Scene 1. *Morning of the next day.* Scene 2. *That evening.* Act III. *Ten o'clock the same evening.*

The Scene. *Daisy Madison's house in Linwood, Pa.*

The Time. *October, 1944.*

The management apparently proceeded upon the theory that one poor playwright multiplied by three might produce a good play. The three it selected were (*1*) Mr. Bush-Fekete, a Central European whose previous local contributions were *The Lady Has A Heart,* which was about as terrifying as they come; a play script that served the Messrs. Hecht and MacArthur for their *Ladies And Gentlemen,* which was little better; and the dramatization of Werfel's *Embezzled Heaven,* a botch; (*2*) Miss Fay (Mrs. Bush-Fekete) who had collaborated on the aforesaid botch; and (*3*) Mr. Sheldon, a music show book fixer and collaborator whose principal gifts to the theatre had been a scene incorporated into a revival of *The Merry Widow* wherein the comedian ate nine bananas and a joke in *Jackpot* wherein a fat comedian in a woods scene said that he would like to look like a slender birch and was apprised by another character that he looked like a big ash. The combined efforts of the distinguished trio, doubtless to the shocked surprise of the hopeful management, amounted only to still another of the returned soldier plays, this one a knock-kneed paraphrase of *Dear Ruth* and without the slightest infection of merit.

The triumph of the amalgamated imaginations of the trio consisted in converting the usual returned soldier into a WAC. Beyond that, their fancy seemed to be unable to reach farther than the customary triangle involving the girl, the civilian who hopes to marry her, and the soldier who appears in due course from overseas and ends up with her. The other characters were the habitual fluttery mother given to tasty cooking, the small brat of a brother who collects money from all and sundry, the lazy old cadging uncle, the country postman who knows what is on all the post-cards and in all the letters, the comic neighborhood fat boy (here named Henry Ford and given to a constant reiteration of "But no relation"), the giggling neighbor girls, and the stencil rest.

The humor included, among similar riches, the joke about ordering a dish from a French menu and learning that it was the name of the restaurant owner, and the line, upon being handed a present, "It's beautiful, but what is it?" And the sentiment achieved its highest development in the routine mush about Paris: "There's something about Paris — it's hard to say just what it is — that's unlike any other city in the world. But Paris isn't meant for one; it's meant for two. It does something to you, to them. It doesn't matter if there are no lights, no heat, no elevator service; there's something in the air that gets you. Ah, Paris, dear beautiful, beautiful Paris!"

The exhibit marked the twenty-seventh of the season inhabited by military uniforms.

THE OVERTONS. February 6, 1945

A comedy by Vincent Lawrence. Produced by Paul Czinner for a beyond the season forced run in, initially, the Booth Theatre.

PROGRAM

CORA OVERTON	*Arlene Francis*	TOMMY	*Donald Kohler*
JULIA	*Mary Lawrence*	MINOT	*Charles Lang*
JUDITH BANCROFT	*Glenda Farrell*	JAMES LAWSON	*Walter N. Greaza*
JACK OVERTON	*Jack Whiting*		

SYNOPSIS: The Overtons' home near New York. Act I. *Living-room. Late summer afternoon.* Act II. *Same. After dinner.* (*Curtain is lowered to denote the passing of half an hour.*) Act III. *Bedroom. A few minutes later.*

At his best, in such plays of two decades or so ago as *Sour Grapes, Among The Married, Spring Fever, A Distant Drum,* and *Two Married Men,* Vincent Lawrence indicated that no comedy writer for our theatre has had a shrewder understanding of the peculiar quirks in the amorous psyches of the male and female of the species. S. N. Behrman, who enjoys a much higher dramaturgical skill and a greater literary grace, was and is to be listed as his closest contender in this respect, but some distance nevertheless has separated them. Behrman every now and then has viewed his men and women through the peach-colored spectacles of a Pinero, but not so Lawrence. That is, to emphasize again, when he has been in top trim.

Pinero was secretly more or less in wayward love with many of his women characters, and hence near-sighted in his contemplation of them. Only in some such rare case as his *A Wife Without A Smile* did he approach one of them fairly platonically. Behrman is similarly, if not exactly in love with his leading female characters, at least somewhat infatuated with them. But Lawrence, while he undoubtedly likes his women, is far from wearing his heart on his playwriting sleeve and appraises them pretty coolly for what inside them they really are.

Having spent the greater part of his life since his meritorious beginnings in the Hollywood factories, a considerable portion of his earlier sagacity has deserted him. One needed only to observe his men and women in *Washington Heights,* which he wrote while out there and which was produced in New York during a very brief holiday trip East some fourteen years ago, to appreciate the bacilli that even so soon began to go to work on him. But though he is far from being the man he was before Hollywood took its toll of him, it is gratifying to learn that, for all his decline, at least some traces of his old seeing-eye still obstinately inhere in him. A look at *The Overtons* sufficiently proves it, though the play itself otherwise has all kinds of things wrong with it and though even what is not wrong with it was made to seem so by poor casting, bad acting, and Elisabeth Bergner's even worse stage direction. The result of these last named botcheries caused the less discerning to lose sight of the author's periodic virtues and outright to condemn the play in its entirety.

Lawrence has often in the past suffered from this critical confusion of misguided stage presentation with the script. And his plays themselves have here and there in part, it must be granted, helped to contribute to their condemnation as a whole. But it remains that, whatever their freely admitted deficiencies, they offer moments and intermittent scenes which for sharp penetration of the sexual and amorous natures of human fowl are uncommon to our native playwriting.

The Overtons, with its feeble first act, mild second and thoroughly ingenious third, though lacking in other respects is not lacking in such moments and scenes which dig hintfully into the esoteric psychology of its characters. Its failure at the hands of most of the reviewers and at the money-till is indeed as much due to these truthful moments and scenes as to its more general obvious weaknesses. For if there is one way to fail in our American theatre it is to deal with uncompromising honesty with men and women beset by the idiosyncrasies of sexual passion and the spidery business called love. The best and most truthful comedies on the subject, like Brieux's *The Incubus,* have invariably failed, as have the best of the somewhat more serious plays, like Porto-Riche's *L'Amoureuse.* (In the case of the two examples named, both have collapsed not only upon their original local productions but upon their revivals.) And in the still more serious approach to the subject, such eminent dramatists as Strindberg, Björnson, Wedekind, *et al.,* have never been acceptable to the public at large.

To achieve eulogy and money, a writer of sex comedy, which is the immediate topic, must make his characters believe not what they honestly by their very natures believe but rather what an audience would believe in their places. Lawrence does not thus condescend to an audience's prejudices, or at least he does not condescend sufficiently, and his reward, over the years, has been preordained failure.

As in most of his plays, *The Overtons* lays hold of a familiar plot scheme and seeks to make it fresh by viewing it through unconventional eyes. In this instance the story is simply the oft-told one of the loving married couple torn asunder by suspicion of faithlessness and eventually reunited. Worse for originality in any such direction, its basic fabric sometimes suggests a mosaic of episodes from a variety of recognizable plays, among them *Bought And Paid For, The Constant Wife,* and *Private Lives.* Yet in detail it frequently achieves the touches of freshness implicit in the author's before-noted close observation and assessment: the wholly innocent and negligible little remarks and acts on the part of a man that drive a woman, however much she loves him, to distraction; the peculiar remaining pull of a sex attraction of which a man thinks he has tired and is done with; the contentful physical weariness that overcomes a man when after too long preparation and too deferred triumph he has subjugated a woman's amatory reluctance; the shoe that remains stubbornly and embarrassingly irremovable at the aforesaid triumphant moment; etc., etc.

While it is true that even a dozen swallows do not make a summer or a dozen or more such little things a play, it seems a pity that criticism has not liberally taken sufficient cognizance of them and more greatly encouraged their author toward the fulfilment of his higher intentions, and has driven him back once again, downcast and discouraged, to Hollywood.

Miss Bergner's direction was predicated on the popular European theory that American audiences will fall asleep save a stage be directed in the tempo of an express train run amuck. The actors were accordingly instructed into so much footwork and so many bouncings up and down on couches and chairs, dashings up and down stairs and scampering exits that the exhibit resembled less a play on a February theatre stage than the Coney Island Subway station on the Fourth of July. As for the acting performances themselves, Miss Francis in the role of the wife offered a succession of imitations of Lynn Fontanne, Gertrude Lawrence and several other actresses, seemingly omitting only one of Cissie Loftus; Mr. Whiting as the husband conducted himself after the musical comedy formula with which he has had so long an experience; Mr. Greaza as the suspicious lover again, as in *The Visitor,* sniffingly prowled about the stage as if shadowed by the crate of puissant cheese; and the personable Miss Farrell for the greater part of the evening poutingly threw her effervescent corpus upon all the chairs, divans and window-seats in sight, on frequent occasion in such cunning wise that the splendors of her hinter contours would not be lost to the audience.

HOPE FOR THE BEST. February 7, 1945

A comedy by William McCleery. Produced by Jean Dalrymple and Marc Connelly for 117 forced performances in, initially, the Fulton Theatre.

PROGRAM

Howard Hilton	*Edmond Ryan*	Sgt. Joe Jordan	*Paul Potter*
Mrs. Bassett	*Doro Merande*	Lucille Daly	*Jane Wyatt*
Margaret Hicks Harwood	*Joan Wetmore*	Michael Jordan	*Franchot Tone*
Professor Wechsler	*Leo Bulgakov*		

SYNOPSIS: Act I. *A Saturday afternoon in spring.* Act II. *That evening.* Act III. *The next morning.*

All of the action of the play takes place in the living-room of Michael's house in Connecticut.

Minus anything resembling real wit, humor, or character drawing — or, for that matter, a sense of dramatic writing — the play gets nowhere, and quickly. The first curtain is not up long before one can ascertain not only its ending, but its finish. After all, if you hope to concoct an interesting play about a newspaper columnist with great potential gifts as a sociological and political expert you can not very safely present him as a cross between the Harold Lloyd of the early movie slapstick comedies and an oaf who hopes to accomplish anything with a pair of women constantly hanging over his typewriter and alternately kissing him on the ear and cheek. And you can hardly persuade an audience to accept the character as worth a second important thought by directing the actor playing him, as Marc Connelly did, to comport himself like Baby Snooks, even though he wear tweeds and smoke a pipe.

Mr. McCleery's further attempt to fascinate his auditors with the doctrine of liberalism is couched in such debutante terms, involving gadgets such as blocks of wood that tumble cardwise into a heap by way of illustrating the necessity of the common man's share in world economy and a globe of the world augurously containing a lot of smaller globes representing countries, states and communities, that one anticipates Ed Wynn to come on and preside over the stage. The net effect of Mr. McCleery's hero's endeavors in the direction of liberalism, accordingly, is any half-way intelligent auditor's immediate complete sympathy with his hypothetically odious character who offers herself as a snobbish reactionary.

The general writing is no less unfortunate. A scene, for example, in which the young heroine stands close to the footlight trough, faces the audience, and for what seems at least twenty minutes indulges in an excited monologue, with gestures, about her father's remarkable baseball pitching achievements, suggests nothing so much as one of the hereinbefore noted old scenes in which the heroine, similarly adjusting herself to the footlights, used ebulliently to describe an imaginary horse race, to the copious throwing of peanuts at the poor girl from the gallery. Nor is that the worst. The fatuous columnist hero, whenever he loses confidence in himself, which properly and finally should have been before ever the first curtain rose, pulls out a map of his home state, Indiana, and visualizes upon it the smiling face of his deceased mother. His conversation, when he is not righteously concerned with correcting the grammatical errors of other persons present or spouting his patent medicine cure-alls for the world's ills, consists in perfectly solemn allusions to the muses that guide his literary efforts. The heroine in love with this mastermind tenderly expresses her philosophy respecting him thus: "I always like to see anything done superhumanly well by a modest little guy, so long as he is very human in all other ways." The general attempts at humor reach their pinnacle in the hero's observation that he once knew a fellow who always wanted to meet a girl who already had a fur coat and had her appendix out. And he eventually sums up his momentous recipe for the betterment of the world in the declaration that every citizen should bear the responsibility for it and should go about his community ringing the doorbells of others to see to it that they are not remiss in sharing that responsibility.

Mr. Connelly's stage direction periodically had Franchot Tone in the role of the columnist perform much like Stan Laurel, of the Laurel and Hardy team; caused the attractive and normally impressive Jane Wyatt to embarrass herself out of any ease of movement; allowed Leo Bulgakov in the role of the inventor of the columnist's gadgets so to mutter his lines that the audience could not make anything of them; and permitted Joan Wetmore in the part of the American reactionary to constitute herself a poker stirring up the cold embers of such a Manhattan-British accent as he apparently believed indicated a very high-toned social station.

ONE–MAN SHOW. February 8, 1945

A play by Ruth Goodman and Augustus Goetz. Produced by Jed Harris for 36 performances in the Ethel Barrymore Theatre.

Program

Lucian Gardner	*Frank Conroy*
A Woman	*Elizabeth Brew*
Tom	*Mitchell Harris*
James Dockerel	*Hugh Franklin*
Racine Gardner	*Constance Cummings*
Emory Jelliffe	*James Rennie*
Blanche	*Kasia Orzazewski*
Francis Kearny	*John Archer*

SYNOPSIS: Act I. *Late afternoon.* Act II. *After dinner. A week later.* Act III. *The next morning.*

Scene is the Gardner Gallery, New York City.

Time. *Spring.*

The play is basically a variant of the silver chord theme with a father in the place of the mother. It treats of what the Freudians describe as a father-daughter fixation, which impels the girl to offer her favors, whether merely flirtatious or more anatomical, to potential buyers of the former's art gallery wares that she may gratify his every wish, and which eventually impels the father in turn to something that seems very closely to approach incest. In their attempt at subtlety in this sexual direction the novice authors have fallen into such studied confusion that some of the earlier portions of their play lose meaning and suggest that it might have been to their dramaturgical advantage had they tutored themselves in such modern playwrights with a similar exotic theme as, for example, Lenormand. In the same way, it would have been better for them had they not so obviously tutored themselves in the problem plays of the Pinero school of the 1890's. It is difficult in this connection not to think at times of Sir Arthur's Iris, Maldonado and Trenwith in the cases of their paraphrases respectively named Racine, Jelliffe, and Kearny.

Several scenes are intelligently handled and nicely phrased, but the others more frequently are invalidated in the mind of the audience by a heavy calculation, taking among other things such transparent dramatic forms as allowing the characters not only to anticipate one another's thoughts but to predetermine what they are about to say, This is often supposed by beginning playwrights to contribute valuably to dramatic economy and quickly to further the action. What it just as often does is to provide any experienced audience contemplating the pseudo-clairvoyant characters with the feeling that it could have foretold the thoughts and speech of the lot of them at least twenty-five years before.

The authors, furthermore, are given to miscellaneous stage pauses, in this instance considerably extended by Jed Harris' direction, which are designed to give the impression that the actors are deep in perplexed thought. This in turn provides the audience with a thought of its own, albeit not so deep and perplexed. To wit, that the pauses are arbitrary on the authors' part and are inserted at such intervals as the latter are baffled in the writing of materials relevant to the actors' immediate articulative purposes. These pauses, even in the instance of much more able playwrights, often lead to disaster, since it is notorious that most actors, even against the polite persuasions of their directors, or perhaps with the latter's despairful concurrence, are disposed under the circumstances to privilege themselves a Roman holiday of such anatomical *tours de force* and such face-makings as would frighten the virtuosity of even an Oscar-endorsed motion picture performer.

Some of the authors' humor is sufficiently cultivated, but more is of an impaired nature that imposes upon the dialogue such byplay as an ironic observation, following a high price set upon a painting, that the artist must be dead; the request by a man with a substantial highball in his hand that his host add more whiskey to it "to lighten it"; the admiration of a painting that happens to have been hung upside down; the query, following a man's rapt description of the women in South America, if there are not any males among the inhabitants; and a paraphrase of the idea that the surest way to guarantee rain is to carry an umbrella.

In the way of character drawing, the authors are most successful in the instance of the father. The daughter, energetically fashioned as a sympathetic character, emerges, for all their efforts to suggest her otherwise, as half nincompoop, half — in the vulgar expression — pushover, and with a one-finger equipment assiduously addressing itself to the emotional keyboard. The rich, elderly lawyer who hopes to persuade her to be his mistress through favors to her father is directly out of the popular drama of fifty years ago, confected in England by the Pinero-Jones school and later on in America by the Broadhurst-Walter group. The young artist who wishes to marry the daughter is the stereotyped young stage artist down to the rumpled trousers and worn tan raincoat. And the young hero who finally wins her from her father's sinister wing is essentially the familiar "clean" young fellow from the wide, open spaces.

The acting in the cases of Frank Conroy, as the father, and John Archer, as the open-spacer, was satisfactory, but in the cases of several of the others, notably Miss Cummings, far from that. While moderately convincing in her lighter moments, save for the omnipresent belief that amiability is most effectively to be expressed by a firmly tethered smile, the latter's performance in the serious passages much too regularly suggested that she had rehearsed her role with a stock company Scarpia.

Mr. Harris' direction varied from the first-rate in certain details (his handling of the adjoining room dinner table with the identity of the guest hidden by an only partly opened door was excellent theatre) to the overly pretentious in the matter of the stage in general. He seemed to have subscribed to the Herman Shumlin directorial theory that a slow and ponderous tempo heightens the air of a play's importance. What it more commonly does is rather to show up the play's tenuousness. His insistence upon actors seated down stage and facing the audience contributed further to artificiality. And his conversion of the daughter role into a duet played by Julia Sanderson and Lady Macbeth, presuming that he and not the actress in it was responsible, was, in view of his past sagacity, an eyebrow lever.

THE STRANGER. February 12, 1945

A melodrama by Leslie Reade. Produced by Shepard Traube for 16 performances in the Playhouse.

PROGRAM

Napoleon Mickalieff	*Engene Sigaloff*	Mrs. Gregory	*Eva Leonard-Boyne*
Jean Prunier	*Alfred Hesse*	Maggie MacAndrews	*Wendy Atkin*
Bill Humphreys	*Kim Spalding*	David Mendelsohn	*Eduard Franz*
Police Constable Hood	*Stanley Bell*	A Gentleman	*Morton L. Stevens*
Christina Thomson	*Perry Wilson*		
Liz	*Stella Todd*		

SYNOPSIS: Act I. *An autumn night.* Act II. *Night, about a week later.* Act III. Scene 1. *Saturday night, the following week.* Scene 2. *Next morning.*

The entire action takes place in the meeting room of the International Workmen's Educational Club in London. The time is 1888.

This is an even poorer excursion into the familiar Jack-the-Ripper theme than *Hand In Glove* (*q.v.*). Not content with writing a simple and possibly effective melodrama, the author has followed the later day grim determination of playwrights to lend their exhibits an air of greater importance than any really buoyant melodrama should properly possess. One does not demand that melodrama necessarily include a lot of gunfire, or pugilism on high cliffs, or the East River docks at midnight, or even a saw-mill or horse race. But one has the right to ask that it concern itself principally with affording one a few spinal vibrations, and they are hardly forthcoming when, as in this case, the playwright takes the attention from what should be the business in hand with belated William Archer quotations of Bernard Shaw, disquisitions on slum conditions, and justifications of economic revolutions, along with some fancy psychology, sociological philosophy, and other such matters more relevant to an entirely different species of drama.

Mr. Reade, an Englishman, according to the program holds a degree from Oxford and, thus probably considering simple, unaffected melodrama beneath his intellectual status, has sought further to minimize his peccadillo by hanging a picture of Karl Marx on its wall, merchanting psychopathic apologies for his villain, and indulging in such facetiæ about his fellow Britons, Russian opera singers, and French morals as even George Kaufman would hesitate to incorporate into *The Late George Apley*. He additionally considers himself so superior to his audience, and the latter such an utter simpleton, that he believes it sequently will possibly believe that a character whom he has laboriously built up as a sympathetic figure may, for all the evidence he piles up against him, turn out to be guilty of the crime with which the play concerns itself. He condescends yet more greatly to the audience by making this figure a persecuted Jew, and if there is another playwright who doesn't know that a present-day audience in turn knows that no Jew shown on the stage is ever finally disclosed to be other than an admirable character, and not even a tenth cousin to Jack-the-Ripper, he has not been heard from in some time. Mr. Reade, for all his Oxford training, doubtless in this connection had his eye on the popular box-office quite as hopefully as such past American night-school alumni as Harry James Smith, Aaron Hoffman, Anne Nichols, *et al.*

Even aside from these considerations, Mr. Reade fails to reveal himself as a competent hand at melodrama. His dialogue descends to the outworn "Why should I be telling you all this?" business; his idea of shock reposes in such innocent old Guignolisms as the murderer's impudent challenge to the police that he will cut off the ears of his next victim and send them along as a present and as a police officer's shout to an assistant off stage, upon peering out of the window at the body of a slashed victim, "Mind you 'er 'ead don't drop off!"; and his chief reliance upon suspense is vested in an old crone fortune-teller who shrinks from the suspected party as one possessed of the evil eye and as a criminal of most sinister hue, thus fooling the audience as to his guilt not in the slightest.

The Jack-the-Ripper theme, in short, has by now been done to death by inept playwrights. Some years ago Mrs. Belloc-Lowndes contrived still to entertain audiences with Jack's idiosyncrasies in *The Lodger,* but since then his carving virtuosity has become steadily less fascinating in the hands of less imaginative writers, and the theatre seems to be willing to relegate him permanently to the left-wing Hall of Fame.

Boris Aronson's fearsome set was sorely disappointed by what was played inside it.

In short, the fifty-eighth failure out of sixty-five attempts.

SIGNATURE! February 14, 1945

A melodrama by Elizabeth McFadden, based on a short story, Naboth's Vineyard, *by Melville Davisson Post. Produced by Richard Skinner and Dorothy Willard for 2 performances in the Forrest Theatre.*

PROGRAM

Judge Simon Kilrail	*Frederic Tozere*
Zeke	*Morris McKenney*
Charles Borse	*Lawrence Fletcher*
Thadeus Braxton	*Charles Francis*
John Cartwright	*Donald Murphy*
Randolph	*Lyster Chambers*
Abner Davisson	*Judson Laire*
Nora Davisson	*Marjorie Lord*
Lance Moor	*Charles Keane*
1st Guard	*William Forester*
William Taylor	*Bob Stevenson*
Fendler	*Charles S. Dubin*
Alice Steuart	*Anne Jackson*
2nd Guard	*Lew Herbert*
Nathaniel Madison	*George Lessey*
Aunt Sophie Gide	*Nell Harrison*
Dr. Martin Storm	*John McKee*
Hon. Thomas Fargon	*Gregory Robins*
Diccon	*Page Spencer*
Morrey	*Bruce Halsey*
Rev. Rockford	*Peter Pann*
Henry	*Coby Neal*
Arnold	*Harry Kadison*
Dayton	*Charles Kuhn*
Rev. Adam Rider	*Cyrus Staehle*
Alkiri	*Frederic Faber*
Donovan	*Edwin Cushman*
Elnathan Stone	*Glenn Regent*
Ward	*William McMillen*

SYNOPSIS: Act I. *An evening in August, about 10.00 p.m.* Act II. *Sunset, one week later.* Act III. *Morning, two weeks later. The opening day at September term of the Circuit Court.*

The play takes place in a conference room in the courthouse of a hill town of Virginia, about 1856.

Melodrama which discloses the identity of the criminal very early in the proceedings and concerns itself thereafter with fastening the guilt upon him calls for a much shrewder artificer than Miss McFadden. Ingenious invention and action seem to evade her talents and, as if appreciating her weakness in sustaining an air of ominous suspense, she takes refuge in such a repertoire of off-stage sounds, designed to heighten the atmosphere of evil, as would suffice a year's supply of Hollywood horror films. Baying hounds, death-buzzing katydids, stealthy feet, branches that beat against the walls of the house, rising mob noises, howling winds, glass panes smashed by the storm, clanking door chains, and a load of other such villainous *hors d'œuvres* are thus hopefully relied upon to play an obbligato to a mystery that is approximately as mysterious as *Mother Carey's Chickens* and to a thriller that does not thrill. Under the circumstances, it would probably have been more fortunate all around had Miss McFadden permitted her audience to absorb her play from backstage.

Melville Davisson Post, whose story serves as the foundation of the melodrama, in his day concocted some curiously piquant tales, notably in the volumes called *The Strange Schemes Of Randolph Mason* and *The Man Of Last Resort,* both of which deal with the possibility of committing various crimes in the different states of the Union safe, under the peculiar laws of the states, from conviction. The story which Miss McFadden has made use of is of another sort, to wit, the guilty judge who finds himself presiding over the trial of the accused, and in one paraphrase or another has for many years been familiar. To fashion a holding melodrama from it in this later day would not be easy, since even were the preliminaries made interesting, which in this case they are not, the last and what should be the punching act must necessarily resolve itself, aside from the jurist's conventional climactic gasps and totters, into more or less actionless talk, and since the dénouement is theatrically predetermined. Like other contemporary writers of melodrama, Miss McFadden has hoped to infuse her play, and particularly this final act, with some vitality by lugging in what passes for sociological thought, but all her declamations on "the latent power of the crowd for constructive good," "the indomitable will of the people for justice," and "the ordinary democratic citizen's responsibility for the acts of his public servants" succeed in doing nothing other than to emphasize her desperation in the face of sagging drama.

While, generally, the presumably frightening noises are

going on off-stage, the stage itself is occupied by so many outworn devices of melodrama — secret drawers, self-opening creaky doors, the missing papers, etc. — that the noises refractorily lend them an air of travesty, much as might the portentous drum beats of *The Emperor Jones* were Jones to be acted by Hamtree Harrington. And albeit the noises were for the most part well-handled, those supposed specifically to represent the whining of the trees in the night wind sounded so much like something by Rudolf Friml that, when they intermittently went into operation, the audience was to be pardoned for thinking that the judge might at any moment burst into song.

Roy Hargrave's direction was otherwise better than the materials deserved; the acting company was fair enough; and Stewart Chaney's set, ably lighted by Hargrave, here once again offered all the foreboding that the play neglected to realize.

The fifty-ninth failure in sixty-six tries.

AND BE MY LOVE. February 21, 1945

A comedy by Edward Caulfield. Produced by Arthur J. Beckhard in association with Victor Hugo-Vidal for 14 performances in the National Theatre.

Program

Sarah Fenton	*Lotus Robb*	Allen	*Charles Colby*
Henry	*Walter Hampden*	Mr. Fillmore	*Jed Prouty*
Martha Webster	*Esther Dale*	Ada Bennett	*Violet Heming*
Mrs. Spence	*Edmonia Nolley*	Lizzie	*Viola Dean*
Mr. Spence	*Sydney Grant*	No. 2527	*Graham Velsey*
Phyllis	*Ruth Homond*		

SYNOPSIS: Act I. *A late morning in August.* Act II. *Morning. One week later.* Act III. *Afternoon. Five days later.*

The action takes place in the sitting-room of Sarah Fenton's house in Riverhead.

The play was a product of one of the summer theatres and like so many other exhibits in the summer theatres doubtless required the remission of judgment induced by several hundred assiduous mosquitoes and ten or twelve Coca-Colas for its enjoyment, if any. In wintertime New York it required a suspension of judgment induced by enough Old-fashioneds to make one think one was seeing *Harvey* to generate any favorable reaction to it.

Treating of an elderly actor posing as a naturalist and of his amorous adventures with a middle-aged widow whom he has encountered in a matrimonial bureau, the comedy in essence is a distant cousin to such as E. S. Willard and Sol Smith Russell used to appear in. Those similarly involved an elderly fellow, sometimes a professor given to the study of butterflies, sometimes a crusty but lovable widower whose beautiful young ward had come to live with him (and in both cases absent-minded), who didn't realize that the heroine loved him until it was time for the oldsters in the audience to go back home again and fight with their wives. But, though the plays were very innocent and frequently even childish, they were now and again written with some skill and humor and feeling, and they provided pleasant entertainment in their equally innocent and even childish theatrical day.

Mr. Caulfield is undoubtedly a worthy man in other respects, but he has none of the qualities that went to make such comedies acceptable. Aside from one or two fair gags, his specimen travels a corduroy dialogue road and its characters are for the most part descendants of deceased theatrical characters rather than persons freshly out of life. His work, in short, gives the impression not of a comedy that had to be written out of its author's undeniable, eager, and honest impulse but merely out of its author's arbitrary determination to write a play, come hell or high water.

Too many writers these days seem to fashion plays for that and no other reason. They are apparently impelled to dramatic composition not through anything they have experienced which has made a deep impression upon them, not through anything they have observed which has affected them, but simply because the urge to try their hands at playwriting is irresistible. This accounts not only for the surplusage of dramatized stories and novels which absolve the writers from any such personal experience or personal observation, but also for the poverty of the plays which they write independently. Even artificial comedy calls for experience and observation, as the plays of Sheridan, Wilde and Co. fully attest. And certainly comedy that purports to be realistic calls for the qualities at the top of its voice.

Mr. Caulfield further complicates his difficulties in having laid hold of a love story whose solution at the altar was, under its own theatrical terms, both automatic and entirely obvious. His efforts to defer that solution, which in other hands might have been made perfectly acceptable through witty treatment, take rather the stereotyped and dull form of mechanical outside interference on the part of equally stereotyped puppets, the net effect being of a heavy freight train bound for nearby Trenton, New Jersey, which finds itself far in advance of its running schedule and, by way of killing time, stops at Newark, Passaic, Rahway, Paterson, Elizabeth, New Brunswick and Princeton Junction to take aboard an assortment of payless wayfarers.

It is, in short, nothing much against the play that, as the usual complaint goes, one can see its ending from the start. What is against it is that, as intimated, the author does nothing in the way of interrupting the vision with compensatory humors, lively reflections, amusing character traits, or any other such alleviating *pourboires.* While the train of his plot is slowly puffing and pulling its way toward its matrimonial destination, he fails to lift the window curtains, or to sell magazines, or to peddle milk chocolate and ice-cream cones, or to have the porter wipe off one's shoes at intervals, or to do much of anything else to break the monotony.

A play whose ending is clearly in sight shortly after its beginning may, contrary to popular opinion, often be a wholly satisfactory play, provided its author be a sufficiently gifted fellow. In the case of mystery plays, things are different; but in the matter of other species of drama it is less the destination that counts than the nature of the journey. It is as easy to foretell the ending of Maugham's excellent comedy, *The Circle,* as it is to foretell that of this hopeless one of Caulfield's. It is Maugham's nimble mind and uncommon skill that spell the difference.

All kinds of good comedies, while lacking in surprise in connection with their conclusions, make up for the lack in surprises of one sort or another *en route:* shrewd turns of phrase, odd facets of character, apt transitory business, etc. It would be a blind man who could not foresee the endings of a long line of such comedies as Bahr, Capus, Caillavet, Flers, and even the great Shaw himself have periodically written. But it would be a deaf one indeed who did not appreciate the verbal picnic provided by the authors in the intermediate distance.

Even a comedy whose final resolution is readily discernible and whose dialogue leading up to it is not remarkable for any inspiriting wit or humor may occasionally manage to get by on the score of its acting or by virtue of favorite personalities in its cast. A number of comedies, feeble in themselves, have thus been successful with audiences in France when a Guitry or Boucher has appeared in them, in England when a Hawtrey or Du Maurier or Hicks has purveyed them, and in this country when a Drew or Ditrichstein or Lunt has invested them with his presence. Marie Tempest, Mrs. Fiske, Ethel Barrymore, Ina Claire and other actresses have similarly at times lent profitable bounce to essentially bounceless comedies. But a tepid comedy minus such acting or such personal vitamins has an almost impossible row to hoe, and *And Be My Love* found itself in that furrow.

Mr. Hampden is a respected member of the theatrical community, but not only is he hardly in the popular category of pin-up actors; he is hardly one whose forte is comedy. There is by nature an unbending quality in him which, when he essays comedy, gives his stoop to conquer the aspect of Richelieu recovering the dropped handkerchief of Elwood P. Dowd's sister. The ease and lightness and brio vital to the acting of comedy are simply not in him, and what results from his performance is an audience's feeling that the Servant In The House has in a seizure of amnesia wandered into the wrong household. Miss Robb, likewise, does not enjoy the comedy gift, and between the two of them Mr. Caulfield's already crippled play missed the crutches that might conceivably, remotely conceivably, have kept it from falling on its face.

CALICO WEDDING. March 7, 1945

A comedy by Sheridan Gibney. Produced by Lester Meyer and Richard Myers for 5 performances in the National Theatre.

PROGRAM

CAPT. GEORGE GAYLORD *William Post*	BETTY MARLOWE *Patricia White*
LIEUT. JENSEN *Roderick Winchell*	PEG HALL *Barbara Joyce*
NORA *Eva Condon*	ALMA BIDDLE *Joy Geffen*
MARY GAYLORD *Grete Mosheim*	HENDRIK VAN DELDEN *Jerome P. Thor*
HERBERT ABERCROMBIE *Forrest Orr*	"CAP" WILSON *Henry Richards*
MRS. ABERCROMBIE *Mary Sargent*	LOTUS WILDER *Jane Hoffman*
FREDERICK BOYNTON *Louis Jean Heydt*	ALAN PACKARD *Vincent Gardner*
	BOB WILLARD *John Kane*

SYNOPSIS: Act I. Scene 1. *A radio listening post. Alaska. Spring, 1944.* Scene 2. *Bedroom of the Gaylords' apartment, New York City, spring, 1937.* Scene 3. *The living-room. The following morning.* Act II. *The living-room. Late that evening.* Act III. *The living-room. The next morning.*

THE PLAY WAS first produced by one of the summer theatre stock companies ten years ago. In an effort to bring it up to date, the author has incorporated a prologue laid in an Army listening post in Alaska, which haplessly has nothing to do with it. But, even if it had a great deal to do with it, it would hardly suffice to bring up to date any play dealing with such antiquated materials as the wife who thinks her husband is neglecting her for his business and who sets out to make him jealous by way of bringing him to book. Add to this basic plot such venerable adornments as the bedroom scene with the husband going to sleep at the wife's most ardent moment, the subsequent scene in which the dejected wife becomes deliriously inebriated upon downing two ounces of alcohol, the scene in which she then makes love to a bashful young man who has become effulgently intoxicated immediately upon imbibing one ounce, and several other such dramatic souvenirs, and any attempt to lend an air of contemporaneity to the proceedings would have to include no mere Alaska listening post but at least a scene showing the Army invading Tokyo, a *Frankie And Johnny* ballet, and maybe several speeches by Joe Ball, with a big Elsa Maxwell party afterward in the Tavern-On-The-Green.

Under the impression that he had given the necessary fresh life to the comatose materials by allowing the husband to remain uncertain as to just how far his wife had gone with the young man, the Hollywood author apparently had not been informed that, far from being fresh, that idea had served Henry Arthur Jones all of fifty-one years ago in *The Case Of Rebellious Susan.* Under the further impression that he would be esteemed as a man of witty parts, he indulged himself in such humors as the discomfort of a husband's arm slept on by a wife, which apparently nobody had cautioned him was long familiar to readers of Shaw's preface to *Back To Methuselah,* published all of twenty-four years ago. And under the final impression that the idea of a woman so bewildered that she could not know for certain whether she had indulged the night before in sexual intercourse was both novel and extremely piquant (if not idiotic), he apparently missed the advice that the notion had served the play called *The Conquerors* all of a half century ago.

The theory, still indulged in by many playwrights like Mr. Gibney, that jealousy serves invariably as an effective catalyzer is the mark of their immaturity. Jealousy just as often turns eventually into irritation toward the person who originates it, and induces a feeling much more closely identified with profound boredom than with amatory stimulation.

In the role of the wife, the Berlin refugee, Grete Mosheim, described in the program by the Celtic Richard Maney as having been one of the more popular players in "the famous Deutsch Theatre," acted for the entire evening in the manner of an Elisabeth Bergner giving an imitation of Billie Burke before the age of puberty.

SIMON'S WIFE. MARCH 7, 1945

A Lenten play by Francis D. Alwaise. Produced by the Blackfriars' Guild for 15 performances in the Blackfriars' Guild Theatre.

PROGRAM

LEAH	*Ruth Fischer*	JUDAS	*Joseph Boley*
RACHEL	*Helen Purcell*	BENJAMIN	*David Knight*
JOSEPH	*James Kearny*	A BEGGAR	*Robert Hawkins*
SIMON	*W. Hussung*	A PHYSICIAN	*Joseph F. Fox*
ANDREW	*Wilson Brooks*	JOHN	*Frank P. Soden*
MARTHA	*Fran Lee*		

SYNOPSIS: *The action takes place in Palestine in* A.D. 28–30. Act I. Scene 1. *Simon's house at Capharnaum in Galilee – late afternoon.* Scene 2. *The same – some weeks later.* Act II. *The same – one week later.* Act III. *A rented lodging in Jerusalem – afternoon of the first Good Friday.*

THE STORY of the play is of the forsaking of his wife Leah by Simon called Peter that he may join the Nazarene as leader of the Apostles, of Leah's bitterness and doubts even in the face of the Nazarene's miraculous cure of her mother, of Simon's loss of loyalty at Gethsemane, of Leah's gradual acquisition of belief, and, finally, of her restoration of faith to Simon and his going forth into the world to preach the Gospel. The author, a Dominican priest, is a beginner in playwriting and his effort fully betrays the fact. Instead of dramatizing his story, he merely talks it, and the whole takes on the color of a not particularly interesting lecture, without even changing stereopticon slides to lend it a bit of movement.

A Blackfriars' program note observed, "In the Lenten season, the organization is interested in providing dramatic fare for those who generally put aside their theatregoing, and in trying out a script for parochial groups who are looking for a new vehicle." The phrase "dramatic fare" was ill-chosen.

GARDEN OF TIME. March 7, 1945

A play by Owen Dodson. Produced by the American Negro Theatre for 30 performances in the West 135th Street Library Theatre.

Program

Medea / Miranda	*Sadie Brown*	Jason / John	*Dean Newman*
First Woman	*Joan Smith*	Beles / Blues Boy	*William Greaves*
Second Woman	*Edith Whitman*	Aeson	*Lawrence Pepper*
Third Woman	*Doris Black*	Mama Leua	*Elsie Benjamin*
Aetes	*Austin Briggs-Hall*	Little Randy	*Melba Hawkins*
Absyrtus (Medea's Brother)	*Gordon Heath*		

The action is laid in ancient Greece and in a Georgia, U. S. A., cemetery at the turn of the nineteenth century.

The author, quondam head of the drama department at Hampton Institute, has here undertaken something. "I believe," he stated in the public prints, "that the modern drama is too stingy. We don't use it for all it's worth. *Garden Of Time* is told in terms of the fable of the Golden Fleece instead of hard, realistic terms. It uses music and song and dance and poetry. It begins in ancient times in Colchis off the coast of Asia Minor and ends in a graveyard in Georgia, U. S. A., at the end of the nineteenth century. It's the story of one country, Greece, the ruling country of the world, going to a smaller country, Colchis, whose people are a dark people and trying to take its emblems. Jason, the Greek, captures the Golden Fleece, aided by Medea, priestess of Colchis, who has fallen in love with him. They flee to Greece, killing Medea's brother in their flight. Two children are born to them, but eventually Jason deserts Medea. 'You're dark,' he tells her, 'I can't stand you.' Actually he is spurred on by the chance of marriage with Creusa and its promise of new wealth and possessions."

Here, continued the author, "the play switches to the end

of the last century, with Georgia substituted for Greece and Haiti for Colchis, and with the main characters going on and the Greek idea of vengeance and atonement being realized through Mama Leua, a Haitian voodooist, who is like the ancient goddess Hecate." Then, elaborating, "Jason and Medea could have gotten along together, but these passions that move them — ambition, lust, greed — destroy them. They realize what has been wrong when the play comes to its end but it's too late to turn back. The play foreshadows an end of all this, however, as the nineteenth century Medea says:

'The rats been eating at the
  seeds of time,
Eaten full the gullet
But the end's coming.' "

Since Mr. Dodson's previous demonstrations of dramatic composition consisted chiefly in an unproduced play written while at college and in one or two shows executed for amateur performances while he was in the Navy, it is not to be wondered that his ambitious plan, which would come near to frightening even a dramatist like O'Neill, who seems rarely to be frightened by anything, has been too much for him. Like various other tyros, he has attempted to enlarge the scope of the "too stingy" drama without first mastering the stingy scope of such dramatists as, say, Ibsen, Strindberg, *et al.* His process of enlargement resolves itself mainly into fancy rhetorical flights which adorn his story like so many artificial beads; in the kind of experiment, however well-intentioned, which operates upon that story to its serio-comic undoing, like a small boy's improvement upon the telephone by attaching the dinner table bell to it; and in a garrulity which, while it undeniably enlarges the script, reduces to a minimum what active drama his theme may intrinsically possess. He might have profited by taking a cue from Charles Sebree's classical stage settings and by writing his play in equally simple terms.

The performance of a mixed company of Negroes and whites was as confused as the materials, only louder.

IT'S A GIFT. March 12, 1945

A comedy by Curt Goetz and Dorian Otvos. Produced by the Goval Corporation for 47 cut-rate performances in, initially, the Playhouse.

PROGRAM

PROF. THEODORE W. HERRMANN	*Curt Goetz*
MATILDA HERRMANN	*Valerie Van Martens*
ATLANTA, 17	*Julie Harris*
THOMAS, 15	*Robert Muscat*
PETER, 14	*David Green*
LEWIS, 13	*Roland Green*
URSULA, 12	*Sally Ferguson*
OTTO, 11	*William Kinney*
EVELYN, 10	*Yvonne Pothen*
DAN, 9	*Victor Vraz*
SOPHIE, 8	*Winnie Mae Martin*
ELSIE, 7	*Joan Gordon*
SANDY, 6	*Kevin Mathews*
FINNIE, 4	*Evelyn Daly*
EMILY	*Hilda Laufkoetter*
REV. ENDICOTT	*Whitford Kane*
HERBERT KRAFT	*Michael Strong*
MAYOR DOUBLEDAY	*G. Swayne Gordon*
BELINDA	*Marjorie Peterson*
MADAME DE LA JARDINERRE	*Suzanne Caubaye*
ROSITA	*Elaine Carter*
CHIQUITA	*Hope Miller*
LUPE	*Doris Brent*
DOLORES	*Elsa Johnson*
MR. FLYNN	*Morton DaCosta*

SYNOPSIS: Act I. *The home of Professor Herrmann in Hazelton, Pennsylvania.* Act II. Scene 1. *A house in Montevideo, Uruguay. Six weeks later.* Scene 2. *A few hours later.* Act III. *Professor Herrmann's home. One morning several weeks later.*

Time. *1911.*

THERE IS no good reason why it should be so, but let a play come along these days that includes in its cast of characters a State trooper, a Pablo, a Chiquita, or more than one child under twelve years of age and the odds are that it will not be too easy to bear. While *It's A Gift* does not contain either a State trooper or a Pablo, it offers a Chiquita and not merely one child under twelve years of age but all of seven. It also exposes children of fifteen, fourteen, thirteen and twelve, which increases the odds considerably.

For one play like *The Innocent Voyage* which manages to be entertaining despite a liberal supply of youngsters, one may usually count on at least five that will operate toward depression. The explanation is simple. Children are latterly most often the device of second-rate playwrights who resort to them for ready-made sentimental audience reaction or who employ them physically for a humor which is otherwise beyond their capabilities. The result is usually a stage that seems to substitute them, in much the same way and to the same end, for the small dogs which box-office playwrights were once wont to fall back upon.

The story of the item under immediate discussion is of a morally rigid professor, the head of a copious family, whose sister, exorcised long years before for a sexual indiscretion, upon her death tit for tat wills him and his eldest daughter a great sum of money provided he or she gives issue to an illegitimate child. To further the plot, the authors have resorted to such theatre-album materials as the girls' school mistaken for a bordello, the young daughter mistakenly thought to be with child, the discovery by the parents that their marriage was not legal, etc. While several situations, for all the familiarity of the ingredients, are amusing and while some of the lines are comical, the dialogue too often is reduced to such things as speculating on the early bird that catches the worm ("If the worm didn't get up so early," etc.) and to such jocosities on a woman who has given birth to an impromptu baby as the retort, in answer to the extenuation that she committed only a little mistake, "What did you expect — twins?"

What properly should have been farce is treated as straight comedy, to its additional detriment. Mr. Goetz, one of the authors, known to the pre-war Central European stage, and his wife, Valerie Van Martens, also known to that stage, had the roles of the philoprogenitive father and mother and acquitted themselves, under the circumstances, with a measure of credit.

FOOLISH NOTION. March 13, 1945

A play by Philip Barry. Produced by the Theatre Guild for 103 performances in the Martin Beck Theatre.

PROGRAM

SOPHIE WING	*Tallulah Bankhead*	ELSIE	*Maria Manton*
HAPPY HAPGOOD	*Joan H. Shepard*	JIM HAPGOOD	*Henry Hull*
FLORENCE DENNY	*Barbara Kent*	FLORA	*Maria Manton*
GORDON ROARK	*Donald Cook*	FLORA	*Barbara Kent*
ROSE	*Mildred Dunnock*	FLORA	*Mildred Dunnock*
HORATIO WING	*Aubrey Mather*		

SYNOPSIS: The action of the play takes place in the course of a single evening, in the library on the second floor of Jim Hapgood's house in New York. The time is early November, 1944. Act I. *Quarter to nine, according to fact.* Act II. Scene 1. *Later, as imagined by Gordon.* Scene 2. *As imagined by Horatio.* Scene 3. *As imagined by Happy.* Act III. Scene 1. *Later, as imagined by Sophie.* Scene 2. *Later, according to fact.*

IT SHOULD BE the right of playwrights and producers to demand of the Actors' Equity Association that its contracts include a clause forbidding actors to give out interviews on the plays in which they are engaged to appear, and in particular before the plays open. An example of the injury such interviews can do was to be had in the case of Tallulah Bankhead, the star of the play here considered. Miss Bankhead spread herself in the public prints in advance of its New York première and ventilated herself in such wise that any person who read what she had to say subsequently approached the play with highly prejudiced misgivings.

"A Barry play is a joy to act because he writes so well," effervesced Miss Bankhead. "He has such humor and insight. Ideas, too. Why, this play is full of them! There's the idea that if you imagine a thing hard enough — a fear or a wish — you get it out of your system. You're free of it. Then there are those lines in the script about not knowing people, even though they're close to us. 'I'm beginning to believe that no one has more than a glimmer about any one from one minute to the next . . . what they're thinking, what they're hiding . . . what actually goes on in them at all.' Do you see what I mean about the lines being beautifully written?"

The answer was No.

The answer further was No about those great ideas. I for one, for instance, may, my dear Miss Bankhead, imagine as hard as I can the wish that actresses would refrain from such senseless interviews, but the wish still somehow refuses to get out of my system and I am still not free of it. I can also imagine a whole lot of other things so hard that I exhaust myself, but nevertheless my wishes and even my fears stubbornly persist. What is more, that great idea about people not having more than a glimmer of others from one minute to the next, aside from its inordinate age, appeals to me as being sentimental nonsense. The notion that the average person is mysteriously inscrutable is the conviction of persons with brains approximately as profound as those of a correspondence school psychiatrist.

Miss Bankhead, waxing now enthusiastic beyond all bounds, proceeded with her tributes to Barry and his play. What Barry has written in his second act, she bubbled, "are not dream sequences; I hate dreams in a play. They're what some of the characters imagine is going to happen! Then in the last act you see what really does happen." Here, Miss Bankhead paused proudly, apparently convinced that Barry had devised something startlingly new in drama. Miss Bankhead's readers may have been forgiven something of an impolite hiccup. The device has long been familiar in one form or another through use by a variety of playwrights.

While it is true that subsequent attendance upon Barry's effort only re-emphasized the trepidations induced by his discursive star, it still remains that the latter did him an injustice by undoing one's interest in his play some time before its first curtain rose. What one engaged proved, however, that Miss Bankhead had been a first-rate critic of it, albeit in reverse.

The story of the play concerns a famous actress whose writer-husband, missing for five years and believed to have been killed in battle action, has been declared legally dead and who is about to marry her leading man when news comes that the husband is alive and on his way home. Various characters in the play, the actress, the leading man, the actress' father, and her small adopted daughter, thereupon severally imagine what will happen when he appears, the imaginings being acted out upon the stage. When he does appear, it develops that nothing they have imagined approximates the reality. At the final curtain, the husband declares his intention of marrying a young woman who has been hanging around the house, thus leaving his wife free to wed her co-actor.

On this occasion, as against twelve in the previous night's exhibit, two children are involved in the play: one in the cast of characters and the other, the author. The one in the cast of characters, while she does her share in depressing the audience, is, however, not nearly so instrumental in that direction as the author himself, for the mind that he brings to the play is that of an annoyingly precocious youngster and one given, to boot, to an absurd pretentiousness. Undoubtedly convinced, as at times he has been in the past, that he has evolved something fresh, vital, and rather important in the way of drama, all that his effort amounts to is a helminthic paraphrase of Ferenc Molnár's *The Phantom Rival* (original title, *The Fable Of The Wolf*), shown in the local theatre many years ago by David Belasco, with some of the most childish philosophy conceivable injected into it for extra light weight.

What Master Barry has persuaded himself to believe is a novel dramaturgical idea, but which, as noted, has already and long since seen service, consists only in sneaking out of the venerable dream business by labeling it his characters' imaginations. These so-called imaginations, however, are essentially the same old mechanical stage dreams and, worse, are even more destructive to his play, since they impose upon his actors a garrulity often spared characters who are dreaming and since, further, the species of imagination which he has visited upon them is unfortunately bereft of any of the misty fancy and cajolery which are part and parcel of the dream state.

In a dream play, the characters' actions are critically acceptable by virtue of the circumstance that their minds are suspended. But when Master Barry asks us to rationalize the actions of fully awake imaginations and yet makes those actions even more grotesque and foolish than the wanton actions induced by dreams he makes an audience in turn doubly conscious of his play's preposterous quality. It takes a highly imaginative dramatist to substitute active imagination for passive dream, and the playwright's imaginations here contributed to his characters are simply the kind that one finds in the Samuel T. French catalogue under the heading of "Children's Charades For School, Church Festival, and Parlor."

Master Barry's gestures toward philosophical wisdom similarly come under the publishers' catalogues' heading, "Juvenile Department." Incorporated into his play, along with a freight of quotations from Scripture and from Socrates, Shakespeare and other famous authors, in the hope of lending it a semblance of weight and gravity, they consist in such revolutionary profundities as were fulsomely hailed by Miss Bankhead in her interview — that no person can really know what another is like, and that the way to rid oneself of anything is to think it out of one's system — and reach their triumphant climax in the argument that the human imagination is never capable of co-ordinating reality and fancy. As for wit, the young master's further trumps take such forms as "The Metro lot is not a happy one," "Sufficient unto the day is the upheaval thereof," "You're a sight for sore eyes if I ever blacked a pair," "There's quite enough in that little head without the Lone Ranger galloping through it," and "Have a night-cap?" — "No thanks, tonight I'll sleep bareheaded."

Miss Bankhead's considerable resources were lost in the kindergarten maze, and the other players, apart from Barbara Kent in the only well-written scene in the play, were no luckier. John C. Wilson's direction was evidently so baffled by the materials in hand that he even succumbed, in the episode depicting the child daughter's imaginings, to making the little one face the audience, throw her head far back and gaze piously at the ceiling like a travesty Joan of Arc, and recite her fancies to an obbligato by her tortured Adam's apple. Jo Mielziner's spaciously handsome library setting only made its contents seem the more puny.

DARK OF THE MOON. March 14, 1945

A legend with music by Howard Richardson and William Berney, the music by Walter Hendl. Produced by the Shuberts for a beyond the season's run in the 46th Street Theatre.

PROGRAM

John	*Richard Hart*
Conjur Man	*Ross Matthew*
The Dark Witch	*Iris Whitney*
The Fair Witch	*Marjorie Belle*
Conjur Woman	*Georgia Simmons*
Hank Gudger	*John Gerstad*
Miss Metcalf	*Frances Goforth*
Mr. Jenkins	*Gar Moore*
Uncle Smelique	*Roy Fant*
Mrs. Summey	*Kathryn Cameron*
Mr. Atkins	*James Lanphier*
Mrs. Bergen	*Agnes Scott Yost*
Edna Summey	*Millicent Coleman*
Burt Dinwitty	*Robert Pryor*
Hattie Heffner	*Peggy Ann Holmes*
Mr. Bergen	*Allan Tower*
Mr. Summey	*Stanley Nelson*
Marvin Hudgens	*John Gifford*
Barbara Allen	*Carol Stone*
Floyd Allen	*Conrad Janis*
Mrs. Allen	*Maidel Turner*
Mr. Allen	*Sherod Collins*
Preacher Haggler	*Winfield Hoeny*
Greeny Gorman	*Dorothy I. Lambert*
Dancing Witches	*Marguerite de Anguera* *Jinx Heffelfinger* *Peggy Ann Holmes* *Lil Liandre*

SYNOPSIS: Act I. Scene 1. *The peak of a ridge in the Smoky Mountains.* Scene 2. *The central square of Buck Creek.* Scene 3. *The Allen cabin on Chunky Gal Mountain.* Scene 4. *The general store of Buck Creek.* Act II. Scene 1. *A clearing in the woods near Barbara and John's cabin.* Scene 2. *Barbara and John's cabin.* Scene 3. *Same as Scene 1, Act I.* Scene 4. *The Church of God, Buck Creek.* Scene 5. *Same as Scene 1, Act I.*

HERE IS A meritorious contribution to the native drama made to seem largely the opposite by a defective stage production. Though the authors, both still in their twenties, are new to playwriting, they have composed a paraphrastic treatment of the derivative Barbara Allen Carolina hillbilly legend which, for all its occasional lapses and let-downs, manages a combination of eerie fantasy and earthy humor that is frequently impressive and that, in its better portions, achieves a degree of real eloquence.

The story is of a witch-boy of the Great Smokies who craves the love of the human Barbara, who strikes a devil's bargain with a Conjur Woman that in exchange for being himself made human his beloved must remain faithful to him for a year else he return to his original state and she forfeit her life, and who is betrayed through the instrumentality of the superstitious and religious Baptist mountain folk, with the threatened consequences. What any such play calls for is, obviously, adroit staging, shrewd casting, and expert direction. It received none of these. As a result, the inner worth of the script was little perceived by both the lay audiences and a number of the professional critics. Nor were they, considering the obfuscating botch the producers had made of it, overmuch to be blamed.

These are only a few of the things that befell the script. George Jenkins' commendable settings were manipulated in such wise by the careless stagehands that the audience spell was vitiated not only by unscreened guide-lights during what should have been complete darkness while the scene shifting was going on, but by the disconcerting presence of a laggardly stagehand or two on the stage after the lights had gone up on a set. Robert Perry's direction failed to orchestrate the song and ballet numbers with the dramatic text, giving them the aspect of excrescences rather than of an integral part of the play. It also permitted Richard Hart, in the role of the witch-boy, so to shout his lines in the early portions of the fantasy that he had nothing left when it came to his succeeding scenes. The yelling further contrived to make the early scenes seem less part of a fantasy than of the football episodes in George Ade's *The College Widow*. And, even at such points as the director managed relatively better, an amateur note, doubtless as in certain other past instances calculated to impress an audience with the exhibit's naturalness and simplicity (both in quotation marks), was allowed to hover over the whole, with the play taking on the appearance of a liqueur served in a paper cup.

Matters were made worse by the producers' fear of License Commissioner Moss' possible censorship and their excision from the script of the all-important scene wherein, during a revival meeting, Barbara is seduced by the lowland bully, thus returning her witch-boy lover to the eagles and the moon and guaranteeing her own death. The deletion robbed the play of its climactic moment and killed the effect of what came after. The authors, additionally, at the last moment not only were persuaded to alter a number of their original lines, to the weakening of the scenes in which they figured, but of their own volition changed the original ending of their play, depriving both the final curtain and the play of the evening's most tender and significant moment. As first written, the witch-boy upon being exorcised from humanity glances casually at the dead Barbara lying on a mountain rock and, no longer recognizing her, gropes his way slowly upward wondering who she is. Probably nervous lest someone accuse them of having paralleled the curtain in a play by Jean Giraudoux (*Undine*), they saw fit to eliminate it and to substitute for the casual glance a fixed gaze and for the witch-boy's wonder the line, "Barbara, if only you hadn't been human!," which made the conclusion of their play not a little silly. And, as a final production touch, the witches, properly designed by the authors as not of the broomstick variety but as the personable temptresses out of classic imagination, were disclosed as being considerably more suited to the stage of a musical revue than to the exhibit in immediate question.

An intrinsically often valuable play was thus, among other ways, sacrificed to inexpedient theatrical governorship. Although Hart indicates potentialities as an actor, the casting of him in the leading part was ill-advised, since he lacks experience and declaimed the role instead of acting it. Carol Stone, though serviceable in one or two passages, was also unequal to the part of Barbara, which might more sagaciously have been cast against itself, as the theatrical term has it, with an actress pictorially less imitative of a combination Tallulah Bankhead and Mae West. And while some of the minor roles were both aptly cast and played, others seemed to have been filled with actors of the summer theatre genre for the purpose of saving money.

In conclusion and to repeat, what might in original script have been developed into an impressive stage offering was deprived of its due by its susceptible authors and their cicerones. That script remains by and large, however, the single critically creditable one that has emerged in recent years from either the college or the summer playhouses.

HAPPILY EVER AFTER. March 15, 1945

A comedy by Donald Kirkley and Howard Burman. Produced by Bernard Klawans and Victor Payne-Jennings for 12 performances in the Biltmore Theatre.

Program

Charlie Porter	*Parker Fennelly*
Martha Whatcoat	*Kathleen Lockhart*
Sam Jarvis	*George Calvert*
Rev. Homer Whatcoat	*Gene Lockhart*
Alec Dixon	*Warren Douglas*
Rita Collins	*Margaret Hayes*
David Macdonald	*Barry Macollum*
Beulah Robinson	*Dulcie Cooper*
Mack	*William Thomson*
Dinty	*William C. Tubbs*
H. A. Stillwater	*Herbert Heyes*
Stubbs	*Nicholas Saunders*
Stan	*Charles Wallis*
Lil	*Melba Rae*
Sheriff	*Hans Robert*

SYNOPSIS: Act I. *Morning.* Act II. *Early afternoon.* Act III. *Late afternoon.*

The entire action of the play takes place in the living-room of Parson Homer Whatcoat in a small marrying town in Maryland.

Time. *Not so long ago.*

Comedies concerned with either the deferred or immediate discovery by a couple that its marriage was, for one reason or another, not legal are not altogether a novelty in the theatre, one such, indeed, having again made its appearance only four nights before. The main change in the present manipulators' version of the theme is that they have multiplied the usual single couple by 10,000, all but two of whom, however, remain off-stage, which is a benefit. They have also shifted the emphasis from the hypothetically wedded to the party responsible for their woes, which may be a further fresh touch but which somehow does not seem materially to increase the benefit.

Dealing with an unordained minister in a Maryland marrying mill and with, upon his unmasking, the anticipated alarms of his victims, the comedy, which should have been written in terms of farce, harks back thirty and more years ago to the day when Roi Cooper Megrue and other playwrights were assiduously bent upon turning out imitations of the kind of things that George M. Cohan, their godfather, could do so very much better. Yet whatever the relative shortcomings of their exhibits were, they at least enjoyed a certain theatrical ingenuity which provided them with some bounce and life. The authors of *Happily Ever After* indicate no such ingenuity until the latter part of their third act comes along, which is a bit late. The earlier portions of their comedy are heavy with strain and, save for a few comical lines, are visibly hard put to it trying to kill time until the last act gets under full way.

Gene Lockhart was amiable enough in the role of the charlatan, at least up to the moment when he was called upon to deliver a moist monologue on the beauties of married life, which took the season's prize for creepy sentimentality. Parker Fennelly and Herbert Heyes as, respectively, his stooge and his old-time colleague in rascality, were the only other members of the company who demonstrated any slightest ability in comedy acting. The stage direction by Crane Wilbur was more appropriate to *Little Eyolf.*

THE DEEP MRS. SYKES. March 19, 1945

A play by George Kelly. Produced by Stanley Gilkey and Barbara Payne for 71 performances in the Booth Theatre.

Program

Mr. Sykes	*Neil Hamilton*	Ralph	*Richard Martin*
Mrs. Sykes	*Catherine Willard*	Adeline	*Mary Gildea*
Ada	*Myra Forbes*	Roy	*Ralph Glover*
May	*Charlotte Keane*	Ethel	*Gwen Anderson*
Cyril	*Romney Brent*	Mrs. Taylor	*Katherine Anderson*
Myrtle Weaver	*Margaret Bannerman*	Mr. Manzoni	*Tom McElhany*
Mrs. Fentriss	*Jean Dixon*	Mr. Taylor	*Grandon Rhodes*

SYNOPSIS: Act I. *Living-room in the home of Mr. Sykes. An evening in February.* Act II. *Drawing-room at Mrs. Taylor's. After dinner, March 20th.*

The intellectual content of the plays of the average American playwright would, if poured into a one-ounce bottle, leave ample room for the distillations of the combined profundities of Dino Grandi, Lady Astor, and Mortimer J. Adler. Any considerable intellectual content, it is true, is hardly necessary to the composition of good drama, which, it need not be repeated, remains an emotional rather than a cerebral art. The fact persists, however and nonetheless, that a sufficient number of our playwriting friends elect to pleasure themselves with the opposite view and to employ the medium as a gymnasium wherein to exercise their mental muscles.

These exercises, which embrace their sociological, theological, political, economic, racial, and other theories, and which include their philosophies on love and marriage, pretty generally tend to dispirit the judicious. For, if the truth must be told, they think primarily with their emotions and what results approximates logic to the same degree that "Mairzy Doats" approximates poetry, or music.

It is thus that when we get a play which betrays symptoms of adult intelligence we congratulate ourselves, even if the play itself is otherwise not all it should be. This, on both counts, is the case with this offering of Kelly's. As a play viewed critically, it has many things wrong with it. The first of its two acts amounts to little more than toilsome and not too holding exposition and its second, for the most part ably written and interesting, is interrupted to its serious damage by an interminable harangue on the part of a female alcoholic, so screeched as to be exceedingly painful to the eardrums. And the author is hardly to be endorsed for lifting his curtain in the instance of both acts on an empty stage by way of the old Broadway trick of inducing his audience, not knowing what else to do, to applaud the scenery, and for thereafter in each case resorting to the ancient business of bringing on the servants of the household to discuss family and kindred affairs. Yet into much of his play, even when it sags in a dramatic direction, he has introduced character analysis filtered through a shrewd intelligence and he has, besides, treated his basic theme to the ministrations of an alive mind, and these in combination contrive to invest his exhibit, apart from its physical aspects, with a gratifying bounce.

Like Vincent Lawrence a playwright whose purpose it is to explore the easy, superficial character limnings of Broadway drama and to scoop out of their box-office perfumes their constituent less fragrant and less edifying musks, Kelly here digs into the poisonous egotism of the female of the species which, in his words, usually passes for mere feminine jealousy, and analyzes it into the open. If he seems to be bitter, his bitterness does not proceed from himself personally so much as from himself as a kind of scientific dramatist. In this he differs from many of his colleagues who offer us simply their personal prejudices in the guise of profound research, close analysis, and ultimate fact. What he has to say may scarcely be notable for any new discovery, but it at least is sound, which is more than may be allowed of the psychological findings of a liberal share of his contemporaries.

The current passion of various such contemporaries thus

to psychologize their themes and characters is, contrary to general opinion, no later-day development. It got a local head-start toward much of its present absurdity nigh unto forty years ago when Augustus Thomas, an ex-actor who fancied himself as of puissant mind and who was encouraged in his delusion by the critics of the period, had a character in a "psychological" melodrama called *The Witching Hour* think a loaded revolver right off the trigger finger of the man who was about to shoot him. That was the beginning of the psychological gold-rush, and since then playwrights have set themselves to shovel the Freudian, Jung, Stekel and other pay-dirt in carloads.

It is a rare season that does not cough up a sizeable number of plays with a psychological label attached to them, like a tin can to a dog's tail. That the psychology involved is often approximately as convincing as the Schnauser that used to be added to the pair of bloodhounds in an *Uncle Tom's Cabin* troupe by way of making the show advertisable as a "mastodonic" production for the impression of hinterland yokels is borne in upon anyone who ever got beyond Tichenor's sophomore year. And that the probing and revelation of psyches frequently takes on very whimsical forms is lost upon no one but the playwrights themselves.

We accordingly get so-called psychological melodramas whose profound soul surgery rests upon the disclosure, as in *The Stranger,* that a murderer's idiosyncrasies are conditioned on his conviction that prostitutes should be given to more churchgoing; as in *Hand In Glove,* that sexual impotence is alleviated by blood-letting, provided only it be on a big enough scale; and, as in *Sleep, My Pretty One,* that a miscellaneous impulse to murder is a concomitant of motherlove. And we further get plays like *The Perfect Marriage* which gravely argue the sexual coldness which assails wedlock after a long span of years in startling terms of the parties having become a little tired of each other, and still others like *Trio* which betray the staggering psychological news that if a young woman of Lesbian tendencies finally meets a young man whom she passionately loves she will be impelled to forego her previous amatory peccadillo, at least for a while.

Even at such times as the psychology involved in these and other entrechats may intrinsically be not entirely without merit, its performance on the part of the playwrights minimizes that possible merit to the vanishing point, and makes the exercise generally ridiculous. It seems, indeed, that many a playwright who finds himself momentarily bogged by a character and unable to figure out what the character would logically do under the immediate dramatic circumstances takes the easiest way out of the difficulty by attributing some desperately incorporated extrinsic quality in him to a psychologically induced aberration. For what passes as psychology has apparently come to be to these playwrights what sociological, economic and other disputations are to certain of their playwriting colleagues: something despairingly to fall back upon when their plays are running too thin and in the nature of sugar pills fed hopefully in the guise of strychnine to an audience drooping from dramatic anemia.

Kelly is of a far different cut. His psychological operations are uniformly honest, well-grounded, and sound.

The theme of *The Deep Mrs. Sykes* is developed from a mere bunch of white lilacs sent anonymously to the attractive wife of a neighbor, and demonstrates how the much-vaunted and bogus intuitions of women play havoc with those whom they wrongly suspect and with their own lives. The final touch of the play is fetching theatre. The accomplished concert pianist with whom the youngest of the husbands is infatuated, after playing in the off-stage music room, leaves the scene. The young husband is alone on the stage. Presently from the music room is heard the immature playing of his young wife who deeply loves him and who, aware of his love for the other woman, tries thus pathetically to find a little of that other woman's place for herself in his heart. The playing stops and she comes into the room. The husband's eyes are still on the one who has gone. The young wife comes to him and gently, very gently, tells him that, whereas married others, like him, can find solace only in their love for someone else, she is content and happy in her love for him alone.

The play suffers, I think, from being cast in the mold of drama rather than high comedy, which might have glossed over the weaknesses it betrays as drama. Its thinness strains dramatic treatment. But that a grown-up mind presides over the stage simultaneously with an inadequate dramatist is obvious.

Of the acting company, Catherine Willard, as the pseudo-intuitive older wife, was much the best. The ordinarily able Jean Dixon, as the vituperative female given to drink, was, largely due to the author's ill-considered direction, a caricature and wholly out of key with the play's tone. That general stage direction, furthermore, was altogether too ponderous and suggested at times an organ playing the *Miserere* at a tea party. It also neglected to caution the actors that the proper pronunciation of the name of the flowers does not happen to be "lilocks."

KISS THEM FOR ME. March 20, 1945

A play, originally called The Lovely Leave, *by Luther Davis, based on the novel,* Shore Leave, *by Frederic Wakeman. Produced by John Moses and Mark Hanna for a beyond the season run in, initially, the Belasco Theatre.*

PROGRAM

F. Neilson	*John McGovern*	Tailor	*Harold Grau*
Lt. Comdr. Wallace	*Edward Crandall*	Chief	*George Cory*
		Nurse Wilinski	*Virginia Kaye*
Mississip	*Dennis King, Jr.*	Chief Nurse	*Amy Douglass*
Mac	*Richard Davis*	Gunner	*George Matthews*
Ensign	*Douglas Jones*	Hedrick	*Dudley Sadler*
Crewson	*Richard Widmark*	Charlie	*Daniel Petrie*
Turnbill	*Robert Allen*	Mr. Hardy	*Paul Ford*
Wac	*Sonya Stokowski*	Mrs. Hardy	*Patricia Quinn O'Hara*
Alice	*Judy Holliday*		
Gwynneth	*Jayne Cotter*		

SYNOPSIS: Place, San Francisco. Act I. *The living-room of a suite in the St. Mark Hotel; noon.* Act II. *Officers' solarium in a naval hospital; the following afternoon.* Act III. *The living-room of the suite again; a few hours later.*

Still another in the line of Navy servicemen-on-leave plays, the layout follows, save in minor detail, the usual pattern of boozing, wenching, and the juke-box drama like. Almost everything that has become familiar from plays of a kind is again in evidence: the impudent bravado of the boys with women, the heroine who yields patriotically to a sexual affair with the hero, the comic-relief floozie, the wounded returned hero who delivers himself of the customary affecting monologue, the miscellaneous saucy slaps on female posteriors and the affectionate ditto on male backs, the difficulty of adjustment to civilian surroundings, the boys' nonchalant depreciations of their heroism, etc.

In the present case, there has been an effort to give the old materials a seeming significance, but the significance signifies only that the author has some very eccentric and mighty silly ideas. For example, he heatedly criticizes civilians in connection with the war effort and chooses as his especial target for ridicule a ship-builder who has served the effort loyally and handsomely. He derides this competent man and presents him as his play's villain simply because he wishes a naval aviator on leave and bent solely on getting drunk and consorting with loose women to take an hour or so off, talk to the shipyard workers about the war, and thus help to discourage absenteeism. He also sneers elaborately at what he dubs the "paper Navy" for its red-tape (the red-tape in his mind being strict attention to registry documents, careful methods of hospitalization, and the like) because it sometimes gets in the way of servicemen's good times when on leave. It is his significant conviction, apparently, that the Navy would be a lot better if it were run like a Chicago night club.

To bespeak an audience's sympathy with three flyers out for a hot time who insult honest and faithful civilian effort and necessary and important Navy routine and who accompany their derogations with constant booze swilling and fornicatory gestures at womenfolk seems to be asking almost as much as bespeaking that audience's distaste for a valuable ship-builder simply because he doesn't relish a flyer's suggestive passes at his fiancée and for a hospital staff for thoughtlessly preventing servicemen from sneaking away and getting drunker than ever.

I had believed that the venerable final curtain on the heroine's "I'll be waiting" had long since gone into the discard for all time but, sure enough, here it was again.

The presenting company was in the aggregate personally satisfactory. Herman Shumlin's direction varied from good to very bad. Certain passages he handled well enough, but the conduct of the flyers in the first act suggested too greatly that they were members of a *Boys Of Company B* cast and their conduct in part of the last act that they must be members of the *Russian* Navy.

The play marked No. 32 in the series of the drama in uniform.

SWEET GENEVIEVE. March 20, 1945

A comedy by Mary G. and Marchette Chute. Produced by the authors plus Joy Chute and Mina Cole for one performance in the President Theatre.

PROGRAM

Mrs. Quigley	*Grace Kleine*	Mrs. Martin	*Ruth Grubbs*
Joel	*Sam Banham*	Mrs. Rutherford	*Nolia Trammel*
Genevieve	*Rosilyn Weiss*	Mr. Rutherford	*Hal Hershey*
Mr. Quigley	*Jay Davis*	Mr. Larchmont	*Paul Rapport*
Daisy	*Ruth Manning*		

SYNOPSIS: Act I. *A room on the third floor of Mrs. Quigley's rooming house on the lower East Side of Manhattan. A June evening in 1886.* Act II. *The same. The following morning.* Act III. *The same. The afternoon of the following day.*

THE THREE Chute sisters and a friend of the family's, Miss Cole, hired the little President Theatre in the West Forty-eighth Street spaghetti and delicatessen belt for the display of two of the sisters' maiden dramatic effort. The effort, termed a "romantic comedy," related the elopement in 1886 of a young couple, their honeymoon in a rooming house on the lower East Side of Manhattan, and the manner in which the bride's mother, who had objected to the marriage, became reconciled when she learned to her relief that a neighbor's baby was not, as she had feared, the illegitimate consequence of an act participated in by her daughter. Neither the playwriting Chutes nor the producing Chute and her associate girl friend indicated the faintest degree of talent for anything even remotely connected with the theatre.

ETERNAL CAGE. MARCH 21, 1945

A play by Jules Denes. Produced by C. Sherman Hoyt for 9 performances and a total intake of 296 dollars in the Barbizon-Plaza Theatre.

PROGRAM

ROBERT DUNCAN *Frank Gibney*	FRANCES HARRINGTON *Johanna Douglas*
MARION DUNCAN *Sheila Bromley*	DON ANTONIO RODRIGUEZ *William Forrest*
WALTER WHITFORD *George Blackwood*	
VIVIAN LAKE *Frances Dale*	

SYNOPSIS: The entire action takes place in the Duncan living-room, New York City. Time. *The present.* Scene 1. *Afternoon.* Scene 2. *The dream.* Act II. *The dream continued.* Act III. *Again that afternoon.*

THOUGH MR. DENES, a Hungarian, is alleged to have had experience in both dramatic authorship and stage production in his native land, there was here no evidence of either. His play, dealing with the wife of a physician who rebels at his dictatorship over her and who drinks herself into a dream wherein she fancies what she would do if she were rid of his influence, is a strictly amateur performance, and minus merit in any direction. And his staging of the script was no more professional. Mr. Hoyt, the producer, is a wealthy yachtsman and Mr. Denes' friend. Friendship could go no farther, though wisdom might have shortened the distance to the profit of both.

THE FIREBRAND OF FLORENCE
March 22, 1945

A musical show originally called Much Ado About Love, *derived from Edwin Justus Mayer's comedy,* The Firebrand, *by Mr. Mayer, Ira Gershwin and Kurt Weill. Produced by Max Gordon for 43 performances and a loss of 225,000 dollars in the Alvin Theatre.*

PROGRAM

HANGMAN	*Randolph Symonette*	CELLINI	*Earl Wrightson*
TARTMAN	*Don Marshall*	CAPTAIN OF THE GUARD	*Charles Sheldon*
SOUVENIR MAN	*Bert Freed*	OTTAVIANO	*Ferdi Hoffman*
MAFFIO	*Boyd Heathen*	ASCANIO	*James Dobson*
ARLECCHINO	*Jean Guelis*	EMELIA	*Gloria Story*
COLUMBINA	*Norma Gentner*	ANGELA	*Beverly Tyler*
PIEROT	*Eric Kristen*	MARQUIS	*Paul Best*
FLOMINA	*Diane Meroff*	DUKE	*Melville Cooper*
PANTALONE	*Hubert Bland*	PAGE	*Billy Williams*
FIORINETTA	*Mary Alice Bingham*	DUCHESS	*Lotte Lenya*
GELFOMINO	*Kenneth Le Roy*	MAJOR-DOMO	*Walter Graf*
ROSANIA	*Mary Grey*	CLERK OF THE COURT	*Alan Noel*
DOTTORE	*William Vaux*		
MAGISTRATE	*Marion Green*		

Locale. *Florence and Paris.*
Time. *1535.*

IT WAS Compton Mackenzie, I believe, who years ago employed the title, "Florence On A Certain Night," for a book of verse. The management might well have negotiated for its use, since *The Firebrand Of Florence* altogether too much suggests Laura Jean Libbey with her sequent particles and invokes the temptation on the part of the show's critics to dub it *The Firebrand Of Florence, or Max Gordon's False Step,* which, though very sound criticism, would be deplorable in the habitually polite.

This marks the second unsuccessful attempt to convert Mayer's amusing comedy of two decades ago about the rivalry of glandular Benvenuto Cellini and the arid Duke into the musical form. Some seventeen years back the late publisher, Horace Liveright, aided and abetted by the late banker, Otto Kahn, offered a version called *The Dagger And The Rose* that never got beyond its try-out in Atlantic City. The culprits on that occasion were Isabel Leighton (book), Edward Eliscu (lyrics), and Eugene Berton (music).

With on this occasion enough money invested in the exhibit to float a battleship, Gordon has floated only a towboat, desperately chugging away and pulling at nothing. He here demonstrates that an infinite capacity for taking pains and genius have nothing at all in common, for though his production indicates all kinds of hard work he gets barely nearer to what a musical show should be than the hereinbefore noted Mrs. Dresselhuys, which may be allowed by those who suffered the latter's *Rhapsody* to be some distance. A few fair tunes are there, and the period costumes have sufficient color, and Melville Cooper and the attractive Gloria Story help in so far as they can. But otherwise, from book to John Murray Anderson's stage direction, from principals to small-part actors, and from Jo Mielziner's scenery to this and that, Mayer's comedy has been turned into something that lacks only a little music by Wagner in Weill's stead to constitute it a first-rate funeral.

While Ira Gershwin's lyrics here and there offer a momentary hint of his erstwhile skill, they more often descend to such stuff as "I know where there's a nosey cook — My lord, you mean a cozy nook." A lyric, furthermore, in which the singer strives vainly for a rhyme with Angela the while, after theoretically hilarious pauses and triumphant looks at the audience, he succeeds in negotiating such rhymes as needeth for Edith and so on, is hardly more to the credit of the talented lyricist of *Of Thee I Sing* and a half dozen other shows than such souvenirs of the musical stage of the early nineteen hundreds as are sufficiently suggested by titles like "There Was Life, There Was Love, There Was Laughter," "When The Duchess Is Away," and "Come To Paris."

The book, though Mayer himself worked on it, has lost

all trace of the entertainment value of its source and plods its heavy way like a *The Vagabond King* in water-soaked boots. Poor Cooper, a nutritious comedian when given half a chance, is condemned in his attempts at a little relieving humor to such lines, in reply to a pert girl who describes herself as a lady-in-waiting, as "Well, you won't have to wait long." Though he earns double his salary by bequeathing it a final hiccup and by trying to make the audience forget it in allowing his elbow to miss the edge of the table at which he is seated (both gratis), his virtuosity avails him not, and the evening continues on its *Rhapsody* course.

It surely is not too much to ask of a show treating of the amours of Cellini that it have something of a romantic air, and that air is scarcely to be achieved with a stageful of people, excepting only the aforementioned Story girl, who look and act like a *Night Must Fall* company dressed up for a Garibaldi birthday celebration, in Peekskill. Earl Wrightson, as the famous lover, has a good baritone voice which serves the occasion when it is devoted to song but which, when it lapses into dialogue, sounds considerably less like the hypnotic Benvenuto than like Benay Venuta. To the role of Angela, Cellini's beloved model, Beverly Tyler, imported for the event from Hollywood, brings a voice notable chiefly for flatting the higher notes and a stage demeanor still so awkward that she must needs heavily finger her skirts this way and that in order to conceal the woodenness of her gait. The ladies of the ensemble, furthermore, for the greater share resemble Mr. David O. Selznick, and many of the males would provide perfect illustrations for the tales of the Brothers Grimm.

Costume musicals are frequently, even at their best, fertile in stage embarrassment. From theatrical time immemorial, tights have had an obscene way of wrinkling at the knees and making any impassioned love duet wherein the heroine proclaims their wearer the peer of Apollo rather less convincing than one might wish. The motion pictures enjoy an advantage in this respect. The camera can cut off the Apollo at the waistline and thus to a degree sustain the illusion. But the stage is helpless in the situation and unavoidably has to pay the price. The movies, too, can similarly maneuver the unsightly hooks and eyes and zippers on the women's costumes out of audience vision and so encourage the fancy that in the theatre has trouble reconciling such eye-sores with a squad of hypothetically ethereal Beatrices. And the films can manipulate further trivialities in such a manner that they do not invade the romantic mood. That the costume pictures themselves are otherwise generally much worse than their stage counterparts does not obscure their superiority in these minor details, which should provide an almost colossal satisfaction to the hereinbefore mentioned Mr. Mamoulian and other of their enthusiasts.

It takes music of an uncommon sort to make any stage costume show capture the necessary fragrant mood. Even the best book has a time of it competing with the waywardly realistic mood of later-day audiences. And when the book is as sour as that of this *The Firebrand Of Florence* it would require the services of Lehár, Eysler, Kalman and Victor Herbert operating in combination and at the top of their form to win over those audiences to it, or to get them, at the least, to suspend judgment regarding it. Weill is a lightly pleasant composer who at times, notably in *The Three Penny Opera,* has written proficiently. But he hasn't the strength or the fulness of musical imagination and resource to work any such miracle in this case. Some of his melodies, indeed, not only do not distract their auditors from the yesterday aspect of the show but fix their attention grimly on the yesterday aspect of the melodies themselves. I have in my day engaged so many musical shows that I can't remember all the songs in them, but if I haven't long since heard some that sounded very much like some of these of Weill's my ear is less reliable than I think.

THE BARRETTS OF WIMPOLE STREET

March 26, 1945

A revival of the play by Rudolf Besier. Produced by Katharine Cornell for 87 performances in the Ethel Barrymore Theatre.

Program

Doctor Chambers	*Russell Gaige*
Elizabeth Barrett Moulton-Barrett	*Katharine Cornell*
Wilson	*Brenda Forbes*
Henrietta Moulton-Barrett	*Emily Lawrence*
Arabel Moulton-Barrett	*Patricia Calvert*
Octavius Moulton-Barrett	*Erik Martin*
Alfred Moulton-Barrett	*Stanley Parlan*
Charles Moulton-Barrett	*Howard Otway*
Henry Moulton-Barrett	*Roger Stearns*
George Moulton-Barrett	*Keinert Wolff*
Edward Moulton-Barrett	*McKay Morris*
Bella Hedley	*Betty Brewer*
Henry Bevan	*Roger Stearns*
Robert Browning	*Brian Aherne*
Doctor Ford-Waterlow	*Ivan Simpson*
Captain Surtees Cook	*Chester Stratton*
Flush	*Himself*

SYNOPSIS: This comedy was played in Elizabeth Barrett's bed-sitting-room at 50, Wimpole Street, London, in 1845. Act I. Scene 1. *The evening of the 19th of May.* Scene 2. *The afternoon of the following day.* Act II. *Three months later.* Act III. Scene 1. *Some weeks later.* Scene 2. *The following week.*

SURROUNDED BY virtually the same company that was associated with her in the one hundred and forty performances of the play for American troops in Italy, France and the Netherlands, Miss Cornell's reception on the opening night was but slightly less thunderous than that accorded the late Admiral Dewey on his triumphant return from the Philippines. Accepting it with a gracious, if faintly whimsical smile, she then entered into the role of Elizabeth Barrett in which she had made so agreeable an impression all of fourteen and, in revival, ten years ago and attested to the fact that, when it comes to romantic parts of a kind, she still possesses that quality of dark fascination and vocal harmony which so satisfactorily adorns them. As the Robert Browning of the familiar romance, Mr. Aherne, again in his old role, indicated that the intervening years he had spent before a Hollywood camera had taken their customary toll of a dramatic actor and offered a performance bordering on travesty. And the support in the aggregate was mediocre.

Besier's exhibit, it need hardly be repeated, is a theatrewise treatment of the two poets' love affair which unfolds on the stage with considerable greasepaint brio. It remains as efficient a star vehicle, if as critically dubious a play, as when first shown. Since it deals with celebrated literary figures it is naturally accepted by the preponderance of theatregoers as a literary play, which it is only superficially. But it so "humanizes" its protagonists that what in less skilled hands would emerge merely as historically labeled ventriloquial dummies here emerge as moderately alive figures, albeit with a heavy splash of purple makeup on their faces.

YOU CAN'T TAKE IT WITH YOU

MARCH 26, 1945

A revival of the farce-comedy by Moss Hart and George S. Kaufman. Produced by Frank McCoy for 17 performances in the City Center Theatre.

PROGRAM

PENELOPE SYCAMORE	*Daisy Atherton*	HENDERSON	*Edward Kreisler*
ESSIE	*Dorothy Stone*	TONY KIRBY	*Richard Maloy*
RHEBA	*Eula Belle Moore*	BORIS KOLENKHOV	*Charles Collins*
PAUL SYCAMORE	*John Souther*	GAY WELLINGTON	*Emma Bunting*
MR. DE PINNA	*Donald Keyes*	MR. KIRBY	*John Clubley*
ED	*Lance Cunard*	MRS. KIRBY	*Dorothy Scott*
DONALD	*Charles Benjamin*	THREE MEN	*Spencer Sawyer* *Charles Foley* *George McLain*
MARTIN VANDERHOF	*Fred Stone*		
ALICE	*Lucile Marsh*	OLGA	*Ulla Kazanova*

SYNOPSIS: The scene is the home of Martin Vanderhof, of New York. Act I. *A Wednesday evening.* Act II. *A week later.* Act III. *The next day.*

THE CITY CENTER pursued again its second-hand road show policy with the display of the 1936–37 farce-comedy in a performance so inferior to the original that its humorous quality was largely lost. While Fred Stone has long been held in affection by the theatre public, and properly, that affection has been for him as an individual rather than as an actor. As an actor, whether in musical shows or in his occasional later ventures into straight plays, he has always been and remains little more than a vaudevillian with a limited equipment. Take away the acrobatics and mechanical props with whose aid he rose in older days to celebrity and his lack of a real comedian's resources are laid bare. His talents, in the literal sense, have need of a springboard.

His assistants here, including his daughter Dorothy and his son-in-law, Charles Collins, were no better fitted to distil the laughter from the script, and the eccentric Sycamore household, which once had its audiences roaring, acquired the flavor less of the gay lunatic asylum it previously was than of a Sunday school with a few tacks on its benches.

The City Center concluded the season with a showing for two and one-half weeks beginning on May 2 of the originally admirable *Carmen Jones* in a cut-down producton designed for the road which, while it could not obscure its virtues, materially reduced its former theatrical power.

LADY IN DANGER. March 29, 1945

A comedy-mystery by Max Afford, adapted by Alexander Kirkland. Produced by Pat Allen and Dan Fisher for 12 performances in the Broadhurst Theatre.

PROGRAM

Bill Sefton	*James Gannon*
Monica Sefton	*Helen Claire*
Miss Hodges	*Elfrida Derwent*
Dr. Francis Gresham	*Alexander Kirkland*
Sylvia Meade	*Vicki Cummings*
Andrew Meade	*Rodney McLennan*
Karl Kurt	*Paul Fairleigh*
Chief Inspector Burke	*Clarence Derwent*
Detective Dennis Marsh	*Ronald Alexander*
Constable Pogson	*Hudson Faussett*
Frederick Smith	*Gary Blivers*

SYNOPSIS: Action of the play takes place in the Seftons' apartment, Villa Flats, Melbourne, Australia, during a summer evening. Act I. Scene 1. *6 p.m.* Scene 2. *11.30 p.m.* Act II. *About 1 a.m.* Act III. Scene 1. *One hour later.* Scene 2. *Immediately following.*

Mr. Afford is an Australian radio script writer whose play, his first, was produced successfully Down Under. In its original form its scene was laid in London and its knave was a Nazi spy. In Mr. Kirkland's adaptation the scene has been shifted to Australia and the knave converted into a Japanese spy. In both cases it remains largely the conventional espionage mystery number, if much worse and much duller than usual, in which miladi, her visage permanently wrinkled in apprehension, is murderously stalked by the villain and in which the creepiness is that of a small child on all fours rather than anything associated with adult foreboding. It is, further, the sixtieth mystery play failure out of the previous dozen seasons' plus this season's sixty-seven attempts.

The nonsense involves the following:

Item. A cat with poisoned claws that scratches the victims to death.

Item. The body that falls out of the closet.

Item. The heroine who is a writer of mystery stories.
Item. The dumb detective.
Item. The wise-cracking female friend of the heroine.
Item. The newspaper reporter whose appetite for gin does not blunt his great sapience.
Item. The circumstantial evidence against the heroine that wouldn't fool anyone but the Messrs. Afford and Kirkland.
Item. The eavesdropping female servant.
Item. The doused lights and the flashlights in the dark.
Item. The scream.
Item. The heavy comedy-relief consisting chiefly of jokes about the lavatory.
Item. The Japanese agents who speak with a thick German accent.

The members of the acting company, though given to such locutions, in reference to the corpus of the deceased, as "the prostate body," did not, however, like various such otherwise illiterate acting companies, fail in the customary pronunciation of the word "record" with the painstaking precision of the president of the fashionable Negro country club in *Carmen Jones.*

THE GLASS MENAGERIE. March 31, 1945

A play by Tennessee Williams, with incidental music by Paul Bowles. Produced by Eddie Dowling and Louis J. Singer for a far beyond the season run in the Playhouse.

PROGRAM

THE MOTHER	*Laurette Taylor*	THE GENTLEMAN CALLER	*Anthony Ross*
HER SON	*Eddie Dowling*		
HER DAUGHTER	*Julie Haydon*		

A play in two parts.
An alley in St. Louis.
Part 1. *Preparation for a gentleman caller.*
Part 2. *The gentleman calls.*
The alley.
Time. *Now and the past.*

IT HAS BEEN MORE or less clear for some time now that if our stage hopes for anything approaching dramatic delicacy and beauty it will have to look largely to a one-time soft-shoe dancer and song writer, of all people, to supply it. For if there is another producer like Eddie Dowling who is willing to risk things like *Shadow And Substance, The White Steed, Love's Old Sweet Song, The Time Of Your Life, Magic, Hello, Out There,* and this *The Glass Menagerie,* let me have his name and I shall be delighted to indite a testimonial like this to him, too. But I myself can not at the moment think of him, and I have been thinking hard. I can, in short, think of no other present producer, despite his periodic touching tributes to himself, whose honest and closest desire is to bring to our theatre that type of drama which possibly departs the security of the box-office for a brave flight into those upper reaches of a human spirit far removed from Broadway.

He has been a poor man in worldly goods, this Dowling, and at times, having less than two hundred dollars in the bank to support his wife and child, has been compelled to undertake pitiable side jobs for others, such as *Madame Capet, Manhattan Nocturne* and *This Rock,* to get a little living money. But let him find a play that no other producer would touch and which his critical sense tells him has some qualities of worth and loveliness and, if he has a spare nickel to his name, he will go out and beg, borrow or steal the rest of the money needed to get it a hearing.

It has often been heartbreaking for him in a lot of ways. The Shuberts, who helped him out with the necessary funds to produce *Shadow And Substance,* lost all faith in the play when it was tried out in Pittsburgh and it was only his pleadings that kept them from closing it after the one week's engagement there. The Theatre Guild, whose dollars helped him to put on *The Time Of Your Life,* horned in on the production and made such a scenic mess of it that all seemed lost until Armina Marshall judiciously countered the masterminds into letting him have his own way. His adventures in the instance of *Love's Old Sweet Song* were enough, before he finally got the first New York curtain up, to drive another man to suicide. His troubles with Schuyler Watts, who backed him in the production of a program of delightful short plays by O'Casey and Saroyan and who had ideas of his own as to how they should be done, were so great that he found it impossible, after a Princeton, New Jersey, try-out, to bring the production into New York. And now most lately in the case of this *The Glass Menagerie,* which has turned out in the majority opinion of the reviewers to be the year's finest theatrical adventure, his hope to persuade the Theatre Guild to lend the play its subscription audiences was firmly blasted by Theresa Helburn, who, even after viewing it during its successful Chicago run, said that it was much too dangerously fragile to be sure of making money in New York and, besides, that the Guild had another play already scheduled, which peculiarly never materialized.

But that was only a drop in the overflowing bucket of Dowling's trials and disappointments. In its opening week in Chicago, the play took in a mere 3,300 dollars at the box-office, which represented so heavy a loss that Singer, Dowling's co-producer who had put up the money for the production, was all for closing it then and there. Supporting him in his decision was not only Alex Yokel, the company manager, but even Harry Davies, the press-agent. And once again Dowling had to argue, shout and implore that the play be given another week's chance to prove itself. To his aid came Ashton Stevens, Claudia Cassidy, and several other Chicago critics who admired the play, and the week of grace followed, and the receipts slowly climbed, and prosperity came to a production that, if the others had had their way, would have been summarily consigned to the storehouse. Moreover, when Dowling subsequently tried to book the play into the Playhouse in New York while it was still running in Chicago, Harry Fromkes, that theatre's owner who previously had booked a steady succession of prompt failure rubbish like *Sophie, Sleep, My Pretty One, A Goose For The Gander, Hand In Glove, The Stranger,* etc., hesitated for almost three weeks to give the play, after seeing it and liking it though believing it not to have box-office possibilities, the longed-for booking and did so at length only when contracts giving him sufficiently rewarding terms were agreed upon.

I sometimes hear it said that I am prejudiced in Dowling's favor. What I hear said, believe me, is damned true. I am prejudiced in Dowling's favor as I would be in the case of any man who, like him, places the pride of the theatre above a potential fat purse, who is not afraid of risky but meritorious plays, and who is willing for weeks and even months to subsist on doughnuts and tea if it will allow him eventually to realize some little dream he may have.

The Glass Menagerie, not as a play but as a production, marks the high-light thus far in this Dowling's career. It provides by long odds the most imaginative evening that the stage has offered in this season. Originally written as a rather freakish "experiment" and replete with such delicatessen as the moving picture titles of silent cinema days thrown intermittently on the scenery, it has been metamorphosed under Dowling's guidance into the unaffected and warming simplicity that it should have had in the first place.

Deficient in any touches of humor, since Williams forthrightly confesses himself to be a playwright with none, it has been embroidered under that same guidance with suggested flashes of humor. Its narrator character, like most gratuitious and faultily incorporated narrator characters originally the routine wooden *compère,* has similarly been rewritten into a measure of reason and plausibility; and little things like, for example, the final illumination of the grinning father's portrait, the final tossing of the play into the lap of the audience's imagination, etc., have transformed the script into a medium over which the arts of the theatre can and do play their most hypnotic colors.

The play, which is intrinsically rather less a play than a palette of sub-Chekhovian pastels brushed up into a charming semblance of one, has had everything possible brought to it for its production effect, which is demonstratedly pretty fine. Jo Mielziner's setting of the St. Louis alley and dowdy flat, with the latter's draperies and scrims ingeniously fashioned to catch his unusually expert lighting, itself catches perfectly the mood of a play that also consists almost entirely in mood. Dowling's direction, with some assistance from Laurette Taylor and, to a considerably less extent, Margo Jones, orchestrates the whole in key with Paul Bowles' engaging musical obbligato. And the acting is the best example of ensemble work that has been observable on the season's stage. Miss Taylor hits her peak as the now frowzy Southern belle of other days desperately set upon achieving a husband for her lame daughter; hers is a rare performance. Dowling, bereft of his occasional pietistic manner, is completely natural and at ease as the son with his father's wanderer's feet. Miss Haydon's crippled daughter is not the usual, standardized limping Broadway actress with the greasepaint brave smile but a creature crippled deeply in inner spirit. And Anthony Ross as her lost lover rounds out the acting quartet with a healthy believability.

The play received the award of the New York Drama Critics' Circle as the season's best.

A PLACE OF OUR OWN. April 2, 1945

A play by Elliott Nugent. Produced by John Golden, in association with the author and Robert Montgomery, for 8 performances in the Royale Theatre.

Program

Margie Johns	*Toni Favor*	Mary Lorimer	*Mercedes McCambridge*
Pete Reis	*John Howes*	Augusta	*Lotta Palfi*
Nancy Monroe	*Jeanne Cagney*	Henry Barfuss	*Jack Howard*
Charles Reddy	*Robert Keith*	Mike McGroarty	*Anthony Blair*
Jesse Ward	*Seth Arnold*	Joe Kaplan	*Wolfe Barzell*
David Monroe	*John Archer*	Mrs. Brandt	*Helen Carew*
Sam Reddy	*J. C. Nugent*		

SYNOPSIS: Act I. *The living-room in the Reddy home. March.* Act II. *An evening in September.* Act III. Scene 1. *Three weeks later.* Scene 2. *Late November.*

The action takes place in the town of Calais, Ohio, in the year 1919.

The play is the old one about the young, idealistic newspaper editor in conflict with villainously selfish interests who try to do him in. The author has sought to give it a little renewed life by basing the conflict on the latter's opposition to Woodrow Wilson's plans for world peace (the scene is laid in 1919) and by belaboring the obvious later day analogy, but he can not hide his script's betraying crow's-feet. As if disappointedly conscious of the fact, he abandons the Wilson hocus-pocus half-way through his play and thereafter frankly peddles the other old stuff about the hero's marital difficulties (his wife suspects him of intimacy with another woman, etc.) and the troubles he and his wife have with his father-in-law. Both sections of the play are equally bilious.

The dramaturgy is no better. If the author has to get a character off the stage and knows no way in which plausibly to manage it, he has a telephone bell ring for no honest reason in the adjoining room. In order to establish the period of his play, he fumblingly resorts to such business as having a character read a popular novel of the period, or jokingly allude to Mark Hanna, or refer to the dubiety of Prohibition liquor, or play a 1919 tune on the phonograph. And his attempts at humor take such turns as having a character observe that Virginia is the mother of Presidents and causing another to ask, "Virginia who?"

The acting company, excepting John Archer as the pro tem. Wilson crusader and J. C. Nugent as a comic-relief grandfather, harried the already harried script, as did the author's stage direction.

The play was the thirty-fourth that included the military uniform.

STAR SPANGLED FAMILY. April 5, 1945

A play, originally called Star Spangled Widow, *by B. Harrison Orkow. Produced by Philip A. Waxman and Joseph Kipness for 5 performances in the Biltmore Theatre.*

PROGRAM

Gwen Purchase	*Dennie Moore*	"Bud" Jones	*Donald Devlin*
Messenger	*Byron Griffith*	Margaret Jones	*Jean Adair*
Sally Jones	*Frances Reid*	Harry Lupinsky	*Stephen Morrow*
Paul	*Harlan Stone*	Victor Gunther	*Leon Charles*
Harold	*Franklin Allen*	Glen	*Jimmy Sommer*
Mervin Mitchell	*Lewis Charles*	Nurse Craig	*Mary Best*
Dr. Richard Morley	*Edward Nugent*	Dr. Newton	*Bram Nossen*

SYNOPSIS: Act I. *A late spring afternoon during the first year after we have won the war.* Act II. Scene 1. *A week later.* Scene 2. *One month later.* Act III. Scene 1. *Four days later.* Scene 2. *Two hours later.*

The Scene. *The entire action takes place in Sally Jones' living-room in a mid-Manhattan apartment.*

WHO THE AUTHOR IS, the available records this side of Hollywood do not reveal. One thing, however, is certain, and that is that he is not a playwright. Judging from this whatnot, he is rather a person who believes that all that is needed for dramaturgy is to write a pulp magazine story, scissor out of it the "he saids" and "she replieds," and put it on a stage with a constantly ringing door-bell. His dialogic splendor is to be perceived from such specimens as "That can not be Dr. Morley ringing the buzzer as men of science are always precise," "It is too delightfully utter," and "Intellectuals seem always to crowd one's living-room these days"; his humor concerns such things as the magazines in dentists' offices; and his contribution to character analysis consists in the belief that whenever a person is nervous or distraught he will invariably drop whatever he may be holding in his hand.

For his theme, Mr. Orkow has dug into the bottom of

the warehouse chest and pulled out the plot of the child who resents his mother's second marriage, which has served at least two dozen plays in the *Wednesday's Child* catalogue. Thinking to give it a contemporary countenance he has made the deceased father a war hero whom the child worshipped, but the play remains its old self nonetheless, if infinitely poorer than any previously displayed. The direction by William Castle, another Hollywood genius, simply stood the actors on the stage and had them recite their speeches as at a high-school commencement exercise. And the actors in the aggregate were the kind who mistook an appearance of personal apathy for histrionic naturalness and who articulated the phrase "at all" as if a noun regularly followed it.

CAROUSEL. April 19, 1945

A musical play, based on Ferenc Molnár's Liliom, *book and lyrics by Oscar Hammerstein II, music by Richard Rodgers. Produced by the Theatre Guild for a far beyond the season run in the Majestic Theatre.*

PROGRAM

Carrie Pipperidge	*Jean Darling*	Jennie	*Joan Keenan*
Julie Jordan	*Jan Clayton*	Virginia	*Ginna Moise*
Mrs. Mullin	*Jean Casto*	Susan	*Suzanne Tafel*
Billy Bigelow	*John Raitt*	Jonathan	*Richard H. Gordon*
Juggler	*Lew Foldes*	Second Policeman	*Larry Evers*
First Policeman	*Robert Byrn*	Captain	*Blake Ritter*
David Bascome	*Franklyn Fox*	First Heavenly Friend (Brother Joshua)	*Jay Velie*
Nettie Fowler	*Christine Johnson*	Second Heavenly Friend	*Tom McDuffie*
June Girl	*Pearl Lang*	Starkeeper	*Russell Collins*
Enoch Snow	*Eric Mattson*	Enoch Snow, Jr.	*Ralph Linn*
Jigger Craigin	*Murvyn Vye*	Louise	*Bambi Linn*
Hannah	*Annabelle Lyon*	Carnival Boy	*Robert Pagent*
Boatswain	*Peter Birch*	Principal	*Lester Freedman*
Arminy	*Connie Baxter*		
Penny	*Marilyn Merkt*		

SYNOPSIS: Time. *1873–1888.* Prelude. *An amusement park on the New England coast. May.* Act I. Scene 1. *A tree-lined path along the shore. A few minutes later.* Scene 2. *Nettie Fowler's spa on the ocean front. June.* Act II. Scene 1. *On an island across the bay. That night.* Scene 2. *Mainland waterfront. An hour later.* Scene 3. *Up there.* Scene 4. *Down here. On a beach. Fifteen years later.* Scene 5. *Outside Julie's cottage.* Scene 6. *Outside a schoolhouse. Same day.*

It is now some years since Jerome Kern, who succeeded Victor Herbert as the first composer of the contemporary theatre, dispossessed himself of all his books and thus prepared himself for acceptance by Hollywood, where he has posthumously quartered his talents. Along with the books, which constituted one of the most valuable private libraries in the country, he dispossessed himself of his quondam theatre collaborator, Oscar Hammerstein II, who with him had written, among other things, *Show Boat* and *Music In The Air,* two of the most valuable of all American musical plays, and who, as has since been attested by *Oklahoma!, Carmen Jones,* etc., has become the first music show bookman and lyricist of the contemporary stage. With Kern's disappearance, Hammerstein has allied himself with Richard Rodgers, who now in turn seems to be taking over Kern's place in the compositional van. Together, they form an uncommonly able team.

Carousel follows their remarkably successful *Oklahoma!* and follows it with exceptional credit. Hammerstein's treatment of the Molnár play happily abstains from any inclination to reduce it to the whims of Broadway; he allows it with but minor amendments to retell its lovely and affecting story of the bully who can express his inarticulate love only by beating the woman of his heart, of that woman's deep, silent, and infinitely patient love for him, and of his day's release from the purgatory whence death in a planned robbery has dispatched him by way of permitting him at length to do one good act on earth that may redeem his soul. The scene has been shifted from modern Hungary to the New England coast of the 1870's and 1880's, but the essence of the fantasy remains. Only in the unfortunate inclusion of two or three specimens of Broadway humor such as, for example, a girl's pleading with a man to say something sweet to her and his rejoinder, "Boston cream pie," and in the occasional careless employment of such anachronistic slang as "drip" and the twentieth-century sort has Hammerstein lapsed. His lyrics, furthermore, are of a simple flavor in keeping with the tone of the book, avoiding any of the over-tricky and strained rhymes so close to the vanity of his lyric writing contemporaries and resolving themselves into the pleasant innocence of songs like "This Was A Real Nice Clambake," "Geraniums In The Winder," "When I Marry Mr. Snow," "When The Children Are Asleep," "June Is Bustin' Out All Over," and the kind.

Rodgers' score is one of his very best. His "If I Loved

You" is as good as Kern at the top of his old form, and his "You'll Never Walk Alone" and others are exactly what the fable calls for.

Rouben Mamoulian's staging forgives him for the affectations and euthanasian ormolu with which he overlaid *Sadie Thompson,* though his undue prolongation of the death scene in the second act induces in the restive audience the feeling that it is attending the joint demise of Camille and Little Eva, and though he privileges Agnes de Mille's beach ballet, albeit original and attractive, some twenty-three long minutes when twelve would be ample and would materially improve it. The color background provided by Jo Mielziner's settings and Miles White's costumes helps effectively to etch the play as a whole into the audience imagination.

As the Julie of the Molnár-Hammerstein love story, Jan Clayton reveals herself as the best of the Holywood escapists who have newly braved the musical stage in recent seasons. Shaw once wrote, "As virtuosity in manners was the characteristic mode of eighteenth century smart society, it follows that we get nothing of the eighteenth century at Her Majesty's except that from time to time the persons of the drama alarm us by suddenly developing symptoms of strychnine poisoning, which are presently seen to be intended for elaborate bows and curtseys." The average Hollywood actress, whether on the dramatic or the musical stage, usually alarms us by similarly betraying unmistakable and very realistic symptoms of catatonia complicated with a violent inflammation of the grin muscles, which are presently observed to be intended for volcanic sex appeal and buoyant *joie de vivre*. Miss Clayton is a relief. She comports herself like a normal young woman; she abstains from screwing up her features like a village idiot under the Hollywood impression that it will overwhelm an audience with its implication of bonhomie and jolly camaraderie; she acts simply and naturally and honestly; and she can sing.

The Liliom, or rechristened Billy Bigelow, of John Raitt, while vocally fair, relies altogether too much on the protrusion of a sweatered chest to depict the unquenchable masculinity and bullying nature of the character. The rest of the troupe, while nothing calling for individual mention, is, however, in the main sufficient unto the occasion.

In sum, a show which might be paced more quickly to its advantage, which contains a little too much Agnes de Mille for comfort, and which misses some of the ironic enchantment of its original's purgatory and heaven episodes, but one which nevertheless is a cheering change from the more usual Broadway tuned-up merchandise.

COMMON GROUND. April 25, 1945

A play by Edward Chodorov. Produced by Edward Choate for 69 performances in, first, the Fulton Theatre.

PROGRAM

Aide	*Arthur Gondra*
Buzz Bernard	*Philip Loeb*
Kate DeRosa	*Nancy Noland*
Geegee (Genevieve Gilman)	*Mary Healy*
Nick DeRosa	*Joseph Vitale*
Alan Spencer	*Donald Murphy*
1st Italian Soldier	*J. Anthony Selba*
2nd Italian Soldier	*Lou Gilbert*
3rd Italian Soldier	*Rupert Pole*
Ted Williamson	*Paul McGrath*
Captain Angelini	*Luther Adler*
Colonel Hofer	*Peter Von Zerneck*

SYNOPSIS: Act I. *Afternoon.* Act II. *A few minutes later.* Act III. *A few minutes later.*

The action of the play takes place in the music-room of an old Italian castle, between afternoon and evening. The time is that period immediately preceding the capture of Naples.

This marks the author's third try in three successive years to rid himself of the spirochetes contracted in Hollywood and to write a reputable play. Two years ago, the microbes were still in powerful evidence in his *Those Endearing Young Charms,* which dealt with a virgin who defiantly bestowed her favors upon an Army flyer bound for the battle zone, but which wound up conventionally at Will Hays' marriage altar, inc. It amounted to little more than a motion picture acted out on a theatre stage. Last year, the bugs were only slightly less visible in his *Decision,* which had to do with a returned soldier's discovery that the seeds of Fascism were sprouting in his home town and with his high resolve at the final curtain's fall to stamp them out. Since the author's theme was simply another obvious rehash of the *It Can't Happen Here* idea and since his young hero was unintentionally presented as a cretin whose political eloquence consisted chiefly in the expression "O.K." and whose general deportment suggested that he would have been more at ease on a horse yelling "Hi-yo, Silver!," the exhibit indicated that it in turn would have been more at ease in a film theatre. And now this year in *Common Ground* it is apparent that the purge remains still unsuccessful.

On this occasion, Mr. Chodorov employs a troupe of American mimes traveling in Italy as a USO unit and embracing a variety of races and paternal nationalities, along with its capture by the Nazis, to deliver himself of his testimonials to Americanism and Democracy, his exasperations anent anti-Semitism, his opinions of Hitler and Co., and the like. Though his sound track is in good, loud working order, what emanates from it is only what any number of playwrights have aired in past seasons, and for the most part, in view of the passing of time, with considerably more trenchant effect. His compound of denunciations and hornpipes, which suggests Elmer Rice in one of his less inspired moments, finds his audience much in the position of the Peter the Hermit about whom Shaw once wrote. A number of Crusaders on their way to battle the Paynim host encountered Peter sitting by the wayside and implored him to join them, but Peter politely declined. They wanted to know why. "I've been there," he replied simply. The audience has been at Mr. Chodorov's play before, and it has heard his harangues many times before, and it isn't interested.

The customary argument in such cases is that it does not matter how old materials are and that fresh treatment may make them again alive. The customary argument is true, but Mr. Chodorov unfortunately has not done anything about the fresh treatment. He has, in fact, done little more than to paste together elements of a dozen or more bygone plays like *Flight To The West, Idiot's Delight, Glorious Morning,* etc. — and including, as God is our judge, even a morsel from *Camille* — and to accompany the glue-pot with so many repetitious and dramaless speeches that one feels one is not in a theatre but at an indignation meeting in Carnegie Hall, simultaneously holding hands with Samuel Grafton and playing footie with Lillian Hellman.

Mr. Chodorov's conception of dramaturgy is very peculiar. His play consists for the greater part in a mere succession of dialogues at the right or left side of the stage with his disengaged characters standing or sitting about doing nothing but lowering their heads sympathetically or gazing at the speakers with intensely blank expressions presumably indicative of breathless fascination. And all to an obbligato of off-stage bomb-mimicking drums which give off the sound of a bad amateur performance of Ravel's "Bolero."

Various allusions to Darryl Zanuck, Metro-Goldwyn-Mayer, and Twentieth Century-Fox are interspersed through the play in further testimony to its Hollywood genesis, which the author fondly, if unsuccessfully, hopes to conceal by including several self-consciously saucy animadversions on the morals and stupidity of that community.

As his own stage director, Mr. Chodorov permitted himself such an affection for his play's contents that he hovered lovingly over the worst of them and coddled them into extended snores. He evidently esteems his writing as an unbroken string of precious pearls and is loath to tamper with a single gem. Another director might have proved a sounder lapidary.

Two items in the evening provided some speculation. Laying pleased eyes on George Jenkins' setting of a ruined Italian castle, one wondered why it is that, while such interiors are often admirable, the backdrops of sea and hills seen through the rear windows almost always look as if they had been painted by Putzi Hanfstängl on his eighth birthday. Laying less pleased ears to Luther Adler's portrayal of an Italian captain, one further wondered why it was that the audience, as always, enthusiastically applauded a distinctly inferior performance simply because the actor, an American, had learned some lines in a foreign language, the wonder being increased when, upon his exit, another character exclaimed, "That was bad acting if ever I saw it!," and when the same audience thereupon gave itself to an uproarious, concurring laughter.

TOO HOT FOR MANEUVERS. May 2, 1945

A comedy by Les White and Bud Pearson. Produced by James S. Elliott for 21 performances in the Broadhurst Theatre.

PROGRAM

SERGEANT WALTER BURROWS *Dickie Van Patten*
SERGEANT REGGIE WINTHROP *Michael Dreyfuss*
CAPTAIN HAMILTON *Ronald Telfer*
CORPORAL "EINSTEIN" SMETTS *Alastair Kyle*
COLONEL STEVE HADLEY *Richard Arlen*
AMY BURROWS *Helene Reynolds*
CADET "WIMPY" WORTHINGTON *Billy Nevard*
ALEX *Arthur Hunnicutt*
MAJOR PETERS *Jed Prouty*
COLONEL BEDLOE *Lawrence Fletcher*
MAJOR STANLEY *Harry Antrim*
MR. WINTHROP *Fleming Ward*
MRS. WINTHROP *Agnes Heron Miller*
MR. PERKLE *Harry Koler*
PATSY LAVERNE *Eve McVeagh*
COUNTESS ROSINI *Ellen Andrews*
VERONICA *Sheila O'Malley*
HILDA *Edith Leslie*
CADET NO. 1 *Roy Robson*
CADET NO. 2 *Marty Miller*
CADET NO. 3 *Pat O'Rourke*

SYNOPSIS: Act I. Scene 1. *The headmaster's office, at Hadley Military Academy. 9 a.m. Saturday morning.* Scene 2. *The same, 1 p.m.* Act II. Scene 1. *The same, 9 p.m.* Scene 2. *The reception room at Countess Rosini's. 10 p.m. that night.* Act III. *The same as Act I. The following morning.*

The entire action takes place in and around Hadley Military Academy, near New York city, about fifty minutes from Pennsylvania Station.

Time. *Autumn, 1944.*

ELLIOTT, a tender youth with a grim ambition to be a theatrical producer, presided over the concluding week of the 1942–1943 season with an item by Irving Elman called *The First Million,* which was judiciously evacuated from the stage after four performances. What was engaging his gifts in the concluding week of the 1943–1944 season, the records do not reveal. But in the concluding week of this 1944–1945 season he appeared again with an opus which, in respect to authorship and the presence in the cast of at least two movie names, bore all the earmarks of Hollywood, both coming and going.

Concerned with boys at a military academy and the faculty's trials when a spurious Countess opens what is thought to be a euphemistic massage parlor hard by the premises, the transaction is a minestrone of elements derived from such military school comedies as *Brother Rat,* such strip farces as *Good Night Ladies,* such bordello musicals as *Early To Bed,* and a dozen or more of the kind of small budget movies that occupy the double feature bills in the small neighborhood theatres. The writing is of the film scenario species, and the characters are mainly the rubber-stamps indigenous to the routine plot. An intermittent spurt of humor enlivens the script, but the filler materials between laughs are strictly stogie.

Much of the acting, especially that of the cinema's Richard Arlen, additionally pestered the occasion.

The play was the thirty-sixth of the season equipped with the military uniform.

Especially Interesting Performances

ANNA LUCASTA
Hilda Simms
Frederick O'Neal

LOVE ON LEAVE
Bert Freed

SONG OF NORWAY
Irra Petina
Helena Bliss
Sig Arno

WHILE THE SUN SHINES
Melville Cooper
Cathleen Cordell

SOLDIER'S WIFE
Glenn Anders

I REMEMBER MAMA
Oscar Homolka

SNAFU
Billy Redfield

EMBEZZLED HEAVEN
Martin Blaine

HARVEY
Frank Fay
Josephine Hull

SADIE THOMPSON
June Havoc

THE STREETS ARE GUARDED
George Mathews

THE LATE GEORGE APLEY
Leo G. Carroll
Percy Waram
Margaret Phillips

HAND IN GLOVE
Aubrey Mather

A BELL FOR ADANO
Tito Vuolo
Albert Raymo
Charles Mayer

THE SEVEN LIVELY ARTS
Beatrice Lillie
Alicia Markova

LITTLE WOMEN
Mary Welch

DEAR RUTH
Howard Smith
Virginia Gilmore

SOPHIE
Marguerite Clifton

SING OUT, SWEET LAND!
Burl Ives

TRIO
Lois Wheeler
Richard Widmark

THE HASTY HEART
John Lund

LA VIE PARISIENNE
Lillian Andersen

THE TEMPEST
Arnold Moss

ONE–MAN SHOW
John Archer

THE STRANGER
Eugene Sigaloff

THE DEEP MRS. SYKES
Catherine Willard

KISS THEM FOR ME
Judy Holliday

THE FIREBRAND OF FLORENCE
Gloria Story

THE GLASS MENAGERIE
Laurette Taylor
Eddie Dowling
Julie Haydon
Anthony Ross

CAROUSEL
Jan Clayton

Index of Plays

Index of Authors and Composers

A NOTE ON THE TYPE USED IN THIS BOOK

The text of this book has been set on the Linotype in a type-face called "Baskerville." The face is a facsimile reproduction of types cast from molds made for John Baskerville (1706–1775) from his designs. The punches for the revived Linotype Baskerville were cut under the supervision of the English printer George W. Jones.

John Baskerville's original face was one of the forerunners of the type-style known as "modern face" to printers: a "modern" of the period A.D. *1800.*

The typographic scheme and the binding design are by W. A. Dwiggins. The book was composed, printed, and bound by The Plimpton Press, Norwood, Massachusetts.